ENDGAME, 1945

ENDGAME, 1945

The Missing Final Chapter of World War II

DAVID STAFFORD

Little, Brown and Company
New York   Boston   London

Little, Brown and Company
Hachette Book Group USA
237 Park Avenue, New York, NY 10017
Visit our Web site at www.HachetteBookGroupUSA.com

First American Edition: November 2007
First published in Great Britain by
Little, Brown Book Group Ltd. in August 2007

Extracts from *Commando Men* by Bryan Samain
reproduced courtesy of Greenhill Books

Library of Congress Cataloging-in-Publication Data
Stafford, David.
Endgame, 1945 : the missing final chapter of World War II / David Stafford.
p.   cm.
Includes bibliographical references and index.
ISBN-13: 978-0-316-10980-2
ISBN-10: 0-316-10980-0
1. World War, 1939–1945 — Miscellanea.   2. Nineteen forty-five, A.D. — Chronology.
I. Title.
D744.S725 2007
940.54'21 — dc22   2007030126

10   9   8   7   6   5   4   3   2   1

Q-FF

Printed in the United States of America

For Ruth,
who survived,
and
in memory of
Sydney, who fought

CONTENTS

Say no more than *How will it be with me?* for however it be thou wilt settle it well, and the issue shall be fortunate . . . if a great boar appear, thou wilt fight the greater fight; if evil men, thou wilt clear the earth of them. *But if I die thus?* Thou wilt die a good man, in the accomplishing of a noble deed.

EPICTETUS

I am tired and sick of war. Its glory is all moonshine . . . War is Hell.

GENERAL WILLIAM TECUMSEH SHERMAN

INTRODUCTION

W ars do not end when the fighting stops, and military victory in itself is no guarantor of peace. The wounded continue to die. The dispossessed still seek a place to call home. Parents search for lost children among the ruins, and families and friends try desperately to reunite. Soldiers of the defeated forces face weeks, months and even years interned in prisoner-of-war camps often far distant from home. The victors do not suddenly turn their swords into plowshares. They hunt down enemy leaders, confront those who wish to continue the fight, and wrestle hard to establish law and order. Only then can peace come. For this requires more than the absence of conflict, and is harder to build than battering cities to rubble.

Histories of the Second World War in Europe invariably end with the surrender of German armies and the celebration of VE (Victory in Europe) Day on Tuesday, 8 May 1945 (or 9 May in the former Soviet Union). From a military perspective alone this is misleading, because fighting continued in some places well past that date. Yet even where conflict ceased, allied soldiers did not suddenly fling aside their weapons, celebrate wildly, and return home. On the contrary, for most of them, VE Day was merely a brief pause in the continuing and exhausting experience of being in uniform and under arms. Thanks to Adolf Hitler's manic vision, Europe in 1945 was a disaster zone, and the aftermath of war proved as demanding as battle itself.

It required the surrender of millions of enemy soldiers; the urgent quashing of looting, rioting and random violence; the robust and often severe restoration of law and order; the reestablishment of basic services such as electricity, gas, water and sewerage; the restoration of smashed roads, railways and telephone systems; the quest for the proceeds of the large-scale looting of European gold and art treasures; and, not least, the search for Nazi and Fascist leaders fleeing retribution and justice. The participants did not stop writing their diaries or letters home, and neither did they consider that their war was over; for one thing, those directly involved in the fighting expected to be transferred to the Far East to finish the conflict against the still-undefeated Japanese.

Nor did the fighting become less bitter as liberation dawned. Indeed, the final weeks of the war saw some of the cruelest moments of all, providing a terrible climax to a conflict already marked by brutality and death on a scale unprecedented in human history. Since D-Day in June 1944, allied armies had suffered a sequence of bitter setbacks that continually postponed the day of victory. When they finally entered the German heartland, Hitler made it clear that he would fight on to the bitter end. Referring to the armistice sought by Germany at the end of the First World War, he firmly told the Wehrmacht in his proclamation on "Heroes' Memorial Day"— 11 March 1945 — that "the year 1918 will not repeat itself." To rule this out, no price, not even destruction, was too high. A week later, he issued his so-called Nero Order. Nothing was to be kept for the enemy to use: mines were to be blown up, canals blocked, telecommunications wrecked, and Germany's cultural heritage destroyed.

Josef Goebbels, Hitler's propaganda minister, expressed the same chilling nihilism more pithily: "If we have to leave the scene," he wrote in typically theatrical fashion, "we'll shut the door so tight that no other government will ever open it again." What all this meant was that allied soldiers could expect a remorseless fight to the death.[1]

As for civilians, liberation often marked the beginning and not the end of their tribulations, a bittersweet moment of exhilaration and despair. It was only with the overrunning of concentration camps such as Buchenwald, Belsen and Dachau in April 1945 that the full scale of Nazi atrocities became apparent to Western eyes. For the survivors, the trauma of returning home was just the start of a painful process of readaptation to normal life. While, for the thousands of Jews who discovered that they had no homes or families to go back to, the struggle now began in earnest to build their own new state of Israel. For civilians who had not been transported to the camps — the vast majority of Europeans — VE Day was little more than a moment of brief relief in a life of continuing hardship and daily struggle.

This was also a time of retribution and revenge. The Second World

War precipitated the climax of two decades of ethnic rivalry and ideological conflict, and almost everywhere society trembled on the brink of civil war or serious disorder. The end of the fighting permitted the winners to vent their rage on those of their opponents who had collaborated with the enemy. This presented the liberating armies with another urgent problem in the wake of their hard-won triumphs.

It was only after the fighting stopped, moreover, that help could reach the millions of people transported and enslaved by the Nazis in their insatiable search for labor to run the war economy of the Third Reich. For the first time, the army of relief workers who descended on Europe were able truly to appreciate the full scale and depth of the human misery involved. They also confronted a vast new wave of refugees, some fleeing westwards ahead of Stalin's armies, others deliberately uprooted from their homes in Central and Eastern Europe because they were ethnically German. This, the largest forced migration of peoples in European history, took little notice of the celebrations of VE Day and it, too, threatened a new round of instability and conflict.

Even in unoccupied Britain, a political tremor was about to throw the nation's triumphant war leader, Winston Churchill, out of office. In the United States, the inexperienced new president, Harry Truman, struggled hard to master the complexities of the international power game for which he had been ill-prepared by his predecessor, Franklin D. Roosevelt. It is scarce wonder that historians have described the end of the war in Europe as little more than a "semblance of peace," as a "poisoned peace," or most recently as a case of "no simple victory."[2]

In Britain and the United States, the story of the Second World War is invariably told through its military campaigns. This is understandable. Neither country was occupied, and apart from British civilians affected by the German bombing of their cities, the war was most directly experienced by those who took part in the campaigns in Northwest Europe and Italy and the Far East. But the history of war is too important to be left to military historians alone, and in Europe the conflict had its greatest and most devastating impact on civilians. For most of them, it was not an affair of movement and battle but "a daily degradation, in the course of which men and women were betrayed and humiliated, forced into daily acts of petty crime and self-abasement, in which everyone lost something and many lost everything."

More than one recent historian has reminded us of this, and of the fact that for half the continent the peace that came in 1945 was that "of the prison yard, enforced by the tank."[3] How the might of the Red Army smashed westwards to capture the great capitals of Central and Eastern Europe such as Berlin, Vienna, Prague and Budapest, and what this meant for their post-war life, is a story that has been told in a legion of books. It provides all the more reason to be thankful that the continent's other great capitals, such as Paris, Rome and Brussels, were liberated by the Western liberal democracies of Britain and the United States — and that London was never occupied at all. Without that, the history of Europe would have taken a radically different and far more dismal turn.

This is why I deal here with the final weeks of the war and its immediate aftermath in that half of Europe liberated by the Western allies. I make no attempt to offer a comprehensive account but rather a portrait, a partial glimpse of the complex tapestry that was Europe during the endgame of Hitler's war.

Behind and amid all great events lie individuals, their experiences and their actions, and it is only through understanding these that we can fully grasp the larger picture. Historical events, noted the exiled German author and historical journalist Sebastian Haffner in his brilliant memoir of life in Germany during Hitler's rise to power, have varying degrees of intensity. Some barely impinge on true reality — which means the central, most personal parts of an individual's life — while others wreak havoc and leave nothing standing. Only through reading biographies, especially the all too rare ones of unknown individuals, can we appreciate this. "There," writes Haffner, "you will see that one historical event passes over the private (real) lives of people like a cloud over a lake. Nothing stirs, there is only a fleeting shadow. Another event whips up the lake as if in a thunderstorm. For a while it is scarcely recognizable. A third may, perhaps, drain the lake completely."[4]

This explains the approach I have taken here: to present the interwoven narratives of a handful of individuals caught up in the end-of-war storm that engulfed the lives of millions, based on their letters, diaries, memoirs and personal testimonies. The cast includes women as well as men, civilians as well as soldiers, and people of several nationalities. I have chosen them because of the intrinsic interest of their individual stories, the ways in which they illuminate the broader themes I have mentioned, and the light they cast on some particular dimension of the war.

They include a German mother held prisoner by the SS and brutally separated from her two sons; a young British commando who reaches the Baltic coast, only to witness the aftermath of the horrendous and tragic accidental death of thousands of concentration camp victims; an equally youthful American soldier fighting in Italy who tries desperately to overcome his fear of death and preserve his idealism amid the horrors of battle; a middle-aged war correspondent traveling with George S. Patton's Third US Army into southern Germany who descends deep into a salt mine to see for himself the hidden gold reserves of Germany and piles of art looted by the Nazis; a Canadian officer who gets caught up in a bitter, last-ditch battle in Holland; a German-Jewish exile fighting as a British secret agent behind the lines in Austria; a New Zealand intelligence officer whose campaign in Italy ends in confrontation with the communists in the disputed city of Trieste; an American paratrooper whose war against the Nazis elides seamlessly into a struggle against the Russians in Berlin; and a woman with long experience of refugee work helping liberated slave laborers and concentration camp victims in Bavaria.

The narrative begins on Friday, 20 April 1945. This is Hitler's birthday, when the Nazi dictator, trapped in his Berlin bunker, makes it clear that he will fight on to the bitter end and die there if necessary. It ends on Monday, 16 July 1945, when Churchill and Truman arrive in the ruins of the Nazi capital for the Potsdam Conference, the last of the wartime "Big Three" meetings. They make a tour of the devastated city and Churchill, after walking through the rubble-strewn marbled halls of Hitler's once magnificent Chancellery, wanders into the garden to gaze on the very spot where the dictator's body was burned after he killed himself. After several moments, he turns away in disgust. That same morning, thousands of miles away in the deserts of New Mexico, the world's first atomic bomb is successfully tested. Japan's fate is now sealed and the Pacific War, too, is effectively over.

Yet what peace means is far from clear. Some of the characters are exhausted but feel they have done a good and necessary job. One or two retain a battered idealism. Others are simply happy to have survived. At least one feels disillusioned, and another finds herself lost and bereft. All have experienced or witnessed the horrors of war. Each is anxious about the future and what it holds for them personally. No one can see the future for themselves, or for the world. What will happen in Germany? Is there any chance that democracy can take root? Will it be overwhelmed by the catastrophic influx of millions of refugees? Will Nazism return? Indeed, is it even certain that Adolf Hitler is dead? Will civil war break out at any minute in Italy? Will the country fracture into two parts, the north and the south? Will its monarchy survive? And what about relations with the Soviet Union? Can peace be built with Stalin? Or must it be constructed without or even against him?

When the clock stops on this narrative in mid-summer 1945, none of the answers to these questions is obvious. It is starkly apparent that a necessary victory has been won, but also that it has not yet delivered a peace. Indeed, it has created new problems for those who survive. Only one thing is certain: the war, for all its dreadful cost, has prevented Hitler and the Nazis from making an imperfect world into an even worse one. That, by any measure, makes it worthwhile.

I have many thanks to give to those who helped make this book possible. My first debt of gratitude is to those whose stories I tell here, some of whom are still alive and who generously agreed to meet with me, discuss their experiences of six decades ago and help me in various other ways, ranging from providing documents, letters and photographs to putting thoughts to paper in response to my questions. I thank them all: in Rome, Fey von Hassell, along with her son-in-law David Forbes Watt; in Hamburg, Fred Warner, who sadly has since died, and his wife, Annette; in Victoria, British Columbia, Canada, Reg Roy; in Gloucestershire, Sir Geoffrey Cox CBE; and in Suffolk, Bryan Samain and his wife, Helen. Leonard Linton of New York kindly agreed to assist me in telling his story but died before we were able to meet; I am grateful to his daughter Sandy for seeing me there and for answering questions and providing photographs. In London, Elizabeth Horder kindly talked to me about her aunt, Francesca Wilson, and lent me portions of her diary; while in York, Rosalind Priestman, another of Francesca's nieces, guided me to sources about the Quakers and lent me the photograph of her aunt that appears here. Heather Aggins and Russell Enoch also talked to me about their memories of Francesca. To my friend and colleague in Edinburgh, Jeremy Crang, I owe a special thanks for letting me delve freely into the hitherto unexplored papers of his grandfather Robert Reid; while to Robert's daughter Elizabeth I am grateful for further insights into her father's wartime family life.

As ever, I am indebted to many expert and hardworking archivists and librarians, invariably underpaid and overworked, who make all historical research possible. The chief librarian at the Alexander Turnbull Library in Wellington, New Zealand, kindly gave me permission to draw on the papers of Sir Geoffrey Cox, and I am grateful to Peter Cooke for finding the relevant material for me. Also in New Zealand, Dolores Ho of the Queen Elizabeth II Army Museum in Waiouru provided me with further material about Sir Geoffrey Cox as well as photographs by G. Kaye from the photographic collection of the Kippenberger Military Archive. In the Netherlands, Dr. Hans de Vries, of the Information and Documentation Department of the Netherlands Institute for War Documentation in Amsterdam pointed me in the right direction at the start of my researches into wartime Holland; while Monique Brinks, of the Groningen Archiv and curator of the April 2005 exhibition "From Me to May: The First Year after the War in Groningen," kindly found time from her hectic exhibition schedule to talk about the days surrounding the liberation of the city. Local historian Franz Lenselink generously drove me around the Delfzijl area to explore the terrain, gave me a copy of his invaluable pamphlet on the town during the war, and shared his observations about the battle fought there in 1945 by the Cape Breton Highlanders.

At the Imperial War Museum in London Rod Bailey helped me with the Walter Freud Papers, while Stephanie Clarke assisted me in gaining access to the papers of Sigismund Payne Best, along with the generous permission of his widow, Bridget Payne Best. In the United States, Professor Emeritus John Imbrie, veteran and Vice-President of Data Acquisition and Analysis of the Tenth Mountain Division Association, provided me with much valuable material about the division's wartime operations, answered many of my queries, and made valuable suggestions. Debbie Gemar and Dennis Hagen, of the Tenth Mountain Division Resource Center at the Denver Public Library, Colorado, sent me copies of the morning reports of the Tenth Mountain Division 85th Regiment Company F, April–July 1945, as well as photographs.

At the Defence Intelligence Museum at Chicksands, Bedfordshire, Major Alan Edwards OBE gave me enormous help during the initial stages of my research and helped me discover Fred Warner's unpublished account of his SOE mission to Austria. In Berlin, Dr. Helmut Trotnow OBE, Director of the Allied Museum, first drew my attention to Leonard Linton's unpublished memoirs. Sebastian Cox, head of the Royal Air Force Historical Branch at Bentley Priory, Stanmore, provided me with material about the *Cap Arcona* affair and discussed this tragic event with me. Dr. Yves Tremblay, of the Directorate of History and Heritage at National Defence Headquarters in Ottawa, Canada, helped with inquiries about Canadian forces in Holland. The late Sydney Hudson kindly let me consult his useful collection of press cuttings made by his father during the war.

I wish also to acknowledge the generous help given by various staff members at the National Library of Scotland, the Liddell Hart Centre for Military Archives at King's College, London, as well as Ian Martin, archivist at the King's Own Scottish Borderers' Regimental Headquarters in Berwick-upon-Tweed and Dr. Diana Henderson of the Scots at War Trust. As when I was writing *Ten Days to D-Day*, the staff at the Naples branch of the Collier County Library in southern Florida provided an unfailingly excellent service.

I have also benefited from discussions with friends and colleagues in many places. To Professor Terry Copp of Wilfrid Laurier University in Kitchener, Ontario, I am, as ever, indebted for providing material from his own extensive researches on the Second World War that helped me significantly in the early stages of my work. David Ellwood of Bologna University was, as always, generous with his knowledge and contacts, and put me in touch with Professor Giampaolo Valdevit of the University of Trieste, with whom I had an illuminating discussion in Trieste about the complex politics of the city in 1945. John Earle, also of Trieste, was similarly helpful, as was John Shillidy, who wrote to me about his work with British military intelligence there at the end of the war. Lt.-Col. Roderick Mackenzie, formerly of the 178 (Lowland) Medium Regiment RA, sent me the relevant chapter of his memoirs of experiences fighting in support of the Tenth Mountain Division as well as an article by the late Lt.-Col. Hugh Freeth DSO, Silver Star, the regiment's commanding officer. Dr. F. Akkerman of Haren wrote to me about the fighting for Groningen and the capture of the bridge at Oosterhoogebrug that was crucial to the Canadian advance on Delfzijl. Dr. Coen Tamse and Dr. Homme Wedman of Groningen University provided welcome hospitality in the city and filled in some useful details.

Others who helped at various stages along the way include Martin Clark, Richard Aldrich, Tim Naftali, Tony Hepburn, Alastair C. Duke, Bob Steers, Hayden Peake, Ian McGibbon, Dr. Rob Rabel, Fred Judge, A. Struan Robertson, Mark Seaman, Tessa Stirling, Gill Bennett, Mary

Mackie, Beth Slavin, Betty Thomas, Gerry Brent, Seamus Spark, Frank Bright, Madeleine Haag, Tony Williams, Sidney Goldberg of the Normandy Veterans Association, Angus McIntosh, Adrian Gilbert, David Storrie, Matthew Parker, Sandy Gordon, Christopher Woods, Duncan Stuart, Andrew Jeffrey, Tim Carroll, Grant McIntyre, Ian D. Armour, Slawka Mieczyslawa, Joanna Potts, Marion Milne, Dolores Hatch, Jack Granatstein, Christopher Woods, Tom Wales and Sir Tommy Macpherson. My colleagues at the Centre for the Study of the Two World Wars and in the Department of History at the University of Edinburgh, Paul Addison, Jenny Macleod, James McMillan, Jill Stephenson, Donald Bloxham and Pauline Maclean, all helped provide the friendly and supportive working environment every writer needs.

To my agent in London, Andrew Lownie, I am deeply grateful for making the project possible in the first place, and to my editors at Little, Brown in London and New York, Richard Beswick and Liz Nagle respectively, I am profoundly indebted and thankful for their incisive comments, valuable insights, welcome suggestions and unfailing support. To Iain Hunt, Rowan Cope, Bobby Nayyar and Philip Parr, who also helped bring the project to fruition in London, I am very grateful.

Finally, to my wife, Jeanne Cannizzo, editor of first resort and unconditionally supportive companion, once again I can never say thank you enough.

David Stafford,
Edinburgh,
February 2007

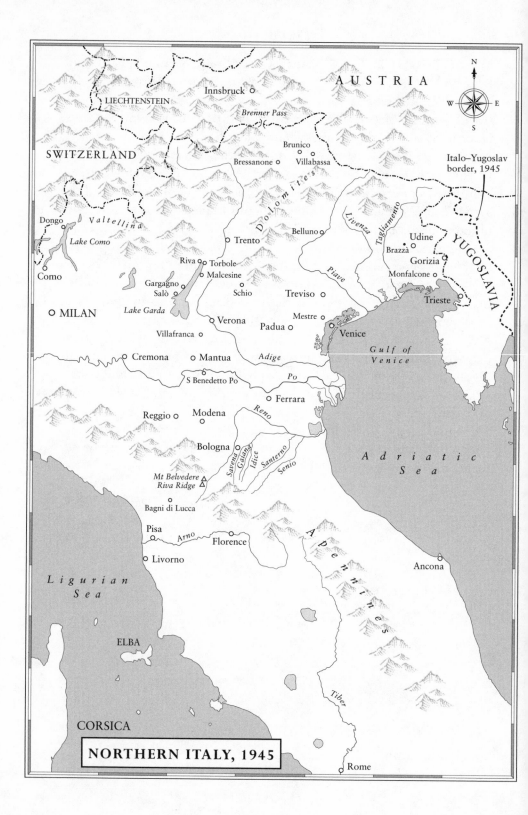

NORTHERN ITALY, 1945

PART ONE

FRIDAY, 20 APRIL 1945

CHAPTER ONE

CRUEL SPRING

Friday 20 April was Adolf Hitler's birthday. Since seizing power in 1933 and making himself Führer of the German people, the anniversary had been celebrated throughout the Reich as a public holiday. Across Germany, the blood-red flag of the Nazi Party, with its crooked black swastika, had festooned private balconies and public buildings alike. Radio broadcasts had played special music and adulatory speeches, schoolchildren had enjoyed the day off, and at his Bavarian home at Obersalzberg outside Berchtesgaden Hitler had smiled paternally as blonde young girls presented him with posies of alpine flowers.

But today, as he turned fifty-six, the mood was distinctly unfestive. Josef Goebbels, the Führer's fervently loyal minister of propaganda, tried to make the best of it all amid the mood of impending disaster. The German people, he announced that morning on the radio, should trust their leader to the bitter end. For this, Hitler himself was now making grim preparation. For weeks he had been in Berlin, living an underground existence in his neon-lit bunker deep below the Chancellery. It consisted of eighteen cramped rooms with a special suite that he shared with his mistress, Eva Braun.

Today, as elsewhere across Europe, it was a sunny spring day in the German capital and the lilacs were in bloom. But throughout the city housewives were desperately stocking up with food in preparation for the battle that everyone knew was coming. Overhead, the once vaunted and feared Luftwaffe was reduced to an impotent weapon, and American and British heavy bombers had been hitting the capital with impunity for months. Only the week before, they had sent the Foreign Ministry and the old Reich Chancellery itself up in flames. Now, overnight, knowing the significance of the date, they had returned for an even bigger raid, and all day the acrid smell of smoke hung heavy in the air. On the ground, Red Army forces had begun their final big offensive against the capital with two and a half million men and were rapidly approaching the eastern suburbs, threatening to surround the city completely. The thunder of heavy artillery was now audible even to those below ground.

Traditionally, the Führer was congratulated first on his birthday just after the stroke of midnight by his personal household staff. But this year he told them the situation was too somber for such ceremonies. Despite this, they persisted. Looking twenty years older than his actual age and his skin a deathly white, he trudged down the line of men and women and limply shook hands with each of them. Then, after sleeping a few hours, in the early afternoon he climbed the steps out of the bunker into the Chancellery garden to take Nazi salutes from selected army units and SS troops. About twenty teenage boys from the Hitler Youth who had been fighting against the Russians were also lined up.

Hitler was wearing his field-gray army uniform jacket with its Iron Cross, awarded for bravery during the First World War. Slowly, he walked down the line, pinching a few of the boys on the cheek and muttering words of encouragement. A newsreel camera recorded the event. Inadvertently, it also captured the violently shaking left hand that he kept firmly behind his back in an effort to conceal it, a mark of his rapid physical decline in recent months. "Here in Berlin," Hitler told the teenagers, "we are facing the great, decisive battle . . . Our belief that we will win . . . has to remain unbroken. The situation can be compared with that of a patient believed to have reached the end. Yet he does not have to die. He can be saved with a new medication, discovered just in time to save him."

What the miracle at this stage might be was anyone's guess. Since the allied landings in France on D-Day the previous June, Hitler and Goebbels had constantly hinted at miracle weapons that would yet win the war, such as the V2 rocket or a new jet aircraft. The week before, it had even seemed that a political rather than a military miracle might save the Reich. Shortly before midnight on Thursday 12 April a

BBC–Reuters flash had announced the sudden death of President Franklin D. Roosevelt at his private retreat in Warm Springs, Georgia.

Goebbels immediately phoned Hitler. "My Führer," he exclaimed, "this is the miracle of the House of Brandenburg we have been waiting for. This is the turning point predicted in your horoscope!" The Minister of Propaganda was referring to a historical event well known to Hitler, with his megalomaniac habit of comparing himself to the great figures of German history. In 1762, King Frederick the Great of Prussia had been saved from defeat in the Seven Years' War against Russia by the sudden death of Czarina Elizabeth. Hitler, who kept a portrait of Frederick in his bunker study, reacted to Goebbels's news with delight. Soon, he told him, the Americans and the Red Army would be exchanging artillery barrages over the roof of the Chancellery.

The euphoria had been fleeting. Few of those now listening to Hitler's promises in the garden placed much faith in his curiously defiant yet depressing message to the assembled faithful about a dying patient. Later that day, below ground again, he greeted assembled luminaries of the Reich — ministers and generals alike — who had come to give him their birthday wishes. He shook hands with each and exchanged a desultory few words. Then, the birthday ritual completed, they turned to the great decision of the day. Would Hitler stay in Berlin, or would he move south to Bavaria to lead some last-ditch resistance from his base at Berchtesgaden? This had long been the plan. Just ten days before, he had sent his servants south to prepare the way.

The decision was now urgent. The Red Army advance was so rapid and so close that it threatened to cut off all routes of escape out of the city. Worse, with the Russians advancing west, and the Americans moving rapidly east in central and southern Germany, the Reich faced being cut in two, with the route south to Bavaria being completely shut off. Everyone present argued that Hitler should quit his capital immediately. Earlier in the day, Field Marshal Wilhelm Keitel, his military chief, had urged this course, but he had been rebuffed. "Keitel," said Hitler, "I know what I want. I will fight on in front of, within, or behind Berlin." Now, after further discussion, he relented a little by saying that he would leave the final decision to fate.

Yet, in truth, he had already made up his mind. In March, Eva Braun had arrived in Berlin from Berchtesgaden. Then, just a week ago, she had descended from her private apartment in the Chancellery to sleep with Hitler in the bunker. Gerda Christian, his senior private secretary, knew instinctively what this meant: Hitler would never flee to Bavaria. Instead, Berchtesgaden, in the shape of Eva Braun, had come to Berlin. Hitler's mistress was a middle-class Catholic girl from Munich. Twenty-three years his junior, she had met him in the studios of his official photographer Heinrich Hoffman, where she was working as an assistant. Whatever else might be said about her, she was loyalty supreme. She would stay at his side until the bitter end.

Gerda Christian's guess was confirmed later that evening when Hitler, as so often, ended his day by chatting with his secretaries in his study. He always liked the company of impressionable young women, and it was to women that he often revealed his deepest feelings. They too wanted to know if he would leave Berlin. If he did, he replied, he would feel like a Tibetan lama turning an empty prayer mill. "I must," he insisted, "bring things to a head in Berlin — or go under!"[1]

To all but the willfully blind, it was now obvious he would do both. Moreover, whatever he said or did in Berlin was increasingly irrelevant to the march of war throughout his beleaguered Reich and beyond.

Of all the bitter months of the war against Hitler, April 1945 was the hardest to bear. It was not just the weather, although this proved true to form, shifting treacherously between days of spring promise and the last gasps of a dying winter that fought back tenaciously with sleeting hard rain and flurries of snow that drove soldiers and civilians alike scurrying for warmth.

Nor was it the fear of allied victory slipping away at the last moment, like some perpetually distant and elusive prize. The end of Hitler's Third Reich was now inevitable and visibly close. Hostile armies surrounded the Nazis in a tightening grip. In the flatlands of Northwest Europe British, American and Canadian armies had crossed the Rhine, the traditional guardian of Germany's western frontier, and were pushing rapidly forward through Holland and towards the great North Sea ports of Bremen and Hamburg.

On the bountiful granary plains of eastern Germany, Stalin's Red Army had crossed the Rivers Oder and Neisse to reach the outer suburbs of Berlin. Further south, the Soviet dictator's forces were poised to link up with the Americans in the center of the country, and in Austria his troops had already taken Vienna. In southern Germany, American troops were driving rapidly up the Danube and deep into

Bavaria, Nazism's spiritual home, with its cities of Munich, the Nazi Party headquarters, and Nuremberg, site of the torch-lit rallies that had mesmerized the world just a few years before. In Italy, allied forces were finally poised to make their crucial breakout into the valley of the River Po with its arrow-straight roads pointing north to the Alps and the Reich beyond.

However, unbearably, despite all this, Hitler refused to surrender. Instead, his armies were fighting on with ferocious tenacity. Soldiers and civilians alike now knew that this would be a fight to the death, with all that this meant for them and for Europe. Liberation would come to millions, but at a price made painfully high because it seemed so needless. More soldiers and civilians would die. More houses would be destroyed by bomb and artillery shell. More fields and crops would be flooded by broken dams and dikes, ruining crops and tightening the grip of hunger that had already reduced millions to starvation. And more refugees would be sent on their way along desolate roads with their pathetic bundles of personal belongings slung on their backs or dragged in carts behind them. This, indeed, was a bittersweet month.

Globally, the end of the war looked no less dark. Japan, like its German ally, was battling back viciously to postpone the day of defeat. The island-hopping advance of the Americans in the Pacific had come to a bloody halt on rocky Okinawa, the last stop before the Japanese mainland. Here, 120,000 Japanese troops supported by 10,000 aircraft were making a suicidal last stand against an army of 155,000 Americans that stormed ashore on the first day of the month. Kamikaze pilots dive-bombed American warships and the Japanese Imperial Navy sent the *Yamato*, the largest battleship in the world, on a desperate last mission to ram as many enemy ships as it could. The battle would end eighty days later with the ritual suicide of the Japanese commander and his chief of staff, and with only 10,000 of the island's defenders still alive. With 50,000 dead and wounded Americans, the fight for Okinawa offered a grim and worrying portent of what could still lay ahead before Japan surrendered.

Politically, too, the shadows were deepening. At his death, Roosevelt had yet to resolve the big question of how to deal with Stalin and the Soviet Union; while his successor, Harry Truman, was virtually unknown even to Americans and had little executive experience. Britain's prime minister, Winston Churchill, was by now full of dark foreboding about Soviet intentions in Europe and was already using the term "Iron Curtain" to describe a Europe divided between communism and democracy. Poland, for whose independence Britain had gone to war in 1939, was already in the grip of the communists. Would military victory turn to dust once the killing stopped?

More than anything, Robert Ellis wanted to sleep. All night he had clambered up the ridge dodging machine-gun and mortar fire. Physically and mentally, he was drained. Now, even though it was only early spring, the harsh Italian sun was scorching his skin. He crouched deeper into his foxhole to escape its relentless glare, but the ground was baked hard and his shelter was shallow.

Earth is the friend and final resting place of the combat infantryman. There he takes cover, shelters and sleeps, but it is also what he must capture and occupy. For six straight days, Ellis, of the Tenth Mountain Division, had been fighting in the last big push by the US Fifth Army to break out of the Apennine Mountains and into the valley of the River Po.

It lay below him now, its fertile green plain stretching far into the distance, representing both promise and threat. The grueling weeks of scrambling up and down rock-strewn hillsides braving withering enemy fire were over. But the river was wide and deep, a natural barrier for the retreating yet stubborn enemy. The last week's fighting had been the heaviest and most costly thus far for the division. Three hundred and seventy men had been killed and some fourteen hundred wounded. In Ellis's battalion alone, almost fifty men had perished in just two days of fighting. He knew all too well that many more men would die before victory came. It still seemed far away.

He was twenty years old. Home was Wooster, Ohio, where his parents had settled after years serving as Presbyterian missionaries in the Persian city of Urumia. They had arrived in Urumia during the First World War. "It was a battleground for Turkish and Russian troops, Kurdish tribesmen, Assyrians, Armenians and other native partisans," he wrote. "Massacres and epidemics were the order of the day. My father's medical services as a surgeon were desperately needed."

In 1918, his parents narrowly escaped a massacre of Christian missionaries by Muslim Kurds. Already they had two small children, both boys. A daughter followed three years later. Robert had completed the family when he was born in 1924, finally arriving in the States in the mid-1930s for more formal schooling.

Now, Ellis was heading a machine-gun squad in Company F of the division's 85th Regiment, having recently been promoted to sergeant. He had covered his helmet with burlap to reduce the reflection and make himself less of a target to the enemy, and had decided not to wear his sergeant's stripes on his shoulder. Like most of his buddies, he assumed the Germans made special efforts to shoot officers and NCOs to disrupt the chain of command.

There had been enough death anyway, without drawing attention to yourself. Casualties were running high and one in particular came shockingly close. On the first day of the offensive, Bill Luth, one of his oldest friends in the division, had been killed. They went back together to training days in Colorado, where they had enjoyed one fabulous weekend's leave with a couple of other buddies in Colorado Springs, singing fraternity and popular songs as they took the breathtaking drive over the mountains in full moonlight. Bill had come from Wisconsin, and Ellis had shared with him the cake his mother had sent for his nineteenth birthday, just two days before Bill's own.

Now, Ellis wasn't at all sure that he himself was going to make it. "The war may seem very close to the end," he wrote to his parents, "but to the men here who watch their comrades die each day the end is far away." Preying vividly on his mind was the final, heart-wrenching scene in *All Quiet on the Western Front*, the 1930s' film version of Erich Maria Remarque's great anti-war bestseller about the First World War. As he waits in his foxhole on the front, the armistice signed but not yet in effect, the soldier hero reaches out to touch a butterfly that has settled on a blade of grass only to be shot dead by an enemy sniper.

No one now was keen to be killed, and self-inflicted wounds, to provide an exit from the carnage, were not unusual. The risks did not diminish because victory was close. Over the last few days Ellis's company, along with others of the division, had advanced slowly from hilltop to hilltop through deadly, often unsuspected minefields as well as towards murderous machine-gun fire that raked the slopes as men desperately scrambled for cover. Mortar and artillery fire also caused dreadful wounds.

"Men were spun to the ground by the impact of bullets," writes one historian of a typical Tenth Division firefight in the Apennines, "sliced open by whirling jagged shards of shrapnel, atomized by direct bursts from artillery and mortar shells, catapulted into the air from the force of explosions, or thrown to the ground in agony, screaming with pain, clutching at torn limbs or spilled intestines, at jaws and genitals that had disappeared."[2] German *Schu* mines, undetectable in their wooden boxes and scattered liberally over the landscape, invariably blew off their victims' feet. In such savage and bitter fighting, where American soldiers saw friends killed or mortally wounded in terrible ways, prisoners, especially wounded ones, were sometimes simply shot. Ellis, like most young soldiers, was careful to self-censor his letters home about such matters.[3]

Round-the-clock marches had left him more exhausted than he had ever been before in his life. The previous day the regiment had captured the last great ridge before the Po Valley. Ahead of him he had glimpsed, on the horizon far to the northeast, the red tile roofs of Bologna. He had not slept for forty hours, but there was still no rest. At midnight his battalion started a rapid march to take control of a small town and then fought hard to capture another strategic ridge overlooking the valley. Now, as he desperately sought sleep, he was close to collapse and full of foreboding. Would he, like the soldier in the movie, die in his pathetic little foxhole at the final hour?

On this same April day, deep inside Germany, another river and its defenses confronted a young British commando, Captain Bryan Samain. His previous two years of military life had almost felt like a continuation of school. After his father died when he was only five, his almost penniless mother had sent him off to a Royal Masonic boarding school in Hertfordshire. But, unlike the other new boys, he didn't mind being away from home. He was an only child — a younger sister had died before he even became aware of her — and he had already learned to be self-reliant. Nor did he unduly miss his mother. "In fact," he recalled years later, "I never cried during those early, lonely days at school — even in the dormitory at night."[4]

Life at the boys' school was spartan and regimented, revolving mainly around a daily regime of sport and the weekly cadet corps, which was compulsory. "Great attention was paid to spit and polish," he recorded, "with much green blanco being applied to webbing." He had also learned to be a team player and to fit in. His father had been Protestant and a Freemason, but his mother was fiercely Catholic and had sent him to the school only because, as a Freemason's son, there were no fees to pay. It meant that he was the only Roman Catholic there, but he was never bullied or taunted because hardly anyone knew about it. Instead, he camouflaged himself by attending the regular morning prayers and Sunday Church of England services like everyone else — even if, during the holidays, he went with his mother to the local Catholic church.

Home was originally in Chelmsford, Essex, but by now his mother had remarried and was moving from place to place in the Midlands, following her accountant husband in various war-related jobs. At first, after leaving school at fifteen, Bryan had fancied going on the stage, like his aunt Kit, who had played in several musicals and revues. But this youthful idea had been firmly quashed, and instead he had signed up in London as a trainee journalist. As his eighteenth birthday approached, he was working in Fleet Street for an Australian paper, the Sydney *Daily Mirror*.

He knew he would soon be conscripted. "Being ambitious," he recalled, "I wanted to go for a commission rather than stay in the ranks." He found out about the "Y" scheme of the Royal Marines, a short cut for potential officers from their volunteers, so one day he traveled to a recruiting office in Croydon, where he was interviewed by a tough-looking, leather-faced sergeant who grilled him about his school, his sporting abilities and his academic record. Above all, he was interested in the fact that Samain had passed the military-based "Certificate A" in the cadet corps. "You'll do, lad," he concluded.

So, on 14 January 1943, the day he turned eighteen, Bryan Samain had said goodbye to the aunts in Wimbledon with whom he had been lodging and took a train to the Royal Marines' reception center in Devon. That had been just over two years ago, but now it felt like a lifetime away.

The day before, he had arrived in Luneberg. This picturesque medieval city, with its spas and gabled Gothic and Baroque façades, was one of the main hospital towns of Germany and was being used by the Wehrmacht for the treatment and convalescence of its wounded. It had been declared an open city and its undamaged houses provided comfortable shelter for the commandos. Like Ellis and the Americans in Italy, the British commandos were pausing for breath after a period of bitter fighting.

The term "commando" was first coined by the Boers to describe their irregular forces fighting the British in South Africa at the beginning of the century. Now, it was used for self-supporting allied units of about five hundred highly trained and mobile men. Although predominantly

British, the commandos also boasted hundreds of men from the occupied countries of Europe, refugees from France, Belgium, Poland, Yugoslavia, and even Germany itself. Samain himself was conscious that his family background was French, his ancestors having been Huguenots who had fled into exile during the reign of Louis XIV. The commandos were trained to the peak of physical fitness, knew how to handle a variety of weapons and explosives, and were able to march at up to seven miles an hour for several hours.

"As expected," wrote Samain, "the Commandos bristled with brave, larger-than-life characters — most of them volunteers, all of them keen to get to grips with the enemy. To wear the green beret of the Commandos, which I was now permitted to do, was a prized honor. To have to leave the Commandos, for whatever reason — when you were 'Returned to Unit' or RTU'd — was bitter personal reverse." His own unit was part of the First Commando Brigade, advancing with Field Marshal Montgomery's Twenty-first Army Group in northwest Germany.[5]

Less than a month before, they had taken part in the great allied crossing of the Rhine close to the city of Wesel. When Samain finally entered it, the town had been so thoroughly pulverized by Royal Air Force Lancaster bombers that he found the carefully prepared maps of German defensive positions virtually useless. In front of him stretched nothing but a maze of enormous craters, smashed-up landmarks and few passable roads. A British war correspondent who passed through the town at about the same time recorded,

> Surely the horror of war, the sheer blanket ruthlessness of it, is shown more vividly in Wesel than in all the towns of Germany . . . there is nothing left except rubble, stinking with the dead beneath it and rotting in the hot afternoon sun . . . so great is the devastation, so great and complete the ruin, that we did not even see that most familiar sight . . . the men and women and children picking in the ruins for what they could find . . . Wesel had ceased to exist.[6]

As Samain and his troop advanced in single file through the ruins, he received a nasty foretaste of what was to come. Around him lay the bodies of countless Germans. All were apparently dead. But suddenly, as the marines' commanding officer neared the corner of a street, one of the "corpses" stood up and fired a grenade launcher at point-blank range. It killed two of the commandos immediately, wounded the officer, and knocked everyone else off their feet.

Surprised, angry and fearful, the men retaliated by emptying their "Tommy" sub-machine-guns into the German. When they rolled over his corpse and looked more closely they were not surprised to find a member of the SS. To be sure nothing similar happened again, they then shot up every apparent corpse they could see. Samain would no longer take anything for granted.

His reaction was typical. There were too many stories of Germans fooling allied soldiers by playing dead to ignore, even if it meant that the Geneva Convention on the treatment of prisoners was fraying at the seams. In the ten months of grueling fighting since the Normandy landings, allied soldiers had honed their instincts for survival. In France, Polish tank crews had driven straight over retreating Germans, giving them no chance either to escape or surrender.

Enemy snipers always received short shrift too, and sometimes it took little more than an arrogant reply from a captured German to trigger a killing. When one British commando lance-corporal — not in Samain's troop — asked a surrendering German general to put his hands up, the Wehrmacht officer answered defiantly that he would surrender only to an officer of a similar rank. Unimpressed, the lance-corporal replied: "Well, this will equalise you," and opened fire with his Tommy gun. His only punishment was to have to dig the grave for his victim. This was what was meant by the glib phrase "the sharp end of war."[7]

Such shootings were the exception, not the rule, but the willing surrender of thousands of German soldiers witnessed by Samain and the other commandos only increased their ruthlessness towards those who continued with what seemed now like futile resistance. Beyond Wesel, one British unit found itself waging a fierce firefight for the possession of a tiny village. First, allied artillery pounded it into rubble, then the infantry moved in. They were met by concentrated machine-gun fire from the basement of a house while German riflemen picked off anyone trying to outflank it. Eventually, a full company of men was required to get close enough for one of their number to reach the back of the house and break in. As he did so, a German soldier rushed up the cellar steps and fired a magazine of bullets from his Schmeisser, killing the intruder instantly. "His death," recorded a British lance-corporal, "was followed a split second later by that of the German as our lads cut him down. Going through the house, they threw grenades into each room and the cellar. No prisoners were taken and several Germans were bayoneted as they tried to surrender."[8]

Montgomery's men were now advancing across the traditional training grounds of the Wehrmacht that covered the vast expanses of the North German Plain. They were encountering not just fanatical yet inexperienced Hitler Youth contingents but the hardened staffs from the army training schools, marines and even grounded Luftwaffe pilots—all now being thrown into the battle to stem the allied advance. British troops were increasingly minded to call for air strikes or heavy shelling to blast aside roadblocks or last-ditch strongholds—anything to reduce the risk of hand-to-hand fighting and encountering death when victory was now certain. The Germans still fighting were prepared to die for their Führer. It was hardly surprising that most allied soldiers were often all too happy to oblige them.[9]

In Wesel, Samain and the other commandos slept in a deserted factory. The next morning, looking out of a window, they spotted a dozen weary German soldiers wheeling bicycles towards the factory. They were chatting casually among themselves and remained oblivious to the commandos' presence. Samain's troop, arms at the ready, watched them come closer and closer, but held their fire. The Germans passed by only a few feet away. Still the British held back. Only when the last of the soldiers finally turned his back on them did they open up. Thirty seconds later, twelve corpses lay spread-eagled on the road.

During the few days of rest that followed, the commandos were well fed and read mail and newspapers from England packed with reports of their exploits. Most were accurate, but highly colored. "Every time I visit these men," observed one of the war correspondents, "there is an atmosphere of death." Samain laughed like the others when he read this. What on earth did the reporter expect? Did he not know, he wrote, that "Death, at that time, was our business?"[10]

It was certainly his. The training he had received on joining the Royal Marines was designed, after all, to transform him into an efficient killing machine. At the basic training school at Lympstone in Devon, the civilian was knocked out of him by weeks of drilling, marching and square-bashing. He learned to shave and wash in ice-cold water, defecate sitting precariously on a long, trestle-supported pole perched over an earthen trench, keep his hair short, and always be immaculately turned out.

Hardened into a human machine, he was then taught everything there was to know about the handheld instrument he needed for the job, the rifle. He learned how it was put together, how to strip it, and how to fire it. The position, he was told, was lying down, legs well apart and heels flattened inwards to the ground. The same went for the Bren light machine-gun, a standard British infantry weapon double the weight of a rifle which delivered five hundred rounds a minute.

Above all, he learned how to use and almost to love the Thompson sub-machine-gun (the "Tommy" gun), an American-manufactured weapon specially issued to the commandos. In Hollywood movies, the Tommy gun was a free sprayer of bullets producing heaps of victims in one lengthy burst. But Samain learned that the proper way to fire it was in short, controlled bursts of two or three .45-caliber bullets at a time. It was essentially a close-quarters weapon, most effective within a range of fifty yards. It had become his personal weapon of choice, and he had carried his through Normandy and Holland, always firing single shots or short bursts, conserving his ammunition.

But he was also taught to survive without any weapons at all. His training included bouts with a professional wrestler, whose first act was to shake him by the hand and throw him over his shoulder — "just to make sure," he quipped, "that you never bloody well trust anyone!" He went on to learn how to kill someone with his bare hands — one skill he had luckily never had to use — how to tackle a knife-wielding adversary, and how to disarm a weapon-carrying enemy soldier at close quarters.

His physical fitness was tested to extremes in the Welsh hills and Scottish Highlands, where he trekked mile after mile with a full pack on his back, practiced night-time attacks by canoe on lonely lochs, and "cat-crawled" on a rope strung high across rushing rivers. "The greatest thrill of all," he said, "was the final 'Tarzan' or 'death slide' when you slid with the aid of a wet toggle (to prevent burning) down a long, taut rope that ran at an angle of 45 degrees from the top of a high tree to the ground below."[11]

In short, by the time he was allowed to wear the coveted green beret, Bryan Samain had been turned into a superbly fit, disciplined, thoroughly trained and skillful young army killer. Three short years before, he had been a fifteen-year-old schoolboy playing as an extra in the film *Goodbye, Mr. Chips*. The MGM studios were only a few miles from his school and he was one of the lucky ones chosen to take part.

For three engrossing weeks he was taken by bus every morning to the studios at Denham, handed a costume, and rehearsed throughout the morning for scenes to be shot in the afternoon. The school was paid a guinea per day per head for their services. The heart-warming tale of an old schoolteacher looking back fondly over a long career while recalling pupils and colleagues was pure feel-good material, and featured not a single villain.

After Wesel and nineteen exhausting hours driving in the back of a truck along rough country roads in heavy drizzle and rain, Samain moved on to Osnabrück, a major industrial and railroad center en route to Lüneberg, and the largest German town so far taken by British forces. It was three-quarters blitzed, thousands of its citizens were cowering in cellars, and the town's water supply, when it worked, mingled with raw sewage.

The main problem here was not fanatical SS resistance, although plenty of enemy snipers had to be picked off. Instead, the commandos found thousands of liberated slave laborers. Deported forcibly by the Nazis from all over Europe to work in factories and on farms, they were rioting and looting in a frenzy of celebration. Laughing Polish women were trying on fur coats, Frenchwomen looted stockings from shop windows, and men of every nationality scavenged wildly for food. Only after imposing a twenty-four-hour curfew did the marines finally manage to post guards on warehouses and bring some order to the city.[12]

Looting was almost universal. Nearby Hanover provided another vivid example. Allied military government officials arrived to find a city of half a million people with no water, no electricity and no working sewers. Even the restrained British official historian F.S.V. Donnison hints at scenes of horror: "It was a town of looting, drunkenness, rape and murder as forced labor broke from restraint," he records. "Shots whistled by from drunken 'slaves' or left-behind snipers. Police were mobbed and their bodies strung from lampposts." Only the brutal enforcement of law and order made possible the revival of basic services and the semblance of normal life.[13]

Now, however, in Lüneberg, everything appeared calm and peaceful. The commandos rested and prepared for the forthcoming crossing of the Elbe, the last important river barrier that stood in their way. There were hot baths and plenty of food. A cinema was rigged up, football matches were played between units, and in the comfortable middle-class house where he was billeted the padre discovered a cache of fine wine hidden in a secret room behind a cupboard, and champagne was enjoyed by all. All around, the town's daily life continued much as usual while doctors and nurses carried on with their normal work. "It was strange," recalled another British officer, "to wander round this lovely old city and meet on every street corner one's hated enemy. Unarmed and engaged in the world-embracing task of ministering to the sick and wounded, they seemed harmless enough."

Yet appearances were deceptive. All too close lay the dark under-belly of Hitler's Third Reich. Next to a row of modern middle-class houses near the city center stood a small hospital made up of crude wooden huts. Packed inside, British soldiers found dozens of Russian slave laborers, both men and women. Most of them had been badly wounded in a recent RAF bombing raid on a nearby factory where they worked. Those who attempted to escape had been shot down by the SS. The morgue was filled to overflowing, and only a single doctor was on duty, helped by a solitary nurse. On dirty gray sheets, bathed in their own sweat and filth, the Russians lay gaunt and weak, too ill to move.

Samain had earlier witnessed similar misery on his final drive to the city. Traveling at speed along dusty rural roads, he more than once found himself held up for hours by crowds of displaced persons recently liberated from concentration or labor camps:

> They would pass us on carts, in stolen German cars (which seemed to run out of petrol all too soon) and on the backs of horses. They drove cattle before them so they could eat; and on their backs were pots, pans, water bottles and old clothes. Every time they met us they cheered in a dozen different tongues, and when we looked at them closely we saw they were little more than walking skeletons, with ribs protruding pitifully from the flesh, faces lined and haggard, and eyes that told of a hundred sufferings.[14]

There were almost twelve million pairs of haunted eyes in those parts of Europe now being overrun by British and American troops. Many were Germans, fleeing in panic from the Russians or made homeless by allied bombing and shelling. But the vast majority were victims of the Nazis' massive uprooting of Europeans from their native countries for racial, ideological or economic reasons. While some had moved voluntarily to Germany in search of work, most had been forcibly transported to labor for the Nazi war effort in factories and on farms.

Known as "displaced persons," or DPs, this witches' cauldron of the desperate and the dispossessed proved a headache to the advancing armies. They blocked roads, demanded to be fed and housed, and frequently vented their anger and desperation in bouts of looting and rioting. To take care of them, hundreds of trained civil affairs officers accompanied the forces in the field. But this military effort was seen as a purely short-term measure and everyone agreed that sooner rather than later civilians would have to take over. And those civilians already had their own organization. In November 1943, the allies had created a special relief and rehabilitation agency, known as UNRRA (United Nations Relief and Rehabilitation Agency), to deal with just such a problem.

At least, that was the plan. But the well-meant intent behind it quickly ran into some unyielding realities. The agency was ill-organized, lacked experienced and competent staff, and was severely short of equipment—above all, its own transport and supplies. Of the two hundred teams requested by the military for use early in 1945, only eight were produced, and in the parts of Germany liberated by the British Army, UNRRA's task was often taken over by the Red Cross. But in the American zone—where the vast majority of the DPs were located—UNRRA eventually managed to field a few dozen teams.

This stuttering effort was dismally apparent at UNRRA's training center near Granville in Normandy. The town was a gray and austere old fortress on the west coast of the Cotentin Peninsula facing the Channel Islands, which were still occupied by the Germans in the spring of 1945. Headquartered in the city's grand old Hotel Normandie, the center did not open until early March, and was both badly administered and located disconcertingly far from where its task was most urgent.

In fact, it was almost abandoned even before it began work. Hardly had the advance team arrived than the Germans launched a daring commando raid on the town from the Channel Islands. They stayed for only thirty minutes, but in that time they succeeded in killing about twenty allied officers and men and capturing fifteen prisoners. Four of these came from the UNRRA team.[15]

UNRRA survived this assault, but to the many relief workers from Britain and across Europe who had enthusiastically volunteered to work with the war's human wreckage Granville proved a dispiriting and frustrating place. Day after day they scanned the noticeboards in vain, hoping to learn they had been assigned to a team for immediate dispatch to Germany. Meanwhile, the newspapers were filled with reports describing desperate scenes such as those being witnessed by Bryan Samain that cried out for action.

One of the relief workers waiting at Granville was a slight, dark-haired Englishwoman in her fifties with blue eyes, aquiline features and a voice like a rusty saw. Francesca Wilson was a veteran in helping the human debris of Europe's twentieth-century upheavals. She had worked with Serbian refugees during the First World War, fed starving children in post-war Vienna, looked after Russian émigrés fleeing the Bolsheviks, assisted victims of the civil war in Spain, and given shelter in her own home to exiles from Hitler's Germany. "The main force driving me," she explained, "has been first of all a desire for adventure and new experience and later on a longing for an activity that would take me out of myself, out of the all too bookish world I had lived in when studying, and even when teaching."[16]

There was plenty in her life and background to escape from. Born on New Year's Day 1889 to a Quaker family in Newcastle-upon-Tyne, her father ran the family-owned hatter's furrier's factory down on the quayside by the River Tyne, a dark, smelly and fortress-like building that always frightened Francesca. It was full of ragged women sitting on benches and shouting or singing in loud voices while they stripped the rough hair from rabbits' skins.

She had two older sisters and a younger brother, and the family was prosperous enough, but her parents led an austere, pious and thrifty life. "Every penny was accounted for," she recalled, "and not a farthing spent in self-indulgence. They smoked no tobacco, drank no strong drink, walked to their work and to meetings or took a twopenny bus." To the end of his life, her father took a cold bath each morning, and every Sunday he handed out slabs of chocolate to the inmates of the nearby Workhouse Hospital.

Like most Quakers of the day, he was an ardent Liberal and supporter of Gladstone as well as a convinced pacifist and internationalist. The only time Francesca ever saw him angry was at the time of the relief of Mafeking, when British troops broke the siege of the town by the Boers. The children's governess had bought them Union Jack flags, red, white and blue sweets, and colored portraits of Generals Buller,

Kitchener and Roberts. "Bursting with chauvinistic pride," she recalled, "we decorated the breakfast room and prepared to eat our patriotic sweets." But at that very moment her father entered the room, swept away all the trophies, and furiously flung the pictures and flags into the fire.

The family house itself was stern, dark and typically Victorian. A three-story stone building standing high on a quiet avenue with a magnificent view over the Tyne Valley and the hills beyond, it included six bedrooms, a schoolroom, and a top-floor nursery that stretched the full length of the house. The rooms were gloomy and claustrophobic, with heavy carpets and curtains, and lace hanging over the windows. There was much heavy furniture and many pictures in gold frames. The Wilsons enjoyed the services of a cook, a housemaid, a weekly char for the washing, and an occasional gardener.

When Francesca was only four years old her mother "defected" to the Plymouth Brethren, an even more strict and severe order whose followers believed in the literal truth of the Bible and abhorred any notion of evolution. After that, Mrs. Wilson became a more pious and religious figure than before, determined to keep her children as cloistered and as far away from worldly temptations as she could. The result was that, until the age of thirteen, Francesca was educated at home by a governess, who was also a member of the Brethren. But finally, at her father's insistence, she was sent to the leading girls' grammar school in the city. Here, the seeds of religious doubt grew rapidly. She had always been a bright and curious girl with little time for traditional feminine fripperies and soon she was going off by herself to the city's Literary and Philosophical Institute to drink in lectures about Dante and other writers, or taking long solitary walks in the rain to contemplate her loss of religious faith. Her father, she recalled, rarely read a book.

At eighteen, she won a place at Newnham College as one of a small and elite group of female students at Cambridge. Life in the university town offered her a stimulating new world of experience and intellectual discovery. Her best friend was an atheist and, even though chaperoned, she was able to meet fascinating men of her own age with whom she could talk frankly about life and the world.

After her First World War work with refugees, she spent most of the interwar years as the senior history mistress at a school in Birmingham. But here, too, she chafed at her restricted life and wanted more. She had had at least one passionate affair during her years in Europe but had no desire to be tied down in a marriage. Instead, she created a family by giving shelter to a succession of homeless exiles. Most were Russian refugees from the Bolsheviks, and she adopted one of these, Misha Sokolov, as her son. Others were Germans who had fled the Nazis, including the future distinguished architectural historian Nikolaus Pevsner.

After war broke out in 1939, she seized the chance to resume her front-line work with refugees and journeyed to Hungary to help Poles and Czechs who had fled their countries after the Nazi or Soviet takeovers. She documented these experiences in a book entitled *In the Margins of Chaos*.

This was the unpredictable terrain in which she flourished. "Like many spirited and capable people," wrote her distinguished contemporary, the historian J.L. Hammond, "she enjoys flinging herself in situations that demand a high degree of resourcefulness, presence of mind, and the power of quick and effective action."[17]

Francesca, as even her best friends admitted, was not the most practical of people, but she was creative and imaginative, and possessed boundless reserves of energy. Now, in Granville, she was impatient to get working. Every so often her face would break into a warm and welcoming smile. She loved being back in Europe and mixing with people from different nationalities, and she found it exhilarating talking with people who had worked so hard to see their countries freed from the Nazis. Only a year before, the Hotel Normandie, with its spacious terrace overlooking the sea, had been occupied by Wehrmacht troops, their laundry being washed and their meals cooked by the staff that were now looking after the UNRRA teams. Victory, she could see, was taking visible shape.

One by one, she met her fellow volunteers. Spending time in Granville didn't bother her as much as it did the others. She was well aware of the center's imperfections, but had already done most of her training in England so they hardly bothered her. For now, she was happy making friends and hearing accounts of life under German occupation. She was keen to liberate the deportees from enemy territory and get them back home. An adventure lay ahead, and she was looking forward to it.[18]

On this April Friday, too, a Canadian soldier named Reginald Roy was on the edge of the IJsselmeer — or what the Dutch used to call the

Zuider Zee, or South Sea, to distinguish it from the North Sea, before they drained most of it dry. Canadian troops had reached the small community of Hoorst the day before after a rapid advance westward from Arnhem to cut the German forces in Holland in two.

It was a day of beautiful spring weather. The tulip fields were a mass of color and the grass tall, green and lush. There was no resistance as the Canadians rounded up fifty German prisoners without a single casualty. After almost a week of non-stop advance, sometimes up to twenty-five miles a day, it was time for a rest. Sleep came first, then the portable showers were brought in, weapons and vehicles were inspected, cleaned and repaired, and mail was distributed. Most of the men also seized the chance to write home with letters of their own. Receiving and sending mail was a fantastic morale booster and the army set a high priority on delivering it. Sometimes it was even brought to the men as they lay in slit trenches just yards away from the enemy.

Roy was a twenty-two-year-old second lieutenant in the Cape Breton Highlanders, one of the many regiments fighting with the First Canadian Army that formed the left-hand flank of Montgomery's advance into Germany. He had even met the great British hero of El Alamein. It had happened a few weeks previously, during one of the prearranged publicity stunts so loved by the image-conscious British commander. Irreverently, Roy and his buddies referred to him as "God Almonty." They had been warned he was coming and coached about what to do: they would be scattered in groups alongside the road, and as the great man passed in his jeep they would "spontaneously" and simultaneously raise a cheer and wave their helmets. Well in advance, Roy's company was trucked to the chosen site, the vehicles were tucked away out of sight, and then he drilled his men thoroughly in their cheering.

When Monty duly arrived on schedule, the Canadians performed so well that he suddenly stopped in front of Roy and fired a barrage of questions at him. Where was he stationed? How long had he been there? When did he join up? Then he asked the average age of the men. Making a lightning guess, Roy replied, "Twenty-five, sir." Delighted, Monty replied that this was exactly what he had hoped, before speeding off again along the road for more orchestrated stops.

But now, Reg was quickly devouring the three letters from his sister Joannie that were waiting for him. Then, in turn, he brought her up to date with an aerogram—a single sheet of thin blue paper that he folded in four, leaving just a small space to write her address. Two days earlier, the Cape Bretoners had liberated Barneveld in the central Netherlands, an agricultural town of a few thousand people. "What a welcome," he enthused. "The town went mad — completely mad — with joy . . . Huge bands of men and women marched through the streets, arms linked and ten to fourteen abreast, singing their national anthem over and over. People everywhere were laughing, singing, shouting for joy. We were mobbed with kindness."

Reg was overwhelmed by the abundant gratitude of the Dutch people. At one point he stopped at a house to brew himself some tea. When he asked the owner, an elderly woman, if she would care to join him, she dissolved into tears. "You can't imagine," he told his sister, "how good it makes you feel to bring such happiness to so many!"

The Highlanders, though, were not all about bringing joy; in fact, they were a notoriously rough-edged outfit. Recruited mostly from miners, fishermen, steelworkers and farmers from Cape Breton Island in Nova Scotia, on Canada's harsh Atlantic coastline, they were a clannish bunch likely to resent anyone "from away," meaning not born on the island. Most had recent Scottish or Irish ancestry, and a few were even Gaelic-speaking. Not for nothing was their Maple Leaf cap badge emblazoned with the Gaelic words: "Stol Na Fearail" — "the Breed of Manly Men."

Roy's own grandfather had left Scotland in the 1850s and arrived in Nova Scotia as a miner. His father had been a First World War sniper and pilot. But even with such a tough and military background, Roy found the men often hard to handle. "Out of the line," he noted ruefully, "they were restless. Many liked the bottle a bit too much . . . and were somewhat quarrelsome." Sectarian Catholic and Protestant rivalries also lay close to the surface and could often erupt abruptly and violently. But when they were well led, they proved fearsome fighters.

Not surprisingly, given their heritage, the Cape Bretoners were famous for their music. The day after liberating Barneveld, they piped their way through the streets followed again by an enormous crowd of enthusiastic townspeople.

For the Dutch everywhere, the arrival of the Canadians brought to an end five years of detested occupation and a regime that became harsher and more intolerable as time passed. Men were forcibly deported to Germany for labor, and underground resistance steadily grew. Increasingly savage reprisals and executions followed. Worse, a significant minority of the population actively collaborated with the Germans.

Liberation sparked spontaneous punishment of the guilty and a rough justice that caught many innocents in its grip. Resistance fighters, now free to emerge into the open and wearing their red, white and blue armbands, sped around the town on bicycles rounding up collaborators. Women who had slept with German soldiers had their hair shaved, were paraded around the streets and were slapped around by other women. A few local Dutch Nazis changed into civilian clothes and tried to slip out of town, but they were caught and forced to crawl on their hands and knees through the main streets to the prison, where they were shot.

Roy saw all of this with his own eyes. Never short of initiative, he promptly commandeered the apartment of one of the Nazis, including the sixteen-year-old maid, and made himself comfortable. Then, exhausted by the week's fighting, he fell deeply asleep.[19]

Also on 20 April, but to the southeast, troops of the United States First Army entered Leipzig in Saxony, Germany's fifth-largest city and a major industrial center. Here, Martin Luther had preached his first sermon, Johann Sebastian Bach lay buried, and Richard Wagner was baptized. The city was also the site of one of Germany's most famous historic memorials, the massive three-hundred-foot stone monument built to celebrate the Battle of the Nations won against Napoleon's forces after his retreat from Moscow.

Here, too, SS troops now fought on to the bitter end, some of them retreating into the cavernous base of the monument for a desperate firefight with the Americans. When the battle for the city was over, the GIs took some twelve thousand prisoners. At the Town Hall, they uncovered a macabre Wagnerian scene. In the Council Chamber, sprawled dead over tables with blood on the floor, lay three members of the *Volkssturm*, the German Home Guard. They had shot themselves. Next to one of them stood a half-empty bottle of cognac.

Upstairs, in the Lord Mayor's luxuriously furnished oak-paneled office, they discovered an even more grisly spectacle. Slumped dead over his paper-strewn desk, his hands sprawled out on the blotting pad in front of him and an empty bottle beside him, lay Lord Mayor Alfred Freyberg. Facing the dead man on the wall was a large oil-painting of Hitler. Beneath it, spread-eagled on her back across a large leather sofa, lay the body of Freyberg's wife, her head on the armrest and her feet stretched out on the floor as though she were taking a nap. In an adjacent armchair lay their dead eighteen-year-old daughter.

Three days before, they had all taken poison after a somber last supper, when it was obvious that the end had come to their Nazi dreams. At about ten o'clock, they went down to the cellar restaurant below the Town Hall and enjoyed champagne and sandwiches with a local high-ranking Nazi. Suddenly, Freyberg announced that they could not possibly survive the occupation of the city and formulated the suicide pact. When the shocked official protested that this was akin to deserting Germany in its hour of need, Freyberg simply shrugged his shoulders. "It's all over," he said, "Germany is beaten forever." At midnight, he and his family went up to his office, locked the door, and carried out the pact.

Behind a closed door leading from the Mayor's office the Americans found three more bodies: those of the City Treasurer, his wife, and their daughter, still wearing her nurse's uniform. They, too, had taken poison. Outside, in an anteroom, lay the body of another *Volkssturm* member who had killed himself. Twenty- and fifty-mark notes lay scattered around his corpse.

Just outside the city, the Americans discovered a small concentration camp. The day before, SS guards had herded its three hundred inmates into one of the wooden barracks, doused it with petrol, and set it alight with grenades. Those who tried to escape from the blaze were shot. The buildings were still smoldering and corpses festooned the barbed-wire perimeter when the GIs arrived. Following what by now was becoming a grimly familiar routine across Germany, the city's new burgermeister was ordered to supply caskets for the dead and to find people to dig the graves. He was also instructed to provide a cross and a wreath for each grave, and all city officials were required to attend the funerals, along with a hundred other prominent citizens. Several hundred DPs dropped flowers on the graves, as did some of the several hundred Germans who voluntarily joined the ceremony.[20]

But the caretaker who had shown the Americans round the Town Hall seemed unmoved by all the deaths. When they had seen enough, he had simply locked the doors behind them and walked down the stairs. A little later, Hitler heard of the Mayor's suicide pact and baldly declared it a "cowardly evasion of responsibility."[21]

*

As British troops nudged forwards to the suburbs of Bremen and Hamburg in northern Germany, Hitler's birthday saw US forces enter Nuremberg in the south.

Hitler had made Nazism a secular religion with himself as God and Nuremberg as its holy shrine. All six Nazi Party Rallies of the Third Reich had been held there, vast ritualized spectacles that were immortalized in Leni Riefenstahl's famous documentary, *Triumph of the Will*. At first lasting four days, then extending to eight, each September they were attended by a quarter of a million people drawn from all over Germany and from every sector of German society. Some fifty thousand were members of the Hitler Youth or the German Girls' League. Two thousand of them walked several hundred miles on a grueling "Adolf Hitler March" to reach the city.

The Rallies saw endless parades, displays of mass calisthenics, continuous music and singing, gala performances of Wagner, solemn ceremonies to honor the party's "martyrs" killed in the failed 1923 Munich *putsch*, and military exercises. Their dramatic high point came on the evening of the "Day of the Political Leaders." As darkness fell and 100,000 spectators took their seats, 110,000 men marched onto the review field and the space was suddenly lit by a ring of lights illuminating thousands of fluttering party banners. Then, at the instant Hitler entered the arena, one hundred and fifty searchlights shot their beams vertically into the night sky to produce a vast "cathedral of light." It was, said one overawed spectator, "solemn and beautiful . . . like being inside a cathedral of ice."[22]

Hitler had deliberately selected Nuremberg because it was a virtually intact walled medieval city with a castle. Unsullied by modernism, it thus linked the Nazi Party with German history stretching back to the First Reich of the Middle Ages. The city, declared its Nazi Lord Mayor proudly, was the "most German of all German cities." To emphasize the point, after the 1938 Anschluss with Austria, Hitler had the regalia of the old Holy Roman Empire — including Charlemagne's bejeweled prayer book and several scepters and orbs — brought back to the city from Vienna, to which they had been removed in 1794 to save them from the marauding armies of Revolutionary France.

It was to Nuremberg, too, that the German Reichstag was summoned during the 1935 Rally to pass the infamous, anti-Semitic "Nuremberg Laws" that deprived Germany's Jews of their basic civil rights and proclaimed illegal — through the "Law for the Protection of

German Blood and German Honor"—all marriages between Germans and Jews. (This law was extended the next year to encompass Roma, Sinti and non-whites.) The city was also home to the Sturmer Publishing House, owned by Julius Streicher, a radical anti-Semite and one-time local Nazi Party Gauleiter (district party leader). His newspaper, *Der Stürmer*, had a circulation of hundreds of thousands and spewed out a diet of undiluted hatred against the Jews. "If one really wants to put an end to the continued prospering of this curse from heaven that is Jewish blood," wrote Streicher on Christmas Day 1941, "there is only one way to do it: to eradicate this people, this Satan's son, root and branch."[23]

The walled city was far too small for the enormous Rally crowds, so in 1934 Albert Speer, Hitler's favorite architect, had been commissioned to design a vast complex of buildings and parade grounds on the southeast edge of the city. Eventually covering some eleven acres, it included the Luitpold Arena, capable of holding some 150,000 people, the Congress Hall, seating 50,000, and the vast Zeppelin Field. This last was designed by Speer personally and was modeled on the Pergamon Altar. With a spectators' tribune some three hundred meters long crowned by a gilded copper swastika, it held some hundred thousand people. A special railway station was constructed close by to deliver the vast crowds to its entrance. Nearby, a sprawling wooden city of halls, open-air theaters, bowling alleys and carousels was built for the Nazi organization *Kraft durch Freude* (Strength through Joy).

In all, the Rally grounds with their vast monumental buildings symbolized the two great, powerful myths of the Third Reich: first that of the Führer—the idea that Hitler was an instrument of Providence sent to save the German people; second, that of the *Volksgemeinschaft*, or national community, founded on shared feelings and experiences. The buildings were all designed so that Hitler would be the sole focus of attention and elevated well above the crowds. The central axis of the complex—the two-thousand-yard-long and sixty-yard-wide "Great Road"—was deliberately aligned by Speer with the city's castle and old town. This again symbolically linked the Rallies, the Nazi Party and the Third Reich with the historic German past.[24]

The shrine-like significance of Nuremberg to Hitler and the Nazis was not lost on allied propagandists. Newspapers, especially in the United States, made much of its impending capture, as did the US Army. "In view of its ranking position as Nazi Circus Town," noted one

US Army map of the city, "its importance cannot be exaggerated." By the time of Hitler's birthday, two-thirds of its 450,000 population had fled, 90 percent of the ancient city lay in ruins, and of its 65 listed artistic monuments, 32 had been completely destroyed and another 18 badly damaged.

But the local Gauleiter promised Hitler that he would fight to the death and there followed a grueling four-day battle. The city's medieval half-timbered streets had already been largely obliterated and burned by allied bombers, with the heaviest raids taking place a few weeks earlier. Over six thousand people were killed and over three hundred thousand made homeless by the bombardments. Now, though, the city's anti-aircraft guns were directed against the US infantrymen on the ground. Disguised as a house painter, Julius Streicher had fled three days before from his home in nearby Steinbach in a limousine driven by his wife followed by a truckload of personal belongings, leaving behind him an extensive library on Jewry, including hundreds of volumes in English. Streicher's successor as Gauleiter of Franconia, as well as the Lord Mayor of the city, were both eventually found dead in Gestapo headquarters, where they had killed themselves.

The Americans faced hand-to-hand fighting through rubbled houses and cellars before finally breaching the old city walls. The next day, in the battered ruins of the Adolf Hitler Platz in the heart of the city, they raised Old Glory while a military band played "The Stars and Stripes Forever." Out on the Rally grounds sprawled a handful of dead Hitler Youth and *Volkssturm* conscripts who had attempted a futile last-ditch resistance. "Over the vast stadium," announced Universal Studio's weekly newsreel shown in cinemas across America, "Old Glory overshadows one of the world's most hated symbols. Here, where once thousands of swastikas flew above goose-stepping troops parading before the Führer, and where he ranted to the assembled thousands, the troops Hitler once laughed at take over."

In the wrecked city, order was only slowly restored. Few city employees took any notice of the order to return to work broadcast from loudspeakers mounted on the back of US Army trucks as they snaked and bumped their way along the narrow tracks cleared through the rubble.

Meanwhile, German civilians and freed forced laborers alike happily looted warehouses stacked with food, undeterred by the two hundred streetcar conductors drafted in by the Americans to act as temporary policemen. Reports of rape and robbery by GIs piled up on the desk of the army's public safety officer. A few days later, watched by a legion of war reporters from around the world, the swastika over the Zeppelin Field was dynamited into smithereens by American troops.[25]

CHAPTER TWO

"SORROW AND DARKNESS"

Hitler's war was fought not just on the battlefield. It was a struggle he waged against enemies wherever he found them. As a totalitarian ideology, Nazism had everyone in its sights, and its opponents were nowhere more obvious and threatening than at home. If Germany was to be renewed, believed Hitler, then he must first eliminate the internal forces he blamed for the catastrophe of the nation's defeat in 1918. This primarily meant the Jews, the Bolsheviks, socialists, liberals, democrats—the list was easily expandable. Since 1933, he had been steadily "cleansing" the Third Reich of these groups' influence with his racial laws and relentless political persecution. Those designated as hostile, alien or degenerate were thrown into prisons or concentration camps, dozens of which had sprung up across Germany since his seizure of power. Since the outbreak of war and Germany's occupation of most of Europe, their population had expanded into hundreds of thousands. Millions of Jews had been shot in mass killings or murdered in extermination camps, such as Auschwitz-Birkenau, Treblinka and Sobibor.

The concentration camps were run by the SS. Its head, Heinrich Himmler, claimed they existed to reeducate their prisoners, who were invariably depicted as criminal, along the paths of obedience, self-sacrifice and "love of the Fatherland." In reality, they were little more than licensed centers of brutality and terror, designed to isolate and break the spirits of their inmates.[1] By April 1945, they had become places of unspeakable atrocity as food ran scarce, disease became rampant, and arbitrary violence and killings took hold. Their existence was no secret; indeed, the SS had been glad to use their reputation as a weapon to terrorize the population into submission. But outside their barbed-wire perimeters, no one had any inkling of the full scale of the horrors that were about to be exposed.

The ancient, small town of Dachau lies about twelve miles northwest of Munich. For centuries it was favored by Bavarian princes as a summer residence, and in the eighteenth century they remodeled its medieval castle into a grand royal palace. By the end of the following century, the town had also become a flourishing artists' colony, a welcome refuge from the noisy streets of Munich.

But this serenity was soon to be broken by the First World War, when the voracious demands of the Kaiser's armies led to the construction of a large munitions plant on the outskirts of the town. After the war ended with the drastic disarmament clauses of the Treaty of Versailles, the factory was closed down. Its acreage became a forlorn and abandoned site crying out for some new development. Salvation arrived just two months after Hitler came to power. On 21 March 1933, Heinrich Himmler announced that it had been chosen as the location of a detention camp for "the enemies of National Socialism."

Dachau was the first of what, over the next twelve years, was to become a vast empire of Nazi prison camps. Its early inmates were members of the German Social Democratic and Communist parties, but soon they were joined by thousands of others deemed enemies of the Reich, such as Jehovah's Witnesses, gypsies, clergymen and homosexuals. After Kristallnacht in 1938, some ten thousand Jews were also shipped there, although most of them were released after a few weeks. Once the war began, the numbers were swelled by such groups as resistance fighters from across occupied Europe, anti-Nazi German émigrés captured in Paris, Amsterdam or Prague, gypsies, Polish priests and dissident Wehrmacht officers.

By April 1945, over two hundred thousand prisoners had passed through its gates, and more than thirty thousand had died. In addition, and unrecorded in its otherwise meticulously kept records, tens of thousands of Russian prisoners of war had been shot en masse. Dachau also played host to medical experiments on live prisoners, such as measuring the effects of rapid decompression and freezing temperatures on the human body.

As Hitler's empire collapsed, the camp ultimately provided a dumping ground for prisoners from other concentration camps. The already appalling conditions deteriorated sharply. By the time of Hitler's birthday, the daily ration for inmates was down to six hundred calories—a starvation diet—and typhus had taken hold; two hundred prisoners were dying from the disease every day. Just the week before, Himmler had told the camp's commander that there was to be no surrender to allied forces. The prisoners were to be evacuated, he ordered, and on no account were any of them to fall into the hands of the enemy.

The camp now held seventy thousand inmates, none of whom knew if they would survive these last few days of the war. Among them was a blue-eyed, twenty-six-year-old German named Fey von Hassell. A few short years before, she could never have imagined she would end up behind the camp's barbed-wire perimeter. After all, she was a child of privilege. Her father, Ulrich von Hassell, was one of Germany's most urbane and distinguished diplomats, with a career stretching back to the days of the Kaiser. He had been posted to Rome as German Ambassador only weeks before the Nazi seizure of power and stayed there until 1938, when he was dismissed by Joachim von Ribbentrop, Hitler's foreign minister, for criticizing Nazi policy towards Britain.

In Rome, Fey had enjoyed all the pleasures of an ambassador's daughter, with an endless round of society balls and glittering parties. In the Villa Wolkonsky, the German Embassy, she had had a beautiful bedroom all to herself. "It has a lovely balcony overlooking the garden," she wrote in her diary. "I feel like a princess!"[2]

But her fate was inextricably tied to her father's. Like many other conservatives and nationalists committed to rebuilding a powerful Germany by reversing the terms of the Treaty of Versailles, he had deluded himself that Hitler could be controlled. So, when his own party, the right-wing DNVP, was dissolved in 1933, he had joined the Nazis. Unlike some other senior German diplomats, he had also stayed at his post.

Yet, long before his dismissal, he had become disgusted with the barbarities of the regime and seriously alarmed by the march to war. On leaving Rome, he linked up with conservative opposition groups, and later in his secret diary railed at the Nazis' persecution of the Jews, the euthanasia program against the handicapped and insane, the savagery of the war in the East, and the general barbarity that now ruled his country. This did not prevent the émigré novelist Thomas Mann from judging him harshly: von Hassell, declared Mann, was "one of the people who should never have served the Nazis and yet who did so out of ambition, cynicism, or ignorance. Too late did they regain their sight."[3]

Perhaps aware of this responsibility, von Hassell also drew close to the conspiracy that culminated in the July 1944 plot by army officers to assassinate Hitler with a bomb planted beneath the conference table at his military headquarters at Rastenberg in East Prussia. The device exploded but failed to kill its target. Nazi retribution was savage and widespread. Colonel Claus von Stauffenberg, the man who planted the bomb, was executed along with dozens of other plotters. Thousands more across Germany suspected of anti-Hitler sympathies were arrested by the Gestapo and sent to camps. Organized opposition to the regime — and with it any hope of ridding Germany of Hitler through internal revolt — was crushed.[4]

News of the bomb plot had filtered through to Fey in Friuli, the region of northeast Italy bordering Yugoslavia. By this time she was married to a young Italian aristocrat, Detalmo Pirzio-Biroli, and was living on his family's estate at Brazzà, close to the snow-covered peaks of the Dolomite Mountains, not far from Udine. His family had an ancient and distinguished lineage: Brazzaville, capital of the Congo, took its name from his grandfather's brother, the explorer Count Detalmo Savorgnan di Brazzà; while his grandmother was the American heiress Cora Slocomb. The estate had been in the family's hands for almost a thousand years.[5]

A few days before the wedding, Detalmo had written Fey a special letter:

> I begin my life as the happiest man on earth . . . As for you, my darling love, I wish you good luck with all my heart! You are leaving your glorious family and your people to follow me! You are coming away with me to a house that is dull [and] empty . . . You are marrying a young man who still has everything to do! Who can present you with absolutely nothing: no cozy home, not much money, no advanced career, really nothing . . . You face the unknown! I understand all this very well, Fey, and I admire you so.[6]

When he wrote these words, he could have had no idea how immense the unknown that she faced was to become.

Brazzà boasted forty-eight rooms and had a little chapel in the grounds. The family always spent the summers there, and here its members were born, married and buried. Fey thought of it now as her home, too. It was, as Detalmo said, "like a huge old hen protecting us with its broad wings." She loved it, especially amid the turmoil of war. "It is standing on a hill far from all the troubles and worries of the world," she wrote to her mother when she first caught a glimpse of the villa surrounded by shaded marble seats, gravel paths and cypress and pine trees. All around lay the vast Friuli Plain, studded with brilliant white houses and poplars that stretched far into the distance. "On one side you look down over a great plain towards Venice," she enthused. "On the other you can see the mountains, still topped with snow."

But a few years later, in the aftermath of the bomb plot, the troubles of the world finally sought her out. Evidence of an active opposition exhilarated her, and at first she pushed aside worries about her father. "The names of the men who had been executed, published in the papers, were all too familiar to me," she wrote. "Even though they were mainly army officers at that point, many were friends of my father. Maybe, I thought, the 'civilian' opposition groups had not been discovered."[7]

Letters from her mother continued to arrive from Germany, but they made no reference to the plot—naturally enough, for everyone knew that mail were heavily scrutinized by the Gestapo. Fey was not overly worried, although several references to "one great preoccupation" concerned her. Nevertheless, when she heard no bad news, she assumed that if her father had been involved, he had not been found out.

However, an undercurrent of worry persisted, especially as she had no one to reassure her. She had hardly seen Detalmo for months. After the fall of Mussolini in 1943, Italy had signed an armistice with the allies. That same day, Detalmo had quit the Italian Army to go underground and work with the resistance in Rome, his native city. As the Germans flooded the north of Italy with troops, his last gesture of defiance had been to throw open the gates of the prisoner-of-war camp he was guarding and allow thousands of allied soldiers to escape into the surrounding countryside.

Now Fey heard from him only through occasional letters. As they had agreed in advance for security's sake, he signed them either "Isabella" or "Giuseppe." Sometimes, though, he was able to arrange for a letter to be delivered by hand to her personally at Brazzà by a resistance fighter. On those occasions he wrote frankly. In December 1943 he had written in English, their common language, to tell her what he was doing for the resistance, which was mostly working with contacts abroad and writing propaganda to be circulated in America about the Italy he hoped to see emerge from the war.

To Detalmo, as to others in the resistance, victory would see a rebirth comparable to the great nineteenth-century Risorgimento inspired by Garibaldi. "My darling," he'd concluded,

> I love you, and you stand out in my thoughts as something extremely great and important in life. I would like to be with you and try to console you a little. This is a great revolution, like the other great ones in history. We must make the new world. Let us only think of this difficult task and especially that we are going to work *together* with the children under the blessing of our great love. Put all other mournful thoughts aside.[8]

But building new worlds was easier said than done. To make matters worse, Brazzà itself had been requisitioned by the Germans. First, a regiment of the SS took it over, and when they left, officers of the German Army's Corps of Engineers arrived. Only after fierce bargaining had Fey got them to agree that she and the boys could use three of the rooms on the first floor. Life became increasingly difficult and stressful. To get through the weeks and months of unaccustomed isolation, she had to draw on all her inner strength.

She was a German living in occupied Italy, where anti-German feeling was rising in leaps and bounds. Daily, she had to negotiate with the officers about tiresome but essential details regarding domestic affairs and the running of the estate. Beyond its gates, Italian partisans were growing in number and daring. They roamed around the countryside, descended on villages and houses to demand or steal food, sniped at German soldiers, and provoked sometimes brutal retaliation against the peasants.

Fey did not have much time for them, believing that a lot of what they did was stupid or counterproductive. Taking pot-shots at German soldiers was easy compared to the far more dangerous and useful work of blowing up bridges and roads, she thought; and it provoked more reprisals.

Behind her reaction lay the knowledge that her brother Hans Dieter was serving with the Wehrmacht in France. He had been seriously wounded fighting against the Russians and was now adjutant to one of the leading generals in occupied Paris, where the French resistance had also begun killing German soldiers. He had visited Brazzà a few months before and had been able to jolly along the officers who were occupying the house, which made things easier for a time. Then, after eight short and wonderful days, he had returned to Paris.

After he left, Fey felt more alone than ever. On several occasions she dealt with pleas from the local populace to intercede to prevent someone being shot or deported. To help, she tried her best to keep on decent terms with the local SS. From time to time she even invited the Udine representative of its security service, a Major Alvensleben, whose family was known to her parents, to tea at Brazzà, and once she successfully talked him into rescinding a deportation order against one of the locals. As a result of these tactics, she was accused of being too cozy with the hated occupiers.

Negotiating her way through the political minefield that had become Brazzà was exhausting. In a rare letter she managed to have delivered by hand to her mother, she wrote:

> The partisans have put me on their blacklist, because they say I'm too friendly with the Germans. On the other hand the local people appreciate me because they know that I help when I can. However, that is only useful to me when dealing with Italian partisans. If the Slavic ones [i.e., Tito's communist partisans from Yugoslavia] should arrive, they will not ask how I behaved or what I did . . . I'm rather at a loss.[9]

The only real comfort she found in this crash course on female independence was with her sons, Corrado, aged three and a half, and Roberto, who was eighteen months younger. She and Detalmo had planned to wait until the war was over to have children, yet Corrado's unexpected arrival in November 1940 had given her quiet satisfaction. His brother's arrival had been less welcome. "It must be the supreme spell of Nature," Detalmo resignedly told his mother-in-law, "which evidently wants to fight death with life." But Fey had quickly adjusted and adored them both: "They are all my joy in uncertain times," she wrote to Detalmo in one of her secret letters. However, even this small oasis of family happiness was to be snatched away from her.

On Saturday, 9 September 1944 Fey was lying in bed. It was 7 a.m. Suddenly there was a knock at the door. Outside stood Lieutenant Hans Kretschmann, the twenty-three-year-old aide-de-camp to Colonel Dannenberg, the officer in charge of the contingent billeted in the house. Fey deeply distrusted him. "Educated by the Nazis and soaked in their propaganda," she recorded, he "lacked flexibility of thought. I do not believe he had a single independent idea in his head. His opinions had been learned in school, in the Hitler Youth, and at military college." His only apparent weakness was a tendency towards melancholia, which he would drown out by drinking. Sometimes, other officers informed her, he'd leap on the table after dining and tap dance "like a man possessed to the wild applause of his audience."[10]

Yet it was a cold and indifferent Kretschmann who now stood in front of her. His face was ashen, and she could read fear in his eyes.

"For heaven's sake what's happened?" she asked irritably as he stood there saying nothing.

"Luckily you are still at home."

"Why shouldn't I be?" she asked.

"You didn't listen to the radio last night or early this morning?"

"No," she answered. "How could I? I have guests; they're still asleep next door. What has happened?"

Without any more preliminaries Kretschmann threw his response in her face. "Your father has been arrested and executed. He has been hanged."[11]

All the self-control Fey had been brought up with was mustered at that instant. Only her body betrayed her as she began to shake. Like most people confronted with shocking news, her mind seemed to close down and focus on the immediate and practical. She asked her guests to depart at once and, as they left, hid some of her diaries in their pockets. If the SS needed any proof of her own anti-Nazi feelings, they would find it in her diaries.

At ten o'clock, a Gestapo official, along with Colonel Dannenberg, arrived to take her to Udine. It was the colonel who had informed the secret police that von Hassell's daughter was living at Brazzà. He looked duly embarrassed and guilty, mouthing apologetic words of condolence. She asked her maids to take the children to their rooms so they would not see her being taken away. As she was led to the waiting car, members of the estate's staff silently watched, frightened and weeping.

They drove to the Gestapo headquarters in Udine in silence, too. There, after some discussion, it was decided to put her in the city prison. The women's section was run by nuns belonging to the order of Ancella della Carita (the Handmaidens of Charity). For years they had been used to handling nothing but common criminals and delinquents, and Fey found their commands "rude and harsh." The Gestapo ordered them to find her a cell to herself, but the prison, built for fifty, now held more than three times that number, and the "politicals" were mixed up haphazardly with the criminals. Some were packed thirty to a room and had to sleep without blankets on wooden boards.

Fey was lucky, though. She was put in a cell with just two other women. Between them they had two iron camp beds and two mattresses, as well as blankets. She was too tired and shocked even to talk to her cellmates. She just slumped down exhausted on one of the beds.

During the lonely months at Brazzà she had begun to pride herself on her power of patient suffering, but quickly she found it being severely tested. There was only one toilet in the whole prison. Twice a day the cells were opened and Fey stood in a long queue awaiting her turn on the filthy, primitive bowl. The cells crawled with insects and buzzed with mosquitoes. All she got to eat each day was a single bowl of disgusting soup.

Meanwhile, the nuns prayed constantly. They prayed in the morning, they prayed before the meal, they prayed after the meal, and they prayed last thing at night. They even prayed during the toilet break, and during the few precious minutes every day when the inmates were let out for exercise in the courtyard. Every morning they all celebrated mass in the tiny chapel. "At least it was a change from being locked up," wrote Fey, who had been brought up as a Protestant. She even recorded that she found the mass quite beautiful.

But she found agonizing the periodic roll-call when the guards would read out the names of the women to be deported to Germany. The prison would fall totally silent, and everyone would wait with dread for their name to be read out. The prisoners unlucky enough to be called would fall to the ground in convulsions and have to be dragged away. It was a frequent reminder to Fey of her father's death, which haunted her waking hours.

Aside from the mass, her only relief came in the form of almost daily visits from one or other of the German officers at Brazzà. Even Kretschmann and Dannenberg appeared, obviously racked with guilt and promising to speak with the SS and get her freed. A long week passed with no news, but after ten days, they succeeded. She could return home until further orders were received.

"I felt like a queen sitting in Kretschmann's car," Fey recalled, "speeding through the countryside under a splendid blue sky. The fresh air, the sun, and the green fields seemed to promise a liberty far greater than I had any hope of obtaining." The children were ecstatic to see her again. Corrado kept hugging her and crawling into her arms, and when she began to cry he shouted, "Mama is crying. Corradino wants to help mama!" Roberto simply rushed crazily from room to room in his excitement. That evening, she said prayers with them before putting them to bed. "Mama must never go away again," Corradino said, "without telling Corrado where she's going and when she is coming back; it's a terrible thing." Elated by the day's events, Fey promised it would never happen again.[12]

But a mere five days later she was woken up again by a knock on the door. This time an officer handed her a letter from Dannenberg. He had unexpectedly been called away to Verona, he explained, but he had been informed that the next day she and the children were to be taken, for the moment, to Innsbruck. He would personally drive them to the station at Udine, where a man in civilian clothes would collect them. "So, Mrs. Pirzio-Biroli," he concluded, "chin up, even if everything is very difficult for you."

Her reaction was despair mixed with anger. Despite the fact she was obviously a marginal figure, had two small children, and was not even living in Germany, she was being sucked into the Nazi terror machine. She had already rejected offers from the resistance to help her escape, mostly because of fears about the reprisals that might fall on her mother, and she now felt angry at herself for turning them down. But she still refused as impractical a last-minute plan by the resistance to attack the train to Innsbruck.

With only twenty-four hours to get ready, family servants stayed up all night busily knitting sweaters for the boys while a local cobbler hurriedly made them shoes. One of the German officers gave her three hundred marks, which he advised her to sew into the lining of her coat. Her baggage consisted mostly of things to eat, including an entire ham and several large salamis.

The news of her transportation quickly spread, and friends and neighbors came with cigarettes, biscuits, tins of meat, tea and condensed milk. That evening more friends came over and they drank some cognac. Before they left she asked them to make sure that Detalmo was told what had happened. She also wrote a hurried note to Lotti, her old governess, who had virtually become one of the family and was living in Rome. After telling her in a few short lines what was happening, she signed it: "Your desperate and worried Fey."[13]

At four o'clock in the morning, while it was still dark, Dannenberg's "big black car," as one of the boys would forever remember it, picked them up and drove them to the station. Here Dannenberg helped carry Fey's suitcase before handing them over to the Gestapo man in civilian clothes. One or two friends came to the station to lend moral support, and Fey burst out weeping. She felt that she was on the verge of losing everything.[14]

After an agonizing wait, the train finally arrived, the Gestapo men led them to a private compartment, and the children fell instantly asleep. The train was slow, they missed a connection, and only the next afternoon did they arrive at Innsbruck. Its Gestapo office was housed in a comfortable villa, but Fey's arrival was far from friendly. "You are the daughter of that criminal whose head we cut off: that dog, that pig! Do you expect to be greeted with kid gloves?" were the first words that greeted her. It was a foretaste of what was to come.

The next day, as Fey was putting the boys down for their afternoon nap, two SS nurses arrived and abruptly took them away. It would be for only a few days, they assured her, and the boys would be kept comfortable and safe in a children's home; meanwhile, the Gestapo wanted to ask her some questions. As calmly as she could, she told the boys: "Mama will follow you very soon, but first you will go for a nice walk." Roberto seemed happy at the idea, but Corrado, sensing that all was not right, began to scream and tried desperately to escape the grip of the nurse. Fey could hear his wailing as it faded away in the distance and she was left alone in the room. She had no idea where they were being taken. Still less did she know what her own fate was to be.

Three weeks later, she found out. An SS officer arrived at the villa and said simply, "We're going on a little trip." "Where to?" she asked. "Silesia," he replied, and her heart sank—this was hundreds of miles away in eastern Germany. "And my children?" she inquired. His response chilled her to the bone. "You've got children?" he asked. "I didn't know that." Nor did he care. That night, as she sat in the chilly Innsbruck railway station between two guards, she wept for her children, abandoned without friends or family in a strange country. She shed tears for herself too, for her father, and for Germany itself, run now by gangsters. It was the most wretched moment in this young twenty-six-year-old's life.

Thereafter, in a nightmare of travels, she was shifted round Germany and the rest of Central Europe like a sack of produce. In a deserted old hotel in the forests of Bohemia, she joined a small group of other prisoners. As soon as she heard their names, she realized they had something in common: they were all relatives of the bomb-plot conspirators. Officially, the SS termed them *Sippenhafte*, or prisoners of kin.

Whatever their ultimate fate, it quickly dawned on Fey that their destinies were now intimately bound up together until the end of the war, or death. Their situation was bizarre—privileged yet precarious. One of the hotel staff politely carried her cases up to her bedroom, which had a pleasant view over the trees. A couple of letters were waiting for her at the reception desk. Outwardly, it seemed as though all was normal and peaceful.

Downstairs, in the paneled old lobby, she quickly got to know the others. They included several relatives of Carl Friedrich Goerdeler, the conservative former Mayor of Leipzig who had been removed by the Nazis and chosen by the conspirators as the head of the post-Hitler government. But the group she was instinctively drawn to was the Stauffenbergs. They included several of Claus von Stauffenberg's cousins, as well as members of his more immediate family. With Mika, the widow of Claus's elder brother Berthold, who had also been executed, she felt an immediate bond. Mika, too, had had her two small children taken away by the SS. Soon, Fey was calling them all by their nicknames and spending most of her time with them. For the first time since being wrenched from her children at Innsbruck, she felt like she had a family again.

Of all the Stauffenbergs, however, she felt closest to Alex, Berthold's twin. "Fey—what a pretty name!" he had exclaimed spontaneously when first meeting her, and she had blushed deep red. He had been arrested while serving with the army in Greece and was still wearing his officer's uniform, but he was no professional soldier. On the contrary, he was an unworldly and melancholy character who had been Professor of Ancient History at the University of Munich. He fitted the stereotype of the vague and untidy academic to perfection, with his hair never properly combed and a gentle dry humor that instantly endeared him to Fey. Smiling, with twinkling eyes, he would sit back in his chair after a meal and refer ironically to their "SS hosts." It always made her laugh.

A few days later she found him reading Dante's *Inferno* in Italian. It was a language he did not know, but he was making sense of it with the help of his Latin and an accompanying English translation. So when Fey decided to offer Italian lessons to others in the group as a way of taking her mind off the children, Alex came along. He picked up the language far quicker than the others, and soon they began taking long walks together, speaking Italian.

It was not long before they were confiding in each other. Alex was still in shock over the execution of his two brothers. In turn, Fey poured out the anguish she felt over Corrado and Roberto, and the grief over her father. Talking with him, she also realized that during her long years in Italy she had become profoundly homesick for Germany. Unlike the Nazis and the SS, Alex personified all that she loved about her native land. Tall and with a handsome profile, he could recite by heart the poems of Goethe, who was her favorite writer. He also wrote poetry himself. The growing friendship between them helped assuage her grief and fear, and gave her some welcome consolation.

Many of the prisoners came from deeply aristocratic families, as did Fey of course, and not just on her father's side. Her mother, Ilse, was the daughter of Admiral von Tirpitz, the mastermind behind Kaiser William II's High Seas Fleet that had contested the naval race with Britain before the First World War. Tirpitz had been a powerful influence on her father, who had absorbed much of the admiral's nationalist fervor.

Ironically for the granddaughter of the man who did so much to turn British opinion against Germany and all things Teutonic, Fey, like many young women of her class, had received some of her education at the blue-chip Cheltenham Ladies' College. She had found England a friendly but strange place stuck in a world more familiar to her grandmother. "We go for long walks through the woods and fields, have picnics in all weather, play tennis, ride bicycles and take afternoon tea on green lawns," she wrote in her diary. "Everyone is kind, although not at all intellectual. I have the feeling," she concluded, "that people in England, living on an island, are very closed." On the other hand, she was impressed by the spirit of democracy she saw in Parliament and everyday life. "I wish we had that, too," she wrote wistfully. "Will Germany and Italy ever be capable of democracy?"[15]

To the Nazis, destroying and humiliating families like the Stauffenbergs and von Hassells was an integral part of their policy of ridding Germany of a reactionary elite that stood in the way of social revolution. "Hitler's speeches are all . . . spiced with sharp attacks on the entire upper class," Ulrich von Hassell had once noted in his diary. "Scum" was the word chosen by Hitler.[16] And Himmler vowed to exterminate *all* the Stauffenbergs after the bomb plot.

Now, only their role as hostages was keeping them alive.

The *Sippenhafte* joined hundreds of thousands of political and other prisoners of the Reich being shuffled endlessly and apparently arbitrarily around a vast closed system of camps. "Dangerous" prisoners who could not be moved were systematically murdered, often just hours or days before allied troops arrived. The Gestapo drew no distinction between Germans or foreigners, and often the victims' crime was no worse than having listened to allied broadcasts.

The rest were continually evacuated in a vain and desperate effort to cover up Nazi crimes — and as a savage act of nihilistic revenge. "If National Socialism is going to be destroyed," Himmler told his doctor in March 1945, "then her enemies and the criminals in the concentration camps shall not have the satisfaction of emerging from our ruins as triumphant conquerors. They shall share in our downfall."[17] Although he quickly backtracked, it was by then far too late to prevent local SS leaders from making lethal decisions on the spot.

In any case, the evacuations almost all became death marches. Even the fittest prisoners had been weakened before they began, and there was little food, poor clothing and no shelter. A low estimate of those who died en route is a quarter of a million. "The marchers, many barefoot in deep snow, were herded about by guards who no longer received orders," writes one historian, "and who shot the exhausted. They also machine-gunned people into the sea, or burned thousands of people in barns, while sometimes taking the most arduous routes so that their captives would die."[18]

Thus, in its end, the Third Reich revealed its true contempt for humanity. Only Himmler's desperate desire to save his own skin and strike a deal with the allies was keeping even the *Sippenhafte* alive. Before Dachau, they first spent two months in Stutthof, a notorious camp outside Danzig (now Gdansk in Poland). Although Fey and the others were nominally privileged and so were housed in special barracks apart from the main body of the camp, they still endured terrible conditions. Stutthof was mostly packed with Poles and Russians and was equipped with a gas chamber that housed one hundred and fifty people at a time.

Fey was not subjected to that, but she did suffer severe malnutrition and cold, and was lucky not to succumb to a deadly typhoid epidemic that swept through the camp. She began to think she might not survive to the end of the war, or see her children again. Alex entered her room each morning and afternoon, bringing wood for the fire. She had done the same for him several weeks before. Exhibiting the proverbial professorial lack of practicality, he had almost cut off his toes while chopping wood and she had visited him frequently during his convalescence. He had shown her some of his poems, which she thought "were simple, in beautiful German, and full of feeling. Even in his weakened state, Alex was becoming more and more a magnet for my wounded emotions."[19]

It was at Stutthof, too, that Alex wrote his first poem to her. "Will you walk with me a little / With me in sorrow and darkness?" it began. Thereafter, through all their misery, they drew even closer together.

The only other comfort came in knowing that Hitler was losing the war. By January 1945, Fey could hear the noise of approaching Russian artillery to the east. But this proved a mixed blessing. The *Sippenhafte* were too valuable to fall into Russian hands, and soon they were heading west. Shipped out of Danzig in below-freezing weather in a cattle truck, several days later they arrived at Buchenwald.

The Ettersberg is a small, thickly wooded hill rising to about 2,500 feet eight miles north of the city of Weimar, the capital of Thuringia. Here, in the eighteenth century, Goethe sought quiet refuge in long, solitary walks among the trees and flowers. Shortly after Hitler came to power, the Nazis chose the Ettersberg as the headquarters of their crack "Death's Head" division of the SS and built a huge concrete barracks for its troops, along with luxurious, half-timbered villas for its officers. Then, in 1937, they began construction of a concentration camp. They called it Buchenwald, or "Beech Forest," so as not to offend the local authorities, who were eager not to be associated with it. Goethe, after all, was being idealized as "the embodiment of the German spirit."

The first prisoners to arrive came as transfers from the Sachsenhausen concentration camp close to Berlin. Mostly they were members of the German resistance, Jehovah's Witnesses, criminals and homosexuals, and they were put to work clearing the forest, laying sewerage pipes, building roads and constructing accommodation for the thousands of inmates destined to follow them. Buchenwald quickly acquired the reputation of being the worst camp in Germany.

After the outbreak of war, like Dachau, it also became a camp for foreigners, and the death toll began to mount. A crematorium was built, lethal injections began to take place, and forced labor in nearby quarries and factories led to hundreds of deaths. In the former stables of the original SS barracks, a special shooting facility was set up where some eight thousand Russian prisoners of war were murdered with a shot through the neck.

Here, too, grotesque medical experiments were carried out on live prisoners, including tests using typhus in which dozens died. In 1943, a large armaments factory was built adjacent to the camp, with the inmates used for labor. There were also several sub-camps, including "Dora," an underground factory at Nordhausen which used forced labor to build V2 rockets, jet aircraft and other advanced Nazi weapons.

By April 1945, Buchenwald was the largest remaining concentration camp in the Nazi system, with 112,000 prisoners, including 25,000 women, housed in the main and sub-camps. A third were Jews, and nearly all had been shipped to Buchenwald in 1944 from camps further east that were being overrun by Stalin's Red Army. The numbers of dying were increasing by the day. In all, some quarter of a million prisoners were incarcerated here by the Nazis, and almost sixty thousand died.

Fey described it as a "small city of tarmac streets," and she and the other *Sippenhafte* were housed in an isolated barracks surrounded by a red-brick wall covered in barbed wire. The group was joined by more relatives of the conspirators, and it was from one of these newcomers that Fey heard the news she had long been dreading.

Despite everything, including the cruel taunts from the SS, she had kept alive the hope that her father might still be alive. But from one of her mother's closest friends, Maria von Hammerstein, the widow of the former Reichswehr chief of staff Kurt von Hammerstein, she heard for the first time the full details of her father's trial before the notorious People's Court in Berlin. He had defended himself brilliantly and won the admiration of many of those who heard him, but the verdict was predictable. Just two hours after being found guilty, he had been taken out and hanged in the Ploetzensee Prison. At last, Fey let the tears flow freely for the father she would never see again.

Two weeks after her arrival, the camp's routine misery was shattered. In the morning, a two-seater Fieseler Storch — the plane used by the Luftwaffe for low-level reconnaissance — circled over Buchenwald several times before landing in a nearby field. Fey and the others rushed out to wave because they suspected they knew who the pilot was. And they were right: it was Alex's wife, Melitta.

Her tale was amazing, even surreal. First, she was ethnically Jewish, her father having come from a middle-class family in Leipzig that had converted to Lutheranism, a fact that to the Nazis would normally have been irrelevant in her designation as racially impure and unfit. She had qualified as an engineer, earned her pilot's license, and in the late 1920s started test-flying aircraft. Since 1937, the year she had married Alex in Berlin, she had test-flown over two thousand missions in Junkers dive-bombers for the Luftwaffe. Only one other pilot, a man, had surpassed her record. In 1943, she was awarded the Iron Cross Second Class along with the Gold Pilot's Badge with Diamonds, and she had recently also been nominated for the Iron Cross Class I.

This vital war work saved her from deportation and the death camps. She had been briefly arrested after the bomb plot, but was released to continue her test-flying. Since then, she had exploited her privileges once before, to visit Alex and bring him and the other prisoners food while they were at Stutthof, providing the group's sole link with the outside world. She had also traced some of the Stauffenberg children, who were being kept in a different camp, and had delighted them with Christmas gifts of medals since she could not find any toys in the shops. "We loved them," remembered one of the children, "she was very exciting. She told the most wonderful stories of flying and her planes."[20]

Only Alex was allowed to go over and talk with Litta after she landed outside Buchenwald. When he returned, the others surrounded him for news. It turned out that Litta had completely lost track of them since Stutthof. The Gestapo had told her that the *Sippenhafte* were probably now in Russian hands. Unwilling to believe this, she had tried Buchenwald on a hunch.

Fey naturally assumed that her family might think that she was now a prisoner of the Soviets, a thought that profoundly upset her. So she was vastly relieved a few days later when several letters arrived for her. In one, her mother told her about recent heavy air raids on Munich:

"Of the Munich we used to know," she lamented, "there is practically nothing left."

To distract herself, she started giving lessons in elementary mathematics and languages to a ten-year-old boy imprisoned in the camp with his mother. But this brought to mind the possible fate of her own children. Were the boys better off in a home, even one run by the SS? Or would they, like this one, have been happier with her in a camp, even one as wretched as Buchenwald?

A month after her arrival she heard the familiar thunder of artillery in the distance, and again the order was barked out to pack a bag and be ready to move. Buses arrived, they were crammed in tightly, and off they went into the night, their destination unknown. Accompanying them were two SS officers. One, Obersturmführer Ernst Bader, was a cold, blue-eyed type known to have worked with execution units. The other, Untersturmführer Edgar Stiller, seemed a bit more human. Their fate now rested in the hands of these two men.

On Tuesday 17 April, just before noon, they arrived outside the big stone gateway of Dachau. But thanks to the Nazis' obsessive paperwork, entering a concentration camp could be almost as difficult as leaving one. The small convoy of buses stood for hours at the entrance while the bureaucrats within wrestled with the files. It was hot, there was no food or water, and despite a rising chorus of desperate pleading no one was even allowed to go to the toilet. In the end, the prisoner sitting next to Fey simply wet the floor. She had become used to such scenes on their journeys, and had long ago abandoned any shame or modesty about bodily functions. The group, men and women alike, were used to sharing a pail hidden behind a rough cloth sheet in the corner of whatever room they inhabited.

Only towards nine in the evening did the buses start up their engines and roll through the gate. Once more, the *Sippenhafte* were segregated from the main body of inmates, and were placed in a large barracks next to the SS hospital. To Fey's immense relief, there was the luxury of hot water. At last, she could thoroughly clean herself and wash her filthy, stinking clothes. There was plenty of hot food as well, brought to them by Russian and Polish prisoners.

The main anxiety now was allied bombing. For months, Munich had been under constant attack, and Dachau itself was also a target. Fey found herself having to run to the air-raid shelter as bombs rained down. The fear she felt brought her barely suppressed worries about

47

her children bursting to the surface. Cities throughout Germany were now in flames. Where were her children? Were they safe? Would she survive, only to find that Corrado and Roberto had been killed? She felt an overwhelming desire to escape and find them, but she knew that this was a futile hope, so she ended up feeling even more trapped and helpless than before.

Sunk in these gloomy thoughts, she spotted one of the female warders from Buchenwald walking towards the SS hospital. The woman's uniform was torn and crumpled, and she looked haggard and exhausted, a far cry from the spruce martinet who had enjoyed lording it over them before. But she was ready to reveal a piece of heart-warming news: she had been transferred just a few days earlier, and Buchenwald was now in the hands of the Americans

On Sunday 8 April, the headquarters of George C. Patton's Third US Army had picked up a radio signal. "To the Allies. To the Army of General Patton," it said. "Concentration Camp Buchenwald calls! SOS. We ask for help. They are going to evacuate us. The SS will exterminate us." The message came from a wireless secretly built in the camp and was transmitted by the prisoners' underground committee. The US radio operators promised them that help was on the way.

Three days later, a tank column belonging to Patton's Third Army was racing down a road at twenty-five miles an hour when, close to Weimar, it encountered an amazing sight. Several hundred former concentration camp inmates wearing tattered rags were marching eastwards. And they were armed. They told the startled Americans that they had come from Buchenwald. Shortly before, they explained, they had disarmed the SS guards, who had fled. Now they were hoping to catch up with them.

Instead, the Americans suggested they return to the camp and sent two of Patton's officers along with them. When they arrived, a white flag was flying triumphantly from the main watchtower. All the remaining SS guards had fled at noon, leaving the camp in the hands of the communist-led underground prisoners' organization. They had run it since 1942, and had acted as trustees to dole out food, assign prisoners to work details, hand out drugs and ration hospital beds. A far less powerful, non-communist organization had been created in 1944. To some extent the two groups cooperated, although each remained deeply suspicious of the other.

Like Dachau, the Buchenwald SS leadership had received orders from Himmler to evacuate the prisoners before the allies reached it. In the four days before Patton's men arrived, some twenty-five thousand had been marched out of the main camp, including nearly all of the Jews. Only a handful had survived.

The Americans found twenty-one thousand prisoners packed into the camp. Many were hovering on the edge of death, suffering from starvation, tuberculosis, dysentery and typhoid. It was not the first of the camps to be liberated by the allies, but it was the largest and the worst yet.

The world's press descended almost immediately. In its vanguard came Edward R. Murrow, the chief European correspondent of the Columbia Broadcasting System. He had made his name reporting live on the London Blitz, using his famous opening and closing catch-phrases: "This is London," and "Good night, and good luck." He had also flown on bombing raids over Europe, making vivid recordings of what he saw, and had assembled an impressive news staff to bring the realities of war to Americans back home.

For the previous week he had been driving hard through Germany, following Patton's forces from Frankfurt to Weimar and beyond. The Germans appeared well clothed, he reported, and in a healthier state than any civilians he had seen anywhere else in Europe. Old men and women were working in the fields, although cows, not horses, were pulling the plows; the horses had been sent to the Eastern Front or Normandy as transport for the Wehrmacht. "But this is no time to talk of the surface of Germany," he abruptly said. "I propose to tell you of Buchenwald." He did so, in the first person, sharing what he had seen when he walked through the gates. He pulled no punches. He talked of people who died at his feet, of children of six with numbers tattooed on their arms, of skeletal people from Vienna, Paris and Prague. Some claimed to have met him when he was a prewar correspondent, but he failed to recognize them. Then he was taken by a Czech doctor to a small courtyard:

It was floored with concrete. There were two rows of bodies stacked up like cordwood. They were thin and very white. Some of the bodies were terribly bruised though there seemed little flesh to bruise. Some had been shot through the head. But they bled very little. All except two were naked. I tried to count them as best I could, and arrived at the conclusion that all that was mortal of more than 500 men and boys lay there in two neat piles.

I pray you to believe what I have said about Buchenwald. I have reported what I saw and heard, but only part of it. For most of it, I have no words. Dead men are plentiful in war — but the living dead, more than 20,000 in one camp! And the country around was pleasing to the eye, and the Germans were well fed and well dressed.[21]

The first British correspondent to arrive at Buchenwald was a short, stocky, dark-haired Englishman in his late thirties. His name was Robert Reid, and he was one of the eight British correspondents traveling with Patton's army. He worked for the British Broadcasting Corporation and was filing regular dispatches for its daily *War Report*, which was aired every evening after the nine o'clock radio news. A friendly figure with an infectious cackle of a laugh, he was known to all his colleagues as Bob.

Despite the insignia of a lieutenant-colonel he wore on his sleeve, Reid at first glance seemed the least likely of war correspondents. Until recently he had been based in Bradford and Manchester, where he specialized in gritty human-interest stories about life and times in the industrial north, much in the fashion of the famous writer and broadcaster J.B. Priestley. The two men had attended the same school in Bradford and spoke on similar themes with almost identical Yorkshire accents — so much so that one of Reid's colleagues later described him as "a pocket Priestley." With his neat dark suit, well-brushed bowler hat and furled umbrella, Reid had been a familiar figure in the newsrooms of northern England. It was hard to imagine him in uniform reporting from the front line.

But he was good at his job and had the born reporter's nose for truffling out the big story. "He never left a job unfinished no matter how late he stayed," said one admiring colleague, "he never looked at a clock." Ink ran in his veins, for both his great-grandfather and his grandmother had worked as journalists in their native Scotland, and his brother was opera critic for *Punch* magazine. "My job," Reid wrote, "is to do what journalism has taught me — to worry the basic facts out of the heat of any problem and give them a man-in-the-street interpretation."[22] Yet, apart from a brief spell reporting from France during its dramatic collapse in the spring of 1940, Reid had done no war reporting at all.

Then, just before D-Day, he had joined the special broadcasting team created by the BBC to follow the allied armies through France and the Low Countries into Germany. Its correspondents were "embedded" with the forces and had their own small censorship unit, which meant that sensitive issues could be discussed freely and quickly. Eventually, Reid got to know by instinct what he could and could not report on air. And anyway, he had little interest in tactical or strategic problems, preferring to focus on the experiences of the ordinary soldiers. Good morale on the home front was vital for the war effort, and here Reid's background stood him in excellent stead: he knew how to report on what was happening to the fathers, sons and brothers of his audience back home.

Ironically, though, what had first made him a household name was a dramatic episode that involved no allied forces at all. It occurred in Paris on Saturday, 26 August 1944, the day that the Free French leader General Charles de Gaulle went to Notre Dame Cathedral for the official Service of Thanksgiving for the liberation of France. The city had been liberated just two days before. More than a million Parisians lined the route from the Arc de Triomphe to the Place de la Concorde as the general walked slowly past, occasionally raising his arm to acknowledge the cheers.

Reid was waiting in the square outside the cathedral. The day before, he had driven into the city from Rambouillet with a BBC colleague. They had been warned to look out for snipers: there were plenty still around, they were told, and they should expect to be fired on from windows or roofs. He had heard the crack of a rifle just the once during the journey, but the bullet had missed them.

He stood ready with his microphone in his hand. Through the open doors of the cathedral he could see a mass of faces turned expectantly towards the entrance. The roar of the vast crowd packing the square swelled to a climax as de Gaulle arrived and was greeted by the waiting group of church dignitaries.

Suddenly, though, a shot rang out, followed by a fusillade of fire. The crowd behind Reid made a sudden rush for the doors. He began to speak into the microphone to record what was happening, but was swept forward and fell to the ground. The microphone and its cable parted company. Reid scrambled back onto his feet and, still gripping the mic, accompanied de Gaulle into the cathedral. The general seemed unperturbed, and had his hands raised, as if to calm everyone around him.

Then came a burst of firing from inside the cathedral. Snipers were hidden high in the galleries beneath the roof. People flung themselves to the floor, or hid behind stone pillars. Gendarmes and soldiers ran inside and exchanged shots with the snipers, lighting up the gloomy interior with brilliant flashes of automatic fire. Amid the din, Reid heard the congregation start to sing the *Te Deum*.

When the service was over, he slipped out of a side door to see what was happening outside. Sporadic firing and sniping was still going on. His recording trailer was parked outside and the engineer had remained at his controls until Reid's microphone had gone dead. The disk on the turntable was covered with dust and chips of broken masonry from the bullets. Reid and the engineer reconnected the microphone, and he sat down and recorded what he had just seen in the church. Even as he was talking, a nearby door opened and a line of gendarmes marched out with four captured snipers. They were, Reid told his listeners, a "raffish-looking" lot.

Although he had no idea of what had made it onto the disk, or indeed any clear recollection of what he had said amid all the confusion, he made sure the recording was rushed to London by air courier. The next night, when he tuned in to the BBC, he heard his broadcast, including the sound of bullets whizzing past his ear. It was one of the most dramatic reports ever aired during the war, "one of the biggest broadcasts, I think, of all time," according to the manager of the War Reporting Unit. In an unprecedented move, it was rebroadcast throughout the USA by both NBC and CBS.[23]

Since then, though, Reid's stories had mostly been about the men advancing into Germany. He was as interested in the engineers building roads and bridges, and the wire men stringing out cables to aid communication, as he was in the front-line troops. Not long before, when Patton's men had overrun a prisoner-of-war camp packed with British soldiers who had survived a forty-day forced march, he had moved from man to man, recording their stories for their families back home. Always, as he interviewed ordinary men doing their jobs, enduring or suffering in the extraordinary setting of war, he bore in mind that his audience back home needed *their* morale boosted, too.

He entered Buchenwald the day after its liberation. Even hard-boiled cynics were weeping at what they saw. Reid, a family man to the core, found it almost too much to bear. He was already exhausted, he had been away from home for almost a year, and he was missing his family badly. Like the soldiers whose stories he was telling to the world, he waited eagerly, sometimes desperately, for letters from home, and even at the end of a long and tiring day he sat down at his typewriter to write a reply. His daily life was one of constant movement and improvisation. He rarely knew in the morning where he would spend the night. Sharing an evening meal with the other correspondents was the closest he came to any semblance of family life.

For months he had been fed up, and ready to go home. "When I think about the future I feel more and more to have a great desire to get out with you and the children in the country," he had told Vera, his wife, back in February, "and I keep on planning imaginary holidays in Wensleydale with our paint boxes."[24]

The night before he journeyed to Buchenwald, he had received three welcome long letters from Vera. But they made him more homesick than ever. Somehow, the fact that it was spring, that the countryside was greening, and that blossom was flowering on the trees made the separation even harder to bear. "I have been thinking all the more longingly of home this last few days," he wrote that night. "I keep sighing and thinking of you and the children and how it would be to be just setting off with you for that favorite walk of mine." He signed off, as he always did, "Love, Rob," and scrawled twelve kisses at the bottom of the page.

Reid's family life was as plain and straightforward as the prose he wrote and the words he spoke. He and Vera lived in a rented house in Bramhall outside Stockport on the fringes of Manchester, and they had two small children: Elizabeth, ten, and Richard, eight. Vera packed her letters with the details of her daily suburban life. She also methodically numbered them. Sometimes, traveling through the vagaries of the military mailing system on a rapidly moving front, they arrived out of sequence. This could be confusing, which made her anxious, hence the numbering. She told him about shopping trips to Manchester, the state of the weather, the plumbers repairing a leaking pipe in the scullery, the steam iron that had been giving her trouble, the sewing she did every night to make or mend clothes, the neighbors and relatives, even the hens she fed in the back garden whose eggs she treasured, keeping a record of their production in a small book. She always reported whenever she had heard his voice on the radio. Since his broadcast from Paris, he had become a local celebrity, and even if she missed a broadcast her friends quickly told her about it. Above all, however, she told him about the children.

In Bramhall, as in Berlin, Lüneberg, Italy and Weimar, Friday 20 April was a sunny day, although in the evening there were a couple of showers of rain. After she had pulled the curtains and put the children to bed, Vera sat down to write Bob letter number 55. The big news was about Elizabeth and Richard. Their daughter had walked in proudly from school bursting with the news that she had been made a prefect. It had been announced that morning in front of the whole school at morning assembly immediately after prayers, and the head-mistress had pinned the navy-blue badge with a big gold "P" onto her dress. Vera, delighted for her daughter, had rewarded her with a ball of wool so she could knit herself some gloves.

It was also a red-letter day for Richard. He was growing taller, and today, for the first time, he had managed to ride his bike while sitting on the saddle instead of standing on the pedals. He had also learned how to get on and off it "in the boy's way," as Vera put it, by putting one leg on the pedal and swinging the other over the seat. He had spent the whole afternoon after school practicing this trick in the street, and Vera had even seen him confidently speeding along with his feet off the pedals. It was time to get the brakes checked, she thought. Then she would allow him to go slightly further afield.

She finished the letter, as usual, by urging her husband to take care. "I wish it would finish soon," she wrote, meaning the war. "But some-how," she added, "the nearer one thinks the end is, yet the further it seems away." She signed it, "All our love, Vera," and she too added twelve small kisses. It was almost as an afterthought that she included a sentence saying she had heard him on the BBC that afternoon talking about Buchenwald.[25]

The contrast with the horrors of Buchenwald might have made the details of daily life in Bramhall seem petty and trivial, but to Reid, the vivid picture drawn by Vera of his children at home had the opposite effect. It made him appreciate his family even more, and in doing so lent his reporting on the camp special poignancy. "Don't you think you bore me," he assured her the next time he wrote. "All this sort of thing is the breath of life for me darling. It brings home right here to me and I can forget what's going on all around."

He filed several reports on the camp, with the most moving and ter-rible about a group of children. In one of the wooden huts the Americans had found nine hundred children between the ages of two and fourteen. Their fathers had been prisoners who had long since died or been murdered. Most were Polish Jews, and they were being looked after by the older prisoners. Reid described them as "pathetic, ragged waifs, looking like little old men with yellow faces and shrunken cheeks." One of them, a fourteen-year-old boy with a shaven head, revealed that the camp doctor used to hold medical parades. He would divide them into groups, and then the sickest would be marched off in the direction of the camp crematorium, never to be seen again.

Another Jewish child in Buchenwald was the sixteen-year-old Elie Wiesel. Transported with his family from their village in Transylvania, he had last seen his mother and sister being directed towards the gas chambers at Auschwitz, before he himself was shipped to Buchenwald with his father that January. Here he had watched helplessly while his father, racked by dysentery and denied any medical help, died before his eyes. Once his father was beaten by fellow prisoners who were sick of him defecating in his bunk. "Don't forget you're in a concentration camp" was the advice the block leader gave Elie when he asked for help for his father. "Here every man has to fight for himself and not think of anyone else. Here," he added grimly, "there are no fathers, no brothers, no friends. Everyone lives and dies for himself."

One night, an SS guard hit his father over the head after he cried out for water. "I did not move," Wiesel later wrote. "I was afraid . . . Then my father made a rattling noise and it was my name, 'Eliezer.' I could see that he was still breathing spasmodically. I did not move." The next morning, Elie awoke at dawn. In his father's bunk lay another prisoner. His father had been taken away in the night to the crematorium. "There were no prayers at his grave," lamented Elie, "no candles were lit to his memory. His last word was my name. A summons, to which I did not reply."[26]

Elie himself was lucky to survive. As the Americans approached, the SS decided to evacuate the children and herded them onto the camp's central square. But that was when the underground resistance decided to act. "Armed men appeared everywhere," recorded Wiesel. "Burst of gunshots. Grenades exploding. We, the children, remained flat on the floor . . . The battle did not last long and around noon, everything was calm again." The SS fled, and by the time the Americans arrived the resistance was in control.[27]

Bob Reid learned more about the camp from another group of prisoners he met. About forty captured British secret agents had been sent there by the SS. Only four were still alive by the time Reid arrived.

One was a twenty-year-old Englishman named Christopher Burney. As a bored junior commando officer, he had written a paper about how to liberate France from within. Then, at a cocktail party a few weeks later, his brigadier beckoned him over. "Ever jumped out of a plane, old boy?" he asked. "I've a feeling you're going to." Not long afterwards Burney was being dropped near Le Mans to join a Special Operations Executive (SOE) network. Unfortunately, though, it had just been arrested en masse, and Burney was quickly picked up by the Gestapo.

"They stuck to boots and fists," he said, "taking care to keep me conscious." But he told them nothing. The following eighteen months were spent in solitary confinement in Fresnes Prison outside Paris. Then he was sent to Buchenwald. The journey was torture. A hundred men, all stripped naked, were pushed into a truck designed for forty. It took them four days, with only one small can of blackish water to drink, to reach their destination. "Half the men in my truck were mad," Burney recalled.

After that, he fought to keep himself alive. One of the worst features of Buchenwald, he found, was the control exercised over other prisoners by the communists in the camp, nearly all of whom were German. "They had absolute disciplinary powers over their fellow prisoners," he wrote, "backed by the SS and the threat of the crematorium behind them. Anybody who savored of a capitalist or an intellectual was promptly marked down as a victim." Indeed, just ten days before the Americans liberated the camp, the German communists had passed a resolution declaring, "It is in the highest degree regrettable that the Anglo-American capitalists should liberate us. We will do all in our power, even under them, to retain the position which we have always held." [28]

In response to this, Burney had busied himself organizing the camp's non-communist resistance cell. This saved his life. In the final days before liberation, word leaked out that the SS was eager to kill the British officers. This was all too believable: only two weeks before, Burney's best friend, another secret agent captured in France, had been taken to the crematorium and hanged. Acting immediately, the new resistance group hid Burney and the others in a secret underground cellar until the danger passed.

Two of the other SOE agents were brothers. Henry and Alfred Newton had been an acrobatic act based in Paris when the war broke out. Subsequently, all their relatives — wives, children, parents — had perished in a torpedoed ship, which had prompted them to join SOE. Nine months after being parachuted back into France, they had been arrested and badly tortured. One day in Buchenwald Alfred saw Henry being carried past on a stretcher: "He managed to give a sign that he had recognized me," said his brother.

The fourth surviving agent, Maurice Southgate, had run a highly successful network in France before falling into a Gestapo trap just six weeks before D-Day following the arrest of his radio operator. Along with the captured wireless set was a file of messages relating to the allied landings. Despite being severely tortured, Southgate held out long enough for the information he had to be useless. He had spent nine months in Buchenwald before Reid arrived. Helplessly and fatalistically, he watched as, one by one, other SOE agents were taken away for execution. This was carried out in a particularly brutal manner, he explained. A butcher's hook was placed under their chins before the trap beneath their feet was sprung. From the execution chamber below ground, their bodies were then speedily lifted to the crematorium.

Reid uncovered other stories of heroism during his time at Buchenwald. Nearby, in a small hospital, he came across a group of young Polish women who had fought as combat troops during the Warsaw uprising of the previous August. Miraculously, the Germans had treated them as prisoners of war rather than as terrorists to be shot. They ranged from fourteen to sixty years old. Altogether, some seven thousand women had been captured. Microphone in hand, Reid broadcast an interview with one of them.

"What part did the women play in that fight?" he asked. Some were in assault groups, the woman replied; others served in the General Staff of the Polish Home Army. They also acted as observers, front-line fighters and couriers.

"What about the courier girls?" he inquired. One of them was only fifteen, answered the woman. She had been a Girl Guide before the war. "She had to go through the canals [sewers]," she continued in her imperfect English, "and as she was little it was easier for her to do that than for a big man or a more higher woman [sic]." The Germans had thrown gas and grenades into the sewers, she went on, and for her courage the girl had been awarded the Polish Military Cross.

Reid was fascinated. The Warsaw uprising was a big story and this was the first opportunity he had had to talk to anyone involved. "How did the Germans treat the people of Warsaw?" he asked.

"Just like wild beasts," came the answer. "We were arrested in streets; arrested in trams; arrested in houses. Nobody knew in the morning if he would live in the evening."

From another woman, Reid learned that even though they had been classified as prisoners of war, the women had suffered severe privations. Thousands of them had been marched out of Warsaw and kept for days without food. "If you could get a piece of dog, meat of a dog," she told him, "you were lucky." Then they were taken to Silesia in cattle trucks and locked in them for three days. "They didn't allow the people to care and give us food and even water," she said. "And they used to shoot the Poles or other people who wanted to bring us food."

Most of the women Reid saw had lost teeth through vitamin deficiency and were thin and haggard, but they had taken care to keep themselves as clean as they could, washing themselves and their clothes constantly to ward off disease.

They had been freed just ten days before. The exact second was etched on at least one of the women's memory: "We are mad with happiness," she told Reid. "We have been freed on 11th April, ten minutes to four. We remember that very well," she added, "when we saw for the first time an American car, and American soldiers."

"How did you receive them?" asked Reid.

"We were shouting and singing and crying with joy, and they were awfully nice to us. They let [sic] us some chocolate and cigarettes."

"No lipstick or powder?"

"No," she answered sternly. "We are not allowed to use that if we are soldiers. Although," she added conspiratorially, "some of us, I think — I will tell you that in secret — dream about it!"

It was a light-hearted moment in what had otherwise been a horrific and depressing few days. When he moved on for his next story, Bob Reid was heartily glad to put Buchenwald behind him.[29]

But at least he had been able to do one good turn that made him feel better.

The four British SOE agents spent the first night of their liberation sleeping in a comfortable bungalow that had belonged to one of the camp's SS officers and his family and had been commandeered by one of the Americans.

The next day, a British major in well-pressed battle dress rolled up to the camp in a jeep. "Get us away from this hell-hole," said Alfred Newton, delighted to see an officer in British uniform, and all too aware that their lives might still be in some danger from the communists still at large in the camp. But his hopes were crushed. They would have to wait until the proper repatriation authorities arrived, the officer told them. He could do nothing to help except make a report when he got back to his headquarters. Then he jumped into his jeep and drove away. He hadn't even offered them a cigarette.

By this time, Reid had finished his interviews and was chatting with Burney. His jeep with his recording trailer emblazoned with "BBC Recording Unit" was parked by the main gate, and the two of them strolled towards it slowly together. As they got close, Reid offered Burney a lift. "Thanks for the offer, old boy," replied the SOE man, "but there are three other officers with me, and I couldn't dream of leaving without them." Then he introduced Reid to the others.

By this time Reid had noticed the inscription above the gate: "*Recht oder unrecht Mein Vaterland*." "Right or wrong my country," translated Reid in his broad Yorkshire accent. He turned to business: "What the hell are we waiting for? Come on, lads! Pile in. If I don't get you away from here, my name's not Bob."

Burney, Southgate and Alfred Newton packed themselves into the jeep, while Henry Newton settled down in the trailer among the recording equipment. As they left, a GI thrust some K rations into their hands.

It was dusk when they reached Third Army headquarters in Gotha. Here Reid dropped off the four men at the guardroom, then put out his hand and gave them a broad smile. "Right or wrong, my country! Nay, I'm not likely to forget that one . . . Well, lads, Ah must go now. Look me up some time. 'BBC Manchester' will always find me. Cheerio!"[30]

CHAPTER THREE

AVENGING JUSTICE

In Italy, across the ragged peaks of the Alps where winter snow was still blocking the highest passes, four more secret agents were preparing for their own mission behind enemy lines. France, the main target for British and American agents before D-Day, had lost its appeal to the shadow warriors after liberation. As Robert Reid was witnessing with his own eyes at Buchenwald, captured agents had paid a terrible personal price in torture and death, but their efforts had paid dividends in harassing and diverting the Germans as they scrambled to react to the landings in Normandy.

Now, even at this last minute, allied agents were parachuting into the Third Reich itself. Here too, perhaps, they could help the advancing allies with behind-the-lines exploits. Germany had been off limits to SOE until after D-Day as too dangerous and unlikely to produce results among a hostile population. But since the bomb plot, with its revelation of an active internal resistance prepared to kill Hitler, views had changed. SOE even put a lot of time and energy into concocting a plan to kill the Führer by dropping an assassin close to his home outside Berchtesgaden, only to abandon it as unfeasible and perhaps unnecessary — Hitler's own mad strategy looked like it was bringing defeat to Germany all by itself.

But allied agents might still find useful things to do and people on the ground to help them. Unlikely though it seemed, Austria was now emerging as a focus of allied efforts to inspire resistance. Hitler had

annexed the country of his birth into the Third Reich, many of the
leading and most fanatical Nazis were Austrian, and for the most part
the mass of the population had welcomed the Anschluss. Soon afterwards, Fey von Hassell had toured the country with her parents, who
were contemplating buying a small house there. Neither of them liked
driving, so their young daughter took the wheel. Apart from a couple
of minor bumps, everything went well, despite the disconcerting fact
that the Austrians, like the British, drove on the left-hand side of the
road. They loved the Austrian countryside, although the housing
proved dilapidated.

But what struck Fey above all was the servility of the Austrians to the
new Nazi regime. "At one point my father said 'Even the dairy maid
salutes and says "Heil Hitler" before milking the cow.' Hitler took
Austria by force," she continued, "but Austria, except for a few, willingly accepted."[1] Yet, recently, signs had emerged of a latent
opposition. And with the end of the war in sight, it might dare to help
the allies.

Austria, therefore, was the target for the four waiting agents. When
the weather was favorable and a plane made available, they would fly
over the mountains at night and parachute to a carefully selected spot.
It would be a "blind" drop, meaning there would be no reception committee to meet them. In places such as Austria, with plenty of Nazis
around, that could be disastrous. Even in more friendly countries, the
Gestapo could penetrate an SOE network and set up a false reception
committee as a trap. This had happened in Holland, where about fifty
agents had been parachuted straight into enemy hands.

Just waiting for the right weather could take days, even weeks. It
had to be good for take-off, at the drop site itself and for the return landing. The moon had to be high enough for the navigator to identify the
landing ground with reasonable precision to drop the agents at the
proper map reference — they would quickly have to identify where they
were and hide before daylight. Unexpected cloud cover at drop points
had forced dozens of secret flights to abandon their missions.

Even if all these things came together at the right time, a plane with
a crew specially trained for these flights had to be available. Precision
night flying was hazardous and required men with steady nerves. They
would have to be ready to take a plane down to low levels over enemy-
held terrain, and if necessary circle around several times for long
dangerous minutes while the exact spot for the drop was located. Such

flights were in high demand by many agencies, both British and American, so there was always a queue.

For ten days the four men had been waiting at the big American air base at Rosignano, south of Livorno on the west coast of Italy. They were living in a small house at the edge of the aerodrome. For the first week, each morning promptly at nine-thirty, a dispatch rider would roar up on his motorbike, screech to a halt, and tell them that they would not be flying tonight. But by now he had given up even doing that: he simply slowed down, hooted, and gave them a thumbs down to tell them they had at least another day to wait.

Still, Fred Warner, one of the group, found that life wasn't entirely unpleasant. He also had to admit to a slight sense of relief each time he knew the mission was off. Like the others, he was well aware of what might go wrong, and could imagine a nasty death at the hands of the Gestapo. Another long day filling in time had its compensations. No one stopped them going for walks in the surrounding spring country-side, and at night there was the local cinema, commandeered by the Americans, which showed a different movie every evening. Afterwards, they would go out for a drink in one of the many temporary, Italian-run cafés that had sprung up like mushrooms round the airfield's perime-ter.

One day they all went into Pisa and played at being tourists, having their photograph taken in front of the Leaning Tower, just as enemy sol-diers had done not too long before. In fact, they had been taken for Germans because of their mountain caps, which had large, stiff peaks — not unlike those of the German mountain troops once stationed there who were now fighting the Tenth Mountain Division to the north. Suddenly, someone shouted, "*Tedeschi!*"—"Germans!"—and before they knew what had happened a crowd of small boys had surrounded them and was throwing stones. Eventually the mistake was cleared up and they returned to base unharmed.

Ironically, though, the young Italians had not been entirely mistaken. For Warner, like all the others in his group, was a native German speaker. And thousands of other refugees from Germany and Austria, not all of them Jews, had taken similar paths and were now fighting with allied forces to rid their homeland of Hitler. Warner had been born in December 1919 in Hamburg, where his father owned a suc-cessful business. The fifth in a family of seven children, he enjoyed a comfortable upbringing, including a nice summer house at

Travemunde, a fashionable resort on the Baltic coast a short tram ride from Lubeck. He always wore gloves for the annual ride there, to keep his hands clean during the journey. Life was genteel.

But ten years later the family's circumstances changed overnight when his father lost all his money in the great stock market crash. "No more houses, car rides, servants, nannies and such like," Fred recorded. Instead, they all moved in with Fred's grandmother, some of whose eight children were still living in her large house in the city. For the children at least, though, life remained pleasant enough, and there was a large garden in which to play.

However, that came to an abrupt end with the Nazi takeover in 1933. At Fred's school, the headmaster was replaced by an ardent Nazi who always wore his Stormtrooper (SA) uniform and continuously screamed abuse at any pupil not wearing a Hitler Youth uniform. Fred saw people being beaten up in the street for not giving the Nazi salute. In cinemas, the German national anthem was generally followed by the "Horst Wessel Song," named after a Nazi youth hero killed in a street brawl. During film shows, Fred noted, the lights would suddenly go up and SA men would shout out "*Juden Raus!*" ("Jews Out!"). No one dared protest.

After the passing of the Nuremberg race laws in 1935 the situation became rapidly worse. Fred's family was Jewish but had converted to Christianity, but this made no difference now, and they were classified as "non-Aryan." One of his uncles was sent to prison for two years for having a liaison with an "Aryan" woman. When he was released, he was immediately rearrested and sent to Dachau. The family never saw him again.

Fred left school at sixteen, but he could not join the hotel business, on which he had set his heart, because this was now closed to Jews. So he joined a Jewish-owned corn merchant's, and took private cookery classes in the evenings — the only male in a group of a dozen or so women. As the Nazi terror intensified, his father took to sleeping in a different place every night. One day, a neighbor in the same apartment house as Fred was taken away by the Gestapo. A few weeks later, his wife received a letter saying he had died and that she could come and collect his ashes. A bill was attached.

By 1938, most of Fred's brothers and sisters had left for such safe havens as Brazil, New Zealand and Britain. His younger brother left for London in a children's transport organized by the Quakers, and the next year Fred followed him to England. In February 1939, clutching a single suitcase containing all his worldly belongings, he waved good-bye to his parents at Hamburg railway station. His plan was to move on to New Zealand, to join his sister there. But war arrived before the visa did, so he was forced to stay. When he arrived on the ferry at Harwich he was nineteen years old. The name on his passport was Manfred Werner.

For a while he stayed with the wealthy great-cousin of his mother in the country who had sponsored his entry into Britain. But he felt guilty about doing nothing and early in 1940 volunteered for the Auxiliary Military Pioneer Corps. At least twenty thousand German Jews, both men and women, fought with the allied forces against Nazism during the Second World War. Most of those exiled in Britain joined the Pioneer Corps, which was created specifically for foreigners. However, those who were German, Austrian or Czech had to pass a rigorous security check. The corps was essentially an unarmed military labor unit, and Fred was one of the first to enroll.[2]

Although at first regarded as little more than a "dumping ground" of the British Army, the corps increasingly gained respect and its members were granted commissions and given weapons training. Obviously, they had valuable linguistic skills, knew a great deal about occupied Europe, and began to play an increasingly important part in the British war effort. Several joined regular infantry and armored units. A few entered the Royal Navy. And dozens joined the commandos — where the bulk of 10 (Inter-Allied) Commando consisted of German and Austrian Jews.

Many of them were now fighting alongside Bryan Samain in Germany. That February, indeed, eleven men of his unit had been killed in Holland during a raid on an island in the River Maas occupied by the Germans. The dead had lain where they fell for two or three days. Then two men were sent out under a flag of truce to ask for their bodies so they could be given a decent burial. The interpreter for the task was a Sergeant-Major Howarth, although his birth name was Eric Nathan, and he was the son of a Jewish lawyer from Ulm who had joined the Pioneer Corps almost as soon as it was formed. The bodies were mostly unrecognizable due to exposure in the snow. "One of the last to be brought across," wrote Samain, "could only be identified by two tattered cloth pips on the shoulders, and a pair of faded parachutist's wings on the right arm." Sadly, it proved to be Samain's best friend in the commandos, Lieutenant Peter Winston. He and Samain had gone through officer's training together, and he had been the main reason for Bryan opting to join 45 Commando. Few knew better than the commandos the part being played by exiles from Germany in ridding their country of Hitler.[3]

By 1942, Fred Warner was desperate to do more for the war effort than swing a pick and shovel, and with good reason. "Friends of my parents," he explained, "who had emigrated from Hamburg to [Sweden] had informed me that my parents and young sister had been deported to Lodz in Poland." Although he did not know it, this was a way station for Jews en route to Auschwitz. Along with his friend Eric Rhodes, who was also from Hamburg, he applied for more interesting and active work. However, for months, nothing happened.

Then, in January 1943, he was summoned to an interview at the War Office. He was one of about twenty who were grilled by a "very old" lieutenant-colonel and a slightly younger woman who wore civilian clothes. "I was asked a lot of questions," he recalled, "finally whether I would be prepared to do a dangerous job. When I agreed, thinking of the commandos, I was soon dismissed and told to rejoin my unit." A few weeks later, he and eleven others were ordered to report for duty. They were met in London by a major in the Intelligence Corps. For weeks, noted Fred, "he slept, worked and played with us. He censored our mail and he wrote reports about us." Finally, they were sent to a special training school. They had officially joined the SOE.

Now he was "Captain Frederick Michael Warner," a precautionary change of name in case he fell into Gestapo hands, although when it came to secret agents they did not much care who they were torturing or executing. The others had done the same and were now "Bryant," "Kelly" and "Rhodes." George Bryant had originally been called Breuer, and he was a former lawyer from Vienna; his grandfather, Dr. Joseph Breuer, had cooperated with Sigmund Freud on *Studies in Hysteria*, published in 1895. Kelly's real name was Koenig. Like Warner and Rhodes, he was German by birth.

Friday 20 April came and went. The men were nervous. Tension had been running high for weeks. Staff from SOE HQ had visited them at all hours. Virtually every request for equipment they submitted was granted, however trivial. One of the group whiled away the long hours of boredom by sawing the legs off some of the easy chairs and fashioning them into handles to fix to their Sten guns to provide a better grip.

Fred even began to wonder if he would be dropped before the war was over. Vienna had already fallen to the Russians and the Red Army was still moving west.

Then, one day, a pretty member of the First Aid Nursing Yeomanry (FANY) arrived and closeted herself for several hours with Kelly, the group's radio operator. This was a clear sign that action was imminent. The FANYs, a corps of female first-aid volunteers originally formed in the First World War, provided SOE with much of its secretarial and support staff, including coders and home-based wireless operators. For one last time, Kelly and the girl were going over the codes, signals and transmitting schedules. These would provide the vital lifeline between the men and home base. The group was also given a code name: "Historian."

By now, Warner had gone over his briefing time and time again and knew it by heart. What would actually happen on the ground, of course, would depend on luck and circumstance, and they had been told to be flexible and imaginative in interpreting the brief. But there were four main points. They would be dropped into the central province of Styria, just west of Judenburg, a small but important regional center. Ironically, it had originally been settled by Jewish merchants, hence its name, and the town's coat of arms depicted a head wearing a Jewish cap. The Jews had been expelled twice from their town: once in the fifteenth century, and again after Hitler seized power. Here, Fred and his group — he was second-in-command — were to try to locate any members of the Austrian underground.

They were also to contact and help the growing number of allied prisoners of war being shifted there ahead of the advancing allied forces. And they were to stop the Germans from destroying the military aerodrome at Zeltweg, five miles to the east of Judenburg, which was earmarked by the British for their own use after they occupied the country, and which had been left deliberately untouched by allied bombers.

Targets such as these three were fairly standard for SOE missions, but the final one was unusual because of its essentially intelligence-gathering, as opposed to action-oriented, goal. Warner and the others were to find out whether the Nazis had prepared a redoubt — a fortified stronghold from which to launch a final, last-ditch campaign of resistance — in the Austrian mountains.[4]

In November 1944, readers of the *New York Times* had opened the magazine section to find a sensational article penned by its correspondent in London. It was entitled "Hitler's Hideaway." Strictly speaking, it was about Berchtesgaden, but it also painted a vivid picture of the extensive fortifications that it claimed had been constructed in the area surrounding his Berghof, consisting of a maze of elaborate tunnels and extensive caves packed with food and military supplies. According to the author, as a final precaution the entire district, some twenty-one miles in length and fifteen miles wide, had been mined to prevent it falling into allied hands. Beneath the Berghof, Heinrich Himmler had an office. On its desk lay a button. All the SS chief had to do was press it, and the entire complex would be blown to smithereens.

Similar stories began to surface elsewhere in the allied press over the following weeks. A month later, the *Daily Worker*, the newspaper of the American Communist Party, predicted that the Germans would make a desperate last stand in the Alps and pointed to their bitter resistance around Lake Balaton in Hungary against the Red Army as a warning. Given the fierce fighting taking place on all the remaining battle fronts, more and more people began to accept the notion of an Alpine redoubt: sometimes it was called the "National Redoubt," named after the huge fortification system known to have been built by the Swiss in the mountains after the French collapse of 1940 to defend their country against a Nazi invasion.

It seemed an entirely plausible idea. After all, Bavaria was both the birthplace of Nazism and Hitler's home, and he had built his famous Eagle's Nest on the top of a mountain peak there. Also, it was frequently pointed out, the SS leadership school was located at Bad Toelz, a Bavarian spa town on the River Isar with spectacular views over the Alps. Here in the mountains, experts knowingly nodded, lay the psychological locus of the Nazis — so it was the obvious place for its leaders and zealots to die heroes' deaths in some magnificent, Wagnerian *Götterdämmerung*.[5]

But it was not just the press that conjured up this mesmerizing image. Behind the scenes, the notion was also taking root in allied military commands. "The advance into Germany may take place in conditions of chaos and disorder and in the face of sporadic and organized resistance by diehard remnants of the German Army and the Nazi Party." So read a secret allied intelligence report of September 1944, written after the allies had swept triumphantly through northern France and Belgium and up to the German frontier after the D-Day landings.[6]

No one knew what to expect when they finally reached German soil. Confidence was running high about an early end to the war — some predicted it could all be over by Christmas. But, whenever it ended, *how* would it happen? With a sudden surrender by the Germans when they realized that defeat was inevitable? In a series of piecemeal surrenders front by front, army by army? With one last great battle, in the mold of Napoleon's crushing defeat at Waterloo? Or in a final, hopeless last stand in which the enemy went down fighting in some heroic, Nazi equivalent of the Alamo?

Central to the allies' deepest fears about the Alpine Redoubt was the sinister figure of Heinrich Himmler, who had always been regarded as the main ideological enforcer in the Nazi state. Then, in 1944, after he took over the Abwehr, the Wehrmacht's intelligence service, and eliminated the thousands of dissidents who were allegedly connected to the bomb plot, he emerged as second only to Hitler in the Nazi hierarchy. His strongman image was further enhanced when Hitler also made him commander-in-chief of the Home Reserves.

With SS ideologues in control, it seemed clear to the allies that a military victory alone would not destroy Nazi Germany. The SS, known for its fanaticism, would simply go underground to fight on. This point was put bluntly to President Roosevelt in September 1944 by William J. Donovan, head of the Office of Strategic Services (OSS) — predecessor to the CIA as the nation's main intelligence service. The allies, predicted "Wild Bill," should expect to have to fight "a Nazi government gone underground and offering resistance . . . by a highly specialized and skilled clandestine army of the SS type."[7]

Hitler's daring counteroffensive in the Ardennes of December 1944 further boosted the notion of the redoubt. Allied intelligence sources in Switzerland also fueled the idea. "It seems likely," reported the OSS chief in Europe, the Berne-based Allen Dulles, in January 1945,

> that the men around Hitler and Himmler are preparing for the possibility of a last stand in the inner German fortress of the Bavarian and Austrian Alps . . . [This] is in line with the Wagnerian complex of the whole National Socialist movement and the fanaticism of the Nazi youth. Hitler and his small band of brigands, who started in the beer-hall of Munich, may find their end not far away in the Bavarian Alps after having laid most of Europe in ruins.[8]

By April 1945, when the Germans still showed no sign of surrendering even after massive losses of men and territory, allied concerns about a Nazi last stand came to a peak. The worst of their fears were graphically embodied in a map hanging on the walls of General Eisenhower's headquarters in Reims. Here, tucked away on a back street, the Supreme Headquarters Allied Expeditions Force (SHAEF) was housed in the three-story Collège Moderne et Technique near to the city's main railway station. Close to Eisenhower's office was his map room, where charts showing the known position of allied and enemy forces were updated daily.

One of the maps was headed "Reported National Redoubt." It depicted a huge area of some 20,000 square miles south of Munich, extending into western Austria, a landscape marked by high mountain peaks and steep valleys filled with deep lakes. At its heart lay Berchtesgaden. The map was dotted with military symbols colored in red showing radio transmitters, barracks, ammunition dumps, food depots, fortifications and chemical warfare stores. Here, it was believed, the Nazi faithful, now pouring out of Berlin and heading south, would make their last stand. And from here, too, intelligence reports suggested, the Nazis would dispatch commando and guerrilla units known as Werewolves. Like Britain's SOE and the Americans' OSS, they would wreak mayhem behind the lines.

Late in March, Colonel William W. Quinn, the chief of intelligence of General Patch's US Seventh Army advancing on the southernmost edge of the Western Front, had issued a stark and somber warning. An elite German force, some 200,000–300,000 strong, was gathering in the redoubt. Every week, five long freight trains were entering the area packed with weapons. An underground factory capable of building Messerschmitt aircraft had been established. Werewolf schools were ubiquitous. Here, claimed Quinn, Hitler was consciously planning a final stand.[9]

British intelligence was picking up similar signals. Even Churchill himself was on the alert. Every day he scoured the pile of top-secret "Ultra" intercepts brought to him in his special locked box containing the transcripts of messages from enemy and neutral powers being read by the code-breakers at Bletchley Park. Ultra had previously produced frustratingly little about Hitler's intentions, but as the spring days lengthened, the code-breakers unearthed an increasingly powerful stream of messages reporting the move by various German headquarters to the area around Salzburg that referred openly to the Alpine Redoubt.

In mid-March, one small item caught the Prime Minister's eye. It was a Japanese diplomatic report from the Swiss capital Berne to Tokyo claiming that considerable stocks of war matériel were being accumulated by the Germans in two main battlegrounds or redoubts. One was the area around Wilhelmshaven, Hamburg and Kiel, on the North Sea and Baltic coasts; the other took in a vast area that included Munich, Salzburg, Vienna and northern Italy. Churchill underlined the passage in red ink and demanded the views of his Joint Intelligence Committee (JIC). Britain's top intelligence experts replied that, as yet, there existed little hard and reliable evidence to back up the notion that the National Redoubt existed. But, they added cautiously, there was sufficient information to support the idea that the Nazis had plans to create one. The War Office passed on some additional intelligence of its own: the redoubt would be garrisoned by sixteen German divisions with food and ammunition stocks sufficient for two years. The food supplies would support 600,000 people, including hostages that the Nazis would take with them. The source of this information, added the War Office, was an agent "more reliable than most."[10]

With reports like this flooding in, what were the allies to do? Should they take the intelligence seriously and try to neutralize the redoubt? Or should they ignore it and carry on regardless? Some of the evidence was thin, opaque and cryptic, but parts of it were precise and definite. And the sources — always vital in deciding the value of intelligence — appeared varied enough to give credence to it all: human agents on the ground, photo-reconnaissance flights by allied aircraft over the Alps, and Sigint (signals intelligence), such as Ultra, always regarded as the most reliable source of all. But any decision about allied strategy was Supreme Commander Eisenhower's alone.

With the chart on his map room wall now covered with symbols, Eisenhower's own intelligence experts had come to a hardened view, and, writes the biographer of Montgomery, concern about the Alpine Redoubt had "grown like a cancer." The Nazis, concluded SHAEF intelligence staff, had definite plans for a redoubt in the Alps stretching from Munich through western Austria to the Italian lakes. Here, they believed, "defended both by nature and by the most secret weapons yet invented, the powers that have hitherto guided Germany will survive to organize her resurrection." And, they added, while the allies from both east and west were directing their main strategy to the north and center of Germany, the main thrust of German defense seemed intent on safeguarding the Alpine zone. Why else were underground stores being built there? And why else was Field Marshal Kesselring fighting so bitterly in Italy to protect the Alpine passes from the south?[11]

Even skeptics were being converted to the need for action. Prominent among them was SHAEF's intelligence chief, Kenneth Strong, a hard-boiled Scot and the most senior British member of Eisenhower's combined allied staff. Intelligence assessments invariably rest on a "worst-case" scenario. No one, least of all an intelligence chief carrying such a weighty burden as Strong's, ever wishes to dismiss such intelligence only to have it later proved correct, even if the chances of that seem minimal. Strong was nothing if not professionally astute and cautious. "The Redoubt may or may not be there," he pronounced, "but we have to take steps to prevent it being there."[12]

Eisenhower's staff sent the report to Washington. Two weeks later, back came a response from General George C. Marshall, who was obviously impressed. "Rapid action," he told the Supreme Commander, "might prevent the formation of any organized resistance areas. The mountainous country in the south is considered a possibility for one of these." His chief's response hardened Eisenhower's conviction that a major strategic decision had to be made. Both Bedell Smith, his chief of staff, and General Omar Bradley, his old West Point classmate and most trusted subordinate, backed him. "Bradley is convinced," wrote his aide Chet Hansen in his secret diary, "that we shall have to fight the Germans in the mountain fastness of southern Germany and there destroy the core of SS units which are determined to carry on battle."

When asked at a press conference in Paris what was likely to happen next, Eisenhower responded that "the German would probably make a stand in the mountains." Privately, he also feared that the enemy might be able to hold out almost indefinitely. Of course, he knew that such a stronghold could always be starved out by a blockade, but it could also spark a costly guerrilla struggle lasting long enough to produce disagreements among the allies that might generate peace terms falling far short of unconditional surrender. Worse, time might yet give the Germans the chance to produce some frightening new weapon.

This was not a nightmare to be dismissed lightly. The Nazis had already produced some nasty surprises, such as the V1 and V2, jet-powered aircraft and a new generation of U-boats that was causing serious concern. He resolved to nip the last stand in the bud.[13]

It had long been assumed that the allies would head for Berlin. Its capture, stated SHAEF planners firmly in September 1944, was their main goal. Yet, by late March 1945, Stalin's Red Army was far closer to the German capital than any of the forces under Eisenhower's command. Soviet troops had crossed the River Oder, just forty miles from Hitler's bunker, whereas the closest British and American forces still lay two hundred miles to the west.

The choice that faced Eisenhower was clear. He either had to get to Berlin himself or leave it to the Russians. In late March he made up his mind and took the difficult and controversial decision to leave Hitler's capital to the Red Army. His own forces instead would make their main thrust along an axis in central Germany towards Leipzig in order to link up with Soviet troops south of Berlin and thus cut Germany in two. Further south, they would make for the Alps.

In the north, British and Canadian armies under Montgomery would head towards the Baltic. Here, fears of a northern redoubt also colored his thinking. Perhaps the Germans would retreat through Denmark and into Norway, where tens of thousands of their troops were still stationed, to make a last stand there. By cutting across the base of the Jutland Peninsula to Lübeck, British forces would kill off any chances of that.

Fears of an Alpine or a northern redoubt were not the only factor in Eisenhower's decision. To get to the German capital meant a two-hundred-mile advance and a major crossing of the Elbe, whereas the Russians' million-plus men were far closer to the city. American casualties might run as high as a hundred thousand. And for what? The "Big Three" allies had already agreed on the post-war division of Germany into occupation zones, with Berlin lying firmly within the Soviet zone yet with the Western powers administering half the city. Why risk thousands of lives for territory that would have to be given up anyway when a post-war foothold in the capital was already guaranteed? Moreover, any advance to Berlin would risk a head-on collision with Soviet forces on the ground and possible deadly friendly fire. Only a clear-cut demarcation line could prevent that. The Elbe, flowing south to north, which each side would agree not to cross, presented an ideal and unmistakable dividing line.

Yet, of all these reasons, the growing threat of the Alpine Redoubt, and possibly prolonged guerrilla resistance, was the most decisive factor in dictating Eisenhower's strategy. Bradley certainly gave it great credence, and his influence on Eisenhower was profound. By cutting Germany in two, the allies would put a stop to the migration south from Berlin of yet more German agencies, both civilian and military. With an additional drive to the southeast to block the Alpine passes, Hitler's National Redoubt would be firmly neutralized.

However, Eisenhower's decision infuriated both Churchill and Montgomery. The Prime Minister was already engaged in a power play with Stalin. Deeply concerned about the USSR's intentions in Eastern Europe, he wanted to capture Berlin and use it as a bargaining tool with the Soviet leader. Montgomery, commanding mostly British troops on the Northern Front, wanted the glory of marching them into the city. Angry telegrams criss-crossed the Atlantic, but Eisenhower, backed by both Roosevelt and Marshall, stood firm.

Then, two weeks later, the issue resurfaced. In a rapid thrust, advanced units of American forces reached the Elbe at Magdeburg, only sixty miles southwest of Berlin. Meanwhile, the Soviets had not yet launched their expected offensive on the city. The prospect of a Western capture of the German capital therefore suddenly became more feasible and attractive.

To discuss the next step in his strategy, Eisenhower flew with Bradley to Patton's headquarters. This was the day that Roosevelt died, although the news only reached the two generals that evening. By then, Patton had insisted on giving his visitors a personal tour of two dramatic discoveries made by his GIs as they advanced into the German heartland. The first was at Merkers, a village in Thuringia, twenty-five miles southeast of Gotha. Here lay the Kaiserrode Salt Works, one of the deepest salt mines in Europe. Just before noon on 4 April, advanced US infantry units had entered the village. The area was swarming with displaced persons who were quickly interrogated by counterintelligence experts keen to gain information about the Nazis. Gold from the Reichsbank had recently been sent to the mine, they were told, but these were just rumors and none of them had seen it for themselves. A day later, the Americans heard the same story from a group of French laborers who had been working in the mine. The area was promptly sealed off.

Early the next morning, two military policemen guarding an access road challenged a couple of women out walking before the curfew was lifted. One was pregnant, she explained, and they were making their way to see the local midwife. After being questioned, they were given a lift back to Merkers. As they drove into the village they passed the entrance to the mine. "What sort of mine is it?" asked the driver. "Oh," they replied casually, "it's the mine where the German gold reserve and some valuable works of art were stored a few weeks ago."

The story soon reached the ears of one of Patton's senior civil affairs officers, and he promptly headed for the mine to interrogate its officials. They admitted that gold and other valuables had been stored there. Even more significant, however, was the presence at the mine of two senior officials from Berlin. One was Dr. Paul Rave, curator of the German State Museum; the other was Werner Veick, the head cashier of the Reichsbank's Foreign Notes Department. A tank battalion was ordered up to guard the mine's main entrance, and armed guards were stationed at other subsidiary entrances. In the meantime, Patton had been told about the rumors. However, he had heard similar ones before elsewhere, and they had all turned out to be false, so he ordered that nothing should be said until it was all confirmed.

Since then, though, the story had leaked out, and rumors of what the Americans had discovered had dominated the headlines.[14]

Robert Reid was one of the first correspondents to reach the mine and tell the story.

It lay two thousand feet below ground. "When the cage made its plummet-like drop," Reid told his BBC listeners, "we found ourselves stepping out into what looked for all the world like one of those imitation fairy grottoes you see at fun fairs." Ahead of him stretched a long, rocky tunnel carved roughly out of the whitish-gray salt with a string of electric light bulbs hanging from the roof stretching into the distance. A small railway line ran along the ground. An American soldier, carbine in hand, checked his credentials. In the timekeeper's office, Reid saw a picture of Hitler gazing down at him from the wall. He heard the hum of air-conditioning keeping the temperature at a steady sixty-five degrees Fahrenheit.

He then walked five hundred yards along the tunnel to a massive steel door set in a rough brick wall. The door was jammed shut, but just that morning a hole had been blasted in the wall by explosives. He squeezed through. In front of him was a chamber some six hundred feet long. The floor was covered with sacks lying knee high arranged in neat little rows. Each sack was sealed and bore a red label. One of the Americans tore one open and lifted out a gold ingot. Clearly stamped on its end, in black-and-white lettering, Reid could see the mint mark and serial number. In total there were four thousand such ingots hidden in the sacks. He was gazing at the total gold reserve of the German Reichsbank. How it came to be in the mine was almost as dramatic a story as the discovery itself.

That February, over nine hundred B-17 bombers of the US Eighth Air Force had dropped nearly twenty-three hundred tons of bombs on Berlin and almost totally demolished the Reichsbank as well as its printing presses. Some of the bank's gold had already been shipped to safety in vaults outside Berlin, but the February raid prompted Hitler's finance minister and Reichsbank head, Walter Funk, to order immediate evacuation of the rest of the reserve. Loaded onto trains, it arrived at Merkers a few days later. It stayed there until late March, but then Patton's lightning advance into Thuringia unnerved bank officials and they decided that it should be moved back to Berlin. However, at this crucial moment they ran into an extraordinary obstacle.

The Third Reich might be crumbling, with the Americans and British across the Rhine and most of the nation's eastern provinces already in Russian hands, but the German railway system still insisted on its Easter break and partially shut down for the holidays, making it impossible to shift the gold. Goebbels was incredulous. "One could tear one's hair out when one thinks that the Reichsbahn is having an Easter holiday while the enemy is looting our stores of gold," he stormed in his diary.[15]

Although they were thwarted in their efforts to remove the gold, the bank officials had succeeded in getting out some of the cash, which was in seriously short supply in some parts of the Reich. Just three days before the Americans arrived they managed to load some two hundred million Reichsmarks and fifty packages of foreign currency onto a truck and drive off towards Magdeburg and Halle. Another load almost made it out, too, but turned back when the officials heard how close the Americans were. They had barely put it back into the mine when Patton's men arrived.

There was much more for Reid to see in this Aladdin's cave of hidden treasure. In side galleries off the main tunnel, he told his listeners, "there were more canvas sacks of wealth lying neatly stacked one above the other in long rows as prosaically as though they were smallish bags of flour and nothing more. In one room alone," he added, "I saw hundreds upon hundreds of sacks, each of them containing one million German paper marks, each sack bearing its scarlet Reichsbank label and the amount it contained." Hundreds more contained US bills — some two million dollars' worth in total — as well as thousands of French francs, British pounds, Norwegian kroners, Italian lire, Portuguese escudos and Spanish pesetas. These were the bags that had been hastily brought back to the mine just days before. "You didn't manage to get any souvenirs, did you?" joked a BBC colleague after hearing Reid's broadcast.[16]

Reid's eye also fell on more than a thousand wooden packing cases that filled every other space inside the vast underground labyrinth. These contained the most precious treasures of the art galleries and museums of Berlin that had also been shipped out of the city just three weeks before. Among them were carefully packed works by Rembrandt, Raphael, van Dyck, and Dürer, among others.

Reid stopped to talk to Dr. Rave, the curator who had traveled down with the cases and was still looking after them. A nervous, thin-faced little man, he assured Reid that none of it was art stolen from foreign countries. What he didn't reveal, though, was that the mine had also been used by the SS to store loot plundered from Jews and other concentration camp victims. Between August 1942 and January 1945, the SS had made seventy-two deliveries of such loot to the Reichsbank, where it was received for a holding account in the name of "Melmer," the SS captain who made most of the deliveries. The gold jewelry was mostly sold abroad, and securities and foreign currency ended up with the Reichsbank. Miscellaneous pieces of jewelry were disposed of through the Berlin Municipal Pawn Shop. The proceeds were then all credited to the account of "Max Heiliger" — a code name for Himmler and the SS.

But not all had been disposed of before January 1945, when it was decided that this, too, should be sent for safety to Merkers. The gold and silver bars filled eighteen bags. The rest, including all kinds of gold and silver items, ranging from dental work to cigarette cases, as well as diamonds, coins and foreign currencies, were packed into some two hundred suitcases, trunks and boxes. They had arrived at Merkers just three weeks before, and the Americans had unearthed the cache only hours before Reid arrived on the scene.[17]

He also discovered that parts of the mine were still being worked for salt, and that about two hundred British prisoners of war had been employed there, with some of them toiling below ground for two years. Several came from the Fifty-first Highland Division and had been captured near Dunkirk back in 1940. Reid stopped to chat with a handful still left. They knew all about the treasures. But Reid assured his listeners back home in Britain that the loot did not thrill them as much as the packet of English cigarettes he gave them.[18]

The American generals were similarly ambivalent. "If these were the old days when a soldier kept his loot," cracked Bradley when he and Eisenhower visited the mine with Patton, "you'd be the richest man in the world." Patton simply grinned.

From Merkers, the three men then drove a few miles to the second place Patton wanted to show them. It lay hidden in a pine forest just outside the small town of Ohrdruf.

A few days before, American soldiers had stumbled on a Nazi camp housing thousands of slave laborers working on railway construction. Nearly all were Russians, Poles, Czechs and Jews. Most had been evacuated by the SS to Buchenwald ahead of the advancing Americans. Many of the rest, mainly the sick, the exhausted and the old, had been massacred and their bodies left behind. Immediately inside the barbed wire, the GIs found dozens who had been shot, bayoneted or had their heads smashed in. In one of the wooden barracks more bodies lay stacked like piles of cord wood. They had been sprinkled with lime. In the woods outside, the Americans stumbled on a deep burial pit covered by a grille formed of rail tracks dusted with the charred remains of human beings. Below it lay a pile of bones, skulls and charred torsos.

A man claiming to be one of the camp's inmates acted as a guide for the American generals. "This was one of the most appalling sights I have ever seen," confessed Patton. First their guide showed them a gallows where men were hanged for attempting to escape. "The hanging was done by a bit of piano wire," said Patton in a special memorandum he dictated immediately afterwards to record what he had witnessed, "and the man being hanged was not dropped far enough to break his neck but simply strangled. It is alleged that the German generals who were killed after the attempted assassination of Hitler in July were hanged in the same manner." He continued:

We then saw a whipping table which stands at a height of just to a man's stomach. The person to be whipped then had his feet fastened in a sort of stocks. He was then pulled across the table by his hands and beaten with a stick, about an inch and a half in diameter, over the buttocks and back. The impresario [the man acting as their guide] claimed that he had received 25 strokes. He was such a well-fed looking man that I had an idea he may have been one of the executioners.

Indeed, he was. Two days after the visit, the man was torn limb from limb by enraged inmates.[19]

The smell of death, urine and feces hung over the camp. Emaciated bodies still lay unburied, lice crawling over their yellow skin. Some of their bellies were covered with coarse black sores of dried blood where starving prisoners had desperately torn out the entrails for food. Bradley was too shocked to speak. Patton briefly disappeared to vomit behind a wall. Eisenhower went deathly pale. "We are told the American soldier doesn't know what he's fighting for," he said grimly. "Now at least he will know what he is fighting *against*."

He had made a conscious decision to see these atrocities for himself in order to quash any future allegations that such horrors were merely propaganda. On his return to headquarters he wired both Washington and London, urging that editors, parliamentarians and members of Congress should be sent out to see what he had seen with their own eyes. He was determined to leave no room at all for cynical doubts about the nature and extent of Nazi horrors, and wanted the evidence to be viewed while it was still fresh.

Later, for the same reason, twenty-four prominent citizens of Gotha were forcibly conducted round the camp to witness the atrocity. Two of the most important were missing, though: that morning, the burgermeister and his wife had slashed their wrists before hanging themselves in their home rather than acknowledge the horrors that had been perpetrated on their doorstep.[20]

That night, over a stiff drink back at Patton's headquarters, Eisenhower gave his orders for the next phase of allied strategy. Patton was all for seizing the moment to strike for Berlin. He distrusted the Russians even more than Churchill did. "Ike," he said, "we had better take Berlin and quick and [then go eastward] to the Oder." But again Eisenhower disagreed. The Americans were already outrunning their supply lines, he said. He would leave Hitler's capital to the Russians.

More than ever, his eyes were now firmly fixed on the Alpine

Redoubt. Patton, he decided, would make a powerful thrust with his Third Army up the Danube towards Linz and Salzburg, while on his right flank Patch's Seventh Army, along with the French First Army, would head for Munich and the Alps. "Even then," noted the Supreme Commander, "the National Redoubt could remain in being and it must be our aim to break into it rapidly before the enemy has an opportunity to man it and finally organize its defenses."[21]

The day's experiences had made an indelible impression. The Americans had stumbled on the Merkers treasure only by accident, not as a result of advance intelligence. This raised an inevitable question: what further unknown resources had the Nazis stacked away in other caves to continue the fight? And with their atrocities now revealed to the world, what else could the Nazis do in their fanaticism than go down fighting? If Eisenhower had any more doubts, a visit to Buchenwald the next morning would certainly quash them once and for all.

"The things I saw beggar description," he wrote to Marshall in Washington. "While touring the camp I encountered three men who had been inmates and by some ruse or other had made their escape. I interviewed them through an interpreter. The visual evidence and verbal testimony of starvation, cruelty and bestiality were so over-powering as to leave me a bit sick." In one room, he added, where between twenty and thirty naked men had died of starvation, Patton had refused to enter. It would make him sick, he told Eisenhower.[22]

The experience shook the allied Supreme Commander to the core. Never, he wrote in his memoirs, had he felt able to describe his emo-tional reactions on coming face to face with this indisputable evidence of Nazi brutality and the Nazis' ruthless disregard of every shred of human decency. It was, he said, "beyond the American mind to com-prehend. I have never at any other time experienced an equal sense of shock."[23]

If this were true for Eisenhower, it was even more so for ordinary American infantrymen who stumbled on the camp and had their eyes opened for the first time to the true nature of the enemy. Never did the shoulder-sleeve insignia worn by SHAEF staff members seem more appropriate. Against a jet-black background representing the darkness of Nazi oppression stood a crusader's sword of liberation. Flames arose from the hilt and leaped up the blade — "a representation of the aveng-ing justice," ran the official description, "by which the enemy power would be broken in Nazi Europe."

CHAPTER FOUR

"A CURIOUS PEARLY COLOR"

On 21 April 1945, Robert Reid was back at Buchenwald reporting for the BBC. The Americans had already erected a temporary plinth to commemorate the fifty thousand–plus prisoners estimated to have died there. This time Reid visited the crematorium, and saw for himself the industrial-size elevator that carried the bodies of executed prisoners directly to the incinerators. Accompanying him were members of a British parliamentary delegation who had responded to Eisenhower's request and flown out to Germany for a short but exhaustive visit to see the horrors for themselves.

As the first major camp to be liberated, Buchenwald was to be visited repeatedly over the next few days by similar delegations, but the British group was the first to arrive, landing within twenty-four hours of Eisenhower's telegram. It included members of all the political parties, both men and women. Soon three members of the United States Congress joined them. The American Party included Clare Booth-Luce, wife of the influential Harry Luce, founder and publisher of *Time* and *Life* magazines.

On the gentle hillside overlooking Weimar, now greening with spring growth, American medical teams had been strenuously at work for days trying to save the dying. But the situation was still dreadful and not all the bodies had yet been buried. Shocked, the civilian observers hurriedly walked through the temporary hospitals, listened to testimonies from survivors, and saw hundreds of emaciated bodies in pits that had been hastily dug by US Army bulldozers. "One of the most horrible things about the whole place," said one of the stunned parliamentarians to Robert Reid after viewing the crematorium, "is the cold-blooded, typically thorough German way in which everything was organized."

They had all seen photographs beforehand, and knew what to expect, but none of the pictures could convey the smell of death and disease that filled their nostrils, or prepare them for the experience of talking face to face with the victims. "Not only were they shown through the rat holes of hutments where thousands of prisoners have lived and died, the starved skeletons of what were once men awaiting a decent Christian [sic] burial, and the crematorium with the charred bones still in the ovens," a somber Reid told his BBC listeners in Britain, "they also had an opportunity of talking with many of the prisoners and all they heard confirms every newspaper and radio reporter's story of the place."

It was in part the vivid and shocking coexistence of the beauty of the landscape and the brutality within the camp that inspired Eisenhower to insist that German civilians from Weimar be forced to witness the horrors that had taken place in their own back yard. He wanted no arguing or protesting about German innocence in years to come. At least a thousand inhabitants of the city, he demanded, were to view the camp and the hospital. Half of them should be women. "Those who are required to make the trip include: men and women from 18 to 45, particularly those who belonged to the NSDAP," read his orders.

> Two thirds of those are to be of the more prosperous classes and one third the less. They must be strong enough to endure the march and the inspection (it will last about six hours; the distance is 25 kilometers). Food is to be brought and is to be consumed before visiting the camp. Nothing will happen to the partakers. The march will be accompanied by trucks of the German Red Cross and doctors in order to give help if anyone needs it.[1]

Reid was there to witness the scene. A dozen or so processions of German men, women, girls and boys were herded through the camp, escorted by US military police and some of the camp's block leaders, and forced to gaze, Reid told his BBC listeners, "on the mound of skeletons covered with their tight parchment of purplish skin." It was a hot afternoon, he explained, "and the dusty compound of Buchenwald stank with the corruption of festering death all around. Some of the more stolid Germans just looked at those bodies and said nothing. It was impossible to probe through their skulls and look into their minds to see what they were thinking."

His anger was partly personal. He and Vera had taken a Jewish refugee from Vienna into their home. He knew from what she had told them how ordinary, respectable people had simply turned their backs on Hitler's victims and chosen not to know what was happening.[2]

Buchenwald made headlines around the world. But British citizens were transfixed even more grimly by a similar horror recently uncovered by their own troops in the pine forests of northern Germany.

Celle is a small town lying on the Aller River about thirty miles northeast of Hanover on the road to Hamburg. Close by, Montgomery's British forces had established a corps headquarters as the front line advancing steadily towards the Baltic. Ahead lay Lüneberg Heath. On Thursday 12 April, a colonel of the Wehrmacht approached the British lines on a motorcycle waving a white flag. He asked to speak with a senior British officer. Blindfolded, he was taken to the headquarters.

The colonel was seeking a local truce. The reason, he explained, was that an epidemic of typhus had broken out in a nearby concentration camp. If the fighting engulfed the camp, it was feared, prisoners might escape and spread the disease. After some discussion and amendments his proposal was accepted. It was agreed that when British forces reached a certain point, a truce zone would come into force.

Three days later the British forces reached the line. Among them was a twenty-three-year-old major in the Eleventh Armored Division, David Finnie. He was leading a troop of half-track guns along a narrow road packed with vehicles towards the village of Bergen. They reached a bridge over the Aller, and then, suddenly, the convoy stopped. On either side was a boggy field; beyond, lay dense pine forests. They were stuck. "We sat still on a pleasant spring day," Finnie recalled, "waiting." Occasionally, a German shell exploded nearby.

Eventually, he was briefed for the first time about the truce. They had reached the edge of the agreed zone. He duly marked the area on his map.[3]

Meanwhile, a small British party had entered the camp. One of the first to arrive was a young intelligence officer, Derrick Sington, who never forgot what met his eyes, or his nose:

> It reminded me of the entrance to a zoo. We came into a smell of ordure — like the smell of a monkey camp. A sad, blue smoke floated like ground mist between low buildings. I had tried to imagine the interior of a concentration camp, but I had not imagined it like this. Nor had I imagined the strange, simian throng, who crowded the barbed wire fence surrounding their compounds, with their shaven heads and their obscene striped penitentiary suits . . . We had been welcomed before, but the half-credulous cheers of these almost lost men, of these clowns in their terrible motley, who had once been Polish officers, land workers in the Ukraine, Budapest doctors and students in France, impelled a stronger emotion, and I had to fight back my tears.[4]

At the main gate, the senior British officer charged with taking control of the camp met with its commander, a Wehrmacht officer, and was then escorted to meet the person who was really in charge, SS Hauptsturmführer (Captain) Josef Kramer, a veteran of Auschwitz. The first thing Kramer did was insist that his men should not be disarmed. If they were, he explained, they would be torn to pieces by the inmates. It was agreed that, for the time being, they could keep their weapons.

Kramer then showed the British around, falling over himself to explain that he had only recently arrived and most of what they saw had therefore been out of his control. He appeared to have no shame, and said he had tried to do his best. But what the British soldiers saw that day they never forgot, and all those who followed, writes one historian, "felt the same sequence of emotions: disbelief, bewilderment, horror and anger."[5]

Bergen-Belsen was in reality two camps within one. In Camp 1 were crammed up to fifty thousand inmates, half of them women; of these, some eighteen thousand were Hungarian, Polish, Romanian, Czech or German Jews, most of whom were the sole survivors of families who had perished in the gas chambers at Birkenau (Auschwitz) or Treblinka. The rest of the women were Russians, Yugoslavs, Poles, French and Belgians who had been arrested for resistance activities. Camp 2 was situated next to a Panzer training school on the same site, and consisted solely of men — some fifteen thousand of them. The largest group was

Russian, who made up some 60 percent of the total, followed by Poles. There were between 1,600 and 1,800 Germans, approximately 500 each of Greeks, French, Belgians and Czechs, and the rest were Dutch and Yugoslavian.[6]

By far the worse of the two was Camp 1. Here, crammed into a hundred single-story wooden huts, or lying around the compound exposed to the elements, lay tens of thousands of sick and emaciated prisoners. Most were racked with dysentery, tuberculosis or typhus. The men were dressed in the standard concentration camp garb of striped material resembling pajamas, or wore filthy rags. The women were in striped flannel gowns. Few of either sex wore shoes. For days, as a result of the approaching battle front, there had been no electricity or water. The sanitation, always primitive at best, was now non-existent. The inmates were dying at the rate of five hundred a day. Outside one of the women's huts lay a pile of unburied bodies. Inside, dead women were lying in the passage, and in the main room was a mass of bodies blocking any further access.

The place stank of rotting flesh, feces and urine. "It was just a barren wilderness, as bare and devoid of vegetation as a chicken run," recorded one officer from an army ambulance unit.

> Corpses lay everywhere, some in huge piles where they had been dumped by the other inmates, sometimes singly or in pairs where they had fallen as they shuffled along the dirt tracks . . . [I] saw women drowning in their own vomit because they were too weak to roll over and men eating worms as they clutched half a loaf of bread purely because they had to eat and could now scarcely tell the difference between worms and bread. Piles of corpses, naked and obscene, with a woman too weak to stand propping herself up against them as she cooked the food we gave her over an open flame. Men and women crouching down just anywhere in the open relieving themselves of the dysentery which was scouring their bodies, a woman standing stark naked washing herself with issue soap in water from a tank in which the remains of a child floated.

This was only the most visible misery to meet the eye. Inside the packed wooden huts the liberating British troops encountered scenes from Dante's Hell. Frantic efforts were mounted to save as many lives as possible, but the task proved almost insurmountable.

The first desperate need was for food and water, and within twenty-four hours convoys of water tanks, food and kitchen equipment arrived on the scene. However, much of the food proved too rich for the sick: many of them simply wolfed it down, were promptly ill, and died. But it was the sheer scale of the medical emergency that overwhelmed the liberators. After a rapid survey, it was decided that some seventeen thousand of the women in Camp 1 required instant hospital treatment, but there was no hospital. An emergency one could be set up in the Panzer training school, but that would take time. And although an evacuation timetable was put in place, there were inevitable delays. Meanwhile, the death toll continued to mount.

Two weeks after entering the camp, the British Army's medical services were still so overburdened that they called desperately on the help of ninety-six medical students from London. Each was allocated a hut and told to make conditions as tolerable as possible while the inmates waited to be transferred to a proper hospital bed. They also had to make sure that everyone got their fair share of rations — otherwise the strong simply stole from the weak.

One student left a vivid account of his hut:

It was full of the most emaciated people I have ever seen in my life. There was supposed to be a loo at the far end but they couldn't get up to go to it. [The hut] was almost up to the top of one's boots in excreta. One just stumped about in it. People by now were too weak to use [the toilet] and were just lying in their own faeces and urine which dripped down from one bunk to the next.

Another student captured a singular moment of horror.

I was standing aghast in the midst of all this filth, trying to get used to the smell which was a mixture of post-mortem room, a sewer, sweat, and foul pus, when I heard a scrabbling on the floor. I looked down in the half light and saw a woman crouching at my feet. She had black matted hair, well populated [by lice] and her ribs stood out as though there was nothing between them, her arms were so thin that they were horrible. She was defecating, but she was so weak that she could not lift her buttocks from the floor and, as she had diarrhoea, the liquid yellow stools bubbled over her thighs.

As the students moved through the huts, women clutched at their sleeves in desperation, crying out, *"Herr Doktor! Herr Doktor!"* and telling them their pitiful stories: "My mother and father were burned in Auschwitz"; "My husband was flogged to death by the SS"; or, they asked them pleadingly, "Will I ever be beautiful again, *Herr Doktor?"* [7]

Registration of the victims had long since been abandoned, or had been non-existent from the start. To make matters worse, relatives were sometimes mistakenly separated in the course of the evacuation, a fact that caused immense distress. Gradually, however, nurses began to make out personal history cards for the survivors, along with details of missing relatives. This process again revealed the shocking inhumanity of the Nazis, as was recalled by a nurse in the Swiss Red Cross who asked a patient to state her name, nationality and place of origin: "The woman did not know what to say. At last she pulled up the sleeve of her nightgown and stammered, 'Me . . . no name — only number — no country, just a Jewess, do you understand? I am only a dog.' " [8]

The most urgent problem was typhus. Thanks to the filthy conditions, it was spreading rapidly through the camp. The louse is the main carrier of typhus, which first reveals itself with a skin rash, followed by fever, acute headache and pain, then renal failure and gangrene. Eventually it penetrates the central nervous system, causing an agonizing, convulsive death. One of its victims was Anne Frank, who had died in Belsen that February.

To stop the disease's spread, the lice had to be killed. So everyone in the camp, prisoner or otherwise, as well as all visitors, was sprayed liberally with DDT. "A squirt up each sleeve. One down the trousers. Two more squirts down the back and the front of the shirt and a final shot on the hair," remembered one visitor. Severe speed restrictions were also imposed on all vehicles in and around the camp to keep down the dust that carried and spread the deadly feces of the lice. Slowly, the death rate came down, and by the end of the month it stood at three hundred a day. As each of the filthy and contaminated huts was emptied, it was burned to the ground.

Meanwhile, as the doctors and nurses tended to the living, the work of burying the dead went on relentlessly. The numbers were too great for individual graves to be dug, or for any dignity to be observed in burial. Instead, as at Buchenwald, army bulldozers excavated great open-air pits and the bodies were manhandled in. At first this grim task was given to the remaining SS guards, who were deliberately fed the pathetic rations handed out to the prisoners before their liberation. After a couple of days, two of them committed suicide, one collapsed and another disguised himself as a prisoner and was shot while trying to escape.

A war correspondent, Alan Moorehead, accompanying the British forces in northwest Germany, observed one of the burial scenes:

> We came on a group of German guards flinging the bodies into a pit about a hundred feet square. They brought the bodies up in hand-carts, and as they were flung into the grave a British soldier kept a tally of the numbers. When the total reached five hundred a bull-dozer driven by another soldier came up and started nudging the earth into the grave. There was a curious pearly colour about the piled up bodies, and they were small like the bodies of children . . . all the normal features by which you know a human being had practically disappeared."[9]

Eventually, it was decided to speed up matters by simply bulldozing the corpses into the pits. A Christian padre and a Jewish rabbi then said prayers over the site.

Belsen had never been an official extermination center, like Auschwitz or Treblinka. Nor was it one of the prewar concentration camps for political opponents of the Nazis, like Buchenwald or Dachau, where Fey von Hassell was still interned. Ironically, it had been built in 1943 as a relatively lenient camp for privileged prisoners, mostly prominent Jews with important connections whom the Nazis hoped to exchange for Germans interned in allied countries. Only a handful were ever traded in this way, however, and by late 1944 the camp had degenerated into just another miserable hellhole in the vast gulag of Nazi barbed wire that criss-crossed Hitler's new Europe, "the terminus, the last station," it has been said, "of the Holocaust."[10]

Soon it was packed with prisoners being evacuated from Poland and eastern Germany ahead of the advancing Russians, the sick from labor camps across the Reich, and thousands of others being shipped around Hitler's disintegrating empire for no clear or obvious reason. The only clear thing that emerged from the chaos was that Himmler hoped to strike a deal that would save his life. In March, one of his principal deputies, SS Obergruppenführer Oswald Pohl, had visited the camp at the pleading of Josef Kramer. Shocked by what he saw, he arranged for the rapid removal of seven thousand of the remaining "exchange Jews," obviously in the hope that they could still be traded with the allies for something that would save his boss. But, even as they left, more transports continued to arrive.

By early April, the number of prisoners had grown to some forty thousand from only fifteen thousand in December, and several more thousand arrived in the following weeks. Conditions were made substantially worse by the transfer of administrative SS staff from Auschwitz, men and women who were well hardened to brutality and death. Kramer was a keen and obedient Nazi whose sheer indifference to the squalor that surrounded him defied belief. One of his first acts was to impose a vicious regime by appointing Aryan "kapos" (trusted inmates) for each of the huts and terrorizing the prisoners with endless roll-calls. Typhus had first broken out in February. By March, efforts to bury the dead had simply been abandoned.

A French musician who had played in the camp's orchestra had fallen ill with typhus just two weeks before the British arrived. She recalled:

> I had the most abominable dysentery. I was just a sick animal lying in its own excrement. From 8 April everything around me became nightmarish. I merely existed as a bursting head, an intestine, a perpetually active anus. One tier above me was a French girl I didn't know; in my moments of lucidity, I heard her saying in a clear, calm, even pleasant voice, "I must shit, but I must shit on your head, it's more hygienic!" She had gone mad; others, equally unhinged, guffawed interminably or fought. No one came to see us any more, not even the SS. They'd turned off the water.[11]

Around the world, broadcasts, press headlines and photographs from Belsen, along with newsreels of the horrors, triggered universal shock and disgust. Kramer and his SS guards, both male and female, were denounced as "The Beasts of Belsen." Within hours of the camp's liberation, Kramer was put under close arrest in his own quarters. The next day, he was removed from the camp and placed in a cellar below the officers' quarters. Here, he was interrogated by field security officers and then—by this time being execrated in headlines as "The Shackled Monster of Belsen"—he was taken to the Celle prisoner-of-war camp.

The female guards of Belsen provoked a special loathing, as their behavior flew in the face of everything women were supposed to represent. "They played their vile part in torturing and starving thousands of helpless men, women and children," read one caption beneath a photograph showing three of the well-nourished women. "They flogged starving women too weak to walk, and whooped with joy round their dying victims." Other captions described them as "she-thugs" who "happily wielded whips for Himmler." If anything were needed to prove that the allies were fighting a just cause, this was it. The Germans, screamed one headline, were "The Beasts of Europe."[12] Clearly, the liberating forces believed the whole nation was collectively responsible for Nazi crimes.

Nine days after the British forces entered the camp, the burgermeisters of Celle and neighboring towns were brought to Belsen and shown around. They were led to the burial pit, still half full of bodies, and forced to line up with the SS men and women. Then the British commandant read out a long denunciation. "What you will see here," he told them, "is the final and utter condemnation of the Nazi Party. It justifies every measure which the United Nations will take to exterminate the Party. What you will see here is such a disgrace to the German people that their names must forever be erased from the list of civilized nations." Above all, he made clear his desire to implicate *them*, too. "Who bears the final responsibility?" he asked rhetorically. "*You*, who have allowed your Führer to carry out his terrible whims. *You* who have proved incapable of doing anything to check his perverted triumphs . . . *You* who did not rise up spontaneously to cleanse the name of Germany, not fearing the personal consequence. *You* stand here judged through what you will see in the camp." One of the mayors covered his face with his hands and wept. Another vomited. Another refused to look at the pit in front of him. They all said that they had never dreamed that this was going on.[13]

Under the terms of the truce, the camp guards remained temporarily on duty. Cooks and other service personnel also remained in their jobs until replaced by the British. Furthermore, it was agreed that no more than six days after the arrival of British forces, any Wehrmacht personnel would be conveyed back to the German lines with their arms, their equipment and their vehicles. This did not, however, apply to the SS.

The six days were up on Hitler's birthday. At eight-thirty that morning, a convoy of British Army trucks rolled into the camp and loaded up four hundred soldiers of the Wehrmacht. Two days before, a roll-call had revealed that only fifty-four of them wished to return to the Reich and that the rest were happy to become prisoners of war. But the British overruled them. One eyewitness recorded:

> In their field-grey uniform they marched, carrying their rifles, bazookas, grenades, mortars, the sweat trickling from under their steel helmets, ploughing furrows of dust on their faces. The men of the Wehrmacht were marching to the outer gates of this charnel house to take up their positions against our troops. Our grim-faced men watched them go by . . . Past the clean, green-walled barracks building which had housed them, they tramped looking very cheerful . . . they firmly believed they were not to be assigned to front line fighting. They had been guards so long, they did not know Hitler was putting his schoolboys into the lines.[14]

As the German troops left the camp, hundreds of those inmates who were strong enough to stand hooted and bayed like animals. One of the prisoners, too ill to join in, dipped a solitary crust of bread into a puddle to make it soft enough to swallow. To add insult to injury, the departing Germans had already deliberately wrecked the water supply in the barracks they left behind.[15]

Close by in Lüneberg, Bryan Samain as yet remained unaware of the horrors at Belsen. His sole previous glimpse of what a concentration camp might mean had come at school when he was only thirteen and so had little interest in politics or international affairs. But one day, at chapel, the service was given by a visiting German pastor. The man was a refugee, and bared his arm. A shocked Samain saw the blue number tattooed upon it.[16]

His main responsibility since landing in Normandy had been as his unit's intelligence officer. He had spent six weeks at the British Army's military intelligence training school at Matlock, in Derbyshire. Housed in a grand prewar spa hotel, it still had potted plants in the reception area and a grand old Victorian conservatory. Its staff included a large number of attractive and distracting young Auxiliary Territorial Service (ATS) girls. Much of the training involved map and compass work, as well as TEWTS, which Samain quickly discovered stood for "tactical exercises without troops." This, he recorded, "usually involved standing about on a hill and discussing the movement and deployment of troops, both 'own' and 'enemy' within the framework of a given scenario."[17]

Most of this work was familiar from his basic training, but there was a lot that was new, too, including how to interrogate prisoners of war, the enemy order of battle, front-line codes, and the skill of writing up crisp, accurate situation reports (sitreps). Samain liked the enemy order of battle course best. It involved learning all about the German Army's organization and its divisions in Western Europe. It had an element of intellectual puzzle-solving about it. "We soon learned," he recorded, "that from the capture of a single enemy POW we could deduce, from the name or number of his unit, the regiment he belonged to, the division that regiment was part of, and so on." Throughout the course he was drilled constantly in the basic reason for his life as an IO (intelligence officer): "This is what I know now, who do I need to inform?"

And that was what he had done for most of the time since crossing the Channel. His unit's original intelligence officer was killed on D-Day, and Samain was chosen as his replacement on the strength of the Matlock course. His team included a sergeant, a corporal and six marines. Their task, as he later described it, was to collate, analyze and pass on operational information as they gathered it to both their commanding officer and brigade intelligence. "For this last-named purpose," he said, "I regularly visited Brigade HQ a mile or so behind us, generally on a bicycle. On one occasion, going down a deserted lane, I was blown off the bike into a nearby ditch by a random shell that exploded close by me." He also had to make sure that the front-line men were kept absolutely up to date with the latest positions of the enemy lines, especially through photo-reconnaissance maps taken just hours before. For this, he frequently found himself crawling forward, delivering the information to the men in slit trenches.

But he had also spent plenty of time crawling about under fire for another reason. This was because his other main area of expertise was as a sniper.

Despite their training, civilians turned soldiers often found it hard to kill. They would try to avoid it, or kill only when it was a matter of one's own life or the enemy's. For preference, they did even this at a distance, so they did not have to see the impact on their victims and acknowledge them as human beings. Only a small minority relished the task, and after the war was over few were willing to talk of it. Many felt guilty. Fairly typical was the recollection of one British soldier fighting with Montgomery's forces:

> I was a yokel, yet they taught me to kill in six weeks. Unbelievable. I would never have killed anybody in a million years. There's no two ways about it, you get acclimatised . . . First of all I killed with a Bren gun — so that was from far away . . . I was squeamish when I first did hand-to-hand fighting — when I did my first bayonet attack. But I was good at closing my mind . . . it's kill or be killed. If you think they won't do it to you, you're dead. So whether he's going to shoot you or not, you've got to be first.[18]

To kill in cold blood was hard. That was what made snipers special. It was their unique task "to line up their sights on a man's head and pull the trigger," notes one historian.

> It had to be approached in a calm manner and there was little room for emotions. A few even went so far as to keep "Game Books" in which they logged their daily "bag." British snipers operating from houses outside Arnhem used pencils to scratch their daily scores on to the furniture or walls of the houses they occupied. Some ordinary infantrymen thought sniping dishonourable and disliked their own snipers as much as they feared the enemy.[19]

Yet the practice had a long and accepted place in warfare; it was, after all, a sniper hidden in the rigging of a French ship who had done for Admiral Nelson while he stood on the deck of the *Victory* at Trafalgar. Historically, the skill had been known as "sharpshooting," but during the days of the Raj in India, bored British officers had developed the sport of shooting at snipe — small, fast-moving birds that tested all their skills and reflexes — and the new term was now standard.

If caught, a sniper's fate was rarely happy. Occasionally, he might provide useful intelligence. More usually, he was finished off without much ceremony. "There was no time to muck around with them," observed Samain, who could not remember a single occasion when an enemy sniper's life had been spared.

To perfect his own shooting skills, which he had first honed in his school's cadet corps, he had been sent on a specialized course run by the British Army at Devizes, Wiltshire, for Americans and Canadians as well as British sharpshooters. "A young Canadian backwoodsman I particularly remember," recalled Samain. "He could hit a tin can with a rifle bullet at a range of 100 yards, then do the same thing to other tin cans with a succession of quickly aimed follow-up shots." But such talent was taken for granted on the course: the special skills the instructors were looking for were patience, stealth of movement and the ability to fire a single, telling shot at the critical moment.

Samain repeatedly practiced the fieldcraft basic to commando training: the skillful use of natural cover such as hedgerows and ditches, the shadows cast by trees and buildings, and so on. But he also learned how to prepare a sniper's hide. Typically, this involved digging a shallow trench in a hedgerow and hiding in it covered by branches and foliage, making sure that he had a clear field of fire. His weapon was a standard British Mark I (T) Lee-Enfield rifle with a detachable telescopic sight that he carried separately in a metal case. He also used a pair of standard British Army binoculars.

He would black up his face and the backs of his hands with mud or black cream, then use green-brown netting to cover his body. One of only four snipers in his unit, he had quickly learned in Normandy that there was little time to dig a hide, so instead he made use of natural cover, or the roof of an old building or a deserted barn. Unlike Wehrmacht or French collaborationist soldiers, though, he did not tie himself to a chimney stack or the top of a tree. To have done so would have prevented him from making the often essential quick escape.

Much of the sniper's life, as his training had stressed, involved long hours of patience. Typical was a patrol he went on with two other snipers. Soon after dawn they set off into no man's land between British and German lines, making for a deserted farmhouse some eight hundred yards away. The approach lay along rough country tracks, stretches of shell-torn woodland and deserted fields. "The air stank of dead and rotting cattle lying upturned in fields," he recorded, "and in the woodlands there were German and British corpses alike, including several of our own paratroopers who had dropped on D-Day, still hanging in the trees." Apart from the occasional bark of artillery in the distance, it was dead quiet.

They found the farmhouse to be empty, so cautiously eased themselves into sniping positions — "up the remains of rickety stairs in the farm building itself," he wrote, "and into the loft where, through the shattered tile roofing, we could gain some view of the enemy lines about 100 yards to our front." For two or three hours they watched, all the time being plagued by swarms of mosquitoes. Then, suddenly, they spotted a slight movement behind a hedgerow that obscured the German positions. It was followed by the brief, dull gleam of helmets. It was a small group of men moving across a gap in the hedgerow.

One of the snipers with Samain fired a single shot. After that, there was no sign of any further movement. The commando team lay silent and motionless for some time longer, despite the mosquitoes, waiting to see if any more targets presented themselves. None did. Finally, they withdrew silently, retreating from the farmhouse as cautiously as they had entered it. They could not for certain claim a kill that day, but Samain could comfort himself with the thought that they had made a small contribution towards making the Germans think twice about launching an attack.[20]

German snipers were in action too, of course, but there were other tricky hazards as well, and Samain was lucky not to have fallen victim to one of them. Shortly after taking over as intelligence officer he had been advancing through a heavily wooded area in Normandy when he walked into a wire strung between two trees and set off a booby trap. The grenade that exploded sent splinters into his chest and lower back and he was quickly stretchered back to a regimental aid post, then transferred by ambulance to a field hospital in Bayeux. He stayed there for two or three weeks, sharing a ward with some badly burned members of a tank crew being fed through straws. When he was well enough to be allowed out, one of the first things he did was attend mass in the local cathedral.

Eventually, he heard that his unit had returned to England for a refit, so he hitched a lift on a US Air Force Dakota. The plane was full of small crates and other packages from Brussels, which had just been liberated. Mostly it was champagne, scent and silk stockings. At Northolt he was given a lift by a king's messenger from the Foreign Office, who was waiting for the plane in a Daimler limousine. As they drove into London, Samain realized that he was traveling with several packages of the Brussels loot, which had been packed in the car's boot.

Even as Belsen was being cleared and deloused, the Nazis were still frantically shuffling concentration camp prisoners ahead of the advancing British forces, who were now rapidly closing in on Hamburg. On the edge of this now bombed-out port, the one-time home of Fred

Warner, stood yet another notorious camp, Neuengamme. Once a sub-camp of Sachsenhausen, it subsequently spawned dozens of satellite camps of its own, and by 1945 held some thirteen thousand prisoners, both men and women. It was always a brutal place, characterized by starvation, physical abuse and a total lack of hygiene and medical care, with inmates forced to do hard labor in quarries and munitions plants. The mortality rate was 50 percent.

On Hitler's birthday, the camp's commander ordered SS Sturmbannführer Gehrig, his head of administration, to go to Lübeck to oversee the loading of thousands of Neuengamme's prisoners onto ships. In their thousands, crammed into cattle trucks, or shuffling along in makeshift footwear or often bare feet, they made their way along roads and railway tracks. Hundreds died of exhaustion, or were shot by SS guards when they collapsed. One group, taken south, was herded into a barn which was then shut and set alight, with the guards shooting through the doors. Only twenty-two of the thousand inmates inside survived.

This day, too, in the early afternoon, a column of trucks drove a contingent of Jews from the camp to an empty school building on the northern edge of Hamburg. It contained twenty-two children between the ages of four and twelve, two women and twenty-six men. All had been used for medical experiments. They were taken to the school's gymnasium and hanged so that none should bear witness to Nazi atrocities.[21]

The day before Gehrig received his orders, the first group of inmates had arrived at Lübeck, packed into cattle wagons. Eventually, eleven thousand Neuengamme inmates were crowded onto the Baltic port's quayside. But where this caravan of human misery was going, and for what reason, none of them knew.

In the week between Eisenhower's traumatic visit to Ohrdruf and Hitler's birthday, episodes such as the bitter SS resistance at Nuremberg and the suicides of the Lord Mayor and his family at Leipzig intensified allied fears about some desperate last stand by Nazi fanatics in the Alpine Redoubt.

Now the very speed of the allied advance itself seemed to be making the threat of a redoubt a reality. By forcing "the German desperadoes back into the hard core of the mountains," declared British War Office intelligence in mid-April, it would make them hard to dislodge. A few days later, the code-breakers picked up a message that appeared to confirm their worst fears. It came from none other than Heinrich Himmler himself. In a message to his chief subordinate in Bavaria, the SS chief ordered: "Collect the SS units militarily under your command. Defend the Alps for me."[22]

The day after Nuremberg fell, Eisenhower's chief of staff, Walter Bedell Smith, held a press conference at SHAEF headquarters. After warning the gathered correspondents that what he was about to say should be kept top secret, he admitted that not much was known about the redoubt. Yet, it was clear that the Germans had been shifting men and matériel there. "Just what we will find down there we don't know," he told them. "We are beginning to think it will be a lot more than we expect. Our target now, if we are going to bring this war to an end in a hell of a hurry, is this national redoubt and we are going to organize our strength in that direction . . . We may find that when we have cut the head from the snake the tail won't wiggle very long."[23]

Unknown to Bedell Smith or allied intelligence, just hours beforehand Hitler had finally issued a directive about the redoubt. In one of the last items of business he took care of on his birthday, he ordered one of his most trusted subordinates, Lieutenant-General Winter, deputy chief of the armed forces operations staff, to fly immediately out of Berlin to Bavaria. With him, Winter carried an order instructing him to organize an "inner fortress" (Kernfestung) in the Alps, designed to serve as the last bulwark of fanatical resistance.

The region, Hitler instructed Winter, was to be closed from now on to all German and foreign civilians, and the SS was to remove all superfluous foreign workers. Supplies for the armed forces and the existing civilian population were to be stockpiled to the maximum extent possible. War supplies of all kinds, especially for mountain warfare, were to be moved into the area by the armed forces. Long-range courier aircraft and other planes suitable for reconnaissance would also be made available. Emergency factories for producing munitions, bazookas and explosives would be set up by the Ministry of War Production and Armaments. The senior military commander in the area would assume the duties of a fortress commander, while supreme powers over the Nazi Party itself and all civil government would be exercised by the existing Gauleiter and Governor of the Tirol, Franz Hofer. Winter's directive was made official on Tuesday 24 April.[24]

That same morning, Fred Warner and the SOE "Historian" party finally got the thumbs-up from their daily dispatch rider for their mission into Austria. Warner spent the day carefully checking his equipment and packing his rucksack. Inside was everything except food that he would need for survival in the mountains: thermal underwear and socks, a sleeping bag, a torch and a specially designed sand-colored waterproof cape that to a casual observer could pass for the innocent garments of a worker or farmer. Underneath, Fred would wear his standard khaki British battle dress. If caught, he would claim combatant status and so hopefully avoid being shot as a spy; this was especially important for returning émigrés like Warner and his group, who would otherwise be promptly dispatched by the Nazis as traitors.

Even more vital items were packed in the pockets of his uniform: compass, maps, a .45 Colt pistol and .22 Belgian Browning, and British Army papers identifying him as Lieutenant Fred Warner. With these items, if the worst came to the worst and he lost his rucksack, he would at least be able to establish where he was and could shoot, threaten or bargain his way out of trouble.

An early dinner followed. It was a somber affair, each man lost in his thoughts, although the chef had done his best to make the meal memorable. It was dusk when they were driven out to a special shed on the edge of the aerodrome used for the final fitting out of agents. The first thing Warner saw, laid out on the floor in front of him, was his jumping suit. This was a huge canvas affair fitted with zippers rather than buttons, gauntlets, a padded hat, and knee and elbow pads. Before putting it on, he carefully fitted his money belt. Concealed inside were two hundred US dollars, six gold sovereigns, and several thousand German Reichsmarks. He decided to do without the fur lining of his jumping suit, which made it bulkier than he liked and uncomfortable. Then he fitted his parachute.

Practicing jumps had formed a large part of his training since he had joined SOE back in 1943. Handling parachutes had begun in Altrincham, a wealthy suburb of Manchester, at a requisitioned private house with peacocks strutting majestically around the grounds. Here, well hidden behind the garden's trees and bushes, stood the fuselage of an old Whitley airplane. Warner had spent hours jumping from the aircraft, learning how to land without breaking a leg or an ankle by tumbling when hitting the ground.

Further practice followed on a functioning Whitley from Manchester's Ringway Airport, with the drops taking place at a relatively low altitude over Tatton Park in nearby Cheshire. Sitting on the edge of a hole cut in the floor of the fuselage, he learned to wait for the dispatcher's command of "Go" before pushing himself into the void at several hundred feet. After several successful drops he earned the right to attach a small parachute badge on the sleeve of his uniform. It was a symbolic moment that meant a lot to him. Finally, he could discard the insignia of the Pioneer Corps with its pick and shovel and all the frustrations and humiliations they meant to him. At last, he felt like a proper soldier doing his bit in the fight against Hitler.

In the darkness of the shed, in their jumping suits, Warner and the others discussed details of the flight with the aircraft's crew. The plane was a B-24 Liberator, the crew American: pilot, navigator, dispatcher and gunners. This came as bad news to Warner: American crews had a reputation for being happy-go-lucky and not very careful or practiced in where they dropped the agents. But there was nothing he could do about that except hope for good luck. There was a final farewell and handshake from a member of the SOE headquarters staff who had come to see them off and a hurried thank-you to the sergeant who had looked after the group during the weeks of waiting at the Villa Rosso. Then Warner was physically hoisted up by strong hands into the body of the aircraft. Already loaded were the containers holding the radio transmitter–receiver, the explosives the party would need for sabotage operations, and the bulk of their ammunition and food. This would be dropped separately, to be retrieved on the ground later.

Suddenly the silence was broken harshly as the gunners opened fire to check that the aircraft's weapons were in good order. Then the pilot started up the engines and revved them to a high-pitched scream to satisfy himself that all was well. As the noise died down, the aircraft slowly bumped its way onto the airstrip and trundled to the end of the runway. Three hundred miles to the north and a couple of hours' flying time across the Alps lay the unknown territory of Hitler's redoubt.

CHAPTER FIVE

"TO FALL HEROICALLY"

A re the Germans never going to crack?" On Hitler's birthday a New Zealand intelligence officer was sitting on the steps of his caravan at divisional headquarters in Italy, an encampment of camouflaged vehicles parked between the rows of vines and poplars. Geoffrey Cox was wondering what to write in his intelligence report for the daily situation conference. It was another gloriously sunny day. A slight breeze was ruffling the trees. Purple and yellow flowers bobbed softly in the grass. High above him in the hazy blue sky he could hear a lark singing. Italy had never seemed more beautiful. Yet he was weary, and the beauty failed to move him.

To the west, US Fifth Army troops, among them the Tenth Mountain Division and an exhausted Robert Ellis in his foxhole, had conquered the worst of the high Apennine peaks and were closing in on Bologna. The Russians had reached the outskirts of Berlin. British and American forces were racing through west and central Germany, where Robert Reid and a small army of other war correspondents were tracking their advance.

But here, along the Adriatic coast of Italy, the British Eighth Army seemed stalled. Arguably, this was the most famous army of the Second World War. Beginning its life in the Western Desert in 1941, it had experienced bitter defeats as well as hard-won victories fighting its way from the valley of the Nile across the North African sands to Tunisia, through Sicily, and up along the spine of Italy to the Alps. It has also been described as the "British Empire at war," because it included numerous and famous divisions and units from New Zealand, Canada, India, South Africa and Australia.[1] Yet, in Italy, its progress seemed labored. But that was hardly surprising. The main allied thrust centered on Germany. To supply it, the armies in Italy had been forced to give up thousands of men and much valuable equipment.

The sharp-featured Cox, with his swept-back dark hair and ever-alert eyes, was a veteran not just of war but of the tough and competitive world of peacetime journalism. He had been born in Palmerston, a small community on New Zealand's South Island, thirty-five years before. Like many of its population, he had Scots ancestry — his mother was a MacGregor. A frustrated career woman, she gave him a burning desire to be at the heart of everything. She sent him as a small boy to read and report back on the captions of First World War photographs in the local newspaper, the *Otago Witness*, and ever since he had wanted to explore the world outside New Zealand.

After graduating in history from the University of Otago, he won a prestigious Rhodes Scholarship to Oxford. History was his passion, but he had no desire to become some ivory-tower academic. "I wanted to be at the sharp end, where history is in the making," he said of his decision to become a foreign correspondent after leaving Oxford. "Journalism?" exclaimed a horrified Lord Lothian, secretary of the Rhodes Trust, when Cox told him he had changed his original plan of becoming a diplomat. "That's no career for a university man!"

But Cox persisted and found work as a correspondent for major newspapers such as the *News Chronicle* and the *Daily Express*. He instinctively headed towards the front line. Scouting out Nazi Germany shortly after Hitler came to power, he spent three weeks with the Hitler Youth draining marshes outside Hanover and was arrested by Stormtroopers in Berlin for failing to give the Nazi salute. He also enjoyed a privileged view of the 1934 Nuremberg Rally thanks to a chance meeting with a pro-Nazi bookseller who let him watch the march from the window of his shop. What he saw made him an ardent opponent of Nazism.

Cox also covered the Spanish Civil War and nearly got himself shot. Challenged by a patrol, he reached in his pocket for a white handkerchief to show his neutrality. Thinking he was reaching for a gun, the patrol leader fired but fortunately missed. Thereafter, he was in Vienna for the 1938 Anschluss, and two years later, traveling north of the

Arctic Circle, he witnessed Finnish ski troops taking on the Soviets in the "Winter War" and giving them a hammering. The following spring he left Brussels just hours ahead of the invading Germans, and escaped from France by the skin of his teeth.

Then he joined up. Being a correspondent in other people's wars was one thing, he decided, but it was different when his own country was involved. He enlisted in the British Army, went through officers' training, and joined the New Zealand Second Division, fighting in Crete, North Africa and now Italy.

When at Oxford he had met and married a fellow student, Cecily Turner, and they had two sons: Peter, aged eight, and Patrick, six. Cecily came from Sussex, but for the first two years of the war she lived in New Zealand with the boys and watched as tank traps were built outside Auckland in case the Japanese tried to invade. Inside his army pay book, Cox carried three treasured photographs of them all. He wrote to Cecily often, and cherished her replies. Often he told her what he had been reading. A few months before, he had been stuck in hospital for a month or so with an attack of jaundice. "Cecily darling," he wrote after receiving one of her more than welcome letters, "I was getting pretty down . . . Reading Margaret Mead on *The American Character* . . . Have read all Shakespeare histories except *Henry VIII* and am halfway through *Hamlet*." Over the previous few months he had finished James Joyce's *Ulysses* as well as *Jane Eyre*. Currently, he was reading a polemic by the left-wing British journalist Michael Foot entitled *The Trial of Mussolini*, an attack not just on the Italian Fascist dictator but on those in Britain who had appeased him before the war.

The New Zealand Second Division had just emerged from a blood-letting battle that prompted Cox to wonder whether he would ever see an end to the killing. The Germans were conducting a stubborn fighting retreat at each of the rivers that crossed the allied path of advance. Just three days before, Hitler had issued an uncompromising order to his commanders and officers in Italy: "Under no circumstances must troops or commanders be allowed to waver or to adopt a defeatist attitude. The Führer expects now as before the utmost steadfastness in the fulfilment of your mission, to defend every inch of the north Italian areas of your command." He ended with a barely veiled threat by pointing out the "serious consequences" for all those who did not carry out his orders to the last word. In other words, anyone who wavered would be shot. His commanders were following orders.

Two nights earlier, on the banks of the Gaiana River, the New Zealanders had engaged in a head-on confrontation with several battalions of German parachute infantry. These were an elite of the German Wehrmacht, tough, brutal, battle-hardened and all too willing to die for Hitler. "I hate these paratroopers," confessed Cox's boss, General Bernhard Freyberg, commander of the division. "They represent all that is worst in the whole Nazi system."

He hated them because he feared them. "Tiny" Freyberg stood six feet tall and was New Zealand's most distinguished military figure. He lacked nothing in personal courage, having won the Distinguished Service Order (DSO) for swimming ashore during the Gallipoli landings in 1915 to light diversionary flares, and a Victoria Cross, Britain's highest battlefield award, for bravery in carrying out an assault during the Battle of the Somme. On the day the First World War ended, he won a bar to his DSO by seizing a bridge in France precisely one minute before the armistice came into effect. But from bitter experience, Freyberg and his men knew the odds they were up against. At Monte Cassino the year before, the most savage of all their battles in Italy, they had been mauled by the paratroopers and suffered heavy casualties. Now it was payback time, a chance to even the score.

"The battle of the Gaiana river," observed Cox, "was to attract little attention in those late April days of 1945 . . . yet we can claim, I believe, that few nails were driven into the coffin of Nazism more thoroughly than this."[2]

The description "river" was something of a misnomer. In reality, the Gaiana was little more than a straight irrigation ditch crossing the road between Ravenna and Bologna, a black muddy stream easily crossed by infantry. But tanks could not traverse it because it was channeled between parallel flood banks fifteen to twenty feet high. Here, the German parachutists had dug themselves in. They were ready to prove that they could hold the line where regular infantry could not.

Two days before the battle, the New Zealanders had held their usual morning battle conference to assess the scene. It took place in a spacious stone farmhouse, and out of the window Cox could see shells bursting on the far side of the river.

"Are you sure the parachutists are there in force?" asked Freyberg.

"Yes," replied Cox, confident that he and his intelligence staff had identified six full German battalions either in the line or held back in reserve, along with half a dozen Panther tanks.

"Are you sure they're going to stand and fight?" asked Freyberg.

Cox was certain they would. They had committed all their reserves and were fighting hard everywhere else in Italy. They had even summoned back a Panzer grenadier division that had earlier set off for the front line in Germany. A breakthrough, it seemed obvious to Cox, would threaten all the enemy's fronts.

"Very well, then," said Freyberg when Cox had finished. "We will break him here."

There was no doubt that they had a serious fight on their hands. There was heavy sniping, and the Nebelwerfers had been hard at work. These were German multi-barreled rocket launchers with a four-mile range. Allied troops called them "screaming meemies" because of the noise the siren-equipped rockets made while in flight. There had also been some fierce counterattacks by the Germans. These had mostly come on the left flank of the New Zealanders and were aimed at the Gurkhas. Cox was glad to have these men close. They had shown their mettle fighting alongside the New Zealanders that winter. "They were pouring into the area already," noted Cox, "their small round yellow faces peering like the faces of children from the backs of their many trucks, their shoulders marked with the badge of crossed kukhri knives, their equipment neat and soldierly."

The long sunny afternoon wore on. Guns steadily moved up to take part in the bombardment while from the clear blue sky allied bombers continued to pound the enemy lines. Dusk came, and the air rapidly cooled. Cox was summoned to Freyberg's caravan. He found the general pacing nervously on the grass.

"Give me your estimate of the enemy strength again," said Freyberg.

"A maximum of a thousand, sir," replied Cox.

Freyberg did a quick sum in his head. "That gives us a hundred rounds for each individual paratrooper from the field guns, without counting the mediums," said Freyberg. "I wouldn't like to sit under that—it's a worse barrage than any other there's been this war." This, he told Cox, "will be the most important battle we have fought in Italy."

At 9 p.m. the allied artillery let loose with a massive barrage. To Cox, it sounded like a hundred thunderstorms. "The trees around us," he wrote, "changed from lumps of soft, slumberous darkness to shapes of green and yellow." He watched from a distance as the flamethrowers went in. It was just after 10 p.m., and dark. "Their spurts of flame, red under the lightning flashes, showed again, again, again," he wrote. "All along the line of the river they glared, red and ugly. The black smoke mounted up into the stars."

At first he feared the attack had failed. Very few prisoners were brought in, and it was above all prisoners that he wanted to see. Not just to interrogate, although to a front-line intelligence officer like Cox they could provide invaluable information about enemy dispositions. It was rather that capturing men, rather than ground, would do the most to destroy Hitler's army in Italy and prevent its retreat to the Alps for a final stand.

Yet, when dawn broke, Cox realized he had been wrong. He drove up to the river bank and suddenly understood why the prisoners' cages were half empty. In front of him lay a scene of utter carnage. "Along the banks, in the stream, in their trenches, in houses and holes beyond," he recorded, lay the massed dead of the German Army's elite. The paratroopers had been burned to death in their foxholes, caught by the relentless curling and scouring flames that "sought them out like vermin." They had been spattered into fragments by the barrage of heavy artillery, decapitated, delimbed and eviscerated. They had been shot and machine-gunned by the advancing New Zealanders. They had died their deaths in a hundred other ways, too.

Now they lay with matted and lifeless hair, eyes staring sightless into the spring sky, or doubled up fetus-like and fast stiffening in the black, oily waters of the Gaiana. It was like a scene from the Western Front, a mini-Somme or Paschendaele, death on a grotesque scale. "There they lay," noted Cox grimly, "in all their ghastliness, the youth of Germany, the pride of Hitlerism . . . they were utter waste, wasted and dangerous in life, wasted completely in death, the final price of Hitler and the forces who had brought him into being."

But was the slaughter enough to make the enemy give up? Or did more of the same lie ahead? Sitting there in the sun on Hitler's birthday, Cox seized on a sliver of hope, a small sign that at last the Nazis were losing faith. Among the handful of prisoners they had taken was one genuine deserter, an officer, and the first from the parachutists the New Zealanders had ever encountered. The man was an old-time Nazi and a veteran of the Condor Legion, the German unit that helped Franco seize power in Spain. Cox gave him a cigarette and chatted to him in the prisoners' cage. The man confessed that the flamethrowers, not the artillery, had broken the back of their resistance.

"What is your strategy?" asked Cox.

"To fight you to a standstill," replied the German. "But if you keep the battle moving, we'll break."

"Why did you desert?" queried Cox.

The man shrugged. Whatever happened in Italy, the war was lost anyway. So why wait and perhaps be sent back to Germany and fall into Russian hands? From here, at least, he might get to America. He had been there as a seaman on board a liner in the 1920s. America, the women, what a country!

After this exchange Cox believed the Nazi spirit was breaking. Even the zealots were finally looking for escape routes. He retreated to the cool of his caravan and spent the next few hours carefully compiling his report. It was finished and typed up by six in the evening. The Germans had already withdrawn towards the Idice River, and everyone in the division expected them to make another stand there. But in the course of the day, as Cox was composing his assessment, two Maori companies crossed the Idice with hardly a fight. Meanwhile, tanks splashed across further upriver. Obviously, reported Cox, the Germans were on the run. Even "parachutist fanaticism" was not enough against heavy artillery and flamethrowers.

Yet, hard-won experience also warned him against complacency. From a code list captured that day, Cox learned that a new parachute division, relatively fresh but certainly experienced, had been moved into the area by the Germans. Moreover, to safeguard their line of retreat, the enemy would have to protect a corridor of territory that lay ahead of the New Zealanders. "We must therefore expect tomorrow stubborn and skilful fighting in true parachutist style," warned Cox.

Obstinate resistance and dogged defense by the Germans had characterized the fighting since the Italian campaign had begun with the July 1943 British and American landings in Sicily. Devised to make the most of the allied victory in North Africa, it quickly got bogged down in the harsh terrain of Italy proper, a land that cruelly belied Churchill's optimistic talk of it being "the soft underbelly of Europe." The long spine of the mainland consists of inhospitable mountains up to 6,500 feet high that are perfect for defense, not attack, with only narrow coastal plains on either side of the peninsula for the allies to exploit. This terrain gave most of the advantage to the Germans and very little to the allies. Swelteringly hot in summer, in winter torrential rain and snow-storms turned the mountains into Hell on Earth.

Hitler and Field Marshal Kesselring, his commander in Italy, resolved to defend every inch of ground and poured in several divisions containing some of the Wehrmacht's best fighting men. Instead of the envisaged rapid campaign that would reach Florence in weeks, the allies found themselves fighting a remorseless and attritional grind over two winters of unforgiving snow, rain and mud. To make matters worse, six allied divisions were withdrawn from Italy for the invasion of southern France following the Normandy landings of June 1944.

It was scarce wonder that by the spring of 1945 the allies had not yet crossed the Po. Robert Ellis, fighting with the Tenth Mountain Division, was relatively lucky as his division had arrived in Italy only that January. But Reg Roy, now fighting in Holland, had originally landed with the Canadians in Italy and had survived bitter encounters with the Germans there. Only in February had he been shifted to Holland. Geoffrey Cox had even more experience of the Germans' fighting abilities in and around the Mediterranean. One way or the other, he had been fighting them there since 1941.

The skills that made him a successful journalist made him an exceptional intelligence officer: a sharp, incisive mind; a keenly observant eye for the revealing detail; an ability rapidly to absorb and synthesize great amounts of material; a rare ability to write clear and uncluttered prose; and a nose that smelled out the action wherever it was. "You always knew," said one of his wartime colleagues, "that when Geoffrey appeared the Germans were just over the hill." It was simply, Cox said, like being the editor of a busy news service.

Except that he was also a star reporter. Little of any tactical importance escaped the scrutiny of his sharp, blue-green eyes. "How level is the military horizon," he jotted down in his notebook,

how lacking in the sense of the size and immediate operation in which one is involved. Alamein, Cassino are just another day's operation. To the man in the field a minor patrol may, for him, contain more of personal drama than any great battle. For an Intelligence Officer the day on which the presence of a new formation is discussed can be of greater note than the victory to which the discovery leads.

Cox found it all fascinating and exhilarating. "It required both intellectual discipline and judgment," he observed, demanding an approach as critical, as cautious and as curious as that of "any scholar approaching a newly discovered classical text." There was no margin for error, either. The slip of a single figure in a map reference, for example, or in some hastily dictated description over a scratchy telephone line, could mean at least wastage of ammunition and at worst accidents and disasters. "It was the best mental training," he admitted, "that I have ever known."[3] He rose rapidly up the ladder, and by April 1945, as we have seen, Freyberg was relying heavily on his advice.

So were others. Everyone gravitated to Cox's "I" truck at night. Well lit and warm, it could comfortably hold half a dozen senior officers — or double that at a squeeze — and Cox kept up a tradition of open hospitality that had been established by his two predecessors. On many an evening it resembled "a blend of a newspaper office and a small Paris bistro," but here, in an atmosphere thick with cigarette smoke and resounding with laughter, officers brought in reams of information that he could never have collected on his own. It made Cox and his truck — "the café" — an indispensable source of intelligence.[4]

The morning after interrogating the deserter, Cox was woken early by Captain Colmore Williams, the Royal Air Force liaison officer with the New Zealanders, who was responsible for calling in air strikes to support the men on the ground. Slowly, as dawn came up and color started to drench the landscape, Cox walked to Williams's truck while the youthful British officer explained the problem. On the road between the Gaiana and the Idice, the Germans' natural line of retreat, lay the small town of Budrio. Would it help, asked Williams, if the RAF bombed it? They had twenty-four fully loaded up aircraft at the ready and could easily block the roads coming in and out of the town to obstruct the Germans' retreat. But it really depended on the enemy's position.

As he stood at the tailboard of the truck, his trouser cuffs still soaking with the morning dew, Cox pondered the question. The only way the bombers could block the road was by destroying the houses on either side of it. On the grounds of military need they had done this repeatedly in other Italian towns, and the route of the allied advance now formed a great scar of devastation across the landscape. But now Cox thought of the civilians cowering in their cellars, wondering if their homes would survive and whether they would even emerge alive.

Was it really necessary? "I found it hard to believe that it was," he confessed. "I could not honestly say that we could damage the enemy to any extent by going for those roads." He saw in his mind's eye again the misery of war. In his own hands he held the power to smash yet more homes to pieces. He had only five minutes to make up his mind.

He rapidly ran through the options, factoring in everything he knew about the Germans. Most of their heavy artillery would already be across the Idice. Moreover, the hardened parachutists would hardly be stopped by a few piles of rubble littering the road. So why bother to send in the bombers and make even more misery for innocent civilians?

Was this simple sentimentality? He was a hard-nosed realist with no illusions about Nazism and the perils it posed, but he was also exhausted and sickened by the destruction of war. He had not seen Cecily and the boys for more than a year. He thought about them constantly and wondered how their life together would turn out after the war. What sort of world would his children inherit? He had dedicated the book chronicling his experiences during the bitter fighting of the Winter War to his children "in the hope that they may grow up to know struggle but not war."

A few months before, he had written the boys a touching letter trying to explain what the war was about: "You must both work hard at school and learn all your words so that when you grow up you can learn to make all sorts of things. There are thousands of things to make — houses which have been knocked down by bombs, bridges which have been blown up, ships which have been sunk. We will all have to work very hard to make them all." Just three weeks ago he had sent another letter to Peter: "This war is nearly finished," he told his son, "and we will soon be able to be all together and start building our new house together. We will have to work very hard."[5]

Was this emotional side now getting in the way of a decision that might be vital to save the lives of his own men? That, after all, was his first and overriding duty.

Williams was obviously wrestling with the same dilemma. "What do you say to this alternative target," he suddenly asked, "plaster the main lines north of the river?"

Cox seized on the idea with an overwhelming sense of relief. "Yes," he answered. "Let Budrio stay put."[6]

The decision made, the two of them drank their morning cups of tea from chipped enamel mugs. Then Cox returned across the grass for his morning shave. Budrio was saved. One town and its inhabitants, at least, would be spared from joining the lengthening list of Italy's victims of war.

That same day in Milan, in makeshift offices on the first floor of the city's prefecture in the Palazzo Montforte, Benito Mussolini, the man who had taken his country so eagerly into the war in 1940, was meeting for the last time with his cabinet. Outside, German SS sentries stood guard.

The Fascist dictator and long-time ally of Adolf Hitler was now aged sixty-two. Gone was the bluff and bluster that had marked his great propaganda victory over Abyssinia in 1936, his triumphant proclamation of the "Pact of Steel" with Hitler in 1939, and his ebullient and cynical declaration of war in June 1940 as France collapsed: "I need several thousand dead to be able to take my place at the peace table," he had declared. Since then, Italy had suffered defeat after defeat, and the numbers of dead ran into the tens of thousands. Now, far from being an ally of Hitler, he had become a hopeless dependent.

In July 1943, after the allies had landed in Sicily, King Victor Emmanuel and the Fascist Grand Council removed him from office and he was briefly held prisoner. Then, in a daring raid by German paratroopers led by the legendary Otto Skorzeny, he was rescued and installed in northern Italy as head of the newly formed "Italian Social Republic." Its offices were scattered along the shores of Lake Garda near the small town of Salò, from which it derived its popular designation as the "Salò Republic." Mussolini himself took up residence nearby, in the Villa Feltrinelli, in the pleasant lakeside town of Gargagno.

The writ of the Salò Republic, such as it was, only ever ran in the part of Italy controlled by the Germans. Not entirely a German puppet, but certainly far from independent, Mussolini spent the next eighteen months as "head of state with neither power nor authority" and pretending to govern, a habit that came easily to the former journalist who had a weakness for words and rhetoric. He washed his hands of tough decisions, such as the execution in Verona of his son-in-law and heir-apparent, Count Galeazzo Ciano, husband of his favorite daughter, Edda, for having voted against him in July 1943; he failed to control the many Fascist militias that sprung up to wage an increasingly brutal war against his domestic opponents; and although he occasionally raised himself to protest, he was unable to prevent the Germans from deporting a hundred thousand workers to Germany, shipping out the country's Jews for mass murder, and looting Italy's gold reserves and art treasures. The Germans also accompanied his every move, spied on him constantly and tapped his phones.

By the spring of 1945 Mussolini was alternating between despair, resignation, self-pity and frantic outbursts of hope. At times he appeared calm and composed; at others apathetic; and at others almost manic. "He lives by dreams, in dreams, and through dreams," said one of those close to him. "He does not have the least contact with reality." Sometimes he exploded in rage against the Germans; sometimes he railed against the British and Americans. Invariably, he blamed others for his fate. "I am like the captain of a ship in a storm; the ship is broken up and I find myself in the furious ocean on a raft which it is impossible to guide or govern," he told a journalist, forgetting that it was he who had launched his vessel into the storm in the first place. "No one hears my voice any more."

His departure from Gargagno, along with other members of his government, was precipitated by the imminent breakthrough of the American and British armies across the Po. In the garden of his villa he said farewell to his wife, Rachele, promising he would return for her later, and then left with an escort of German troops led by two SS officers. But his mistress, Clara Petacci, who had been living in a nearby villa, was determined to remain at his side. She too left for Milan that night, along with her own SS guardian.

Heading the agenda for the cabinet meeting in Milan was the question of what to do next. Various schemes had been discussed endlessly over the past few days without any decision being taken. Alessandro Pavolini, the secretary of the Fascist Party, was all in favor of making a last stand in Milan, and talked enthusiastically of turning the city into "the Italian Stalingrad." But Marshal Rodolfo Graziani, the commander of Mussolini's army and the most reliable and loyal of his senior officers, brushed aside Pavolini's idea by brusquely pointing out that American and British bombers would simply obliterate the city. Instead, he suggested a direct approach to the allies for an end to the conflict. Graziani was a former Viceroy of Abyssinia and commander in Libya, and had suffered several bruising defeats in the desert at the hands of the British. He was all too aware of the devastating nature of allied power.

But by this stage Mussolini had already secretly tried a direct approach to the allies through the mediation of Cardinal Schuster, the

Archbishop of Milan, and had been rebuffed. So the idea of a last stand now held a powerful attraction for him. "Whatever the place," he declared, "Fascism has to fall heroically." At first he thought of Trieste for the honor. The city on the Adriatic was a potent symbol of Italian nationalism. Ceded to Italy after the First World War as a reward for joining the conflict on the allied side, the former Austro-Hungarian port had been showered with subsidies and rewards by Mussolini after he came to power in 1922 as a bastion of "Italianness" against the sea of Slavs in neighboring Yugoslavia and the rest of the Balkans. But the Germans had knocked this idea firmly on the head. They had their own claims on the city, which was now under German administration. They had even established a concentration camp in an old rice factory, San Sabba, on its southern suburbs.

Mussolini's second choice was the Valtellina, a slice of Italian territory close to the Swiss border, north of Lake Como. This idea had already garnered some support in the cabinet, and now Mussolini confirmed that at the right moment he would retreat there. Pavolini, thwarted in his designs for Milan, promised three thousand troops drawn from the most enthusiastic Fascist militias.

At 10 p.m. that night, an apparently cheerful Mussolini received an Italian journalist to whom he had promised an interview in his office. "What can I do for you?" he asked.

"I would like a signed photograph," replied the visitor.

Proudly, Mussolini handed one over, signing and dating it, in Roman numerals, "Year XXIII of the Fascist Era." Then he launched on a lengthy self-justification of his political life, claiming to have done everything he could to defend Italy's interests in difficult circumstances. He finished by declaring that while his own career was over, neither Fascism nor Italy would die.

The journalist asked if this meant that there were German miracle weapons.

"There are," replied Mussolini. "I had news a few days ago."

Face-to-face meetings between Il Duce and the Führer had by now become rare, but the two dictators still kept in touch, bolstering each other's illusions with increasing doses of fantasy. Indeed, two days later, Mussolini received a private telegram from the Berlin bunker full of similarly empty rhetoric. Bolshevism and Judaism had brought destruction to Europe, declared Hitler, but the "unparalleled heroism" of the German people would yet change the course of the war.

Yet, in his more rational moments, Mussolini believed none of this, and knew full well that the end was close. Increasingly, he talked of death. The last stand in the Valtellina was not designed to fulfill any useful military purpose. Instead, it would act as a "moral triumph" of Fascism: his political philosophy would go down fighting. Angrily, he rejected proposals from colleagues and friends to flee to Spain or Switzerland. No, he insisted, he would die gloriously in the Valtellina. In the meantime, though, he stayed put in Milan, awaiting events. Now that Rome was lost, he declared, the northern city, where he had first formed his Fascist squads a quarter of a century before, and where — to his and the Germans' admitted surprise — enthusiastic crowds had cheered him on an impromptu visit the previous December, was the only true capital of the Italian Republic.[7]

Meanwhile, in Rome, the official capital from which Mussolini had been expelled so ignominiously a year and a half before, Italian politicians were already jostling for power. Geoffrey Cox had witnessed the liberation of the city in June 1944, just hours before allied forces had stormed ashore on the Normandy beaches.

Early in 1943, he had been briefly seconded to Washington, DC, to serve as First Secretary and Chargé d'Affaires at New Zealand's newly established legation. It was a prestigious position that led him to the White House to meet Roosevelt, placed him at the heart of deliberations of the Pacific War Council, and gave him a front-row seat at the opening conference of the United Nations Relief and Rehabilitation Agency. Then, in April 1944, Freyberg had urgently asked for him back in Italy, where his son had escaped from a prisoner-of-war camp and found refuge in the Vatican. Freyberg wanted Cox to make certain he was safe.

The question on everyone's mind about Rome had been whether the Germans would defend the city. There were plenty of signs to suggest that they would and it could become a bloodbath: the Wehrmacht was fighting a bitter rear guard retreat towards the city, and the Fascist police and the SS were massacring prisoners. Then, suddenly, the columns of men and artillery which had been streaming south out of Rome reversed their direction and headed north. German officers started checking out of their Roman hotels, while partisans began oiling their rusty carbines. Some two million people waited, the city's population swelled by half a million refugees. All were hungry. Water and electricity were in short supply.

Then an ULTRA intercept revealed to the allies that Field Marshal Kesselring was seeking Hitler's approval for an evacuation without a fight. Hitler agreed, but to keep the withdrawal secret, Kesselring ordered several of his more prominent officials to attend the opera, where Gigli was singing in *Un Ballo in Maschera*.

A few German units and stragglers were still in place when the Americans arrived. Some had to swim across the Tiber while others commandeered Rome's horse-drawn cabs to make good their escape, and a few snipers remained on rooftops. The Fascist chief of police sped off north in his Alfa Romeo, taking with him a quantity of jewelry, watches, pound notes and lire.[8]

Several allied advance parties, scouts and spearhead units claimed to be the first into the city. General Mark Clark, commander of the US Fifth Army, drove his jeep up to St. Peter's and posed for his photograph alongside a priest. Crowds of flag-waving Italians swept up the Corso, hoping to meet the commander-in-chief, and many more paraded with Old Glory, the Union Jack, the Tricolor or the Hammer and Sickle. Mussolini had hoped, it was said, that the Romans would die defending the city. They did not, although there were a few acts of vengeance and some immediate retribution in the streets.

Hitler had put the best face on it all by assuring his people that in truth the loss of Rome was an advantage, as the Germans no longer had to feed two million Italians. In Washington, President Roosevelt beamed, "One up and two to go!" referring to Berlin and Tokyo, and the *New York Times* announced that the Tiber had shrunk almost to insignificance as "the rivers of power flow elsewhere."

Cox had landed on the Anzio beachhead on 4 June 1944 and raced up the road towards Rome in one of Freyberg's staff cars. On the way, passing through towns that were now little more than stinking heaps of rubble, he overtook advancing American troops. He arrived in the city on the morning it was liberated, quickly finding himself surrounded by people surging out into the streets in wild celebration, cheering, clapping and throwing roses. Some were rejoicing at the prospect of peace. Others were glad to see the back of Mussolini after two decades of Fascism. One young man jumped onto the running board of Cox's car and flung his arms around his shoulders, shouting, "We are free, at last we are free!" An older man wept. "Free at last," he sobbed, "after twenty years we are free again." At the Palazzo Venezia, Cox saw civil guards taking over the building from which, eight years before,

Mussolini had declared war on Abyssinia. The next day he met a woman whose son had filmed the arrival of American troops at the Vatican. She asked him to write his name in the back of a book. He noticed on the flyleaf, translated into Italian, Abraham Lincoln's words: "Government of the people, by the people, for the people."

Afterwards, he described the scene in a letter to Cecily, who by now had moved with the boys to Massachusetts to teach at Dana Hall, a girls' liberal arts school connected with Wellesley College, where she was also trying her hand at writing short stories. He typed:

> Darling, I know I have seen this at its flood tide, and that these people are destined for disillusion and much bitterness, but even so we are a stage further in life by having fought and freed them to this extent. Please darling believe that, and tell it so to the boys when they can understand, for though they cost us dear it is something to have helped liberate these people from what they have been through—something to us as well as to them.[9]

In the mountains of Italy, though, Robert Ellis was less sure it was all worthwhile. He had started off with a romantic view of war, dreaming of being a dashing fighter pilot. He passed all the tests but was then discovered as being red-green color blind, and rejected.

Next he fell for the glamour of fighting on skis. Like millions of others, he had been beguiled by newsreels from the Winter War showing daring Finns on skis dressed in white hoods swooping down on Soviet columns, overwhelming them with their skill, and then speeding away to safety. There had been a flood of magazine articles and documentaries on the subject, and all too easily Ellis had been seduced by the images of tanned young men, as he put it, "skiing down sunlit trails in defense of their country." With some skiing experience from his year in Switzerland, he eagerly volunteered for the newly formed Mountain Division.

But dreams of individual combat while speeding down slopes quickly dissolved, especially after he became a machine-gunner. He imagined the weapon would give him some powerful personal protection on the battlefield with its high rate of fire, but initially failed to recognize that it made him less mobile and more vulnerable than ever. "It impeded one's movements in combat because of its weight," he quickly learned, "and it [was] a preferred target of answering fire from artillery and mortars."[10]

This explained why he spent so much of his time in Italy dodging hot steel and sheltering in foxholes. His first few weeks of combat were almost a literal baptism of fire that tested his youthful ideals to the extreme. "War is certainly a shock when you first face it in its stark nakedness," he wrote home to his sister Margaret.

> For instance the first time you step over an old friend lying there bloody and still as you press forward in the attack. You wonder if you'll be next . . . you think of all your hopes and dreams, memories, the things you want to do—your awful love of life—hang there unprotected, all to be lost with the whine of a '88 and the rain of shrapnel death. This is when you wonder if anything, any ideal, is worth to you the price of life.[11]

One of his dreams concerned his girlfriend, Pat, the sister of one of his fraternity brothers at the University of Chicago and now in her sophomore year at Oberlin, a distinguished private college in Ohio. He wrote to her regularly, even though he could not see them getting engaged or married for another four years or so. "She's pretty independent and has strong ideas, and I admire that," he confided to his mother. He was keen to get back to her and his family.

But that would come only when the fighting ended. And what sort of peace would that bring? On the day he wrote to his sister, he also sent a letter to his elder brother, Paul, who was in a Chicago seminary. He used some Indian ink he had found in a German foxhole. "I think we should hurry now and make the world safe from all future threats of war and pestilence," he penned. "To use the foxhole as a simile, we should build, construct, and dig deep into solid foundations of brotherhood, and be protected like the walls of Mother Earth by cooperation and amicable discussion."[12]

Amicable discussion remained a distant possibility, though, and his idealism was wearing distinctly thin. Back in early February, when he had only just arrived, he had heard news from the "Big Three" conference at Yalta between Roosevelt, Stalin and Churchill that seemed to promise a brave new world through the establishment of a United Nations organization to replace the ill-fated League of Nations. "Looks like we're on the road to lasting peace," he scribbled in his diary. "I feel as though if I'm killed I've at least died for something worth while."

Yet, after his first experience of battle, the savage assault to capture

Mount Belvedere, he was already starting to question that. He was praying and reading the New Testament, which he kept always in his pocket. Phrases such as "Scared to death" and "Horrible slaughter" began to pepper his diary. Once, as men died around him and he cowered from heavy German artillery, he became convinced the end had come. "I had my Bible in my hand," he told his parents, "and read Paul's letter to the Galatians."[13]

Could this scale of slaughter ever be worthwhile? Afterwards, he was not sure. "I remained uncertain whether the horror I had experienced," he later wrote, "given its effects on those who had lost their lives or suffered such terrible wounds, justified a continuation of the insanity we had encountered." At the very least, he vowed that he would never let time or memory falsify or soften the grisly reality of war.

CHAPTER SIX

"*ICH WAR IMMER DAGEGEN*"

Cautiously, he walked along the footpath. It was pitch-black ahead. Breaking the commonsense rule always to go with a buddy, he was patrolling alone. That was why people called him a risk-taker. He was also getting careless. Instead of carrying his M-1 rifle at the ready, firmly with both hands across the front of his body, it was dangling casually from his right hand. Above him to one side was the railway line, running parallel to the path, the occasional dull shine of the steel his only visual guide. From time to time, a distant searchlight lit up the clouds. He could hear the thump, thump of heavy artillery in the background.

Suddenly, something brushed his lip. He heard a slight noise, and felt moisture on his mouth. Licking it with his tongue, he tasted blood. He stood still for a few moments, listened intently, and then, hearing nothing, he moved on slowly. When he finally reached the railway station he walked carefully around it several times. Finally satisfied, he concluded that no German troops were hiding in the buildings.

Dawn was breaking when he set off back down the track. Then he spotted the source of the blood. Across the path at head height was a single strand of barbed wire suspended between a concrete post on one side and a wooden pole on the other. Attached to the pole was a hand grenade. When he had walked into the wire it had tugged at the release string of the grenade, but by some miracle, it had failed to explode. Looking closer, he saw that the barbed wire was badly rusted, so presumably the detonator had got damp as well and not gone off. The grenade was only six feet from his head. He was a lucky man, this time.

Leonard Linton was twenty-three years old. A paratrooper with the American Eighty-second Airborne Division, he was on duty outside Cologne. Germany's fourth-largest city, on the banks of the Rhine, was little more than a pile of rubble with hardly a building undemolished.

It had been entered by the US First Army early in March. Over a hundred thousand of its inhabitants had died in allied bombing attacks, and a similar number were now living like troglodytes among the ruins. The city, wrote Janet Flanner, one of the first American correspondents to arrive, "is now a model of destruction . . . [It] lies recumbent, without beauty, shapeless in the rubble and loneliness of complete physical defeat. Through its clogged side streets trickles what is left of its life, a dwindled population in black with bundles — the silent German people appropriate to the silent city." One of the last orders issued by the departing Nazis was still plastered on posters over the city: "*Schweigen siegen*" — "To keep silent is to win." Having lost the war of arms, concluded Flanner, defeated Germany was counting again on the psychological victory it had won after the last war — "the victory of silence, lies, whining, energy, devotion, and guile." She could only hope that the US military government running the city would not fall for it all.[1]

Most of the buildings of architectural interest had been destroyed, including at least two of its magnificent Romanesque churches. By some miracle, however, the great Gothic cathedral, with its twin towers reaching over five hundred feet into the sky, was still standing. Its smoke-blackened stone was pitted with shrapnel, and a burned-out Tiger tank still guarded its entrance. The Eighty-second Airborne had moved into the city in early April after the collapse of the Ruhr pocket, when 325,000 German troops had been surrounded and trapped by allied forces before they surrendered and their commander, Field Marshal Walther Model, walked off into a forest and shot himself.

Now the paratroopers were regrouping, awaiting the orders for their next mission deeper into the German heartland. In the meantime, the division set itself up in buildings along the riverfront of the Rhine and established listening posts to detect any movements by Germans on the other bank. From time to time, patrols were sent out to capture prisoners for interrogation by intelligence officers. To the rear, military police and other units stood guard over bridges and factories to prevent sabotage.[2]

The episode with the grenade was Linton's third piece of luck in as many months. The first had been a matter of timing. That January, he had been shipped out of New York aboard a luxury Cunard liner, the *Aquitania*, along with sixteen hundred other GIs. A few days out, he could tell by the stars and the balmy weather they were passing close to the equator. Some of the men thought this meant they were in the South Pacific, heading to fight the Japanese, but he knew that for this they should have already have passed through the Panama Canal. Then the weather grew cold again, and from the Polar Star Linton could tell they were heading north. "We had many drills with life jackets," he recalled, "and spent hours in food and other lines which whiled away the time. I read everything within reach. Many played poker, and a rumor spread that several women on an upper deck were making a fortune every night off men who came from the lower deck for numerous short visits."[3]

January 1945 was a bleak month for the allies. The euphoria of D-Day just six months before had long since evaporated. Paris had been quickly liberated, followed by Brussels, and in September 1944 there was wildly optimistic talk of the war being over that Christmas. But then things started to go badly wrong. The Germans fought back ferociously, there was a spectacular failure to land parachute forces behind the lines at Arnhem, and in December there was almost a major catastrophe for the allies. Back in 1940, Hitler had surprised everyone by launching his attack on France through the heavily forested and hilly area of the Ardennes. Now he fooled the allies again by launching a massive counteroffensive in the same place with the aim of recapturing the vital port of Antwerp and driving a wedge between the American and British armies. It caught them completely off guard. The result was a month of bitter and desperate fighting in appalling winter conditions.

With the stakes enormous for both sides, this "Battle of the Bulge," as it became known, saw the conflict frequently descend into savagery. Losses were heavy, especially for the Americans, who lost several thousand dead and twenty thousand men taken prisoner in the largest surrender of GIs on foreign soil. Eventually, the allies won, but with no sign yet of the long-promised Soviet offensive on the Eastern Front, pessimism took hold in London and Washington. All the talk was suddenly of war extending to the end of 1945.[4]

When Linton saw the lights of Manhattan disappearing behind him, all that he knew was that the Americans were still taking heavy casualties. The Eighty-second Airborne was in the thick of the fighting, and he assumed he would soon be joining what was known as the "All-American Division." It was the US Army's first airborne unit, and along with its rival, the 101st — the "Screaming Eagles" — it formed the elite of American forces, wearing their coveted jump boots and silver parachute badges. "Devils in baggy pants!" one petrified German soldier had yelled when he first confronted the paratroopers — and they had happily adopted the title.

The *Aquitania*, which had done similar troopship duty in the First World War, was fast enough to cross the Atlantic without convoy protection. But one day a sudden alert sounded, and the ship abruptly changed course and veered to one side. Linton found himself running for his emergency station. Then the captain came on the loudspeaker. He told them that a U-boat had just fired a torpedo at them, and from now on they would be taking a zig-zag course into port. To his surprise, Linton could see land on the horizon on all sides. Everyone stayed in their life jackets, ready for orders, but they all remained calm. The captain came back on the loudspeaker to say ("in very British fashion," thought Linton) that they had picked up a German broadcast claiming that the *Aquitania* had been sunk outside Glasgow. Then he welcomed the Americans to Europe. Shortly afterwards, two British tugs appeared and stayed close as they came into the Clyde. A twelve-hour rail journey later, the GIs were in Southampton, boarding a much smaller vessel to cross the English Channel to the French port of Le Havre.

It was a trouble-free crossing, with not a Luftwaffe plane to be seen, but by this time the mood of the paratroopers was sober and quiet, and they could see some heavy destruction in the port. Waiting on the quayside was a steam locomotive and a long line of empty freight cars. Each was stenciled with the numbers 40/8. This meant either forty men or eight horses. The Americans were privileged, though, and only twenty men were assigned to each car.

Linton lucked out. Somehow he managed to wangle himself a place in the "luxury" car, two or three back from the locomotive, and equipped with a jerry can of fresh drinking water, a portable Coleman stove to heat up coffee or soup, and a hole in the corner. This small comfort meant he did not have to wait for the so-called piss stops that the train made from time to time to allow the men to relieve themselves beside the tracks. To avoid boredom, he sometimes rode in the locomotive and got friendly with the crew, from whom he eventually learned they were bound for Verviers. But no one had yet officially revealed their destination, and the officer in charge kept his maps securely by his side. Linton decided not to tell him he knew.

Several hours and many halts later, the train arrived at Verviers in eastern Belgium, on the edge of the Ardennes. Here Linton was issued with an M-1 rifle and an escape kit: a high-quality map printed on silk, a small hacksaw blade in a waxed cardboard container small enough to be hidden in some item of clothing and a tiny, round compass. Given the instructions on where best to conceal it, Linton crudely named it his "asshole compass." His final pieces of kit included a gas mask and ammunition. Having received them, he clambered aboard a truck, part of a long convoy, and drove off into the cold, foggy night. Some hours later they stopped in a small village and he and twenty-five other men were marched to a nearby farmhouse and told to bed down. Looking around, Linton found a pile of old newspapers and magazines and a box of letters and other documents. All were in German, and many bore official stamps with the Nazi insignia of the German eagle clutching a swastika in its claws.

From this, he concluded he was on German soil. By now, the Battle of the Bulge was officially over and won, but the Americans had suffered their heaviest casualties of the war in Europe so far. He hoped that the fight might have finally gone out of the Germans, but he had hardly arrived before finding that the Germans still had plenty of fight, and his luck was tested again.

He and a few other men were sent out on patrol to locate the enemy. Trucked out to the edge of a forest, they set off on foot through the trees, line abreast, keeping each other in sight so they could communicate silently with hand signals. There was snow on the ground and the tops of the trees had been shredded by low-flying shells and their trunks scarred savagely by shrapnel.

They reached a small ravine, and Linton and two companions were ordered to move around to the left while the others headed off to the right. After a while, they arrived at a small clearing and an abandoned German dugout. As they were looking around, they suddenly heard the low rumbling of a tank coming towards them, and the cracking sound of small trees and undergrowth being crushed beneath its tracks. Quickly, they jumped into the dugout. It was L-shaped, and sturdily reinforced with timber — excellent, thought Linton, for taking cover from artillery fire, and better built than most GIs would have bothered to dig. One of the others readied a wine bottle he was carrying in a sock, filled with oil and gasoline. If he got the chance, he would throw it into the grille of the tank's rear air intake.

"I was amazingly calm," Linton wrote. Then a German Tiger tank broke out of the trees and headed straight towards them. Linton got down as low as he could and waited. Everything suddenly went dark. The tank was directly above them. "It was driving right over our emplacement," he remembered, "when suddenly it made some loud crunching noises and our dugout caved in; obviously the tank alternated its right and left treads into forward and reverse directly above us to collapse the dugout. The sandy earth pulled me downward. I sank with it a little and was buried into immobility but heard the tank move on until all was silent." Luckily, as the earth poured over him, his helmet slipped over his face, creating a pocket of air. He heard the tank move off into the trees and then lost track of time, but the clammy earth began to chill his body and he realized he might die. He still could not move. Ages seemed to pass before he heard a scraping sound above him. The rest of the patrol had returned to find out what had happened. Luckily, one of them had spotted Linton's rifle barrel sticking out of the ground.[5]

Soon after this narrow escape, the Eighty-second was sent back for refitting to its main base outside the small town of Sissonne, a few miles from Reims and SHAEF headquarters. Casualties were replaced with fresh GIs and equipment was repaired or replaced from the vast and seemingly inexhaustible stock of supplies pouring in daily to the armies in Europe from the United States. Linton was issued with a brand-new gas mask. Obviously, the chemical weapons experts were expecting the Germans to start using poison gas sooner or later.

Linton's tent was pitched close to the building that housed divisional HQ and its commander General James ("Slim Jim") Gavin. Close by, always at the ready for take-off, stood his personal C-47. At thirty-seven, Gavin was the youngest general in the American Army since the Civil War, a Brooklyn-born son of impoverished Irish immigrants with handsome good looks, oodles of glamour and a driving, aggressive desire to hit the enemy fast and hard. One day, at dusk, Linton saw Gavin's plane take off; it returned the next morning. Almost immediately, rumors swept through the base that Gavin had met with Eisenhower to receive the All-Americans' new assignment: an airborne assault on Berlin.

To most of the paratroopers, this came as a relief. Many had parachuted into Sicily, Italy, Normandy — where they had jumped just a few hours before the ground forces landed on the D-Day beaches to seize a vital bridgehead — and Holland. But since then, they had seen action only on the ground. It seemed like a frustrating waste of all their hard training. What was the point of wearing their treasured and distinctive jump boots? True, German propaganda had built them up as a force to be dreaded, and their tough reputation alone worked wonders — many an enemy unit threw in the towel just knowing they were coming, whether they parachuted behind enemy lines or not. On the other hand, thought Linton more practically, the boots had not been very warm nor sufficiently sturdy for the tough winter conditions they had just endured.

So the rumors about Berlin electrified everyone at the base. In a carefully sealed office and with maps concealed behind covers, Gavin secretly briefed a handful of his senior officers in a vain attempt to keep it under wraps. The drop would be part of Operation Eclipse, he told them, a plan that would be activated if the Germans appeared to be on the edge of imminent collapse. The All-Americans' target was Tempelhof airfield; the rival Screaming Eagles would capture Gatow, another airfield in the city. Then they would both hang on until the ground forces arrived.[6]

Intensive parachute training began, and at an abandoned airfield close to Sissonne rehearsals started for the landings. Linton, though, decided on some preparations of his own. Paris was only three hours away if he hitch-hiked, easy enough to do given the hundreds of military vehicles going to and from the liberated French capital, fun city for thousands of GIs. So off he went, partly to enjoy himself before the assault on Berlin, but also, so he told himself, to get hold of some street maps of Hitler's capital more detailed than those provided by the US Army.

After tracking down a suitable one on the Left Bank, he found a girl and enjoyed what Paris could offer. Two or three times a day he phoned back to a buddy at Sissonne to ask whether an alert had been issued. His leave was unofficial, and strictly speaking he was AWOL, but everyone did it — Paris was too close to resist — and his buddies were covering for him. If the order came to move, or his absence was noted, he would get back immediately.

This he promptly did after being told his name had been called out to

123

report to personnel. He raced back to base, where he was asked about his knowledge of Russians and of Soviet society. It all came to nothing, but confirmed to Linton that the rumors about Berlin were true. Yet, despite his best efforts, he could find out nothing more. Eventually, the rumors subsided and Berlin disappeared altogether as a talking point. Linton knew nothing, of course, of the great row that had erupted between Montgomery and Eisenhower over the fate of the city.

Instead, he was soon sent to Cologne. By the time he reached the city, he was almost a hardened veteran of battle. He had learned how to distinguish between the sounds of shells screaming overhead, either from US artillery behind him or from the Germans ahead. At first, he always dived for cover, but then, like the old timers, he just went about his business if the sound told him the shells were not going to land close by. Even when the dreaded "88" German shells whizzed fifty yards overhead, he kept on moving. Occasionally, he heard V1 missiles flying overhead, bound for the Belgian cities of Liège and Antwerp.

He also learned how to translate everyday army slang into the language of his training school back in the States. Before his close encounter with the Tiger tank, the sergeant had told Linton's patrol: "Everything is f-cked up and no one knows where the f-cking front or the f-cking rear is. We are going into the f-cking forest in a f-cking skirmish line to find the f-cking Krauts and come the f-ck back to report that." In other words, realized Linton, this was a reconnaissance patrol.

He was hardened now, too, to the sight of death. Once on a side road, he had come across two burned-out tanks, one American and a German Tiger. The latter's feared armor-piercing gun was pointing sideways at the American tank, whose own gun was aimed at the Tiger. They had fired at each other simultaneously, each with deadly effect. Linton clambered on top of the Tiger and peered inside. "I could clearly see the light gray powdery remains of the crew burned by the large amounts of gas and oil these tanks contain as well as from the explosion of their cannons and machine gun ammunition," he wrote. "Nothing recognizably human remained except a metal belt buckle with charred remnants of leather." He chose not to look inside the American tank. Eventually, such sights became normal and he stopped looking inside because he always saw the same thing.[7]

He also now knew that in the heat of battle the rules of war were quickly bent. By the time he arrived at the front, everyone had heard about the Malmédy massacre. It had occurred during an especially desperate moment during the Battle of the Bulge, when an American unit rushing to reinforce the beleaguered town of St. Vith was captured at Malmédy by troops of the First SS Panzer Division. The Germans herded the Americans into a field and opened up with machine-guns. When the firing stopped, SS men walked among the bodies and shot anyone still alive. Eighty-one bodies were later recovered, their hands still tied behind their backs. It was one of several such atrocities carried out by the same SS division during the battle. Most of them also involved Belgian men, women and children murdered in cold blood in their own homes.

The reaction to Malmédy was predictable and immediate. As Linton observed, "these and innumerable other German brutalities simply did not bring out the milk of human kindness in our troops." One US unit, according to an American war reporter, was issued with the blunt and unmistakable order: "No SS troops or paratroopers will be taken prisoner but will be shot on sight." Soon afterwards, when twenty-one German soldiers were forced by a firefight out of a cellar being used as a first-aid post, they were cut down by machine-gun fire at the doorway. One GI remembered another act of revenge for Malmédy: "We were bringing in casualties. The captain said, 'Take them out and shoot 'em.' And they did. It was awful. He murdered them."[8]

Often such crimes were committed in the heat of battle, but this was not always the case. Captured German soldiers had to be marched back to the prisoners' cages in the rear, sometimes a distance of several miles, and afterwards the men detailed for the task had to return to their unit. This made for a journey of several miles, sometimes through heavy snow, and always at considerable personal risk. Especially if the German prisoners belonged to the SS, their chances of arriving alive at the cages were slim. Frequently, instead, they were reported as "shot while trying to escape." Undoubtedly some did try to escape — SS officers had every reason to worry about falling into allied hands — and it was not unknown for German POWs to hide grenades on their bodies then blow up their allied escorts. You could never be too careful, and survival was the name of the game. But it was common knowledge among GIs that the march to the cage often meant an automatic death sentence.

Nor was it any different on the British and Canadian front. Since the Normandy landings, they too had learned to be wary of German prisoners, especially those pretending to surrender. There were dozens of examples of allied soldiers being killed by Germans feigning death or capitulation, then suddenly opening fire—as Bryan Samain had learned. Inevitably, survival instincts kicked in. "When the Jerries came in with their hands up shouting 'Kamerad,' " said one Canadian soldier happily during the bitter battle for Caen, "we just bowled them over with bursts of fire."[9] Here, too, SS prisoners were the most likely to be slaughtered, often as a result of their own wanton disregard of the laws of war. On the Belgian–Dutch border a group of SS prisoners was being walked through the streets of a town when one of them threw a grenade at a group of British officers and killed a regimental commander. Every one of the SS prisoners was shot. Sometimes, allied soldiers also responded to requests for revenge from civilians. "There were a lot of areas where [the SS] had killed the people in the towns and villages and we'd get to hear about it," said one allied veteran. "There weren't too many prisoners taken in a place like that."[10]

In the end, though, the shooting of German prisoners proved counterproductive. "The POW cages were not getting any significant inflow and the interrogators not getting the raw material they needed for good battlefield intelligence," Linton recorded. And, as Geoffrey Cox was finding out in Italy, first-hand and up-to-date information from prisoners could prove vital for hard-pressed intelligence staff.

So, without acknowledging that illegal shootings had ever occurred, orders were issued to increase the flow of prisoners to the cages. Everyone knew what this meant. Linton was unfazed by the shooting of captured SS men, but like the vast majority of GIs, he avoided getting involved himself, and when the heat of battle had died down, he spoke out against it.[11]

As for interrogation, this too proved a flexible concept. Under the Geneva Convention, a prisoner of war was obliged to give only his name, rank and serial number, and should not be subjected to any violence. But one day Linton witnessed a blatant breach of the rule. His unit had brought in a prisoner, a Wehrmacht captain who was determined to give only the minimal personal information required by the Convention. Yet, from other prisoners already captured, the American interrogators knew that the captain was the artillery fire coordinating officer of his unit. This meant that he certainly knew the location of the German artillery batteries and could pinpoint them ahead of the forthcoming American attack. "Time was short, tensions high, life was cheap, human feelings absolutely worthless [but our] troopers' lives on the other hand were the only precious thing," noted Linton, who was sitting in on the session.

Finally, after the German once again insisted on his rights, the frustrated interrogating officer picked up the phone on his desk and muttered a few quiet words into the mouthpiece. Almost immediately from the next room in stormed another IPW (interrogator of prisoners of war). He was unshaven and exhausted, his trench coat wet and muddy. He rushed up to the German officer and smacked his fist right into the man's face. "Talk or you'll get more since the Wehrmacht buried the Geneva Convention," he snarled. The German smartly began to talk. But, he insisted, "only under protest."[12]

This, too, was no isolated incident. Again, it boiled down to the survival instinct trumping the rules of law drawn up in peacetime by lawyers sitting at a table. One British soldier witnessed a scene involving a captured German sniper brought in for interrogation by a brigadier. "An officer held a pistol at his temple as the brigadier tried to interrogate him," the soldier recorded. "He said nothing. I watched horrified in case the officer pulled the trigger. I can still see the expression on the prisoner's face as he expected to have his brains blown out."[13]

Then there was looting. This was strictly forbidden under army regulations, but under the guise of "souvenir hunting" it was widely practiced by all armies. This was especially true during the first few hours after a town or city was captured. Popular prizes for British, American and Canadian troops were Wehrmacht or Nazi memorabilia, such as Luger pistols, Nazi flags and other party insignia, medals, Schmeisser machine-pistols, daggers, cameras and other easily transportable items.

Here again, definitions varied according to time and circumstance. Linton shared the general view that the SS was a legitimate target for "souvenirs." The wallets of captured SS men would be emptied and family photos thrown into one pile; ID papers and orders into another; German money into another; and French, Belgian or Dutch currency shared out by the GIs. But while this was thought to be legitimate "liberation" on the battlefield, later it morphed into illegitimate looting— especially if it was directed against civilians at roadblocks, for example.

Soon, Linton was deeply enmeshed in dealing daily with civilians. After they learned that he spoke fluent German, staff at the Eighty-second Airborne HQ sent him to Romilly in France for a short course on military government. MG units, as they were called, were attached to combat units to enforce occupation policy in the immediate wake of the advancing front line. Linton was taught how Germany was divided into provinces, counties, cities, towns and villages, and which authorities were in charge of which services. He learned how the civil police and the fire services operated, how postal and telephone services functioned, who provided water supplies, and how the railways, canals and other waterways were organized. All these services would come under allied control once the fighting passed on. He also discovered that the entire Nazi Party apparatus would be abolished and the secret and political police dissolved, along with all the German armed forces, while Nazi officials at every level of German administration would be immediately removed from office.

The basic idea was to keep German society functioning in spite of all this. People like Linton were being trained to fill the vacuum caused by the removal of the Nazis, in part by quickly finding suitable replacements from among the German population who were untainted by Nazism. Following immediately behind the combat troops, MG units (known as G-5 units in the US Army) would arrive in a town, set up office and start issuing orders to local German officials. Their first act was invariably to post up a large notice in prominent places marked "Proclamation No. 1." Written in German and English, and signed by Eisenhower as Supreme Commander, it announced that he was assuming all control and establishing military government. After any Nazis in the "automatic arrest" category had been identified and locked up, replacements were appointed.

This was a massive challenge in itself. To make it more difficult, however, it all had to be done under the strict rule, controversial from the start and more often than not simply breached, of "nonfraternization." "There must be no fraternization. This is absolute! . . . you will not visit German homes or associate with Germans on terms of friendly intimacy, either in public or private. They must never be taken into your confidence," read the US Army guide handed out to all GIs as they crossed the frontier into Germany. To make sure they always had it handy, they were instructed to carry it securely inside the liner of their steel helmet. The *Stars and Stripes*, the GIs' newspaper, put it more colloquially: "Don't get chummy with Jerry," it urged. "In heart, body and spirit, every German is a Hitler."[14]

The pocketbook given to British and Commonwealth troops contained similar advice. Much of it read like an elementary travel guide for backpackers, with a lengthy introduction on German history and the Nazis followed by chapters on society, food, beer, sport, money, weights and measures, religion, literature, music and health, along with a glossary of useful words and phrases such as "*Bitte,*" "*Danke sehr,*" "*Guten Morgen,*" and "*Wie heissen Sie?*" But its main objective was to warn the British soldiers against being soft or sentimental about the Germans. "You may see many pitiful sights," it warned. "Hard luck stories may somehow reach you. Some of them may be true, at least in part, but most will be hypocritical attempts to win sympathy. For, taken as a whole," declared the handbook, "the German is brutal when he is winning, and is sorry for himself and whines for sympathy when he is beaten." It continued in this style, generalizing that all Germans "adore military show" and "love melancholy songs."

The reader was repeatedly warned that this was the second time in thirty years that the Germans had started and lost a war in Europe. This time, however, unlike before, they had to have it made unmistakably clear that they had been well and truly beaten. "We were taken in by them after the last war," the handbook declared, "and so we let ourselves in for this war." It acknowledged that there were many sincere anti-Nazi Germans, but many would pretend to be, and almost all would have some axe to grind. That was one of the reasons, the book explained, for the order not to fraternize.

It ended with a list of dos and don'ts. Among the former, it urged troops to remember that they were representatives of Britain and the Commonwealth, to set an example, to be smart and soldierly, firm and fair, to go easy on the schnapps, and to remember that in Germany "venereal diseases strike at every fourth person between the ages of 15 and 41." Next to that, the injunction to "KEEP GERMANS AT A DISTANCE, even those with whom you have official dealings," seemed almost redundant.

Among the don'ts were injunctions not to be sentimental—"the Germans have only themselves to blame"—not to believe German accounts of the war or the events that had led up to it, not to believe tales that were critical about Britain's allies or the dominions—"They are aimed at sowing ill will between us"—and not to be taken in by superficial resemblances between the Germans and themselves. It concluded by reminding the reader of the fundamental need for security. The war was not over even if there was no fighting where the reader found himself, and Germans must still be regarded as "dangerous enemies" until the final peace settlement was reached. Nazi agents, propagandists and saboteurs were still at work, the book warned. Life in Germany, it declared, "will demand your constant vigilance, alertness, and self-confidence. Each one of you has a job to do . . . See that you carry it through . . . The more thorough we are now the less likely are we to have trouble in the future."[15]

It all made sense, up to a point. As long as the fighting continued, mixing with enemy civilians could compromise vital security and give away useful information—especially if, as the allies feared, there was a serious Werewolf movement to worry about. But the main purpose of the ban was to make it clear to the Germans that they were a nation guilty of aggression and criminality and had made themselves pariahs and outcasts of the civilized world.

The policy worked—more or less—in dealings with local officials appointed by the allies to carry out basic administrative tasks and keep things running. They were simply issued orders and had to comply. But once the fighting stopped, and troops felt increasingly secure, non-fraternization rapidly began to break down. Not being friendly to small children, being forbidden from handing them chewing gum or candies, and from even smiling and talking with them, proved almost impossible for most soldiers from the start.

But what really broke the "frat ban" was sex. This was especially true after the fighting stopped and the initial horror over the discovery of camps such as Buchenwald and Belsen had faded. To the delight of allied soldiers, German women proved little different from the women of France, Belgium and Holland. The standard fine for breaking the ban in the American sector was sixty-five dollars; so, inevitably, propositioning German women became known as "the sixty-five-dollar question." Thousands of allied soldiers thought the price well worth it—even if they *were* caught. Sex could be had for little more than a packet of cigarettes, which in the general breakdown of society acted as basic currency. As did chocolate. It has been estimated that some 90 percent of GIs ignored the frat ban when it came to sex.

Indeed, a whole vocabulary of slang grew up around the ban. Non-fraternization became known as "nonfertilization." Simply to go out with a Fräulein was known as "Goin' fratin'," while to sleep with one was "to frat"—a convenient alternative to the more familiar four-letter word for the same activity. In the British Army, the standard-issue cheese or corned-beef sandwich—a proven way to "catch" a woman—was known as a "frat sandwich." And to the tune of "Lili Marlene" allied soldiers sang, "Underneath the bushes/You take your piece of frat."[16]

One American soldier recorded his experiences of fratting in Brunswick, which became the headquarters of the US Ninth Army when the fighting stopped. A peacetime psychologist, he was given the mission of exploring "the German mentality." He took his task seriously and roamed the city's streets. Everywhere, he recorded, "women, some of them beautiful and most of them young, accosted us and whispered invitations. They would pass slowly, give us a long sideways look and murmur, "I live all by myself; would you like to come up and see me?" There was virtually no competition from German men, who were nearly all still in the Wehrmacht, in prison or in hospital.[17]

German women were now the sole breadwinners for millions of families and survival was the name of the game. "Women from all walks of life," writes one historian, "flocked to the barracks and billets of British soldiers where they traded their bodies for coffee, cigarettes, and food. Some of the more desperate individuals at many camps wore nothing more than shoes and coats, always ready to pleasure another man in order to save her family from starvation." Late in 1945, a German police official reported, "It is impossible to distinguish between good girls and bad girls in Germany. Even nice girls of good families, good education and fine backgrounds have discovered their bodies afford the only real living. Moral standards have crashed to a new low."[18]

Leonard Linton's life as a corporal in G-5 began outside Cologne, when his commanding officer ordered him to find a billet for the unit. Scouting around in his jeep, he spotted a suitable-looking villa that had suffered no obvious damage. In he marched and handed over a pocket-sized copy of Proclamation No. 1 to the elderly occupant. The man was visibly trembling with fear. Standing over him, Linton made him read it. Then he told the German he had thirty minutes to pack his bags and get out. He never saw the man again.

Soon, though, he was overwhelmed by a pile of problems that kept him and the other G-5 personnel working well past curfew hours. There were anxious relatives querying the fate of family members in the automatic arrest category, individuals protesting their dismissal from office, others seeking jobs, and yet more proclaiming that their membership in the Nazi Party had meant nothing serious. Claimants lined up outside his office requesting extra food rations, seeking permits to travel outside the restricted zone around their residence, asking for medical help, looking for a roof over their head, and an abundance of other requests. Wherever he could, Linton referred them all to the local German civilian administration, some of which was still being run by Nazis. Theoretically, such officials should have been dismissed, but practical considerations sometimes led to a waiving of that rule. Such was the case with the local water supplies, where the only competent technician was a party member. Until someone else could be found, he was left in place.

In Linton's dealings with German civilians, two main refrains dominated the conversations: "*Ich war immer dagegen*" ("I was always against the Nazis") and "I had [or helped] a Jewish friend." If he added up the professed anti-Nazis, he noted wryly, the vast roaring crowds that had once greeted Hitler must have been a mirage. As for the Jews, to go by the number that kindly Germans had claimed to help, they must have totaled fifty million. Sometimes, before he learned not to bother, he would ask for the names and details of the Jews involved. "Oh, they disappeared without trace," would come the response. To which Linton would crudely riposte, "No, they left in a cloud of smoke, perhaps at Auschwitz." Rarely did this evoke anything but silence, except for the occasional disclaimer: "I knew nothing about that." Such disavowals were even harder to take after Linton's commanding officer arranged for explicit photographs from Bergen-Belsen to be posted in the unit's reception area. Here, German civilians waited, sometimes for hours, for their problems to be addressed. When a few of them suggested the pictures were nothing but allied propaganda, Linton's anger bubbled over in a way he later regretted.

One day he stopped to have lunch at an army street kitchen. Standing in line, he got the usual generous GI serving slapped on his plate. But this time, instead of one large steak, he received two, along with the usual pile of mashed potatoes, a dollop of rich steaming-hot gravy, and for dessert canned peach slices. He found he could eat only half of the meal, so he scraped what was left into the rubbish bin, which was already half full. As he did so, a few blond and blue-eyed skinny German boys aged about seven or eight tried desperately to scoop up some of it. Furious, he made sure none of them got their hands on any of it. "I hated their looks only because they were German and somehow responsible for the . . . misery we saw," he confessed. It took several months for such feelings to subside. He was far from alone, and lording plentiful food over starving Germans was a common way of behaving, but in the future he remembered the moment as "probably the blackest day of my life."[19]

A fellow All-American who shared Linton's view tried to enforce the ban when it came to relations between his men and German women. He fully understood the men's sexual needs, but he found it hard to accept the willingness of the German women to sleep with their enemy for either sexual pleasure or material gain. One night on patrol he opened a barn door, lighting up the scene inside with the powerful beam of his motorcycle headlight. What met his eyes, he wrote, was "a love fest in a haymow." The men quickly scattered, but he rounded up three of the women for breaking the dawn-to-dusk curfew and locked them in an unlit cellar for forty-eight hours without food or water, to make an example of them.[20]

All this might have kept Linton hard at work until the day of German surrender, but then Eisenhower made a decision that was to affect every single man in Gavin's division. The issue of Berlin was still simmering in the background, poisoning relations between the allies. To resolve it once and for all, on Hitler's birthday Eisenhower flew to the headquarters of Field Marshal Montgomery for yet another tête-à-tête about strategy. Montgomery was still smarting about Eisenhower's Berlin decision, one made even harder to bear because he had also taken the US Ninth Army away from Montgomery's Twenty-first Army Group to be used by Bradley in the drive into central Germany.

So difficult had things become that before seeing Montgomery, Eisenhower had made a special flight to London to talk personally with Churchill about the issue. Reluctantly, the Prime Minister finally accepted that the Russians should be the first to enter Berlin and that it made little sense for the allies, who were not yet across the Elbe in much strength but had advanced beyond the range of fighter support, to make an attempt. As an alternative, they agreed that another German city now urgently merited their attention: Lübeck, on the Baltic coast. "Our arrival at Lübeck before our Russian friends . . . would save a lot of argument later on," Churchill told Anthony Eden, the British Foreign Secretary, after his talk with Eisenhower. "There is no reason why the Russians should occupy Denmark, which is a country to be liberated and to have its strength restored. Our position at Lübeck, if we get it, would be decisive in this matter." This was not the only political matter decided between Eisenhower and Churchill. The

Prime Minister also agreed with the Supreme Commander's decision to capture the German atomic research facilities near Stuttgart before the French First Army arrived.[21]

When Montgomery greeted Eisenhower he was in his usual tetchy mood: he felt hamstrung, his campaign had stalled, and his forces, unlike those of the Americans, were not yet across the Elbe. For his part, Eisenhower felt Montgomery was plodding and needed firm encouragement to speed up his progress. His view was reinforced by Bradley, who intensely disliked the British Commander and, as he scathingly wrote later, believed that he was reluctant "to go for the jugular, to make the kill, take risks."

So the Supreme Commander spoke frankly. Unless the British speeded up and reached Lübeck and the Baltic soon, he warned, the Russians might beat him to it, reach the Danish border, and perhaps even keep on going into Denmark itself. For political reasons alone this was undesirable, but strategically it could be disastrous. Failure to close off the base of the Jutland Peninsula might enable the Germans to evacuate a large number of their forces through Denmark to Norway for the establishment of a northern redoubt. This prospect did not play such a large part in SHAEF fears as did its southern counterpart, but Eisenhower was worried enough about the possibility for it to color his calculations.

To encourage Montgomery, who made noises about the Elbe being almost as bad a challenge as the Rhine, Eisenhower offered him additional help in the shape of Matthew Ridgway's XVIII Airborne Corps. Reluctantly, Montgomery accepted the offer — but only after several days of wavering. Ridgway's corps included the US Seventh Armored and Eighth Infantry divisions, the British Sixth Airborne Division, and Gavin's Eighty-second Airborne.

Within a matter of days, Gavin's men received their orders to quit Cologne and go like hell for the Elbe.[22]

For Linton, though, there was time for one last mission. He was called into the office of his commanding officer and told that information had just come in about a significant arms and ammunition dump concealed by the Germans in the Ruhr. The informant was a Russian from a nearby recently liberated slave labor camp. The Americans had been prepared for just about every occupation problem except the vast number of such Nazi victims, and they were almost overwhelmed by the task of dealing with them, but here, it seemed, was something promising, a lead that demanded to be followed up.

Linton was detailed to interrogate the man further. The Russian was about twenty-four and explained that he had been working on a farm digging potatoes and beets when, over several nights, he saw the Germans burying their supplies: weapons, ammunition and radios.

"Did you see any Leica cameras?" asked Linton.

"Yes, quite a few," replied the Russian.

"I always wanted a Leica," said the commanding officer dreamily when Linton reported back, and promptly ordered a raid. The Russian jabbed his finger at a point on a map, and off roared Linton and a squad of GIs in a couple of jeeps with the man in tow. It was not so much the prospect of some personal loot that excited them — any Leica they found would obviously become the CO's — as the hope that at last they had received some solid information about a persistent problem: the Werewolves.

Shortly before the First World War, a north German writer named Hermann Lons had published *Der Wehrwölf*, a novel based on the semi-mythical "Werewolves"—peasant guerrillas of the Lüneberg Heath who had fought the Swedes and foreign mercenaries during the Thirty Years' War. Their bloodthirsty vigilantism and sadistic killings were legitimate "folk" justice, argued Lons, because normal law and order had broken down. Close to the soil and roaming through the forests, he constantly compared them to wolves. It was an image that resonated deeply in a nation brought up on the dark and frightening tales of the Grimm brothers. (Significantly, when Hitler chose an alias for himself in the 1920s it was "Herr Wolf," and his Eastern Front headquarters hidden in the forests of East Prussia was known as the "Wolf's Lair.")

Lons's book was a bestseller in Germany and inspired at least one of the Freikorps groups that waged guerrilla warfare against the Poles in post–First World War Upper Silesia. In 1944, as the Western allies crossed into Germany, the Nazi Party published a special edition of the novel and excerpts also appeared in several newspapers. The SS also began to organize special Werewolf units. Because all talk of defeat was strictly forbidden, their task would be to harass enemy forces in areas "temporarily" occupied by the allies, and, as befitted guerrilla warfare, they were to form and fight in individual and highly decentralized cells. Their national coordinator was SS Oberstgruppenführer Hans Adolf Prützmann, a Freikorps veteran from Upper Silesia.

The allies were significantly worried about Prützmann's Werewolves, as well as other behind-the-lines German resistance groups that might cause trouble. After all, they had themselves successfully created the SOE and OSS to create murder and mayhem behind the German lines. This concern deepened after a Werewolf group assassinated the American-appointed Mayor of Aachen in March 1945 and intensified with the first broadcast at the beginning of April of "Werewolf Radio."

This was a last-ditch effort by Goebbels to inspire behind-the-lines resistance against the British and Americans, something that had so far been conspicuously lacking. "Hatred is our prayer and revenge is our war cry," announced the station in its inaugural broadcast. "Woe to foreigners who torture and oppress our people, but threefold woe to the traitors among our own people who help them." Naming and shaming Germans who collaborated with the allies was as much the station's purpose as targeting allied soldiers.

But how extensive and serious was the threat? Allied counterintelligence staff circulated endless warnings to units at the front and ceaselessly urged caution. If what the Nazis threatened was true, then a serious danger still lurked ahead for the allied armies. Typical was a nineteen-page report issued five days after Hitler's birthday. After accurately identifying Prützmann as the movement's leader, and reminding readers of the Aachen Mayor's murder, it concluded that the Werewolf danger could "hardly be over-rated," especially as early successes might catch the imagination of fanatical members of the Hitler Youth.[23]

Almost every day a similar intelligence bulletin from SHAEF headquarters crossed Linton's desk, warning him to keep an eye open for any sign of Werewolves. They were supposedly highly organized: arms and ammunition, for example, might be concealed in cans disguised to look like tinned goods, and were coded with certain letters and numbers. Fortunately, learned Linton, SHAEF had secured copies of all the codes and could identify which cans were innocent and which suspect.

He also received a bulletin detailing an almost diabolical cleverness on the part of the Werewolves. The Germans, claimed the SHAEF experts, were able to transform a high explosive into threads, out of which they could fashion overcoats. It would be possible for a man to wear such a garment and pass undetected through a control point. All he would need to do later was take it off, roll it up tightly, attach a conventional detonator, and he could blow up a bridge.

This and other similar dirty tricks seemed highly plausible to Linton.

After all, the Germans were still fighting on despite all the odds against them. So why would they not have put in place an organized resistance that they could mobilize after their surrender? France and Norway had been defeated, and look what had happened there, he reasoned. The bulletins were circulated to all units. GIs were warned not to wander out alone, to keep weapons at the ready and to report all sabotage.

Now, it seemed, as Linton and the jeeps headed off into the German countryside, they were at last on to something concrete. At first, their Russian guide appeared disoriented by all the rubble and debris from the recent fighting. Then, suddenly, he pointed at a large farmhouse with a high stone wall. The jeeps roared in, surrounded the building and screeched to a halt. The GIs leaped out with their machine-guns at the ready. Linton walked into the building behind the Russian. Inside, huddled against a wall, he saw ten to fifteen Germans, mostly men, but some women and a girl of about eight. The Russian was shouting and pointing at them, tugging at Linton's sleeve and pleading with him to let him shoot them. Linton calmed him down, then read out Proclamation No. 1 to the farmer and asked him if the farm contained any hidden weapons. "No," replied the man. Linton therefore asked the Russian to point out the spot where he claimed to have seen the equipment being buried.

He went straight to a barn, opened the door, and stomped on the ground close to a cart. It sounded hollow. Linton asked the farmer for the truth this time. The man said they had hidden some family items for safekeeping. It was true as well, he admitted, that the Russian was one of more than twenty field workers assigned to him by the local Labor Office for help with the harvest. But, he insisted, all the Russians had been very well treated and ate the same food as his own family. He even asked why the man was so angry, and concluded by saying that farming people had never been for Hitler, that most of them had never heard of the concentration camps, and that they were glad the war was over so they could all go back to their work in the fields. To Linton, it all sounded drearily familiar.

While the farmer coolly talked, the GIs were breaking through the floor. It looked highly suspicious. Down below they found an oblong room lined with shelves. Many were piled with household items such as sheets, towels and clothing. There were also a number of cardboard boxes. To save time, the GIs simply ripped them open with their bayonets and within minutes the place looked as though a tornado had torn through it. But, to their increasing fury, they found not a single weapon, not a single radio and not even a single Leica, only a battered old Brownie box camera that belonged to the little girl.

The whole affair, it was suddenly clear, had been a wild-goose chase caused by the Russian's bitter if understandable desire to visit revenge on his former German boss. He barely got back alive. The GIs threatened to kill him, and twice Linton had to stop them. But once back in Cologne he was happy to deliver the man to his camp, which was now being firmly and roughly administered by Red Army officer POWs. Here, Linton assumed, the man would be court-martialed, and perhaps even shot. But he was far too busy to return there so never found out the man's fate. He continued to remain on the alert, however, for any signs of real Werewolf activity.[24]

Other units did likewise. One of them moved into Bonn specifically to neutralize the potential resistance threat by intensive house-to-house searches for illegal arms dumps. "We carried out this search in a manner designed to convince the local population that we meant business," recalled one of the paratroopers involved.

> After dividing the city into sectors, the sectors to be searched were sealed off. The first day, I led a team that searched Bonn City Hall and its adjoining air raid shelter. The shelter, which rose several stories above ground, was also a flak tower. There were four or five underground levels . . . [where] . . . we discovered room after room filled with oil paintings and other art objects. I reported this to the US military government authorities.

The next day, the unit searched every building in the center of the city. When owners complained that the keys had been lost, the paratroopers shot a few locks to pieces until they "got the message." But the only find of any significance was a cellar full of wine and spirits. After some civilians moved the stash to another location under cover of darkness, the paratroopers quickly located it, brought up a truck and drove it away.

But of Werewolves, there was not a sign.[25]

PART TWO

20–30 APRIL 1945

CHAPTER SEVEN

"A SORT OF ALICE IN WONDERLAND AIR"

Still waiting patiently in Normandy, Francesca Wilson was becoming acutely aware of UNRRA's fumbling start in getting to grips with the vast problem of Europe's refugees. Many of the recruits seemed either inexperienced or even cynical. "To many Frenchmen," she noted, "its set up seemed a bewildering, though rather jolly, joke." One of the recruits was a former member of the French Foreign Legion who had been appointed as a warehouseman, although he knew nothing about keeping stocks. Others were messing officers, who told her cheerfully they knew nothing about cooking—except, they joked, "to eat as Frenchmen." Others were in supply. "That was popular," she remarked sharply. "Both in the Army and the Resistance they had learned to help themselves . . . They were ready for a jaunt under whatever label, and the salaries were high."

But she tempered her skepticism with realism. UNRRA was a great experiment—the first international body trying to do something concrete and constructive about refugees. There was much, she admitted, that seemed amateurish, but the agency had been working in the field for less than a year. It also had a budget of several million pounds. This, she noted optimistically, marked an enormous advance in attitudes towards the vast human needs created by modern war from those that had prevailed a mere generation before.[1]

Meanwhile, in Bavaria, Robert Reid was having problems keeping up with Patton's tanks. "This is surely the fastest advance in the history of war," he told his BBC listeners, "an advance where divisional command posts make big jumps forward two or three times a day." And that was even before they had reached Buchenwald, during Patton's impressive and daring push eastwards from the Rhine into Thuringia.

While Reid was reporting on Buchenwald's horrors, the thrust of Patton's advance turned sharply and rapidly southwards towards the River Danube. Here, read the general's plan, his Third Army would probably link up with the Soviets advancing from the east, before pushing on to Salzburg and the Alpine Redoubt beyond. To feed and fuel his men and vehicles, a million tons of food and a million gallons of gasoline had already been stockpiled. In preparation for the contact with the Red Army, he circulated recognition data for Russian vehicles and equipment to all his corps commanders. No one wanted any damaging incidents of "friendly fire" with Stalin's forces.

In his rapid advance deep into Germany, Patton was in his element. A flamboyant, profane and aggressive figure wearing polished boots and ivory-handled pistols strapped to his hips, not for nothing was he known widely as "Old Blood and Guts." He idolized his Virginian and Confederate forefathers, and he loved the army and its men. "No American general had a better grasp of the human element in war," writes one biographer, "no one realized more profoundly that morale is never constant [and that] troops in contact with the enemy should never be allowed to remain quiescent . . . action, and offensive action at that, alone brings release."[2] Even Montgomery, who disliked and denounced Patton as a "sabre-rattler," conceded that he was the most aggressive "thruster" in the allied camp.

Whether riding in a jeep, standing at attention, or simply listening to a briefing, he always dominated the scene. "His polished exterior glistened," writes another biographer. "He was always on display, his energy coiled like a cat's . . . he inspired excitement and awe, as well as loyalty and trust." Yet, behind this aggressive exterior lay a man who cared passionately for the welfare of his men. "No commander," writes a third biographer, "ever devoted more time to training his troops to such a high standard that would *save*, not waste, their lives."[3]

As personalities, Patton and the mild-mannered Robert Reid could have hardly been more different. Not surprisingly, perhaps, the British correspondent kept his views on the controversial American strictly to himself. But they had at least one thing in common: both believed instinctively in the vital importance of morale, and each had a profound sympathy for the ordinary GI.

The German defenses proved a fragile crust, and the Americans found opposition light or non-existent. They encountered plenty of blown bridges and roadblocks, but few were defended. Most of the Wehrmacht's Panzers had been lost in the Ruhr pocket, its normally efficient administration was in disarray, replacements were not reaching the front, and makeshift units of low-grade troops, including the elderly and teenagers, both girls and boys, were being thrown into an increasingly frantic defense. Faced with Patton's tanks, the Germans were surrendering in large numbers. In the first three weeks of April, his army took almost a quarter of a million POWs.

Also helping was the weather. Apart from one or two days of wintry squalls of freezing rain and sleet, clear skies provided first-rate conditions for hundreds of tactical air support missions to help the men on the ground. Behind them they left hundreds of wrecked locomotives, destroyed aircraft, pockmarked runways, burned-out trucks and ruined bridges. By now, the Luftwaffe had virtually ceased to exist, and allied aircraft operated almost at will.

Practically the only brakes on Patton's advance were the supply of gasoline for his tanks and the congestion on the roads as support convoys frantically tried to keep pace. However, food was also becoming a problem. Capturing and storing German food supplies suddenly became a high priority, not least because hundreds of thousands of allied prisoners of war and displaced persons were known to be in this zone of operations, and all would have to be fed.

Reid was even feeling the pinch himself. Normally, press correspondents could expect to eat well, often sharing the officers' mess at divisional headquarters. But now the situation was a far cry from the first few weeks with Patton's army before the crossing of the Rhine. Then, Reid had enjoyed the comforts of a hotel room with constant hot water, an excellent mess with good food, a professional chef and civilian waiters, and plenty of free time in the evenings when he could quietly sit in a corner and read or write letters home. Recently, though, "It has all been very hard work and I think we are all getting tired again," he wrote home to Vera in one of his increasingly rare and hastily typed letters. "Our food has not been quite so good as it was earlier on, simply because of the supply question . . . when an army is on the move you have to fall back on hard tack and tinned stuff." So it came as a welcome relief when one of his fellow correspondents made a foray into the country one day and returned with a batch of fresh eggs. It was even better when another managed to find a rifle and ventured out to shoot a hare.[4]

Third Army units were now regularly making advances of thirty or forty miles a day. On Tuesday 24 April, they finally reached the Danube near Regensburg in Upper Bavaria. Here, a mere three weeks before, Fey von Hassell had been kept in a small, filthy cell. The city, one of the oldest in Germany, had survived seventeen sieges and had suffered a long and bloody history of violence. A Roman fortress, a bishopric since the eighth century, a way-station for Crusaders on their way to the Holy Land and a prosperous medieval port city, it had served as seat of the diet of the Holy Roman Empire until it was abolished by Napoleon. It was also the site of one of his victories during his advance on Vienna in 1809, and here too the French Emperor had been slightly wounded during the fight to breach its ancient walls. It had been home for the medieval astronomer Johann Kepler, and much later for the industrialist Oskar Schindler, who saved hundreds of Jews from the Holocaust.

When Patton's men entered the city they found it mostly intact, although allied bombers had flattened its railway stations, freight yards and Messerschmitt aircraft factory. Its twelfth-century bridge, the Steinerne Brücke, had been all but destroyed by SS troops trying to halt the American advance. And there was another example of Nazi disregard for cultural heritage. Hidden in the vaults of the city's Reichsbank, the Americans found a vast collection of art stolen from all over Europe: paintings, precious stones, bracelets and watches taken from extermination camp victims, silver bars formed from melted-down jewelry, and solid gold items removed from churches in Czechoslovakia, including a solid gold tabernacle from a Russian Orthodox church in Prague. Most valuable of all, however, were three billion dollars' worth of Austrian securities, as well as the major part of Bavaria's paper assets.[5]

Meanwhile, some units of Patton's army were skirting the Czech border, while others soon crossed the Isar River, which flows through Munich to join the Danube at Platting, and headed into Austria.

It was no wonder that Reid was breathless at the pace of it all. Each morning, he and his radio technician, Bill Costello, clambered into the back of their open jeep and were taken by an army driver for several hours in search of a story. April was still cold, and Reid bundled up well. Over his leather jacket he piled on a greatcoat, and around his feet he wrapped a warm, fleece-lined coat that was his personal piece of loot "liberated" from the Germans.

Reid's task differed from that of the many press correspondents who were also tracking Patton's advance. They were print men and women. By contrast, he was working for BBC radio, so had to bring the *sounds* of battle and of the front to listeners back in Britain. He was acutely aware, and fiercely proud, of being on the cutting edge of a development in communications that made reporting in this war radically different from how it had been in the First World War.

"The modern miracle of wireless," he wrote, "was about to bring the sounds of the battlefield to the domestic fireside." This marked a revolution, and like all revolutions it encountered initial suspicion and resistance. During the Battle of Britain in 1940 the BBC had broadcast an eyewitness account of a dogfight over Dover between RAF fighters and the Luftwaffe that had been widely criticized. A cricket match or horse race was one thing, but to report on an event where men were losing their lives was thought tasteless.[6] By now, however, opinion had completely changed.

Mostly Reid's reports were broadcast on *War Report*, which went out each night after the nine o'clock news. This meant that he was always working frantically against the clock. When he spotted something interesting, he could quickly grab a hand microphone and describe the scene in front of him, or do an impromptu interview while Costello concentrated on making sure that everything was being recorded properly in the little trailer that was towed behind the jeep.

Sometimes, when they could not reach a site by jeep, they would carry a portable box of recording equipment to the site. This was a standard piece of equipment developed by BBC engineers and first used successfully during the Anzio landings in Italy the previous year. Weighing forty pounds, it included twelve double-sided disks which were good for an hour's recording, a microphone with a small clip that could be attached to almost anything handy, and a dry battery unit. It was so simple that Reid could work it himself, unlike the much more sophisticated unit in the trailer.

When he returned to the press camp each evening, Reid was obliged to play the disk recordings to army censors, who were listening for anything that might be militarily sensitive and of use to the Germans.

This meant he had to censor himself carefully as he made the recordings. It was easy enough to strike out an offending word or sentence from a written dispatch, but doing the same with a disk was almost impossible. When he had joined up with the BBC for war service, he had been sent on some pretty rigorous training courses where he learned about the pitfalls of censorship.

That wasn't all he had endured. In the mountains of North Wales, he had painfully ridden a mule to watch an artillery exercise, and on the Yorkshire moors he had lain flat on the ground pretending to write a dispatch while live bullets whizzed overhead and land mines exploded around him, showering him with clods of earth. He also learned how to drive a heavy truck, a grueling experience for a man who had never even driven, let alone owned, a car. This was made even worse by having to practice in the country lanes around Portsmouth that were crowded with tanks, mobile guns, bulldozers and ambulances heading for the D-Day beaches. Once, when he encountered a convoy of the famous Desert Rats with the message "Alamein to Berlin" chalked on the turrets of their tanks, he sensibly handed over the wheel to his instructor.

Yet the most important training of all, apart from the purely technical aspects of broadcasting from the field, concerned censorship. To highlight the problems of handling disks, correspondents were taken to a fake German HQ where a "Nazi" intelligence officer played specially prepared recordings supposedly made by careless British correspondents, and then extracted seemingly innocent remarks into militarily significant intelligence. They were then given a course on how to avoid such mistakes. All this helped Reid think pretty rapidly on his feet when recording his stories.[7]

After the disks were passed by the censor as fit for broadcast, they were carefully packed up, addressed to the BBC, and put on a courier plane. Sometimes, if he was lucky, Reid found a telephone line he could use to speak directly to the BBC. In that case, a special machine in London known as a telediphone recorded his words onto a wax cylinder. This was then played back to a typist who produced a written script that could be read by a censor. This saved time.[8]

Now, the very speed of events itself was providing good, dramatic copy. "I drove for several hours yesterday in blinding rain and hail storms along some of the roads heading southeast packed with supply trains, through a countryside where the engineers have once more worked miracles in the way of bridge construction across rivers and railways," he told listeners breathlessly three days after his Buchenwald dispatch. Suddenly, he drove into a town still stunned at being over-taken by Patton's steamroller advance. In front of him, German civilians were cycling, apparently casually, alongside a railway line where a freight train loaded with twenty or thirty trucks was still ablaze following an allied air attack.

American tanks thundered through the streets bound for their next destination. Reid stopped to look in the window of the local Nazi Party headquarters. The out-of-date news bulletins on display were still reporting the fighting on the Rhine. As he stood there, two young women walked up and became annoyed to find the office closed. One of them was returning a small booklet, so she simply stuffed it behind the drainpipe next to the front door. Reid gently took it from her. "It was an impressive bit of work," he told the listeners, "telling of the invincibility of the German Reich and particularly the impregnability of the west wall complete with illustrations." The booklet was well thumbed and obviously much read. With a laugh, the girls happily let Reid take it. "Just propaganda," they said contemptuously. "All propa-ganda and nothing more."[9]

By this time Reid, like many war correspondents—and certainly the troops on the ground—had little time for any Germans, especially after witnessing the atrocities of Buchenwald and other concentration camps. As far as he was concerned, he confessed to Vera, he saw no dis-tinction between Germans and Nazis, and all had to take responsibility for the horrors the allies were uncovering. He detested them all, but particularly the servile ones. To make his point, he gave her an illus-tration. He had been listening to a newly appointed burgermeister talking to an American officer. When the German finished, he absent-mindedly wound up with a "Heil Hitler." "You can't beat that sort of thing," Reid insisted. "It's the principle of running with the hare and hunting with the hounds all the time."

Some of his BBC colleagues back home shared his views, and wrote to tell him so. One, from Broadcasting House in Manchester, warmly contrasted Reid's opinions with reports from some newspaper corre-spondents who had remarked on the friendliness of the Germans being overrun by allied forces. "I simply do not believe it," he told Reid. "Of course, they are friendly now that they are conquered, but that is their nature . . . I am glad that our BBC correspondents, at any rate, are more balanced."[10] Vera felt much the same. Like her neighbors in Stockport, she had seen photographs of Belsen in the newspapers, and heard her husband's account of Buchenwald on the BBC: "I'd sterilize the lot from four years of age upwards," she told him bluntly.

It all made her worry about him more than ever. How was he dealing with it? Was he eating properly? "I have seen so many pictures and having read so much of the horrors you have seen and knowing what your tummy is like," she wrote, "I felt sure you have not had a good meal this past week." She also knew he had recently been vaccinated, presumably against typhus. She missed him badly and wanted him home. So did the children. It had been three and a half months since they had last seen him. And despite the excellent news about Patton's advance, Vera remained skeptical about claims that the end of the war was close. Symbolically, the war had finished in Britain that very week with the lifting of the blackout. She would not have to pull the curtains any more just because it got dark, she told him, although in practice she would continue to do so because she did not want people seeing her alone in the house at night. London's lights were now happily ablaze again. But she was not getting her hopes up. The war still had many weeks to go, she felt.[11]

Hardly had the ink dried on her neatly handwritten letter than her husband was taking a look at the ruins of Nuremberg. It had been heavily bombed that January, and its ruins were still smoldering from the bitter battle that had seen the Americans capture it just three days before. The Germans had mounted a staunch defense of the home of the Nazi Party Rallies, relying heavily on the fixed ring of anti-aircraft guns that encircled the city, which they turned against the American ground troops. Once the Americans broke through the ring, writes the US official historian of the campaign, "the fight developed into the slow and often costly business of clearing one crumbling building after another, one more heap of rubble, one more cellar, defeating one more futile though dangerous counter attack launched by a few men, a squad, a platoon." All the while, American fighter bombers and artillery kept pounding the wrecked city. It took the ground troops three grueling days to reach the ancient walls around the heart of the old town. Before daylight the next morning, the Nazi Gauleiter directed a final, doomed counterattack. Except for a few zealots who still had to be rooted out of the rubble, that was the end of it.[12]

Reid and his wife had passed through the city by train early one morning on their way to Munich just before the war, only half awake as they peered through the carriage's window. "Do you remember?" he asked. "The place looks in a shocking mess today."

To his BBC listeners, he painted a far more graphic scene. The Nuremberg known to tourists no longer existed and the city of Hitler's torchlit rallies was still without electricity, water or gas. Three days before, when they had entered its ruins, American forces had found an underground tank factory and eighteen air-raid shelters packed with dead, dying and wounded German soldiers. Some ten thousand Russian, Polish, French, Belgian and Czech slave laborers were wandering through the streets, scavenging for food and shelter.

Bombing and shelling had reduced the city, Reid reported, to "one vast wilderness of tumbled and tumbling ruins, tottering walls, huge mounds of debris and still burning and smoking skeletons of buildings." The population of two hundred thousand was living a troglodyte existence in cellars and tunnels. Reid spotted a stove-pipe sticking out of the rubble and went to take a closer look. He found a tiny entrance in the wreckage. Peering into the depths below, he spotted some shadowy figures half lit by candlelight. When they sensed his presence, they began to scream at him in terror. Only when they realized that he was neither a Russian nor a Pole did they stop. More than anything, German civilians now faced the pent-up anger of the slave laborers in their midst, whom they had once ignored, tolerated or exploited.

Everywhere, gangs of children and youths scuttled like rabbits over the ruins. In the wreckage of a church Reid stumbled on a surreal scene: clips of bullets littered the floor, and he spotted a bloody bandage; on a plate lay the congealed and hardening remains of a half-eaten meal; and, perched on the top of a vacuum cleaner, were piled several unopened packets of hair dye.

But the most fantastic scene he witnessed occurred in the historic center of the old city, in the cellars of a warehouse storing wine. People were streaming towards it from every direction carrying pots, pans, bottles and jugs, and fighting and shuffling their way through the ruins to the cellar door. "Old men and women," Reid reported, "the harlots and the sluts, the boys and the girls of Nuremberg." Inside, huge casks of wine were being tipped and poured into jugs and pails. In a courtyard outside, workmen were tilting them to their lips and letting the wine slop freely all over themselves. Even as he watched, a man reeled over and collapsed in a puddle of mud and wine. He spotted some boys rolling casks out of the building and away over the debris.

Nearby, a freed deported laborer, a Frenchman, had devised a simple way of getting his fair share of the booty. As the citizens of Nuremberg passed by laden with their loot, he gently tapped each one on the shoulder. "German?" he asked, and when they replied in the affirmative he levied a bottle of wine on each of them. None dared protest.

Already, American forces were hard at work improvising emergency shelter for the thousands of freed laborers who were roving the streets, singly or in predatory gangs. They chose a site that not long before had witnessed a totally different sort of spectacle. In a magnificent stroke of poetic justice, the Nazi Party Rally grounds were being transformed into a camp for the homeless.

"From the look of the place today," concluded Reid after he had finished his tour, "it might be better to wipe Nuremberg off the records and start again."

Flying over the city two days later, Patton described it as "a pathetic sight." On the day of Reid's dispatch, the losses to the general's army were the lowest of any day of its operations since it had landed in Normandy — just three men killed, thirty-seven wounded and five missing. And on that day they captured 8,878 enemy troops.[13]

The fall of Nuremberg was rich in symbolism. But the eyes of the world were focused on a strategically and politically much more significant event — the long-awaited meeting of American and Soviet forces.

Torgau is a picturesque medieval town lying on the River Elbe. Close by, at 4:40 p.m. on Wednesday 25 April, leading elements of the United States First Army rendezvoused with Red Army forces of the Fifty-eighth Guards Division. Germany was now cut in two. Truman and Stalin were both immediately informed, newsmen rushed to the scene, and the Soviets organized a splendid alcohol-fueled banquet replete with plenty of attractive female soldiers in neatly pressed fresh uniforms. Reid's BBC colleague Edward Ward arrived shortly afterwards. "I saw soldiers of the First American and the Red Armies throw their arms around each other's necks and kiss each other on the cheeks," he told his audience. "I even had to undergo this greeting myself from a burly Ukrainian soldier . . . The whole scene was one of the gayest fraternization. A Russian lieutenant sat on a wall playing the accordion and singing Russian songs, and the Doughboys joined in. Drinks were passed round and everyone was happy."

That night, Churchill marked the historic moment in a broadcast to the nation: "After long journeys, toils and victories across the land and the oceans; across many deadly battlefields, the Armies of the great Allies have traversed Germany and have joined hands together. Now, their task will be the destruction of all remnants of German military resistance, the rooting out of the Nazi power and the subjugation of Hitler's Reich."

Yet the scenes of warmth and the generous talk of "hands together" masked a much harsher reality. "Take no initiative in organizing friendly meetings," Soviet front commanders ordered their units, "[and] give no information about operational plans or unit objectives." The Red Army was quickly to reveal itself as a far from cozy ally.[14]

Nevertheless, with this meeting up of US and Soviet forces, the war appeared all but over. In Moscow, over three hundred guns fired a twenty-four-shot salvo in celebration. In Times Square, a vast crowd of New Yorkers sang and danced into the night. At Torgau itself, cameras popped and flashed, and pictures of American and Russian soldiers in close and happy embrace sped around the globe. It was a moment the world's media — not least the BBC — had been waiting for. Mistakenly thinking it might be Patton's army who would link up first with Stalin's forces, they had told Reid that capturing this story should be his top priority. The telegram from London had pulled no punches. It had come while he was still filing his Buchenwald stories. "Grateful dispatch from you present control and relief Buchenwald camp following Murrow story," it read in telegramese. "This only secondary for military coverage stop any Russian linkup maximum priority stop."[15]

In the event, neither Patton's army nor Reid made the day. Instead, one of his great BBC rivals, Frank Gillard, who was traveling with the US First Army, got there first. Reid was philosophical about it, though. He was driven by no great personal ambition, and had no lust for the limelight. He knew that his own biggest story, that from Notre Dame, had happened almost by accident. But Vera was furious. She hated the fact that her husband was constantly being trumped by Gillard. The BBC radio star had become her personal *bête noire*, and she frequently wrote to tell her husband so. Still, she contented herself, "your prize may be Hitler."[16]

*

After Nuremberg, Reid resumed his helter-skelter pursuit of American forces as they penetrated deeper and deeper into Bavaria. He passed through an idyllic green landscape spotted with yellow fields of mustard, where farmers were working as if nothing unusual were happening around them. "An air of complete and unbalancing unreality envelops a nation which is disintegrating before our very eyes . . . a sort of Alice in Wonderland air," he reported.

> In many of the towns and villages through which I drove today it was obvious that the local grapevine had been at work bringing news of stupendous events, for main streets were thronged with townsfolk and prisoners of war and deportees—unusually amicable affable throngs in what might have been liberated rather than conquered territory.

American troops had even been greeted with cheers, offered wine and given directions by the local populace.

Reid himself experienced their solicitude. "When my own jeep stalled with engine trouble outside a bomb-shattered garage," he told his listeners, "it was the German proprietor who came to my driver's rescue and put in half an hour's work on the engine before we set off again."

Only occasionally did the Americans run into isolated pockets of resistance, whereupon they quickly wiped it out with overwhelming firepower. Some American columns forged ahead without firing a single shot, and casualties were so low that the medical units almost ran out of work. But the POW cages were still filling to bursting point. "Patience and good humor . . . pervades an army which knows that the victorious end of this campaign is now a matter of days," Reid recorded with satisfaction.[17]

Patton passed his own blunt and inimitable verdict on events at a press conference he held at Erlangen outside Nuremberg on Friday 27 April. He had just been promoted to a four-star general and was in a particularly ebullient mood.

"Do you expect the Germans to try to hold [out]?" asked one war correspondent.

"I hope they do . . . I really don't know," replied Patton, obviously still itching for a proper fight. "I don't see what the fools are fighting for . . . There is nothing of interest happening. I was down there today and crossed the [Danube] river, and it wasn't worth even pissing in."

Three days later, he prerecorded his victory speech to be broadcast along with those of other allied commanders when VE Day finally arrived. "The war," he confided to his wife in a letter home, is "very dull."[18]

Boring it may have become to the bellicose Patton, but even as he was recording his speech, several thousand prisoners of war nearby were celebrating their liberation at the hands of his Third Army men.

Moosburg is a small town twenty-seven miles northeast of Munich. Here, twenty-four hours before, some thousands of allied prisoners of war had ecstatically cheered as American forces entered Stalag VIIA, the official name of the POW camp built on its outskirts. It was originally built for ten thousand men. Now it was overflowing with some eighty thousand prisoners. They were predominantly French and Russian, but the camp also contained some fourteen thousand British and American airmen and soldiers, both officers and men. Many had recently arrived there after exhausting days-long marches, or on train transports, from other camps in eastern Germany that were threatened or had already been overrun by Soviet forces.

The camp was squalid, discipline was poor, and parts of it were positively dangerous "no-go" areas. The wooden huts were packed full, and other men slept in tents where the April thaw had turned the ground into a sea of mud. A long trench served as an open latrine, and dysentery was rife. Food was scarce. In recent weeks, ever fewer Red Cross parcels had been getting through. Briefly, a rumor ran through the camp that all the prisoners would be marched off to the Alpine Redoubt, but it had come to nothing, thanks to a last-minute agreement between the Germans and the Red Cross that they would move on no more prisoners.

Now the camp was liberated. The guards had quietly slipped away during the night. A few of the SS troops dug themselves in by the river to defend the town, and for a while there was heavy firing. Then it stopped. Soon, a column of Sherman tanks rolled in through the camp's gate flying Old Glory.

Shortly afterwards, Patton himself arrived in a jeep. Wearing his famous pearl-handled six-shooters, he pointed to the Nazi flag still flying from the camp's flagpole. "I want that son-of-a-bitch cut down, and the man who cuts it down," he said, "I want him to wipe his ass with it." At least, that's what the legend quickly claimed. True or not, Old Glory was duly raised, and men wept and cheered and waved. The Union Jack quickly joined the American flag.

Many of the British prisoners had been captured as far back as 1940—"old kriegies" of many years' standing, as one of them put it. He and his mates watched as the mostly younger Americans went wild. Then, he said, "we celebrated quietly on our own with a peaceful brew of tea in the sun." Another British officer celebrated by sharing a tin of canned salmon with his mates, and followed it with a good draft of Scotch whisky donated by a couple of Americans. "God bless the bastards," he scribbled in his diary, "I am wild, happy and mad. After five years, free at last. May be home next Sunday."[19]

Reid arrived on the scene two days later. Moosburg was the center of a wide area, stretching as far as Munich, that was dotted with dozens of smaller camps and outdoor working parties of POWs. As he drove towards the main camp, hundreds of prisoners watched and cheered from side roads at the passing cavalcade of tanks, trucks and men. Here and there he spotted huge farm buildings with the letters "POW" painted in white lettering on their roofs. At one point, he passed hundreds of Indian troops shivering with cold as they waved him on. Moosburg was a global camp with nine thousand British forces representing all the dominions, including nearly all the Canadian officers who had been captured during their ill-fated raid on Dieppe in 1942.

Reid interviewed the senior British officer, Royal Air Force Group Captain Willetts, in his personal quarters. Adopting a breezy and light-hearted tone, Willetts minimized the problems of food: the Red Cross supplies were now flooding in, he assured Reid, and would keep the men comfortable for the week or two before their evacuation home.

"What is the general condition of all the prisoners?" asked Reid.

Willetts continued with his upbeat message, no doubt bearing in mind the prisoners' families listening back home. "They're fit as fleas," he joked, "even those who've got a few fleas on them! They're happy. In fact, there's a move to change the date of Christmas to 28 of April when the tanks rolled in at the front door."[20]

Victory brought jubilation to thousands, but for other victims of Hitler's Third Reich, liberation dawned amid death and despair. And Reid was determined that in the flush of victory this story should not be lost. It offered a somber and sobering counterpoint to the otherwise benign scenes he had been reporting recently from the lush Bavarian countryside.

"There is a trail of death one hundred and twenty-five miles long across Germany — not the death of soldiers killed in combat but the murder of those luckless inmates of the concentration camps of Buchenwald and Flossenburg who were forced by their Nazi jailers to take to the road when the Americans approached both camps," he told his BBC audience after interviewing one of the six thousand survivors out of eleven thousand prisoners who had begun the walk of death.

The interviewee was a thirty-four-year-old Frenchman who had been thrown into a camp after his arrest in Paris in 1941 and had ended up in Buchenwald.

He had a terrible story to tell. The killings had begun almost as soon as they left the camp's gates, with SS men posted every five yards or so clubbing the prisoners as they were force-marched the short distance down the hill into Weimar. Here, they were put on a train, packed eighty-five men to each freight car with virtually no food. By the time they reached Dachau four days later, four hundred of them had died.

After a short stop in the camp they were marched off again, along with five thousand prisoners from Dachau itself. "The shootings began again," the Frenchman told Reid. "They shot when a man stopped to tie his shoe laces or when a man tried to pick up grass to eat." When they eventually arrived at Flossenburg concentration camp, close to the Czech border, only half of the prisoners who had left Buchenwald remained alive.[21]

Best described as a factory producing death, Flossenburg was a main camp with forty-seven satellite camps for men and twenty-seven for women. In many of them, the work was carried out underground. There was an appalling death rate: during the previous twelve months, almost fifteen thousand men and over a thousand women had died. Hunger, sadistic treatment, inadequate clothing, medical neglect, disease, beatings, shootings, suicides and hangings all attributed to the death toll. That Christmas a number of prisoners had been hanged in front of the others. By the side of the gallows had stood a gaily decorated Christmas tree.[22]

Hardly had they arrived there, however, when the order came down for Flossenburg to be evacuated as well. So off they went again, the guards still trigger happy and shooting stragglers left and right. This went on for four days. Then they heard an American Piper Cub spotter plane circling overhead, and a column of American tanks suddenly arrived on the scene. Instead of giving up, the SS guards decided on a last-ditch stand. "They turned their automatic weapons pointblank into the half-dead prisoners, killing two hundred of them outright in an effort to make a roadblock of human bodies," Reid reported. "Then the guards attempted to escape into the woods with the tanks opening fire and killing more than a hundred of them."

During the death march, some of the prisoners were forced to dig shallow graves for the bodies of their dead comrades. Eisenhower ordered that these bodies, and those who had simply been left to rot beside the road or in ditches, should be given decent burials. During this last week of April, Third Army chaplains officiated at hundreds of such burials. In some towns MG officials ordered local German civilians to dig up the bodies, make coffins and prepare proper graves.

Reid recorded the events at one Bavarian village where men, women and children were forced to witness the burial of some two hundred victims. An American press correspondent also witnessed the scene. It was Sunday 29 April. "Under a bright blue sky with the spring sun slanting down on the green shrubbery of [the] cemetery," wrote John R. Wilhelm of the *Chicago Sun*,

> several hundred of the most prominent citizens of this German village today buried 204 battered bodies of Polish Jews who had been beaten and shot to death near here by their SS overlords. I watched as these German burgers, clad in their best Sunday clothes, some with stiff white collars and neat black ties, picked up those emaciated, mutilated corpses and placed them side by side with their own German ancestors in the village cemetery. Several women were weeping. Many shuddered. Others turned away in a faint. But the burial went on.

Not all the victims, in fact, were Jews, but, as Reid reported, those who were received a special burial from Jewish survivors. "They refused to allow the Germans to touch their dead," he told his listeners. "Instead they themselves [laid] the remains of their comrades in their caskets. Then, with four Germans carrying each coffin and with a Jewish survivor walking ahead of them praying in Hebrew the procession turned slowly towards the local cemetery."

The villagers, wrote Wilhelm, had "shame in their eyes." Yes, they said, they had heard of the concentration camps, but they had never seen such things with their own eyes. "They also plainly felt," added the reporter, "that their little village was connected with the massacres only by accident."

Like all those who witnessed such scenes, Reid was determined to make sure the story was told. There were still skeptics at home who were reluctant to accept the truth or were ready to make excuses. He knew this from Vera. "Various neighbors have asked if you are alright, they have all heard your stories," she wrote to him after his Buchenwald reports. "Most people are very shocked by it all, though two remarks made to me this week have been 'of course I don't believe it all' and another about the prisoners 'Perhaps they deserved it.' These are people around us," she reminded him.[23]

While Patton's southerly columns were penetrating into Austria, other Third Army units crossed the Czech border and headed in the direction of Pilsen. Here, too, it was open season for allied aircraft. About twenty miles east of the city, American reconnaissance planes spotted a huge German convoy of tanks, mobile guns, armored cars and horse-drawn vehicles heading slowly southwards, away from the Russians who had already captured Brno. Over the next three hours, successive flights of Thunderbolt aircraft bombed and strafed the column at will.

Reid interviewed one of the pilots, an American from Miami, on his return to base. "They were . . . all jammed up together," said the airman, "and when we attacked them and the cars and trucks began to burn the flames spread from one to another then to the nearest buildings until whole villages were set on fire."[24]

The entry of allied troops into Czech territory posed an immediate problem. Czechoslovakia was an occupied nation and its government-in-exile in London an ally in the war against Hitler. Yet the region that Patton's men were capturing was the Sudetenland, which was heavily and historically populated by Germans. Demands for autonomy by the Nazi-supported and subsidized Sudeten-German Party under its leader Konrad Henlein had led to the Munich Conference in 1938. There, in a futile attempt to appease Hitler, Neville Chamberlain had handed over the territory to Germany. Most of the Sudetenland's population had cheered Hitler's troops when they immediately marched in. Henlein, who then merged his party with the Nazis and became an SS Obergruppenführer and Reichstag deputy, was appointed Gauleiter, a position he held throughout the war.

Now, the question was whether the Sudetenland should be treated by the allies as conquered enemy territory or as a liberated land.

Technically, the answer was clear: it was liberated territory, even if this meant tearing up the Munich Agreement. Yet most of the local population had supported Henlein, and so formed a potentially hostile force that might spark serious problems. "A casual visit to the Sudetenland," reported Reid, "gave the impression that full military government was being applied. Some of the Eisenhower Proclamations, for instance, were posted in the streets of such towns as Asch." Lying right on the Bavarian border, Reid explained to his listeners, this was the former home of Henlein and "the hatching ground of the Sudetenland plans and plots."

The Americans had also posted flyers demanding the handover of firearms, but as these did not produce acceptable results, they launched raids on hundreds of houses and posted a final warning, colored in bright scarlet. Such signs sat oddly next to others addressing the Czech nation as allies.

On the whole, Reid reported, the attitude of the Sudetens towards the Americans was apathetic. Asch, a town with a normal peacetime population of about twenty-five thousand, had swollen to forty-eight thousand thanks to a huge influx of displaced persons, but of this total only about fifteen thousand were Czech. Reid's unspoken question hung heavily in the air. What would be the fate of the Sudeten Germans in the nation they had come close to destroying? For one man at least, the answer was clear. Henlein was soon captured by Patton's men, and shortly thereafter he committed suicide by slashing his wrists in the prison at Pilsen.[25]

There remained one final, unanswered question. When Reid had reported a few days beforehand on the flight of Julius Streicher from his home near Nuremberg, he noted that the notorious anti-Semite had headed south. Presumably, speculated Reid, he was "heading for the Nazi redoubt in the Bavarian mountains." Yet Patton was now rubbishing that scenario. Asked about the redoubt by another war correspondent, he dismissed the notion out of hand: "I think it is a figment of the imagination," he said. "It's just a good word."

But was it? When April ended, the threat of the Alpine Redoubt still seemed very real to many.[26]

CHAPTER EIGHT

"THE MOST DEGENERATE
SPECTACLE"

While Patton's forces in Bavaria sliced through the fragile crust of German defenses, in Italy the allied armies completed their long-awaited breakthrough, out of the Apennine Mountains and into the valley of the Po. At last, noted a war-weary Geoffrey Cox, "the fruits began to tumble from this tree." On the evening of Hitler's birthday, Germany's commander-in-chief in Italy, General von Viettinghof, ignored the dictator's demand to stand firm and ordered a general withdrawal from the Bologna area. Early the next morning, the city was entered by Polish forces, followed soon afterwards by Americans and Italians.

At around the same time, General Freyberg issued orders for his Second New Zealand Division to continue their advance northwest in the direction of the River Adige. Acting as motorized cavalry, armored cars of the 12th Lancers would lead the way, while the rest of the division followed. Now, he promised, it would be like the way they used to do it in the desert: an advance so rapid that they would have to keep in touch by wireless. Only at night, when they stopped to rest, would the signalers have time to lay down the land lines they had been relying on recently.

In his intelligence truck parked at divisional headquarters, now safely across the Idice River, Cox took out his maps to examine the route ahead. Meanwhile, one of his unit's photographic interpreters sought out aerial shots up to the Alps. Cox worked alongside four other intelligence specialists. Two of them were aerial photography experts with a specially equipped caravan of their own. Both belonged to the Mediterranean Air Interpreters Unit-Western Section. Its initials at the bottom of the steps to their caravan — MAIU (West) — gave rise to inevitable jokes about Mae West and "coming up to see them some time." When visitors did, instead of the Hollywood bombshell, they encountered two bespectacled Englishmen. One was a peacetime furniture dealer from the Lake District, the other a former member of the Milk Marketing Board. But both were expert analysts. Between them, they spent hours poring over their maps to identify gun pits, slit trenches, vehicle tracks and hazardous topographical features of the landscape. Their calculation of river widths was so exact that the engineers trusted them implicitly when building the improvised bridges they had to throw across the numerous watercourses encountered by the New Zealanders.

Cox also studied maps of northern Italy captured from the Germans. Here, the Adige was called by its German name, the "Etsch," and he recalled the line in the German anthem "Deutschland Über Alles" urging Germans to guard the Reich "from the Etsch to the Baltic." The second-largest river in Italy, it was more than a hundred yards wide and too deep and fast flowing to be forded. Along parts of it the Germans had constructed their last defensive barrier in Italy before the Alps, the so-called Venetian Line, which ran from just south of Venice to Lake Garda. Designed to close the forty-mile gap between the Adriatic and the Dolomites that provided the gateway into northeastern Italy, it could block the allied advance for days.

For the moment, however, the New Zealanders pushed on with little to stop them. If the only real problem facing Patton in Bavaria was the supply of gasoline for his tanks, for the allies in northern Italy the main brake on their advance now was the rate at which the engineers could build bridges. There was little sign of the gray-uniformed enemy, except for the occasional handful waiting patiently by a roadside to surrender.

Morale among the Germans was sinking fast. By late April, across the entire Eighth Army front, allied interrogators were reporting the same thing. Cox summarized the scene in one of his daily intelligence bulletins:

> The fact that they [the Germans] are continuing to fight — and sometimes fight well — is not in general due to any conviction but rather to lack of initiative, general mental stagnation, and moral cowardice.

Even though it is obvious to the vast majority that Germany has lost the war, they are quite prepared to fight on so long as it is the easiest thing to do and so long as there is somebody there to tell them to do it. The thought of mutiny does not occur to them — though as soon as the tactical situation makes surrender an "honourable" course to take and the easiest way out they are only too glad to do so. They have little stomach for the last man and last round theme.[1]

Sometimes the Germans appeared simply to evaporate. One of the New Zealand units consisted entirely of Maoris — the 28th Battalion, created in 1939 at the direct request of Maori Members of Parliament. A purely volunteer force, it was quickly joined by many Maoris who had already volunteered for other units. Maoris were keen to prove that they were the equal of their *pakeha* (white) comrades, as well as to earn the full benefits and privileges of New Zealand citizenship.

The battalion was organized on tribal lines under tribal leaders, although most of its senior officers were *pakeha*. It had acquired a fierce reputation in Greece and Crete, where the Maoris had once petrified the Germans with a bayonet charge after being taken by surprise while they were resting. "The instant Maori reaction — a *haka* [a traditional war dance accompanied by chants and gestures] followed by a charge made more terrifying for the hapless enemy by the sound of war cries," writes one historian, "typified the Maori style of fighting throughout the war." On that occasion, they killed about a hundred Germans and put the rest to panic-stricken flight. Similar episodes in North Africa had caused the German commander Erwin Rommel to complain bitterly that they were "scalp hunters."[2]

Since the previous November, the battalion had come under Maori command in the shape of thirty-five-year-old Lieutenant-Colonel Peter Awatere.

In peacetime, he was an accountant, but now, with his heavy and athletic figure girded with weapons like a Wild West sheriff, he belied every stereotype of the cautious, desk-bound pen-pusher. He was a strong leader with a close and thorough knowledge of both his own people and the *pakeha*. "Indeed," wrote Cox, "I often wondered if he did not deliberately overstress his Maori characteristics in a sardonic belief that that was what the *pakeha* liked, and so he would give it to them in good measure." If so, it worked. There was no doubting Awatere's courage. He had already been awarded the Military Cross and the

Distinguished Service Order for bravery, and he and his men were never reluctant to take on the Germans. "After all," he once said to Cox while explaining the Maoris' reputation, "my father's generation was the first in Maori history which had not spent most of its life under arms."[3]

Now, aerial reconnaissance reported that there was no sign of the enemy for the next few miles ahead. But Awatere insisted that the Maoris should advance on foot and search every building on the way. About twenty Germans had, in fact, holed up in one of the houses, but as soon as they saw the Maoris coming, they fled before they got close.

Awatere, though, was still not satisfied. By this time, his men were wet to the skin from wading through canals, and because of the mud in their socks they had slung their boots over their shoulders. All around, houses had hung out white sheets from their windows. The Maoris finally clambered onto tanks and any other vehicles they could find and swept forward to the next river obstacle, the Reno. But still Awatere refused to give up. "Anxious to throw a company over," records the official New Zealand history of the campaign in Italy, "he waded across and examined the empty [German] trenches. Then he yelled in Maori, 'There's no one here. Come over B Company.' "[4] By that evening, the New Zealanders were all safely across the river and Cox was elated. That afternoon — Monday 22 April — he felt as if they had just come out of a long tunnel, or a dark green forest, into the sunlight. "The end of it all," he wrote, "seemed suddenly in sight."[5]

After a day's regrouping, the Eighth Army and the New Zealanders resumed their advance, and the next day they reached the southern bank of the River Po north of Bologna. It was dead-flat country now, the roads lined with poplars and an occasional plantation of oak or pine. As the tanks and trucks rolled forward in the bright April sun, they raised clouds of yellow dust that reminded many of the New Zealanders — as Freyberg had promised — of the North African desert.

Yet this was a lush and heavily populated land dotted with villages and the towers of churches. "Every ditch was gay with yellow buttercups, white daisies and blue snapdragons," recorded one poetic diarist of the campaign, "every field fenced with mulberry, poplar, elm, chestnut and oak trees, all supporting grape vines in full leaf. The populace waved to the speeding trucks or crowded around with flowers and wine at the frequent and unpredictable halts." It sounded like a pleasant Sunday picnic.[6]

Cox saw it all with a different eye, though — that of the intelligence officer shrewdly calculating the damage inflicted on the enemy's strength. He instantly noticed that the approaches to the Po were littered with mile upon mile of the abandoned matériel of an army, some deliberately destroyed, some just abandoned. The Germans had been under constant attack from allied aircraft in "a hundred local Dunkirks, each worse in its own way than the 1940 evacuation." Trucks, horse-drawn wagons, cars, caravans and guns lay tipped into ditches or along the edges of fields. Hundreds of draft horses used by the Germans and their accompanying Hungarian units ran wild and free through the fields. Soldiers, along with civilians, hunted for loot among the wreckage and rounded up hundreds of the horses before bartering or selling them to the locals. Any of the German vehicles that could be repaired joined the column of northbound traffic heading towards the Alps.

Here, even at its narrowest point, the Po was three hundred yards wide and far too deep and rapid to ford. Allied aircraft had destroyed every bridge across it to hamper the German retreat, so the New Zealanders were faced with a crossing by assault boats, amphibious tanks and "ducks" or DUKWs (specially constructed six-wheel trucks equipped with propellers).

They did it at night, under cover of heavy artillery, and ran into only very slight resistance. Then followed the engineers to build a pontoon bridge for the heavy Sherman tanks and the other supplies and men that would carry the division north. "In the sunshine," recorded Cox, "it was like a Regatta." It was Wednesday 25 April, ANZAC Day, the thirtieth anniversary of the day when Australian and New Zealand forces had landed at Gallipoli in the First World War. "The enemy showed no stomach for a fight on the Po last night," Cox reported with satisfaction.[7]

Meanwhile, American units of Mark Clark's US Fifth Army advancing further west had reached the outskirts of Verona, and the Tenth Mountain Division was closing in on Lake Garda and the roads leading to the Brenner Pass, the last line of escape over the Alps for the Germans. The two allied armies in Italy had finally linked up, and their advance was gaining rapid momentum. "If we don't stop now," Freyberg told the New Zealanders, "the enemy won't be able to fight again."

That morning, Cox was called over to talk to the second-in-command of Divisional Signals. The man had just intercepted a radio message he wanted Cox to hear. He walked over to where the radio expert was bent over a small receiving set and put on the earphones. Through the static, he could hear a voice talking rapidly in broken English: "This is Genoa. Patriotic Radio Genoa. The patriots this morning captured all of Genoa. The German garrison has surrendered. We have many prisoners. Send help quickly. Allies send help quickly."[8]

This was just a start. All over northern Italy, the partisans were rising in open revolt ahead of the approaching allied armies. In Genoa, the German commander had finally received orders just two days before to withdraw from the city into Lombardy, and had sought a promise through an intermediary that the partisans would let him retreat without a fight. But the secret was betrayed before any agreement could be reached, and the partisans immediately launched an insurrection. After two days' fighting, the Germans had surrendered and the partisans had broadcast their appeal for help.

Until now, Cox had had little to do with the partisans, although he had seen plenty of signs of their presence. In the town of Forli, through which he had frequently traveled that winter on his way to and from the front, the Germans had hanged the local partisan hero in the town square along with his mistress, and the walls of the houses were plastered with their names, hailing them as martyrs of the resistance. North of Bologna, he had slept by the road where notices warned German convoys that they were traveling in a zone "infected with bandits." Clearly, the partisans were a serious nuisance to the Germans, but Cox, like most regular soldiers, had given little thought to how they could provide significant help to the allies.

Now, though, things were changing. The partisans were starting to emerge from hiding and were helping the New Zealanders in practical ways. A few days before, they had built a bridge for the Maoris and taken part in a firefight against the Germans. Many New Zealanders who had previously been captured in Italy began filtering through the lines and singing the praises of the partisans, who had hidden them or helped their escape. Along with such stories came ample evidence of the frequently generous and self-sacrificing assistance given to evaders and escapers by the local peasantry, often at the risk of their own lives. The German Army was ruthless and murderous in dealing with Italian civilians it suspected of helping the allies, or of being involved in any way with the "bandits." On the allied side, derogatory jokes about the Italians (the "Eyeties") had at last begun to give way to a dawning appreciation of their value, as well as of the suffering they had endured at the hands of their erstwhile allies.

Cox felt an instinctive sympathy for the partisans, who were mostly drawn from the poor and dispossessed. As a boy and student, he had spent school and university holidays working on a farm on New Zealand's North Island as well as on sheep stations in the mountains of Otago. This had given him an insight into the hard-working and outdoor pioneering life of farmers who were, as he put it, "the heart and soul of the New Zealand of the 1920s." He had also learned to appreciate nature, observe details of the topography, and find comfort in the landscape around him.[9]

He was a man of strong egalitarian conviction. In the 1930s, like many of his contemporaries, he had been drawn towards communism. Indeed, during the Spanish Civil War he had come close to joining the party. "If Harry Pollitt [the leader of the British Communist Party] asks me to join, I shall," he had once sworn. But the call never came, and the Soviet behavior he witnessed later in Finland transformed him quickly into an ardent anti-communist. Now, he thought of himself as a pragmatic social democrat.[10]

The evening they crossed the Reno, Cox talked with a New Zealand sergeant who had been hiding with the partisans north of Venice since 1943. The man was eager to join them in the final battle. For an hour, he and Cox pored over the maps while he pointed out where the partisan formations could be found. Along with the sergeant was an American officer who had fought with another partisan group near Venice. "Wait till you see them," he told Cox. "We've a whole army waiting for you. These guys are good."[11]

Allied escapees such as these two also provided Cox with excellent intelligence about the state of the retreating Germans. Another New Zealander ex-POW he interrogated that week, an NCO, painted a vivid account of the scene he had witnessed along the road ahead: "Petrol was so short that each lorry hauled at least three or four others. Tanks and even horses and oxen were hauling MT [motor transport]. There were horse drawn and oxen drawn carts in great numbers, but few guns . . . The enemy took to the ditches the moment a plane came over." The NCO had been there when allied artillery fire came in. "The enemy panicked and ran wildly into the fields," he reported, "or fought to get aboard vehicles which were already packed to overflowing. Those on the vehicles fought savagely to keep the others off. It was plain that all the German troops felt the war was utterly lost."[12]

A few days later, Cox saw with his own eyes what well-organized partisans could do. On Sunday 29 April he awoke to a cold, gray morning and the sounds of shots. The weather had turned, and heavy rain had begun to transform the ground to mud, hampering the work of the engineers and sucking at the wheels of trucks. Cox had not yet got used to the sound of partisan sniping so close, and had slept uneasily.

He was on the edge of Padua, the city that held the keys to the approach to Venice and beyond. The day before, the New Zealanders had breached the much feared Venetian Line with barely a skirmish to advance twelve miles north of the Adige — "enemy country," Cox called it. Verona was already in American hands, and somewhere in the hills ahead lay the German parachutists. But exactly where, what they were doing and what they planned to do remained unclear. That they were getting desperate, however, was obvious. In one village the inhabitants told him that the Germans had demanded bicycles, and brutally shot half the menfolk to get them.

After dawn, he acquired a much clearer picture, thanks mostly to the partisans. The Eighth Army liaison officer with the Italian resistance fighters was a Montenegrin who spoke fluent Italian. He had caught up with the New Zealanders the day before, and Cox sent him ahead to find out what was happening. He returned with reports that the city was now in partisan hands. "Are the messages reliable?" asked another senior officer. Hoping they were, and taking a deep breath, the Montenegrin replied, "Yes." On the strength of this assurance, the tanks edged slowly into the city, with the liaison officer clinging to the turret of the leading vehicle. In a small square, shadowy figures emerged carrying rifles. The Montenegrin shouted out some words in Italian, and back came the reply, also in Italian. These were the partisans. They had already seized control of the city, forced the Fascist authorities to surrender, and taken some five thousand German prisoners.

Inside the tank, the radio operator reported back: "City in partisan hands," and soon Cox himself was debriefing the Montenegrin outside his caravan. Shots could still be heard from patrolling partisans, while in the small square in front of him women were calmly walking to mass and troops were quietly shaving in front of mirrors propped up against the sides of their tanks. The partisans were eager to hand over all their German prisoners, but the New Zealanders had the manpower to take only a handful of senior officers.

Cox sent his radio expert off to fetch the officers. He returned mid-morning, sitting on the front of a Sherman tank, Tommy gun in hand. Behind him sat four German officers hanging on with one hand and waving large white flags with the other. Clinging precariously to other parts of the tank were eager partisans wearing the red scarves of the mostly communist Garibaldi Brigades. Behind them walked a crowd of cheering civilians. Cox recognized one of the Germans as General von Alten, commander of the Ferrara area. He and others were then locked in a disused office building.

When he returned to arrange their transfer south, the Germans arrogantly gave Cox a Nazi salute, and he heard von Alten's aide-de-camp making sneering remarks about the "Neger" outside the door— meaning the Maori guard. Angered by this, Cox curtly refused von Alten's request that he be allowed to take with him a basket of cognac bottles. Instead, he gave the basket to the guard.

His dislike for the Germans had been running high since the Libyan campaign of 1941, when he had first started interrogating prisoners. "I don't hate them," he recorded, "I just dislike them as I dislike rats and snakes. They have been corrupted by Nazism into a hateful people . . . They are perverted by Hitler." But now, his dislike had turned to anger which had finally reached boiling point. A few days before, his driver had appeared holding copies of the *Union Jack* and *Eighth Army News*, news-sheets produced for the troops. "There's some real horror stuff this morning, sir," he said. On the front page, Cox saw pictures from Belsen of corpses piled high like logs. Even with his knowledge of Nazism garnered from his prewar work as a foreign correspondent, he was shocked. "Stick this up in your truck," he said to his chief inter-rogator, "and ask them what they say about it."

Still angry, Cox went over to the POW cage to talk to a new group of prisoners among a batch of some two hundred recently captured parachutists—four Russian women and a German officer speaking per-fect English, who claimed to be an anti-Nazi. The women were said to have worked in a hospital, but to Cox it seemed obvious they had formed a traveling brothel for the Germans. Aged between eighteen and thirty, three of them sat on the ground, red-eyed and weeping. The fourth was standing with her back to a tree, staring at the Germans in the cage and running her hands through the tangled mass of her unruly black hair. "All the fury of an enslaved and despised continent," wrote Cox, "glowered in the eyes of that one Russian peasant girl."

As he watched, the German officer approached him. He was a lecturer in English from Hanover, and Cox decided to test what he meant by being anti-Nazi, so he showed him the photographs from Belsen. The man shook his head, as though he thought them fake. "Why did you do nothing against Hitler?" demanded Cox. The German asked what he could have done. "My friends and I were not Nazis. We hated the Nazis. But we were powerless. We had to do what we were told. But you must realize," he added, "that all Germans are not bad."

Cox knew this well enough, but he was not going to let the man off that easily, so he goaded him about his service in the German Army. Why had he helped the Nazis? The man replied that he had never fought and had just been in charge of a ferry-boat across the Po. But that, responded Cox, simply meant he had helped other men, soldiers who had killed New Zealanders, his friends. The man said nothing, and his eyes dropped back to the photographs of Belsen. Suddenly, in front of Cox's eyes swam a kaleidoscope of images he had witnessed in Italy: the blackened and swollen corpses of hostages shot outside Arezzo; the tiny pieces of flesh and clothing spattered in pine woods, where the Germans had blown up three partisans after tying them to a tree; and the scarred wall of a church outside Siena where, one Sunday, the Germans had pulled all the men out of mass and shot them.

As he turned to leave, the German officer asked what would become of them all. Overcome by an irresistible desire to strike back, Cox deliberately lied: "You will be handed over to the Russians," he replied abruptly. As he walked away, he saw fear spreading rapidly across the man's face.

Days later, he was still unable to control his feelings. Victory was now obviously close and an end to the killing was in sight. Defeat for the Germans was inevitable but still they kept on fighting. "Cecily darling," he wrote in a brief, handwritten letter to his wife penned quickly on the outskirts of Padua:

We can see the Alps ahead of us, which is most encouraging. I find my contempt for the raw material of the German race grows as they keep docilely obeying the orders of a corrupt and beaten regime. Day after day I interrogate scores of young [Germans] whose minds have been shut to any fresh thought but Nazi obedience since Hitler took over. They are the most degenerate spectacle I have ever encountered.[13]

By the time they reached Padua, the New Zealanders had received their next set of orders. The target now was Trieste, at the head of the Adriatic a hundred miles beyond Venice. The capture of this major port, once the maritime gateway to the Austro-Hungarian Empire, could provide a vital lifeline for supplies to the allied armies as they headed across the Alps and into Austria. The Yugoslav partisans under Marshal Tito, who were now organized as a regular army, were also advancing on Trieste from the south. Between them, they would squeeze out the Germans. Venice was a mere sideshow and could be largely bypassed, leaving perhaps just a small squadron to make it secure. The quicker the New Zealanders could get to Trieste, the better. "We can get there in a day!" promised Freyberg.[14]

Cox was rapidly on the road again. While he was dealing with the obnoxious von Alten and his ADC, the tanks had headed off in the early morning darkness towards Trieste. On the Brenta River just outside Padua, they took the Germans by surprise, captured the bridge intact, and rolled on in the direction of Venice, twenty miles ahead. At one o'clock in the afternoon Cox heard a message come crackling in over the wireless: The 12th Lancers had crossed the causeway over the lagoon and entered the city.

He was already packed and ready to go with the rest of the divisional headquarters. Off they sped through the streets of Padua, lined with green, red and white Italian flags and banners, and civilians shouting, waving and cheering as they passed. The rain began again, lashing the windscreen of his jeep, and occasionally they stopped while ahead they heard the thump-thump of tanks or the rat-a-tat-tat of machine-guns twenty minutes ahead as they pushed aside some last-ditch and futile defiance from the Germans.

Here the country was flat and criss-crossed with canals, the roads lined with large houses and walled gardens belonging to the wealthy merchants and noble families of Venice. Partisans were rushing around in trucks, and as the sun came out again people streamed out of the houses to greet the New Zealanders. In one place, Cox stopped outside a small park and a man came out through the wrought-iron gates with his wife and two small daughters. His face had the pallor of the sick. "This is my first day out of hiding for a year. A year in a cellar," he said. Then he repeated it: "a year."[15]

This was joyful liberation. But death still traveled as its companion. At a small bend in the road Cox stumbled on a scene of carnage. Twenty minutes before, a group of retreating German coast guard troops had fired on the leading New Zealanders, who had retaliated with their heavy machine-guns. The fight was over in ten minutes. Propped against a tree by the side of the road lay a badly wounded German. His face was gray with pain, his lips barely moving. Fifty yards on, others lay in a ditch. "They lay as they had been hit," noted Cox, "dying and wounded in a crumpled gray muddle . . . fifteen or twenty of them. The partisans had already taken away their weapons. One man looked up imploringly, saying nothing. Another, a middle-aged man, formed with his lips the words '*Ich habe Schmerzen — Schmerzen* [I'm in pain, in pain].' The face of another, lying on top of two dead men, was gray already with death." An Italian priest arrived to administer the last rites. Then a jeep full of photographers roared up and took pictures of the priest bending over the bodies. When they asked him, he changed his position so that the sun was just right for a better shot. Behind them, from a red-bricked campanile, a bell rang out with the sounds of liberation. Beyond, Cox could see the pale blue line of the Alps. Slowly, a wooden cart packed with straw trundled across the field to collect the wounded Germans.

Then Cox was off again. Within minutes, he spotted the dome of St. Mark's away to his right across the Venice lagoon. But instead of taking the causeway into the city he swung inland towards the industrial city of Mestre and the road to Trieste. The streets were again packed with cheering Italian civilians and the partisans were out in force with their red scarves and neckties. Cox was mesmerized by the women. "Were there ever such girls as those of Mestre on this Sunday of liberation?" he asked.

Brown faced, aquiline, sunburnt, lithe girls with shiny hair and with greeting and invitation in their eyes . . . The Italian men greeted us warmly enough, with relief and thanks. But in the eyes of the girls there was something akin to ecstasy. Some threw us kisses, some threw their arms wide as if they would embrace us all, in their exultation; others smiled quietly, and called to us "Ciao, Ciao" as we moved eastwards through the winding streets. We smiled till our muscles were stiff, we held out our hands till they were almost tugged off. It was no mean reward, the greeting of these people of Mestre in the April sunshine.[16]

Out of the city, he drove on down the road that paralleled the Adriatic to his right. To his left rose the jagged, snow-covered peaks of the Dolomites. Between the sea and the mountains lay the Friuli Plain and Brazzà, the home of Fey von Hassell. He passed through a village, where the children were sitting on a grassy bank and chanting *"Viva—i—nostri—liberatori"* (Long live our liberators). He saw a group of terrified-looking German prisoners being escorted somewhere, possibly to their deaths, by partisans. And in the late afternoon, his eyes fell on a white-painted stone by the roadside announcing that Trieste lay just 125 kilometers ahead.

That night, the leading New Zealand units crossed the Piave River by boat. Once again, the hard-worked engineers, the true heroes of this Italian campaign, set about building a bridge to carry the rest of the division towards their final destination. "There should be only light resistance," predicted Cox that night, as he reported that the Germans were now retreating north to the Alps rather than east to Trieste. "Once across the Piave, we should therefore have straightforward going until the [River] Tagliamento or the [River] Isonzo which should be crackable with one good blow."[17]

The brief delay while the engineers built yet another bridge across yet another river gave Cox the chance to drive back into Venice. There was a partisan intelligence group in the city and he could pick up some useful intelligence there. It also gave him the opportunity to see the famed city of water at yet another milestone in its history.

With its maze of twisting canals, Venice sits on an archipelago of islands in a huge saltwater lagoon at the head of the Adriatic. The Venetian Republic, home of the great explorer Marco Polo, had once been the most prosperous city in Europe and the greatest sea power of its day. Its powerful merchant families dominated Mediterranean trade, built great palaces, and subsidized artists such as Titian, Tintoretto and Canaletto.

But Napoleon had put an abrupt end to its independence and handed it over to Habsburg control. Since then, as part of the new Kingdom of Italy, it had continued its long and slow decline into a backwater that drew increasing numbers of well-heeled tourists to its melancholy attractions. "Nothing in the story of Venice is ordinary," writes one historian, "she was born dangerously, lived grandly, and never abandoned her brazen individuality."

This, though, had not prevented the city from being "obediently Fascist" under Mussolini, and although there had been some sporadic resistance it had provided a safe and popular resting place for German officers and high-ranking Italian Fascists throughout the war. Nearby industrial Mestre had been heavily bombed more than once, but allied planes had left Venice intact. Almost the only casualties of war were its two hundred citizens who had fallen into canals during the blackout.[18]

At four o'clock in the afternoon of Sunday 29 April, two allied tanks raced along the causeway that linked the city to the mainland and parked by its railway station. The local population came out in force to greet the New Zealanders, and partisans rounded up almost three thousand German troops still remaining in the city and interned them in a huge garage. In Rome, Freyberg had been furious at being cheated by the Americans of the Hotel Excelsior as the New Zealanders' officers' club, and driving up from Trieste, US Army trucks had been noticed carrying placards for Venice's premier hotel, the Danieli. Determined not to see a repeat of what had happened in the capital, Freyberg ordered his troops to seize the hotel and keep out the Americans. They did just that and it quickly filled up with New Zealand and British officers.

The Danieli was now Cox's own destination too. After crossing the causeway, he boarded a gondola and proceeded majestically down the Grand Canal and past the city's finest palazzos to St. Mark's Square. The canals were eerily quiet. Here and there, people waved or cried out at them from a window, or looked down as they passed under a bridge, but it was hard to feel like a liberator seated in a gondola, and Cox felt rather embarrassed. He was glad when he arrived at the hotel.

In Venice, as elsewhere, the partisans had risen in revolt as the Germans left, and there had followed two days of fighting against the SS and the Fascist blackshirts. Some of Mussolini's supporters were still being rounded up, and Cox saw one of them, surrounded by an excited crowd, being escorted by armed partisans across a canal near the Bridge of Sighs to the city's prison. He was a thin man in his late thirties and was wearing a blue cap that made him look like a railway porter. "He carried a paper parcel under his arm and his face was white," recalled Cox. "He grimaced constantly, either from fear or indifference."

Apart from this, however, Venice appeared to be making a seamless transition from one set of occupiers to another, as it had done so often in its history. In St. Mark's Square, things were astonishingly normal. Women were already selling food for the pigeons to a handful of New Zealand soldiers, and at the foot of the campanile someone was taking down the German price list and putting up another in English. All the shops were shut, but huge crowds were out walking, and the large flags of Venice and Italy flew in front of the church.

The city's partisans, assisted by agents from the OSS, had set up their intelligence headquarters in a suite at the Danieli. Here, overlooking the Grand Canal, Cox spent the next few hours getting first-hand and up-to-date reports about German positions and the state of the bridges from towns and villages along the road to Trieste. As he plotted the details on his map, it seemed clear that the partisans had seized control of all except one.

Before night fell he drove back to his tent on the banks of the Piave to prepare for the next day's advance. But he carried with him a scene from the Danieli that was lodged indelibly in his mind. That day at lunch, he had watched as suave dark men in smart linen suits accompanied well-coiffured women to tables glittering with cut glass and silverware. "To Venice," he reflected, "the Republican Fascists had sent their wives and their mistresses for safety from the bombing. Here had gathered the wealthy of Northern Italy. Here, boldly enough, they waited to see what action we would take now that we, and not the Germans, were the masters."[19]

Several hundred miles to the west, though, what was to become of collaborators in France was already pretty clear. Just days before, in the chill air of early morning, a convoy of nine cars had swept out of Austria and into the Swiss frontier town of St. Margarethen, close to Lake Constance. In the back of the lead car sat an elderly man with a bald head and a drooping white moustache. Beside him sat his wife, wearing a black coat and hat. In the car behind rode their daughter and her husband. The following five cars were packed with the man's personal doctor, his aide-de-camp, his advisers and his household servants.

Bringing up the rear came two cars filled with suitcases, trunks and personal belongings. As the frontier barrier came into sight, a supercharged Mercedes which had been escorting the convoy turned back. Inside sat several black-uniformed SS troopers and a couple of Gestapo officials.

Once past the barrier, the convoy stopped outside the small Swiss customs house. The elderly man was helped out of the lead limousine. He was bareheaded and wore a dark gray overcoat. A young Swiss girl handed him a bunch of fresh purple lilac and bobbed a curtsey. "For your eighty-ninth birthday, Marshal Pétain," she said simply.

Philippe Pétain, marshal of France and national hero of the great First World War Battle of Verdun, was going home. He had signed the humiliating armistice of 1940, met personally with Hitler at Montoire in Touraine to shake the Nazi dictator's hand, promised him full French collaboration in building a new Europe, and ruled France as the Vichy government's head of state for four years.

Then, three months after D-Day, the Germans had bundled him into a car and driven him to Germany. He had spent the last few months incarcerated as a virtual prisoner in a castle at Sigmaringen on the upper Danube. Now, he had decided to return to France to face whatever justice awaited him. He had long deluded himself that he had served as the protector of France against the Nazis and his role as a true French patriot, he believed, would be recognized.

"The fact that I find myself on Swiss territory is the most beautiful birthday present I could have wished for," he said as the girl presented him with the blossoms, and he shed a few tears. After insisting that he had been taken to Germany against his will and that he had refused an offer to form a "French Quisling government," he was kept waiting in his car while the frontier guards phoned through to Bern seeking instructions.

The Swiss authorities had already refused entry to Pétain's first prime minister and arch-collaborator, Pierre Laval. The previous autumn, Laval had been condemned to death *in absentia* by a court in Marseilles. Desperate to escape French justice, every day over the last week he had tried frantically to cross into Switzerland. Each time, he had been turned back. He had even begged a Swiss Red Cross official to intercede for him. When the man explained it was beyond his authority, the increasingly panicky Laval burst into tears. "You condemn me to death," he cried.[20] The Swiss had also refused entry to Marcel Déat, another pro-German French collaborator who was seeking asylum.

But Pétain was not seeking refuge. He merely wanted transit across the country into France. Eventually, after an hour and a half's waiting, permission was telephoned through. An escort of motorized Swiss police drew up and the convoy headed off westwards, in the direction of France. As they left, Pétain waved to a silent crowd of curious Swiss onlookers.

Eventually, the convoy arrived at the border crossing into France. His entry had been agreed at an emergency meeting of the French cabinet, which had also fixed the exact time and place where he should turn up.

As Pétain stepped out of his car, he was formally arrested, and a customs official began to search his luggage and count his money. Waiting
for him was General Pierre Koenig, de Gaulle's faithful Free French
chief of staff, commander of the Free French Forces of the Interior, and
now the military governor of Paris. Pétain held out his hand in greeting, but Koenig impassively ignored it. Beside him, a representative of
the French High Court read out the summons for the marshal's trial.
With the rituals completed, Pétain and his party were ushered aboard
a special train. It was heavily guarded, and as it steamed out of the small
frontier town its estimated time of arrival in the French capital
remained a tightly kept secret. [21]

The France that awaited Pétain was very different from the one that
had fêted him as the nation's savior just five years before. De Gaulle
and his Free French followers had rejected the 1940 deal with Hitler
from the start, and the wartime resistance had long demanded that
Pétain and other collaborators be brought to justice and purged from
French society. Eventually, the harsh rigors of the Nazis and the
excesses of their local collaborators had also led millions of others to
give up on him. Now that he was a beaten man and a lost cause, they
wanted nothing of him. Yet there were still plenty of supporters who
argued that he had indeed shielded France from the worst and
remained unapologetic about their allegiance to his regime.

Since the D-Day landings in Normandy, France had been liberated
in stages and purges and trials had been under way for months. They
had been accompanied by plenty of "rough justice"—unorganized
reprisals against collaborators—and thousands of suspects had been
lynched, murdered or beaten up. Hundreds of trials had already sent
dozens of collaborators to prison or to the guillotine. However, even
some ardent Gaullists were beginning to tire of the purges and were
complaining about their often arbitrary and selective nature. For the
sake of national unity, they argued, it was time for greater understanding and leniency to be shown. But now, in April, as the allies
overran the concentration camps, their inmates were returning home.
Thousands were French, and many had been denounced by their own
neighbors and taken off to Germany for months of incarceration
behind barbed wire. France was shocked to the core by what it was
starting to hear.

Two weeks before, de Gaulle had personally headed a reception
committee at the Gare de Lyon in Paris to welcome back the first

group of almost three hundred women liberated from the camps. Some members of the welcoming crowd carried lilac blossoms to welcome them. Others brought lipstick and face powder to hand out.

None of them was prepared for what greeted their eyes as the train disgorged its emaciated and traumatized passengers. "Their faces were gray-green with reddish brown circles around their eyes, which seemed to see but not take in," recorded one journalist at the scene. A diarist noted that the returning deportees had a "greenish, waxen complexion, shrunken faces, reminiscent of those little human heads modeled by primitive tribes." Some of the women were so weak that they were unable to remain upright. The rest remained standing, shakily, while they sang "The Marseillaise" in thin, cracked voices to the devastated audience.[22]

One of those who'd become most critical of the excesses of the purges was François Mauriac. The sixty-year-old novelist and playwright had spent much of the 1930s attacking fascism in the columns of *Le Figaro*, and he was an ardent supporter of de Gaulle and the Free French, but even he now recognized a distinct and harsher mood in the country. "The allied advance into Germany," he wrote, "has suddenly become a descent into hell." Now, witnesses to inhumanity on a gargantuan scale were making their voices heard, and collaborators who had taken refuge in Germany were being captured and brought back. "All resentments," he continued, "have been awakened or aggravated against those Frenchmen who collaborated with the authors and the accomplices of these crimes, and who favored their victory."[23]

Haunting images of the returning victims from Buchenwald, Ravensbruck and Bergen-Belsen were plastered across every newspaper in France and the debate about what to do with the collaborators had grown more intense than ever.

In Normandy, Francesca Wilson was hearing first-hand accounts about Nazism and its collaborators from their victims. Eager to learn and voraciously curious, she talked to as many people as she could about life under occupation. She encountered a kaleidoscope of views.

Almost everyone she met had a relative in Germany, either as a prisoner of war or as a deportee. She talked to one woman she met on the sands gathering cockles and mussels. The beach had been out of bounds to civilians until very recently, so this was a tangible fruit of liberation. The woman told Francesca that one day a German officer had asked for her spare room. "But that is the room of my son, monsieur," she had protested. "He is a prisoner of war in your own country; I cannot give it up." The officer had not insisted.

Another woman was already disillusioned by the liberation. She had worked for a transport company in Paris, daily shipping out goods bound for Hitler's Reich that were paid for with francs printed in Munich that cost the Germans nothing. After the Germans left Paris, she worked for the Americans. The trouble with them, she complained, was that "they thought France was a night club which never shut." They appeared blind to the fact that most French people were profoundly shocked by drunkenness and licentiousness.

Others among the locals had done well out of serving the Germans. More than one contrasted the old occupiers' "correct" behavior with that of the rude and robust Americans. But others offered an acutely different angle on the previous four years. "Boche politeness?" protested one Frenchman in astonishment. "Fifty innocent hostages seized in their beds, bundled through the town, made to dig their own graves and shot into them!"

Francesca also met a forty-year-old engineer whom she described as a "small, lean, dark, active realistic and true Latin." He had evaded labor conscription to Germany by going underground and had got hold of a gun dropped by a British plane for the resistance. Most of the time he had ferried arms by night from Paris. Once, he had been shot at by German sentries but had managed to get away. "Men with children could not do that sort of thing," he told Francesca. His wife had helped him and they were never caught. It had been a time of "risk, adventure, and a goal."

A student fighter with de Gaulle's Free French Forces of the Interior deplored the fact that most of their losses were due less to the Gestapo than to the treachery of his fellow citizens in the hated Milice, the Vichy paramilitary police force. He pungently described them as men tempted by high pay who "hunted in packs."

Another young man had been arrested for helping downed allied airmen escape. He had been saved from the firing squad only by the arrival of British forces. During his months of solitary confinement, he confessed, his greatest source of consolation had come from reading Pascal. "I don't understand it now," he told her, "but while waiting for the Gestapo to haul me out for interrogation, I found comfort which I could not now . . . Perhaps because Pascal pours such scorn on 'the perpetual agitations and tumultuous occupations of man' . . . Why, [he] asks, does man fear of all things to be alone with himself? Does he not realize that the whole visible world is a prison cell?" He would recommend Pascal, the man said with a wry smile, for anyone facing solitary confinement.

Francesca was particularly struck by the testimony of a handsome middle-aged man who told her he had retreated to his estate to avoid seeing or having any dealings with the Germans. This, he told her, was akin to how Montaigne had retreated to his library because he could not bear the civil wars between Catholics and Protestants, stained as they were by treachery and inhumanity. Three hundred years later, he told Francesca, the Nazis had made a science of inhumanity and "put a premium on treachery." She was lucky to be English, he pronounced. She had not had to see her friends making accommodations with the Nazis, or denouncing others for venal advantage.

This was sobering stuff, but there was much worse. One day, a group of Red Army soldiers came to sing Russian songs at one of the center's impromptu Sunday concerts. They had been captured by the Germans, dragooned into forced labor or the Wehrmacht, and were now being held by the Americans in a nearby camp.

After they had sung, Francesca talked to one of them. He had what she described as a "tragic" face: "It had that half-animal look that the endurance of brutal treatment and long privations gives," she wrote. Having fallen into German hands at Odessa, he had been marched in the snow through Romania and into Germany. The weak who could not make it were simply shot. But the scene he could not get out of his mind was that of seven sailors from the Soviet Black Sea Fleet who had been marched to the gallows naked except for a shift with their hands tied behind their backs. They waited in line as they were hanged, one by one, each watching his comrades die at the end of the rope. "And they sang," the Red Army soldier told Francesca, "they sang till the last moment, with their hands tied behind their backs." [24]

CHAPTER NINE

DEATH OF A DICTATOR

W e've really been having a madhouse here — you can read more about it in the papers, I guess, than I can tell you. But I've certainly been having experiences and I'll tell you about them some day soon, I hope. It looks as though we'll still have some stiff fighting though if these Heines hole up in the Alps."

It was Wednesday 25 April. Robert Ellis and his company of the US Tenth Mountain Division had just crossed the River Po near the Italian town of San Benedetto Po, and he was seizing the chance to write to his parents. His father had quit Iran and was now working in Ohio as a country doctor. His mother had always believed firmly in perfecting all of one's God-given gifts, and as a result his school days had been rigorously scheduled with piano lessons, violin practice and homework. But she remained, as always, generous in her praise and affection, replying to his letters whenever she could and circulating his responses proudly around the family.[1]

Alongside the family's ethos of stern self-improvement flowed a powerful internationalist spirit. Like millions of others during the dark decade of the 1930s, they had pinned their hopes on collective security as the guarantor of peace. One of the high points of a year he spent at the International School in Geneva had come when he and his mother sat in the great hall of the General Assembly of the League of Nations to hear Emperor Haile Selassie of Abyssinia appeal for help against Mussolini's invasion of his country. "I watched in awe as the tiny figure of the emperor came to the podium," he remembered. "In an impassioned cry for help, he gave one of the great speeches of history . . . Alas, the great powers were too concerned with 'peace at any price' to rescue Selassie . . . Collective security was doomed," he concluded, "and World War II became inevitable."[2] This historic moment made a profound impression on Ellis. He signed up for courses in international relations at the Universities of North Carolina and Chicago before his education was cut short by his induction into the armed forces in 1943.

Since the division had broken out of the mountains he had hardly had time to catch breath as the American forces raced north to reach the Alps before the retreating Germans were able to turn the mountains into their final redoubt. At dawn four days before, he had begun a forced march to reach the river some fifty miles ahead. In addition to his normal pack and other gear, in each hand he carried a fifteen-pound box of belted machine-gun ammunition. The handles were made of steel, and they dug so fiercely into his palms that whenever he tried to uncurl his fingers they felt as if they would never be normal again. They marched rapidly through endless small villages in the blazing sun. Everywhere peasants showered them with flowers, wine, water, food and kisses. For the first time since arriving in Italy, he began to feel that what they had been through recently was worthwhile. He had been mostly trained for the bitter slog of mountain fighting, but now the division was spearheading the rapid advance across the flat valley of the Po and catching the Germans off guard by their sheer speed.

Like the rest of his comrades in the Tenth, Ellis had survived weeks of grueling training at Camp Hale, 9,500 feet up in the snowy mountains of Colorado outside Boulder. It was a legendary period in the division's short history that was etched sharply on the memory of every ski trooper. "Sung of and cursed at once," writes one historian, "[it] was a wild, terrible place, where each year half the men dropped out because of the rigors of climate and exercise."[3]

Ellis admitted to finding the training fierce. "So far," he wrote home soon after arriving, "the life here has been Hell. For a few days I thought I'd go AWOL . . . Everyone here has asthma, or rheumatic fever, or colds, etc." Soon he fell sick, too, and was hospitalized for several days with a high fever. When he recovered, his daily regime proved punitive. "Up at 5:30. Breakfast at 5:45. Inspection from 6:30 to 7:00," he reported home about one typical day. But that was merely the prelude to half an hour of calisthenics, an hour's lecture on military discipline, and other lectures on such subjects as guarding prisoners. After lunch came a lecture and practice in digging foxholes, an hour's drill, a mile-long run and, after supper, a two-mile march to observe a demonstration of night firing by machine-guns. Then they all walked back to barracks, took showers to kill off the Rocky Mountain fever ticks, and were in bed by eleven.[4]

Tough though this was, he could stand it. Sometimes he even enjoyed it. But, unlike British commando Bryan Samain, he loathed the loss of autonomy that joining the army involved. "This is a completely new existence," he complained in only his second letter home. "I can hardly believe that it is actually me in an olive drab uniform sitting on an army cot. It seems so irrational for me to be here, with no will of my own or freedom of action . . . I hate regimentation and the crushing of individuality . . . I'll certainly be glad when this war is over."[5] Although he adjusted—he had no choice—he continued to resent his existence as a mere cog in the greater military machine. For a sensitive and educated young man who liked nothing so much as to curl up quietly with a serious book, life in the infantry was something to be endured, not enjoyed.

Now, however, he was finally beginning to feel free and exhilaration set in, especially after he downed a glass of grappa handed to him by a roadside family, which he mistook for water. Then he and his buddy Larry Boyajian miraculously stumbled on an open-topped German staff car abandoned by the roadside. With Boyajian at the wheel and Ellis riding in the back seat, they roared up the road, stirring up clouds of whirling white dust, feeling like Erich von Stroheim in some Hollywood movie, and cracking jokes about the duty of saluting officers as they sped past footsore fellow infantryman.

When the car ran out of gas, they found an abandoned motorcycle and sidecar. It started up straight away, and off they sped on the next installment of their madcap ride. Theirs was typical of many such escapades, well captured in the laconic entry by the company sergeant in his official morning report that day: "In action. Racing across the Po Valley. Using German horses and vehicles."[6]

Here, as Geoffrey Cox and the New Zealanders were finding further east, the Germans had left the roads littered with vehicles of every kind. Ellis and Boyajian passed trucks, cars, bicycles and horse-drawn wagons, as well as forlorn columns of German prisoners being marched to the rear. Bands of partisans were roaming everywhere, too, cutting German communications and supply lines, rounding up snipers and isolated pockets of resistance, destroying German equipment and installations, and seizing Fascists.

Blackshirts behind the lines could still prove a menace. Civilians in San Benedetto reported that someone in the tower of the church was ringing the bell as a signal. Whenever American troops moved up to the river's edge to make a crossing, the bell rang out and German artillery batteries began firing. So the bell was silenced, and the artillery fire tapered off. The same day, two local Fascists were arrested while sending up flares.[7]

Outside Modena, other Tenth Division units overran Fossoli, the largest concentration camp in Italy. A former POW camp, it had been transformed by the SS after the Salò Republic's savage anti-Semitic law of December 1943 into a transit camp for Jews on their way to extermination camps in Germany or Poland. It was through Fossoli that the Turinese writer Primo Levi had passed in February 1944 on his way to Auschwitz. "There were twelve goods wagons for six hundred and fifty men," recorded Levi. "In mine we were only forty five, but it was a small wagon . . . The train did not move until evening. We had learnt of our destination with relief. Auschwitz was a name without significance for us at that time, but it at least implied some place on this earth."

The train traveled slowly, with endless halts, and they all grew desperately thirsty. Through the slats they eventually spied the tall, pale cliffs of the Adige Valley and the names of the last Italian cities disappeared behind them. "We passed the Brenner at midday of the second day and everyone stood up but no one said a word," he wrote, "and I looked around and wondered how many, among that poor human dust, would be struck by fate." By the time the Americans reached Fossoli, only four of those in Levi's wagon that day were still alive. A full third of all the Jews deported from Italy had left the camp for extermination.[8]

Even in full retreat the Germans could prove a nuisance, trying the temper of the infantry now exhausted by their long march and impatient for the end. Outside the villages and towns of the Po Valley the countryside was flat and open, but it was dotted with substantial farmhouses that provided excellent bases for rear guard action. Often the Germans were driven out by artillery fire, but if they dug in their heels the infantry had to flush them out. These fire fights could be expensive in casualties given the open nature of the ground and the lack of cover. Sometimes, having killed or wounded several American attackers, the Germans would put up a white flag at the last minute and try to surrender. Not surprisingly, the Americans seldom emerged with prisoners.[9]

When their motorcycle also ran out of gas, Ellis and Boyajian hitchhiked a ride on a tank. "The Ities are mad with joy to see us," he managed to scribble in his diary as they rumbled along. "Give us eggs, milk. Some girl just threw flowers on me and the church bells are ringing in freedom. People hug you." A special task force of the division speeding ahead of Ellis reached the Po so rapidly that General von Senger und Etterlin, the German commander of the XIV Panzer Corps—and, like New Zealander Geoffrey Cox, a former Oxford Rhodes scholar—was forced to swim across at dawn to escape capture. "I had tried repeatedly to drive . . . stragglers back to their units still fighting at the front," he plaintively recorded, "[but] when whole major units have been disbanded and the infantry troops are exhausted from long marches, swimming across rivers, and sleepless nights, there remains for psychological reasons but one alternative: to act in accordance with the instincts of the ordinary soldier and order the units to withdraw."[10]

After two long days of marching Ellis was also dead beat. "The never-ending dust, the perpetual movement with no chance ever to settle down, and the food snatched on the run . . . all combined to form a depressing tapestry which seemed to have no end," he remembered. Even the unbridged Po offered little chance for a rest. Just twenty-four hours after reaching its low sandy banks he found himself scrambling into a small canvas assault boat to paddle across the river at night. The water was just below the gunwale and the boat felt flimsy and unstable, so he loosened his boots and removed his backpack and ammunition belt in case it tipped into the water. Close by, another of the boats capsized, but it was too dark to see who was in the water, or exactly where, and he heard terrified screams and cries for help until they fell chillingly silent. Once ashore, they dug in, expecting a German counterattack, but it never came. It was then, during a precious few hours of sleep and relaxation, that he found time to write to his parents.

He also took the opportunity to make a personal confession. He kept it short, just a simple sentence of some fifteen words: "The other day, I killed a sniper at about 15 feet with my .45 revolver." Several weeks later, he felt able to describe the details in a letter to one of his brothers. It had happened eleven days before, in the mountains, at the start of the division's big push. He had been pinned down with Boyajian for hours on a mountainside by murderous shell and mortar fire when one of his platoon was shot in the foot. For some reason this made Ellis angry. It felt almost personal. So he crawled through the underbrush to try to locate the spot from where the shot had come. Just twenty yards ahead he saw two log bunkers. Keeping flat to the ground, he crawled to the first and found it abandoned. Then he edged cautiously towards the blind side of the second.

Suddenly, he saw the head and shoulders of the German sniper. His back was half turned, and he was bobbing up and down in a peculiar way. Ellis could not see a weapon, but if the German was unarmed, why had he not surrendered? Could Ellis risk calling out to him to raise his hands, only to have the sniper turn and either shoot or lob a grenade at him? He had to make a split-second decision. Everything he had absorbed from his missionary parents told him not to assume the worst about another human being, but his army training, not to mention his own fear and excitement, led him in the opposite direction. He rested both elbows on the ground and readied his .45 pistol in both hands.

The German must have heard him, because he turned. As he moved, Ellis pulled the trigger and shot him through the head. The man dropped straight out of view. Rather than investigate more closely, Ellis signaled to the others in his platoon to continue the advance. With a single shot, he had crossed his own personal Rubicon. Now he was a fully fledged member of what the famous American war correspondent Ernie Pyle described as the "ghastly brotherhood of war."[11]

Pyle had made his name through his vivid front-line reporting from Italy the year before, doing nothing to sugarcoat the brutal realities of life for the infantry, or to disguise the fact that clean-cut American boys were being transformed into killers. The boy next door, he constantly reminded his readers back home in the United States, had made "the psychological transition from the normal belief that taking human life is sinful, over to a new professional outlook where killing is a craft." His most moving and effective dispatch was about the body of a company commander being brought down a mountainside on the back of a mule and the effect that this had on his men. Only four days after Ellis's encounter with the sniper, Pyle was shot dead by a sharp-shooter near Okinawa in the Pacific.[12]

The Tenth Division's orders were to advance as quickly as possible from the Po to Verona on the River Adige, cutting the roads north of the city leading to the Brenner Pass and the Germans' line of retreat into the Alps. To spearhead the advance, General George P. Hays, commander of the Tenth Mountain, formed a mobile task force. As its head, he appointed Colonel William Darby, who had previously led an elite force in North Africa and Sicily known as Darby's Rangers, which was modeled on the British commandos. Ellis's regiment was to follow immediately behind, mopping up any bypassed German forces and acting as a reserve in case the task force encountered heavy resistance. Hays's plan was for his three infantry regiments to leapfrog one another. Each would march as rapidly as it could for eight hours, and then rest for sixteen while the others were brought up by trucks. This way, he hoped, they could advance about sixty miles a day and twenty at night.

The leapfrogging began that Friday from Villafranca, a town just south of Verona, and by six o'clock that evening Ellis had reached the shores of Lake Garda, Italy's largest lake, thirty miles long and varying between two and eleven miles wide. Further ahead, advance units had run into a roadblock and fierce fighting with SS troops had followed. By now, northern Italy's partisans were in open revolt and most of the German escape routes over the Alps had been closed off. The one exception was the road running up the east shore of the lake. Here, the Germans decided to put up as much resistance as they could, and it was ideal terrain for defense.

On the left of the narrow road lapped the lake itself. On the other side, at its northern end, loomed steep, gray, granite Alpine cliffs several thousand feet high into which the road had been cut, often disappearing into tunnels several hundred yards long. Ellis was familiar enough with recent history to know that thirty years before, during the First World War, the area had been bitterly fought over by Italy and Austria-Hungary. For very little territorial gain, casualties on both sides had mounted to more than two hundred thousand. So far, Ellis had avoided injury, and he certainly did not want to end up being shot during what, surely, was the last chapter of the war. But he had no choice. He had to do his duty.

It was cold, and raining heavily, when he and the rest of his regiment started its march along the lakeside. Quickly he discovered a trick that helped him along: if he walked behind a tank, its exhaust sent out gales of hot air that kept him relatively dry and warm. At midnight he reached the small town of Malcesine, two-thirds of the way up the side of the lake. Having completed their eight-hour stint and marched seventeen miles, the men were at last allowed to sleep. "Morale high," recorded the company sergeant.

When Ellis awoke the next morning, he saw rugged mountains rising from both sides of the lake, reminding him of a Norwegian fjord. He had finally reached the Alps. "The Tenth Mountain Division, trained and equipped primarily for mountain warfare," recorded the division's historian proudly, "had outraced all other units of the Fifth Army to seal off the German escape routes." [13]

Ellis was a lucky man. His regiment was due to set off again the next day, but stiff German resistance along the lake's edge slowed the advance, and he remained in reserve for the next two days. The fighting yet to be done, notes the official American history of the war in Italy, "would in no way affect the outcome of the long campaign, but it continued nonetheless to exact a bitter toll of dead and wounded men." It was not that the Germans at this stage of the war held out any hope of victory. On the contrary, the strategy of Field Marshal Kesselring, commander of all German forces in Southwestern Europe, including southern Germany, Yugoslavia and Italy, was to salvage what he could from inevitable defeat. The longer his forces held out, the more German forces retreating in the face of the Russians could reach American and British lines and surrender to them, rather than to the Red Army. [14]

Advance units of the Tenth Division pressed north to the top of the lake and the towns of Riva and Torbole. To make the advance as difficult as possible for the Americans, the Germans began blowing up the road tunnels, but the Americans foiled them by ferrying their men around the blocked-off sections of road. They repeated the process all the way north, and by the afternoon of 30 April, fighting off some fierce German counterattacks, they entered Torbole.

Here, the hand of fate intervened. Colonel Darby, head of the task force that had so successfully spearheaded the advance, was climbing into his jeep which was parked outside a hotel in the town when shrapnel from a shell fired by Germans across the lake hit him in the chest. He died an hour later.

Several others also perished in these final hours of the war when a German shell exploded ten yards inside one of the road tunnels. There was a crushing concussion, shell fragments ricocheted off the walls, and the blast turned fragments of rock into deadly shrapnel. Five of the Americans were instantly killed, and fifty wounded. To make matters worse, as the wounded crawled to the tunnel's exit, they found themselves clambering over the dismembered bodies of German soldiers and horses killed just hours beforehand when the demolition charge they were laying had exploded prematurely.[15]

To Ellis, however, Malcesine offered a welcome safe haven. In peacetime, Lake Garda was a lush resort area dotted with villas, beautiful gardens, olive groves, citrus and palm trees, and comfortable hotels. The village itself was a picture-postcard fishing port dominated by a thirteenth-century castle, an idyllic spot where Goethe had lived and worked between 1786 and 1788.

Ellis luxuriated in a room on the ground floor of one of the hotels. After he caught up with sleep, he strolled around the town with buddies looking at boats in the harbor and talking to the locals. Not even the firing of enormous guns from the courtyard of his hotel disturbed him once he grew used to the noise. They belonged to an artillery unit of the British Army that was providing support to the division. Sometimes relations between the British and American allies could be difficult, but one of the artillery officers, a Scot, had nothing but admiration for the Americans of Ellis's division. "We are having a magnificent time chasing the Hun," he wrote home enthusiastically. "We are supporting some first class troops and, with them, have met with some amazing successes. I am sure the Hun has had it now and everything should be over, bar some guerrilla fighting, within the next fortnight."[16]

Across the lake and a few miles to the south, Ellis could see the town of Gargagno. But by now its most famous recent resident, Benito Mussolini, was dead, shot by partisans on the shores of Lake Como.

Mussolini had passed his few days in Milan in a miasma of indecision. Surrounded by the tattered remnants of his supporters, he dithered about what to do next as the allies swept north from the Po and, one after another, the cities of northern Italy fell into the hands of the partisans. Sometimes he talked of surrendering in order to avoid the evils of a civil war. On other occasions, he reverted bombastically to his idea of making a last stand in the Valtellina. His actions appeared chaotic, and he seemed "to drift like a leaf in a storm." From all parts of the country came news of the massacre of Fascists.[17]

At last, on the afternoon of Wednesday 25 April, with local partisans poised to seize control of Milan itself and a general strike already under way in the city, the situation came to a head. After an intermediary arranged for him to meet a delegation from the Committee for the Liberation of Northern Italy (CLNAI), the partisans' controlling body, he made his way through the eerily quiet streets to the palace of the Archbishop of Milan, Cardinal Schuster. Having once endorsed Fascism as a bulwark against Bolshevism, the cardinal was now keen to avoid any further needless bloodshed.

The resistance delegates arrived late, so Mussolini spent an hour awkwardly making small talk with the cardinal. The stilted chat did not raise his spirits. The Catholic prelate reminded him how the defeated Napoleon had found comfort in God during his exile on St. Helena, and when Mussolini mentioned his plans for the last stand in the Valtellina with three thousand supporters, Schuster observed gently that three hundred seemed a more realistic figure. To this, Mussolini smiled weakly and agreed. He seemed, recalled the cardinal, a man bereft of will, listlessly accepting his fate.

Finally, the partisans arrived. After a stiff exchange of handshakes they made it clear that they expected nothing but unconditional surrender. Mussolini seemed close to agreeing, provided that his soldiers were guaranteed proper treatment as prisoners of war under the Geneva Convention. Then Marshal Graziani suddenly interjected that nothing should be decided without first informing the Germans. They were, after all, Italy's allies, and a unilateral surrender would be dishonorable.

This prompted a startling reply from General Cadorna, commander of the partisan forces. "I'm afraid," he said, "the Germans haven't been troubled by the same scruples." Mussolini's allies, he revealed, were already in negotiations for an unconditional surrender to the British and Americans.

This news came as a bombshell to Mussolini, who had been kept completely in the dark by the Germans. The SS in Italy had sent out feelers to the allies as far back as February. Discussions had been lengthy, tortuous and complex, but by this time they were on the point of fruition.

Mussolini exploded in fury. He abruptly stood up, denounced the Germans roundly for having always treated the Italians as slaves, and stormed out of the archbishop's palace, declaring he needed an hour to think things over before resuming the talks. In a rage, though, he decided to leave Milan immediately and head for the Valtellina. Dressed in the uniform of the Fascist militia — gray-brown jacket and gray trousers with red and black stripes down both sides — and with a sub-machine-gun slung over his shoulder, he drove off in the back of his open-topped Alfa Romeo. Behind him followed a convoy of thirty or so cars packed with his supporters and the ubiquitous contingent of SS guards, who refused to be shaken off. Bringing up the rear came his mistress, Clara Petacci, and his son, Vittorio.

That night, he reached Como. The next day, instead of the three thousand Fascist fighters he had been promised and hoped for, fewer than a dozen joined him. His journey up the shore of the lake, once imagined as the prelude to a glorious last stand, descended into the disorganized shambles of an ignominious flight. At Menaggio, the dispirited group linked up with a German military convoy of about two hundred men heading north for the Brenner Pass and the safety of Austria. They were now in mountainous partisan country, a land where rough justice traveled hand in hand with liberation. As a precaution, Mussolini exchanged the comfort of his Alfa-Romeo for the safety of the convoy's armored cars. Only twenty-four hours before, in the nearby town of Dongo, the funeral of four partisans whose bodies had been retrieved from the mountainside after being dumped by Fascists had been disrupted by members of the Black Brigades, a Fascist Militia force, who had fired wildly into the air.

Suddenly, just outside Dongo, the convoy was halted by a partisan roadblock and a brief exchange of gunfire took place. But at this late stage of the war neither side was keen for a serious fight, and there followed several hours of tense negotiation. Finally, it was agreed that the convoy could proceed, but without the Italians, who would be handed over to the partisans. Mussolini promptly disguised himself as a German soldier, donning a helmet and a military overcoat. Then he clambered into one of the trucks at the rear of the convoy and pretended to be asleep.

The ruse failed. When the convoy was stopped in the town square of Dongo for a more thorough search, he was quickly recognized by one of the partisans. Hauled out unceremoniously, he was held for several hours in the office of the Mayor. Later, to ensure that there would be no repeat of his 1943 rescue by Otto Skorzeny, he and Petacci were secretly moved to the farmhouse of a partisan sympathizer in the hills nearby. It was not just German efforts to liberate Mussolini that were feared by the partisans. The allies — or at least the Americans — were also interested in getting hold of him. "We made strenuous efforts to intercept and rescue him," claimed General Lucian Truscott, the Commander of US forces in Italy, "but without success."[18]

Mussolini and his mistress finished the last stage of the journey on foot, scrambling up a steep and stony mule track from the village of Giulino di Mezzegra below. It was raining heavily and soaked the blanket Mussolini was wearing to keep himself warm. That night, amid a violent thunderstorm, he and Petacci slept in a double bed in the loft of the simple building.

At about four o'clock the next afternoon — Saturday 28 April, while Robert Ellis was enjoying his break from fighting on the shores of Lake Garda and Geoffrey Cox and the New Zealanders stood poised to enter Padua — a tall man wearing a brown raincoat arrived at the house. He was carrying a sub-machine-gun. "I have come to rescue you," he declared. "Hurry up." Petacci began rummaging around among her clothes. "What are you looking for?" asked the man impatiently. "My knickers," replied the thirty-three-year-old brunette, who was well known for her heavy make-up and smart appearance. "Don't worry about that," snapped the man. "Come on, hurry."

They stumbled down the rough mountainside to a car parked on the road below and climbed into the back seat. In addition to the driver and the man in the raincoat, there was another man seated in the car. It drove a few yards down the hill, then stopped in front of the wrought-iron gates of a villa. The two passengers were bundled out and pushed in front of a low stone wall.

What happened next remains in dispute. According to their "rescuer" — in reality their executioner — he read an official death sentence in the name of the Italian people and then shot them. Mussolini, he claimed, said nothing, but cowered in terror in the final seconds of his life. However, a later report by another member of the death squad recorded that Mussolini rose to the occasion, defiantly tugged open the collar of his coat, and shouted, "Aim for the heart!"

Irrespective of whether Mussolini died bravely or as a coward, what followed next is undisputed. The bodies were bundled into the car and it drove off at speed towards Dongo. Here, fifteen of the Italian group that had traveled with Mussolini up the lakeside had already been shot, and their leader's and Petacci's corpses were added to the pile. It included several ministers of the Salò Republic, top Fascist Party officials, and Petacci's brother, Marcello.[19]

The man who shot Mussolini, Walter Audisio, was a peacetime accountant and communist member of the CLNAI who went by the name of "Colonel Valerio." On hearing the news of Mussolini's capture, a hurriedly convened and partial gathering of the CLNAI in Milan had agreed that he should be shot, and it sent Audisio and another dedicated communist, Aldo Lampredi, to carry out the mission. Ever since the murder by Fascists of the left-wing member of parliament Giacomo Mateotti in 1924, the dictator's assassination had been high on the agenda of his opponents, the price he would have to pay for the criminality of his regime. He survived several attempts to kill him during his two decades in power.

The bodies remained overnight in Dongo. Then they were loaded into a removal van and driven to Milan, the birthplace of Fascism a quarter of a century before. Dawn was breaking as the vehicle entered the Piazzale Loreto and the corpses were unceremoniously dumped in a heap on the ground. The site was electric with symbolism. Eight months before, fifteen political prisoners had been dragged from Milan's jails and shot by a Fascist squad on SS orders in reprisal for a suspected partisan attack. Their bodies had then been dumped in the piazza for everyone to see, a practice of displaying the political dead that had become almost routine in Fascist Italy. The square had since become highly significant for the resistance and a place that cried out for vengeance. A wreath of flowers covered the spot where the bodies had lain, and a hand-lettered sign read, "Square of the Fifteen Martyrs." The Fascists, Mussolini had declared presciently at the time — and more accurately than he could ever have imagined — would "pay a high price for the blood of Piazzale Loreto."

In the square, his corpse now lay next to that of his mistress. Her dark hair and the lace ruffles of her blouse were caked with mud. As the news spread, a huge crowd gathered, pushing, shouting, screaming; people began to kick, spit and urinate on the bodies. Mussolini's skull took several heavy blows, and shots were fired into his body.

Milton Bracker, a *New York Times* war correspondent, arrived in the middle of it all. Mussolini's eyes were still open, he reported, "and it was perhaps the final irony that this man who had thrust his chin forward for so many official photographs had to have his yellowing face propped up with a rifle butt so as to turn it into the sun for the only two Allied cameramen on the scene." Their photographs were flashed around the world, presenting irrefutable proof that the Italian dictator was dead.[20]

After a while, Mussolini, Petacci and two others were strung up on a rusty iron bar in front of a petrol station in the corner of the square. As the ultimate insult, they were hung upside down by their heels, like animals in an abattoir, their names on paper pinned to their feet. Petacci's dress fell down over her head. In a fleeting act of decency, someone tucked it back up. This, though, did not prevent the crowd from continuing to rain blows at Mussolini's skull until his head was a bloodied mess, spattered with pieces of brain.

Not long afterwards, at about 10:30 a.m., an open truck made its way through the crowds and pulled up in the square. Standing in the middle of it, surrounded by armed guards, was a lithe, square-jawed and surly figure wearing a black shirt. This was Achille Starace, one-time secretary-general of the Fascist Party as well as chief of staff of the hated Fascist militia. The truck paused for a second in front of Mussolini's corpse, and Starace shot it a rapid glance. He appeared to sag forwards, until the guards roughly pulled him up. The truck edged further forward and then stopped.

Starace was taken out and placed near a white wall at the back of the petrol station. Beside it were some baskets of spring flowers — pink, yellow, purple and blue — that people had placed in memory of the anti-Fascists who had perished there a few months before. Then a firing squad of partisans shot Starace in the back. Another partisan, perched on a beam high above the crowd, made a broad gesture of finality with his arms.

"There were no roars or bloodcurdling yells," reported another American war correspondent who witnessed the scene. "There was only silence, and then, suddenly, a sigh — a deep, moaning sound, seemingly expressive of release from something dark and fetid." Two minutes later, Starace's corpse was strung up alongside that of Mussolini. "Look at them now," an old man standing next to the journalist kept saying. "Just look at them now!"[21]

Eventually, the American military authorities, who had just entered the city, ordered the bodies cut down and taken to the city's morgue. Yet still onlookers followed to watch while a US Army photographer carefully placed Mussolini and Petacci in each other's arms to make a better shot.

The date was Sunday 29 April 1945. That same day, at allied head-quarters in Caserta near Naples, the tortuous weeks of behind-the-scenes negotiations finally came to an end when two German delegates formally signed the surrender of all German forces in Italy. It was to come into effect at noon on Wednesday 2 May.

Robert Ellis heard the news of Mussolini's death over the radio while he rested on the shores of Lake Garda. The next day he found time to jot down some notes in his diary and write a longer letter home, giving a thumbnail sketch of his recent march across the Po Valley and the frenzied welcome they had received from the local population. "At first the newly freed are a little frightened," he told his parents, "but the moment they realize we're Americans their joy reaches no bounds." In short, he noted, the war news was sensationally good. That, and the fact that Lake Garda was the most beautiful place he had ever seen, made him almost euphoric. Yet the upbeat mood also heightened his sense of the fearful proximity of death. Men were still dying in Italy, he reminded his father and mother, and "the load will be lifted from none of our soldiers until the last shot is fired."[22]

That same day, another company in Ellis's regiment was dispatched on a potentially hazardous mission across the lake to its western shore. Its target was the Villa Feltrinelli, Mussolini's recent personal home at Gargagno, as well as the nearby offices of ministers and officials of the Salò Republic. After taking control of these buildings, along with any remaining Fascists they might capture, the company would head north to neutralize any German forces still occupying the far side of the lake.

Shortly after midnight, the small force of two hundred men crossed the open waters of the lake in twelve DUKWs, cutting the engines as they approached the shore and gliding in silently to land two miles north of Gargagno. Roadblocks were quickly set up, and at dawn the entire force headed on foot into the town. By eight-fifteen they had occupied Mussolini's villa and his office in the town. They met with no resistance, and a dozen or so German prisoners were handed over by the partisans.

The Villa Feltrinelli stood on the lakefront, a spacious building with three dozen rooms and a bomb shelter. In the garage the Americans found two limousines, but the engines had been blown up by grenades. Inside the villa, there was a room stuffed with pills and medicines, as well as a large kitchen. Very quickly, the villa became the temporary billet for one of the American platoons.

Two American agents had accompanied the small task force to the villa. These were members of the US Army's Counter-Intelligence Corps (CIC) who were looking for any of Mussolini's personal files that might substantiate criminal activity by him and the Fascist regime. Since Italy's surrender in 1943, finding Mussolini and war criminals in Italy had been an allied priority, and even as he fled from Milan American and British agents were actively hunting him down. In this search, they were thwarted as much by the partisans as by Mussolini sympathizers. The reason was simple: the partisans would deal with Il Duce themselves, in their own way. "In no case," admitted General Cadorna, the partisan military commander, "would I voluntarily have proceeded to bring Mussolini into the hands of the allied forces for him to be tried and executed by foreigners."

But whatever form post-war retribution took, and whoever delivered it, documents could prove vital in establishing innocence or guilt.

The Americans were not alone in considering the capture of such documents important. During his three-day odyssey between Milan and Dongo, Mussolini had carried with him two leather briefcases that he never let out of his sight. Inside were several files he hoped to use in his defense, documents that would establish how hard he had tried to avoid civil war in Italy and to resist German pressure.

Before he left Milan, he also withdrew a large amount of cash from the Salò Republic's bank account. This, too, traveled with him in the convoy up the side of Lake Como. Even when he transferred to the German armored car outside Menaggio, he took the suitcases with him, and after his arrest in the town square at Dongo he managed to carry at least one of them into the Town Hall with him. But he was not permitted to take it any further. On the last night of his life, in the simple farmhouse bedroom at Giulino di Mezzegra, he slept in the knowledge that the last slim evidence for his defense had finally been taken from him.

The documents in the suitcases, however, represented only the "cream of the cream" of Mussolini's files. Before quitting the Villa Feltrinelli, he had filled two large tin trunks with files that were sent to Milan, and it was from these that he extracted those that were in the suitcases. The trunks themselves followed on a truck in the convoy to Como, but this was intercepted by partisans, and at least one of the trunks disappeared. This, as well as the suitcases captured at Dongo and the money, ultimately fell into partisan hands.

So it was hardly any surprise that the American agents uncovered little of interest at the Villa Feltrinelli. Apart from some dossiers on Fascist Party personalities, a few items of historical interest, and some useful and up-to-date intelligence about Fascist organizations in Turin and Milan, the vast bulk of the files had, in the words of one of the agents, "all been cleared out." Here, again, it was clear that the Italians themselves were determined to deal with Mussolini and his legacy in their own way.[23]

Back on the other side of Lake Garda, Robert Ellis finished off his letter home. He had learned that his brother Edwin was about to be inducted into the armed forces, and he was sorry about that. On the other hand, he did not see why any of the Americans serving in Europe had to go and fight the war in the Pacific. Ellis's division had suffered one of the highest casualty rates per combat day of any American division during the war. Approximately one of every three infantrymen who had landed with him at Naples had been killed or wounded in action. "Those of us who have been lucky enough to survive," he told his parents, "should get a break."[24]

CHAPTER TEN

HIMMLER'S BID

Robert Ellis's dread that he might survive the war in Europe only to be shipped out to the Pacific was shared by most other allied soldiers in Germany and Italy. The Japanese were showing no sign of giving in. Instead, they continued to fight back furiously and were causing heavy casualties. In the Philippines, the Americans finally cleared Japanese defenders from the small islands in Manila Bay but on the main island of Luzon resistance remained strong. Heavy fighting continued on Okinawa, and kamikaze attacks were becoming more frequent. On the small adjacent island of Ie Shima — where Ernie Pyle was killed on 18 April — it took five days of battle and five thousand Japanese dead to finish off matters. Only the invasion of Japan itself, it seemed, would put an end to the killing. At Eisenhower's headquarters in Reims, his staff busied themselves identifying units for transfer to the Pacific.

The war against Japan was also much on the mind of the new American president, Harry Truman. Roosevelt had done little to brief him on strategic and diplomatic affairs, and he was having to learn fast. "I felt as if I had lived five lifetimes in my first five days as President," he later confessed. And the frantic pace continued. Thirteen days after taking office, he received the most important briefing of all from Henry Stimson, the Secretary for War. Making sure the two men were alone, Stimson took out of his briefcase a typewritten memorandum several pages long, and handed it over. "Within four months," read Truman, "we shall in all probability have completed the most terrible weapon ever known in human history, one bomb of which could destroy a whole city."[1] The new president took the news in his stride and agreed that the project should continue. Two days later, a special "target committee" set up to consider on which Japanese city the atomic bomb should be dropped dismissed Tokyo on the grounds that it had already been smashed to smithereens by American bombers. The largest Japanese city so far untouched was Hiroshima. It, noted the committee, should be considered for the list.

After his midday briefing from Stimson, Truman went over to the Pentagon to talk directly on the private transatlantic telephone to Churchill in London. Something had just come up that urgently needed discussing. It was nothing less than a secret German offer to capitulate, made two days before to the vice-chairman (and effective head) of the Swedish Red Cross, Count Folke Bernadotte. The man making the offer was none other than Heinrich Himmler, head of the SS. After Hitler, he was the most feared member of the Nazi hierarchy.

Folke Bernadotte was a nephew of Sweden's King Gustav V and a direct descendant of Jean-Baptiste Bernadotte, one of Napoleon's most controversial marshals. After marrying a former lover of Bonaparte, Jean-Baptiste eventually fell out with the French Emperor, became Crown Prince of Sweden, joined the allied coalition that defeated him at Leipzig, and in 1818 became King Charles XIV of Sweden.

Married to a wealthy American, Folke Bernadotte was well connected internationally, and had already helped negotiate exchanges of disabled German, British and American prisoners of war. Since February, he had also met Himmler several times in or near Berlin to discuss a scheme to have all Norwegian and Danish prisoners in concentration camps evacuated to Sweden. "He had small, well-shaped, delicate hands, which were carefully manicured," noted Bernadotte after his first meeting with the Reichsführer SS. Himmler also proved extremely affable. This did not prevent him from rejecting the Swedish scheme, however, nor from telling Bernadotte that "every German would fight like a lion before he gave up hope."[2]

Nevertheless, he agreed that the Danes and Norwegians could be collected together in the Neuengamme camp outside Hamburg to receive help from the Swedish Red Cross. Soon afterwards, a column of Swedish buses, painted white and bearing large red crosses, drove across the Danish border into Germany. Over the next few days, they collected some 4,500 Scandinavian prisoners from Sachsenhausen, Dachau and other concentration camps, and took them to Neuengamme. Here, in a specially prepared area, the Swedes worked hard to improve sanitary conditions and bring in urgently needed medicines.

To see things for himself, Bernadotte visited the camp on Good Friday, becoming the first representative of a neutral humanitarian agency to enter a Nazi concentration camp. Its SS commander had had plenty of notice to make conditions at least appear good, but Bernadotte still found the overcrowding appalling and the discipline "barbarous," and he could well imagine what conditions must have been like beforehand. He also caught a glimpse of the other sections of the camp, to which he was not permitted entry. Beyond the barbed wire, he spotted "human wrecks, wandering aimlessly about . . . apathetic, vacant-minded, incapable of ever returning to normal existence."

Within days, Himmler agreed to a further major concession: all sick Scandinavian prisoners, all women, all Norwegian students, and all Danish policemen — interned after the Nazis had dissolved the Danish police force — could be evacuated to Denmark for eventual transport to Sweden.

The exodus from Neuengamme finally began on Hitler's birthday, with more than four thousand grateful Danes, Norwegians and other nationalities clambering aboard the white buses for the Red Cross ride north to safety. This was also the day that the SS camp leadership decided to evacuate the rest of the camp. Hurriedly and brutally, the unlucky ones were herded aboard cattle trucks, forty prisoners to a wagon, and then disappeared towards the east.

This time, Bernadotte was not present to witness the scene. Instead, he was in Berlin, hoping to push Himmler into making more humanitarian concessions. The Swedish Red Cross headquarters during this mission of mercy was based at Schloss Friedrichsuh, outside Hamburg, the former home of Count Otto von Bismarck, Germany's nineteenth-century "Iron Chancellor." But it was from another Bismarck estate closer to Berlin, Schonhausen, Bismarck's birthplace, that Bernadotte made his regular trips by car into the German capital. By now, he had grown hardened to the sight of female prisoners from Ravensbrück being marched along the roads to work camps, and accustomed to the pathetic sight of endless columns of German refugees from East Prussia fleeing from the Russians who had entered the region in January and were now pillaging and raping their way westwards. Most of the latter were women too, the rest aged over sixty-five, or children. If lucky, they were traveling in covered wagons similar to those used by American pioneers to cross the prairies.

The less fortunate simply walked, with rags often all they had to cover their feet, and many wore traditional peasant costume. They represented a vast reversal of history, the undoing of several hundred years of German colonization to the east. This month, April, some eight million German civilians were on the road, fleeing from East Prussia, Pomerania and Silesia. Three million alone passed through Berlin, where many died. The price of coffins in the capital soared.

"They appeared worn and weary," observed Bernadotte, "and utterly hopeless. There was no future for them, and the present was an inferno. Whatever they had possessed was lost, material goods as well as any belief in life. Silently the pitiable procession moved on, along roads lined with the carcases of emaciated horses that had drawn the primitive vehicles until their strength gave out." Rarely had he been able to complete the hundred-mile drive without having to leap out of the car and into a ditch as allied aircraft dive-bombed the road.[3]

Hitler's birthday proved no exception. As a precaution, Bernadotte traveled with two chauffeurs. One of them sat on the boot of the car to act as an observer: his job was to bang loudly on the car's roof if he spotted allied planes. On the outskirts of Nauen, just twenty miles west of Berlin, they suddenly heard the loud drone of approaching bombers and jumped into a nearby anti-aircraft trench. It was a sunny and cloudless day, and for an hour or so Bernadotte watched as wave after wave of planes dropped their bombs. Not a single German aircraft appeared on the scene — yet another sign of the utter collapse of Goering's once vaunted and feared Luftwaffe.

When he finally reached Berlin, the noisy festivities that had once marked Hitler's birthday were noticeable by their absence. The city seemed eerily silent, with people drifting about as though waiting uncertainly for instructions. No sooner had he arrived than more allied air raids forced him down for hours into the shelter of the Swedish legation. When he resurfaced he learned that Himmler had abandoned the city for Hohenlychen, a sanatorium ninety miles away which he had made his temporary headquarters. As he left the capital, Bernadotte could hear the thunder of Russian artillery in the suburbs.

It was not until six o'clock the next morning that Himmler finally turned up. He was exhausted and distracted, and nervously tapped his front teeth with a fingernail. All that Bernadotte could extract from him was an agreement that if Denmark became a battlefield, the Scandinavian prisoners from Neuengamme would be moved out of harm's way to Sweden, and that all female prisoners from Ravensbrück could be removed immediately by the Swedish Red Cross. "The military situation is very, very grave," admitted Himmler, before cutting short the meeting.

Back at Friedrichsuh to arrange for the Ravensbrück releases, Bernadotte was awakened at three o'clock the next morning by a phone call. In every meeting so far, Himmler had insisted that the war would go on and that, because of his personal oath of loyalty to Hitler, he could contemplate no other course. The Führer had made the path ahead clear in his so-called Nero decree of March, when he demanded that German soldiers and civilians must resist to the end and announced a "scorched-earth" policy to deny the allies the fruits of victory. "No German city will be declared an open city," Himmler had loyally told the SS as recently as 12 April. "Every town and every village will be defended at all costs." Throughout Germany, local SS forces were enforcing this policy, ordering local town officials to stand fast, organizing last-ditch resistance, and shooting or hanging those who disobeyed.

Yet it appeared now that Himmler had abruptly changed course. He told Bernadotte that he urgently wanted to meet Eisenhower to arrange for the capitulation of all German forces in the West. However, Bernadotte had had some long conversations with Eisenhower and knew full well that the allied Supreme Commander would refuse a German surrender on the Western Front alone. The total and unconditional surrender of all Nazi forces, including the overthrow of the Nazi regime, was an axiom of allied policy. Anything less was out of the question, opening up as it would the prospect that Germany, as it had done after the Treaty of Versailles, would once again rise from the ashes of defeat. As far as Eisenhower was concerned, the Soviets were allies to the bitter end of the Nazi regime. Nevertheless, Bernadotte agreed to see Himmler one more time. The place agreed for the meeting was Lübeck.

The Baltic port was characterized by labyrinthine streets, red roofs and majestic brick churches with towering copper-green spires. The novelist Thomas Mann, whose father had been a wealthy merchant and influential senator in the city, had been glad to leave its stuffy bourgeois provincialism before the First World War. "Our Lübeck is a good city," he noted ironically. "Yet it often makes me think of a grassy plaza, covered with dust, that needs the storm of spring which powerfully nudges life from the suffocating shell." But it was a death-delivering and man-made tempest that had finally woken the city from its medieval torpor. In March 1942, the Royal Air Force had chosen it as the target of its first area-bombing raid.

The result was that the crooked symmetry of its ancient streets lay wrecked, grass grew amid the ruins, and the great Marienkirche stood as an empty shell, one of the two great bells from its tower firmly embedded in the floor of the nave. The city had been the site of one of Jean-Baptiste Bernadotte's all too rare military victories for Bonaparte, when he had forced the surrender of the Prussian forces of General Blücher. Now, on Monday, 23 April 1945, in a building inhabited by the Swedish consulate, his descendant met again with Himmler. It was half an hour before midnight.

"I shall not easily forget that night with its uncanny feeling of disaster," Bernadotte later remembered.[4] Himmler had barely arrived when the air-raid sirens started, and they had to rush down to the shelter in the cellar. Several people were already there, including some German civilians, but Himmler went unrecognized as he chatted with them and tried to gauge their reaction to events. After an hour, the all-clear siren sounded and they trooped back upstairs to the conference room. The power was still out, so the talk took place illuminated by nothing more than a couple of flickering candles.

Himmler was obviously nervous and struggling to maintain a façade of calm. "I admit that Germany is beaten," he confessed. As far as he knew, he told Bernadotte, Hitler might already be dead. Even as he uttered the words, he almost certainly knew that this was not true, but the events in the bunker on Hitler's birthday, as well as a manic outburst by the Führer two days later, had finally convinced the SS leader that it was safe to break his oath of loyalty. Maneuvering—in the words of one of his biographers—with "serpentine secrecy,"[5] Himmler now hoped to save his own skin, as well as to buy precious time for Germany by dividing the West from the Soviets.

He reiterated that he was prepared to capitulate in the West, but not in the East. "I have always been, and I shall always remain, a sworn enemy of Bolshevism," he declared. Again, Bernadotte repeated his reservations about the chances of the West agreeing, but he said he would forward the idea to the Swedish government on condition that the surrender of German troops in Denmark and Norway was included in the deal. To this, Himmler instantly agreed.

It was half past three in the morning when the meeting broke up. Himmler insisted on driving his car himself as he was in a hurry to return to the Eastern Front. But he was so nervous that he immediately crashed into the barbed wire surrounding the building, and it took several frantic minutes to get the car back on the road. To Bernadotte, the accident seemed symbolic of the whole bizarre and chaotic episode. Himmler, he learned later, had entered into such a fantasy world that he had been speculating with his aides on whether he would have to bow to Eisenhower, and if he ought to shake hands.

It was this offer from Himmler that Truman now discussed by phone with Churchill, the first occasion that the Prime Minister and the President talked directly with each other. Already, Churchill had formed a clear opinion of his partner in Washington. "The new man is not to be bullied by the Soviets," he told Foreign Secretary Anthony Eden.

In reality, though, there was little of substance to talk about, and Truman was adamant: "I don't think we ought even to consider a piecemeal surrender," he said bluntly. Still, given the Soviet dimension, it was a highly sensitive issue, and they needed to agree on the correct wording in their response to the Swedes. A German surrender, they informed Stockholm, could be accepted only on all fronts. And if, after signing, German resistance continued anywhere, allied attacks would be ruthlessly continued until total victory was gained.[6]

Bernadotte handed over this predictable reply to Himmler's right-hand man in the talks, SS Brigadeführer Walter Schellenberg, in Sweden on Friday 27 April. It seemed as though things had come to an end. But in the hope of still striking a deal about German forces in Denmark and Norway, Bernadotte organized one more meeting with Himmler in Lübeck.

However, it never took place. The next day, news about Bernadotte's previous talks with Himmler broke in the world's press and the Reichsführer SS flew into a rage that his secret was out. His fury, though, was trumped by that of Hitler. Radio Stockholm broadcast the news, and it was picked up by Goebbels in Berlin. For the first time, the Führer learned of what had been going on behind his back.

This, he raged, was the ultimate betrayal. Worst of all, it had been committed by the "*treue* [loyal] *Heinrich*."[7] He immediately ordered Himmler's arrest, expelled him from the Nazi Party and stripped him of all public offices.

While the top Nazis turned furiously against each other, Truman and Churchill kept faith with their Kremlin ally and sent a telegram to Stalin informing him of their reply. The Soviet dictator signaled his approval, and outwardly the allies remained in step.

Yet, since Yalta and even before, Churchill's fears about ultimate Soviet political and territorial goals had been growing darker by the day, and incontestably ominous evidence that Stalin was intent on imposing a communist government on Poland was leading the Prime Minister to talk gloomily about the "shadows of victory."[8] Only four weeks before, he had insisted on crossing the Rhine to gaze for himself on the fruits of victory, and had visited what remained of Wesel, which Bryan Samain just days earlier had passed through with the commandos. Seeing the destruction prompted Churchill to think hard about the future of Germany. He would never agree to the country's dismemberment, he declared, until his doubts about Russian intentions were assuaged.

By the time of Himmler's offer, the division of Europe between East and West was taking concrete form, with imminent occupation of Prague by the Red Army and a tightening Soviet grip on Austria. Together, Churchill and Truman protested to Stalin that in Vienna the Russians were making decisions that excluded the Western powers. Churchill's desire to have allied troops advance on Berlin had also been thwarted, of course. But since Eisenhower had flown to London for their talks in mid-April, the Prime Minister had been gratifyingly reassured on another point of great political concern: the Supreme Commander would not let the Red Army beat him to Lübeck, and he was determined to block their advance into Denmark.

Given the pace of the Soviet advance westwards along the Baltic coast, this now seemed a plausible threat. And Eisenhower's proposed move would have the added benefit of preventing a retreat by the Germans into Jutland to establish a northern redoubt. Since his meeting with Churchill, Eisenhower had been prodding Montgomery to hurry up with his projected crossing of the River Elbe. Even as Bernadotte was agreeing to meet with Himmler to explore the chances of a separate surrender of German forces in Denmark and Norway,

SHAEF telephoned Montgomery to point out the urgent need to reach Lübeck ahead of the Russians, and Eisenhower himself followed it up with a personal telegram making the same point. But by this time, Montgomery had already issued his orders. The Elbe would be crossed on the night of Saturday 28 April.[9]

Montgomery's orders brought British commando Bryan Samain's comfortable ten-day sojourn in Lüneberg to an unwelcome end. His unit was slated to cross the Elbe close to the town of Lauenburg, which lay on the other side of the river. It would not be easy. The town was on top of high, thickly wooded cliffs, along which the Germans had built a series of defensive trenches reinforced with machine-gun posts. Outside the town, a battery of heavy guns dominated all the likely crossings of the river. Intelligence suggested that the Germans were grouped in considerable strength in the area. The river was the last great natural barrier to the allied advance. Around Bremen just three days before, British forces had faced a last-ditch, suicidal German stand including boys as young as eight. Along with everyone else, from Montgomery down, Samain was convinced that the Germans would again try something desperate.

At six o'clock on the Saturday evening, he left his billet and clambered aboard one of a convoy of buses that would take the commandos to their jumping-off point. At a crawl, the convoy moved through small village after small village. Out of the window, Samain could see the massive preparations under way for the offensive. Artillerymen were piling up great stores of shells alongside their guns; light anti-aircraft batteries were being trained on their targets; and alongside the buses marched two long columns of Scottish soldiers — Samain's commando brigade came under the command of the Fifteenth (Scottish) Division.

Two hours after setting out, the convoy reached the concentration area and everyone de-bused. Samain tried to catch a bit of sleep in a field, but an hour later the sky suddenly lit up as British artillery began a barrage to "soften up" the enemy defenses. It reminded him of the crossing of the Rhine a few weeks before. "The rumble of heavy guns heralded the shrill whine of shells hissing through the air," he recorded, "and once more the sky was filled with a fantastic pattern of orange-colored lights as ack-ack shells 'pepper-potted' Lauenburg. Already the town was beginning to glow ominously as one building after another caught fire."[10] It began to drizzle as the commandos awaited the order to advance. Soon, Samain's battle dress was soaking wet. It would be a long wait. Two other commando units were leading the assault with the task of establishing a bridgehead. Only then would Samain's troop move forward.

It was two o'clock in the morning when the order finally came. Samain clambered out of his trench and jumped into one of the boats that would ferry the men over the river. The advance commandos had already made it across. Faintly, above the roar of the vessels' engines, he could hear the crackle of machine-gun fire and the whining burst of grenades in the town. But the crossing proved easy. A few machine-gun bursts whizzed harmlessly overhead then, suddenly, he heard the Buffalo grate on the shingle and he quickly leaped out. Ten yards ahead loomed the cliffs, and they began to climb. The rain had made the single track tortuously muddy and slippery, and it took them twenty minutes to reach the top. Here, they spotted the line of white tape laid by the advance units to guide them through the darkness ahead.

Over the next few hours, Lauenburg was steadily infiltrated by British troops, and by daylight the town was secured. Apart from occasional heavy firing, opposition was slight and the speed and daring of the commandos' assault up the cliffs caught the enemy off guard. Several hundred frightened German soldiers were soon dragged out of cellars and basements in the town.

The main task now was to erect a bridge across the river. As Folke Bernadotte had painfully experienced on the roads outside Berlin, the Luftwaffe had virtually ceased to operate, but here its remnants made some effort to hinder the engineers. It was the first time Samain had seen German aircraft at work since Normandy. The attacks were noisy but ineffectual, hampered by fire from a battery of light flak guns hastily abandoned by the Germans overnight and now manned by commandos. The Stukas, Focke-Wulf 190s and Messerschmitt 109s, flying in low over the river, came in singly, one every half hour, and dropped a bomb apiece in an effort to hit the bridge that was already carrying tanks and vehicles. They caused delays, but failed to strike the target. One suffered a direct hit from the flak guns that sent it hurtling to the ground. By evening, the planes had ceased their attacks altogether.[11]

That night, Samain slept peacefully. When he awoke the next morning, it was to find that the armored divisions were already across the river and heading rapidly north. Montgomery was jubilant. "I have every hope," he cabled London, "that we shall reach the Lübeck area in two days' time." Privately, he now felt confident that at last the Germans were about to surrender. "They are hard pressed," he recorded, "they keep on fighting only because every German soldier has taken a personal oath to Hitler and so long as he is alive they must keep on fighting. Once it is known that he is dead, or has cleared out, there will be a big scale collapse."[12] The Red Army was now in the suburbs of Berlin, but no one outside the walls of Hitler's bunker had any idea of his fate.

Not until two o'clock in the afternoon of the next day was Samain's commando unit ordered to move on. Its task now was to "clear out" pockets of German resistance left behind by the spearhead of the advance. The first targets were two small villages, Lutau and Wangelau, lying twelve and fifteen miles, respectively, east of the Elbe. Again, Samain found himself on a bus, then continuing on foot to get close to the target. But Lutau was already a smoking ruin thanks to the British gunners, so they moved on cautiously. His troop, E (Easy), led the way. They advanced in single file along hedgerows and the edges of woods and then up a small lane until they got within sight of Wangelau. A hundred yards short of the village they stopped. Reports had come in of large numbers of Germans carrying weapons there. A section of the troop was sent ahead to investigate a large farm on the right-hand side of the lane. They entered the farmyard unopposed and peered through the windows. Inside, a large party of SS officers and men were calmly sitting down to a meal. "*Handes hoch!*" (Hands up!) shouted the commandos, and leaped into the room. Taken totally by surprise, the SS men dropped everything, stood up and obediently raised their hands.

Meanwhile, the rest of the troop had surprised another group of German soldiers preparing a meal in the farmhouse kitchen. The commandos proceeded calmly to sit down and enjoy it. Shortly afterwards, another group of oblivious German soldiers marched into Wangelau from the north, and straight into a commando ambush. Those not immediately killed or wounded ran for cover in nearby houses or farm cottages. A twenty-minute firefight followed, but after British heavy guns began shelling the Germans, several dirty white handkerchiefs appeared at the windows of the buildings. The commandos had been caught by this trick before and lost men, but this time the Germans were serious and genuinely wanted to surrender. Within half an hour the commandos had added 135 prisoners to their tally. Only one

British soldier, a sergeant in Samain's own troop, was killed in the operation.

The next morning, Samain witnessed perhaps the last aerial dogfight of the war in Europe. In the bright blue sky of a brilliantly sunny day, he watched a lone duel between a Spitfire and a Messerschmitt, and he cheered with the others when the Luftwaffe plane took a direct hit and plunged to the earth in flames a mile outside the village. When the commandos sent out a party to look for it, he reported, "we found the usual gruesome wreckage of fuselage, with the pilot lying a few yards from his machine, a battered mass of flesh." They removed his identification papers, then buried him. That afternoon, they also buried their sergeant in the shadow of the farmhouse where he had fought his last battle. "It seemed an ironical twist of fate that the two men, one British and the other German," wrote Samain, "should die almost as the last shots of the war were being fired. To us it symbolized the stupidity of the whole business."[13]

Also driving east across the Elbe were the paratroopers of Gavin's Eighty-second Airborne Division. Leonard Linton was among them. As a member of a military government unit he enjoyed the privilege of having a jeep all to himself, and he was speeding down a side road towards the division's first target beyond the Elbe, the town of Neuhaus. Unexpectedly, he came to a T-junction on the brow of a hill. As he wondered whether to turn left or right, he spotted a black hole in the middle of a bush straight ahead. With a sudden lurch of his stomach he realized he was staring into the muzzle of an 88mm gun. The bush moved, and he found himself confronted by several Wehrmacht soldiers.[14] One of them shouted in English, "Hands up!" Almost without thinking, Linton answered back in German.

It was a language he knew well, having learned it after his father had moved to Berlin on business when Leonard was still a babe in arms. His brother Val was born there, and the family lived in the comfortable Schoneberg quarter of the city. Leonard was schooled in the German capital until he was eleven.

Like many prosperous Berliners, the family spent their summer vacations in resorts along the Baltic coast. Once, they rented a house at the Pomeranian resort of Swinemunde. With the son of the house, a boy of his own age, Leonard spent endless hours in the sand dunes playing games inspired by stories of the famous German North Sea pirate, Klaus Stortebecker, who had terrorized Hanseatic shipping during the fourteenth century and was renowned for imprisoning sailors in herring barrels. Linton could not get hold of enough paperbacks about his hero to keep himself happy.

Back in the capital's streets he was a bit of a tear-away. Once, he joined up with a gang of rowdy Hitler Youth, mindlessly dropping stink bombs in Jewish shops and throwing stones through their windows. He soon dropped out, but in a juvenile show of bravado joined a militant Zionist boys' organization instead before quitting that, too. He found it all too serious. And in any case, he did not know Hebrew.

He had, though, acquired a thick Berlin accent, and he resurrected it now to instant effect. "*Seit nicht doorf, wir sind Tausende*" (Don't be stupid, we're thousands), he said, boldly removing the Mauser rifle pointed straight at him before its startled Wehrmacht owner had time to react. After that, it proved easy. Linton took possession of a Luger pistol, a precious piece of war booty highly prized by all GIs, ripped out a field telephone and its wires he found in the soldiers' dugout, and handed out several packets of Lucky Strike cigarettes. After telling them they would be safe if they raised their hands when the paratroopers arrived, he sped off into Neuhaus.

So rapidly had he moved that he was convinced he must be the first American into the town. So he was bitterly disappointed when he saw scribbled on a wall a sketch of the familiar All-American patch with the distinctive white letters "AA" on a red and blue background and underneath it the immortal words, "Kilroy Was Here." He was also sobered by a sight on a nearby street where the façade of a house had been ripped off by shell fire. The rooms inside were completely exposed, like those of a doll's house, and in the dining room he saw an entire German family sitting dead at the table, killed by the blast.

A few miles on he drove into the small town of Ludwigslust. It was physically untouched by war. On its outskirts, surrounded by vast English-style parkland, stood the baroque palace of the grand dukes of Mecklenburg. In no mood to sightsee, Linton drove straight on to the Town Hall. He arrived in the middle of a meeting of town officials, who were discussing what to do when the Americans arrived. Taken completely by surprise, some of them jumped up and stood to attention. Others began trembling with fear. Brusquely, Linton read out Eisenhower's Proclamation No. 1 and told the Mayor he was to continue running the town until further notice.

He then commandeered several buildings, including the palace, which became Gavin's headquarters. For his own unit's use, he took possession of a house owned by two sisters, who moved into the servants' quarters. In one of the wardrobes he found the brown uniform of a high official of the Todt Organization. Named after its founder, Hitler's chief engineer Fritz Todt, and using forced labor and mostly Russian prisoners of war, it had consumed millions of tons of cement in building bridges, roads, rocket ramps, U-boat pens, bunkers and defense installations, including the coastal defenses of the Atlantic Wall, for Hitler's Reich. The uniform belonged to the husband of one of the sisters, who had fled.

After a couple of days Linton also discovered that a small bust of Hitler which he had taken from another house as a souvenir had gone missing. After searching high and low, he found it smashed to bits in the backyard. After a grilling, one of the sisters confessed that she was responsible. She was afraid, she claimed, that one of their enemies had planted it in the house to incriminate them as Nazis. Shortly afterwards, Linton caught two haggard-looking men rummaging through the women's belongings and harshly ordered them out. The sisters, already badly scared, were profoundly grateful. They had good reason to be: the men were survivors of a nearby concentration camp, and few of such victims of Nazism felt benevolent towards German civilians — and especially those so clearly implicated with Hitler's regime.

CHAPTER ELEVEN

"BOULEVARD OF BROKEN DREAMS"

Deep in the Berlin bunker, the ten days after Hitler's funereal birthday celebrations witnessed the final disintegration of the Nazi regime. The Red Army relentlessly tightened its grip around the city, its tanks nosing ever closer to the center and its heavy artillery lobbing shells with increasing accuracy at the Chancellery.

Two days after his birthday, Hitler's fantasy of halting the Russians came crashing to the ground. Learning that a counterattack he had ordered by General Felix Steiner's SS Panzer Corps on which he was pinning all his hopes had failed to take place, he flew into a violent rage. Screaming that he had been betrayed by everyone, and now even the SS, he strode up and down the bunker's conference room pounding his fist into his palm, his face white with rage, and wept tears of fury and frustration. His tirade lasted for a full half hour, shocking all those in the room and reaching the ears of everyone outside.

Finally, exhausted, he fell whimpering into a chair. The war was lost, he declared. He would now stay in the city to lead its final, doomed and defiant defense. But he would never fall into the hands of the enemy. Instead, at the last minute, he would shoot himself.

Afterwards, he retreated to his private quarters. "It's all lost," he told his staff, "hopelessly lost." He urged them to leave the city immediately for the south and told them that an aircraft was fueled and ready to fly them out. But his secretaries all refused, as did Eva Braun, who had already declared she was not leaving. "Ah," responded Hitler wistfully, "if only my generals were as brave as my women." Later, he gave orders for his personal papers to be burned. His aide hurriedly began the task of carrying them up to the garden and setting them alight.

Goebbels, the ultimate Nazi loyalist and public spokesman for Hitler, now announced that he, his wife and all six of his children would move into the bunker to be at the Führer's side. Soon after, he and his family left his official residence near the Brandenburg Gate and were driven to the nearby Chancellery in two Mercedes limousines. Before leaving, he made one last radio broadcast: "The Führer is in Berlin," he announced, "and will die fighting with his troops defending the capital city." In the final editorial that day for his weekly mouthpiece, the newspaper *Das Reich*, he demanded resistance at any cost. Even children should hurl grenades and anti-tank mines at the Russians, regardless of the danger.

Hitler now abandoned all pretense at leadership, and left his subordinates free to make their own choices. "Do whatever you want," he told them, "I'm not giving any more orders." Nearly all, except his personal staff, chose to leave the city. Some opted to continue the fight from elsewhere, others to salvage what they could from the debris. With Germany effectively cut in two, separate Northern and Southern Commands were created. Grand Admiral Karl Doenitz took control in the north, Field Marshal Albert Kesselring in the south. Both decided to fight on for as long as they could with the forces at their disposal. Steadily, the bunker emptied.

In these last few days, too, Hitler appeared personally to decompose. He became a shuffling, hunched-up figure with shaking hands whose clothes, once immaculate, were now spattered with food stains. His pale, gray-blue eyes were bloodshot, with drooping black sacks of fatigue hanging beneath them. Heavy lines creased his yellowing face. Increasingly, he retreated into himself, brooding on the treachery and cowardice he believed explained the approaching *Götterdämmerung*.

Himmler had not been the first of Hitler's inner circle to abandon him. Over the winter, Hermann Goering had sent his wife and children south to the relative safety of Bavaria. Along with them went several loads of mostly looted works of art from Carinhall, his palatial house outside Berlin. He also began to talk of the need for negotiations with the Americans. It was urgent that he leave for Bavaria to command the Luftwaffe, he told Hitler on the night of the Führer's birthday. Hitler seemed almost indifferent, as if he expected nothing better from his heir-apparent. He merely muttered a few words and perfunctorily shook Goering's hand.

After this cool farewell, Goering gave orders for Carinhall to be blown up and headed south in his chauffeur-driven and armor-plated limousine to join his family in their lavish mountainside villa close to Hitler's Berghof. Here, numerous other Nazi Party stalwarts, top government officials and Wehrmacht officers also retreated during these last days of April.

Three days later, word reached him of Hitler's furious declamation that he had no more orders to give. Effectively, it seemed to Goering, the Führer had resigned. After seeking legal advice, he sent a telegram to Hitler suggesting the time had now come for he himself to assume the "total leadership" of the Reich. If he received no reply by ten o'clock that evening, he added, he would assume that Hitler had lost his freedom of action and proceed as planned.

Imposing a deadline proved a bad mistake. Inside the Berlin bunker, Goering had many enemies. Goebbels, for instance, had long detested the corpulent and high-living head of the Luftwaffe as a man who loved the privileges of high office but had proved an utter failure in his primary task of defending German cities against allied air raids. "Medal-jangling asses and vain, perfumed dandies don't belong in the high command," he scoffed. Hitler's private secretary and gatekeeper Martin Bormann, who by now was one of the most influential figures in the bunker, was an even more bitter opponent. "He's only waiting to get me," noted Goering. "If I act, he will call me a traitor. If I don't, he will accuse me of having failed at the most crucial hour." [1]

He was right. Bormann skillfully manipulated Goering's telegram to make it appear like an impatient and disloyal grab for power. Hitler had long been struggling against his own growing doubts about his veteran comrade-in-arms, and Bormann's spin finally tipped the balance. "None of this is new to me," he raged. "I have always known that Hermann Goering was lazy. He let the Luftwaffe fall apart. The man was a monumental crook . . . He has been a drug addict for years. I have known all these things all along." [2] Then he stripped his old ally of all public and party offices, and within hours the man who had once been the most powerful figure in Germany after Hitler himself was placed under arrest and his house in Bavaria was surrounded by SS guards.

Worse was to come. Twenty-four hours later, Goering woke to a deafening roar sweeping up the valley from Berchtesgaden and the villa's windows began to shake. It was the Royal Air Force making a massive bombing raid on the Berghof. As the Lancasters dropped their bomb loads, Goering and his family were pushed hurriedly by the SS guards into the air-raid tunnels that had been built beneath the building. They were dank and dismal, the lights failed, and they had to use candles.

Goering tried to send a telegram to Berlin, but his captors refused even to handle it. In the meantime, hungry and unwashed, Hitler's erstwhile successor fell into a slough of self-pity. Above, the allied bombers systematically destroyed Hitler's residence, and when Goering was finally able to emerge into daylight he found his swimming pool destroyed, the roof of the house torn off, and his study completely wrecked.[3]

Hard on the heels of Goering's defection, the news of Himmler's betrayal was the last straw for Hitler, the final, undeniable signal that all was truly lost. When the evidence came through, writes Eva Braun's biographer, "he raged like a madman, his face so suffused with blood as to be unrecognizable, beside himself with fury and, strange as it sounds, grief."[4] For Hitler had defended Himmler many times from those in his inner circle who loathed him. Now, he had been proved wrong.

In his anger, he ordered the instant execution of Hermann Fegelein, Himmler's liaison officer in Berlin and, through his marriage to her sister, the brother-in-law of Eva Braun. Despite Eva's desperate pleadings, Fegelein was taken up to the Chancellery garden and shot. Then Hitler ordered two of his most faithful acolytes, the air aces Ritter von Greim and Hanna Reitsch, to fly out of the city in their small plane to Plon, where they were to instruct Doenitz to have Himmler immediately arrested and shot.

By now, the Soviet bombardment of the Chancellery had reached a climax and shells were falling regularly on the very center of the building. Below ground, those who were left rehearsed their plans for suicide, and ghoulishly discussed how their bodies should be disposed of. Hitler was now planning his own heroic demise. "It's the only chance to restore personal reputation," he told the über-loyal Goebbels. "If we leave the world stage in disgrace, we'll leave for nothing . . . Rather end the struggle in honor than continue in shame and dishonor a few months or days longer."[5]

Determined to give the Soviets neither the pleasure of killing him in battle nor of defiling his body, he made careful plans for his suicide. To test the poison he planned to swallow, he first had it given to his beloved Alsatian, Blondi. When he saw that it had worked, remembered his secretary Traudl Junge, his face "looked like his own death mask."

He also made sure that there was a large enough stock of petrol for his corpse to be thoroughly burned in the garden. The news of Mussolini's fate had reached him just hours after his one-time ally's corpse, along with that of Clara Petacci, had been strung up in Milan. This only cemented a decision he had already made, that he would never end up as a public spectacle to be crowed over by his enemies.

Shortly after the departure of Greim and Reitsch, at about 11:30 p.m. on Saturday 28 April, he dictated his last will and testament to Traudl Junge. In his private will, he disposed of his personal possessions to the Nazi Party, and expressed the hope that his collection of paintings would go to a gallery in Linz. He appointed Martin Bormann as executor, to ensure that his relatives and long-serving staff did not go unrewarded. But the more significant document was his political testament, a long, rambling piece of self-justification that revealed, even now, the depth of his hatred for the Jews and his inexhaustible ability to blame all but himself for the catastrophe he had brought to Germany and Europe.

It was a drearily familiar litany of claims, complaints and delusions: he had never wanted war, which had been instigated by international statesmen who were either Jewish or working for Jewish interests; the Jews would have to pay for all the destruction that Europe had suffered through the previous six years of "murderous struggle"; the German people's fight against the Jews would eventually go down in history as "the most glorious and valiant manifestation of a nation's will to existence"; at some point in the future there would be a renaissance of National Socialism; and, finally, he exhorted, the struggle must continue, even after his death — there would be no surrender.

In the final part of his testament, he appointed a successor government, with Doenitz as head of state and of the armed forces, Goebbels as Chancellor, and the Munich Gauleiter Paul Giesler as Minister of the Interior. Gauleiter Karl Hanke, who was still leading a fanatical last-ditch fight against the Russians in Breslau, was named as Himmler's successor. If any further proof were needed of Hitler's racial fanaticism, he concluded with these final words of exhortation to this new, last Nazi government: "Above all I enjoin the government and the people to uphold the race laws to the limit and to resist mercilessly the poisoner of all nations, international Jewry."[6]

With the bunker shaking from nearby explosions, he now married Eva Braun. He had always declared he could never marry, as he was already wedded to his country, but now Germany was no more, so he was free. Besides, it could no longer cause him any political damage. Bormann and Goebbels were witnesses, and the ceremony was conducted by a Berlin city official who was hastily brought in for the task. Hitler was frail and stooping, his hair turning gray, but beside him Eva Braun was smiling rapturously in an elegant navy-blue dress embroidered with sequins, and black suede shoes from Ferragamo. Afterwards, there was champagne. Only at 5 a.m. did everyone finally go to bed.

By this time, Soviet troops had fought their way to the Potsdammer Platz, just a few hundred yards away, and at dawn Red Army artillery opened up with a massive bombardment of the Chancellery. Later, Hitler ate an informal lunch with his secretaries, perching at the small table in his study known as the map room, and toying with spaghetti and tossed salad. Afterwards, he shook hands with the remaining staff and said his farewells. He was wearing his usual black trousers and uniform tunic with a white shirt. Beside him, Braun wore a black dress with roses around the neckline, his favorite. "Please do try to get out," she said, smiling, to Traudl Junge. "You may yet make your way through. And," she added with a hint of a sob, "give Bavaria my love."[7]

Then the two of them retired to his study. Ten minutes later, one of his aides opened the door. Inside, Hitler and his wife of just a few hours were sitting side by side on a small blue and white sofa. Braun was slumped sideways, her feet tucked up snugly beneath her body. She had bitten on her capsule of potassium cyanide and the air smelled of bitter almonds. Hitler's head drooped lifelessly, and from a bullet hole in his right temple blood dripped onto his tunic. At his feet lay his powerful Walther pistol.

It was approximately 3:30 p.m. on Monday 30 April. Just an hour before, and less than a mile away, a Soviet soldier had waved the red flag from a second-floor window of the Reichstag. As arranged, the bodies were taken up from the bunker into the Chancellery garden, doused with petrol and set alight.

One of the few people to have seen Hitler following his manic outburst the previous Sunday had been Obergruppenführer Gottlob Berger, head of the Waffen SS. Berger had arrived shortly after midnight, having driven in from Himmler's headquarters in response to an order from Hitler, who wanted to see him before he traveled south to Bavaria. Inside the bunker, he found Hitler still railing against those around him. "Everyone has deceived me! No one has told me the truth!" he shrieked. "The armed forces have lied to me!" At the end of their talk, the issue of the *Prominente* came up—the politically or socially well-connected prisoners in SS custody being held as hostages for negotiations with the allies. Recently, they had been moved to Bavaria from camps elsewhere in Germany. The two men also talked about growing evidence of separatist sentiment both there and in Austria.

As Berger took his leave, Hitler rose to his feet, his body trembling and his hands and head shaking. "Shoot them all! Shoot them all!" he shouted. But as he left the beleaguered capital to fly to Bavaria in Himmler's plane, Berger was unclear whether the Führer meant the prisoners, the separatists, or both.[8]

In Berlin, however, the SS knew exactly what to do.

Situated in the middle of the capital stood the Moabit Prison. A grim, five-story brick building, it was constructed in the shape of a star with several wings containing a total of some five hundred cells. Hundreds of political prisoners had passed through its doors since 1933, including Fey von Hassell's father who had lain in one of its cells for several days en route from Ravensbrück to the Gestapo interrogation cells on the Prince Albrechtstrasse. Others had been there for years.

Heavy allied bombing had damaged the building and recently the prisoners had been taken deep down into the cellars. Late that night, two groups of eight prisoners were summoned from the cells and handed back their personal effects. Twenty others had been released earlier in the day, and the mood was hopeful. Many of the sixteen men—there were no women in the prison—were distinguished lawyers or military officers who, one way or another, had fallen foul of the regime. One or two were merchants or industrialists, and the group also included a young German communist, a Soviet prisoner of war, and Karl Bonhoeffer. He had been a legal adviser to the national airline Lufthansa but more significantly was the brother of Dietrich Bonhoeffer, the Lutheran theologian and tireless opponent of Nazism. Another of the sixteen was Professor Albrecht Haushofer. The son of the man who had virtually invented the "science" of geopolitics, which gave Hitler some of the key ideas that appeared in *Mein Kampf*, such as the notion of *Lebensraum* ("living space"), Haushofer had suppressed doubts about the Nazis and served as an adviser to Hitler's deputy Rudolf Hess, as well as carrying out special missions for both Ribbentrop and Hitler himself.

Too late, he woke up to the dangers of war and tried frantically to send out peace feelers to Britain. Behind the scenes, he also played a role in Hess's flight to Scotland in May 1941 to seek a peace deal with Britain, and suffered as a result by being briefly grilled by the Gestapo. Three years later, he was rearrested during the massive round-up of everyone and their families implicated in the July bomb plot. He had been in Moabit since December 1944.[9]

Having been given their effects, the prisoners returned to their cells to pack. Haushofer was sharing a cell with a German communist, Herbert Kosney, and he gave him a loaf of pumpernickel bread to take with him. Then the prisoners were marched up to the prison yard. Here they were given the rest of their valuables, such as cigarette lighters, watches, rings and wallets. They signed receipts for the items, completed forms stating they had been released, and were told as much by the prison governor, who made a brief appearance. One of the SS guards told Kosney he would soon be at home with his wife. Cheerfully, they marched towards the prison gate through a narrow hallway. Suddenly, a light was switched on. Lining the passageway they saw over thirty SS Sonderkommando soldiers armed with machine pistols — two for every prisoner. Then they were told that they were not, after all, being released. Instead, they were being transferred to another prison by train. If they tried to escape, they would be shot.

It was now after midnight. Flashes from approaching Soviet artillery occasionally lit the sky. Ominously, the prisoners were now ordered to hand back all the valuables they had just been given. They marched for a while down the street, then were directed towards a huge bombed-out and cratered exhibition site with a ruined building in the middle. The guards explained that this was a short cut to the train station, although they all knew it was not. Once inside the building they were divided into two: Haushofer's group was ordered to the left; the other men to the right. They all were made to face the wall. Then Kosner and Haushofer heard the sound of shooting and stared at each other for a split second before they, too, were mown down by a volley of shots to the backs of their necks from the guns of their SS guards.

Kosner was very lucky. He had turned his head and the bullet had somehow passed right through his skull but had failed to kill him. Nevertheless, he fell with the others. Then, still conscious, he lay as still as he could while one of the SS men put bullets through the heads of all those he thought might still be alive. Eventually, when everything fell silent, Kosner managed to drag himself home before collapsing. When he regained consciousness in hospital several days later, he still had in his pocket the piece of pumpernickel given to him by Haushofer, although it was now covered in blood.

It took Heinz Haushofer until Saturday 12 May to find his brother's body, still lying where he had been shot. Clutched in his hand were scraps of paper containing poems written out in longhand.

During his weeks in Moabit, Haushofer had had plenty of time to meditate on Germany's fate and his role in its downfall. Like many Germans who had flirted with Nazism or believed they could influence Hitler in the direction of peace, he had been proven badly wrong and was consumed with guilt. He accepted that he had been fooled by "criminals and murderers," and sought solace in composing the poems found by his brother. "A host of gray rats eats the land," began one of them, depicting a group of maddened rodents laying waste to the fields before a piper [Hitler] leads them over an abyss to their deaths in the sea.[10]

In the dying days of Hitler's Reich, life remained cheap and the fate of prisoners in the hands of the SS was an arbitrary affair. Since at least March, Himmler had been looking for a way to survive the approaching disaster and ingratiate himself with the allies. This explained his dealings with Folke Bernadotte over the Scandinavian prisoners as well as some other selective releases, such as that of certain Jews to Sweden.

However, he remained determined to hold on to others as hostages. But as the Reich disintegrated, his personal grip on SS affairs seriously weakened. Not all his SS subordinates agreed with him, while some, such as Heinrich Müller, the Gestapo chief who ordered the murders of Haushofer and the others in Berlin, actively opposed his line. To its many hardened zealots, there was simply no room for negotiation or mercy towards prisoners. If their revered Reich was to perish, so should its enemies.[11]

Few prisoners were more aware of their personal peril during these last few days of April than Fey von Hassell. In Dachau, surrounded by the other *Sippenhafte* whose relatives had perished at Nazi hands, her father's brutal death still festered like an open wound. She also had no idea what had happened to her two boys.

More than once on her recent forced odyssey the hand of fate had reached out apparently arbitrarily to pluck one of her fellow prisoners for execution. The latest victim had been Dietrich Bonhoeffer. The dissident theologian had recently joined them in the schoolhouse at Schoneberg along with several other new arrivals. There he spent a good deal of time with Soviet Foreign Minister Molotov's nephew, trying to instill in the young communist the foundations of Christianity while learning some Russian in return.

But he was already doomed. The Nazis had recently discovered the secret diary of Admiral Canaris in which the former Abwehr chief had confided his contacts with the anti-Nazi resistance. This enraged Hitler and he ordered the Austrian Nazi Ernst Kaltenbrunner, Himmler's deputy, to see to the immediate disposal of Canaris and any other plotters who had so far escaped execution.

On Sunday 8 April, Fey had attended morning service in the schoolhouse. It was held by Bonhoeffer, who read the texts for the day, said prayers and spoke of the thoughts their captivity had prompted among the prisoners. Suddenly, the door opened, and two civilians brusquely called out: "Prisoner Bonhoeffer, get ready and come with us!"

Subsequently, Fey heard his footsteps going down the stairs and saw him being bundled into a black Gestapo car. A few hours later it reached Flossenburg. Here, a summary court was already waiting and Bonhoeffer joined Canaris and the other Abwehr conspirators in front of it. It was well after midnight before the prisoners reached their cells. Canaris knocked on the wall to signal that they had all been condemned.

In the gray of dawn next morning, they were taken from their cells. The camp doctor saw Bonhoeffer kneeling on the floor and praying fervently before having his prison garb removed. "I was most deeply moved by the way this lovable man prayed," he wrote, "so devout and certain that God heard his prayer." At the foot of the gallows he said another short prayer, then he climbed the steps, calm and composed, readied himself, and the trapdoor opened. Amid a small pile of the condemned men's possessions left in the guardhouse, another prisoner unearthed a volume of Goethe illustrated with etchings and inscribed with Bonhoeffer's name. All the remaining possessions were burned, as were the corpses.[12]

Now in Dachau, the surviving members of the *Sippenhafte* group were still under SS control, led by the sinister Ernst Bader. Almost every night, the air-raid sirens sounded and bombs rained down on the camp and its surrounds. As the days passed, the thump of artillery grew ever closer.

Then, on Wednesday 25 April, Fey heard the order she had been dreading: "Prepare to leave! Bring only what you can carry in your hands!" The camp was being evacuated before the Americans arrived. Two days before, all the Jews in the camp had been kept standing overnight and several dozen had died. The rest were locked into box-cars but were still waiting for a locomotive to haul them away.

Fey finally abandoned the battered old suitcase she had kept with her since leaving Brazzà, made a careful selection of essentials, and wrapped them all in a small rucksack fashioned from a stolen blanket. The others did likewise. Soon, the weary human convoy was trudging its way through the camp with pots, pans, tins and cups hanging from their backpacks, as though they were off on some carefree hiking trip.

Outside, they were pushed into heavily overloaded trucks covered with rough canvas roofs. As always, Fey stuck with the Stauffenbergs. She felt closer to Alex now than ever before. Two weeks earlier, tragedy had struck: when piloting an unarmed Bücker-181 trainer plane, his wife, Litta, had been shot down by an American fighter. She landed the plane successfully but died shortly afterwards from bullet wounds. Alex heard of her death four days later when Edgar Stiller called him into the corridor. Fey was there when he came back. His face was white with shock, and they were all so horrified that they left him alone for a while to absorb the devastating news. Then he beck-oned Fey and his cousin Elisabeth to his side and told them he needed people close to him who understood. Thereafter, the tragedy subtly altered the balance between them: previously, she had felt that she needed him; now, it was clear that he needed her, too.[13]

For what seemed like hours, they stayed parked in the trucks to make way for long columns of other prisoners being marched out of the camp, shuffling along in their crude wooden clogs and wearing their striped camp uniforms. Some were too weak to walk, and fell despairingly to their hands and knees. The guards poked and prodded them to get up. Even as Fey watched, horrified, a few who could not rise to their feet were shot in the back of the neck.

After the last of the prisoners had passed through the gate, the truck began to move and she looked around its gloomy interior to examine her new companions. In addition to the familiar faces there were some new ones. The *Prominente*, those privileged hostages of the SS slated three days before by Hitler to be shot, had joined the *Sippenhafte* for the next stage of their bizarre journey. She had already met some of them during a brief stay at the municipal prison in Regensburg. Others had joined the group at Dachau. Altogether, the convoy that now headed south towards an unknown destination carried almost a hundred and fifty people.

One of those she instantly recognized was Kurt von Schuschnigg, the former Chancellor of Austria. He was only in his forties but was a man of old-world courtesy. Dressed in his native Tirolean costume, he sat next to his much younger wife, Vera, who was cuddling their three-year-old daughter, Sissy, on her knee. Like many prewar European politicians, Schuschnigg had badly underestimated the ruthlessness of the Nazis. As a minister in the government of the right-wing strongman Engelbert Dollfuss, he had been happy to repress the Social Democrats, and when Dollfuss was assassinated in 1934 by SS thugs, Schuschnigg replaced him as Chancellor and virtual dictator of Austria.

But he was unable to oppose Hitler's annexation of the land of his birth, and a treaty he signed with Berlin guaranteeing Austrian sovereignty proved worthless. Summoned to Berchtesgaden, he was browbeaten by Hitler into bringing the Austrian Nazi Party leader Artur Seyss-Inquart into his cabinet as Minister of the Interior. In a desperate last effort to regain his authority, he called for a plebiscite on Austria's continuing independence, but two days before it took place Hitler sent in his troops, annexed the country, and had Schuschnigg arrested. For almost a year and a half the Chancellor was kept in a tiny room at Gestapo headquarters in Vienna's Metropole Hotel, where he was humiliated by being forced to clean the latrines of his SS guards with the single small towel issued to him daily for his personal use.

He had lingered behind bars and barbed wire ever since, although secretly he was writing a journal recording his experiences, as well as his thoughts on the future of Austria and Europe.

At first, Fey found him taciturn and reserved, but slowly he thawed, and had much to say about the prospects for post-war Europe. His main concern was the Soviet Union, whose Red Army had already occupied Vienna. Schuschnigg predicted that they would never leave.

Vera, the former Countess Czernin, was much closer to Fey in age. She had been permitted to marry her husband in prison but was still traumatized by the few weeks they had been imprisoned together in Flossenburg. From inside her cell, she told Fey, she frequently heard the shouted order, "Take off your clothes!" followed by a chilling volley of shots outside. There was also a gallows in the corner of the little yard where they were allowed to exercise for half an hour each day, and her husband noticed how frequently the sawdust beneath it was changed. "Whoever has been condemned to this hell here," he scribbled in his diary, "has done penance enough for any mistake of the past." [14]

Fey also recognized one of the Nazis' most outspoken German opponents, the Protestant pastor Martin Niemoller, who was sitting close by, propped up against the side of the truck with an empty pipe in his mouth. A highly decorated First World War U-boat commander, he had been a convinced German nationalist and officer in the post-war right-wing Freikorps. For him, the fourteen years of the liberal democratic Weimar Republic represented "years of darkness." He, too, was taken in by Hitler, in this case by Nazi Party claims to stand for "positive Christianity," voted Nazi when the party first ran in national elections in 1924, and welcomed Hitler's assumption of power in 1933. Germany's national rebirth, hoped Niemoller, would lead to the nation's Christian renaissance.

Of course, he was quickly disabused. Almost immediately the Nazis attempted to take control of the churches and imposed a pro-Nazi "Reich Bishop" on the Protestants. Within months, Niemoller was setting up the Pastors' Emergency League to resist them and later he inspired the creation of the dissident Confessional Church. From his pulpit in Dahlem, one of the most fashionable districts of Berlin which was heavily populated by the Nazi elite, he began to preach overtly rebellious sermons that increasingly enraged Hitler.

Fey's father heard one of them during a visit to the city in 1937. She recorded his reaction in her diary. "He just stood there like a fearless prophet, speaking with total conviction," she noted her father telling her. "His message was clear. It was everybody's duty to fight the evil that was spreading through Germany."[15] Weeks later, Niemoller was arrested, along with several hundred other dissident pastors across the country. Since then, he had spent most of his time in prison or concentration camps, ending up in Dachau.

Beginning on Christmas Eve 1944, he was permitted to conduct religious services in a small cell. The last sermon he delivered, on Easter Monday just three weeks before, bleakly reflected his despair over the previous eight years. Warning against any facile optimism inspired by the arrival of spring, he promised that God's mercy "knows nothing of a universal natural law according to which life is stronger than death, good is mightier than evil, or other such idealist dogma, whatever they may be — in which at any rate," he added, "no one really believes any more." Only through a belief in Christ's resurrection, he concluded, could hope be found.

Fey did not find him the most cheerful of company. Niemoller's was an uncomfortable message for any German, especially one with a father such as hers who had, after all, served the Nazi regime until his forced dismissal. All Germans, Niemoller had come to believe, should share the guilt for Nazism. Later, the epigram he coined about this would become famous: "First they came for the Communists, but I was not a Communist so I did not speak out. Then they came for the Socialists and the Trade Unionists, but I was neither, so I did not speak out. Then they came for the Jews, but I was not a Jew, so I did not speak out. And when they came for me, there was no one left to speak out for me."[16] It could have applied to most of those traveling on this end-of-war odyssey into the unknown.

But of all the *Prominente*, the one who was to prove most important for Fey, as well as for the other prisoners, was Captain Sigismund Payne Best. Physically, he was the perfect caricature of the Englishman. "Very tall, very gaunt, and even stooping a little through emaciation," wrote a fellow prisoner, "with hollow leathery cheeks, prominent teeth, a monocle, flannel trousers, a tweed jacket, and a cigarette, [and] always showing his big false horse's teeth in an obliging smile and displaying that trustworthy discretion which engenders deep confidence."[17] This confidence was well placed. Payne Best spoke fluent German and was to prove an indispensable link and negotiator with their captors in the tense days ahead. He was quickly accepted by everyone as unofficial spokesman of the group.

From bitter experience, Payne Best also had a shrewd understanding and knowledge of the SS. For while being a stereotype, he was also a senior officer in the SIS, Britain's secret intelligence service, and he had once helped run its Western European networks from an office in the Netherlands. But in November 1939 he was seized by the Germans at Venlo on the Dutch-German border while exploring supposed peace feelers from Berlin that the Chamberlain government was keen to advance. In reality, these were nothing more than a Machiavellian ploy by German intelligence — masterminded by none other than Walter Schellenberg, who was now negotiating with Folke Bernadotte — to capture him and his SIS colleague Major Richard Stevens, who was also in the prisoner group, and interrogate them about British networks in Europe. Best then spent five and a half years in Sachsenhausen before being moved to Buchenwald.

He first spotted Fey in the prison at Regensburg. "A very pretty girl whom I took to be about sixteen years of age," he recorded, who "was distracted with the fear that she might never find [her boys] again." With his fluent German and friendly manner, he quickly became a valued father figure to the young German mother.[18]

After leaving Dachau, the convoy of trucks passed through Munich, lurching like a ship at sea as it bumped through the pot-holes. The city had recently been heavily bombed and the air was still thick with smoke. Payne Best, who had lived and studied in the city, could see little more than the ruins of gutted buildings behind a wall of rubble. Trams were still running, but their shattered windows were patched with cardboard. It was hard to believe that anyone in the city was still left alive. "Not a living being, not a light, not a noise," observed another of the prisoners. But Fey was prepared for what she saw: "Of the Munich we used to know there is practically nothing left," her mother had written after a major air raid the previous January.

As they headed towards the mountains, the road narrowed and grew steeper. At one point, they were all ordered out of the trucks to push, and Fey joined in with the others. During one stop she recognized another of the *Prominente*, a short, elderly man with spectacles, a bushy moustache and a mane of white hair. He was carrying a cane and walking with a limp. This was Léon Blum, twice Prime Minister of France in the 1930s as head of its left-wing Popular Front government. A life-long socialist, he had introduced the forty-hour workweek and collective bargaining as well as nationalized the Bank of France and the

French munitions industry. After the collapse of France in 1940 he was arrested by the Vichy regime of Marshal Pétain and hauled before a show trial on cooked-up charges of "war guilt." Amid the glare of the world's press, though, he turned the tables on his accusers, the trial collapsed, and he emerged with his stature enhanced.

But as a socialist, a Jew and a convinced supporter of General de Gaulle as the personification of French resistance, he was triply suspect to the Nazis. After they took over unoccupied France in November 1942 he was sent to Buchenwald as a potential hostage. There he had at least one narrow escape and he remained keenly aware of death's daily presence. Rightly so, for Hitler had personally approved Blum's name being placed on a list of hostages to be killed in reprisal for the execution of French collaborators by de Gaulle's Free French. This was not an idle threat. For several months, Blum had shared quarters with Georges Mandel, the French Minister of the Interior at the time of the French collapse and noted for his hostility to Nazi Germany. But in July 1944 Mandel was returned to France and murdered by the collaborationist Milice. Blum's brother, René, the former director of the Ballet of Monte Carlo, had already perished in Auschwitz.

Kept with his wife in special quarters, Blum was permitted to read French newspapers and listen to the radio, so he saw little of the barbarities being committed elsewhere in Buchenwald, although occasionally he caught the whiff of a strange odor in the air — that of the crematoria hard at work.

After being evacuated from the camp, he kept a daily diary. It was full of dark forebodings of death, although outwardly, for the sake of the others, he maintained a brave front. He was convinced of the reality of Nazi plans for an Alpine Redoubt and was sure that all the *Prominente* would be crushed in the final collapse of the Third Reich. Hitler would perish, he wrote, "but like the despots of the East — like Sardanapalus in the Delacroix painting — piling on his funeral pyre his companions, his slaves, his hostages." Blum was referring to the French romantic artist's portrayal of the legendary King of Assyria, who preferred to die with his harem rather than surrender to the Persians.

The trucks continued to jog their way through the night and at dawn passed through the sleeping streets of Innsbruck. Shortly outside the town they turned down a side track and stopped in front of a gateway where SS sentries stood guard. This was "Police Education Camp

Reichenau," which meant, as Payne Best wryly noted, that it was the police who did the educating.

Fey could hardly wait to get out of her cramped truck, and she happily clambered down into the sun to stretch her legs. It was already warm, and she found herself in a beautiful valley surrounded by mountains. But this was a sharp contrast to the sordid, lice-infested camp with open cesspools as toilets that greeted them.

For hours, the dozens of prisoners milled around in the hot sun. Best discovered that there were several British officers in the camp. Some were survivors of the massacre inflicted on RAF officers who had escaped from Stalag Luft III in the "Great Escape" of March 1944. (Fifty of those recaptured after that escape had been shot on Hitler's personal orders.) Another was Lieutenant-Colonel Jack Churchill, who had been dramatically captured in a raid on the Dalmatian coast.

But the most prominent of this British group was a handsome man in his mid-thirties named Captain Peter Churchill. Neither he nor Jack Churchill was related to the British Prime Minister — or to each other — but they had both been careful not to disabuse their captors of the idea. Peter was an SOE officer who had been captured in France. He had operated for two hundred days behind enemy lines before being betrayed to the Gestapo along with his female courier, Odette Sansom. Thereafter, he spent several months in Sachsenhausen before being evacuated with the other *Prominente* to Dachau.

In an effort to protect her with the Churchill name, he claimed that Odette was his wife, but they were separated shortly after their arrest, and now he had no idea where she was. In fact, she was in Ravensbrück, where, as he hoped, the Churchill tag had spared her from death. Instead, she was kept in solitary confinement in a small cell next to the execution ground. Every day, she heard the volleys of shots that told her of the continuous killings in the camp. Here, writes one historian, "in moods of sadism or Anglophobia her captors would starve her, or subject her to extremes of light or darkness, heat or cold." It was as well Churchill remained ignorant of all this, for he had fallen deeply in love with her.[19]

Among the other *Prominente* emerging from the trucks were Mario Badoglio, whose father had negotiated the Italian armistice with the allies, and General Garibaldi, a sixty-year-old partisan commander from northern Italy and grandson of the great nineteenth-century Italian liberator. In Dachau he had been made to clean out the latrines. There was also Colonel Ferraro, his right-hand man, a tall, powerfully built character with a ruddy complexion and curly brown hair who was placidly puffing on a pipe amid the hubbub. To Peter Churchill, he looked for all the world like "a champion golfer waiting patiently in a crowded club house for his turn to tee off."[20] There were several more Italian partisans, too. Fey found them kind and generous, although their behavior sometimes embarrassed her. They strutted around "like peacocks," she noted scornfully, "as if they, and only they, could save Italy."

More well-known faces from Germany had also joined the convoy. One of them was the industrialist and steel magnate Fritz Thyssen, who had helped finance Hitler's rise to power but later fell foul of him and fled to France, where he was turned over to the Nazis by the Vichy regime. Another former prisoner was Prince Philipp of Hesse, a great-grandson of the British King George V and a nephew of Kaiser Wilhelm II. Fey was surprised to find him there because he was a well-known supporter of the Nazis, a personal friend of Hermann Goering, and a man who had helped procure many looted works of art from Italy for Hitler's projected Führermuseum. But he was also married to Princess Mafalda, the daughter of the Italian King Victor Emmanuel, and after Hitler held him responsible for Mussolini's overthrow he and his wife were incarcerated in separate concentration camps.

Fey knew that Mafalda had been killed in an allied air raid while in Buchenwald, but when Hesse asked her if she knew what had happened to her, she could not bear to tell him. Besides, she felt profoundly uncomfortable around him. As she later confessed to Best, he had been a solid Nazi full of lies, unfaithfulness and dishonesty, and had behaved "disgracefully" in regard to her father.[21]

The best-known figure among all the Germans was Dr. Hjalmar Schacht, the former president of the Reichsbank. He was another one-time but now disillusioned ally of the Nazis. "Germany's future is dark," he moaned, "because megalomaniac fools and mountebanks have gambled away the capital of her good name, her trustworthiness." The best thing for Germany, he declared, would be British dominion status.[22] Also in the group was Colonel Bogislav von Bonin, a General Staff officer still in his Wehrmacht uniform, who had been dismissed by Hitler for disobeying his orders never to surrender even untenable positions to the Russians.

Fey spent most of the day trying to find out if any of them knew anything about the fate of children in SS hands. All she could glean was that some were being held in special institutes and that others had had their names changed and been given to German families for adoption. After a while, she dropped the subject because no one seemed very interested. What worried them now was their own survival.

Whatever their fate, though, this mini–League of Nations were now all in it together. As Blum put it, they had been deposited like a filtered residue of all Nazism's "most detested adversaries, subjects and vassals the most gravely suspected of treason . . . the last battalion of enemies and hostages." Blum, the socialist and secular Jew, could only nod when Schuschnigg, devout Catholic and scourge of Austrian socialism, observed dolefully that they had both sought the welfare of their countries and peace, but now only had the same opponents. It had taken the Nazi horror to make both men realize the values they held in common. "I must say I am obliged to the Gestapo," wrote Schuschnigg, "for having arranged the acquaintance with Léon Blum, in whom I have met a great European and — even more important to me — a fine and noble character. Perhaps this is the same thing."[23]

Blum, indeed, had become a powerful living symbol of the democratic Europe destroyed by the Nazis. When he and the others were marched out of Dachau, they were recognized by the vast crowd of emaciated prisoners standing watching them. He heard his name being pronounced, along with that of Schuschnigg and others, rolling in a powerful whisper all around them. In turn, they started whispering their nationality: French, Austrian, Russian. Then this came back to them from the crowd, until to Blum it felt like the ringing of a great and powerful bell calling out for victory.[24]

Blum's personal dignity amid the squalid conditions impressed all of Fey's fellow prisoners. "I think most would agree," wrote Peter Churchill, "that the elderly Léon Blum was an outstanding example of an alert mind, an unquenchable spirit, and a uniform charm of manner that could have made all French hearts glow with pride, whatever their politics."[25]

To everyone's relief, five large buses were eventually brought from Innsbruck to replace the trucks. Like some prewar Cook's party of tourists they clambered in, thankful to put the vermin-infected Reichenau behind them. At sunset, they set off towards the Brenner Pass and the Italian frontier. Now and again they were forced to stop while allied fighter-bombers strafed the road to block large-scale movements of German troops and munitions bound, presumably, for the

Alpine Redoubt. Outside, it was hard to see anything, but Fey noticed the drop in temperature as they reached the wintry heights of the mountains.

As usual, she stuck close to Alex and the other Stauffenbergs. Packed in with them were the Blums, the Schuschniggs and Pastor Niemoller. The mood was somber. Bader and Stiller were now accompanied by about twenty SS guards, and ominously they hauled a crate of hand grenades aboard. What on earth for? The war was all but over. Everyone feared the worst.

In another of the buses the prisoners decided to cheer themselves up by singing. It was known as the English bus, although it contained quite a few prisoners beyond the British group of officers. One of them was a German woman the same age as Fey. She, too, was a *Sippenhafte*. But she had a radically different past.

Isa Vermehren was an accordion-playing cabaret singer from Berlin who had cut several records and featured in half a dozen films. As a rising young talent in the 1930s she made her name with a succession of love ballads and sea songs, one of which became a bestseller, and in the early years of the war she went on tours to the front to play to the troops.

But, like Fey, it was the activities of a family member that caused her to fall victim to the Nazis. In her case it was her brother Erich who had marked himself as politically unreliable when he repeatedly refused to join the Hitler Youth and was blocked from taking up a coveted Rhodes scholarship at Oxford on Hitler's personal order. He, too, joined the Catholic Church by way of protest but later managed to get himself posted as a member of the Abwehr to Istanbul. Eventually, in February 1944 he defected to the British along with his wife and fellow agent, the glamorous Countess Elizabeth von Plettenberg, a member of one of Germany's most traditional and distinguished Catholic families.

This double defection finally snapped Hitler's patience with the Abwehr, which he had long suspected — rightly — of harboring dissident sentiments. Coupled with his mounting suspicions about the loyalty of the man who ran it, Admiral Canaris, this prompted him to dissolve the service and turn its functions over to Himmler's SS.

To protect his family from reprisals, Erich carefully disguised his defection as an abduction and arranged in advance with British intelligence agents to be openly "kidnapped" on a public street before being secretly spirited away to safety. But the SS was not fooled. Rumors spread — mistakenly — that the Vermehrens had fled with the Abwehr's codes and an infuriated Himmler decided to set an example. Isa, her parents and another of her brothers were arrested and became the first of the *Sippenhafte*. In April 1944 her parents were sent to Sachsenhausen, while Isa was imprisoned in Ravensbrück before ending up in the bizarre convoy now heading up the Brenner Pass.[26]

Peter Churchill had met her a few days before. She had sought him out after hearing there was a Churchill in the group and asked if it was his wife she had met in Ravensbrück. From his description, Isa immediately knew that it had indeed been Odette. She told him that because of orders issued by the camp's commandant she was known as Frau Schurer, but everyone knew who she really was. Odette was in excellent health and high spirits, she assured Churchill. However, she suggested he should also speak to another of the prisoners who had been in even closer contact with Odette at Ravensbrück. So he did, pulling out of his pocket a photograph of Odette to show the man. It took him some time to recognize her. "Yes, yes . . . it might be she," the man eventually admitted. "People can change so much in prison . . . Forgive me, my dear Churchill." It was like a blow in the stomach. Now, alone with his fears for Odette's safety and health, he could only imagine the worst.[27]

Isa still had her accordion, but she did not lead the singing. Instead, that role was taken by another member of the British contingent, a red-headed Irish sergeant named Thomas Cushing who had been captured at Calais in 1940 during the British Army's frantic retreat to Dunkirk. The larger-than-life "Red" Cushing was a soldier of fortune with a rich Irish brogue and the gift of the gab. "With three or four Guinnesses down my gullet I'm the greatest storyteller since old Paddy Flynn of County Sligo," he once boasted, "and that's gospel."[28] He claimed to have fought for the Irish Republican Army as well as with the US Army in China, Nicaragua and the Philippines. For a while, he said, he had also been a guard at Alcatraz before joining the Lincoln Battalion and fighting in Spain for the Republicans.

After his capture in Calais he had escaped three times before being recruited by the Abwehr, who trained him as a secret agent to be dropped into Britain, where the Irishman planned immediately to turn himself in. But eventually the Gestapo learned of his double game and threw him into a concentration camp. Here, he claimed, he shared his Red Cross parcels with Jacob Stalin, the Soviet dictator's captured son.

Now, he led his bus in a bravura show of carefree confidence while Isa accompanied him on her accordion. The Irishman also proved to be a brilliant drummer, beating out his rhythm, recalled Isa, "on whatever came to hand, suitcases, windows, cooking pots, the heads of the people in front of him and other solid objects." Whenever he ran out of objects he simply shouted, "babababababa . . ."

The bizarre concert reached its climax as the bus arrived at the summit of the Brenner Pass and two dozen voices sang a lusty rendition of "The Boulevard of Broken Dreams," a hit from the 1934 Hollywood musical *Moulin Rouge*. "I walk along the street of sorrow," they sang with feeling, "the boulevard of broken dreams/Where gigolo and gigo-lette/Can take a kiss without regret/So they forget their broken dreams." For Isa, the words carried a special poignancy. For her fiancé was a prisoner of war of the Russians and she had no idea where he was, or even if he was still alive.[29]

Near the top of the pass, Fey's bus broke down, and again they all had to get out and push. There was a full moon, and shrouded by the eerie light, hundreds of dark, silent figures trudged past her along the road. "Some were Italian workers who had been released from their work camps [in Germany]," she recorded, "others had probably escaped from concentration camps. All were slowly making their way back to freedom, shuffling along through that most desolate mountain land-scape." Over the next few weeks, this stream of refugees heading home over the Alps would become an almost unmanageable torrent, with up to six thousand men, women and children crossing over the Brenner each day.[30]

Eventually the bus was fixed and reached the summit, crossing the frontier into Italy and beginning its long, slow descent into the South Tirol. This was territory given to Italy by Austria-Hungary after the First World War but it remained mostly German-speaking.

In the predawn light, even the English bus fell silent. For Isa Vermehren, seeing the inhospitable mountain landscape through the windows only worsened a deepening sense of apprehension. Even the smallest reduction in the speed of the buses spread a feeling of alarm. There was a tangible sense that the hour of decision had come. When they spotted an inn or a village, the mood lightened, but a lonely and desolate hollow inspired dread.

Stiller had assured Best that they were heading for a hotel in the Tirol, where they would be kept until allied troops arrived. But Best

231

was suspicious. If that were true, he wondered, why were Bader and his SS contingent still with them? These were men with a sinister record of eliminating prisoners. And what about the box of grenades?

Sitting close to Fey, "Onkel" Moppel, one of the elderly Stauffenberg cousins, was still wearing his cavalry officer's uniform. He was convinced they were bound for Bolzano, the provincial capital of South Tirol. Here, he assured her, the Nazis would make their infamous last stand.

CHAPTER TWELVE

ALPINE REFUGE

As dawn broke on the morning of Saturday 28 April, the convoy of buses carrying Fey and the others completed its crossing of the Brenner Pass and continued to head in the direction of Bolzano. Then it turned onto a side road and trundled through several small villages before abruptly stopping. After a while it veered right along a narrow road and over a railway crossing before coming to another halt. It was now almost nine o'clock in the morning. They were about a mile outside the small town of Villabassa. Neither Bader nor Stiller appeared to know what was happening. Fey saw the two SS men arguing on the road before they stamped off in the direction of the village. Ominously, sentries armed with automatic weapons took up positions along the road at ten-yard intervals. Léon Blum was convinced their end was imminent. Where? When? How? seemed the only valid questions left to ask.[1]

Fey sat in the bus for hours. Midday came and went. Outside, it was pouring with rain. She had had nothing to eat or drink since leaving the camp at Reichenau the day before. Nor had anyone else, including the guards. As the time passed some of them relaxed and talked about how much they were looking forward to being reunited with their families now that the war was almost over. They appeared to have no more idea than Fey of what was going to happen next. Everyone grew hungrier and thirstier. In late afternoon, the atmosphere changed again. The prisoners were becoming impatient and the guards nervous and restless. What were the SS men up to in the village?

One of Fey's companions was already busy finding out. During the interminable overnight drive through the mountains, Colonel von Bonin had overheard a whispered conversation between two of the SS men sitting at the front of the bus. Thinking that all the prisoners were asleep, they had been discussing what they were going to do about those on their list who had to be liquidated. "Well," said one, "we were ordered to put the bomb under the bus either before or just after the—" Then the noise of the bus drowned out the rest of the sentence. But von Bonin had heard enough. Shortly after Bader and Stiller had set off for Villabassa he used his status as a uniformed Wehrmacht officer to browbeat some of the younger guards into letting him off the bus. Then he followed the two SS officers into the town to find out what was going on.

In another of the buses, Captain Payne Best was also convinced that something sinister was afoot. So he suggested to Thyssen and Schacht that the time had come to try some bribery and asked if they would put up a hundred thousand Swiss francs, which could be offered to the more pliant Stiller to take them to the Swiss frontier. The former industrialist and the ex-Reichsbank director agreed to act as bankers, but then they balked at putting the deal to Stiller. This angered Payne Best, who felt it was time for some of the Germans in the group to take the initiative.

Amid these discussions, a group of cyclists on a morning outing passed by, and they recognized Schuschnigg. (The ex-Austrian Chancellor was a well-known and revered figure in the region.) The cyclists quickly spread word of the convoy and its passengers, and the news reached the ears of the local resistance leader, Dr. Antonio Ducia. Before long, he was organizing billets for the prisoners in houses and inns around the village.

Meanwhile, Bader, Stiller and most of the SS guards were stuffing themselves with sausages and beer at the Hotel Bachmann, a small inn located on the main square. Their plan still was not clear. But whatever they had in mind was suddenly disrupted. Von Bonin had already decided that he had to get word to General von Viettinghof, the commander of German forces in Italy and a friend of his from his days on the General Staff. As he was wondering how to do this, though, he glanced across the square and spotted a group of German officers talking together. It did not take him long to persuade them to allow him to telephone von Viettinghof and alert him to what was happening. The last thing the German commander needed on the very day that he was negotiating the surrender of his forces in Italy was a massacre, so he promised von Bonin that he would take all "appropriate measures."

An hour later, the SS men were still enjoying their lunch when the door of the inn flew open and in walked a Wehrmacht major with a pistol in his hand and a squad of armed soldiers behind him. The astonished SS men had no time to react as the major shouted at them to hand over their weapons. Bader flew into a fury, but he was told abruptly to shut up and make sure his men were disarmed. Sullenly, he obeyed.

With the Wehrmacht now in control, at last the prisoners were safe. The German Army would act as their guardians, not their captors. But they still needed protection in case the SS attempted to recapture them.

Soon afterwards, the other prisoners arrived in the village and bedded down in the various comfortable places found for them by Ducia. Fey and several of the younger women in the group slept on mattresses on the Hotel Bachmann's floor, their stomachs contentedly full after a delicious, piping-hot traditional Tirolean meal served by its staff.

Celebration was in the air. Over the course of the evening, groups of excited German soldiers heading for home drifted into the inn. But some, noted Fey, seemed convinced that the war was not yet over. "Churchill and the Americans are going to join us in an attack on the Russians!" they shouted. Fey felt sure that they knew this was not going to happen, but they were desperate about the fates of their wives, daughters and mothers at Russian hands. "Besides everything else," she wrote, "this pathetic ranting brought home to me the criminality of Hitler and the Nazis against the Germans themselves." As if to confirm this, now that their ordeal was over, Stiller finally confessed that an order had been sent from Himmler's headquarters that on no account should the prisoners be allowed to fall into allied hands. The date for their elimination had been set for 29 April—the very next day.

Payne Best, too, made himself comfortable in the inn. Later in the evening, he slipped down to the kitchen in search of a drink. A couple of the SS guards had remained in the inn, and they were sharing a bottle of wine, so he decided to join them. One of them, Fritz, was already well in his cups and had not yet absorbed the turn of events. Being in turn lachrymose and truculent, he talked sentimentally about his wife and children and about how he would never allow himself to be taken alive.

Then, out of his pocket, he took a piece of paper. "Here is the order for your execution," he told Payne Best: "You won't be alive after tomorrow." He waved it wildly in Payne Best's face. Then, in another emotional turn, he confided, "Herr Best, you are a friend." The plan, he revealed, was to set fire to a building that would eventually be found for the prisoners, then they would be shot as it burned. But shooting was a messy business, Fritz confessed. It was not always quick, as he knew from personal experience. So, when the time came, he would give Payne Best a sign so that the Englishman could get close to him. Then he would give him a quick "*Nackenschluss*"—a shot in the back of the head—and it would all be over in a second.

By this time, Fritz's SS companion had passed out and was lying with his head on the table, while Fritz himself was getting increasingly glassy-eyed and ever more melancholy. His dear wife and children had no idea, he admitted, how many hundreds—no, thousands—of people he had shot during the war, and that was a terrible thing. But it was all the fault of the Jews and the plutocrats in England and America. Hitler was a good man and only wanted peace . . .

As he rambled on, Payne Best slipped out quietly and returned to his room. Fey slept on blissfully, gloriously comfortable on her mattress on the floor.

Their peril was by no means over, however. Other SS units were roaming around in the vicinity, the war was officially not yet over and a safe and secure place still had to be found for the prisoners. To his alarm, early the next day, Payne Best discovered that General Garibaldi and Colonel Ferrero were planning a rising by the local Italian partisans that very night to capture the village and spirit the prisoners away to safety in the mountains.

The idea had already won support from a few members of the British contingent, including Peter Churchill and the RAF escapees, but Payne Best could see only disaster in the plan, which he denounced as "absolutely mad."[2] Garibaldi's local partisans seemed little more than youths who had quickly wrapped red scarves around their necks. They would have no chance at all against the professional and well-armed Wehrmacht contingent.

So he took Garibaldi aside and stressed the dangers. Suppose that things went wrong and people like Blum or Schuschnigg were killed, he pointed out. Imagine the international outcry, and who would be blamed. What would then happen to the South Tirol, only recently handed over to Italy? Such an episode, if seen to be the fault of

Garibaldi and his men, could seriously backfire and affect the future of the region as part of Italy. Besides, added Payne Best, the Wehrmacht had no interest at this stage of the war in harming the prisoners, so why try to move them?

This impassioned appeal persuaded Garibaldi to call off the plan, although not without the bitter disagreement of Colonel Ferrero, who flounced out of the room. At noon, as Fey and the others gathered in the dining room, Payne Best clambered onto a tabletop and announced that they could now all consider themselves free, but he cautioned that for the time being they should remain where they were while arrangements were completed to take them to another hotel, higher up in the mountains. With only a single narrow approach road that could be easily guarded, this would be a safe place to wait for the arrival of allied forces and the official end of the war.

It was Sunday 29 April—the day marked for their death by the SS. Already, Fey was feeling less among strangers and more with friends. The Wehrmacht officer guarding them turned out to be a Major Werner von Alvensleben. Fey quickly discovered that he knew her family and had once even stayed with her parents on the family's estate. By grimmer coincidence, he was also the brother of the SS officer in Udine who had refused to help her after her arrest at Brazzà. "Let's not talk about him!" said von Alvensleben bitterly. "As you can imagine, he's the black sheep of the family. He has always been a Nazi and I only hope for his sake that he doesn't make it through to the end of the war."[3]

In France, meanwhile, Francesca Wilson was finding it a relief occasionally to escape from Granville and forget about the war. One of the UNRRA directors was a retired general and, like herself, from Northumberland. They drove out one day into the countryside. It was even more beautiful than she had expected. "Beech, lime, plane and poplar leaves were shining in the enamel of their fresh leaves," she remembered, "and the air was full of the faint songs and rustles of a spring warm as midsummer." They passed convoys of German prisoners of war out collecting firewood and guarded by black GIs. The countryside of orchards, pastures and plowed fields was placid, dotted with picturesque stone villages and graceful churches that reminded her of her native county and of towns such as Hexham, with its ancient Saxon abbey, and Corbridge on the River Tyne, with its historic Roman connections. As a child, she had spent regular family holidays up on the lonely moors and found comfort in the landscape, with the desolate Roman wall, the sound of complaining plovers on the wind, and the echoes of Meg Merilies from Walter Scott's *Old Mortality*.[4]

Most of her fellow British recruits at Granville were retired army officers, many of them Indian and colonial army men, and there was much talk in the bar at night about Poona and the good old days of the Raj. Others came from local government or civil defense organizations. Given that UNRRA duties involved a great deal of social work, she was surprised to find she was one of only a handful of women.

"It is difficult," she had written earlier that year in a pamphlet for the Quakers, "to choose the right people for relief work abroad. Upheavals attract the unbalanced as well as those with constructive powers. People who have made a mess of their own lives in their own country are eager to leave it," she warned, "and they may get excellent testimonials from friends who think they will make good somewhere else — and prefer to see them there." Drug addicts, alcoholics, criminals fleeing from the law, all "worm their way into relief agencies, along with a miscellany of adventurers desperate to escape the confines imposed on them by the war." A spirit of adventure was all very well, she added, as well as the obvious need for specialist qualifications, but what was required above all, she stressed, was charity, "in its old-fashioned and Biblical meaning."[5]

But at Granville, for the most part, the women she met had been well chosen. Mostly between the ages of thirty and forty-five, they brought valuable experience as billeting officers for evacuees, welfare workers in factories, child guidance experts, and organizers of rest homes and shelters during the Blitz. There were also a large number of Frenchwomen. Some had worked with refugees during the great debacle of the French collapse in 1940; others had helped the resistance; and yet others had valuable experience behind the lines of the First French Army in Alsace. In addition, there was a handful of Americans. Few knew any foreign language, which was a handicap, but Francesca had to admit that they had far more professional experience in social work than most of the others and proved first-rate administrators.

However, as April drew to an end and the hour for action got closer, anxiety grew among all the UNRRA volunteers. Francesca wondered if the others in her team would prove congenial. And as there were more than a dozen nationalities being trained at the camp, she had doubts that she would even be able to talk to her teammates.

By now, in preparation for an imminent departure, they had been moved five miles south to the small seaside town of Jullouville. Instead of the comforts of the Hotel Normandie, Francesca found herself immured in a bleak and squalid old school building. There was no privacy, they all slept together in huge drafty spaces that resembled dismal train station waiting rooms, and the toilets without seats distressed the Americans. Team lists began appearing on the noticeboards and were eagerly scanned. Afterwards, Francesca heard murmuring and rumbles and sometimes muffled sobs in the corner of the room. Occasionally, faced with rebellion, the center's staff would reluctantly shuffle the teams. All in all, Francesca was glad to put April behind her.[6]

On Sunday 29 April, four days after Fey von Hassell had left the horrors of its concentration camp behind her, advanced elements of General Patch's US Seventh Army moved into Dachau. In Milan, Mussolini's battered and mutilated body was hanging next to that of his mistress in the Piazzale Loreto. In Berlin, Adolf Hitler was preparing to dictate his last will and testament.

It was a gray, sunless and freezing morning as the American infantry cautiously advanced through the town of Dachau, keeping a lookout for snipers. But its streets were deserted and there was no resistance. Advanced patrols pushed on towards the camp itself. One of them approached it from the south, bypassing the main gate.

Dachau was the largest concentration camp to be liberated by American forces. By now, the horrors of Buchenwald were known to virtually everyone, but what the GIs next discovered was even worse than any of them had expected. On a spur off the main rail line to Munich they stumbled on thirty-nine stationary boxcars. Usually they were used for transporting coal. As they neared, they were overwhelmed by the stench of death. All the cars were piled high with rotting human corpses. In total, they contained the bodies of some 2,300 men, women and children. All were either totally naked or clad in their striped blue-and-white concentration camp clothes smeared with blood and excrement. Most had starved to death while being transported from Buchenwald nearly three weeks before. The train had reached the siding only two days prior to the arrival of the Americans, and the few prisoners who had survived the journey had been shot or clubbed to death by the SS.

The GIs were stunned into silence and disbelief by what they saw. "We had seen men in battle blown apart, burnt to death and die in many different ways," recalled one of them, "but we were never prepared for this. Several of the dead lay there with their eyes open. It seemed they were looking at us saying, 'what took you so long?' " Some of the infantrymen wept. Others began screaming and shouting with rage. "It's haunted me for thirty six years," another GI recalled long afterwards. "I mean, who are they? What's their name? What nationality are they? What is their religious faith? Why are they there?"[7] Cries of "Let's kill every one of those bastards" and "Don't take the SS alive" went up.

Most of the SS guards had slipped out of the camp the day before, but a few remained. Four emerged from a hiding-place, their hands raised, but an American lieutenant simply herded them into one of the boxcars and emptied his pistol into them.

Meanwhile, other American units approached the main gate of the camp. As they got close, though, machine-gun fire broke out from the watchtowers. Excited prisoners milling about in the large square began to charge the towers and for a few moments the guards turned their fire on them as well. In the end, the US infantry rushed the towers and most of the guards were killed. The official history says that American soldiers tried to protect the guards from the prisoners, but at least one eyewitness account claims that in their fury they shot them.

Close to the camp's infirmary, another SS group was rounded up. The Americans stood them against a wall while a machine-gun was set up to keep them in order. Thinking they were about to be shot, the SS men panicked and started to run. Someone shouted, "Fire!" and the machine-gun burst into life. In the hail of fire, seventeen of the SS men were killed.

The camp still housed some thirty-one thousand prisoners existing on a meagre six hundred calories a day. In compliance with Himmler's orders, the Germans had begun to evacuate the camp several days before the Americans arrived. Just two days earlier, a group of over six thousand prisoners had been marched out, supposedly to help build the Alpine Redoubt. But only about fifteen miles from Munich, in a secluded area, their guards opened fire and massacred them. Only sixty survived.

Now, the remnants in the camp were close to death from starvation and typhus. There was no electricity or water, and sanitation was non-existent. Eventually, though, the firing died down. In front of the main gate, with its arched motto "*Arbeit Macht Frei*" (Work Makes You Free), the commandant of the camp officially surrendered to the Americans. After this, the prisoners were told they were free. "First American comes through the entrance," scribbled one of the prisoners in his note-book. "Dachau free!!! Indescribable happiness. Insane howling."

Many desperate inmates tried to rush the barbed wire, but an American officer told them that they would have to stay in place until food, water and medicine arrived. "Then I saw bodies flying through the air with the prisoners tearing at them with their hands," he reported. "[They] were killing the informers among them. They actually tore them to pieces with their bare hands."

Just beyond the prisoner enclosure stood the crematoria and torture chambers. In one of these buildings lay the rotting corpses of another twelve hundred prisoners, and beyond the crematoria the Americans found another two thousand bodies. They had been thrown into a ditch by the SS men, who had not had time to burn them before fleeing. Only after a war crimes investigation team visited the camp a few days later were all the bodies that had been found in the camp removed for burial.

One of the first US war correspondents to enter Dachau was the twenty-four-year-old *New York Herald Tribune* reporter Marguerite Higgins. "Are you American?" shouted out one of the prisoners, and she nodded. Pandemonium broke out. "Tattered, emaciated men weeping, yelling, and shouting 'Long Live America' swept toward the gate in a mob," she wrote.

She then inspected a crematorium. It contained hooks on which the SS had hung their prisoners to flog them, as well as a grotesque mural painted by the guards themselves depicting a headless man in uniform with the SS insignia on his collar sitting astride a bulbous pig into which he was digging his spurs. She was also shown the exact spot where pris-oners had knelt to be shot in the back of the neck. There, just ten days before, General Charles Delestraint, the head of General de Gaulle's Secret Army in France, had been executed. He had been captured by the Gestapo in the summer of 1943 and kept in quarters close to those housing Léon Blum and his wife. He was led to his death believing at first that he was simply being transferred to another camp.[8]

The American troops who liberated Dachau had been temporarily diverted from their primary mission of occupying Munich — what

Eisenhower described as "the cradle of the Nazi beast"—which lay fifteen miles to the south. "I am more attached to this city than to any
other spot of earth in this world," Hitler wrote in *Mein Kampf*. Since the
party's birth there in the revolutionary aftermath of the First World
War, the city had assumed paramount ideological and emotional
importance for the Nazi movement. After coming to power, Hitler had
bestowed two honorific titles upon it—*"Haupstadt der Deutschen Kunst"*
(Capital of German Art) and *"Haupstadt der Bewegung"* (Capital of the
Movement)—a move that reflected Hitler's love for the city where he
had spent so much of his youth, and which helped transform it into the
central pilgrimage site of the Third Reich's political religion. The hon-
ors were physically embodied in several new monumental buildings,
such as the Haus der Deutschen Kunst (House of German Art) and the
Nazi Party offices, which were constructed as vast neoclassical palaces
on the Konigsplatz. In 1937 the city was also declared one of the Third
Reich's five *"Führerstadte"* (Führer Cities). If not interrupted by war, the
project would have resulted in a massive program of urban renewal,
including the building of Hitler's own mausoleum.[9]

So far, the American advance through Bavaria towards the city had
met with little resistance because the German forces were under-
manned and ill-equipped. In many of the picturesque villages the
inhabitants flew white flags and the American tanks simply roared
through and on to the next small dot on the map. But where the
Germans did make a stand, tanks, artillery and planes simply and
instantly reduced buildings to rubble. The message quickly got
through. Soon, virtually all of the villages were flying the white
flag.[10]

The pattern of no resistance also appeared in the towns. At
Memmingen, the Americans sent ahead a contingent of burgermeisters
from towns that had already been captured to warn that only white
flags would save the city from instant destruction. No one fought back.
At Landsberg, where Hitler had written *Mein Kampf* after being imprisoned following the abortive 1923 Munich *putsch*, the Hungarian
garrison simply lined up in parade-ground formation to surrender—
and there was no struggle at all. At Augsburg, the German commander
was given five minutes to surrender, and he dutifully marched his
forces in good order out of a city already bedecked with hundreds of
white flags. Here too, for the first time, evidence began to emerge of
some internal resistance to the Nazis. A group calling itself the

"Freedom Party of Augsburg" had managed to reach an American regiment by telephone to announce that the city wanted to surrender, and some other civilians had even led a US column to the bunker housing the German commander and top city officials.

Bavaria, the cradle of Nazism, appeared to be crumbling without protest. But Munich proved a tougher nut to crack, although even here some internal resistance to the Nazis manifested itself.

On Saturday 28 April, two days before the first US troops reached the city, an attempted coup took place spearheaded by a small group calling itself "Freedom Action Bavaria." Led by a Wehrmacht captain from a company of army interpreters, it also included a handful of lawyers, professors, civil servants and physicians. Joined by other groups, some genuinely anti-Nazi, others simply war weary, and yet others purely opportunistic, the uprising began at dawn.

At first, it met with success, capturing two radio stations, and the group's leader was able to broadcast an appeal for citizens to join them. Suddenly, the white and blue flag of Bavaria appeared all over the city and people began to pour into the streets amid rumors that Hitler was dead and the war was over. Within hours, however, the uprising collapsed. The rebels failed to capture the Gauleiter of Munich, Paul Giesler, and could not even persuade General Ritter von Epp, the chief Reich executive in Bavaria, to support them. Nor did they succeed in seizing the city's military or Nazi Party headquarters. Meanwhile, from an SS barracks in the north of the city, loyal Nazis offered fierce resistance. By two o'clock in the afternoon Giesler had reasserted control over the city, and the leaders of the coup fled in a car bearing SS number plates.[11]

Yet Munich was in no position to defend itself against four American divisions. The Wehrmacht had left the city to its fate, and it was now only hard-line Nazi zealots who were ready to resist. "For most of the day," writes the official historian of the Americans' last offensive,

it was a question of pouring in heavy artillery fire, attacking behind smoke across city streets, dodging deadly fire from anti-aircraft guns or persistent machine guns—all the usual accoutrements the men had come to expect in clearing rubble-strewn German cities. Even as a big white streamer flew from the highest building in Munich, troops from the 45th Division were fighting from room to room in the SS caserne to dislodge die-hard defenders.[12]

In the chaos of these last few hours, a mob stormed Hitler's Führer Museum, where more than seven hundred mostly looted paintings from all over Europe were stored, including the entire Schloss Collection, taken from a private collector in France.[13]

The city that American forces entered early on Monday 30 April was the hollowed-out ruin glimpsed briefly by Fey von Hassell as she was driven through its streets in the back of the truck evacuating her from Dachau. Like most German cities, it had been hit hard by allied air raids. In the previous two years alone it had been bombed at least sixty-six times. Between a third and a half of all its buildings were heavily damaged or destroyed. In the city center, the Altstadt, the figure rose to 60 percent. Its oldest church, the Peterskirche, built in 1169, had suffered severe damage to its tower, roof and nave, as had the Frauenkirche (Cathedral of Our Lady), with its famous twin onion domes. The historic seat of the Wittelsbach dynasty that had ruled Bavaria until 1918, the Residenz, had lost most of its roofing, and on the city's main square, the Marienplatz, the old City Hall lay completely wrecked. The Wittelsbacher Palais, built by King Ludwig I for his son, the Crown Prince Maximilian, and used during the war both as Gestapo headquarters and as a satellite camp for Dachau, had been completely gutted by fire; only its outer walls remained standing. The central railway station was little more than a tangle of twisted metal.

"I had imagined it would be terrible, but it was even worse," recorded the writer Klaus Mann, eldest son of Thomas, when he returned to the city a few days later for the first time since going into exile in 1933, "Munich no longer exists. The entire city center from the main train station to the Odeonsplatz is composed only of ruins . . . all the streets that I knew so intimately had become . . . horribly disfigured." The futile last-ditch resistance by SS troops had made things even worse, as the only way to flush them out was by concentrated heavy shelling.[14]

One of the first US soldiers to enter the city was a twenty-seven-year-old lieutenant who spent much of the morning with his company advancing at a snail's pace through deserted streets and edging cautiously round buildings not knowing what to expect. "Even if we didn't see anybody at all," he noted, "we never knew what was hiding around the next corner. We didn't have any dogs or tanks or anything like that. Just jeeps. My soldiers had rifles. I had a pistol. That's all."

It was two o'clock in the afternoon by the time he reached the Marienplatz.

There was a bunch of people. Really quite a few. Most of them were made up of very old people who were too old for the *Volkssturm*. We were greeted as the great liberators of the city, which, to be honest, really made me angry at the time. This was, after all, the capital of the movement. It was where the Nazi party got its start and where its main propaganda organ the *Volkischer Beobachter* was headquartered. And they were now happy to be "liberated"?

On the opposite side of the square stood a police station, and the American lieutenant marched in to confiscate their weapons. Prepared for the worst, to his surprise he was greeted with military salutes and found that the weapons had already been boxed up and were ready to be taken away. With immaculate efficiency, each of the more than a hundred surrendered pistols carried two tags, one bearing its number, the other the name of the officer to whom it had been issued. The official handing over requested, with scrupulous bureaucratic formality, a receipt.

It was an ironic moment. For with just such bureaucratic nicety, the lieutenant, born in Hamburg and brought up in Berlin as a Protestant, had been identified as a Jew, expelled from the Boy Scouts when it was transformed into the Hitler Youth, and forced to flee his native Germany for America after the Nazi seizure of power. Now, at virtually the same moment, Hitler, still obsessed by the Jews, was about to pull the trigger on his Walther.[15]

The day Munich fell, the British newspaper the *Daily Telegraph* published a report by its special correspondent Noel Panter from the Swiss town of St. Margarethen, across the border from Bavaria. Headlined "Nazi Chiefs' Wild Flight to Southern Germany," it told of confusion and panic as fleeing Gauleiters ran out of petrol and desperately sought hiding-places in small Bavarian villages. One SS official sought sanctuary with a Catholic priest but made the mistake of choosing one who had been interned in Dachau for several months. "I can only hear your confession," said the priest, whereupon the SS man knocked him unconscious with the butt of his revolver before fleeing on a bicycle. Meanwhile, an angry crowd slashed all the tires on his car. Bejeweled and well-dressed wives of Nazi officials tried desperately to barter their wealth for peasant clothing to disguise themselves. The entire border area, reported Panter, was packed with German officers who now regarded the war as finished.[16]

South across the Alps, the weather in Villabassa was cold and unpleasant. Fey von Hassell spent most of the day keeping warm in the cozy comfort of the Hotel Bachmann, enjoying her first day of freedom. Except that it was a strange, hybrid kind of freedom. Thankfully, Bader and his dangerous contingent of SS men had finally disappeared. But now she felt trapped by circumstance. She had no money or food, no news from home, and only a very shaky idea of what was happening in the wider world. Separated from her children, she found her predicament agonizingly hard. She was desperate to start looking for them, but how? At this stage of the war, with Germany in total collapse, postal and telephone communications across Europe were non-existent and she had no independent transport of her own. In any case, most land routes were impassable, either smashed or roadblocked. And virtually no trains were running anywhere.

To Captain Payne Best, trying to reassure her and the other 136 men, women and children whose ages ranged from four to seventy-three, they resembled passengers in an old sailing ship crossing the ocean. "We had mutinied and removed the officers and crew," he wrote, "but did not yet know how our further course was to be set nor who would navigate."[17]

Shortly after five o'clock in the afternoon some buses arrived. Once again they all clambered in. Then they set off up into the mountains. It was a short, steep drive that eventually deposited them in front of a large resort hotel on the edge of a lake. They were five thousand feet above sea level and it was snowing lightly. The hotel, a huge, rambling, old chalet-style building, was the Prager Wildsee — or, to give it its Italian name, the Lago di Braies. It had been closed for the winter, and was consequently freezing cold. On closer inspection it was discovered that the heating plant was frozen solid and consisted of a mess of burst pipes. Anyway, there was no fuel. Log fires were quickly lit in the dining room and kitchen, but they made little difference — the place still felt like a refrigerator.

Nevertheless, to Fey, it appeared like bliss. An advance group had arrived earlier to assign everyone a room, trying as best they could to keep national groupings close together. For the first time in what felt like a lifetime she had a proper bed and a room all to herself. It overlooked the lake, which was still and silent, with not a ripple troubling its pure, glacier-fed, emerald-green waters. All around stood magnificent pine trees. Beyond rose jagged peaks that seemed to enclose her in a safe and comforting embrace. She could hardly tear herself away from the window. As she gazed, entranced at the scene, she realized that her beloved Brazzà was little more than sixty miles away. Briefly, she was tempted to set out for home on her own, but she found she lacked the courage. She had been captive too long. For the moment at least, she had lost the nerve to act on her own.

CHAPTER THIRTEEN

"DEATH FLED"

Fred Warner and his SOE group had now reached the heartland of the feared Alpine Redoubt. They had taken off from the airfield in Italy on the day that Fey von Hassell left Dachau in her convoy of covered trucks. It was now two o'clock in the morning, a bright and moonlit night, and Warner had been flying for three hours. Below him, he could see incredible snow-capped peaks. At any other time he would have enjoyed the view, but tonight he was lost in his thoughts, wondering what dangers awaited him on his mission and whether he would even come out of it alive. It was freezing cold inside the Liberator but he tried to get some sleep.

Apart from the aircrew and the dispatcher, whose job was to see that their parachutes were properly fixed and that they jumped at the right time, there were seven men in the plane. One was an American OSS agent bound for a solo mission unknown to the rest of them. The Americans ran their own separate operations and had recently sent two teams to search for evidence about the Nazi last stand, one of which was at work close to Innsbruck.[1] SOE had nine similar groups in waiting.

The rest of the plane's passengers were British agents on two separate missions: Fred's group of four, code-named "Historian," and a two-man team code-named "Duncery." This was led by Hans Schweiger, who had once been a lawyer in Vienna and now went by the name "Stevens." Its other member was a younger man who had just recently celebrated his twenty-fourth birthday. Alone among the SOE agents he had declined to change his real name. There were two reasons for this: first, he believed that if he was caught by the Nazis blowing something up he would be executed regardless of what name he gave them; and second, he was proud of his heritage. He had good reason to be, too. For Walter Freud was the grandson of Sigmund Freud.

Along with the rest of the Freud family he had been forced to leave Vienna after the Anschluss of 1938. Eventually, he joined his father — the eldest of Sigmund's sons — and the rest of the Freud clan in Highgate, London. Like Fred Warner, he was briefly interned as an enemy alien before joining the Pioneer Corps and then being recruited by SOE. He qualified as a wireless operator and was sent out to Italy, where he continued his training alongside Warner and the others. In his pocket he carried vital radio codes. The transmitter-receiver he would be using to keep in touch with base would be dropped in a separate container.

The red light came on. They were approaching the target and would parachute in two groups of three. Warner watched as the first trio took up their positions round the hole in the floor of the plane, their legs hanging down into space. Then on came the green light. The dispatcher shouted "Go!" and they disappeared, one by one. Freud went first. When they landed, they would signal with a torch if it was safe for the others to follow. The plane made a short turn and headed back to the drop zone. Fred readied himself by the hole. The green light came on again. He jumped.

Above him, he heard the familiar and comforting swish of his parachute flapping. A little later he heard the engines of the plane getting louder and closer again as it circled a third and final time to drop the containers with all their heavy equipment and wireless sets. Then the noise faded away and he was alone in the sky.

He looked down and had his first shock. He had obviously been dropped at a higher altitude than planned. It should have been at about a thousand feet but he estimated he was at seven or eight thousand. The second surprise came when he tried to get his bearings. In the clear moonlight he could see a river running through the valley into which he was drifting. There was also a railway line running alongside it, and he could see a fair-sized village close by. He had spent hours poring over detailed aerial reconnaissance maps of the dropping zone, and none of the things he saw now should have been there. He was in the wrong place.

Worse was to follow. He made a nice, soft landing, collapsed his parachute quickly, then hid it and all his unnecessary gear, such as the jump suit, under a nearby tree. So far, so good. No one had spotted him and not a dog had barked, even though he had landed close to a large farmhouse. But where were the others? He had no idea. He climbed a small hill but it was covered with trees and he could not see anyone or anything close by. Quickly he realized that he was not only in the wrong place but on his own. He decided that he had to move quickly to put as much distance as possible between himself and the dropping zone. Evidence of their arrival was bound to be found soon, and farmers rose early.

Freud was in a similar position. He had drifted a considerable distance away from all the others and did not even bother to try to find them, or indeed any of his equipment, in the dark. Instead, he found some shelter, unrolled his sleeping bag, and tried to get some sleep.

Fortunately, the others had all landed close together. But some lost their personal gear, and to their horror they discovered that the containers with their demolition kits and wireless sets had got entangled in the chimney stack of a house in a village which should not have been there. They would have to be abandoned. The four men decided that the only thing to do was to combine forces. For a while, they searched for Warner, but then gave up. They did not bother to look for Freud, who had last been spotted drifting far off course. Having lost their demolition material, they abandoned any ideas of sabotage and chose instead to seize the aerodrome at Zeltweg.

Meanwhile, Warner had to decide on his next move. The best idea was first to find a safe hiding-place higher up, away from the village, so for the next few hours he climbed straight up through the heavily forested mountainside. Now he understood why the SOE training had been so tough.

He had realized pretty quickly that he had been drafted into SOE and not the commandos when he was sent to Arisaig House, a grand old lodge on the rugged coast of the Scottish Highlands. Sure enough, the course was physically demanding and included most of the commando skills learned by the likes of Bryan Samain, but it also focused on sabotage skills, such as how to handle and make explosives, and he and his fellow trainees were encouraged to speak German among themselves.

They were also supplied with the latest German Army magazines to keep them up to date with the Wehrmacht slang. Once, he was even sent on a burglary course.

Most of the time he stayed close to his friend, Eric Rhodes. Although born in Hamburg, his teammate was more Scottish than German as his mother was a Scot, his father an ex-German naturalized Briton, and he had spent most of his life in Aberdeen. Their last large exercise had been a "secret mission" to Birmingham in April 1944. Provided with false papers and fake personal stories, they were ordered to penetrate the railway yards and "destroy" key installations using a minimum of explosives. Afterwards, they reported back their results in code via a Dead Letter Box (DLB) which they set up in a public lavatory. In the lucky event that they were not arrested after five days, they had permission to report back to an agreed "safe house."

Warner and another trainee stayed in a boarding house, survived for five days and were feeling pleased with themselves. Then, in the middle of the night, they were rudely awoken by two hard-faced detectives who gave Warner a good grilling and made him undress before subjecting him to a thorough body search. They were looking for his codes. Cleverly, though, he had rolled them up into a tight little ball and hung them outside his window at the end of a length of black thread. In the dark, he reckoned, no one would find them. He was right. Afterwards, he was heartily congratulated and given a slap-up breakfast. It had, he decided, "been a most useful exercise."

Finally, he went to London to be kitted out with continental-style clothing with no tell-tale labels of any kind. One evening, he and the others went out for a meal at a Chinese restaurant in Leicester Square. They were all wearing uniforms displaying the parachute badge on the left sleeve of their battle dress. They ordered, and after a long wait asked the Chinese waiter when they would be served. "Don't you know there's a war on?" he replied cheekily. As one man, they lifted him off the ground and shouted, "We know!" When they let him down, he fled outside and they did not see him again.[2]

Now, behind enemy lines in Austria, he stumbled on a small wood-cutter's hut in a clearing. Here he rested, dried out his clothes and boots, and nibbled on his emergency rations. The sun came up, it grew hot, and his confidence began to return. Later in the day, he felt even better. Far above him, glinting in the sun, he spotted scores of allied aircraft heading into Germany.

When darkness fell, he took off his boots and jacket but kept on everything else, including the belt with his .45 Colt automatic and a small ammunition pouch. This was basic SOE training — stay prepared. He had also been at work with his compass and calculated they had been dropped about twenty miles away from the designated dropping zone. He worked out the location of the prearranged emergency rendezvous point and so knew in which direction he would take off the next day. Then he fell deeply asleep.

Suddenly, in the pitch black, he was wide awake. Outside, he could hear men's voices. Then someone tried to open the door. In no time he was out of his sleeping bag, flat on the floor, gun in hand. "Who's there?" he said in German, trying to sound as nonchalant as possible. The reply came back immediately and to the point in a volley of shots.

"I heard the bullets hitting the wooden rear wall of the hut behind my back," he recorded. "Dust and bits of bark were flying all around me. Staying on the ground and not getting up had saved my life." He answered the first volley by firing two or three rounds straight ahead, out of the door, which was now partly open, then a couple more out of each of the hut's side windows. He could hear the shots echoing around the mountainside, and saw flashes spurting out of the barrel of his Colt. Then the firing stopped. He quickly reloaded his weapon and heard the sound of running feet. For a split second he thought they were heading towards him. Then, with relief, he realized they were fading away.[3]

As soon as he felt safe, he left the hut and headed as rapidly as he could for several hours through the trees in the direction he had planned the day before. Once again, he found an unoccupied old hut. This one was full of dry hay. He unrolled his sleeping bag and soon fell asleep.

Several hours later he awoke to find that it was snowing heavily. It kept on falling for the next few days, but it was warm in his shelter and he decided to wait there until the snow stopped. The only visitors he had were a few deer that appeared one evening on the edge of the clearing. Eventually, though, he began to run out of food. Far below him he could see through his field glasses a road with plenty of traffic including military vehicles mingling with horse-drawn carts. By now, he had abandoned any thought of making it to the emergency rendezvous. Too much time had passed and there was little chance of meeting up with the others. With no radio, no food and in enemy country, Warner was definitely on his own.

So was Walter Freud. He had spent the week looking for the others, sheltering every night with a different peasant family in isolated mountain farmhouses. Sometimes, people were afraid of him, offering him soup with shaking hands. On other occasions, they welcomed him almost as though he were expected. No one ever questioned his identity and he never offered any explanation. But it was obvious he was a stranger — if nothing else, his strong Viennese accent made that clear. In every farmhouse where he stayed or begged a meal, he encountered only young mothers with their small children, and grandparents. Everyone else had been mobilized into the German war machine. All the men of military age, which by this time in Nazi Germany meant between sixteen and sixty, were serving with the armed forces or in the *Volkssturm*. Single women were working in munitions factories, and adolescents were on anti-aircraft duty. It seemed obvious to Freud that this was not the material for any resistance force — Nazi or otherwise.

Once, he made a bad mistake. On one of the paths through the woods he encountered a truck collecting wood. He asked the driver for a lift and the man agreed, indicating he should climb into the back. Freud responded with a cheerful "OK" in English. Immediately he knew he had made a possibly fatal slip of exactly the kind that SOE training had tried to eliminate. But the man merely gave him a long and curious look before driving on. Freud took extra care to say "*Auf Wiedersehen*" when they finally parted company.

At another time, he panicked after thinking he had lost his rucksack. He put it down under a tree while he clambered to the top of a small rise to get his bearings. When he came down again, he could not find it. Everything he needed to survive was in it, principally his sleeping bag. Without that, he would freeze to death. He began to dart from tree to tree looking for the kit, getting more and more frantic. Then he got a grip on himself. He returned to the top of the rise and made his way slowly down, walking backwards. At last, to his immense relief, he found the rucksack. He never let it out of his sight again.

With him, he had a small radio receiver, a much less sophisticated piece of kit than the transmitter-receiver the others had abandoned close to the drop site. However, with it he was able to keep up with news from the war and learned about the rapid allied breakthrough in northern Italy. Guessing that British troops would soon be entering Austria, he also abandoned any idea of making it back to find the others. Instead, he decided to head for the aerodrome at Zeltweg. If nothing else, he could claim it on behalf of His Britannic Majesty.[4]

By the last day of April, one thing was becoming transparently clear to all those in the mountains: the Alpine Redoubt was a mirage, and it was dissolving as rapidly as the snows in the strong spring sunshine. Fey von Hassell and her fellow ex-hostages, who had long feared elimination during some desperate last-ditch stand by the Nazis, were now securely in the hands of Wehrmacht forces in Italy, who in turn were awaiting official implementation of the already-signed surrender. During his week in the Austrian mountains, Fred Warner had encountered little more than a frightened and trigger-happy woodcutter and a herd of grazing deer. Walter Freud had seen mostly women and children keeping home and hearth together. And while the rest of the SOE groups had been warned by locals of individual SS or Nazi Party zealots, they were also meeting local resistance leaders who were willing to help them.

Soon after setting off, they met a friendly farmer who warned them about Nazis in the neighborhood and suggested a route they could take. It took them past a hut in the woods being guarded by three German soldiers. As George Bryant thought it might be a Werewolf hideout, they gave it a wide berth. Eventually, going ahead to scout out the ground, he found a woman who proved friendly and anti-Nazi and said all she wanted was to have her daughter back home from her anti-aircraft duties in Linz. But, she warned him, she worked at a local inn where the family was Nazi and ran another inn nearby where Himmler had dined a short time before. The SOE men decided not to linger and moved on.

In general, they found the civilians friendly and definitely sick of the Nazis. Indeed, they could see that the momentum for restoring an independent Austria was gathering pace. Already in Vienna, Karl Renner, the Social Democratic Chancellor of Austria after the First World War, had proclaimed the creation of an independent Austrian government. And in northern Italy, Fey von Hassell had seen with her own eyes the enthusiasm that greeted Schuschnigg, Austria's last independent Chancellor, in South Tirol. Nowhere was there any serious sign of a Nazi last stand.[5]

It was, indeed, a chimera. Despite Hitler's last-minute instructions from the bunker, he had never entertained any serious plans for an

254

Alpine Redoubt. Even to talk of one, he frequently thundered, smacked of defeatism. Yet the idea had caught fire with the allies and significantly affected their strategy over the last two months of fighting. Why had that happened? The answer lay in a sequence of events that had begun several months before.

The small Austrian town of Bregenz lies on the frontier with Switzerland close to Lake Constance, a historically and strategically important road and rail junction. Here, throughout the war, the SS maintained a branch of the Sicherheitsdienst (SD), its security and intelligence service. Its principal task was to act as a courier station for secret reports coming into the Third Reich from Switzerland.

In September 1944, the office received an especially rewarding package. Inside was a lengthy American diplomatic report that had been intercepted on its way from Zurich to Washington. Its content was similar to the OSS report filed that same month by "Wild Bill" Donovan to President Roosevelt: namely, an extended discussion of the dangers of an Alpine Redoubt. The report soon ended up in Berlin, and was followed by others in a similar vein.

Himmler immediately spotted an opportunity. If the allies could be induced to believe in the reality of the redoubt, and the fact that it could hold out for a couple of years, this could be hugely beneficial to the Nazis. There was even the chance that the Americans and British would seek a negotiated peace, which would in turn provoke a split with the Soviets. In that way, Himmler fantasized, victory might yet be seized from the jaws of defeat.

Goebbels also got in on the act, although for very different reasons. Here, he saw an opportunity to reinforce Hitler's public vow never to surrender—a promise that was targeted as much at the German population as against the allies. Early in 1945, he set up a special unit to spread rumors about the redoubt and feed tantalizing tidbits to a hungry allied and neutral press. The themes of the stories were always the same: "impregnable positions, massive supplies carefully hidden in bomb proof caves, underground factories, and, of course, elite units of troops to man the whole bastion."[6] A credulous Western press, not to mention receptive allied analysts, fell for it. The SD joined in, leaking phoney blueprints and bogus intelligence to sources it knew were feeding the Americans.

These Nazi maneuvers worked exactly as planned. One typical result appeared in *Collier's* magazine in January 1945. In a detailed article, the author outlined a gigantic post-defeat guerrilla warfare campaign being planned at Bad Aussee, high up in the Austrian Alps, about fifty miles from Berchtesgaden. Here, he claimed, the cream of the SS and the Hitler Youth were being trained as Werewolves. Eventually, ran the story, a secret headquarters would be set up even higher in a special redoubt in the mountains. It depicted the mastermind of the scheme as Ernst Kaltenbrunner, Himmler's deputy.

Like the Alpine Redoubt, a Werewolf movement designed to fight on after a German defeat was nothing but an illusion. But this idea, too, began to corrupt intelligence assessments at Eisenhower's headquarters. As the allied armies seriously began to penetrate Germany in 1945, the myth of the redoubt and fears of the Werewolves gathered almost unstoppable momentum. Himmler invariably appeared as the mastermind, the complex and well organized provisions typical both of his demonic skill and the last-ditch fanaticism of his SS followers.[7]

In truth, however, by the spring of 1945 Himmler and the SS were neither of these things. By now, the SS chief was indecisive and close to being a nervous wreck, talking feverishly one minute of negotiations and the next wildly promising a determined campaign of eleventh-hour fighting. Ironically, having fostered the myth of the redoubt to fool the allies, he appeared sometimes to be seduced by it himself as he desperately sought a way out of the coming collapse. As for the SS, it was far from being the precision tool imagined by the allies that Himmler could wield at will. It was riven by intrigue, plots and counterplots. For instance, two of Himmler's principal subordinates, Schellenberg and Kaltenbrunner, were firmly at each other's throats.

After briefly flirting with the idea of the Alpine Redoubt, Kaltenbrunner had promptly abandoned it after a meeting with Hitler, who had mesmerized him, not for the first time, with his fanatical conviction that victory was still possible, if only he had the will. "You need do nothing more than believe," he told his faltering fellow Austrian, "I still have the ways and means to conclude the war victoriously!"[8]

Unfortunately for the allies, their intelligence, while normally excellent, failed to identify these inner divisions and the desperate scramblings of Himmler and his SS deputies to save their skins. The reason for this was that despite many brilliant triumphs in breaking German ciphers, by April 1945 the Bletchley Park code-breakers lacked any clear insider knowledge of what was happening in the inner councils of the SS. The intercepts of Abwehr communications, which had proved so valuable earlier in the war, had dried up after it was subsumed into the SS and new ciphers were introduced. All that allied analysts could do was feed small snippets of intelligence, sometimes accurate in themselves, but also manufactured by the Nazis, into a largely predetermined picture of what was happening—and that included badly mistaken assumptions about the place the Alpine Redoubt held in Hitler's mind and the hard-line ideological commitment of the SS leaders.

There were skeptics among the allies, even at the highest level, but after the costly intelligence failure over the surprise attack in the Ardennes in December 1944, no one was prepared to discount the possibility and risk another disaster. Once the image of the redoubt had been planted in allied minds, it festered and grew like a cancer. Nazi opportunism fueled a major allied misconception.

Ironically, though, during these last days of April, explicit references to the Alpine Redoubt began to appear for the first time in messages decoded at Bletchley Park. These stemmed not from the SS, but from General Winter. The Wehrmacht officer had loyally proceeded to Bavaria as instructed by Hitler to prepare an "inner fortress" in the Alps as a last bulwark of fanatical resistance. This was the only time that Hitler himself ever mentioned the notion, and it was clearly a hurried improvisation that was hopelessly too late.

As soon as he reached Bavaria, Winter realized that all hopes of creating a redoubt were useless, but he still tried to implement some of the measures that Hitler had ordered, either out of conviction or because he wanted to appear loyal to the last. His radio messages reporting back to Berlin were intercepted by the allies and of course reinforced their belief in the redoubt's reality. On Sunday 29 April, the day that the German armies in northern Italy and western Austria capitulated, Winter warned Hitler that a fighting withdrawal of the German Army from Munich would involve the loss of troops intended for the redoubt. The following day, he told Kesselring about various locations he had chosen to serve as headquarters for the fortress.

As if this were not enough, intercepted messages from Himmler appeared to clinch matters. The day after the allies rejected the SS chief's peace offer, he sent a message to Gottlob Berger, his deputy in Bavaria, calling on him to collect together all SS forces in the south of Germany. He followed it with a second plea: "Collect the SS units militarily under your command and head them yourself. Defend the entrance to the Alps for me."[9] The next day, the allies intercepted a report to Himmler from none other than Ernst Kaltenbrunner. It appeared so important that it was sent immediately to Churchill.

By this time, Kaltenbrunner had left Berlin and retreated to Alt Aussee in Austria, where Countess Gisela von Westarp, his blonde twenty-two-year-old mistress, had recently given birth to their twin boys. His message to Himmler referred to the "Fortress Tyrol" and he acknowledged growing evidence of opposition to both the Nazis and any continuation of the war. But, he added, "nowhere else do terrain as well as the political atmosphere provide more favorable prerequisites for the continuation of a lasting resistance than the Tirol. Various interests of [the] allies and neutrals come into conflict here. A skilful political game and military energy will make more acute the conflicts."[10]

This strongly suggested that the allies could still expect some serious fighting in the Alps. In the meantime, Kaltenbrunner and other SS figures hoped, not to win the war, but to postpone defeat long enough to provoke a fatal split between the allies.

On the last day of April, the tiny Dutch village of Achterveld witnessed a meeting that proved momentous for the people of Holland. Nowhere in Western Europe was the end phase of the war more bitter than in the Netherlands. Vast areas of the country had been deliberately flooded by the Germans. In the west, bypassed by the allied armies in their advance northwards into Hitler's Third Reich, much of the population still under Nazi rule — including the great cities of Rotterdam, The Hague and Amsterdam — were starving or dying.

The last few months had been so bad that they would forever be remembered in the Netherlands as the "Hunger Winter."[11] But April was even worse. The official ration was now down to four hundred grams (less than a pound) of bread per week per adult. Forty people a day were dying of hunger in Rotterdam and food was predicted to run out completely by the end of the month. In Amsterdam, there was famine. "There was no food and no fuel," remembered one of the city's residents. "We collected wood from houses that had been deserted by Jews [i.e., Jews forcibly deported to the death camps] and from the streets that had wooden blocks instead of paving. Every day we got a ladle of soup from the municipal kitchen and a piece of bread — horrible gray stuff. We were so hungry we ate tulip bulbs."[12]

In the city's gutters, feces bubbled up from the grates because the sewerage system had broken down. There was no wood for coffins, so bodies lay unburied in churches. There was nothing to sell and shops were closed. The city was racked by looting and crime. One of Amsterdam's citizens who was living illegally underground as one of the thousands of Dutch citizens known as "divers" saw two children dying in the street. "They looked like small dead birds in winter," he said, "so sad and helpless."[13]

Here again, the final weeks of the war had proved the most bloody, with German terror reaching its peak with the mass execution of hostages. "You saw them lying everywhere in groups of twenty — and they left them there as a warning," wrote one Dutchman. To heighten the impact, the Germans shot the hostages in public, in squares and on street corners. The biggest bloodbath of all had come less than eight weeks before. It followed an attack by a resistance group on the second-highest-ranking Nazi in the Netherlands, Hans Rauter, that left him badly injured but still alive. By way of reprisal Himmler ordered the execution of five hundred hostages. In Amsterdam, seventy men were shot, and across the country groups of between five and ten were killed. The worst massacre took place at the site of the attack on Rauter. Three coaches brought 117 hostages from the prisons in Arnhem and Apeldoorn and unloaded them by the roadside. Then they were formed into a long row and gunned down by members of the green-uniformed German Order Police.

The reprisals did not end there. Rauter's successor embarked on a rampage of killing that reached far beyond hostages. A week after the attack, one Rotterdammer found himself looking at the bodies of twenty men and boys on the Hofplein who had been shot there that morning. "Somewhere else in town," he recorded, "another twenty men were shot in public . . . They were lying there as they had fallen, higgledy piggledy, next to each other and half over each other, unbelievably still . . . One man had his lunchbox under his arm and there was a boy of fifteen, picked up on his way to school."[14]

Achterveld lay five miles east of the town of Amersfoort, just inside Canadian lines. It had a small school, St. Josef's, with several empty classrooms. Here the allies had agreed to discuss with Nazi officials how to save the Dutch. Red, white and blue Dutch flags were flying in the streets. It was the birthday of Princess Juliana, the Crown Princess and heir-apparent to the nation's monarch, Queen Wilhelmina, who had spent the war in exile.

Eight years before, Juliana had married a German count, Bernhard von Lippe-Biestefeld, who had once worked for IG Farben as secretary of its board of directors in Paris, and even been a member of the Nazi Party and the Reiter SS (SS Cavalry). Finding a wartime role for him that was acceptable to the Dutch people had proved difficult, but in a stroke of genius, the previous year Wilhelmina had appointed him commander of the Dutch Forces of the Interior, a move that united all Dutch resistance movements behind the Crown and gave them official status as combatants. It also meant they could be controlled more effectively by the allies and prevented from launching some disastrous, premature uprising. Bernhard took Dutch nationality and proved such a loyal citizen that he became popular with the people of Holland.

Now, he was among the first to arrive to the cheers of the villagers. "How's the Princess?" some of them shouted, and he smiled. He was followed by Eisenhower's chief of staff, Major-General Walter Bedell Smith, and an allied team that included Lieutenant-General Charles Foulkes, commander of Canadian I Corps, Major-General Francis de Guingand, Montgomery's chief of staff, Eisenhower's chief of intelligence Major Kenneth Strong, and a Soviet representative.

But all eyes were on the bespectacled and balding man with a slight limp who stepped out of the convoy of limousines flying white flags that arrived last of all. Reichskommissar Artur Seyss-Inquart was the most hated figure in the Netherlands, for he was the man sent by Hitler in 1940 to rule the Dutch. "The Führer wishes me to plant tulips," he quipped to his wife. But Nazi rule in the Netherlands had never been a joke. Instead, Seyss-Inquart had bent his lawyerly skills to ruthlessly exploiting the country for the benefit of Germany as eagerly as he had delivered his native Austria to Hitler at the time of the Anschluss. Now, though, he was busily saving his skin and defying Hitler's "scorched-earth" order of March to destroy anything in occupied Europe that could help the allies.

As he stepped out of his limousine he saw Prince Bernhard leaning against a large Mercedes and taking photographs of the historic scene. With a shock, Seyss-Inquart recognized the car, with its distinctive number plate RK1 (Reichskommissar 1), as his own; Bernhard had found it in nearby Amersfoort and could not resist the temptation to drive it to his meeting with the top Nazi. He had always liked fast cars and had only just escaped with his life in a high-speed crash six years before that broke his neck. Disguising his reaction, Seyss-Inquart turned coldly away and led his delegation into the school. Here, the Germans were locked in a classroom under armed guard. Meanwhile, in another room, the allied leaders mingled with the Dutch and enjoyed a hearty meal. For many of the Dutch, it was an emotional encounter. Some of them had been underground for years and this was their first meeting with compatriots who had been in exile in London and elsewhere.

At exactly one o'clock, the two sides finally met across the table. Their business was to finalize a plan that had emerged after almost a month of behind-the-scenes discussions prompted by relentless pressure from Churchill and Roosevelt. Two days before the latter's death, Churchill had alerted him to the impending Dutch "tragedy"; he had later sent a similar warning to Truman. Two days before, in the same small schoolhouse, lower-level German officials and Dutch representatives had sketched out details of the plan. It was understood by everyone that the war was all but over and that the allies would not be attempting to liberate western Holland by force. In return, the Germans would allow the allies to send in emergency food supplies. They would also halt all further flooding and destruction, as well as the execution of hostages and resistance fighters.

With the groundwork well prepared, agreement came quickly at the schoolhouse. Then the delegations broke into separate teams to discuss practical arrangements on how the food would be brought in by air, land and sea. Meanwhile, over several stiff gins, Bedell Smith told Seyss-Inquart that Eisenhower would hold the Reichskommissar personally responsible if anything went wrong. The Austrian lawyer agreed that Germany was essentially defeated, but he refused to surrender Nazi forces in Holland. That, he said, was a matter for General Blaskowitz, the Wehrmacht commander in Holland.

"If you're pigheaded about it," responded an irate Bedell Smith, "[and] cause more loss of life to allied troops or Dutch civilians . . . you know what that will mean — the wall and a firing squad." Slowly, Seyss-Inquart turned his watery eyes to gaze across the table at his interlocutors. "I am not afraid," he replied softly, "I am a German."[15]

Meanwhile, "Manna," the operation to save the Dutch from starvation, had already begun. The day before, after a delay of twenty-four hours caused by bad weather, the first of hundreds of Lancaster and Flying Fortress bombers loaded with food had taken off from airfields in Britain. Flying low through a blizzard across the choppy North Sea waters they entered Holland. Green flares lit up designated dropping zones for the packages. Keeping close to the ground, the aircrews could see hundreds of people waving and cheering as they pushed out the parcels.

It was a striking contrast with just days before when Holland lay on the bomber route into Germany and the Ruhr. "I recall so vividly many of our [bombing] operations," said one Canadian pilot who took part in Manna,

> the wake-up call at two o'clock in the morning, then the drive to the dining hall for breakfast, and the table talk which was usually nothing more than bickering over who would have the extra bacon . . . [But] when we flew over the occupied part of Holland I was so relieved that I myself no longer had to be destructive that I was not too concerned about the possibility of being fired upon by the German ground installations. I remember watching the German ack ack guns and I can recall them following our progress, making absolutely sure we obeyed the terms and conditions of the operation.

The crew were all eating roast-beef sandwiches in the plane, recalled another pilot, "and we felt it as an improper luxury. One of my men was so carried away that he threw his own tin of cigarettes down and others followed his example."[16] In all, some eleven thousand tons of food were dropped by the allies into Holland over the next ten days.

Four drop zones had been agreed with the Germans and the rescue operation was announced to the Dutch by radio. As zero-hour approached, tension among the civilians reached a peak. As soon as they heard the planes' engines people rushed out to watch them. "We left our meal," wrote a journalist in The Hague,

> raced outside, waved with hats, shawls, flags, sheets, with anything to the planes which by now were thundering over our streets in an interminable stream. In a flash our whole quiet street was filled with a cheering, waving crowd and elated people were even dancing on the roofs. Many had tears in their eyes, others could not utter more than a few inarticulate cries.

In Amsterdam, one of its residents wrote simply in his diary: "Death fled."[17]

But in reality, death took its time in departing. The food had to be carefully sorted into balanced diets, properly and carefully weighed, then distributed throughout Holland to special centers so that everyone received their fair share. This was also true for the food now being brought in by trucks and ships following the plan agreed with Seyss-Inquart. It was a full ten days after the first air drops that the food finally began to reach the starving. For many, it proved too late.

These were long days for the Dutch that stretched far beyond liberation. People continued to die in the hundreds; in fact, the death rate rose. The wild celebrations at greeting allied troops disguised desperate conditions, for the men and women dying in their beds remained invisible. "It is an empty country, inhabited by a hungry, and in the towns a semi-starved, population," wrote one observer from Eisenhower's headquarters. "The people, especially in the big towns, are exhausted both physically and mentally . . . more children are dying per month *now* than per year in 1942." The black market was rampant, with many middle-class people having sold all their possessions so that they could buy essentials. There was a huge illegal traffic in coupon (ration) books and a total lack of many of the basic staples of life: no coal, hence no heat or light, no soap, and no new clothes since 1940. One British nutrition expert sent into western Holland reported seeing hundreds of people of both sexes and all ages "as emaciated from starvation as any we had seen at Belsen concentration camp."[18]

Five days after the meeting at the Achterveld schoolhouse German forces in Holland surrendered and the fighting stopped. But a new battle lay immediately ahead: to combat starvation, typhus, typhoid fever and dysentery. And, as Canadian officer Reg Roy was soon to discover, the occupation of even a grateful and friendly population could very rapidly wear thin.

CHAPTER FOURTEEN

"THE BITTEREST BATTLE"

In northern Holland, Reg Roy was about to sample the effects of the obstinate German refusal to give in.[1] Everyone knew him as "Boy Roy" because he signed up with the Cape Breton Highlanders when he was only sixteen. "Boy" was an old rank in the British Army inherited by the Cape Bretoners. Boys did just about everything that privates did, but they received only half the pay and had to have their parents' permission to join up. Reg eagerly enlisted in the spring of 1939 along with his older brother Bob. When war broke out that September he was issued with his kilt, sporran and brightly colored half socks, or "hose-tops," over which his white spats were to be worn. He also received a Glengarry hat, headgear that was later replaced with the flat tam o'shanter for which the Cape Bretoners became famous. Now, though, he was wearing his standard khaki-colored Canadian battle dress and a helmet.[2]

Until a few days before he had been in charge of the Pioneers platoon, the regiment's mini-engineering outfit that cleared minefields, "de-nutted" booby traps, and did everything from making small bridges to sand-bagging the quarters of the commanding officer. They were also responsible for handling protection measures against enemy poison gas if it were ever used. He was now an expert in handling explosives and in laying and clearing mines, knew how to drive anything from a motorcycle to a Bren gun carrier, and could fire almost any weapon, from pistols through Sten and Tommy guns to mortars and anti-tank guns. The one thing he had not done thus far was drive or ride in a tank, even though he was serving in an armored division. "Big, noisy brutes," he thought of them, targets that attracted unwelcome enemy fire and that once they were hit or had a track blown off became certain and fiery death traps. Personally, he preferred the freedom of the slit trench.

Now, he was in charge of a platoon in "D" (Dog) Company. At twenty-two, he still had a youthful look about him, despite the small, almost Hitler-like moustache he had been sporting since becoming an officer. When he had sailed back to Canada a couple of years before to take his officer's training course, he had become engaged to Ardith Christie, a girl from Sydney. Recently she had moved with her parents to Canada's west coast and he was looking forward to building their post-war life in British Columbia. But in Holland, as in Italy and Germany, April 1945 was to prove a bitter month, with more than a thousand Canadian names added to those already interred in temporary graves and military cemeteries scattered across the country.[3]

On Sunday 29 April Roy snatched a few moments to jot down some notes in his diary. The Cape Bretoners had been shelled on and off all the night before and he knew he would be back in action once darkness fell. In the meantime, he caught up with news about the war on the radio. The big item was Himmler's peace offer and its rejection by Truman and Churchill because it excluded the Soviets. "Hitler is reported very sick," Roy scribbled. "Goering is reported as having left the country. Himmler is the real Joe in command at present." Like virtually everyone else on the allied side, Roy had little idea that Hitler had already stripped "the traitor" Himmler of all his positions.

Allied forces seized on Himmler's offer as a sign that German morale was finally cracking. That same day, around noon, Canadian artillery fired smoke shells at twenty-two suspected enemy positions ahead of Roy. The shells were packed with thirty thousand specially printed leaflets referring to the offer and urging the Germans to surrender. They were followed soon after by several hundred safe-conduct passes.

However, this battlefield propaganda offensive had little or no obvious effect. It had long been clear to Roy, as to every other Canadian fighting in Holland that April, that "Jerry's goose is cooked," yet here he was, still fighting. And for what? About a mile ahead of him, across a dead-flat landscape bereft of virtually everything except an occasional farmhouse or windmill, he could see the Dutch port of Delfzijl. There lay the answer.

Tucked away in the northeast corner of Holland, Delfzijl nestled behind its sea wall on the west bank of the River Ems just a few miles across the estuary from the German port of Emden. Its history was intricately bound up with the North Sea and Baltic shipping trade, and for centuries it had thrived as a busy, if small, port going about its unremarkable business exporting dairy products and potato flour and importing wood, coal, grain and chemicals. A few years before, a prodigious Belgian novelist still in his twenties named Georges Simenon had tied up in harbor there while trying out the *Ostrogoth*, the yacht he had bought with the proceeds of his phenomenal early successes. He hung out in cafés, observed the local scene, and out of the experience crafted his legendary fictional detective, Inspector Maigret. He also made the port the setting for one of his novels, *A Crime in Holland*.[4]

But apart from this brief cameo, Delfzijl had passed largely unnoticed on the world's stage. Its mostly Protestant population of ten thousand people had the reputation of being silent, sober and unemotional. In 1876, the building of the Eems canal linked it with Groningen, northern Holland's largest city, just eighteen miles to the south, making it the principal terminus for inland shipping in the northern Netherlands, and the country's third-busiest port.

The Second World War, however, gave it a sudden, unexpected significance. Although its contact with Britain and other allied nations was severed, it attracted new trade that had been diverted from Dutch ports closer to Britain, such as Flushing and Rotterdam, which were more vulnerable to allied air raids. Its harbor became a regular port of call for German minesweepers, torpedo boats and other coastal surveillance craft.

More important, though, was that no sooner did they occupy the town in May 1940 than the Germans constructed a battery of four heavy guns on top of the town's sea wall. These were less for the defense of Delfzijl itself than to protect Emden as part of its anti-aircraft defensive perimeter. Linked by canals to Germany's industrial heartland in the Ruhr, the German port was fated to become a major target for allied bombers with its ship-repair docks, U-boat construction yards and moorings for a wide variety of naval vessels.

Just two minutes' flying time away from Emden, Delfzijl took several accidental hits from allied bombers jettisoning their surplus

Robert Ellis, Camp Hale, spring 1944.
(Denver Public Library)

Attack in the Apennines by Tenth Mountain Division infantry on a German position
in an Italian house. *(Denver Public Library)*

Mother of two and concentration
camp prisoner Fey von Hassell.
(Collection of Fey von Hassell)

Fey von Hassell with Corrado and Roberto (right
at Brazzà, 1943. *(Collection of Fey von Hassell)*

Alex von Stauffenberg, with whom Fey von Hassell fell in love while in SS captivity.
(Collection of Fey von Hassell)

BC reporting . . . Robert Reid interviews two American GIs on the road in Germany, 1945.
(Robert Reid Papers)

Secret agent Fred Warner parachuted into Austria in the dying days of Hitler's Third Reich. *(Fred Warner Collection)*

April 1945. Liberated slave laborers
scour through a German freight yard
for anything they can find to eat,
trade or use. *(NARA)*

Bavaria, May 1945. A German woman
is ordered by US soldiers to view the
bodies of eight hundred murdered
Russians and other slave laborers
exhumed for burial. *(NARA)*

Belsen: a survivor.

Belsen, 19 May 1945. The last of the typhus-infected huts is torched by a British flamethrower.

Geoffrey Cox, front-line intelligence officer, witness to the battle of the Gaiana River, northern Italy. "Few nails were driven into the coffin of Nazism more thoroughly than this," he wrote. *(University of Otago)*

The body of a German soldier, the Gaiana River, April 1945.

(G. F. Kaye, Kippenberger Military Archive, Army Museum Waiouru, NZ)

Leonard Linton reads a letter from home. *(Family of Leonard Linton)*

Milan, April 1945. Wearing a bloodied white vest, Fascist dictator Benito Mussolini's battered corpse lies next to that of his mistress, Clara Petacci. *(IWM, NA24672)*

Fascist woman with "M" for Mussolini painted on her forehead being marched through Milan by Italian partisans. *(IWM, IA66354)*

The San Sabba rice factory in Trieste, used by the SS for the detention and murder of political prisoners.
(Author photograph)

A New Zealand machine gunner covers the road between Trieste and Miramare, May 1945.
(IWM, NA25262)

Italian civilians cutting up a dead German horse for food. *(Denver Public Library)*

Near Linz, Austria, 6 May 1945. Prisoners pull down the Nazi eagle over the entrance to Mauthausen concentration camp, liberated by troops of General George S. Patton's Third Army. *(NARA)*

Austria, May 1945. Cossacks surrendering their weapons before being handed over to the Red Army. *(IWM, NA25021)*

Berchtesgaden, Bavaria, 4 May 1945. An American GI watches as Hitler's Berghof burns. *(NARA)*

Cape Breton Highlander Reg Roy (far right) poses with other Canadian officers on the sea wall at Delfzijl, May 1945. *(Collection of R. H. Roy)*

Canadian soldiers killed in the battle for Delfzijl lie neatly bound ready for burial, May 194
(Collection of R. H. Roy)

Retribution. Dutch Nazis held in a former internment camp are marched to their meal
guarded by a Dutch resistance fighter. *(IWM, Bl2058)*

The end of Fey von Hassell's odyssey at the hands of the SS: the Lago di Braies hotel, reached by US forces on 4 May 1945. *(IWM, NA24872)*

Wearing a trilby and smoking a cigarette, the gaunt SIS officer Sigismund Payne Best poses with other freed prisoners in front of the hotel. On his right, in Wehrmacht uniform, is Colonel von Bonin. *(IWM, NA24871)*

The end of the last Nazi government, 23 May 1945: Albert Speer (left), Admiral Doenitz (center) and General Jodl (right) in a courtyard after their arrest. *(IWM, BU6708)*

Berlin, 16 July 1945. Churchill, with his cigar, is shown the spot outside the bunker where Hitler's body was burned. Note the empty petrol cans. *(IWM, BU8966)*

high-explosive loads on their way home. Frequently, incendiary bombs would also land in or near the town. During the worst such incident, several houses were damaged, a warehouse burned to the ground and a twenty-year-old woman mortally wounded.

Equipped with searchlights and radar, by 1945 the Delfzijl battery was manned by well over a hundred German marines and protected on its landward side by heavy entanglements of barbed wire and minefields. To all intents and purposes, the town was a naval garrison governed by the German commandant.[5]

During most of the war its civilians had endured an existence typical of hundreds of Dutch towns. At first, normal life continued except that German soldiers patrolled the streets, with people going about their normal jobs, children walking or bicycling to school, and the town's Mayor continuing with his civic tasks. But the more obvious it became that most of Delfzijl's citizens disliked the occupation, the more the Germans resorted to force and intimidation. Censorship was introduced, most political parties were banned, and any sign of loyalty to the Dutch royal family, which had gone into exile in London, was fiercely stamped out. In 1942, the Mayor was removed and held as a hostage, to be shot in case of serious trouble in the town. A more pliant successor was installed in his place.

Delfzijl was more suspect to the Germans than many Dutch towns because, as a North Sea port, it offered a natural link with Britain and neutral Sweden. Britain's SOE more than once considered using Delfzijl as an entry point for smuggling agents into Holland.[6] Not surprisingly, the SD arrived early in Delfzijl. Here it set up office in the old Town Hall on the Markstraat, with a subsidiary office in the lockmaster's residence next to the locks of the Eems Canal. It busied itself with searching ships, regulating the ferry service that continued to run between the town and Emden, and keeping an eye out for people and goods being smuggled to Britain. It also stamped down on any sign of resistance. This meant anything illegal such as listening to the BBC, reading illegal newspapers, or making offensive comments about the Germans. Relatively minor offenses were taken care of in the Markstraat office. Suspects were called in, questioned, intimidated and occasionally beaten up. More serious cases were sent to the SD headquarters on the main square in Groningen. Anyone who ended up there ran the risk of being beaten to death or receiving a bullet in the head.

The SD was especially feared in Delfzijl because half of its members were Dutch, insiders in the society they were repressing. Some were just natural opportunists or mercenaries. Others were outright supporters of Nazi ideology or members of the Nationaal-Socialistische Beweging, or NSB, the Dutch equivalent of the Nazi Party led by Anton Mussert, Holland's most notorious collaborator. Thanks largely to bad economic conditions in the 1930s, Groningen Province had a relatively higher percentage of NSB members and supporters than most other parts of the country, and Delfzijl was no exception.

By April 1945, their numbers had increased considerably thanks to collaborators fleeing there as southern parts of the country were gradually liberated by the allies. In Groningen itself, a notorious SD team arrived from southern Holland in the autumn of 1944 and for the next few months, until the liberation of the city, it imposed some of the worst repression on the civilian population of the entire war. Throughout the Delfzijl area, intimidation by collaborators was widespread.

It was mostly Dutch informers who kept the SD in business. Such was the case with the town's main resistance group, the "Zwaantje," or "Little Swan," named after a café frequented by the group's founder elsewhere in Holland during his prewar military service. His name was Allard Oosterhuis, a local physician, who owned a boat that he used for smuggling out intelligence information and escapees to Britain via Sweden. In exchange, he received radio transmitters, money and propaganda material, such as photographs of Queen Wilhelmina and the rest of the royal family.

Alerted to its existence by details that were carelessly revealed on American radio by an escapee who had reached the United States thanks to the group's efforts, the SD managed to infiltrate one of their informers, a Dutch ship captain, into the Little Swan. It also succeeded in pinpointing the resistance group's secret transmitter by means of a radio-detection van, a disguised vehicle stuffed with sophisticated equipment that traveled through the streets listening in to the airwaves and locating the source of unauthorized signals. In July 1943, after monitoring its activities for several weeks, it pounced on the group and arrested the ringleaders. Several months later, in June 1944, they were sentenced to death.

This was the same month that a Dutch traitor also betrayed the hideout of the family of Anne Frank in the secret annex of their house in

Amsterdam, condemning the teenager to her miserable and tragic death in Bergen-Belsen. The hundred and fifty Jews of Delfzijl had already suffered the fate of the majority of their fellow Dutch Jews. In March 1942, they were taken to Amsterdam by train and later deported to the dreaded transit camp of Westerbork, several miles south of Groningen in the eastern part of the country. From there, they were sent in cattle trucks to the death camps of Auschwitz and Sobibor in Poland. For the rest of the war, the Germans used the Delfzijl synagogue as a handy place to store coal. The Jews of Groningen followed soon afterwards. Here, the local police chief, a Dutch Nazi, briefed his men about the "enjoyable" task he had for them — to reunite, he sneered, the many separated Jewish families.[7] The trains that transported the Dutch Jews to the death camps from Westerbork traveled back through Groningen on their way to the East. As they passed through the station, the inmates would drop hastily scribbled messages onto the tracks. Sometimes, these were found and kept by local residents.

Only ten of Delfzijl's Jews survived the war. The Dutch military police force obediently followed SD orders in sealing off the town's railway station to ease their removal from the town. In wartime Holland, informers and collaborators were plentiful, trust and courage scarce commodities — some 66,000 Dutch citizens were later to be found guilty of collaboration.

Reg Roy had already witnessed the rough justice being handed out to those who had helped the Germans. He also knew that the local resistance was proving helpful: it was no use as a fighting force, but it sometimes possessed useful details about German military installations. Recently, it had passed on details of a German ship offshore that was shelling the Canadians, and the next day the Royal Air Force turned up and sank it. Roy was also aware that Dutch informers were still around, equally ready to pass on information about Canadian positions to the enemy.

Just three weeks before, Hitler had ordered Emden, and along with it Delfzijl, to be declared a "fortress." This meant that they were to be defended to the last man and the last bullet. Emden had already suffered from dozens of allied air raids and 85 percent of its buildings lay in ruins. A fortress commander was appointed, and a few days later his representative arrived in Delfzijl equipped with full powers over all German forces in and around the town. By the time Roy and the Cape

Bretoners arrived on the scene, the fortress was on the alert, ready for its last stand. For the town's inhabitants, their liberation was to prove the most perilous time of all.

Two days before Roy scribbled the lines about Himmler being "the real Joe" in charge, the Cape Bretoners had learned they would lead the final assault into the town. Planning for the attack had begun the previous week. On Hitler's birthday, while Roy was resting on the shores of the Zuider Zee at Hoorst, General Harry Crerar, commander of the 1st Canadian Army, prerecorded the message he would deliver to his troops on VE Day. Later that same day, he put his fifth Armoured Division—known as the "Mighty Maroon Machine" because of the maroon patch worn by its soldiers on their sleeves—under the command of General Bert Hoffmeister, who was in charge of clearing up affairs in northeast Holland. Among Hoffmeister's instructions were orders "to clear the Delfzijl pocket."

Both tactical and strategic reasons lay behind this order. Groningen, the last significant center of communications for the Germans in the region, had already fallen to Canadian and Polish troops after a four-day battle that severely damaged the city center. This left the area round Delfzijl as the only part of northern Holland still in German hands. From here, German troops and equipment were being evacuated across to Emden, and every enemy soldier who escaped meant yet another defender for the German town, which was a major target for the Third Canadian Division that had recently crossed the German border. Strategically, capturing North Sea ports had become a top allied priority during this final chapter of fighting in Northwest Europe. They were to prove essential for shipping in badly needed allied supplies. And as long as they remained in enemy hands, they posed a serious threat because of the persistent danger from U-boats and other German naval craft.

Since the end of March, the Bletchley Park code-breakers had been intercepting German naval messages reporting serious preparations to resist allied advances in the Ems Estuary, as well as in Schleswig-Holstein, using midget submarines, explosive motorboats, one-man torpedoes and teams of frogmen. Allied intelligence reported that even at this stage of the war seventy-five Seehund (midget) submarines were patrolling Dutch and Danish waters, posing a threat that deeply worried the British Admiralty.

The land campaign might be going well, but allied ships were being sunk at a higher rate in the first three months of 1945 than for any single quarter in the previous year. Next to U-boats, E-boats (fast torpedo boats known as *Schnellboots* to the Germans, or *S-boots*) ranked high on the list of threats. Between thirty and forty were estimated to be still at large along the Dutch coast. Anything that could make their work more difficult, such as capturing Delfzijl, was given high priority.

The port was important for another reason, too. This had nothing to do with the fighting, and everything to do with the humanitarian disaster that now threatened to engulf the Netherlands. Provided it could be captured intact, its harbor could prove vital for the import of food that was essential to save the lives of hundreds of thousands of starving people. Swedish Red Cross ships had already unloaded hundreds of crates of food during three separate trips to Delfzijl, to be transported south to the starving parts of the country through its extensive network of canals. Even now, as Canadian forces readied themselves for the attack, another Swedish food ship was lying offshore, waiting to enter the harbor.[8]

No one expected the attack on Delfzijl to be easy. Canadian Army intelligence estimated that the task would prove as tough as taking the "Breskens Pocket" on the Scheldt Estuary the previous October—a battle to clear the southern approaches to Antwerp in which the Canadians had lost hundreds of men. The ground around the port was flat, exposed and soggy, and criss-crossed by countless drainage ditches and canals. Vehicles would have to stick firmly to the roads and there was virtually no cover. The entire area was also riddled with minefields and trenches. Several small hamlets dotted the approaches to Delfzijl. Each was built on a small mound to protect it from the sea, providing dangerous vantage points for the defending Germans. Adding to these problems, the heavy guns of the Delfzijl battery had been turned to fire inland. Once the Canadians came within their range it would be less deadly to keep on pushing forward than to pause and attempt a siege: "Three or four days mucking about would cost us more in the end," declared Hoffmeister. Anxious to capture the port intact, he opted for a rapid assault and surprise attack at night.[9]

At Hoffmeister's disposal for "Operation Canada," the official code name for the attack, were several Canadian regiments in addition to the Highlanders, such as the Westminsters, the Perths, the Irish Regiment, the British Columbia Dragoons, the 8th New Brunswick Hussars, and a couple of field artillery regiments. Hundreds of acres to the west of the town were under water, and thus any attack from that direction was blocked. Instead, the Canadians would take the town in a two-pronged pincer movement from the north and southeast. After they had squeezed the pocket tight, the Cape Bretoners would administer the *coup de grâce* and capture the battery.

The weather had turned nasty by the time Reg Roy arrived to take part in the attack. After a couple of days by the Zuider Zee, he had been trucked rapidly north towards Delfzijl, covering a lot of ground very fast and passing through village after liberated village where the red, white and blue Dutch flag hung from every window and lamppost. Parts of the route was sign-posted by units recently transferred from Italy: hand-painted markers such as "Sangrio Route" or "Coriano Route" were nailed haphazardly on trees and telegraph poles, and once he crossed a bridge named "Oh Mama Mia," which gave him a good laugh.

He had fought himself in Italy for several months before being transferred in February along with the rest of the Canadians to reinforce Montgomery's hard-pressed forces in Northwest Europe. The fighting in Italy had been tough enough, but the conditions of civilian life were what had really shocked him. "Dirty, filthy, old Italy," he described it in a letter to his fiancée, where children with cigarette butts drooping from their mouths mobbed and begged from the troops, and everything looked shabby and neglected. Being shipped out of there through France, he told his parents, had felt like "coming from the city dump to a lovely flower garden."[10]

But in Holland the Germans had broken many of the dikes to flood the land, and the relentless rain had turned the rest of the ground even boggier than usual, making it almost impossible for tanks. Low cloud ruled out air strikes. So it was up to the infantry and their light artillery. If he was worried about getting killed at this late stage of the war, Roy was not letting on. His letters home retained their consistent upbeat, joky and often flippant tone, almost as though he were trying to cheer up himself as much as their recipients. In marked contrast to Robert Ellis's letters home from Italy, Roy's were remarkably devoid of the gritty and gruesome details of infantry fighting, and he showed none of the doubts felt by the American about whether it was all worth it. But, devoid of introspection though his letters were, he knew the Cape Bretoners could expect a tough fight. He had come to respect the Germans in Italy. Sometimes, when faced with his own unruly men, he even envied German officers for the discipline they could expect from their troops.

For the opening shots of Operation Canada, the Cape Bretoners stayed back in reserve in the small village of Bierum. Then, on the night of Sunday 29 April, they fought their way to another small town, Uitwerde, less than two miles from Delfzijl. Just a few days before, the local resistance in Bierum had planned to help the Canadians by attacking a nearby enemy watch-post, but a local woman betrayed their plans to the Germans, and five innocent people from the village paid the price. Seized at random by the Germans, they were forced to dig their own graves at the foot of a dike, then shot.[11]

Now, on the last day of April, Roy was poised for the final assault on Delfzijl. After dark, at ten o'clock, the Cape Bretoners launched their attack, but it was not until three hours later that D Company got the signal to go. No sooner did they move out than the Germans sent up flares. "They had us cold," recorded Roy, and his first thought was that they had been betrayed by Dutch civilians. But this was not the worst of their problems. "Down came shells—big ones. KEERIST! [Christ]," he scribbled in his diary as soon as he could. That was not all: the roads also proved too bad for any of the supporting vehicles and they had to abandon them.

Nevertheless, Roy and his platoon managed to reach a small dike. "Was pinned down by snipers and that cursed SP gun [a self-propelled gun that the Germans had mounted on a tank chassis]," he noted hurriedly. "Saw 'C' [Company] go in with tanks and doing a good job. My God it was terrible to see our fellows cut up so."[12] By five o'clock in the morning, D Company were in deep trouble. At this stage, Roy was convinced he was finished.

They were almost out of ammunition, and the Bren gun carrier was stranded far behind them. The flamethrowers, used to flush out enemy troops, were unable to travel on the narrow, heavily damaged roads. Roy found it almost impossible to figure out where he, or the enemy, was because it was pitch black. "It was VERY difficult to know who was shooting at you and from where," he confessed. "Odd, but true. If you knew there was a spot handy for the Jerries, probably the firing was coming from there. Exactly where, though, was a very hard thing to pinpoint." Sometimes, he added, "if there was a covered approach to the German position the Jerries would loose a string of bullets along the brush-covered ditch, even if there was nothing there. A smart move

273

on his part!" By now, the entire company was pinned down by Panzerfausts and Spandau machine-guns. The fire was so heavy they could not even send a guide back to bring in a relief party from another company. Surrounded by the din and confusion, and lost in the dark, Reg found it almost impossible to work out what was going on. But as light began to filter through at dawn, there followed one of those surreal moments that occurs in every battle.

> I remember going on the road approaching the sea wall when we stopped for a moment. I glanced about and noticed a German helmet, apparently sitting on nothing. I looked closer and there was a German soldier, sound asleep, a machine gun curled in his arms, wearing the helmet! We woke him up, took the machine gun from him, and sent him to the rear . . . The enemy was somewhere ahead and we went forward hugging the side of the dyke and wondering what was around the corner.[13]

When daylight came, Roy was still pinned down with the others on flat, open ground, just a few hundred yards outside the town. Heavy, relentless fire was coming from the dozens of pillboxes and huge reinforced bunkers that protected the battery. Too late, Roy realized that the pre-battle intelligence briefing had been pretty useless: the German resistance was far heavier than predicted; he had no idea that there were concrete bunkers or that they would be so well defended—he had thought of the battery merely as a "nasty strongpoint" to be eliminated; and the number of enemy troops was obviously higher than anyone had expected.

Nor had he been briefed to expect glass mines. He had plenty of experience at uncovering ordinary mines with the standard handheld mine-detector. (Even then, though, the Germans—"nasty bastards as they were"—had developed a mine with a bottom detonator that would blow up and kill anyone trying to remove it.) But that detector could not find a new type of mine the size of a soup plate, made of glass and containing two chemicals. When pressure was applied to the mine, the chemicals came together and a flame shot into an explosive slab of gun cotton to detonate it. "That," explained Roy, "was the end of a useful steel tread for a tank . . . Praise be that they did not invent them earlier." Still, that was no comfort now. The invention was a nasty piece of work which he had never experienced before.[14]

For the first time since arriving in Holland, the Cape Bretoners' commanding officer was seriously worried, and sent in a tank, but it was quickly shot to pieces by heavy German fire. In the end, it took desperate flanking action by other units to save the day. They captured the railway station, took a few hundred prisoners, and by mid-morning had finally relieved the pressure on the beleaguered D Company. By this time, too, Roy and his exhausted comrades had finally been resupplied with ammunition. They resumed their advance, and at 11 a.m. at last captured the four big battery guns and took nearly three hundred prisoners. The harbor, although prepared by its defenders for destruction, was captured intact.

To the Cape Bretoners, the battle for Delfzijl proved costly: twenty of them were killed and over fifty wounded. Half of the dead were from D Company. "I hope I never have to see another battle like it," Roy scribbled in his diary just hours later. "It was murder . . . the bitterest battle I've been in." He himself was extraordinarily lucky. Just before the start of the attack, he had been replaced as the leader of the platoon by a newcomer to the regiment, a twenty-three-year-old lieutenant who was keen to get a taste of battle. "I didn't mind one bit!" confessed Roy, who brought up the rear in the fighting. The newcomer was killed while leading his platoon towards the sea wall.

By the time Roy reached his target he was exhausted. "Am dead tired and cold and stiff and hungry," he scribbled down. "Found four bottles of champagne!"[15] But he wasn't quite finished. Eager to capture some more war booty, he bagged several German flags and then volunteered to go into the town to look around. On his way he passed a German quartermaster's building that was blazing fiercely. Quickly, he nipped inside, seized a handful of swastika pins, and got out just as the ammunition began to explode.

When he returned to the sea wall, he had time to take a closer look around. Clearly marked around the concrete rims of the heavy German guns were the positions of local landmarks, such as houses and churches, along with distances, so that the artillerymen could judge the range. He also discovered that the gun positions were linked by underground cables to the blockhouses, where a periscope jutting up out of the roof had given the German commander an excellent view of the battlefield—except, of course, at night. The bodies of Roy's dead comrades had already been wrapped in blankets. Neatly, they lay in a row on the ground, awaiting burial. Twenty-nine of Delfzijl's citizens were also killed in the attack.

PART THREE

HITLER'S DEATH TO VE DAY

CHAPTER FIFTEEN

DEALING WITH NAZIS

Hitler was dead, but the war went on. The smell of victory was in the air and the once feared and mighty Wehrmacht was shattered beyond repair. Yet determined remnants fought on and fears about the Alpine Redoubt still darkened the horizon. Blind to the frantic machinations in Hitler's underground bunker, many allied observers believed that the man now pulling the strings was Heinrich Himmler.

One of them was a BBC colleague of Robert Reid. Chester Wilmot was traveling with British forces in their drive up the North Sea coast towards Hamburg and the Baltic. "Here in the north, there's still an army to be reckoned with: an army whose fighting power Himmler may still regard as a bargaining weapon," he told listeners in a radio broadcast the day that Hitler killed himself. "We have smashed the German Army as a whole and its Air Force; but we haven't yet broken the power or spirit of the German Navy."

Indeed, as Reg Roy and the Canadians were experiencing that same day at Delfzijl, the Germans were fighting hard in defense of ports and naval bases all along the North Sea and Baltic coasts. In Kiel, Wilhelmshaven and elsewhere more than a hundred thousand German naval personnel were being poured into the land battle, reinforced by units from Denmark. "We can't afford at this stage of the war to pause in the task," emphasized Wilmot. "So long as there are pockets of resistance as well organized as this one, the Nazis may be encouraged to fight on elsewhere. And so here in the north," he concluded, "the

[British] Second Army is striking at what amounts to Himmler's last hope."[1]

A potent source of such fears was the recent bitter fighting in Bremen. This ancient, red-bricked city was one of the most important German North Sea ports and a major U-boat base. The Nazis were determined to cling on to it as long as possible. As British forces closed in on the city, Himmler made a personal visit. Traveling in his special armored train, he demanded a tightening of SS control over the city's defenses to ensure that neither the city authorities nor the local commander weakened and surrendered. For days, Bremen was pounded by RAF bombers, mercilessly shelled by artillery, and fought over bitterly by infantry. Finally, after several days, British forces entered its shattered remnants.

Among them was a soldier fighting with a Scottish division. "The civilian population was beyond resisting," he recorded,

> [I]t was psychologically in the desperate state of crazy abandonment that so often came on a people who cannot bring themselves to stare the bleak face of defeat in the face. They had gone wild, looting, drinking, fighting among each other for what are called consumer goods; their frenzy was complicated by the presence among them of large numbers of utterly demoralised Displaced Persons from internment camps in the countryside round about. For two or three days towards the end of April 1945, Bremen was probably among the most debauched places on the face of God's earth: all sanctions broke down among those Germans who rioted in their shocking inability to accept the consequences of their own political stupidity.[2]

Wynford Vaughan Thomas, another of Reid's BBC colleagues, gave a vivid account of the aftermath. He spoke from the center of the North Sea city, where army bulldozers driven by men with handkerchiefs over their mouths as makeshift protection against the clouds of dust were already hard at work clearing away the rubble. Bremen, he reported, was a "rubbish-heap."

"There are walls standing, there are factory chimneys here and there, but there's no shape and no order and certainly no hope for this shell of a city that was once called Bremen," he went on. It was a landscape of great blocks of flats with their sides ripped open and their personal household goods blown into bomb craters. Most of Bremen's citizens had survived by retreating into the city's many giant air-raid shelters. Some of them, Vaughan Thomas added, were beginning "to potter about in that seemingly aimless way that bombed-out people do among the dusty rubble." Thousands of foreign workers deported to work in the city were already heading back to their homes in France, Italy, Holland or Poland. "But the inhabitants of Bremen," he ended with grim satisfaction, "have got to stay in the ruins of their city. And they now have ample time to walk around us and see the results of total war."

As April gave way to May, the prospect that other German cities, such as Hamburg, Lübeck and Kiel, might offer similar obstacles to allied forces seemed all too likely.[3]

One of those most alert to the possibility of last-ditch Nazi resistance was Winston Churchill. By now, he had virtually no influence over the allied armies, and events on the ground, both military and political, lay beyond his control. But he still had the ability, the will and the bulldog determination to follow closely what was happening day by day. He did this by reading the never-ending flow of top-secret intercepts produced by Bletchley Park.

More often than not, these were brought to him personally by Sir Stewart Menzies, the head of Britain's Secret Intelligence Service. But on 30 April, Menzies decided that with the war almost over, it was time to reduce the amount of detail and papers being sent to Churchill. "Prime Minister," he wrote, "in order to save time in reading I am preparing, until such time as you direct me to the contrary, Boniface Reports as Headlines, in the same form as Naval headlines as submitted to you daily."

The note appeared innocuous enough. Naval "headlines" were short one- or two-line summaries of naval intelligence, and Churchill had always seemed quite content with these. Menzies was now proposing that similar brief summaries be made of the military and diplomatic messages that, by contrast, the Prime Minister had always received in full. The term "Boniface" had been concocted early in the war to suggest they came from a spy rather than from the code-breakers. But Churchill reacted angrily to the idea. How could the SIS chief possibly think he had any less need to read such material now, just because the war was nearing its end? This was the very time, indeed, that he wanted to know *exactly*, and in detail, what was going on. Picking up a thick red pencil on his desk, Churchill boldly wrote the word "No" underneath the suggestion, then underlined it for emphasis. "Certainly not," he added, and instructed Menzies to continue sending him the full intercept messages.[4]

Like everyone else, Churchill was trying to penetrate the fog that surrounded the last few days of Nazi resistance. Just two weeks before, he had read an intercept of an order from Hitler himself that ominously called for an increased level of resistance against allied forces precisely because they were so obviously winning. "The peak of activity must be maintained in action, only by attacks against the flank and rear of the enemy, the disruption and interruption of his supply communications can success be guaranteed," dictated Hitler. "The success of the whole is won by the total of counter blows to be dealt with at all times and in all places in the enemy's rear, combined with guerrilla warfare."[5]

From personal experience, Churchill knew what damage could be inflicted on regular forces by determined guerrillas. In his youth he had seen the Boers at work in South Africa. In Cuba, he had reported for British newspapers on the success of insurgents fighting Spanish forces during the island's struggle for independence. More recently he had poured British support onto Tito's forces in Yugoslavia, to the maquisards in France and to the partisans fighting behind German lines in Italy. His fear now was that, along with fanatical determination and loyalty to Nazism, this sort of warfare could wreak terrible damage on the allied armies.[6]

His fears can only have been reinforced by a decrypted message he read from Himmler to Kaltenbrunner in Salzburg on the day that Hitler died. The Reichsführer SS was now desperately trying to undo the damage caused to him by the leaking of news about his talks with Folke Bernadotte. Denouncing such reports as a "malicious perversion," he attempted to stiffen his deputy's resolve to carry on with the fight. "It is clear," he told him, "that to fight on is the only possibility since the other side is at present absolutely against us!"

Over the next forty-eight hours, the Bletchley Park team cracked several more reports written in similar vein. All presented the unambiguous message that the Nazis would fight on until the last possible minute. On Wednesday 2 May, the very day that German forces in Italy surrendered, the code-breakers produced an Order of the Day from Field Marshal Kesselring, the commander of all German forces in Southern Europe. "Man who [gives] in now [sins] against people, [loses] his honor, and [forfeits] his life," it read. Immediately afterwards, they decrypted an equally ominous order from Grand Admiral Doenitz, the commander-in-chief of the German Navy. In it, he urged all U-boat crews to fight on against Bolshevism "in order to save thousands of Germans from destruction and enslavement." As long as the "Anglo-Americans" tolerated the destruction of Germany by Bolshevism, exhorted Doenitz, the fight was to go on, unrestricted.[7]

This second message was particularly chilling. For that same day, it was announced to the world by Radio Hamburg that Hitler had fallen "in the defence of Berlin" and that he had named Doenitz his successor as Reichspresident and Minister of War. It appeared as though Hitler's death had done nothing to lessen the Nazis' willingness to fight on to the bitter end.

Karl Doenitz was a tall, stern, thin-lipped man of fifty-four. He was not a member of the Nazi inner circle, but by April 1945 his influence over Hitler was almost second to none. As a First World War submariner and the man who had created the Nazi U-boat fleet, he now held in his hands the promise of the final secret weapon that might yet save the Third Reich. This was an electric-powered U-boat, the 1,600-ton Type XXI, which Hitler eagerly embraced as a new and aggressive weapon of war. The Luftwaffe under Goering had palpably failed in its task and the Wehrmacht was staffed by generals who constantly pleaded for strategic withdrawal. In Hitler's eyes, Doenitz by contrast was loyal, committed and efficient. Born into a strict, middle-class, Lutheran family in Prussia, he had been instilled with an absolute sense of duty and obedience to the state. Even the normally acerbic Goebbels described him as "a very cool and realistic calculator."[8] Thanks to Doenitz's efforts, as well as those of the energetic Minister for Armaments Albert Speer, U-boat production had risen steeply throughout the previous year.

In March 1945, despite all the efforts of allied bombers to smash German factories and shipyards, the U-boat fleet still numbered 459, the highest total of the war. The Type XXI could cruise as far as the Pacific without needing to recharge its batteries, and when sprinting at depth it could easily match the speed of the fastest of allied escort vessels. Along with other new types of U-boat, this "streamlined harbinger of the future" posed a formidable potential threat that promised to inaugurate a second, and to the allies catastrophic, Battle of the Atlantic.[9]

As a serving officer, Doenitz was not a member of the Nazi Party, but in every other respect he was the most loyal and trustworthy of

Hitler's paladins. Completely mesmerized by the Führer's magnetic personality, he spoke warmly of his "enormous strength" and shared Nazi views about "the disintegrating poison of Jewry." More than any other senior commander, he insisted that the interests of the armed forces and the state were one and the same. "The idle chatter that the officer is non-political is sheer nonsense," he declared. "The whole officer corps must be so indoctrinated that it feels itself co-responsible for the National Socialist state in its entirety." Post-war, even after a decade in Nuremberg Prison for war crimes, he held firmly to the view that it was only through National Socialism that Germany had truly established its unity.[10]

As the Soviets advanced on Berlin, Doenitz ordered his officers to be hard and strict with their men. "If circumstances demand making a quick, horrible example of someone, let us not shrink from the task," he demanded. The navy was to stand like a "rock of resistance" as an example to the rest of Germany. To this end, he happily cooperated with Himmler and the SS, and effectively sent his U-boat crews out to sea on suicide missions. In Doenitz, then, Hitler had found a true companion spirit.[11]

Nevertheless, Doenitz was stunned by his appointment. However, he readily accepted it. As far as he was concerned, his task now was to save as much as he could from the debris. "When I read the signal," he wrote, "I did not for a moment doubt that it was my duty to accept the task." In his eyes, the greatest threat now to Germany and Germans came from the East. In his inaugural address to the German nation as Hitler's successor, broadcast over Hamburg's North German Radio on 1 May, he told them that his first task was "to save German men and women from destruction by the advancing Bolshevik enemy." Thus, his strategy was to hold back the forces in the West for as long as possible in the hope that this might encourage a split in the allies.[12]

By this time, he had left Berlin and established himself in the small town of Plon, in Schleswig-Holstein, safe from the Red Army but close to the great naval base of Kiel. Here, on the edge of a lake, the Nazis had constructed a huge naval barracks that was transformed during the war into the Third Reich's Number 1 U-boat Training School. To Plon had also come the headquarters of the German Navy when it moved out of Berlin that March. This made it a natural base for Doenitz, and here he assembled a new German government, the last of the Third Reich. As Foreign Minister he appointed Count Schwerin von Krosigk, a member of an old noble family and a former Oxford Rhodes scholar and Fabian socialist. But he had also served Hitler loyally as Finance Minister and helped loot the property of Jews.

After a few days, though, even Plon seemed vulnerable. British forces were rapidly approaching from the south, so files and documents were hastily bundled into trucks which headed north along chaotic roads choked with thousands of refugees and dozens of military convoys packed with wounded soldiers. Driving in his armored limousine, Doenitz was frequently forced off the road to take shelter as British fighters, their lights ablaze, strafed the roads. He finally reached his destination at Murwick, just north of Flensburg next to the Danish border, at 2 a.m. Here, for the next two weeks, the final act of the Nazi drama was played out.

In the vanguard of British forces moving up into Schleswig-Holstein and pushing the last Nazi government ever further north was commando Bryan Samain. Having crossed the Elbe, his brigade moved rapidly northeast. They bypassed Hamburg and on Wednesday 2 May entered the small port of Neustadt, on the Baltic, twenty miles north of Lübeck.

Along the way, Samain witnessed all the signs of a defeated nation. "We passed column after column of weary, travel-stained prisoners," he recalled, "confused civilians, often in small family groups with women and children, carrying what was left of their belongings and walking on the side of the road in the opposite direction to us; all reminiscent of the familiar pictures of French families and other refugees seeking safety on the roads of France soon after the German breakthrough in 1940."

At one point, the commandos stopped to help some released and exhausted British prisoners of war who had been walking for hours from their camp. One of them, a middle-aged officer, burst into tears when he saw them. "We offered him and his comrades an immediate 'brew-up' of tea and cigarettes," recalled Samain, "whilst our unit cooks prepared egg and chips for them."[13]

Other British units headed into Lübeck. Contrary to fears of desperate last-ditch resistance, they met only token opposition and a society in disintegration. In the nearby town of Molln, huge numbers of forced laborers had broken out of their camp and were roaming the streets and looting wine stores, so that wine literally ran in the gutters.

A prisoner-of-war camp had been liberated and ecstatic RAF personnel had commandeered any transport they could find: some rode on top of great cart horses, others seized traps and gigs and with chalked slogans on their sides were happily heading to the rear.

In the midst of this carnival of chaos, thousands of bewildered and despondent but fully armed German soldiers simply sat by the roadside or wandered about aimlessly. "Soon," remembered one British soldier, "the fields began to fill with vast herds of field-gray like cattle, silent, tired, and beaten. Panthers [tanks], all brand-new, were abandoned by their crews at cross-roads; gunners manning their 88s watched the tanks go by with their hands in their pockets. The SS was pretending to be something else, and trying to slip away without any idea where to go."[14]

Some of the defeated enemy, though, had a very clear notion of where they should go. At the Baltic seaside resort of Travemunde, where SOE agent Fred Warner had spent many happy hours as a child, a British unit spotted a motorboat trying to slip out to sea. They stopped it with a burst of fire that put its guns out of commission. On board, they found a German major-general who admitted he was off to Scandinavia with his staff officers, his mistress, a large stock of cigars and thirty bottles of Kummel liqueur.

The vessel of another far better-known Nazi sybarite was also captured by British forces during the drive to Lübeck. Among the more lavish items accumulated by Hermann Goering during his profitable career of indiscriminate looting and exploitation of state and private coffers was his personal yacht, the *Carin II*. During the 1930s, he regularly sailed her along inland waterways from Berlin to the Elbe and down through canals to the Rhine to the applause of Germans lining the banks. Dressed in a white uniform and languidly sprawled in a deck chair, he would beam as the boat's loudspeakers blared out gaudy popular songs such as "Blame It on Napoleon" or Wagner operas. Once, he sailed her up to Copenhagen to see a performance at Elsinore Castle of *Hamlet* and purchased some of his beloved Danish pastries. During the war she was moored on the Oder, but that February she had been removed from her moorings to save her from the Russians and brought to Molln. Here she now lay, a desolate symbol and reminder of a venal and corrupt regime in its final death throes.

There were plenty of other sights, too, revealing the true nature of the Nazis. As the British commandos continued their advance, Bryan

Samain's youthful and impressionable eyes were taking it all in. "In fields that we passed," he recorded, "we saw concentration camp victims newly freed from somewhere, wandering about, confused and seemingly aimless, clearly identifiable with their shaven heads, shrunken faces and bodies and striped rag-like prison clothes." On reaching Neustadt, he remembered, "We did not expect any resistance and we did not encounter any." Instead, there was a mass of German soldiers trying to surrender, and, as in Molln, freed slave laborers were roaming the streets. Samain's first task was to head a small advance party into the town and secure billets for all 450 members of his unit, 45 Commando. He leaped into his jeep and headed down one of the town's principal roads until he reached two large blocks of flats facing each other on opposite sides of the street. As far as he could see, they were undamaged. "Together with the rest of my party I jumped out of the jeep and ordered all the occupants of the left-hand block to leave their flats within half an hour and 'double up' across the road with the occupants of the block on that side," he recalled. "The people concerned were all civilians, mainly middle-aged or older, both couples and small families, and they rapidly complied. All of them were (understandably) very scared." But he had a job to do, and there was no room for sentiment: he had to find billets for 450 battle-weary men, and quickly. "I had no qualms," he admitted, "and when the rest of my unit arrived in transport I was able to direct them all into vacant flats."[15]

This was standard procedure wherever the allied armies advanced. The rules were simple but strict: the Germans were given a short period to collect "personal belongings" and then told to leave. Where they went was their business, not that of the occupying troops. And what comprised "personal belongings" was entirely up to the whims of the officer concerned. It usually meant basic bedding and clothing that could be carried by hand. Kitchenware, food, fuel and radios — anything wanted or deemed necessary by the occupying soldiers — had to be left behind. Essentially, occupied property belonged to the occupiers. Often, much of it was carted off for use elsewhere.[16]

The civilians in Neustadt knew the rules. They were defeated and had no choice. For himself and the other five men in his intelligence unit, Samain commandeered a flat on the top floor of the block. Inside, they found an old wind-up gramophone and a single, worn record of Tchaikovsky's *Capriccio Italienne*. "We played that record over and over, at all hours of the day and night. Ever since, and even after so many years," he wrote over half a century later, "I cannot hear it without immediately recalling the days in Neustadt."[17]

To all appearances, Neustadt was a port whose trade had been crippled by the war. In reality, though, Samain quickly discovered that it was also "a hothouse of enemy atrocities."[18]

Even before entering the town, British troops had received a foretaste of what was to follow. On the march up from Lübeck, another group of commandos had spotted, hiding in a copse of trees, a small party of starved and filthy people dressed in the by now grimly familiar striped concentration camp uniform. They were frightened and in poor physical shape. A British officer handed over a piece of his rations from his haversack, and one of the prisoners broke it into small portions and distributed it to the others. "I am an English soldier," said the officer in broken German, "where are you from?" The prisoner replied, "Ruskie," and gestured out to sea. Out in the bay the commandos could see a ship moored at anchor. The Russian also managed to convey the information that SS guards had kicked, clubbed and shot prisoners to death.

Meanwhile, advance British units were reporting that close to Neustadt slave laborers, mostly Poles, Russians and Jews, were being shot on the beach by regular German military personnel as well as by SS troops. Further on, in the town itself, the commandos discovered a small concentration camp. It was a mini-Belsen, with hundreds of corpses littering the ground and mounds of excreta.

In charge of First Commando Brigade was Brigadier Derek Mills-Roberts of the Irish Guards. A Liverpool solicitor in peacetime, he was a combative personality known to his men as "Mills Bomb," after the standard egg-shaped British hand-grenade. "He spoke with a deceptive drawl," recalled Bryan Samain, "for as anyone on the receiving end of his tongue could testify, he was not a man to be trifled with." He had led the brigade's four commando units throughout the fighting in Normandy, Belgium and Holland, and was a holder of the Military Cross and two DSOs as well as the Légion d'Honneur and the Croix de Guerre. He had seen the sharp end of war with all its horrors, but even he was shaken by what now greeted his eyes.

As he entered one of the sheds of the camp to see the evidence for himself, he saw the skeletal figure of a tall man lying on the ground in front of him. He lifted the man up while an army doctor liberally sprayed the living skeleton with anti-tetanus powder. "You are all right now," said Mills-Roberts, "the British Army is here." The doctor slowly shook his head. Starvation had done its work and the man was beyond saving.

Shocked by this, Mills-Roberts returned to the temporary headquarters set up in a restaurant in the town square. Hardly had he arrived than he was told that a high-ranking German officer was waiting to see him. It turned out to be none other than Field Marshal Erhard Milch. A First World War fighter squadron commander and a former chief executive of Lufthansa, Milch was an early Nazi supporter. Appointed Goering's deputy at the Air Ministry in 1933, he later became Inspector-General of the Luftwaffe. As the man in charge of the technical directorate of the German Air Force for most of the war he oversaw the tripling of aircraft production and was elevated to field marshal after commanding the 5th Luftwaffe Air Fleet during the 1940 attack on Norway.

A few days before, as the Red Army approached Berlin, Milch had fled from his hunting lodge close to the capital and taken refuge in Sierhagen Castle, just outside Neustadt. Here, he put on his full dress uniform and his medals from both world wars and calmly awaited the end. It came with the arrival of two British soldiers who knocked at the door of the castle. He put on his black leather overcoat and peaked cap. Then he stepped into his chauffeur-driven Mercedes and was driven to meet Mills-Roberts. Expecting red-carpet treatment befitting his rank, and carrying his field marshal's baton — a black, silver-headed ebony stick inscribed with his name — he marched arrogantly into the restaurant. Instead, he encountered a silent Mills-Roberts, who barely gave him a glance. "He spoke English and his first words consisted of a self-congratulation that he had not surrendered to the Russians," recalled the short-tempered brigadier. "In fact he had been careful to move out of their area of occupation or influence and was glad to surrender to us." But after his experience at the concentration camp, the fiery commando officer was in no mood for pleasantries. Instead, he cut Milch short by asking him abruptly about the prisoners in the camp. Milch appeared surprised that Mills-Roberts seemed so upset. The prisoners were not soldiers but Poles or Russians, he replied. Then, as if by way of explanation, he added that "they were not human beings by our standards." This reply infuriated Mills-Roberts, who grabbed an empty champagne bottle from one of the tables and thumped it down hard while demanding a proper answer. At this, Milch seized hold of the bottle and tried to take it from Mills-Roberts, which simply prompted the enraged commando to seize Milch's baton and break it over the head of its startled owner. Then he ordered Milch to be taken under escort around the concentration camp. This had the desired effect: Goering's former right-hand man was shocked. "It was an abominable spectacle," he recorded in his diary, "dead, diseased camp inmates . . . lying about in the open air and in the exercise sheds."[19]

Later, Milch would allege that he had been roughly manhandled by one of his escorts while being shown around. This escort was possibly one of the several anti-Nazi German exiles wearing British uniform and bearing Anglicized names fighting with the commandos. Mills-Roberts had sixty or so such soldiers fighting under his command, and they were no lovers of the Nazis. "I certainly took no trouble to give Milch a special escort," recorded Mills-Roberts, "there were more important and urgent matters at hand."

CHAPTER SIXTEEN

THE *CAP ARCONA*

It had been a week since the prisoners from the Neuengamme concentration camp near Hamburg were evacuated by their SS guards
ahead of advancing British forces. Some marched on foot; others were
packed into cattle wagons. As they passed the outskirts of Hamburg,
those closest to the wagon doors peered through the wooden slats.
Outside, they could see a landscape covered with ramshackle huts
where thousands of the city's inhabitants had taken refuge from allied
bombers. Eventually they reached Lübeck. Two ships were moored at
the docks, the *Thielbek* and the *Athen*. The former was a freighter that
had been badly damaged the year before during an air raid on the River
Elbe and brought to the city's shipyards for repair. The latter was also
a freighter, but smaller. Both ships had been commandeered by the SS.

Over the next few days, the prisoners were transferred in batches
from the dockside railway siding to the ships. At first, the captain of the
Athen refused to take them, but he quickly gave way when he was
threatened by the SS. "They drove us on board the ships with shouts
and blows," said one Polish prisoner. "We climbed down steep ladders
into the holds. In the rush, many prisoners fell from a great height into
the depths of the hold and were severely injured, suffering contusions
and breaks. We could hardly move below. It was dark, cold, and damp.
There were no toilets. No water. It began to stink."[1]

Boarding the *Thielbek* proved no less arduous. The prisoners entered
through a narrow door in the ship's side and clambered down several

iron ladders into the hold. Here, in total darkness, they were kept for several days. There was an open tub in the center of the hold that acted as a latrine. Soon it was overflowing with excrement. Every other square inch of space was occupied by a human body. The prisoners were so tightly packed that many of them had to balance precariously on the curved surface of the hull. From time to time, a hatch was opened and containers of soup roughly handed down. But no bowls were provided, so much of it ended up on the floor. Otherwise, the prisoners survived on American Red Cross parcels they had smuggled with them from Neuengamme. Conditions were no better on the *Athen*.

One of the prisoners on the *Thielbek* regularly braved beatings to clamber up the ladder and take a peek outside. French resistance fighter Michel Hollard had been betrayed to the Gestapo after providing secret intelligence to the allies about V1 rocket sites in France. He endured months of beatings and torture at Fresnes before being sent to Germany. Outside, on the quayside, he saw two or three freight wagons. One of them was apparently being used as a sick bay. Beyond, he spied a revolving bridge crossing a canal. Once, he spotted a tram pass over it full of men and women on their way to work before it disappeared into a tree-lined street towards the center of Lübeck. Back in the darkness of the hull, the atmosphere became increasingly fetid and heavy with the sense of impending doom.[2]

A few days later the main hatch was opened and ropes lowered to permit the long-overdue removal of the tub. But the effort only yielded more degradation for the prisoners. "As it reached the level of the upper deck," recalled Hollard, "the thing tipped up, emptying its revolting contents on the heads of the prisoners who had gathered underneath for a glimpse of the open sky." Nobody tried to clear it up — there was nothing to do it with anyway — and thereafter they were forced to move around in ankle-deep excrement.[3]

After a few days, the *Athen* steamed out of Lübeck with orders to transfer the prisoners to a large passenger ship moored offshore. This was the *Cap Arcona*, a 28,000-ton former luxury liner of the Hamburg–Sud (Hamburg–South America) shipping line. Often referred to as the "Queen of the South Atlantic," she spent her prewar years carrying passengers on the Hamburg–Rio de Janeiro route. Many were Germans emigrating to South America. An elegant, three-funneled ship, she was commandeered for war service in 1939 and her once brilliant-white superstructure and red-and-white striped funnels were now painted camouflage dark gray. She spent most of the war moored at Gotenhafen (now Gdynia), near Danzig, providing accommodation for naval personnel.

This was all a far cry from the glowing transatlantic career envisioned twelve years before, when she left the Hamburg shipyards of Blohm and Voss for her maiden voyage to Buenos Aires, watched by waving crowds along the banks of the Elbe. "From the waters of the Baltic, in the north of the dear island of Rügen, there rise steep cliffs, crowned by a lighthouse . . . which beams its light out over the sea every night," spoke the owner's daughter eloquently when she officially launched the liner. "The name of these cliffs, the only Cape which graces Germany's coast — Cape Arcona — will, from now on, be your name. May you sail the seas, to the honor of our dear German fatherland and to the joy of your Company, and be a further bond between the new world and the old."

On each trip, the *Cap Arcona*'s thousand passengers were cared for by a small army of masseurs, physicians and chaplains, and fed by fifty kilos of caviar and six thousand kilos of chicken and venison. The Hamburg poet Hans Leip, author of the iconic soldier's song "Lili Marlene," which he wrote as a poem while serving as a soldier during the First World War, spent his honeymoon on board the liner. "A crossing is like this," he said, "a short whistle, a blown kiss. We ate well and danced. Slept beside each other in the dancing ship."[4]

Briefly, in 1942, she regained at least an ersatz taste of glamour thanks to Joseph Goebbels, who dreamed up the idea of a major disaster film with a toxic anti-British slant, and chose the *Cap Arcona* as the location for the shooting. Based on the story of the *Titanic*, the film told how the luxury liner's owners and shareholders forced it to sail at full speed in order to break the transatlantic crossing record and thus boost the company's ailing share price. In doing so, they willfully disregarded the warnings about icebergs given by the ship's first officer and the film's hero, the only German crew member on board. The hundreds who perished, concluded the film, were all victims of "English greed."

But the project proved as ill-fated as its subject. Frustrated by the constant flirtation of the naval officer extras with female cast members, the director uttered some bad-tempered comments about the German Navy and was arrested by the Gestapo. Shortly afterwards, in August 1942, he was found hanging in his cell, although whether by suicide or murder was never established. His replacement finished the film, and it was given a test screening, but when Goebbels saw it, he quickly changed his mind about its suitability as inspirational propaganda. The panic as the ship went down too closely resembled the all too real stampedes now happening regularly in German cities during allied bombing raids. In the aftermath of Stalingrad, the film might also, Goebbels feared, be seen as a metaphor for the future of the Third Reich. So he restricted its showing to a premiere in Paris in November 1943, and it was never screened inside Germany itself.[5]

After this hapless sortie into filmmaking, the *Cap Arcona* resumed her sedentary life at Gotenhafen until late 1944. Then, along with hundreds of other ships, she was urgently mobilized to help with the massive sea operation mounted by the German Navy to evacuate more than two million Germans from the Baltic states and the eastern provinces of Germany being overrun by the Red Army. She made three separate runs, zig-zagging at top speed to dodge Soviet submarines and air attacks, and ended up in Lübeck Bay with her turbines exhausted and unfit for further service.

Like the captain of the *Athen*, the *Cap Arcona*'s skipper at first refused point blank to accept the concentration camp prisoners. He had accommodation and sanitary facilities for only a few hundred people, he pointed out, and his ship was undefended. But he too changed his mind when the SS told him he would be shot if he did not obey. For three days, the *Athen* then transferred prisoners to the luxury liner. Finally, there were some 4,600 prisoners crammed aboard, along with approximately 600 SS guards. As usual, the worst treatment was reserved for the Russians, most of whom were prisoners of war. They were held on the lowest deck — the so-called banana deck — without fresh air, light or food. Occasionally, the guards opened the hatches to let in a bit of air but then they quickly closed them. The shortage of oxygen grew steadily worse. Even to the end, the SS kept to its perverted sense of racial hierarchy.

All the life belts were removed from the ship to prevent escapes, except for a few put aside for the crew. Each day, a launch brought out water from Neustadt, and returned to port carrying the corpses of those who had died overnight. These were then buried in mass graves in and around the town.

Meanwhile, still trapped in the fetid darkness in Lübeck, Hollard and the other prisoners on the *Thielbek* heard the sound of gunfire in and around the city from the advancing British troops. Soon afterwards, they heard the winches begin to turn and the sound of grinding chains. Vibrations from the ship's engines told them they were about to leave. In the blackness, they thought they had begun the end of their journey and they all fell silent.

Hollard was the first to say anything. "My friends," he said, speaking in French more calmly than he felt, "our turn has come to set out for the unknown. We are all afraid, and I must admit that the prospect is far from reassuring. Is not this the moment to show what sort of men we are?" Then he called for them to pray. "We shall now make a chain with our hands," he said. There was a movement in the darkness as some of the other French prisoners shuffled towards him and formed a circle. "Oh God, from the depths of our agony, we beseech you," he spoke out strongly, "whatever happens to us, protect, we implore you, our wives and children and guard them against all evil." For a few lingering seconds, the hands remained linked. Then the circle broke, and the prisoners felt their way back to their positions in the hold.[6]

Shortly thereafter (although without Hollard and his compatriots), the *Thielbek* sailed out of harbor and steamed close to the *Cap Arcona*. The two ships were still there when Bryan Samain and the commandos reached Neustadt. No attempt had been made to paint either of them white, or to display Red Cross insignia or flags. The *Athen* was also still moored close by, as was another former passenger liner, the 20,000-ton *Deutschland*, which had been converted into a hospital ship. Aboard were a couple of dozen nurses and a surgeon. Only here had any effort been made to protect the vessel against attack from the air. A single red cross was painted on the side of one of the two funnels, both of which were painted white. But even it had not been registered as a hospital ship with the Red Cross

Why the prison ships were there, and what their destination was, remained a mystery. Some of the ships' crews were told that the prisoners would be taken out to sea and transferred to Swedish Red Cross ships, but this seems unlikely and it is unsubstantiated by any Swedish source. Probably, the SS simply regarded the ships as convenient holding pens for prisoners towards whom they were pathologically indifferent, a group of people whom Himmler had decreed should not fall into allied hands. Perhaps they intended to sink the ships with the prisoners aboard and thus eliminate inconvenient witnesses to the atrocities at Neuengamme. Whatever the case, the ill-fortunes of war were soon about to intervene in a tragic and terrible way.

The morning of Thursday 3 May dawned misty and overcast across northern Germany. The day before, Major-General Wolz, Hamburg's military commander, had agreed to surrender the city to the British. Thus, he eliminated the nightmare vision of a street-by-street and house-by-house battle for the great port that Hitler had ordered to be defended to the last. British forces were scheduled to enter the city shortly after noon.

Yet, elsewhere, there was no sign of surrender. Across Schleswig-Holstein allied reconnaissance planes spotted endless convoys of Wehrmacht vehicles heading north. In and around the great port and naval base of Kiel, they reported the presence of hundreds of vessels, including warships and U-boats. In the general chaos, it was next to impossible for allied intelligence to determine the significance or otherwise of all this.

But one thing seemed clear: there was a general movement of shipping and U-boats towards Norway, which was still occupied by some eleven German divisions, and whose long, deep fjords provided welcome shelter for dozens of U-boats. Was all this activity destined to create the infamous Northern Redoubt? Intelligence reports had frequently hinted at this possibility, and the risk could not be ignored. The situation was not unlike that in the spring of 1943 at Cape Bon in Tunisia. Here, after the defeat of Rommel's army in North Africa, the Germans had attempted to evacuate men and supplies across the Mediterranean to Italy. In the event, they had merely provided sitting-duck targets for the allies.

The main difference now was that the British had no naval vessels in the Baltic because minefields in the Kattegat blocked the way. So it was all up to the Royal Air Force. Allied aircraft were ordered to launch all-out air attacks across the region.

"No quarter was given or asked for in the air today," reported the RAF intelligence summary that evening, "and operations proceeded at full blast . . . All aircraft carrying bombs or R/P [rocket-propelled missiles] were diverted to deal solely with the large concentrations of shipping making their way from Lübeck, Kiel and Schleswig in the general direction of Norway . . . Full results will doubtless show that a very satisfactory score was achieved."[7]

Back in Lübeck, however, someone had already sensed an impending tragedy. Four days before, an anonymous letter had been dropped through the letter box of the Swedish Red Cross office in the town, reporting the presence of the *Athen* and its human cargo of prisoners. As a result, one of the Red Cross doctors went to the ship and talked with the officer in charge. The SS man told the Swede that 250 of the prisoners on board came from France, Belgium and the Netherlands. The others were mostly from the Soviet Union. The doctor said he could do nothing for the Russians, but he offered to take care of the others by sending them to Sweden on board two Swedish Red Cross ships that were also moored at Lübeck. The SS officer agreed to this and the next day, when the Swede returned, he found the 250 prisoners, as promised, waiting on the quayside to be shipped to Sweden, delighted at their rescue.

Among them was Michel Hollard, from the *Thielbek*. Along with all the French, Belgian, Swiss and Dutch prisoners, shortly after leading the prayers he was suddenly ordered up to the deck. Fearing the worst, Hollard deduced that all was well only when a hose was turned on and they were told to wash the filth off their bodies. Then a gangway was placed in position for them to disembark.[8]

Now, the doctor asked the SS officer what would happen to the prisoners who were left on board. The officer admitted he had no idea, and frankly he did not know what to do with them. The doctor suggested they should be turned over to the British forces when they arrived in the city. Assuming this would have been done, the day after the British entered the city he returned to the harbor. But he found that the *Thielbek* had sailed and was now moored close to other prison ships off Neustadt. As soon as he could, he reported this to a senior British Army officer in the city, emphasizing especially the dangers to the prisoners from air attacks. Later that same day — Wednesday 2 May — this information was passed to the intelligence officer at 83 Group RAF headquarters, to which the Typhoon squadrons were attached.[9]

The next morning, four squadrons of RAF Typhoons took off from bases recently vacated by the Luftwaffe across northern Germany and flew towards Lübeck Bay. The powerful, single-engined Typhoon carried either a thousand pounds of bombs or eight rockets, each with a sixty-pound high-explosive warhead. They had delivered devastating attacks on German tanks, armored vehicles, trains and troop formations over the past few weeks, and the Germans described them as "*shreckliche Jabos*," terrifying fighter-bombers.

"We flew along the coastline," recalled one of the pilots. "It was unbelievable how many ships were there. Until that day, we had seen hardly any. Now suddenly we saw ships of every kind, transports, patrol boats. I can remember seeing a long line of submarines, one behind the other."[10]

However, the cloud proved too low to carry out any attacks, and the pilots returned to base. But early in the afternoon, the weather cleared and they sortied out again. Their task, explained to the pilots in their briefings, was clear: the ships in Lübeck Bay were part of a huge congregation of enemy shipping that might be headed for Norway and could include high-ranking Nazis and military personnel.

"We were on 'readiness' when we were told by Operations that a very large ship loaded with SS troops was leaving to continue the fight from Norway and had to be sunk," said the leader of one of the squadrons involved in the attack. "We were not too happy, as the war was obviously ending and we had experience of SS flak." To another of the pilots, their task "was to prevent the enemy escaping to Norway thus prolonging the war." Yet another remembered that they had received "secret information days earlier that Nazi leaders wanted to move to Norway . . . They wanted to continue the war from there." At all costs, this last escape of the Nazis must be blocked.[11]

This seemed straightforward enough, but the pilots were unaware of one crucial fact: someone at headquarters had failed to pass on the report about the human cargo that the SS had packed into the hulls of the ships in Lübeck Bay.

Shortly after midday, four Typhoons belonging to 184 Squadron swept in low and launched their first rocket attacks on the packed prison ships. A second attack followed three hours later led by Group Captain Johnny R. Baldwin, a skilled and much decorated pilot who had led the attack that wounded Field Marshal Erwin Rommel in France the previous July.

On board the *Thielbek*, Bogdan Suchowiak, a thirty-eight-year-old Polish prisoner from Posen, was sharing a rare meal of soup containing pieces of meat with a friend who had managed to steal a tin of beef from the crew's provisions. At first, when the planes appeared, he paid no notice, but when the first of the rockets smashed into the hull panic broke out. Prisoners on the lower decks frantically tried to clamber up the four steep iron ladders. In the pushing and shoving, many fell back down into the hold. Prisoners on deck threw down ropes for others to clamber up, but when the Typhoons came round for a second attack they hurriedly abandoned the effort to take shelter.

Then the ship began to list. Suchowiak recalled:

> It was clear to me that if we did not jump overboard immediately we would all be drawn into the deep by the suction of the sinking ship. I undressed to my shirt and let myself down slowly on a rope. The water was damned cold. I clung to a wooden plank. It must have been about 3.30 in the afternoon. The sun was shining but then there were passing clouds and rain showers. The sea was relatively calm, with small waves. It was about five kilometres to the shore. [12]

Somehow, he managed to stay afloat for a couple of hours. Then he spotted a minesweeper fishing out survivors and swam as fast as he could towards it. When he got close, he saw a young officer speaking to the crew through a loud hailer: "Don't pick up any prisoners," he was instructing them, "only SS personnel and sailors."

Luckily, though, Suchowiak spoke German, and he talked himself aboard:

> I crept into a bunk and covered myself with everything I could find. Two Soviet prisoners followed my example. The bunk collapsed. A sailor came in and ranted at us. Then one reported to him that we were foreigners. The sailor drew a bayonet. I ran up to the deck and hid myself in a hawser locker. The boat was moving very quickly. A sailor found me and shouted Get Lost! And pushed me and sent me overboard.

Again riding his luck, by this time he was close to the shore and managed to swim to the beach.

He was one of the few survivors. Forty-five minutes after the first rockets hit, the *Thielbek* suddenly overturned and sank. Of the 2,800 prisoners on board, only 50 survived. Most went down with the ship before they had time to get out of the hold.

The *Cap Arcona* suffered a similar fate. Forty of the sixty-two rockets fired from the Typhoons hit the liner, penetrating the superstructure and exploding in the accommodation area. Fire quickly broke out, but the firefighting equipment was damaged and pumping seawater proved impossible. Prisoners from the lower decks rushed madly up the main stairway to reach the upper deck, but it suddenly collapsed in flames, taking hundreds with it. Soon the whole super-structure was ablaze from bow to stern.

Along with eleven others, a German prisoner named Heinrich Mehringer was lying on the floor of a luxury cabin on C Deck when the Typhoons struck. The prisoners had eaten nothing for twenty-four hours except for a single slice of bread, and obviously they were weak. "The ship shuddered as if hit by an earthquake," said Mehringer.

> People rushed out of the cabins. Prisoners lay in the passageways, their clothes on fire. We threw covers over them. A Frenchman came up the companionway, his clothes were also burning. He stam-mered "Water everywhere! Fire everywhere! Everything gone!" Then he collapsed. Beneath our cabins the fire must already have been raging—the cries stopped suddenly. The floor was very hot . . . everyone beneath us was dead and burnt. [13]

Prisoners rushed frantically towards the rails, but most of the lifeboats were ablaze or fell into the water when the manila ropes that held them in place burned through. Somehow, though, three boats were successfully launched. Prisoners stood tightly pressed together. Others floundered in the water, clinging to the sides. Two of the boats almost immediately capsized, and those who were thrown into the water swam to the third. But as they grabbed hold of its sides, or fran-tically tried to clamber aboard, it too turned over.

The water was freezing and hypothermia quickly claimed the starv-ing and the emaciated. Some of the victims managed to find life jackets but simply died on the surface, their arms outstretched and their heads bobbing up and down in the waves. Most, however, just sank silently beneath the waters of Lübeck Bay.

Meanwhile, on shore, a squadron of British tanks was approaching Neustadt along the road from Lübeck. To one of the tank commanders who had driven all the way from the Normandy beaches, the experi-ence was markedly different from that in France and Belgium. Instead of jubilant and cheering flag-waving crowds, they were met by silent, sullen and fearful knots of people, and the only flags visible were white. "Struggling groups of people, and the vehicles, cyclists and weary foot-sloggers," he wrote, "were turned off the road by a wave of my hand." After passing through several picturesque resort towns, the squadron crested a rise overlooking the bay. Its arrival coincided with the attack of the Typhoons. "In harbor several submarines could clearly be seen," continued the tank commander, "and as the tanks deployed three RAF Typhoons went in to attack them. Anti-aircraft fire opened up from the U-Boats and other shipping in the Bay. The squadron including myself joined in the fun, opening up on all the vessels we could see."

Then they continued on their way towards Neustadt, which they reached at four o'clock that afternoon.[14]

Back on board the *Cap Arcona*, the roar of the inferno quickly drowned out the cries of the prisoners. "My back and head were burning," recalled Heinrich Mehringer, "but because of my agitation I did not feel the fire hot, but cold." He managed to grab an iron pipe and pull himself and a friend up above the seething mass. "We ran for our lives on the heads of our comrades as if on a pavement," he continued. "The people beneath us were standing so close together that we could not fall through." At the ship's rail they clambered over the side and down onto the rudder deck. "On the deck above," he said, "all our comrades burned. After a while there was nothing more for the fire to burn. It was deathly silent."

The fire raged for three hours, then there was a massive explosion that ripped open the hull. The *Cap Arcona* turned on its port side, and sank. Of the 6,400 on board, 4,250 of the prisoners were drowned, burned or killed, including nearly all of those from below decks, such as the Russians on the "banana deck" and those kept in the once glamorous "Winter Gardens" saloon. Of the five hundred SS members aboard, some four hundred were saved, including twenty female helpers.

The waters of Lübeck Bay are shallow, so after the ship sank half its hull remained above water. About 350 of the prisoners managed to cling to it and wait for rescue. All had severe burns or other injuries, and they were cold and shivering. Nevertheless, one of them managed to cling to the ship's brass nameplate.

Heinrich Mehringer was among them. After a long time, a small motorboat came alongside. "We were aft and had to run along the hot hull towards the bow," he recalled. "The surface was so hot that we had to lay planks one in front of the other, taking the rear one and putting it in front so that we could walk over them. Everybody helped, gradually the weakest were also transferred." When he was put ashore at

Neustadt, he found that two British tanks had driven onto the pier. "The Tommies came up to me and shook my hand," he said. "I did not understand a word, but I felt that these people were well disposed towards us." Then, suddenly, he realized he was on his own and began walking. "It was like a delirium," he explained. "On and on. Suddenly I was freezing because my clothing was still wet. The houses were blacked out." He was turned away from one or two, then a woman pointed him in the direction of the submarine school. It was guarded by a British soldier, but when Mehringer managed to explain he had come from the *Cap Arcona* he was shown inside to a room containing linen and blankets. "I made myself a thick lair," he said, "and sank into my heavenly bed."[15]

In two subsequent attacks, the Typhoons set fire to and capsized the *Deutschland*. None of the pilots saw the small red cross on one of its funnels. The *Athen* miraculously escaped. Her captain had earlier decided to return to Neustadt Harbor, possibly for water, and the ship avoided attack. All its 2,400 prisoners made it safely ashore.

After the war, the British launched a war crimes inquiry into Nazi atrocities at the Neuengamme concentration camp, and in it they also tried to find out what had happened to the prison ships. Among a large number of witnesses was the intelligence officer for 83 Group RAF, who admitted that on 2 May a message *was* received that the ships were loaded with concentration camp prisoners. "Although there was ample time to warn the pilots of the planes who attacked these ships on the following day," read the report, "by some oversight the message was never passed on."

The report also noted that no such message had been forwarded to the naval liaison officer attached to the British troops who entered Neustadt, and therefore that he had no idea that prisoners were aboard the ships. As a result, and believing that escape efforts by fleeing Nazis were still the main problem, he vetoed any attempts to send craft out from the port to help survivors. Only at six o'clock on the evening of the attacks did he finally learn about the prisoners and countermand his order.

The attack on the prison ships was a tragic, unnecessary and avoidable accident of war, which would not have happened had the information from Lübeck been passed on to the Typhoon squadrons. The British report came to an unambiguous conclusion. "Primary responsibility for this great loss of life must fall on the British RAF personnel who failed to pass to the pilots concerned the message they had received concerning the presence of KZ prisoners of war on board the ships." However, it failed to provide any explanation for the lapse, instead suggesting an official inquiry into the disaster. Despite its urging, though, no such inquest was ever held.[16]

But equal if not greater moral responsibility for the tragedy clearly lay with the Nazis and the SS. The deaths did not result from a knowing or deliberate attack on undefended prison ships, and the pilots learned only afterwards about the human cargoes their targets were carrying. By contrast, the SS knew full well that they were sending unmarked prison ships into a battlefield. They also behaved callously before, during and after the attacks, and made no effort to save the prisoners. The conditions in which the prisoners were kept, the state of the ships, the removal of many life-saving devices, the failure to paint the ships white or to give them Red Cross protection were all consistent with the standard treatment being handed out by the SS to concentration camp inmates across Europe in these last cruel days of the war.

If anything were needed to illustrate the point, it lay in the savage treatment meted out to many of the survivors who finally struggled onto dry land. As we have seen, Bogdan Suchowiak miraculously survived to reach the shore. He had won, he thought. He had saved his life. The war was behind him, as was the disastrous September 1939 campaign in which he had fought to save Poland from the Nazis. He had survived being a prisoner of war and fifty-seven months in a concentration camp. "I had in the end," he thought, "been saved by the beef soup which I had eaten shortly before the attack and which had given me some strength."

But a rude shock awaited him. The first words he heard when he struggled to his feet on the beach were "Bandit, do as you are told or else I shoot!" His captor was a sixteen-year-old cadet from the nearby Neustadt naval school. Along with fifteen or so others who had managed to scramble ashore, Suchowiak was force-marched by the young cadet and several of his cohorts to a nearby hut. Nervously, they constantly prodded the prisoners with their rifle butts and then locked them up.

What his fate might have been had he remained in German hands seemed obvious. But once again, benevolent fate intervened:

> After a long time, a navy truck arrived. We were ordered to climb in — in the distance we could hear machine-gun fire. Suddenly the

truck stopped. We were afraid we were going to be executed. Someone opened the rear door of the truck. I did not believe my eyes. In the middle of a group of German soldiers stood a British captain — a German infantry major was saluting him.

Dozens of others were not so lucky. Instead, they were brutally shot along the beaches by SS troops as they staggered ashore. One such atrocity was still under way when the first of the British commandos arrived on the scene. "The Germans who saw that the tables had turned stopped firing and ran to our soldiers to seek protection," recalled one British officer. "Many displaced persons, who were about to be shot, wanted to avenge their executioners and encircle them. It was the first time that [the commandos] did not hurry to intervene."[17]

Other SS massacres also took place in Neustadt. This time the victims were not prisoners from the Neuengamme camp; they came from Stutthof, one of the concentration camps survived a few weeks earlier by Fey von Hassell. A week before, three huge barges towed by tugs had left the Hela Peninsula, at the mouth of the Vistula near Stutthof, packed with prisoners being evacuated from the concentration camp ahead of the advancing Russians. Each barge held about a thousand men, women and children. They were emaciated, shaven-headed and dressed in tattered clothes. Most were Jews, although one of the barges carried large numbers of Norwegians. No food was handed out during their voyage along the Baltic coast, and there was nothing to drink. In desperation, some of the prisoners drank salt water. Many died as a result. Others simply perished through hunger and exhaustion. Two Jewish women tied themselves tightly together with towels and jumped overboard, their combined weight guaranteeing that they would rapidly sink.

On one of the barges, the SS guards called for volunteers to shove people into the sea. According to one eyewitness, a few Ukrainians stepped forward. "They picked out some people from among us," she recalled, "whom they threw overboard. Those selected were undressed, dragged up a steep iron ladder, and thrown through the hatch into the sea. This was their method of relieving congestion."[18]

Eventually, the ghastly odyssey, minus one of the barges that was deliberately sunk in the Baltic by the crew of its tug, ended up in Neustadt. It was the eve of the *Cap Arcona* disaster, the day that Samain and his commando unit reached the port. As they approached the town harbor, SS men began beating prisoners with the butt ends of their rifles and pushing them over the rails into the water. Once in the harbor, the captain of one of the tugs, horrified by what he had seen, cut the rope of his barge. The guards had already abandoned it, and the Norwegian prisoners on board, mostly policemen who had fallen foul of the occupation regime in their country, took control. They raised a makeshift sail of blankets, managed to maneuver the barge ashore, and were able to greet the British forces when they entered the town.

The prisoners in the other barge were simply dumped ashore. Most were shot. According to some sources, the killing was carried out by marines from the Neustadt U-boat school. "The beaches for a good few hundred yards were covered with bodies," recalled one British officer who visited the scene shortly afterwards. "the two Dutch [*sic*] barges, which were very deep, had had their ladders removed and it was impossible for the victims to escape. These people had been mown down by machine guns . . . The children had been clubbed to death and judging by the shape of their wounds, rifle butts had been used."[19]

Busy with his billeting duties elsewhere in the town, Bryan Samain saw none of this at first hand, but he quickly heard about it. Most of his time was taken up patrolling the town and stamping out any looting or disorder — although, unusually for a German town, this did not prove a major problem in Neustadt. However, his most important job was helping Field Security.

The job of British Army Field Security units was similar to that of the American Army's Counter-Intelligence Corps (CIC) — the protection of the army against intelligence and sabotage threats. In practical terms, this meant hunting down Nazi officials and suspected Gestapo agents who might try to continue the war and attack allied forces by underhand and clandestine means.

Leading the task in Neustadt was a Belgian aristocrat, Major Arthur de Jonghe, a tall, lean, sinister and wolf-like figure who had worked as a British agent in Belgium before fleeing to Britain after being identified by the Gestapo. Now, the hunted had become the hunter. De Jonghe proved an enthusiastic tracker of SS and Gestapo men. Armed with a list, he and his team set ruthlessly to work.

"Like the Nazis themselves," recalled Samain, "we operated in the dead of night — crashing into the houses and apartments of our targeted suspects, hammering on their doors and breaking them down if necessary — usually in the early hours of the morning when they were asleep in their beds." Only one of the suspects caused any trouble, a woman. Woken from her bed, she reached for a derringer under her pillow and tried to fire, but she was quickly overpowered and taken away.

The work gave Samain a deep sense of satisfaction: "We dealt with a number of Nazis," he recorded, "in precisely the same manner that they had dealt with Jews and others during their days of power."[20]

Meanwhile, many grotesque scenes greeted the British tank crews when they arrived in Neustadt and rumbled into the town square. "Into the square, at first a trickle then a stream then a flood, there staggered the emaciated half-naked remnants of a huge number of political prisoners, the survivors of the two [sic] large ships still blazing in the bay," recalled the British officer who had earlier witnessed the Typhoon attacks. "Some, unable to walk, sank to the ground, while others tried to drink from the puddles in the road."

He and the tank crews did all they could to help by giving the victims a sardine on a biscuit each from their rations, but it was not enough. So German soldiers' food, clothing and blankets were requisitioned, and civilians were ordered to produce bread and cheese. So ravenous were the prisoners that they began to fight over scraps of food. It took a volley of shots over their heads to restore calm.[21]

There now remained the task of burying the hundreds of corpses that littered the beaches on both sides of Lübeck Bay. These included the victims of the attacks on the ships and of the SS massacres of the survivors, along with the prisoners from Stutthof.

"Under instructions not to retaliate," recalled one British commando on the scene, "we called out the Germans to bring their spades and shovels to bury the corpses. When they saw the handiwork of their compatriots they assumed that they were called out to dig their own graves and to be shot in retaliation, and some tried to run away. In the end, they dug the graves to bury Himmler's victims."

At dusk, the bodies of hundreds of men, women and children were laid to rest. In the distance the commandos could see the gun flashes of Russian artillery approaching from the East.[22]

CHAPTER SEVENTEEN

"THE DEAD-END OF HITLER'S REICH"

By now, the Russians were in Berlin. Even as the bodies of SS victims were being buried along the shores of Lübeck Bay under the watch-ful gaze of British soldiers, their Red Army counterparts were busily scouring the Berlin bunker for signs of Hitler's corpse. They had to search for two more days before they found his charred remains in the Chancellery garden.

What they did discover straight away, however, were the bodies of Josef Goebbels, his wife, Magda, and their six children. In his last will and testament, Hitler had nominated the über-loyal Propaganda Minister as the new Chancellor of Germany, with Doenitz as President. But Goebbels and his wife chose suicide rather than life in a world without their leader. First, they arranged to have their children mur-dered by cyanide inserted into their mouths by Hitler's personal physician as they slept. Then, they climbed out of the bunker into the Chancellery garden and bit on their own suicide capsules. An SS man put bullets through their heads to make sure they were dead. The Russians found the children still tucked under blankets in their bunk beds, as though they were sound asleep.

Hitler's death did not put an end to the fighting. German forces sur-rendered in Italy, but they continued to resist the Red Army in Austria, Czechoslovakia and eastern Germany. Along the Baltic coast, the Russians continued to race towards Lübeck.

On the night of Wednesday 2 May, far in advance of his own columns, a Red Army scout officer arrived in his jeep at the port of Wismar, barely thirty miles east of Lübeck. This was another small medieval port of patrician gabled houses and huge red-bricked Gothic churches. In 1922, its labyrinthine streets had formed the backdrop for F. W. Murnau's classic Expressionist vampire film, *Nosferatu*. Now they lay in ruins, smashed by recent allied bomber raids. Only one of the town's three steepled churches remained intact. Over the winter, the freezing population had resorted to burning the remains of the wooden statue of St. George and the Dragon from the fire-gutted church of the same name.

To his surprise, the Soviet officer found that Wismar was already occupied by troops from the 1st Canadian Parachute Battalion under the control of General Matthew Ridgway's American XVIII Airborne Corps sent to secure the east flank of the allied advance. With this meeting of the two allied armies at Wismar, both sides now halted their advance. "It's the end, the dead-end, of Hitler's Reich," reported an exultant Wynford Vaughan Thomas while standing beside the wooden barrier across the road that marked the demarcation line between the British and Soviet armies. Shortly before, a few German prisoners had been stopped as they desperately tried to cross to the British side. "The Russian guard gave a wink to me," Vaughan Thomas told his British listeners, "and said 'Siberia.' "

Evidence of widespread German terror about the advancing Russians was plentiful on the road to Wismar. At one point, the Canadian tanks had stopped to refuel. In a small wood they came across a German workshop detachment numbering some three thousand troops. They were eager to surrender. "German civilian women, men and children were there with the troops," reported one of the Canadians, "and when the troops were lined up three deep on the road many had their wives and children with them to accompany them on the trek back to [the prisoner-of-war] cage. This was because the rumor was rife that the Russian army was only nine miles away. They wanted only to be taken by us." The Canadians' advance to Wismar was so swift because the Germans wanted them to get as far east as possible to head off the Russians. Thousands of German troops lined the roads and crowded the villages. Some even cheered on the Canadians.[1]

By this time, Gavin's Eighty-second Airborne Division was also across the Elbe. Still driving his jeep, Leonard Linton rushed ahead to Neuhaus, the first small town east of the river, convinced he would be the first American there. To his dismay, though, when he drove up to its main hotel scribbled on its walls was "Kilroy Was Here"—the motto daubed throughout Europe by GIs to announce their arrival. He pressed on into the town of Ludwigslust.

The town's name translates as "Ludwig's Joy." It acquired it in 1754, after Ludwig II, the Grand Duke of Mecklenburg-Schwerin, established a hunting-lodge there and gradually transformed it into his main residence and the capital of his duchy. Later, he built a grand Baroque palace, or *Schloss*, which was situated in the middle of a vast park laid out in the English style with canals, fountains and artificial cascades. The town also boasted a church that resembled a Greek temple with Doric columns, built at the same time. Although it now lay on a railway line, when Linton arrived its population was only about ten thousand and it had long since lost its status as the state's capital. The palace and its gardens had become a municipal park. Yet some locals still thought of their town as the "Versailles of the North."

Barely two miles to its north, outside the tiny village of Wobbelin, the Americans discovered a small camp packed with some 7,500 emaciated, dying, diseased and starving prisoners, both men and women. The swastika was still flying from the flagpole. "One could smell the camp," wrote a disgusted Gavin. Most of the prisoners were from Russia, Poland and Czechoslovakia, but many came from France, the Low Countries, Spain and Greece, as well as from Germany itself. Fewer than half were Jews.

Linton decided to see the scene for himself:

> The gate was wide open, and all the German guards were gone, so I asked the [prisoners] why they were not leaving. Their pathetic answer was that they did not know where to go, and my Latvian guide pointed to the barracks and said "most of those there will not see sun tomorrow." It had not yet dawned on me that I was about to enter the gates of hell. I went to my jeep and gave them the few chocolate and candy bars that I had and saw that my Latvian was too weak to tear open the papers, and most of the others were just holding them and not eating them.

He asked how the Germans had been killing them, since he saw no signs of any gas chambers or crematoria. "They said in a sad voice," he recorded, " 'simply by not giving any food.' "[2]

The SS guards had fled the day before. Bodies lay strewn about in the open. Linton walked into a small building that served as a cross between a first-aid post and a hospital. "Inside," he wrote, "was a pile of skinny and naked corpses piled against a wall with other smaller stacks of corpses here and there." In the brick barracks buildings, skeletal prisoners dressed in the standard concentration camp garb of black-and-gray striped clothes still lay in their three- or four-tiered bunks. Some of them were dead, but most were mute, staring and silent. "I talked to a number of other survivors ambling around, asking where they were from," Linton continued. "Almost all said they were Russian farmers and [had been] several years in various concentration camps." Gradually it dawned on him that these were relatively hardy peasants and that was why they had survived. Prisoners from towns and cities had quickly died from the rigors that faced them.

Almost the worst thing of all was the smell, both inside the barracks and outside. "I can't describe it adequately," Linton wrote, "nor do I think better writers would be able to. It had a smell of dead human flesh but drier, more fungus-like, somewhat sweetish — quite unlike the smell of well-fed corpses rotting under bombed buildings we often smelled — mixed with the smell of putrefaction and dirt." He drove out of the camp leaning over the side of the jeep to let the wind clean away the tiny particles of the stench that he imagined were physically clinging to him.

The camp was a satellite of Neuengamme and had been built only that February. Conditions deteriorated so quickly that by the time the paratroopers arrived prisoners were eating the livers of those who had died. It was Linton's first experience of Nazi horrors. "I went back to our office," he recalled, "with the hatred of everything German even more accentuated, if that was possible."

The atmosphere was grim and quiet. Major Seward, Linton's commanding officer, summoned the Mayor to come and see him. He proceeded, Linton wrote,

> to give him a tongue lashing that should have been recorded for posterity. I translated it . . . Deep emotional indignation poured out of [him], without any four letter words, but in the most erudite terms I had heard since entering the army. It filled me with pride and humility at the mere fact of being alive and wearing the uniform of

the US Army. On finishing, my CO turned away in disgust from the silent Mayor.

Linton took the man outside. He did not want to see a moment's hesitation, he told him, from the Mayor himself or any other German from Ludwigslust in helping save every one of the camp's survivors. Later that same day, the Mayor was taken out to the camp to witness the scenes of degradation and death. The next day, he committed suicide by taking poison along with his wife and daughter.[3]

For the American GIs, Wobbelin was as much of an eye-opener and had much the same effect as Belsen had for the British. It revealed the worst horrors of the regime they were fighting, and gave vivid shape to the cause they served but had never fully understood. "It was a defining moment in our lives," wrote one of the All-Americans, "who we were, what we believed in, and what we stood for."[4]

The Mayor's was not the only self-inflicted death in Ludwigslust. A woman of the town who believed her Luftwaffe husband had died on the Eastern Front shot herself and her two small children when she heard a rumor that the Russians were moving into the town. Linton saw the blood-spattered cribs and learned that the children had survived and been taken to a hospital. A few days later, the husband walked into his office asking where they were. Linton tried to find out, but they had been moved on somewhere else and he was unable to help. The man joined the thousands of others across Europe searching for the remnants of his family.

Linton and his detachment did their best for the Wobbelin survivors by moving most of them to a nearby hospital, but he lent a special hand of his own when he came across a small group of prisoners speaking French. Dressed in their striped uniforms, two of them were clearly "zombies," captives so mentally inert that they had lost the will to survive.

They will never survive in the crowded hospital, thought Linton. So he loaded them into the back of his jeep and took them to an empty and undamaged office in the town's railway station. Then he drove around, found some food, and took it back to the leader of the group, who was in the most reasonable condition, warning him to hand it out in only small amounts. Every now and again he returned to see how they were doing, and gradually he saw a change. The eyes of the zombies began to follow his moves and they seemed to listen to his words.

"After a few more days of intermittent visits," he recorded, "the former zombies started talking and I admired the one responsible for saving his colleagues' lives."

On one of the visits, the leader asked Linton where he had learned to speak such excellent French. "I told him a little about my life in Paris and my going to the Lycée Claude Bernard," remembered the American. "I was amazed to learn that one of the former zombies was a classmate of mine in that Lycée. He became a journalist, writing for several years for some Parisian newspaper that was a mouthpiece of the German propaganda organization." But, Linton went on, the man had been arrested and thrown into the notorious Drancy prison camp "because some other Frenchmen denounced him to the French censors explaining that this journalist was writing in fine innuendoes which the Germans failed to grasp, ridiculing [them] right under their noses."[5]

Meanwhile, other members of the division were accepting the local surrender of an entire German army. Only hours after Gavin had set up his command post in the Ludwigslust palace, he was visited by Lieutenant-General Kurt von Tippelskirch, commander of the German Twenty-first Army Group. Although his army had been fighting the Russians, von Tippelskirch, like most of the Wehrmacht at this point, was eager to surrender to the Americans. After some initial haggling over terms, he agreed to the unconditional surrender of the 150,000 men under his command.

The next morning, the Germans began pouring through the American lines. They passed in reverse order, beginning with General Staff officers and ending with the front-line combat troops. The headquarters staff included ten generals. As they rode past in their large, chauffeured limousines, they seemed, noted one amazed American paratrooper, "to have prepared for the grand finale. Clean shaven and groomed, uniforms clean and neatly pressed, boots shined, with monocles and medals, they were proud to the very end." Bumper to bumper, it took several hours for all the vehicles to pass.

At last, on foot, came the weary front-line troops. Some were as old as sixty, others as young as sixteen. "All were dirty and unkempt with shoes held together by rags," observed the same witness, "[and] there seemed no question they were a soundly beaten force, with no fight left in them."

But Linton had a very different impression when he ran into a battleship-gray convoy of trucks packed with Doenitz's unrepentant men on the northern outskirts of the town. The Kriegsmarine officers, like their army counterparts, were immaculately dressed in gray, ankle-length leather overcoats and gold- and silver-decorated caps. But the sailors were truculent and hostile, sitting in their trucks with rifles and fixed bayonets, and far from cooperative. When Linton ordered them to remove the bolts from their rifles, they simply jeered at him and ignored his instructions. Only after the order was transmitted through their captain did they obey.[6]

Two Hungarian cavalry units also proved an exception to the dispirited mien of the German Army front-line troops. Surrendering with hundreds of beautifully groomed horses and immaculately kept and polished equipment, they offered to join forces with the Americans to fight the Russians. Instead, they were relieved of their arms and their mounts. For days afterwards, the Americans enjoyed riding the thoroughbreds in makeshift races around the town.

There was only one minor hitch in the otherwise peaceful proceedings. This came when a company of SS troopers hiding out in nearby woods refused to surrender. A company of paratroopers was sent in with orders either to capture them or wipe them out. Feeling that they had already done their bit in the war, defied all the statistics and come out the other side alive, the paratroopers went in fast and heavy. After they had killed about forty of the SS men, the rest came out waving white flags and pleading, "*Bitte! Bitte!*" (Please! Please!). They were marched off roughly to the cage.[7]

Linton was confronted with a tidal wave of work as military government and counterintelligence units toiled hard to bring order out of the general chaos. They struggled to find a new mayor untainted by either Nazism or communism but eventually unearthed a white-haired socialist who was willing to take on the task. Linton also had to deal with the local *Kreisleiter*, the highest official in the area. He found him to be a "master of silent deception" who merely feigned cooperation while subtly resisting. Before long, the man was arrested by the Counter-Intelligence Corps.

Thousands of items of weaponry and military equipment littered the streets. The debris looked like seaweed left on a beach after a storm, thought Linton. Simply supervising its collection to make the roads safe for children, pedestrians and vehicles took up much of his time. There was also the urgent matter of food. For a few days, he devoted most of his energy to supervising the three or four bakeries in town, ensuring they had ample supplies of wheat, and looking after the distribution of loaves to the most needy. He also found a garage piled high with brand-new medical equipment, and made sure that it went to help the concentration camp survivors. Between times, he scoured the town and surrounding countryside for souvenirs to take home, especially small weapons, cameras and any optical instruments he could lay his hands on. He was a keen amateur astronomer and photographer.

Like most young American troops, he struggled hard to live by the rule of nonfraternization. At least once, he enjoyed a brief fling with a girl from Schleswig-Holstein. But most of the time, unlike the combat troops whose job was now over, he was simply too exhausted by the demands of his job for much fun. After rising each dawn to cope with a range of unpredictable emergencies and problems that took up most of the day, he usually keeled over in bed each night and fell fast asleep.

He also had to deal with cases of rape—although not by fellow GIs but by Red Army troops. Thousands of terrified German civilians had reached the town from the East, where Red Army troops had raped and looted their way through East Prussia and Pomerania. "Red Army soldiers don't believe in 'individual liaisons' with German women," wrote a Russian marine officer in his diary. "Nine, ten, twelve men at a time—they rape them on a collective basis."[8] The Red Army had crossed into East Prussia in January. By April, stories of the mass and systematic rape of German women and girls were causing panic everywhere threatened by Stalin's forces. Goebbels and his propaganda machine exploited them to the full.

The stories were only marginally exaggerated. Not all Soviet soldiers joined in, and occasional efforts were made to stop it. But on the whole, rape and indiscriminate looting accompanied Stalin's men in their advance into Germany as a matter of course. Mostly, it was explained or justified as vengeance for the destruction wreaked by the Germans in Russia. Typical was the response of Marshal Vasilevsky, commander of the Third Byelorussian Front, when he was told of looting by his troops. "I don't give a fuck," he said after a moment's pause, "it is now time for our soldiers to issue their own justice." But even this was to put a gloss on what was usually the spontaneous explosion of a potent mix of testosterone and alcohol-fueled desire to humiliate and dominate. By April, the Red Army's soldiers "tended to regard

German women more as a casual right of conquest than a target of hate."[9]

The town of Schwerin lay close to Ludwigslust and had just been sacked by the Soviet Eighth Guards Army. The Russian novelist and war correspondent Vassily Grossman was there. "Terrible things are happening to German women," he wrote. "A cultivated German man explains with expressive gestures and broken Russian words that his wife has been raped by ten men that day." He also reported that a young mother had been continuously raped in a farm shed until her family was finally forced to ask the soldiers to take a break to allow her to breast-feed her baby to stop it crying. All this, noted Grossman, was taking place in full view of the officers supposedly responsible for discipline.[10]

Linton had to deal with at least one similar case. One day, a seventy-two-year-old farm woman came to ask his help. Ten Red Army men had raped her the previous day and then thrown her down a flight of stairs. All he could do was direct her to the hospital.

At night, across the canal that formed the demarcation line agreed with the Russians, the American paratroopers frequently heard the screams of German women. "When mankind sends their young men off to wars to kill one another," wrote one of the paratroopers, "the victims extend beyond the battlefield."[11]

Thousands of German women committed suicide to escape being raped. In one small German village, a whole unit of Hitler Youth girls perished in a group wrist-slashing. Others who were raped killed themselves later. Altogether, it is estimated that up to two million German women may have been raped by Stalin's conquering armies. Of those who became pregnant, it has also been estimated that some 90 percent obtained abortions.[12]

Five days after Linton's arrival in Ludwigslust, a symbolic reburial ceremony took place in front of the palace for the victims of the Wobbelin camp. First, leading civilians from the town were forced to exhume two hundred bodies from the common pits behind the barbed wire and bring them to the palace. There they were made to dig an individual grave for each one and wrap them in sheets. Then the division's chaplain, Major George Wood, read out a simple burial service. The camp's registry had disappeared just before it was liberated, so none of the names of the dead were known, but of the 200 graves, 179 were marked with crosses and 21 with stars of David.

It was Monday 7 May. Several hundred miles to the west, in Reims,

France, representatives of the Wehrmacht were putting their signatures to the unconditional surrender of all German forces in Europe.

Meanwhile, high up in the Italian Alps, Fey von Hassell was enjoying her first few days of liberation. The hotel to which they had been brought felt like an "earthly paradise." She took walks in the woods, delighted in jumping across crystal-clear mountain streams, and enjoyed lashings of good food and wine. Yet, inside, anxiety slowly began to eat away at her relief at being finally free. The last desperate cries by Corrado as he was wrenched from her grasp by the SS nurse rang incessantly in her ears. What had happened to her boys? Would she ever see them again? If so, when? And would they even recognize her? Now that she had little else to worry about, the torment of her lost children began to give her sleepless nights.

Fey's lifeline, as so often, was Alex von Stauffenberg. He had been her constant soulmate during their ghastly forced odyssey of the last few months, and since the tragic death of his wife they had drawn even closer together. Liberated but still trapped in the mountains, they whiled away the time by taking long walks together through the woods. "Although the loss of the children weighed heavily on my mind and would often dampen my spirits," she confessed, "I found a kind of inner peace being with Alex, who, after all, had lost practically everything."[13]

The few days in the mountains provided others in the group with the chance of some quiet time and intimacy, too. Watching over the scene, the eagle eye of SIS officer Sigismund Payne Best missed little. "Although I may have seemed unobservant," he admitted later, "there was really little . . . which escaped my notice. I was, however, overjoyed when I saw flirtations and incipient love affairs starting, for that proved more than anything that people were on the high road to recovery."[14]

After one of their excursions, Fey and Alex returned to find several camouflaged jeeps parked in front of the hotel and people milling about. It was Friday 4 May. A company of American infantry had finally arrived. Close by, troops of the US Seventh Army advancing from Germany had also driven over the Brenner Pass and linked up with the Fifth Army heading north through Italy. In the process, they had finally put paid to any notion of the Alpine Redoubt. The American troops had already disarmed the German soldiers who had been guarding the group and were also trying to control a bunch of Italian partisans who had arrived on the scene eager for some action. Eventually, they got rid of them.

So, at last, true liberation had come. Most of the American soldiers had never heard of Blum, Schuschnigg or indeed any of the others from the polyglot group that now greeted them, although they knew they were important and loaded them with gifts. This in itself was enough for Blum and his wife. The idea of death had been a constant companion for months, and the Americans' arrival produced in him a feeling akin to ecstasy. "For several days," wrote the former French Prime Minister, "we had known we were alive. Now, we knew we were free."

Food, medicine and clothing materialized overnight, and the group was showered with cigarettes and chocolate. Payne Best had a similar response to Blum: "It was simply astounding," he remembered, "what trouble they took to promote our comfort and security, and what nice fellows they were, too." A couple of days later, a flock of allied journalists, photographers and war correspondents descended on the hotel. They interviewed the big names, and the lobby and corridors popped and flashed with the sounds and lights of their cameras.[15]

Fey was thankful that she still had a few days of quiet in the mountains before having to adjust to the real world, and to say her slow, inevitable goodbye to the group who had become her surrogate family over the last few terrible months. The following day, a Catholic priest from Munich who had been with the prisoners most of the way said mass in the small stone chapel next to the hotel. Fey, along with many of the others, was Lutheran, but they all went to the service anyway. The priest "thanked God for having protected and saved us," she wrote. "His sermon was so simple and touching that everyone was profoundly moved in that forlorn mountain chapel, so far from the rest of the world. It was a place perfectly adapted to such a service."

By contrast, she was irritated by the Protestant service held by Martin Niemoller, the one time U-boat commander. "He marched up and down in front of us as if he were still standing on the bridge of a ship," she wrote. She recognized well enough that in Britain and the United States he had become a powerful symbol of Christian resistance to Hitler, and that he had shown great personal bravery. But in the circumstances, when she was just thankful to be alive, she did not feel like boasting about personal suffering.[16]

*

Fey's children were only two among the millions of lost and displaced victims of the war. Now that the fighting was ending, the lucky ones were beginning to return home. Some walked, others were carried by truck, but most were transported by rail. Not long before, the Reichsbahn had been busy shunting millions of troops to the front and millions of Jews to the death camps. Now, in May, it started ferrying displaced persons (DPs) back to their homelands.

Many of the liberators suddenly found themselves overwhelmed with tasks they could never have imagined when they had first donned their uniforms. One such was a British officer who was seconded to Patton's army to set up a feeding center for DPs. Like Francesca Wilson, he had worked with refugees after the First World War, feeding the starving in Silesia.

On the main line between Munich and Frankfurt lay a small hamlet near to Bamberg named Stullendorf. The station had a couple of sidings and a branch line that could take three trains at a time. Nearby, there was a river where the DPs could bathe. "I had five or six trains each day, 40 trucks to each train, 30 to 40 people to each truck," recalled the British officer. "And I had trains come through at night, as well. I worked out I had to feed between 12,000 to 22,000 people each day." Heading north were Russians, Poles, Lithuanians, Latvians, Estonians and Hungarians. Going south were Italians, Greeks and Yugoslavs. "I had six big boilers holding 500 liters of soup," he said, "and bread and cheese and American army ration packs, and little packs of sweets for the children. Some of the people had been on the line for two or three days and were very hungry . . . Some of them were still in their concentration camp clothes. Some of the people out of the camps were in a very bad way, dying or too ill to move." Once, he had to summon a medical team to look after a trainload of people who were seriously ill and covered in sores. More than once, he buried some unfortunate soul.

One day, he received a phone call from Nuremberg. "You've got trouble coming," an American voice said. "Two thousand Russians on a train. They've got guns from somewhere and they're shooting at people as they pass by." The Russians were also drunk. Almost immediately, a military government officer from Bamberg tore up in his car. "I hear you're going to have a lot of trouble," he said. "I couldn't sleep in my bed and leave you to face all this trouble alone. I've alerted some troops. They'll be here any minute. We'll lay each side of the track. We'll put the lights out and give them a reception."

They waited in the darkness. Then they heard the train approaching. The Russians were shouting and firing their guns. As the locomotive pulled into the station, the Americans suddenly switched on the lights and the Russians found themselves staring at two lines of US infantry pointing automatic weapons straight at them. "That soon sobered them up," said the British officer, and they gave him no trouble.[17]

CHAPTER EIGHTEEN

HITLER'S LOOT

It was a long, piece-by-piece surrender — peace with a whimper. Out of the debris of Germany's military collapse, Doenitz hoped to salvage enough of Hitler's Reich to permit a quick national rebirth. He kept some of Hitler's cabinet in his government, neither banned nor dissolved the Nazi Party, and made no changes at all in the Wehrmacht High Command.

His military tactics during the first week of May were also motivated by this objective. At first, he tried desperately to offer capitulation in the West only, while continuing to fight on in the East against the Soviets. When this effort failed, and the Western allies insisted on surrender on all fronts, he determinedly dragged his heels to gain time. His goal now was to permit as many German troops as possible to withdraw to the West and not fall into Red Army hands.[1]

On Wednesday 2 May he sent Admiral Hans-Georg Friedeburg, his successor as commander-in-chief of the German Navy, to Montgomery's headquarters on Lüneberg Heath, about sixty-five miles south of Hamburg. His mission was to offer the surrender of German forces in Holland, Denmark and northern Germany, including those fighting the Russians. Montgomery refused. The latter should surrender to the Red Army, he replied, and if the Germans rejected this, he would go on fighting. Twenty-four hours later, Friedeburg returned to Lüneberg after conferring with Doenitz. This time he signed the terms dictated by Montgomery.

But Doenitz had not given up. He now sent Friedeburg to Eisenhower's headquarters in Reims to offer the surrender of all German forces in the West, but *only* in the West. This offer, too, was refused. Once more, Friedeburg said he would have to consult with Doenitz. Meanwhile, the delay was permitting thousands of Wehrmacht troops to stream west towards the allied lines and for local surrenders to take place. On Sunday 6 May, Doenitz ordered Jodl to fly to Reims and get out of Eisenhower what Friedeburg had failed to achieve. He had firm instructions: he was to try once again for a partial surrender in the West. But, if that failed, as was likely, then he should endeavour to win as much time as possible by having the surrender implemented in two phases. The first would lead to the cessation of hostilities; the second would permit German troops liberty of movement for as long as possible after the fighting stopped.

Predictably, Eisenhower insisted on unconditional surrender on all fronts. He further demanded that it be signed that very night. But he threw the Germans one bone: he would leave his lines open for forty-eight hours. In other words, if any German troops fighting the Red Army could make it through the Western allies' lines within that time period, it was fine by him.

Doenitz realized that this was about as good as he was going to get. At 2:41 a.m. on Monday 7 May, General Alfred Jodl, chief of the operations staff at the German High Command, as well as Friedeburg, put their signatures to the unconditional surrender on all fronts of German forces in Europe. It was to come into effect just before midnight the following day. A similar ceremony took place at Marshal Zhukov's headquarters at Karlshorst, Berlin, shortly after midnight on Tuesday 8 May.

Thanks to Doenitz's delaying tactics, almost two million German soldiers were able to avoid Soviet captivity.[2] But Hitler's successor could not have succeeded in securing this without the tacit consent of the Western allies. The German army group whose surrender at Wismar Leonard Linton had witnessed several days before had been fighting the Red Army, not the Americans. Strictly speaking, it should have surrendered to the Russians.

To the south, in Austria, BBC correspondent Robert Reid was reporting on a similar scene.

After interviewing the liberated prisoners of war at Moosburg, he had stayed with Patton's Third Army, pushing through Bavaria towards Austria. Poor roads, roadblocks and rough terrain were virtually the only things now slowing them down. Occasionally, some local diehard Nazis would mobilize resistance, but the Americans simply blasted it away. Reid saw what happened when the enemy tried to delay their crossing of the Isar River: the howitzers got to work, he told his BBC audience, and "fruitless opposition was blown away like chaff before the wind by this hail of steel."[3]

Back home in England, his wife, Vera, was fighting battles of her own. Like millions of other women on the home front, she was keeping the house running, paying the bills, looking after their children, making repairs, darning clothes, keeping the garden tidy, feeding the hens, and doing myriad other daily tasks on her own.

With the end of the war in sight, she also worried continuously about their future housing. They were renting the house they lived in, but she had heard on the grapevine that the owners were keen to have it back. What would she and Robert do then? Would they have to fight a court order for repossession? Or would he come back from Europe with enough money saved for a down payment on a house of their own?

For the previous twelve months some people at the top of their road had been vainly trying to get a house, and they had recently been given a month's notice by their landlord. What if this happened to the Reids, too? After all, no one, she reminded her husband, "will have children."

She anxiously scrimped and saved, but recently the bills had seemed to come in thick and fast. Above all, though, she was lonely. The last weekend of April was wretched, "one of those horrible weekends," she complained. The war seemed to be dragging on forever, and a news report that it was over turned out to be cruelly false. The weather did not help, either. It was a typical spring—treacherous, bright and sunny one minute, snowing the next. There had even been a small blizzard, and it was still cold. Her spirits were low as she poured out her frustrations and worries in two long, handwritten letters to her husband. One nightmare was that when the war in Europe finally finished he would be sent to Burma. But, worst of all, she had not heard from him for several days. Occasionally, she heard his name mentioned on the radio, but there had been nothing personal. "I seem to have lost touch with you altogether," she complained. "I know so little of where you are or what you are doing. Are you alright, keeping out of trouble?"[4]

He was. In fact, he spent the night that Hitler killed himself in a cozy farmhouse close to Braunau-am-Inn, the small Austrian border town where the Nazi dictator had been born and into which Patton's tanks were to roll the next day.

The farmer and his wife were eager to ingratiate themselves with the BBC correspondent, so they fed him a good, hearty dinner and brought out photographs of relatives living in Seattle and Chicago. Then, in the flickering candlelight over a bottle of beer, they told him how much they disliked Hitler and all he stood for, probed him on how long the Americans and British might stay, and wondered whether Bavaria might, once again, become a sovereign state.

The evening was all very *gemütlich*, but it severely tested Reid's patience and good nature. He had seen Buchenwald only a couple of weeks before and was profoundly skeptical about any Germans claiming to have opposed Hitler. Only the future, he assured his listeners, would tell how deep and sincere such overnight conversions by the Germans really were.

He was far from alone among allied war correspondents in caustically noting how keen Germans now were to distance themselves from the Nazis. Like the war-correspondent-turned-soldier Geoffrey Cox, the American writer and novelist Martha Gellhorn had reported on the Winter War of 1939. She then went on to cover the war in Europe. In May 1945, she wrote scathingly about the Germans in an article for *Collier's* magazine:

> No one is a Nazi. No one ever was. There may have been some Nazis in the next village . . . Oh, the Jews? Well, there weren't really many Jews in this neighborhood. I hid a Jew for six weeks. I hid a Jew for eight weeks. All God's chillin hid Jews. It would sound better if it were set to music. Then the Germans could sing this refrain. They all talk like this. One asks oneself how the Nazi government to which no one paid any allegiance managed to carry on this war for five and a half years.[5]

On the morning of Monday 7 May, Reid was back at Patton's headquarters in Regensburg. Suddenly, he and the other correspondents were summoned to a special conference. As an American colonel read out a statement, Reid scribbled the words in his notebook. "The war ends officially at one minute past midnight tomorrow night," he recorded, "cease fire went at eight o'clock this morning."

Hurriedly, he and a couple of the others grabbed a few boxes of rations and ordered up their jeep. The recording gear and their bedding rolls were hitched to the back and off they tore in a frantic rush towards Austria and the front line. The bad weather of the previous few days had lifted, and it was under a clear blue sky that they crossed the border. Small children ran out of roadside cottages and threw lilac branches into their laps. The country's red and white national flag was fluttering everywhere in the bright sun for the first time since Hitler's troops had marched into Vienna in 1938.

Reid spent the night in the small village of St. Martin. From a window high up in the nearby castle he looked down on a courtyard and saw the local German commander and his staff step stiffly out of their cars and surrender to the Americans. Early the next morning, he woke to the sound of church bells. Peering through the lace curtain of his tiny room, he saw villagers passing by dressed in their Sunday best on their way to a thanksgiving service. He shaved at a well in an orchard under blossoming apple trees, much as he had almost a year before in Normandy. Then he sped off again in his jeep along dusty roads in the direction of Vienna. At times, it almost felt like a touring holiday.

He soon reached Linz, on the Danube. This was Austria's third-largest city and the capital of Upper Austria. It was also Hitler's home town. Here, the future Nazi dictator had attended high school; and, as an eager and impressionable twelve-year-old, perched high up on the cheapest seats in the gallery of the city's opera house, he had heard his first opera, Wagner's *Lohengrin*. This experience proved "a transcendent aesthetic experience" that awakened the future dictator's deepest artistic and cultural feelings.

Years later, Linz was the first stop on Hitler's triumphal procession to Vienna following the Anschluss. Soon afterwards, he selected it as one of his five "Führer cities." It was marked out to become the most imposing city on the Danube, surpassing even Budapest, the epicenter of European culture with a complex including a library, opera house, cinema and concert hall. For Hitler, the Nazi revolution was above all a cultural revolution that would awaken the deepest longings of the German *Volk*. At the heart of the Linz project would be a museum of European art rivaling the Uffizi in Florence, featuring Hitler's own vast collection of paintings which he was rapidly acquiring through looting and forced purchase. A model of the new city was even installed in the

Berlin bunker. Here, he spent hours poring over the details while the German capital above him collapsed in flames and ruins. The Linz Museum, noted one of his secretaries in the bunker, was "one of his favorite conversations at late afternoon tea."

Linz was also powerfully linked with Hitler's favorite composer, Anton Bruckner, who had been born close by and had served as Linz's cathedral organist for many years. A Bruckner piece always featured at cultural sessions of the Nuremberg Rallies, and Hitler even paid a reverential visit to the composer's monument in the famous Valhalla hall of fame to German heroes outside Regensburg, where he stood mute while the Munich Philharmonic played the adagio of the composer's Seventh Symphony. This piece, the Nazi leader once declared, was equivalent in greatness to Beethoven's Ninth.

During the last desperate days in Berlin it was rumored that when the Berlin Philharmonic chose to play the composer's Fourth Symphony, it meant that the final days of the Reich were near. Ominously, it was included in the orchestra's program on Friday 13 April. As the audience filed out, uniformed members of the Hitler Youth handed out free cyanide pills at the exits to the party faithful.[6]

That was just three weeks before, but Reid had no time to sightsee or waste time pondering the ironies of history and Hitler's cultural ambitions. In any case, by now Linz was mostly a pile of rubble packed with refugees huddled in cellars. So, he pressed on. About twelve miles south of Linz he reached his destination, the town of Enndorf, on the River Enns at its juncture with the Danube. Here, as the jeep traveled down the main street, he ran into his first column of surrendering Germans. The driver swung over a bridge into open fields beyond, and ahead of him Reid saw a crowd of some sixty thousand German soldiers streaming down the road in his direction, a vast cavalcade of defeat containing the remnants of the southern group of German armies. Supervising it all was a handful of GIs, a line of field guns dug in a mile or so to the rear and overhead a spotter plane which rocked and wobbled in the air, swooping low every so often to take a closer look.

As far as Reid could see, German vehicles were jammed bumper to bumper, and everywhere he looked wooden horse-drawn carts rumbled past carrying supplies and weapons. Occasionally, an American military policeman directed a truckload of discarded rifles, bazookas and automatic weapons into the field from where Reid stood and watched, microphone in hand, recording the scene on a telediphone for his audience back in Britain. Many of the vehicles were packed with women, civilians as well as nurses and army auxiliaries, camp followers of the troops from Vienna and Eastern Europe now fleeing the Russians. Some vehicles carried troops on their bumpers or mudguards, or lying deadbeat on their bonnets, and alongside them trudged columns of exhausted infantrymen. A few soldiers on bicycles wobbled past the half-track vehicles, avoiding the ruts that they gouged in the road.

Remnants of the SS Hitler Youth division strode arrogantly past Reid into the field. "Have you had any trouble with them?" he asked the young American major in charge, a native of Pittsburgh. "No," replied the officer. "They ask us for cigarettes; they just seem happy to get away from the Russians."

"So this was VE Day as I saw it," concluded Reid in his special dispatch to Britain, "an amazing unforgettable day . . . a sight I wish I could have shared with everybody whose home has been bombed, and with everyone who's lost some loved one in the war, and with those untold hundreds of thousands of Europeans who were tortured and sacrificed on the altar of Nazism since 1933." Down on the banks of the swiftly flowing Danube, young boys and girls bathed and splashed in its pale green water, watched by wounded German soldiers and nurses from the decks of hospital paddle ships berthed against its banks.

As he drove back to Regensburg, Reid passed weary GIs resting by the roadside, the gunners cleaning their weapons, the tank crews gazing down from their turrets, the sappers building bridges. None of them waved, cheered or made wisecracks to give Reid a good story. The chill shadow of war, he concluded, still lay too close to their hearts.[7]

By now, the world knew that Austria concealed no National Redoubt and that the threat from Nazi Werewolves was purely mythical. To the south, still in the mountains of Styria, SOE agent Fred Warner had reached the same conclusion.

Having spent a week in his mountain hideout sheltering from the snow, when it stopped he set off in search of a house occupied by civilians who might help. He found it the next day. It was a typical wooden Austrian farmhouse with a large balcony running along the entire front of the first floor. High up on the mountainside at the top of a small footpath, it was also nicely secluded. The occupants proved friendly and hospitable. The owners were an elderly couple sharing their house with their daughter and her small baby, as well as another woman and her two young children. The daughter's husband was in the Wehrmacht, fighting somewhere against the Russians.

They gave him a comfortable bed and a delicious meal of bread, butter, bacon, sausage, bottled pears with creamy milk, and a large jug of home-made red currant wine. After a night or two, with no one having sneaked off to inform on his presence to the local police, he felt safe with the family. They were thoroughly fed up with the war and wanted nothing more than the end of hostilities and the return of their menfolk to get on with the farming. He explained who he was and why he was there, and a couple of days later was taken down the mountainside to the nearby village to meet members of the local resistance group. It consisted of an army captain convalescing from a severe leg wound sustained on the Eastern Front, and a few friends who listened secretly every night to the BBC while compiling lists of the local Nazis. Warner discovered that the captain had to make regular visits to a hospital close to the SOE's drop site. As he was keen to find out what had happened to their wireless set, he decided to accompany him on his next visit.

As they rode into town in a comfortable trap drawn by a beautiful horse, he found himself surrounded by columns of German soldiers in full retreat from the advancing Russians, including troops of the SS Viking Division. It was obvious that the war was almost over. At the local police station, he was able to establish that the group's radio set had been taken by the Gestapo to Murau, the nearest big town. More interesting, however, was the rumor that British or American paratroopers had captured the aerodrome at Zeltweg. As this had been one of his group's targets, he decided to head that way.

But first he needed to find a vehicle. Like everyone else, the local top Nazi official was eager to keep out of Russian hands and ingratiate himself with the British and Americans, so it was no great surprise when he volunteered the use of his personal car, and Warner was happy to accept. Sitting next to the Nazi official, a few hours later he arrived at the entrance to Zeltweg aerodrome. Sure enough, a large number of American trucks were parked beside the barrier. A closer inspection, however, revealed that they carried Red Army markings. The Russians had arrived, and within minutes Warner was introducing himself to a

Soviet major who told him that the rest of his group were already there. News of his arrival spread rapidly. Even before he had reached the main building, the others were crowding around him and patting him on the back.[8]

Bizarre though his own journey to Zeltweg had been, he now learned that George Bryant and his group had an even more extraordinary tale to tell. They had heard the news of the surrender of Army Group South in Italy on their small receiving set. Assuming that it also applied to forces in Austria, they descended from their mountain hideout to the nearest village, put through a call to the German military headquarters in Judenburg, and identified themselves as British officers.

Shortly after midnight, two German officers with an escort of soldiers turned up and told the SOE group that the surrender did not apply in Austria. However, explained one of them, they would happily surrender to the Western allies, but under no circumstances to the Russians. In the meantime, he politely invited the group to stay as guests of the German Army.[9]

They set off in convoy, and it was only when they pulled up at the headquarters of General Rendulic at Schloss Thalheim on the outskirts of Judenburg that Bryant recognized it as the former home of one of his uncles, where he had spent many happy holidays as a boy. It was not yet clear whether they were being taken prisoner, so, as a precaution, once Bryant was comfortably installed he tore up the small notebook he carried with him and flushed it down the toilet. The next day, it was agreed with Rendulic that the group would contact their SOE base in Italy to seek instructions about the proposed surrender. But for that, they would need their receiver-transmitter set, which was now in Gestapo hands in Murau.

Getting it back could prove tricky because Wehrmacht/Gestapo relations were often hostile. The most Aryan-looking of the SOE group was Eric Rhodes, who was blue-eyed, blond-haired and six-foot-two tall. So he put on German Army uniform and, accompanied by two genial intelligence officers, drove off to Murau. To his relief, the Gestapo officers were too busy saving their skins to worry about the set, and they happily handed it over. Back at Schloss Thalheim, Kelly, the group's radio operator, sent an encoded message to SOE Italy reporting what had happened.

While they waited for a response, the group headed for the aerodrome at Zeltweg. But here they found a truculent German colonel in charge who refused to hand it over. He had already dealt abruptly with Walter Freud, who had turned up at the aerodrome a couple of days earlier and tried to get the colonel to surrender. But Freud was unable to contact the base in Italy, and he was so obviously junior that the colonel sent him packing to Linz. Although none of the others yet knew it, he eventually reached American lines and was about to be flown out to Paris.[10]

Possibly irritated by the appearance of yet more British agents offering deals, the German colonel now threatened to have them imprisoned as POWs. With things getting sticky, Bryant decided to appeal to higher authority. This time it was his turn to don a German uniform. Throwing on a Luftwaffe jacket and cap, and accompanied by a Wehrmacht officer, he drove off towards the Salzgammergut.

Many top Nazi Party officials had already retreated to this spa-studded region of towering needle-like peaks and shimmering lakes, which was supposedly the heart of the National Redoubt. The road twisted past mountain streams cascading down the rocks, and bright spring flowers were in bloom. After the spa town of Bad Aussee, they climbed steeply up towards Alt Aussee, a smaller town of some four thousand inhabitants nestling on the shore of one of the most beautiful Styrian lakes and framed by snow-capped peaks. This was Bryant's destination — the Austrian base of Himmler's henchman Ernst Kaltenbrunner.

Housed in the Villa Kerry on the outskirts of the town, Bryant discovered a number of Kaltenbrunner's top staff. Among them was Dr. Werner Gotsch of the SD. A fresh-faced thirty-year-old wearing civilian clothes, Gotsch was busily trying to cobble together a "Free Austria" government, a last-ditch SS-inspired effort to rival the government already established by the Russians in Vienna under the leadership of Karl Renner. Known fondly as "Grandpapa Renner," the white-bearded seventy-five-year-old Social Democrat was now heading a coalition of all the major Austrian parties. Gotsch was virulently anti-Soviet and told Bryant that he would like to work for British intelligence against Moscow. Clearly desperate to save his own skin, he suggested a place where the British agents could safely hide out until the situation calmed down.

Later, back at Schloss Thalheim, Bryant learned that an officer attached to the Zagreb headquarters of General Lohr, the commander of German forces fighting against the Russians and Yugoslavs in the Balkans, also wanted to explore the possibility of surrendering to the

Western allies. As the SOE group had still received no instructions from Italy, he decided to meet the officer at Klagenfurt, the capital of Carinthia. There, on the outskirts of the town, they discussed surrender and agreed to refer it back to their respective headquarters. Fred Warner claimed that the person Bryant met in Klagenfurt was SS Obergruppenführer Odilo Globocnik. If so, the encounter must have bristled with tension, for Bryant was an Austrian Jew who had been forced from his homeland by the Nazis, and Globocnik was one of those directly responsible for his misfortune.

Described by one historian as a man "whose energy and ruthlessness distinguished him from the run of his SS associates," Globocnik was born in Trieste. When the Adriatic port was transferred to Italy after the First World War, he moved to Klagenfurt, where he emerged as one of the leading Austrian Nazis behind the Anschluss. For this, Hitler made him Gauleiter of Vienna. Later, Himmler sent him to Lublin as SS and police leader in Poland, where he helped mastermind *Action Reinhard*, the mass murder of several million men, women and children, by overseeing the construction of the killing camps at Belzec, Treblinka, Sobibor and Chelmno. Later, he transferred his homicidal skills to his home town of Trieste. By May 1945, though, he was back in Carinthia, and on the run.

In the Klagenfurt Town Hall, claimed Warner, Globocnik "begged" Bryant to pass on to his superiors the urgent need for the Western allies and Germany to fight together against the Russian "hordes." But if he did so, the SOE officer made no mention of this in his after-action interrogation report two weeks later. It seems most likely that Warner's memory here let him down.[11]

Whatever the truth about Globocnik, both Warner's and Bryant's accounts agreed that two days later they got their answer from Italy. The Germans would have to surrender to the forces against whom they had last been fighting—which meant to the Russians and the Yugoslav armies of the communist partisan Marshal Tito. But the Germans in Schloss Thalheim refused point blank to do this. Within twenty-four hours they left, heading west towards the American lines. At Zeltweg, the commander suddenly turned friendly, invited them into his office for a Scotch, and readily agreed to make the aerodrome usable for the Royal Air Force by lifting the demolition mines laid under its runway. He also provided lists of all the available aircraft, stores and equipment, which the group passed on to Italy by radio.

Comfortably installed in the officers' mess, they waited for British forces to arrive. The first plane to land was an American Mosquito, where the pilot revealed that the British units advancing over the mountains from Italy were being held up by SS troops and that the Russians were getting close. He suggested that the Germans quit the aerodrome immediately and make for the American lines near Linz, taking their planes with them. They promptly did so.

The SOE men therefore found themselves alone at the aerodrome, except for a few Hungarian troops who stayed behind with their families. A day later, on Thursday 10 May, the Russians arrived in force with tanks and infantry. It was hours later that Warner turned up.

Shortly afterwards, the SOE group and several Soviet officers sat down for dinner together in the mess. It was a typically robust and genial affair. The usual endless toasts were drunk to Stalin, to Churchill, to the Red Army and to the British forces. Warner was glad that it was wine, not vodka, that filled their glasses. Still, it was not long before the Russians dropped the usual niceties of using corkscrews and simply knocked the tops of the bottles against the edge of the table. Each of the officers had a bodyguard equipped with a machine-pistol standing behind him during the entire meal. Trained though he was for secret war, it all made Warner feel distinctly ill at ease. He was also taken aback when he asked the lieutenant sitting next to him how he liked the American jeeps and trucks parked outside and the officer replied that he had not seen any. Warner pointed out of the window. "But they have Russian marking on them," the officer replied, clearly believing they had been made in his homeland. Afterwards, when Warner pointed out the English writing on the instruments, the man replied, "Oh, yes, they were meant for export." Such, concluded Warner, was the power of Soviet propaganda.

He and his group spent three or four more nights on the aerodrome. They were "pretty awful," he remembered. "The Russians seemed to go wild once it got dark. Many were drunk, fired tracer bullets into any window showing a light, and, worst of all, went round raping any female in sight. It [was] a pretty horrible situation to hear the screams and to be quite unable to do anything about it."[12] The violence was completely indiscriminate. In a nearby town, the local communist leader who had only recently been released from prison had his house thoroughly looted, and his wife was raped.

It was not just Red Army soldiers who ran out of control. As the

Nazis fled, thousands of forced laborers poured out of their camps and joined in the general plunder. Among them were hundreds of starving Russians, many of them POWs, who had been kept for months or years in savage conditions. On the whole, battlefield death was often better than imprisonment for Red Army soldiers who fell captive to the Wehrmacht. Captured, they were treated like slaves, shot for the slightest misdemeanor, or just killed out of mischief, for fun. Only a fraction of the millions of prisoners taken by Hitler's forces on the Eastern Front were still alive in May 1945.[13]

In Judenburg, Russians — soldiers, prisoners of war and civilians alike — broke into houses and shops and threw out of windows into the arms of their compatriots anything that took their fancy, useful or not. Warner saw scores of Russian soldiers wearing women's fur coats and hats and people using broomsticks as yokes over which dozens of pairs of shoes were slung. He later found a lot of this loot floating in the river that ran through the middle of the town.

Warner was appalled by these scenes, but he found it hard to condemn them out of hand. "Who could blame these people," he asked, "who had been oppressed for such a long time?"[14]

Nowhere in Austria was the systematic cruelty and barbarity of the Nazis, and the savage retribution now visited on them, better illustrated than at Mauthausen concentration camp. This lay just a few miles east of Linz on the banks of the Danube. Three days before Robert Reid sped past on his way to report on the VE Day surrender, American forces had arrived at its gates.

After Ohrdruf, Buchenwald, Belsen and countless other camps, the sight that greeted the GIs was now sickeningly familiar. The camp had been built soon after the Anschluss for twelve thousand prisoners. Now it held some twenty thousand. Food was scarce, typhus rampant, and several hundred inmates were dying each day. At least twelve hundred bodies lay out in the open, unburied. Only a handful of the inmates were Jews. Initially, most were German socialists, homosexuals, Jehovah's Witnesses and gypsies. A second wave consisted of Polish artists, scientists and intellectuals, followed soon after, in 1941, by a large number of Red Army prisoners. After the Germans marched into southern France in November 1942, thousands of Republican refugees from the Spanish Civil War fell into their hands and they, too, ended up in Mauthausen. For these Spanish anti-fascists, the camp became their

Auschwitz. Just hours after its liberation they erected a huge banner over the main gate: "The Spanish Anti-Fascists Salute the Liberating Forces," it proclaimed in Spanish.

Throughout the Mauthausen complex — the main camp and its 49 sub-camps — had passed a total of 335,000 prisoners, of whom 122,000 had perished. Brutal hard labor accounted for most of the deaths. The camp's *raison d'être* was a vast granite quarry close by, raw material for Hitler's grandiose construction projects. Leading from the quarry floor to the top were the notorious "stairs of death." Prisoners were forced to carry huge stone blocks on their shoulders up the almost two hundred steps. If they failed or faltered, they were whipped, shot, pushed off the cliff or transferred to other camps for medical experiments.

Almost as soon as the Americans arrived, fighting and chaos broke out among the starving prisoners. Informers, collaborators and kapos were beaten to death. Most of the SS staff had disappeared, but at least one guard was caught, then hanged naked except for his corporal's hat from the rafters of one of the barracks. Soviet prisoners used his body for target practice, taking turns to throw a long kitchen knife at it. It remained there for two days until the Americans cut it down. Other Red Army survivors roamed the countryside, terrifying the local Austrians.

One of the camp's survivors was a Polish Jew named Simon Wiesenthal. "It was ten o'clock on the morning of May 5 1945 when I saw a big gray tank with a white star on its side and the American flag waving on the turret," he said. "I do not remember how I got from my room into the courtyard. I was hardly able to walk. I was wearing my faded striped uniform with a yellow J in a yellow-red double triangle." He wanted to touch the star on the side of the tank, but he was too weak — his knees gave way and he fell to the ground. The next thing he remembered was someone picking him up. "I felt the rough texture of an olive-drab, American uniform brush against my bare arm. I couldn't speak. I couldn't even open my mouth. I pointed toward the white star, I touched the cold, dusty armor with my hands, and then I fainted."[15]

When Wiesenthal finally recovered, he vowed to start the work that would occupy the remainder of his life — hunting Nazi war criminals.

Another Mauthausen inmate was a Greek political prisoner, Iakovos Kambanellis. He also watched as a battered US tank rammed its way through the gate. As he joined the crowd kissing its charred metal and beating their heads against its sides with tears pouring down their faces, he felt someone grab at his ankles. He bent down to look. Two of the Spanish prisoners had thrown a kapo face down on the ground. With pent-up fury, they were skinning him alive with their knives.[16]

Elsewhere, Patton's armies were uncovering other secrets of the Nazi state. As Reid made his VE Day broadcast, a couple of American jeeps and a truckload of Patton's GIs were cautiously nosing their way up the twisting mountain road to Alt Aussee. They were especially alert because fears about the Alpine Redoubt still loomed large, and none of them was yet sure that it was just a mirage. Nor was it obvious that news of the surrender had reached this remote and secluded spot. Even if it had, there was no guarantee it would be heeded. For the Americans were searching for one of the most valuable prizes of Hitler's Third Reich, one that might well be defended to the bitter end.

By 1943, Hitler had amassed a vast hoard of paintings and other art objects for his projected museum at Linz. Most were looted or purchased at knock-down prices from private collections, mainly Jewish, as well as from dozens of European galleries that had fallen under Nazi control. Stored in museums, galleries and monasteries, they lay scattered across the Reich. But as allied bombers launched increasingly devastating raids on Berlin, Munich and other major cities, the loot was coming under serious risk of damage or destruction. It needed to be hidden in a safe place. After months of searching, a refuge was finally found at Alt Aussee. Here, a labyrinthine salt mine cut deep into the mountain contained a multitude of chambers a mile from the surface. This remote site was ideal because it was constant in temperature and humidity, had few entrances or exits, and was worked by a closely knit group of men whose families had run the mine for generations. The galleries were reached by tiny trains running along miniature winding tracks.[17]

With Hitler's personal approval, workers were exempted from military service to transform the mine into a vast underground gallery equipped with storage racks, wall and ceiling covers, proper floors and electricity. Thousands of paintings were shipped from all over Europe to be housed there. Access was difficult: the only road was narrow, winding and closed in winter, and even when the weather improved oxen and tanks were needed to haul the heavy crates laden with Hitler's loot. The job took months, but when it was complete the mine's guardians felt sure it would be safe from the allies.

The last delivery had been made only weeks before. The crates held several thousand paintings and other art objects, including some of Europe's greatest treasures. In the early days, the Nazis kept a meticulous record of the loot, piece by piece, as it entered the mine. These records were voluminous and filled dozens of ledgers. But by the end, the volume of material became so great that the system broke down, and most pieces were simply labeled with numbers indicating in which shipment they had arrived. Some of them did not even get a number.

Nevertheless, the German curators did as good a job as they could under the circumstances. Hitler's personal collection of Old Masters alone included fifteen Rembrandts, twenty-three Breughels, two Vermeers, fifteen Canalettos, fifteen Tintorettos, eight Tiepolos, four Titians and two Leonardos, not to mention dozens of paintings by Cranach, Rubens, Holbein, Goya and others. One of the most fragile items was the famous Ghent altarpiece by Jan van Eyck, the *Adoration of the Mystic Lamb*, which had a special room inside the mine built for it. Its many panels were shipped to Alt Aussee in a special convoy. The collection also included dozens of Goering's looted paintings, not all of which he wanted to be found in his own collections.[18]

It was far from clear that any of this precious legacy of centuries of European culture would survive the war. Hitler had recently issued his scorched-earth decree and after hearing it the local Gauleiter, SS Obergruppenführer August Eigruber, decided that the Alt Aussee treasures should never fall into the hands of the "Bolsheviks" or "International Jewry." Accordingly, the fanatical Nazi took steps to blow the mine and its contents sky high.

In mid-April, several crates, suspiciously labeled "Marble — Do Not Drop," were delivered to the mine. They arrived along with a huge escort of heavily armed SS troops who then stood guard at the entrance. This provoked high anxiety among the curators looking after the treasure. Some of them, horrified by Eigruber's plan, tried desperately to sabotage or thwart it. Workers at the still-functioning salt mine, who were most concerned about safeguarding their continuing livelihood, joined in these plans. Finally, after their increasingly desperate efforts failed, they appealed directly to Kaltenbrunner himself. Fortunately, by this time, the SS intelligence chief was desperate to establish his credentials with the Western allies. The five-hundred-pound bombs from the "marble" crates had been placed strategically throughout the mine's myriad galleries. In a delicate two-day operation, on Kaltenbrunner's orders they were carefully placed on the tiny trains, moved back along the miles of tracks, and hidden in a pile of brush outside. Then, on Saturday 5 May, the entrance to the mine was blasted shut.[19]

Meanwhile, a British agent had also been active in trying to save the treasure. Albrecht Gaiswinkler was a native of Bad Aussee, a trade union activist and a Social Democrat. Shortly after the Anschluss he joined a resistance group, but with the Gestapo on his heels he enlisted in the Luftwaffe. Posted to France, he deserted shortly before D-Day and soon afterwards was recruited by SOE.

Two weeks before Fred Warner and his group were parachuted into Styria, Gaiswinkler and his three-man team had been dropped into the Salzgammergut. Here, on familiar home terrain, his primary mission was to report on the situation at the mine. Even as he and his team of "Bonzos," as they became known, arrived, convoys of trucks were still toiling up the mountains, bringing loads of looted art to the mine. Just two days after they landed the SS trucks carrying the "marble" also turned up.

Word and rumor quickly spread about their purpose, so Gaiswinkler and his team set about making life as difficult as they could by raising a force of some 350 men and harassing the Germans. They used a variety of methods, including dressing up in SS uniform and issuing orders and counterorders that thoroughly confused the enemy. Gaiswinkler also made contact with Kaltenbrunner. On 6 May, the Bonzos, along with members of the local resistance and some friendly miners, secured the area.

The Americans reached the entrance to the mine two days later, on VE Day. They were prepared for the worst, but instead of meeting a hail of fire, they were greeted by machine-gun-toting guards who surrendered like lambs. Mine and cultural officials, as well as Gaiswinkler and his men, quickly clustered around the Americans. Eagerly, they fell over themselves to claim they had saved the art, showed the GIs the "marble" bombs, and posed for photographs.

Soon afterwards, a small group of experts arrived to explore the contents of the mine and arrange for its removal. They were members of an American team known as the "Monuments Men," an agency set up to protect and recover art and cultural treasures in war-ravaged Europe.

It was cold below ground, so they wore heavy jackets and mufflers.

They boarded one of the small trains, which comprised an engine and half a dozen miniature flat cars, or "dollies." These were each about five feet long and were laden with heavy wooden boxes about two feet wide and two feet high. The Americans squeezed in like sardines. The miners, thought one of them, resembled "a troop of Walt Disney dwarfs."

After a couple of false starts the small train rumbled into the cavern. For the first few yards the irregular walls were whitewashed, but soon they entered a narrow tunnel cut into the natural rock. Sometimes there was a foot or more on either side and a high ceiling, but elsewhere the roof descended sharply until there was hardly any head room and the walls closed in menacingly. In parts of the tunnel there were electric lights, but they were strung at irregular intervals and cast only a dim light on the walls.

The train suddenly branched off the main track and after a few minutes stopped beside a heavy iron door set in the walls of the passageway. This was the Kaiser Josef Mine. There were no electric lights here, so they lit a few carbide lamps. One of the Americans produced a heavy key and unlocked the door. The scene was illuminated only by the flickering lamps and torches they had brought with them. One of the Monuments Men described what they saw amid the gloom:

> Ahead of us we could make out row after row of huge packing cases. Beyond them was a broad wooden platform. The rays of our flashlights revealed a bulky object resting on the center of the platform. We came closer. We could see that it was a statue, a marble statue. And then we knew it — it was Michelangelo's Madonna from Bruges, one of the world's great masterpieces. The lights of our lamps played over the soft folds of the Madonna's robe, the delicate modeling of her face. Her grave eyes looked down, seemed only half aware of the sturdy Child nestling close against her, one hand held firmly in hers . . . The incongruous setting of the bare boards served only to enhance its gentle beauty.[20]

This was only the beginning. In other galleries, the Americans feasted their eyes on similar pieces from the rest of the vast hoard. They had been picking up tips about the Alt Aussee mine ever since landing in Europe, but they had never dreamed of the scale of its treasures. An inventory drawn up soon afterwards listed the mine's contents as

"6,577 paintings, 2,300 drawings and watercolors, 954 prints, 137 pieces of sculpture, 129 pieces of arms and armor, 122 tapestries, 78 pieces of furniture, 79 basket objects, 484 cases thought to be archives, 181 cases of books, 1,200–1,700 cases apparently books or similar, 283 cases contents completely unknown." Over the next few weeks, well into the summer, night and day, the Monuments Men and the mine staff rode backwards and forwards on the miniature trains as they loaded up truckloads of treasures destined for Munich.[21]

Where to store them all safely had presented the Americans with a major problem. The most obvious place was the Haus der Deutschen Kunst, Hitler's first major building project. One of the Monuments Men arrived early in June to look it over, and found it still draped in its billowing dark green, fishnet-like wartime camouflage. But Hitler had looted far too much: the building was simply too small for the purpose.

Close by, next to each other on the Königsplatz, stood the Führerbau and the Verwaltungsbau, Hitler's personal offices as well as the headquarters of the Nazi Party itself. After the arrival of US forces in the Bavarian capital, these had been thoroughly ransacked and the floors were strewn with fancy framed portraits of Hitler, books, stationery emblazoned with Nazi emblems, and reams of party records. Most of what had been stored in the vaults had been stolen, including paintings by Kandinsky, Nolde and Klee that had been confiscated by the Nazis from the Schloss Museum in Weimar after they came to power in Thuringia in 1929.

The Monuments Men decided that the Verwaltungsbau was the best site for the looted art. However, Patton already had his eye on the building for his own headquarters in the city, and a bureaucratic battle for possession broke out. For once, the combative general lost. By the middle of the month the building had been made secure, surrounded by a barbed-wire fence and guarded by armed military policemen.

Patton's men instead took over the Haus der Deutschen Kunst, site of the Nazis' infamous exhibition of "Degenerate Art" just eight years before. Here, with exquisite irony, the Americans turned the cradle of purified Nazi art into an elegant mess and officers' club. "Inside, a transformed German oompah band played the latest 'degenerate' American hits during cocktails and dinner."[22]

If Ernst Kaltenbrunner thought that his role in thwarting Eigruber's demolition plan would save his skin, he was wrong. All across Europe, the victors were now hunting down their prey. Possessing a war record steeped in criminality and inhumanity, the SS Chief still ranked high on the list.

With the hardcore Nazi leaders supposedly holed up in the redoubt, a team of American counterintelligence agents attached to Patton's Third Army arrived in the Salzgammerkut early in May in hot pursuit of human big game. In the fashionable spa town of Bad Ischl, the home of Franz Lehar, the composer of Hitler's favorite operetta, *The Merry Widow*, and the former summer residence of the Austro-Hungarian Emperor Franz-Josef I, they received a tip-off from a member of the Austrian resistance that Kaltenbrunner was hiding out in nearby Strobl. But when they arrived it was too late: the quarry had flown, although they managed to catch his wife. After a further tip-off, they headed up to Alt Aussee with a task force of tanks and infantry.

On Wednesday 9 May, the agents reached the small lakeside spa. Thanks to Gaiswinkler, they were led straight to Kaltenbrunner's SS team at the Villa Kerry, where they arrested them. Among them was Werner Gotsch (the SD officer who had earlier met with George Bryant), a number of lesser Nazis and camp followers, and Walter Riedel, the construction chief for Hitler's V2 rockets. They also found Norman Bailey-Stewart, a notorious British supporter of Hitler, who was imprisoned in the Tower of London in the 1930s after a spectacular trial for espionage. After his release, he returned to Germany and worked in Berlin with William Joyce, "Lord Haw-Haw," broadcasting English-language programs to Britain.

Their most promising captive, however, was Gisela von Westarp, Kaltenbrunner's mistress and the mother of his twins. To the Americans, her presence suggested strongly that the SS leader was hiding very close by. Then they got a tip from a forest ranger, and headed for an isolated cabin high on the snow-covered slopes of a nearby mountain. Inside, they found four men, a large quantity of ammunition, and some burned SS identity papers. Two of the men admitted they were SS guards, but one of them insisted he was merely a doctor discharged from the Wehrmacht, and had papers to prove it. Although he was obviously Kaltenbrunner, instantly recognizable because of his facial scars, the Americans could not prove it.

But he was betrayed by his mistress. When the group was marched into Alt Aussee a few hours later, she broke from the watching crowd to embrace him. Before long, he was heading for an interrogation center.

Back in Alt Aussee, "Wild Bill" Donovan's OSS opened a special interrogation center of its own, staffed by officers of its specialized Art Looting Investigation Unit (ALIU). Its initial mission was to identify Nazi agents who might be using the looting of art and associated activities as a cover for espionage. Now, under the code name "Project Orion," its job morphed into tracing and preventing the flow of assets from the looting to places of refuge where they might be used to finance the post-war survival of Nazism.[23]

CHAPTER NINETEEN

"THE DAWN HAS BROKEN THROUGH AT LAST"

It is over at last, thanks be to God." It was Thursday 3 May, on the edge of Lake Garda. Robert Ellis was in Malcesine, finishing his diary entry for the day. Twenty-four hours earlier, he had heard the news of the German surrender in Italy on the BBC radio news. He was both relieved and sad. "The dawn has broken through at last," he wrote home, "the Nazi beast has finally given himself up and this terrible holocaust of suffering and sacrifice is almost at an end." But he wished that those who had been killed could be there to rejoice. "I feel that very much," he added, "for many of my oldest and best friends of Camp Hale days have given their lives." It was a day of quiet reflection rather than wild celebration. The latter was mostly for the civilians.[1]

For Ellis, as for most front-line troops in Europe, the end of the fighting was not the end of his war, and it offered little more than a brief hiatus in his daily routine. The next evening, Company F was ordered to Bolzano, the headquarters of both General von Vietinghoff and SS General Karl Wolff. Here, high up in the Alps, their job was to assert a US Army presence and prevent attacks by Italian partisans on the Germans. As he left the vineyards and cypresses behind him and ascended into the clear, cool air of the mountains, Ellis passed German roadblocks with guards wearing white armbands. Some carried long poles with straw tips to indicate the right road. In the dark, the yellow straw showed up brightly.

Bolzano was the gateway to the Brenner Pass. Just a few days before, troops of the American Seventh Army coming from the north had met up there with Mark Clark's Fifth Army advancing from the south. Even to the most ardent believers, the link-up meant the end of any possible Nazi last stand. Yet loyalists to Hitler remained easy to find.

The city was still under control of the local Committee of Liberation, and public order was being kept by joint patrols of Germans, still under arms although they had surrendered, and partisans. It was obviously an odd situation. German troops outnumbered the Americans by about sixty to one and some found it hard to accept they had been defeated. At first, the Americans even had to beg for accommodation while Wolff, the German commander, slept in a luxurious villa with some twenty-seven cars at his disposal. "German officers," reported *The Times*, "were driving about everywhere in fast cars, accompanied by women, as if they were still masters."[2]

Walking around the town with his camera, Ellis photographed several German soldiers giving each other the "Heil Hitler" salute, and SS-uniformed men strolled the streets. One morning, hearing the noise of marching, he looked out of his window and saw a troop of burly German women in Stormtrooper or similar uniform heading off in formation for an assignment. He could not help thinking of the female concentration camp guards whose pictures had been plastered in newspapers ever since the liberation of Belsen. Along with most others in the Tenth Mountain Division, he helped himself to some booty and took a couple of pistols from the Beretta factory in the town.

He was back in Malcesine for VE Day. There seemed little to celebrate, as he wrote home:

> Maybe if we were in the States we could get into the mood, but here, far from home, it seems a little flat and meaningless. Not that we're not all terribly relieved. It's just that we have given so much, and seen so many suffer and die, that even the end doesn't seem worthy of cheering . . . I feel like a runner who ran as hard and fast as he could and won the race, but was so exhausted that he couldn't celebrate.

Besides, the end of the war in Europe simply meant he might now be sent to the Pacific. "I lived through this fight through the skin of my teeth," he wrote to his sister, "I know my luck will never hold out there if I'm in a line company . . . Maybe," he joked, "I'll desert to Persia."[3]

In this mood of exhaustion and pessimism, news that he had been awarded the Bronze Star for heroism on the day he had shot the sniper gave him little comfort. It did not help, either, to be shown a War Department film, *Two Down and One to Go*, about the surrenders of Germany and Italy — with that of Japan still ahead. The future weighed heavily on his mind. Cynicism also set in after he was asked by his company commander to take on the job of writing recommendations for military awards. A medal generated a number of points, as did length of service, months overseas, being a parent and the number of campaigns in which the soldier had been involved. Once a certain total of points was reached, the soldier was eligible for discharge. Ellis found it difficult enough to accept the inevitable arbitrariness of a system that gave battle stars to support troops who had never been in the front line, but worse was that "the army brass saw to it that some high-ranking officers who had little exposure to shot and shell were given Bronze Stars" while men who undoubtedly deserved rewards were excluded. Even harder was the daily reminder that, with only forty-four points himself, he was far from the eighty-five he needed for his discharge. So it was with dread that he waited to hear if he would be shipped out to Japan. The vicious and suicidal fighting on Okinawa was a chilling sign of what to expect.[4]

Meanwhile, he found himself on duty locating, disarming and assembling German troops for evacuation to prisoner-of-war camps. Soon this meant exchanging the large villas and pleasant swimming of Lake Garda for the grimy and bustling industrial city of Brescia in the Po Valley. Here, thousands of German soldiers were being gathered in huge compounds before being sent home. It was now scorching hot, with the temperature hitting 100 degrees Fahrenheit. His billet was a stifling two-man tent pitched in a field next to the airfield.

It felt as though he might be trapped there forever. Then, out of the blue, less than a week later, the division received startling new orders: they were to move rapidly two hundred miles northeast, close to the town of Udine in Friuli. The apparently unbelievable suddenly seemed possible: fighting might break out again. But this time the enemy was not the Wehrmacht but the Yugoslav Army of Marshal Tito, who was threatening to seize Trieste and its surrounding region. Open armed conflict was being seriously discussed.

Three days later, Monday 21 May, at 2:30 a.m. Ellis found himself pitching a tent on the muddy banks of the Torre River outside Udine.

It was pouring with rain and he and his tentmate tried to build an earthen dike to keep out the water, but without much luck. Soon, everything was soaked. It was miserable. The next day, each of the division's regiments was formed into a combat team, everyone was fully armed, and the GIs were ordered to be on the alert for any hostile acts. It seemed to Ellis like a hell of a way to end a war.

Forty miles to the southeast, in Trieste itself, Geoffrey Cox felt exactly the same way. For most of May he had been a front-line witness to a rapidly developing crisis between West and East.

The world learned of Hitler's death on Tuesday 1 May. That same morning, Cox and the New Zealanders left Venice and the River Piave behind them, and their armored cars sped rapidly towards Trieste along a deserted road against little opposition. "No road blocks, no craters checked them as they raced forwards at thirty five miles an hour," Cox recorded, "wireless masts swaying like saplings, their tires sizzling on the wet road surface, their commanders upright in the turrets, earphones over their soft black berets."[5]

The only obstacles were crowds of ecstatic, flag-waving, cheering Italians, lining the roadside all the way towards the border with Yugoslavia. Italian partisans were already in control of most of the villages. They were mainly from the "Osoppo" brigades, non-Marxist, mostly Christian Democrat groups wearing green scarves or shirts who took their name from a mountain near Udine famed for an uprising against the Austrians when the region was part of the Habsburg Empire.

Cox gave one of them a lift in his jeep. A lean young man wearing a loose gray smock-like jacket, Sam Browne belt and Bersaglieri hat with a feather on the side, he was the chief of staff of the Osoppo group in Udine. He was also a relative of Fey von Hassell's husband, Detalmo. Although he had fought with the Ariete Division against the allies in North Africa, he had just escaped from the Germans, who had arrested him as a partisan. It was good to have him along. When the crowds saw his partisan outfit they cheered Cox even louder. It was pouring hard— a cold, driving rain straight from the Alps—but that did not seem to matter amid the genuine warmth of Italians glad at last to be free.

Then the mood changed. Across the Isonzo River and into the industrial shipbuilding town of Monfalcone, seventeen miles short of Trieste, the partisans wore red, not green, with red-starred blue caps and scarves. Portraits of Tito lined the road and the walls were scrawled with the slogans "*Zivio* [Long Live] *Tito*" and "*Zivio Stalin*." Now and again, Cox noticed the words "*Tukay je Jugoslavia*" (This is Yugoslavia). The New Zealanders had crossed an invisible boundary.

This was disputed territory, a no man's land inhabited by both Italians and Slovenes. Tito was determined to seize it for Yugoslavia and make the Isonzo his country's frontier with Italy. Already, his partisans had entered Monfalcone, which they called by its Slovene name, Trzic. Outside its town hall, blazing with electric light bulbs, hung a huge red star. That same day, they also entered Gorizia, fifteen miles to the north, on the banks of the Isonzo.

For the time being, though, the welcome remained outwardly friendly. Cox had no feeling that he and the New Zealanders were engaged in some hostile race with the Yugoslavs to reach Trieste first and General Freyberg held discussions with two senior Yugoslav officers and declared how proud he was to meet up with Marshal Tito's "magnificent troops who had fought so long and bravely in the common cause." The next afternoon, the New Zealanders continued their advance to Trieste. At midday, the German surrender in Italy became official, but it did not apply to German troops east of the Isonzo: in Trieste, the German garrison was still holding out against partisan troops who had arrived the day before. The New Zealanders also encountered some isolated resistance, especially on the parallel road running along the Carso, the vast white limestone plateau looming just inland. But nothing serious detained them.

By mid-afternoon, they reached Miramare, a peninsula within sight of the city sporting a white fairy-tale castle on its promontory. The small German detachment readily surrendered and Freyberg decided it was a good place to set up his divisional headquarters. Cox soon had his intelligence truck parked beneath a spreading olive tree on the edge of the castle terrace. Meanwhile, the New Zealanders' Sherman tanks pushed on along the narrow coastal road and entered Trieste to a tumultuous welcome from the city's inhabitants.

Miramare Castle was an idyllic place to end the war. Built by the Archduke Maximilian of Austria as a personal retreat for himself and his wife, Charlotte, it was a typical nineteenth-century turreted confection of the Gothic, the medieval and the Renaissance, and rich in historical poignancy. Shortly after moving in, the Archduke reluctantly accepted the position of Emperor of Mexico and sailed with his wife to

Vera Cruz, only to perish in front of a republican firing squad four years later. Charlotte, his widow, spent the next sixty years of her life in an asylum in Belgium. Afterwards, the castle was used as an occasional residence by the Habsburgs, and in the 1930s, with Trieste under Italian sovereignty, it became the official residence of the Duke of Aosta. He, too, left it for an ill-fated mission, dispatched by Mussolini as Viceroy of Ethiopia only to fall into British hands in 1941. During the war, the Germans used it as an officers' training school.

Behind Cox's truck spread the park. It had been lovingly planned by Maximilian and was studded with pines, magnolia and cypress trees, with the occasional palm or yucca imported from Mexico. Sixty feet below, the waters of the Adriatic lapped gently on the rocks. There was a small harbor, from which the Archduke and Archduchess had set sail for Mexico. Now, from its solid stone jetty, New Zealand soldiers happily dived into the water and splashed about in the clear blue sea.[6]

The Germans had quit in a hurry, and on his first night Cox enjoyed Danish butter, fresh ham and a good Rhine wine. After settling in, he finally found time to write a letter to his wife. As he sat in the evening light, peacefully gazing at Trieste across the bay, it reminded him of far-distant Wellington with the hills behind it. But home now meant England, where they had decided to make their post-war life with their children. He was in a confident, forward-looking mood, planning for their future and proud of the part he had played in bringing the war to an end. Now, he felt, there was nothing left to do in Italy and he was eager to leave. All that remained was for Cicely to move back to England from the United States and for him to find a job in London. He was sure, he told her, that he would be there by the end of June. On the way, he would stop off in Venice to buy some glass and silk stockings. "It is all over," he wrote, "and . . . we can begin life again . . . I love you my darling and I will be with you again soon."[7]

Cox had reason enough to feel confident. Relations with the Yugoslavs and partisans were obviously tricky, but they seemed manageable. True, the New Zealanders and Yugoslavs arrived in Trieste at about the same time and there was a medley of confusion as they sorted themselves out. They both sought to prize the enemy out of his last-ditch stronghold in the city's fortress, the Castello San Giusto, and the Germans' readiness to surrender to the New Zealanders rather than the communists meant the New Zealanders were forced to run a gauntlet of Yugoslav fire to reach its gates first.

Later that evening, as they sat down with the captured Germans to share a meal, Tito's men tried more than once to enter the castle, and from houses above partisan snipers constantly fired on anyone moving inside its walls. The next morning only the New Zealanders' presence protected the Germans from a jeering and hostile crowd as they were marched off to captivity. Yet, elsewhere in the city, Yugoslavs and New Zealanders worked in tandem to pry the Germans from the Law Courts, where an SS officer had decided to make a stand: New Zealand tanks blasted holes in the walls and the Yugoslavs rounded up the defenders. But complicating the scene was the arrival behind allied lines of several thousand of Tito's political enemies fleeing Yugoslavia — Chetniks loyal to his royalist resistance rival, General Draza Mihailovitch, as well as bands of Serbs who had served the collaborationist regime in Belgrade.[8]

But these problems had either already been sorted out or were under active discussion. Cox personally met General Drapsin, commander of the Fourth Yugoslav Army which had fought its way up 120 miles of the Dalmatian coast against bitter German resistance and now occupied the whole area. He held forthright views about Yugoslav rights to the city and the Isonzo frontier, but Cox found him easy, cheerful and intelligent, a man he felt they could do business with. He felt much the same way about Tito's chief of staff, the convinced Stalinist Arno Jovanovic, who was also present.[9]

Unfortunately, though, Cox's confidence proved misplaced. In his admiration and sympathy for the bravery of Tito's men, he underestimated their ruthlessness in attempting to achieve their political goals. The warm welcome given to the New Zealanders by the people of Trieste reflected not just thanks for the departure of the Germans, but relief that they were being liberated from their Yugoslav oppressors. Cox knew that large numbers of anti-German and pro-allied citizens had already been arrested in Trieste, but, like others on Freyberg's staff now surveying the scene from the comforts of Miramare Castle, he was lulled by the outward civility and friendliness of Tito's men. Moreover, the New Zealanders had merely been told that Trieste was needed for military reasons. They knew little of the tangled politics.

Typical of the New Zealanders' response to the imbroglio in the city was the comment of Brigadier Gentry, commander of the troops jointly occupying the city: "Whether there is anything political behind it I don't know," he confessed in reference to the arrests at a staff conference held in the castle. "Games of soccer," suggested Freyberg, might help ease the tension. "There we were from the other side of the world, in all innocence, blithely unaware of the hot pot of political intrigue and worse," observed Gentry many years later.[10]

New Zealand and Yugoslav troops jointly patrolled Trieste, but Freyberg decided to leave the Yugoslavs in control of civil affairs, which meant that power lay in the hands of the pro-Yugoslav liberation movement, the Italo-Slovene Council of Liberation, supported by the Yugoslav military governor who had been installed in the prefecture. Many of the city's Slovenes, discriminated against and persecuted by Mussolini, also backed this organization. Its agenda was clear—Trieste's future lay inside Yugoslavia.

For a majority of the predominantly Italian population of the city, however, this was not a future they wanted. Their voice was represented by a rival liberation movement, the Comitato di Liberazione Nazionale (CLN). Like similar committees throughout Italy, this was linked through Milan with the government in Rome, but unlike the others it excluded communists, who in Trieste supported the pro-Yugoslav group in the belief that a socialist Yugoslavia promised a brighter future than a bourgeois Italy. But they deluded themselves. The red star imprinted on the green, white and red Italian national colors meant little. "The only red star that counts here," reported *The Times*'s special correspondent in the city, "is on a background of blue, white, and red, the colors of Marshal Tito's supporters."[11] They were not alone in their illusions and, as they were soon to realize to their cost, "the proud and rightful rebirth of a nation oppressed by the Fascists [Yugoslavia] was in its turn becoming a savage and oppressive nationalism." Factions existed within factions, and the whole, Cox later wrote, resembled a "witches' cauldron" of conflicting politics and nationalisms.[12]

Nevertheless, one thing quickly became clear: pro-Italian groups, of whatever political persuasion, were under threat. Although the CLN had launched a successful insurrection at the end of April, Yugoslav pressure almost immediately forced it underground and its members once again started meeting secretly and circulating samizdat pamphlets and newspapers. No immediate help was offered by the allied forces: when a CLN delegation sought Freyberg's help he refused to see them, and a busload of Italian *carabinieri* dispatched to help police the city was refused entry.

Despite promises to the contrary, little was done as the Yugoslavs began their purge of the city. Six of the CLN leaders were arrested, along with hundreds of civilians. A crowd flying the Italian flag was fired on by Yugoslav sentries and several people were shot. Windows displaying the flag were also fired at, and a decree forbade any demonstration of national sentiment. But with Yugoslav flags flying from public buildings, and with the red star prominent on the cap of every Yugoslav soldier, this was a blatantly one-sided measure. Fear was spreading like a miasma through the city.

The Yugoslavs claimed they were merely rounding up Fascists and ridding the city of German collaborators. They certainly were doing this, and it was necessary work. Mussolini had poured public money into vast building projects aimed at transforming the city into a cutting-edge architectural symbol of modern Italy and Fascists there had prospered and enjoyed the fruits of office. And, despite later efforts to distance themselves from the Germans, Italians had also collaborated in the running of the notorious camp in the city, the Risiera San Sabba.

Its origins lay in Hitler's response to the defection of Italy to the allies in September 1943 when he seized the northeastern part of the country and combined it with parts of Slovenia to create the "Adriatisches Kuestenland" (Adriatic Coast), a region including the cities of Fiume, Trieste, Udine, Pola, Gorizia and Ljubljana. This he placed under the police control of Odilo Globocnik, the SS officer who maybe later met with George Bryant at Klagenfurt.

Globocnik, by the time of his appointment, had largely completed his extermination work in Poland. Similar tasks now awaited him in his home town and new headquarters, Trieste, where Jews, partisans and political opponents of the Nazis and their Fascist ally swarmed into his eager sights. The San Sabba factory was quickly converted into a combined police detention, torture, transit and concentration camp. Run by Germans with Ukrainian auxiliary guards, it depended on help from the local Italian Fascist police and militia. Over the following year and a half, several hundred of Trieste's Jews, as well as many from the Veneto, were shipped from the factory to the gas chambers in Poland. A far greater number of its eventual three to four thousand victims (the precise death toll remains unknown) comprised Slovene, Croat and Italian political prisoners, partisans, and hostages, often including their spouses and children.

The most sinister side of San Sabba was the arrival in September 1943 of a specialized German killing team made up of veterans of the notorious "T-4" euthanasia unit responsible for the gassing of thousands of mentally ill and handicapped Germans inside the Third Reich itself. They brought with them a "gassing van," and also built a large crematorium inside the factory to burn the corpses of their victims. In San Sabba, writes one historian, "death came in the night, muffled with music blaring out of loudspeakers. It came in the form of a Ukrainian guard wielding a club, or strangling the victims with his powerful hands. If the victim was small enough, he or she was stamped to death. The stench of burning bodies polluted the entire area."[13] In a futile effort to hide their crimes, the SS blew up the crematorium and its chimney seventy-two hours before the New Zealanders arrived in the city.

Yet the "honest" purge of those who had been complicit in such crimes and atrocities as San Sabba, or had actively supported the Fascists, was also exploited to mask the neutralizing of Tito's opponents. Flyers officially posted on walls proclaimed, "Democracy means the will of the people, not the liberty of the enemies of the people." Within the city, a bitter civil war was raging. And the day after Cox told his wife that his work was now completed, a significant new development took place.

On Monday 7 May, at the bridge over the Isonzo, a black hearse escorted by a British Army jeep approached sentries on the Yugoslav side of what had become an unofficial frontier. A uniformed chaplain explained that he was taking the body of a British soldier to Italy. Piled beside the coffin was a heap of old blankets and military gear. This was the man's kit, explained the chaplain. The Yugoslav guards waved him through, and the somber convoy trundled slowly across the white concrete bridge. Once it was well inside Italy and out of sight of the guards, it stopped, and from underneath the blankets stepped three members of the Trieste CLN. The prime target of Yugoslav hostility, this was now being publicly denounced as a "Trojan horse" inside the city. By that afternoon, the CLN members were in Venice, telling the government in Rome about the efforts to subsume the city into Yugoslavia. In a matter of days, charges that pro-Yugoslav "quislings" were playing a treacherous role in the city hit the world's headlines. A political storm in Italy now erupted into a full-fledged international crisis.[14]

The long-term future of Trieste had been such a potential minefield that the allies had put it aside for most of the war. But by April 1945, with allied armies advancing on the city from both directions, this had become impossible. For the West, powerful military and political reasons existed for capturing the city. Control of the port and its lines of communication northwards would help the British advance into Austria. Meanwhile, keeping Tito out of the city would also send a clear signal to Moscow that while Stalin might trample over Poland, the West would stand firm over Italy and its frontier.

This was Churchill's feeling especially. "Our inclination should be to back Italy against Tito," he had declared in March. Now, he felt even more strongly. Stalin's ruthlessness in Poland was becoming clearer by the day. Vienna was already in Red Army hands, and Berlin was about to join it. The key lay in Washington, for without the Americans the British could do nothing. "The great thing," Churchill urged Truman on Friday 27 April, "is to be there [Trieste] before Tito's guerrillas are in occupation . . . Possession is nine points of the law." The President instantly agreed and the next day allied forces in Italy were ordered to race for Trieste. It fell to the New Zealanders to take on the task, which was why Geoffrey Cox now found himself at Miramare Castle, where, he learned, the New Zealanders' telephone lines were already being tapped.[15] Only two days after telling Cicely he would soon be home, he found himself hard at work in his intelligence truck and taking part in tense daily conferences in the castle. This time, though, instead of plotting the positions of the Wehrmacht, he was identifying the whereabouts of Yugoslav Army and partisan units.

And this was how he spent VE Day. As civilians across Europe celebrated the end of the war, New Zealand and other allied troops in Trieste prepared themselves for a new round of fighting. Never before during the war had they had to go on leave armed. Now, when they went to the movies or sunbathed on the beach, they carried their rifles or Tommy guns under strict instructions to avoid any rows or incidents in the city that could spark a conflict. Even when they saw civilians being beaten up or harassed by the Yugoslavs, they were forbidden to intervene. The mood had grown distinctly sour.

That night, there were no allied celebrations in Trieste. Cox listened to Churchill's VE Day speech hunched over the wireless in his truck, with maps of the Yugoslav positions laid out in front of him. Victory had brought an uncertain peace.[16]

In the heart of the city, the crisis steadily deepened. Four days later, official posters went up proclaiming Trieste's future as an autonomous city inside a federated Yugoslavia and denouncing any opponents of the plan as Fascists. The Council of Liberation, reformed with a communist secretary and People's Militia aide by the Yugoslav secret police, intensified its search for political enemies, closed down newspapers, and took over the radio station. Similar developments took place throughout Venezia Giulia, and people continued to disappear without trace. The worst single episode of retribution, or victors' rough justice, took place at Bassovizza, a town on the Carso close to Drapsin's headquarters.[17]

On Wednesday 2 May, Don Virgilio Sceck, the priest in the small village of Corgnale, made his way to officiate at the burial of some partisans in nearby Bassovizza, whose own priest was not available. Close by, herded together in a field, he noticed about 150 civilians. Most, he later claimed, were members of Mussolini's Fascist police. People in the village were clamoring to get to them and administer "summary justice," but the unit of Tito's forces who had occupied the village, from Drapsin's Fourth Army, insisted on a more formal procedure, although this distinction in itself was little more than a formality. "These persons were questioned and tried in the presence of all of the populace, who accused them," reported the priest.

> As soon as one of them was questioned, four or five women rushed up to them and accused them of having murdered or tortured one of their relatives, or of having burned down their houses. The accused persons were butted and struck, and always admitted the crimes ascribed to them. Nearly all of them were condemned to death. Those who were not were however left together with the others.

All—seemingly with no distinction between those condemned and those not—were then shot by a group of partisans en masse. "The partisans were armed with sub-machine-guns," claimed Don Sceck, "and afterwards, as there were no coffins, they were thrown into the Bassovizza pit." This "pit" was the local *foiba*, one of hundreds of caverns that pitted the limestone rock of the hills behind Trieste, known locally as the Pozzo della Miniera. The priest claimed not to have been present when any of this happened.

But, according to others, at least some of the victims were thrown into the *foiba* while still alive. Moreover, it was claimed, the priest gave them succor in their final moments. If so, it must have been a peculiar type of comfort, for Don Sceck was reportedly rabidly anti-Italian and pro-Slovene. "You have erred until now, you have amused yourself by torturing the Slavs," he is alleged to have told one of the Italian police victims, "and now nothing remains but for you to commend your soul to God. The punishment now to be given to you has been fully deserved."

The priest returned to Bassovizza the next day. This time an even larger group, between two and three hundred, had been corralled into the field. Most, like the first batch, were civilians, arrested in Trieste by Tito's forces immediately after they entered the city. But about forty were German soldiers. "These people were also killed by machine-guns," swore the priest, adding that they too were nearly all members of the Fascist police. The bodies were again thrown into the pit, along with several dead horses.

Other witnesses painted an even more graphic scene, claiming that some of the dead had been made to jump alive into the pit. "[They] were ordered to jump across the pit (about 12 feet wide) and were told that their lives would be spared if they succeeded," claimed one, "[but] although some people did manage to jump over, they were later shot and thrown in." According to another source, more than five hundred living people were thrown into the *foiba*. Afterwards, explosives were dropped into its depths.

Most of the locals had little sympathy for the dead. But what a pity it was, complained one elderly local woman, to waste good clothing. The Fascists should have been undressed before being thrown in, she bluntly declared. Local children who claimed to have witnessed the scene expressed sentiments that were, if anything, even more blood-thirsty: "How the Fascists screamed," said one girl, with obvious relish.

Precisely who the victims of the Bassovizza massacre were remains obscure and controversial to this day, a subject of intense political con-troversy. Undoubtedly, many *were* members of the Italian Fascist police. Another local pro-Slovene priest declared that, whoever they were, they "richly deserved the end they met," and claimed they were shot by Yugoslav Army troops on the explicit orders of General Drapsin. Others accused the partisans of doing the shooting. "The Yugoslavs made good use of the [*foibe*] to get rid of Fascists and anybody else they thought inconvenient," recalled one British intelligence officer stationed close by at the time. "Diplomatic attempts to put a stop to the practice came to nothing . . . Certainly, the prospect of getting the War Office to send out grappling gear [to find out how many had died] came to nothing."[18]

Altogether, it has been estimated that some two thousand people in the region disappeared for good in the days following the arrival of the Yugoslav troops. It is certain that not all were Italians or Fascists, for not all Slovenes were allies of Tito. Undoubtedly, as well, the massacre provided a welcome opportunity to settle some personal scores.

The same day that the posters went up in Trieste's street announcing its Yugoslav future, Churchill sent a somber message to Truman placing the city's fate in the wider context of communist and Russian action throughout Europe.[19] Truman, though, needed no convincing that something had to be done. He had already instructed his chiefs of staff to tell Tito to hand over Trieste and its hinterland to allied military control. He would have nothing to do, he said, with "uncontrolled land grabbing or tactics which are all too reminiscent of those of Hitler and Japan." In Moscow, Stalin was informed of the demand.

It took Tito a week to respond. When he did, it was with a forthright "no." Truman decided the time had come to flex American muscle, so Patton's troops in Austria were instructed to move up to the Brenner Pass, and naval forces headed for the Adriatic. A British naval force steamed into Trieste itself, and on 19 May Field Marshal Alexander issued an order of the day to all allied troops to prepare for battle. Three days later, he instructed allied forces in Venezia Giulia to move forward at key points to improve their tactical positions. General Mark Clark, commander of the allied Fifteenth Army Group, moved up a significant number of US infantry and tanks through Gorizia to higher and more defensible ground to the east, nudging aside Yugoslav checkpoints as they went. "Fighting might break out," Freyberg warned his government in New Zealand from Trieste. "If it does, we may expect a number of casualties." On the evening of Sunday 21 May, as tension mounted, twenty-five Russian-built T34 tanks with Yugoslav Army markings rumbled ostentatiously along the waterfront and dispersed into the city.

Outside Udine, Robert Ellis had spent the previous two weeks getting ready for the possible new fight. Accompanied by an officer in a jeep, his task was to visit various groups of partisans and find out the location of any Yugoslav units. There was little love lost between the "reds" and the "greens," and in the Udine area violence and killing between groups of partisans was not unusual. There was also at least one Fascist band still at large in the mountains. When it fired on an American patrol, two partisan bands were dispatched to wipe it out.

Another of his assignments was to locate the defensive positions used by the Italians in the First World War against the Austrians and Germans. Repaired and reconditioned, they might soon be needed against Tito. Ellis found the task "hardly believable," but it gave him a fantastic opportunity to play the tourist. As for the old defensive lines, the few he found proved so eroded as to be obviously useless.

He also found that few of the locals welcomed the imminent arrival of the Yugoslavs: most of them wished simply to be left alone after years of war and confusion. One day, he met a young woman from France, who said she would like to go to America. Jokingly, he told her he was terribly wealthy. No, she replied, all she wanted was plenty to eat, a home and happiness.

None of it seemed real, but he was not unhappy. It was interesting driving around and talking to the locals; and being detained in Italy had one much greater bonus. The Battle of Okinawa was in its eighth bloody week — 8,300 Americans had already been killed and more than 20,000 wounded. And the Americans had not yet even broken the main Japanese line of defense on the island. As long as Tito was causing trouble in Trieste, the Tenth Mountain Division would not be heading out to the Pacific any time soon.

A few hours after General Jodl put his signature to Germany's unconditional surrender, the fifty-two-year-old Hermann Goering turned himself in to the Americans. After the RAF bombing of his villa, he had been transferred by his SS captors to Mauterndorf Castle, forty miles from Salzburg, the former home of his godfather, where he had spent part of his childhood. His wife, Emmy, and daughter Edda were with him. Life became easier: he enjoyed some fine wine and cigars from the cellars, and even fetched the family genealogy to show his captors. It showed, he claimed, that his family bloodline went back to the German emperors as well as to Goethe and Bismarck.

With Hitler dead and Himmler vanished, Goering now hoped he could emerge from the debris to play a major role in the surrender negotiations with Eisenhower. "I consider it absolutely vital . . . that parallel to Jodl's negotiations I approach Eisenhower unofficially as one marshal to another," he radioed Doenitz, blind to the fact that Hitler's successor was placing as much distance as he could between himself and the Führer's political cronies. "I might create a suitably personal atmosphere for Jodl's talks." Then he sent a message to Eisenhower, suggesting they meet at Fischhorn Castle at Zell-am-See. His role, he suggested, might be compared to that of Marshal Pétain, who in 1940 had similarly sought talks to save his country in its hour of need.[20]

At midday the next day, dressed in his pearl-gray marshal's uniform, and with a Mauser pistol tucked firmly into his belt, he clambered heavily into his Maybach limousine and set off with his family for what he hoped would be a historic rendezvous in which, at last, his historic greatness would be recognized, this time as a peacemaker. But halfway to Zell-am-See he was stopped by an American convoy headed by Brigadier-General Robert Stack, deputy commander of the Thirty-sixth (Texas) Division. Stack saluted smartly and motioned Goering into a waiting American sedan. In he stepped, and the convoy led him to Fischhorn.

Here, he was allocated a room. He took a welcome hot bath and then joined the US general for dinner. Afterwards, standing in front of the Lone Star flag of Texas, he posed for photographers. "When do I get to meet Eisenhower?" he asked Stack impatiently. The American was evasive, so Goering raised the issue again with the interpreter. "Ask General Stack whether I should wear a pistol or my ceremonial dagger when I appear before Eisenhower," he urged. Stark's reply was brief and to the point: "I don't care two hoots."

The next morning, still convinced that he would be seeing the allied Supreme Commander, Goering was driven to the Texas Division's headquarters in the Grand Hotel at Kitzbühel, where he was mobbed again by waiting photographers. This time it was the divisional commander, Major-General John E. Dahlquist, who invited Goering to join him for a meal, although on this occasion it was a more modest affair, with the two of them sharing the general's lunch of chicken, potatoes and peas eaten from a mess tin. Afterwards, having changed into his Luftwaffe uniform and donned some of his favorite bejeweled cufflinks, he posed on the hotel's balcony for yet more photographs. "Things are looking good," he had told Emmy before bidding her farewell that morning, but he had also taken care to ensure that his two blue suitcases traveled safely with him. Inside were hidden three small brass capsules of cyanide.

For the next few days, the Americans kept him in Bavaria, even flying him to Augsburg to meet General Spaatz, wartime commander of the US Strategic Air Force, who grilled him about the Luftwaffe and the impact of allied bombing. He also gave a press conference to a group of over fifty allied newsmen.

Only gradually did it begin to dawn on him that he was never going to meet Eisenhower, that there were no negotiations in which he could play a part, and that in reality he was no more than a prisoner. He spent a few more days in an American interrogation center at Wiesbaden and then, towards the end of May, was flown to Luxembourg to join the other top Nazis who had been rounded up.

"The cause for which Goering stood is lost," noted an official US interrogation report from Wiesbaden.

> But the canny Hermann even now is thinking only what he can do to salvage some of his personal fortune, and to create an advantageous position for himself. He condemns the once-beloved Führer without hesitation . . . [but] behind his spirited and often witty conversation is a constant watchfulness for the opportunity to place himself in favourable light.[21]

Certainly, he had charmed Generals Stack and Dahlquist, but their open and friendly reception of the man once touted as Hitler's successor flew in the face of the policy of nonfraternization, and as news spread of their cordial meetings a chorus of protest developed, especially in the United States. So bad did the uproar become that George C. Marshall was forced to cable Eisenhower from Washington, ordering him to intervene. The reaction to this regrettable example of fraternization, Marshall admonished the Supreme Commander, had been "bitter." Eisenhower acted instantly to make it clear to all his forces that there should be no repeat of the episode. It had broken his express orders, he furiously told his subordinates. "Senior German officers will be given only minimum essential accommodations which will not repeat not be elaborately furnished, and all prisoners will be fed strictly upon the ration that has been authorized for German prisoners of that particular category," he insisted. "Any such incident in future will be summarily dealt with. After the successful conclusion to this campaign, I am not going to have the public effect ruined in America by such ill-advised actions on the part of any officer."[22] Yet the damage had been done, and over the next three months the disastrous impact of the "Goering Episode" would act as a brake on every effort to relax the policy of nonfraternization.

PART FOUR

VE DAY TO POTSDAM

CHAPTER TWENTY

VE DAY

"I'm as happy as a kitten full of milk." Cape Breton Highlander Reg Roy had every reason to feel content. VE Day found him in London, writing home to his parents, telling them he had survived.

A week before, faced with a barrage of fire from the German fortress at Delfzijl, he would not have given a plugged nickel for his life. After the battle he spent a couple of days helping clear up the Dutch town and scrounging souvenirs to send home, including a huge swastika battle flag from the Delfzijl battery which he mailed to his father in Canada. "Isn't it a dilly," he wrote, joking that it could be used in a window display in his father's car showroom—perhaps with a Nazi dagger stuck into it to get lots of attention. He also "liberated" twenty-five pounds from a captured German soldier.

Then he started his week's leave. You had to clock up at least six months' action to qualify for that, and even then you had to wait your turn. After the recent fighting, he was more than ready. Everything was laid on very nicely. The Canadian Army knew how to treat its men well. The first stop was a transit camp in Groningen, where they picked up dozens of others. Then he was packed in a truck for a five-hour drive to Nijmegen and a luxurious camp equipped with mess halls, recreation rooms, barbers, tailors, clothes presses, shoeshine boys, baths and beds—everything to transform battleground killers into clean and presentable young men. Then a special train pulled in, and after a stop at Lille for tea ("They think of everything, don't they?" Reg joked to his sister) he arrived at Calais at dawn.

Again, the army machinery took over, changed their Dutch guilders into British pounds, and laid on a guide to show them where to wash and get breakfast. Roy found it all "very, very nice." Even better was the luscious meal served by French waitresses and cooked by French chefs. He even got to practice his French a little and bought perfume and silk stockings for his fiancée, Ardith. Then there followed a stormy crossing of the Channel that made him as sick as a dog. He finally reached London on the night of Sunday 6 May.

It was lunchtime the next day that news came through of the final and unconditional surrender of the Germans at Reims. As it was to take effect at midnight, Tuesday 8 May was officially declared Victory in Europe Day.

There were celebrations, of course. Across Britain they began as soon as news of the surrender leaked out. Flags appeared in windows, shops shut down, and people poured onto the streets. At the stroke of midnight, ships in Southampton docks sounded their horns and a searchlight flashed out the letter "V," for "victory," in Morse code across the sky. By midday, huge crowds had gathered in central London, and St. Paul's Cathedral and other churches were packed with worshippers. At three o'clock, Churchill broadcast to the nation and the Empire from his study at 10 Downing Street, declaring the end of the war and finishing with the exhortation: "Advance Britannia! Long live the cause of freedom! God save the King!" Then, standing on the front seat of an open car and giving the victory sign, he was driven slowly through a dense and cheering crowd to the Houses of Parliament, where he repeated his statement to the Commons. When it was over, the crowd outside who heard it over loudspeakers sang the national anthem.

That night, a floodlit West End of London quickly filled with flag-waving crowds of excited young people. Playing his trumpet, Humphrey Lyttelton, still wearing his Guards uniform, brought the sounds of New Orleans jazz to the Mall, led a wild and lusty procession round Piccadilly Circus to Trafalgar Square, and ended up playing "For He's a Jolly Good Fellow" when the King and the rest of the royal family appeared on the illuminated balcony of Buckingham Palace.

In Edinburgh, the focal point of the celebrations was the statue of the Duke of Wellington, the nation's victor over the last great European tyrant, Napoleon Bonaparte. Here, a British soldier stood perilously balanced on the mane of the Duke's horse while he tried to catch dozens of caps being wildly thrown at him by the crowd below. Across the city, the Union Jack flew in force, but plenty of other flags could be seen too: the Scottish Standard with its lion fluttered everywhere, along with the Stars and Stripes, the Hammer and Sickle, and those of many other nations, such as France, Belgium and Poland. By eight o'clock that evening, the pubs were running out of beer.

The same was true in London. A few hearties and the foolish scaled the cladding protecting the statue of Eros in Piccadilly. By the end of the night, many had swum, willingly or not, in the fountains or ridden the lions that guarded Nelson's Column in Trafalgar Square. Inhibitions disappeared. "Strangers kissed," writes one historian, "couples copulated, condoms were blown up as balloons, bonfires blazed."[1] The crowds' exuberance surprised some allied troops who had taken at face value the legendary British "stiff upper lip."

Reg Roy was one of them. He mingled with the crowds in Piccadilly Circus and Trafalgar Square, saw bonfires in the streets, dodged firecrackers, enjoyed the city's lights fully ablaze again, hopped on trams and buses crowded with cheering and waving crowds, noted people wearing funny little paper hats scrawled with slogans such as "Ike's babe" and "Victory," and gazed spellbound as huge groups of Londoners, young and old, arms linked ten abreast, marched along the streets laughing and singing.

Everywhere, he saw soldiers and sailors perched on lamp-posts and monuments roaring and shouting to the crowds below. He checked his bank balance and saw it was healthy, ate and slept as much as he could, relished the "God's amount" of Coca-Cola and tomato juice that was freely available, joined the crowd outside Buckingham Palace as the royal family waved from the balcony, and heard Churchill's broadcast over the loudspeakers in Parliament Square. He watched the Changing of the Guard, attended the thanksgiving service at St. Paul's, and went to see Laurence Olivier's *Henry V* at the movies.

Across the Atlantic, New Yorkers also started celebrating a day early, for news of the German surrender had leaked before the official announcement. Office workers deluged the streets with tons of ticker tape, scrap paper, old telephone books, playing cards and anything else they could find. They were joined by the garment trade, whose workers threw not paper but bales and bolts of cloth of all kinds into the streets. The *New York Times* reported that "every possible remnant in every possible shade and hue turned and squirmed in the thin morning sunlight" until Broadway was ten inches deep in fabric. Boats on the East River sounded their whistles while on land the cabbies honked madly. Macy's department store had a run on flags. Grinning soldiers and sailors in uniform filled Times Square, kissing and being kissed by their own sweethearts or anyone else's who was handy.

These were the images the reporters and photojournalists captured for posterity. There are fewer pictures of the more modest affairs on the streets beyond the centers of the great cities, particularly in Britain. Here, war-worn mothers pooled their ration coupons to whip up a few cakes for tea parties. Their children decked themselves and their dogs in red, white and blue bunting. Thousands of homemade effigies of Hitler and his henchmen were hanged that night or burned on bonfires whose flames rose high into the blackness. The survival of Big Ben and the dome of St. Paul's was revealed to all as floodlights went on, with no thought now of bombing raids or V2 attacks. But twelve thousand people were still squatting or sleeping deep underground in Tube stations or underground shelters.

Everyone was relieved that the war with Germany was over. But for millions of bereft widows and grieving parents whose husbands and sons would never return it was a hollow moment they were glad to see end. "I had lived in dread for VE Day," wrote one woman whose husband had been killed in Italy the year before. "I was so afraid that I wouldn't be brave. But once the tension had snapped and the day itself been met, I felt stronger to go on. Johnny's going must always be an inspiration to go forward with greater courage. Heaven knows, it's hard enough at times."[2] At least there would be no more telegrams informing families of more deaths in Europe, only news that prisoners of war had survived. That day alone, two hundred Lancaster bombers flew back to Britain more than thirteen thousand prisoners of war just liberated from camps in Italy and Germany.

But, of course, the war in the Far East was still not over. In Whitehall, Churchill appeared on the balcony of the Ministry of Health after his speech in the Commons and conducted "Land of Hope and Glory" for the crowd, but he warned them: "One deadly foe has been cast on the ground, and awaits our judgment and mercy, but there is another foe who occupies large portions of the British Empire, a foe stained with cruelty and greed—the Japanese." There were loud boos from the twenty thousand below, although they knew the Imperial

Army to be no pantomime villain. Churchill ended to loud cheering as he finished with a typical rhetorical flourish. "Wherever the bird of freedom chirps in human hearts," he told them, "they will look back to what we have done, and they will say, 'Don't despair. Don't yield to violence and tyranny. March straight forward and die, if need be, unconquered.' "

There would be many more deaths yet. There were diehard Nazis who hoped to fight another day; there were those who were freed from the degradation of the camps only to die in the arms of their liberators; and there were vast armies of the displaced, starving and frightened who would not survive in the chaos that was Europe, now that the war was over but the peace was not yet secure.

For Reg Roy, the VE Day celebrations in London contrasted sharply with the misery he had left behind in Europe. Traveling through Holland, he had looked out of the window and seen thousands of people swarming in all directions: forced Dutch laborers trudging home from Germany, exiles returning from Britain, and Hitler's dispirited troops being marched east. People who had spent years in hiding were now emerging into the light. It was, he thought, as if a big stick had been poked into an anthill.[3]

Robert Reid was also mesmerized by the thousands of wanderers streaming along Europe's roads, a vision that struck him long before he even reached the Rhine. It was one of the most remarkable sights he had ever seen in his life, a spectacle of almost biblical proportions. Indeed, as he told BBC listeners as soon as he got back to Britain, it reminded him "of those colored plates you remembered seeing as a child in the family bible at home," with as many as forty or fifty thousand people plodding along the dusty highways through the Moselle vineyards, their faces lit by the setting sun. He saw parties of Russians — entire families — riding in horse-drawn ammunition carts with Red Flags flying. There were thousands of French deportees ("heaven knows where they got their tricolors"), old men and women, babes in arms, Yugoslavs riding bareback, people pushing their few wretched belongings in perambulators, and never-ending streams of humanity just plodding westwards on foot. As Reid explained, the fate of displaced persons was one of the most serious problems now facing Europe.[4]

But there was a multitude of others. Behind the superficial glitter of the VE Day celebrations lurked a somber awareness of grim reality. It was as though when the fighting ceased a curtain was lifted to reveal the real drama being played out on the stage behind. Europe lay in ruins: its cities were rubble, its factories wrecked, its transport systems paralyzed, its people homeless and traumatized. Millions had died. It was hard to see any future when the present was so hopeless.

The apprehensive and anxious mood was accurately captured by the *Scotsman* newspaper. "At last," it declared on VE Day, "Europe's long nightmare is ended . . . but it will take a long time to assuage and bind up the wounds of war . . . The problems that gave rise to it remain," it continued, pointing its finger at the national rivalries of the prewar continent. "Will the victors be equal to the demands of the great hour? Hitler and Mussolini have perished, but they have left behind them a shattered world."

It ended with a sobering and unanswerable question. "There's no illusion, as there was after the last war, that an era of universal peace will automatically be ushered in. Indeed, the sufferings of war and the bitter hatreds to which they have given rise may complicate the task of the statesmen. The war has been decisively won. Can they win the peace?"[5]

VE Day in the small German town of Bernterode was witness to a scene remarkably different from anything else in Europe. Here, deep in the Thuringian Forest, close to Weimar, lay a salt mine some eighteen hundred feet deep. Nine years before, the Nazis had transformed it into a vast underground munitions plant and storage depot. During the war, a small army of Italian, French and Russian slave labor was employed in its sprawling fourteen-mile-long complex of corridors and chambers. Many of them were now living in a camp in the pine trees outside.

Access to the mine was by an elevator. At the bottom of the shaft, a group of hefty men struggled desperately to fit a huge metal casket into the cage. It weighed twelve hundred pounds and was so large that if it had been just half an inch longer it would not have squeezed in. Finally, after a lot of sweat and an hour's struggle and cursing, the men forced it inside. They closed the doors and gave the signal to another team waiting in a small building at the entrance to the shaft. As slowly as the engines could turn, they carefully began hoisting it to the surface.

Beside them stood a radio. It was broadcasting victory speeches and music from across Europe. As the casket began its careful ascent, the men could hear the strains of "The Star Spangled Banner." Then, just as it reached the surface, the tune changed to "God Save the King." The men smiled at the irony. For inside the casket lay the remains of the greatest of all Prussian kings, the man who had transformed his lands into the most feared and powerful of all German states: Frederick the Great.

His casket had been discovered by accident just ten days before by an ordnance unit of the US Army sent to investigate the four hundred thousand tons of ammunition stored in the mine. After walking five hundred yards down its main corridor they noticed a brick wall with its mortar still fresh. It was five feet thick but they broke through and found a framed lattice door. Behind this, they stumbled on a bizarre and gruesome Aladdin's cave of treasures. It was almost too fantastic to believe.

The room was divided by partitions into a series of bays. In each, piled high against the walls and lined with brilliant banners, were dozens of paintings, boxes and tapestries. But the men's eyes were transfixed by what they saw in the middle of the room: four massive caskets. One of them was decorated with a wreath and a red silk ribbon. It bore the swastika and the words "Adolph Hitler." During these last few days of fighting, the German dictator's whereabouts and fate had remained unknown. Was he dead, and if he was, had they unwittingly stumbled on his tomb?

Shortly afterwards, an American officer named Walter Hancock, one of the Monuments Men, arrived on the scene. In civilian life, he was a well-known sculptor.

When they had begun their work, the main worry of the Monuments Men had not been the Nazis but the allied armies; they were tasked with preventing their own soldiers and airmen from damaging European monuments, fine art, and archive collections by military action. However, despite providing lists of buildings to field commanders in the hope that they might be spared from shelling and bombing, they had only limited success. In the face of the massive air attacks on enemy cities, indeed, theirs was virtually a lost cause so far as Germany itself was concerned. By early 1945, over 180 monuments from a list of 200 in the Third Reich had been hit, with some 120 of them totally destroyed.

As allied forces liberated Western Europe and crossed the Rhine into Germany in the spring of 1945, they remained a threat to European art, and all too many soldiers were only too eager to grab pieces and send them home to family and friends. At first, the Monuments Men attempted to protect captured art galleries and museums with simple "off-limits" signs, but they quickly learned that these minimal measures were simply being ignored, and decided that a far more effective deterrent lay in surrounding the buildings with the skull-and-crossbones sign used to warn of the presence of unexploded mines.

It was only when they penetrated deeper into Germany that the experts began to stumble on hundreds of sealed-off caves and mines, and uncovered vast hidden caches of European art.

At this point, their mission changed. Some of the art they found represented treasures from German galleries that had been stored underground to protect them from allied bombing, artillery fire and looting. But the vast majority had been looted by the Nazis from galleries, museums and private art collections across occupied Europe.

It was vital to protect and repatriate these treasures, and not just for posterity and for the sake of European culture and national pride. No one yet knew whether military defeat would mark a decisive end to Hitler's Third Reich, and the hunt for top Nazis had hardly begun. Would they go underground and begin some clandestine resistance movement? No one knew, not even the allied intelligence agencies. So it was deemed doubly urgent to seize these vast treasures of art before they could be used for the financing of a post-war resurgence of the Nazi regime.[6]

It was with all this on his mind that Hancock now crawled through the opening into the hidden room. Almost at once, he realized that this was no ordinary depository for works of art:

> The place had the aspect of a shrine. The symmetry of the plan, a central passageway with three compartments on either side connecting two large end bays; the dramatic display of the splendid banners, hung in deep rows over the caskets and stacked with decorative effects in the corners; the presence of the caskets themselves; all suggested the setting for a modern pagan ritual.[7]

In each of the compartments, he found a wooden coffin to which was stuck by Scotch tape a hastily scrawled note in red crayon. The labels read, "Feldmarschall von Hindenburg," "Frau von Hindenburg," and — on the casket swathed with Hitler's personal tribute to Prussia's

"Soldier King"—"Friedrich Wilhelm, der Soldaten Konig." Finally, in the last compartment on the left, Hancock found Frederick the Great. The coffin bore no decoration of any kind, merely the simple label, again scrawled in red crayon: "Friedrich der Grosse." Next to it, he found a small metal box containing several color photographs of portraits of German military leaders from the "Soldier King" to Hitler himself.

Elsewhere in the chamber he also found over two hundred Prussian regimental banners dating from the wars of the seventeenth century to the First World War, all unfurled and making the place feel even more like a shrine. Boxes contained numerous items of Prussian royal regalia, including the crown and scepter used for the coronation of Friedrich Wilhelm in 1713. Sixty additional steel ammunition boxes contained precious porcelain and dozens of beautifully bound red leather volumes that proved to be the complete library of Frederick the Great, transported here from his palaces in Berlin and Potsdam.

In the entrance bay and nearby, Hancock found over 250 paintings that had been removed from the Prussian royal collections. Among them were French eighteenth-century masterpieces by Watteau, Boucher and Chardin, as well as pieces by Cranach and later German masters.

Some of the French laborers were still around, and Hancock asked them what they knew about the scene he had just witnessed. They told him that six weeks before, all civilians were abruptly evacuated from the area. Over the following four weeks, shrouded in secrecy, the German Army trucked all the items to the mine. Then, at the beginning of April, it was sealed. The shrine, speculated the Frenchmen, "was intended to preserve the most potent symbols of the German military tradition around which future generations might rally." It had kept its secrets for just twenty-five days.[8]

Only hours after Frederick the Great had been brought up to the surface of the Thuringian Forest, the mortal remains of the Nazi dictator who had kept a portrait of him on the wall of his bunker were being closely examined in the suburbs of Berlin.

On the morning of Wednesday 9 May, the day chosen by the Soviets to celebrate Victory in Europe, Frau Kathe Heusermann, a thirty-six-year-old dental assistant, was in her Berlin apartment on the Pariserstrasse. Like most Berlin women, she feared being raped by the

Russians and was keeping a low profile by staying indoors. Then there was a knock on the door. Cautiously, she opened it. Outside stood Dr. Feodor Bruck, a Jewish doctor from Silesia who had spent several months of the war in hiding and had just arrived in Berlin to take over the dental practice of Dr. Hugo Blaschke. The latter had worked as Hitler's personal dentist since 1933 and was a loyal Nazi Party member and a major-general in the Waffen SS. Bruck explained to Frau Heusermann that some Soviet officers had arrived at his surgery on the fashionable Kurfurstendamm searching for Hitler's dental records among Blaschke's files. They needed to speak to her urgently. Donning her coat, she followed him.

Frau Heusermann knew a considerable amount about Hitler's teeth. Just six months ago, shortly before abandoning his Rastenberg head-quarters deep in the forests of East Prussia ahead of the advancing Red Army, he had developed a seriously infected tooth. Blaschke was sum-moned, and she traveled out with him and helped with the operation to remove it. She knew the details of the Führer's mouth as well as the back of her own hand.

Later, as the Red Army approached, she took refuge in the Chancellery and saw Hitler on several occasions. She was in the bunker when Hitler and Eva Braun killed themselves, and although she did not see the bodies, she was told that they had been burned with petrol. She stayed there until the very last minute. Then, as the Red Army closed in, she joined a group trying to flee west by walking underground along the tracks of the U-Bahn but she was captured by Soviet soldiers at one of its stations. Eventually, she was allowed to return home. Blaschke was still in hiding.

When she arrived at the bomb-scarred surgery, she was met by a Soviet colonel and a female interpreter. But they found nothing relat-ing to Hitler in the files, and moved on to the Chancellery. Here, too, they drew a blank. Finally, the colonel drove her out to the capital's suburbs. Here, she was shown a gold bridge from an upper jaw, a com-plete lower jawbone, a small gold filling, and another bridge from a different lower jaw. She peered at them closely and was able immedi-ately to confirm that the upper jaw bridge and the lower jawbone belonged to Hitler. Less certainly, she identified the rest of the sparse remains as those of Eva Braun.

The dental evidence had been discovered three days before by a Soviet soldier searching the garden of the Chancellery, all that remained of Hitler and his wife. First the petrol, then the relentless bombardment of the building by Red Army artillery, had reduced their corpses to these few blackened fragments.[9]

The Soviets had hoped to catch Hitler alive. SMERSH (the Russian military's counterintelligence department) had even set up a special unit to find him, and Marshal Zhukov, Stalin's top commander, had boasted that he would lock up "that slimy beast Hitler" in a cage and parade him through the streets of Moscow. But now it was clear that he had cheated them. "So, the bastard threw in the towel" growled Stalin when he was told the news.[10]

A few days later, Frau Heusermann was ordered by the Soviets to pack her bag for an absence of several weeks. She was driven away, and nothing more was heard of her for several years as she lingered in captivity in Russia along with other witnesses to Hitler's final days.

VE Day also sealed the fate of the man whose name more than any other had come to symbolize hated collaboration with the Nazis — Vidkun Quisling, leader of the Nasjonal Samling, the Nazi Party of Norway. He was now in fear of his life. Over the winter and spring the underground Norwegian resistance had been busy liquidating collaborators, mostly those working in the Norwegian and German police. They even managed to kill the chief of the State and Security Police in the street while he was on his way to work.

From 1941 onwards, Quisling had been a virtual prisoner in his home, a villa on a fjord just outside Oslo. Originally named the Villa Grande, it was built by a First World War industrialist before becoming state property. Quisling renamed it Gimle, after the old Norse dwelling of the gods. It was large and spacious, with magnificent views over the fjord and the city, and was surrounded by a park. Quisling packed it with his antiques, books and art treasures. At the bottom of the garden, a speedboat was kept moored in constant readiness for a quick getaway across the water.

By spring 1945, Norway was Germany's greatest fortress in Europe. It still housed some 365,000 German Wehrmacht troops, dozens of U-boats were sheltering in its fjords, and there was much talk and rumor about a final last stand by the Nazis here. If Hitler indeed decided to hold out, Quisling dreaded what would happen if the allies invaded. Dr. Josef Terboven, Hitler's Reichskommissar in the country, wanted to fight to the last cartridge, but Quisling hoped to negotiate his way out of trouble, deluding himself that he might strike a deal for a peaceful transfer of power to a new administration headed by members of the government-in-exile in London.

He made no attempt to flee, and turned down the offer of a seat on Terboven's plane to Spain, where he could have sought asylum from General Franco. One passenger who *did* accept that offer was Léon Degrelle, leader of the pro-German Belgian Rexist Walloon Party, who had headed the Walloon Division of the Waffen SS. He had unexpectedly turned up in Oslo on 7 May dressed in an SS general's uniform before jumping on the plane to Spain that night. News of the German unconditional surrender had reached Norway by then, and national flags had suddenly appeared everywhere in the capital. People were openly celebrating in the streets, and Quisling even went out for an unobtrusive evening drive to witness what was happening, relieved that everything was going peacefully.

Shortly after one o'clock the following afternoon a representative of Milorg, the military resistance movement, arrived at Gimle, where some of Quisling's ministers were enjoying the sunny weather and strolling and chatting on the lawn. At a terse and awkward meeting, Quisling agreed to give himself up and in turn received an assurance that he would be given a just and fair trial. "I know that the Norwegian people have sentenced me to death," he said, "and that the easiest course for me would be to take my own life. But I want to let history reach its verdict."

He spent the rest of the day quietly packing up his personal papers and correspondence and preparing for a gentle internment in some agreeable location. But within hours he received a rude and unexpected shock, when he was told abruptly that he should report to Oslo's main police station. Protests and frantic late night telephone calls to various people were to no avail, so at six-fifteen the next morning Quisling and his ministers left Gimle in a convoy of four cars. It was a quiet, gray morning, and the streets were deserted after the previous day's celebrations. In the center of Oslo, an escort joined them, and with Milorg forces armed with Sten guns standing on the running board, Quisling was driven to the police headquarters at Mollergaten. It had been used by the Gestapo to imprison resistance fighters until just a few days before.

After the usual paperwork, Quisling was submitted to a full and undignified body search and then led to his cell. For the next six weeks, he was kept on suicide watch. His diet consisted mostly of salted herrings and rotten potatoes; he was given no knife or fork, so had to eat with a spoon. The light in his cell was never turned off. He was allowed no newspapers.

Eventually, he was transferred to a cell in the tower of Akershus Castle, inside the fortress that for centuries had protected Oslo from enemy attack. Here, the round-the-clock surveillance continued. That summer, while he languished in custody, ninety thousand other Norwegians were investigated for collaboration. Some 46,000 were found guilty of some degree of helping the enemy, and 600 received prison sentences of more than eight years. Twenty-five were sentenced to death.

Finally, in mid-August, Quisling was brought to trial. Found guilty of treason, he was shot by a firing squad in the castle in October.[11]

If the German surrender marked the end of one story, for many people it was the beginning of another. After waiting at Granville for weeks, Francesca Wilson finally received the order to move. At last, she was on her way into Germany.

She was one of a team of eight. Like most UNRRA units, it was multinational. The director and doctor, both male, were Belgians. The two drivers and the assistant welfare officer, also male, were French. The remaining three were British: Francesca herself, the chief welfare officer; Zinaida — or Zina — Russian-born, but married to a British Army colonel; and a nurse.

The director had been in the Belgian Secret Army before being arrested by the Gestapo. Tortured and condemned to death, he was only saved by the arrival of the allied armies. The doctor was a professor of pathology who had once worked in the Belgian Congo. Everyone called him "Tubeeb," an Arabic word meaning "medicine man" adopted by the French. Pierre, Francesca's assistant, had been an air-raid warden in occupied Paris. Marcel and Jacques, the drivers, were solid and dependable men with families. Zina had fled Russia with her mother after the Bolshevik Revolution, but she had long ago become pro-Soviet and worked during the war for Anglo-Soviet understanding. Francesca had trained with her in England and liked her dynamism and Russian warmth.

So far, UNRRA had been receiving a bad press. Why was it still waiting in the wings? When would it get into action? What was it doing? Paris is starving — where is UNRRA? Why is it not helping the

Dutch? Such were the headlines in the press. They did not understand, thought Francesca. UNRRA could enter a country only if it was invited by its government. Both the French and the Dutch were eager to manage their own affairs and did not want to have to deal with an international body. It also could not move without the authority—and, more crucially, help—of the army. So it was being blamed for problems not of its own making, which was very demoralizing.

They set out from Granville on 7 May in two old reconditioned army trucks. The vehicles were packed with their camp beds, blankets, water bottles, personal kits, helmets and gas masks—the war, after all, was not yet officially over for another twenty-four hours. They spent the day trundling through Normandy until they reached the ancient cathedral city of Chartres.

Crowds were out in the streets, already celebrating victory.

Early the next morning, Francesca slipped out to view the famous cathedral, the apogee of French religious architecture. But she found it still clad in its wartime attire. Sandbags were piled high against the main door and obscured the famous Gothic sculptures she remembered from a previous visit. The magnificent twelfth-century stained-glass windows were in storage for safekeeping, and inside the church had been stripped bare of all its finery. She found it all very dismal.

Although it was officially VE Day, her mood did not lighten. She listened to the official announcement of victory in Europe on a small radio in the back room of a café where they stopped for a meal. The innkeeper's wife stoically continued doing the washing up, but her daughter lifted her apron over her head, and sobbed. Her husband had been killed in the fighting a few months before—peace had come too late for her. Instead of feeling elated that the war was over, Francesca was overcome by "the sense of desolation it had brought and of all that was irrecoverably broken and gone."

Two days later, they crossed the frontier into Germany. White flags hung from houses and public buildings, and the streets were strangely silent. US Army trucks rushed past, packed to overflowing with German prisoners of war, dirty, unkempt, unshaven and mostly wearing Wehrmacht field gray, with just the occasional flash of Luftwaffe blue. From time to time, a convoy of freed forced laborers passed by flying French, Dutch or Soviet flags. They were heading home, except for the Russians, who were bound for some temporary holding camp. Zina shouted at them in Russian and they waved back lustily.

After a brief stop at the UNRRA office in Heidelberg, they journeyed on to Stuttgart. The city had been captured by French troops just a month before and was heavily damaged. The German husband and wife in whose hilltop villa on the outskirts of town they were billeted complained bitterly about the French. They had sacked the city, the couple protested, and "not left a treasure or virgin behind." The husband, an elderly, bald-headed man incongruously wearing Tirolean shorts, hovered in the background, suspiciously guarding his elegant furniture.

Finally, on the evening of Saturday 12 May, the team arrived in Starnberg, Bavaria, their destination. They had set out from Granville thinking they were headed for Dachau, but at Heidelberg they were ordered instead to this small, pleasant town on the edge of the Starnberger See, just a few miles south of Munich. It enjoyed lovely views over the Alps and housed dozens of summer homes of wealthy Müncheners. Here, in the lake's dark waters, the mad King Ludwig II had mysteriously drowned in 1886.

It was typical of the end-of-war chaos and improvisation that Captain Paisley, the local US Army head of military government, was not expecting them. In fact, he admitted, he had never even heard of UNRRA. But Francesca found him gentle, gracious and charming. He was also friendly and hospitable, and found them places to stay. Francesca and the two other women slept in a comfortable lakeside villa that had been requisitioned a couple of weeks before. It belonged to the steel baron Friedrich Flick, Hitler's biggest industrialist supporter. Paisley had arrested Flick, and kept his car and obsequious butler for himself.

He explained that the UNRRA team's arrival was a godsend. Just a few miles down the lake was a camp with three or four thousand displaced persons that was being looked after by a solitary American officer who badly needed help. The occupants had been marched out of Dachau just a few days before the Americans arrived — some of the thousands Fey von Hassell had watched through the window of the bus as she too was being evacuated from the camp. They were dispersed into the Bavarian Alps, possibly to be machine-gunned in some obscure valley, but the Americans turned up in the nick of time. They were now being housed at a place called Feldafing.[12]

No sooner had Hitler come to power than he put in place a special secondary school system for the training of future Nazi leaders known as National Political High Schools, military-type boarding schools whose classes were called "platoons." Inspired by the example, the Stormtroopers opened a school of their own in Feldafing in what had been an International Pestalozzi school until it was closed down by the Nazis. Here, children from eight to eighteen received a solid but completely Nazified education including frequent cultural visits to Munich's museums and galleries as well as to the annual Bayreuth Festival of Wagner's music. They were also taken to see such Nazi extravaganzas as the 1936 Berlin Olympics and the infamous 1937 Exhibition of Degenerate Art in Munich.

Feldafing was also well known to Fey von Hassell as the home of her maternal grandmother. She spent many fairly tedious holidays there, including her fourteenth birthday, when she was alone in the house with her grandmother and her governess. Despite the importance of the day, not a single one of her classes was canceled. "I'm dying of boredom," she confided to her schoolgirl diary. Later, the Nazis expropriated the house so that they could build a Nazi school right in front of it. As a result, her parents found a new house at Ebenhausen, about thirteen miles outside Munich.[13]

For a while, the Feldafing *Oberschule* ran exchanges with elite British and American schools such as Rugby and Choate. One American student who spent a year in Feldafing was struck forcibly by the dominance of the theme of the "reawakening of Germany," as well as by the universal belief of the German students that the Jews — among whom they included the Episcopalian Franklin D. Roosevelt — ran America.[14]

Now the Americans were running the school at Feldafing, which had been evacuated by the Stormtroopers just a few days before. The man in charge was US Army Lieutenant Smith, who, by some masterstroke of poetic justice — and as if to validate the delusions of its former students — was Jewish. The school consisted of eight large brick buildings with an excellent kitchen, hospital, baths and workshops — no expense had been spared for the future leaders of the Reich. Like many wartime German institutions, it had relied heavily on forced labor whose makeshift accommodation consisted of some wooden barracks situated close by. These now held some 1,200 Russian prisoners from Dachau. Occupying the school itself were some 2,500 others from fifteen different countries. Most were Jews.

Smith was living a couple of miles past the camp, in the village of

Tutzing. Francesca found him installed in a pleasant villa with a garden running down to the lake. "He is a very energetic, dynamic man," she noted in her typewritten diary.[15] He immediately demonstrated the fact by summoning the Tutzing burgermeister—an anti-Nazi who had been installed by the Americans—and ordering him to find a house for the UNRRA team. Obediently, he led them to the villa next door to Smith's.

It was a modern, Bavarian-style house with a veranda, and a boathouse on the lake. The door was answered by a tall, dark, good-looking woman, who blanched when she saw them. The burgermeister told her politely but firmly that she had three hours to vacate the house. With all the dignity she could muster, she showed Francesca and the team around, then pleaded quietly for her and her three children to be allowed to occupy the top floor, which could be sealed off from the rest of the house. This was agreed, and the five male members of the team moved in downstairs. A similar procedure happened at the house next door, where Francesca, Zina and the nurse would stay. The female owner burst out weeping and wailing as soon as she saw the group walking up her driveway. She, too, was eventually allowed to stay, but on condition that she cleaned for them.

This is what defeat means to ordinary citizens, thought Francesca, a measure of the prostration of the conquered; that, and the fear of being thrown in prison for some Nazi past. The main burden fell on the burgermeister. He had to turn people out of their homes, requisition food and equipment needed by the Americans and the DPs from his fellow citizens, seize textiles and pay carpenters to make hundreds of emergency bunk beds for the Feldafing camp. It had been the forced labor of the inhabitants of the camp, Francesca reminded herself when she began to feel sorry for the German home-owners, which had guaranteed such women an easier wartime life than women in any other European country. Hardly anyone felt responsible for the slave laborers, yet almost every family in Germany had profited in one way or another from the supply of cheap labor they provided.

The next day, Smith showed Francesca around the camp. At first, she was repulsed. She had seen victims of famine before, after the First World War, in Serbia, Russia and Vienna, but what she saw now were people who had also suffered deliberate cruelty. They still wore their blue-and-white striped concentration camp "pajamas," had shaven heads, and bore their tattooed numbers on their left arms. "They had the furtive look and gestures of hunted animals," she noted. "By years of brutal treatment, by the murder of relatives, by the constant fear of death, all that was human had been taken away from them."

Smith at once set the UNRRA team to work. He already had a German staff of almost three hundred toiling for him as doctors, nurses, cleaners, maintenance men and storekeepers—his "slaves," he smilingly called them—and he was determined to make his DP camp the best in Bavaria. "He was like a whirlwind," said Francesca, "in six different places at once, exploding with rage or laughter, threatening and cajoling." It was her job to deal with the Jews. To get to know them, she explored the blocks that only three weeks before had echoed to the sounds of Nazi marching songs and the laughter of teenage boys ready to die for Hitler. The grounds were dirty and unkempt, and the toilets filthy, deliberately fouled by the inmates for the German staff to clean up. All around, small fires were burning and groups of men were frying bits of meat or bread. Near by, Francesca spotted a huge pile of writing desks, tables, shelves and other bits of furniture from the school being chopped up with an axe by a German sergeant.

In the cellars, she found bundles of old skis once used by the students as part of their rigorous keep-fit regime and heaps of smashed cellos, violins, drums and wind instruments. The Nazi school, as part of its extensive cultural education, had once boasted three orchestras. But on the night they arrived, she was told, the Dachau prisoners—specifically the Greeks—had stormed in and broken all the instruments.

Most of the Greeks were young men and they spoke fluent French. They were all from Salonika, and had once run barbers' or tailors' shops or been students there. Francesca knew the city quite well, having visited it soon after the great fire of 1917 that destroyed three-quarters of the old city, and again ten years later, by which time it had emerged phoenix-like from the ruins as a modern Greek city. She spoke genuinely with the Greeks of her affection for their country and its people. "You were our only allies [in Europe] in 1940, when we were fighting alone," she told them warmly. They crowded around her, all talking at once. Some had fought with the British, others had sheltered shot-down British airmen, and some had fled to Crete. These were the remnants of the Greek Jews rounded up by the Germans and deported to Auschwitz and other camps in 1943, mostly from Salonika—where 95 percent of the Jews had been deported—but also from Athens, a total of some seventy thousand in all. The women, children and old men were taken straight to the gas chambers. When the Red Army approached Auschwitz, the remainder were marched off to Dachau. There were now only about five hundred of them left.

"What will become of us?" they asked Francesca anxiously. "If we go back to Salonika — what then? Our relations are dead — everything we possessed has been taken away. No one will want us. What about America? What about Palestine?"

She had no easy answer for them, but she summoned up memories of sun-soaked Aegean visits and did her humane best. They were Sephardic Jews, she told them, and had lived in Greece since being expelled from Spain in the fifteenth century. "Greece is the land of your birth," she said. "If you go somewhere else you will be homesick for the glittering seas of early morning in the Salonika Gulf, and the midday heat, and the taste of octopus washed down with retsina, and of ripe figs and the snapping, black eyes of Greek women. Money does not matter with a climate like that, as it does in America."

Some of them nodded in agreement. They liked the bit about being Sephardim, rather than Ashkenazim from Central Europe "We don't speak Yiddish," they said proudly, "we speak Spanish, Greek, French and Hebrew."

Francesca plucked up her courage. Why, she asked, with their rich cultural background and love of music, had they broken the musical instruments?

"Because they were German," came the answer. "We had to smash things up when we were freed. Never mind," they added. "We can sing to you without instruments. We have the best choir in the camp."

As she walked away, Francesca thought of the children who had been evacuated from London to save them from the Blitz. Separated from their families, alone in the countryside, they had often smashed and soiled things in revenge against the society that had made them feel like outcasts. How much time would it take, she wondered, before these infantile regressions by the victims of Nazism were overcome? And what lay ahead for the thousands now in camps, liberated but not yet properly free?

In Schleswig-Holstein, British commando Bryan Samain also found that VE Day offered little reason to celebrate. That day, his commando unit moved by truck and jeep from the port of Neustadt to the small town of Eutin, midway between Lübeck and Kiel. It was a pretty market town virtually undamaged by the war and home to a large palace with English-landscaped gardens that had originally been built for the medieval prince-bishops of Lübeck and later became the summer residence of the dukes of Oldenburg. Thanks to a massive influx of refugees, its prewar population of seven thousand had almost doubled. "I cannot say that we felt any particular feelings of elation or celebration," recalled Samain. "There was almost a feeling of anticlimax . . . a feeling that—like everyone else involved—we had set out with a job to do and we had finally got it done."[16] Yet, for him, there was still plenty to do. The commandos' job now was to get Eutin and its surrounding region up and running again.

This involved a litany of tasks: rounding up Nazi officials still at large; appointing a town council from a list of officials screened to eliminate Nazis and their supporters; restoring electricity and gas supplies, and getting transport services working; setting up emergency food centers to feed the refugees and deportees flooding the streets; collecting food from outlying rural areas and seeing to its distribution; finding temporary shelter for thousands of DPs; getting the local police functioning again; rehousing German refugees arriving in the area mostly from regions occupied by the Red Army; and reopening the churches.

From their offices in the Town Hall, within a week the commandos got the electricity, gas and local rail services working properly again. Nazi officials were rounded up and food supplies were under control. A new town council purged of Nazis was in place. It took a little longer to get the police reorganized, though, as they had been well penetrated by Nazis. Controlling the thousands of liberated slave laborers proved more of a handful. As everywhere else in Germany, they reacted to their liberation with outbursts of rage and looting, and it required some stern doses of British Army discipline to bring them under control. Samain was also besieged by local residents seeking to get back to normal and needing his help in myriad ways. Besides them, there were the hundreds of refugees from other parts of Germany who had to be put somewhere. All wanted to stay in the British zone, or at the very least not be handed back to the Russians.[17]

Samain also had to help with the reception and management of German prisoners of war. Thanks in part to Doenitz's deliberate delaying strategy, there were now about two million surrendered members of the Wehrmacht in the British zone of Germany. They had been stripped of their weapons and were currently being marched or transported towards Schleswig-Holstein. About half were destined for the peninsula's west coast, including the highly indoctrinated SS and parachute troops, who would be isolated on the rocky and desolate island of Nordstrand. About half a million others were headed for Schleswig-Holstein's east coast, with the rest distributed between the Elbe and Weser rivers. In addition to these two million, about half a million German sick or wounded prisoners lay in hospitals mostly in or close to Schleswig-Holstein.

One particular task for Samain and his unit was to organize the reception of a group of ten thousand POWs who had to be bivouacked in the Eutin Forest. They also had to supervise SS troops as they were marched through the town on their way to the coast. This caused the British occupiers considerable irritation. "We watched them angrily one day," recorded Samain, "a long column of them, perhaps a battalion in strength, defiantly marching through Eutin with military precision, keeping sharp step and singing the 'Horst Wessel Song' as they marched." Eventually, the British ordered them to stop and issued instructions that future SS columns were to proceed silently through the town. Obediently, the next column to arrive did not sing. Instead, it whistled.

What the citizens of Eutin made of this show of defiance is hard to know. Hitler had secured 55 percent of the town's vote in the 1932 presidential election and even more in the following Reichstag election. Even the Nazis' strongest political rivals in the town, the conservative Nationalists, had gleefully beaten the anti-Semitic drum. But now, Samain guessed, most of them simply wanted to return to their former lives.[18]

Eighty miles to the north of Eutin, and behaving as though VE Day were largely irrelevant, the last Nazi government was trying desperately to carry on as normal. It had established itself at Flensburg, close to the Danish border, where the town was overflowing with sixty thousand German military personnel from all three services. It was so full that the British occupation troops were unable to find any accommodation. Major-General J.B. Churcher, commander of the infantry brigade that had been in the vanguard of the British advance into the region, drove into the town two days after Europe celebrated victory. "The situation, to say the least, was bizarre," he recorded. "The streets were crowded with German staff cars filled with German officers. German army buses lurched through the town. The docks were patrolled by German naval and military police, fully armed. The Luftwaffe was still in charge of the airfield . . . Flensburg was the last Nazi bolthole." Desperate to find rooms for his men, he finally gave the burgermeister three days to make space available. He also ordered him to remove the picture of Hitler that still stood prominently on his desk. "I don't want to see that man's face again," he barked.[19]

Yet it continued to adorn walls nearby. Doenitz had established his headquarters at the Naval Cadet School at Murwick, just to the east of Flensburg, a large and magnificent site overlooking the sea, and outwardly business continued as usual. Every morning, Doenitz, immaculate in his grand admiral's uniform, was driven to the school in the large, armor-plated Mercedes given to him by Hitler, to preside over his cabinet. Armed German soldiers stood guard outside the government offices, and the Reich's war flag fluttered from atop the building. Photographs of Hitler still hung in the offices. The government even acquired the services of an official photographer.[20]

Its members appeared blind to the magnitude of Germany's defeat, to the enormity of the crimes of the Third Reich, and to the realities of big power politics. One hope they still nurtured was for an imminent break between the West and Moscow that would force London, Washington and Paris to recognize them as the legitimate German government. The grand wartime alliance was certainly poised to fracture, but believing that the West would accept the men of Flensburg revealed almost willful delusion, or frantic desperation.

Even Albert Speer, the Minister of Economics and Production, who at last was showing some dim awareness of the criminality of the regime he had served, misguidedly believed he could contribute to the post-war reconstruction of his country. He had deliberately sabotaged Hitler's "scorched-earth" decree during the last few weeks of the war in order to save Germany's industry, and now he thought that he was the man who would make it all right again. Deliberately distancing himself from Doenitz and the others, he found himself comfortable accommodation in Glucksburg Castle, a few miles outside Flensburg, where he lived as a guest of its owner, the Duke of Mecklenburg-Holstein, a cousin of Britain's King George VI.

Here he continued to live in the style to which he had become accustomed. In the middle of May, he was visited by several distinguished Americans who wanted to talk to him about German war production. John Kenneth Galbraith, George W. Ball, and Paul H. Nitze, of the US Strategic Bombing Offensive Survey, were trying to establish how effective allied bombing had been in hitting German industry. The meeting was all very friendly and civilized. Speer, still expecting a significant post-war career, warmly, if guardedly, cooperated. Friendly allied officers even invited him on a day trip to Paris.[21]

Doenitz and others certainly tried to make this last Nazi government acceptable to the allies, and deliberately sought to distance themselves from the atrocities revealed in the concentration camps. Foreign Minister von Krosigk even had the nerve to ask Eisenhower if the Reich Court of Justice could be permitted to try those charged with contravening "the laws and basic principles of justice and morality." The German people, he claimed, had known nothing of conditions in the camps, and even "leading German personalities" had remained ignorant of them. Three days after this decree, Doenitz announced that the millions of German soldiers and members of the Waffen SS had also known nothing of Nazi atrocities and had fought "honorably and cleanly."

That the German armed forces had been untainted by war crimes and crimes against humanity was a fantasy earnestly peddled by this last Nazi government. So, too, was the notion that its own members were free of any guilt or responsibility for what had happened since 1933. To support his case, Doenitz ostentatiously dismissed the most notorious Nazis from their posts and made it clear to Himmler that he had no use for him. The SS leader had turned up at Flensburg obviously hoping for a job from the man who had surprisingly taken his place as Hitler's successor, and with whom he had collaborated closely during the previous few weeks in fighting against "defeatists" within the Reich. But Doenitz was nothing if not shrewd. Accepting the SS leader into his government would be a certain political kiss of death. So, on the afternoon of Sunday 6 May, Doenitz received Himmler in his office and confirmed that he had been stripped of all his positions.

Yet he did not throw Himmler completely naked to the wolves: he agreed to provide the Reichsführer SS and many of the SS retinue who had accompanied him to Flensburg with false papers identifying them as German soldiers. "Dive for cover in the Wehrmacht," was Himmler's last order to his followers.

Thus it was that the once most-feared man in Hitler's Third Reich proved himself "far from the ice cool exemplar of Nordic virtues that Hitler had portrayed," leading his men into a last stand against the "Jewish-Bolshevik" hordes, or sacrificing himself as he had sacrificed so many millions of others. Instead, he shaved off his moustache, put on a black eye patch, gave himself a false name, and on 10 May set off southwards with a handful of SS high-ranking officers in four large staff cars.[22]

Later that week an extraordinary episode unfolded in Holland.[23]

There was an old abandoned Ford assembly plant on the outskirts of Amsterdam. Late on Sunday 13 May, a couple of trucks drove up and two men were bundled out. Their hands were tied behind them, and they were roughly handled to stand against the wall of an adjacent air-raid shelter. Then they were blindfolded. A firing squad appeared, the order was given, and a volley of shots rang out. The two bodies slumped to the ground and an officer strode forward and gave the *coup de grâce*. Only hours before, the men had been sentenced to death by an official court martial.

They were deserters, and the shooting of deserters was hardly unusual. But what made this particular execution extraordinary was that both the military court and the firing squad were German, and the victims were anti-Nazis from Hitler's navy. Moreover, the execution took place five days *after* the capitulation of Hitler's forces. Indeed, that same day, King George VI and Queen Elizabeth drove through London's streets to the official thanksgiving service for victory at St. Paul's Cathedral. To add to the surrealism, the whole affair was assisted by the Canadian Army, which provided the rifles, the truck and the escort that drove the firing squad to the execution spot.

This bizarre post-VE Day cooperation between the Canadians and their defeated foe is explained by a decision made by Canadian commanders following the German surrender to Montgomery at Lüneberg Heath. When this took place, some 150,000 German troops were still under arms in western Holland. They controlled virtually every aspect of Dutch daily life and not a single Canadian soldier had yet entered the area. So who was to keep law and order and oversee the surrender? The answer was obvious: the German Army itself.

To make this possible, Eisenhower and the allied High Command decided to bend the Geneva Convention. Instead of declaring the Germans prisoners of war, they labeled them "surrendered enemy personnel." This had two main advantages: first, they would have to feed themselves rather than become dependent on the allies, who were already having critical problems feeding the starving Dutch; and second, they would remain organizationally intact, with the entire German military hierarchy in full authority. The allies could issue their orders and have them carried out through the German chain of command.

As a practical arrangement, it offered a deft solution to a tricky problem and worked exceedingly well, with the Canadians issuing orders and the Germans implementing them with impressive efficiency. In this way, hundreds of German units remained in place for several days after the liberation, fully armed and on Dutch streets, until they marched in perfect discipline under the command of their officers to designated places where they turned in their weapons. For the Dutch, however, it was often hard to understand why they could see fully armed Canadian and German soldiers mingling side by side and not harassing each other.

Even after they turned in their weapons, the German soldiers remained under full Wehrmacht control, with a German commander in charge in contact with his superiors up the chain of command all the way to General Johannes Blaskowitz, the commander-in-chief of Hitler's "Fortress Holland." In this way, two parallel structures, Canadian and German, existed in Holland for several weeks after VE Day. The Germans enjoyed an amazing degree of authority and individual German troops continued to owe their loyalty to their own armed forces, not to the authority of the victorious powers.

It was this cozy deal to which the two German deserters fell victim. At least one of them had strong anti-Nazi credentials, for the twenty-eight-year-old ship's mate Rainer Beck had a Jewish mother and a father who was persecuted by the Nazis for being a Social Democrat. In September 1944, when allied forces first crossed the Dutch border, he had deserted from a harbor defense unit in IJmuiden and taken refuge with his sister, who was in hiding in Amsterdam. When the Canadians finally entered the city, he came out of hiding and along with the other deserter turned himself in to the Dutch resistance. In turn, they handed him over to the Seaforth Highlanders, the Canadian regiment that just a few days before had entered the starving city amid scenes of wild jubilation.

The Canadians immediately placed the two men inside the Ford plant, along with some eighteen hundred captured German marines. In accord with arrangements elsewhere in Holland, the camp had a German commandant, internal staff and code of discipline. Eager to establish his authority, the commandant seized on the arrival of the two deserters and decided to try the "traitors," setting up the court martial while making clear what he expected its verdict to be. Events then proceeded with dreadful and speedy predictability. The trial took place in front of the whole camp, the mood quickly turned ugly, and when Beck tried to defend himself he was shouted down. It all took just fifteen minutes and the judges unanimously agreed on the death sentence.

What followed next was even more breathtaking. The German commandant now asked the Canadians for weapons to carry out the sentence. Flabbergasted, the local Canadian officer in charge phoned higher authority for direction. Eager not to disrupt the parallel arrangements by challenging German authority over their own soldiers, the senior officers refused to intervene. Eventually, Blaskowitz himself decided the issue by agreeing that the men should be shot, and the order was passed down, through the Canadian chain of command, to the camp in Amsterdam. Here, the Canadian officer dutifully arranged truck transport and issued eight captured German rifles with sixteen rounds of ammunition to the execution squad. From the trial to the bodies lying slumped on the ground took less than twelve hours.

Astonishing though this seems, it was far from an exception. Elsewhere in Holland, German deserters continued to be handed over by the Canadians after VE Day, and several were executed. Only a rising tide of disquiet among the Canadians involved eventually forced a change in policy. After that, such prisoners were no longer turned over to the Wehrmacht but instead to allied field security units.

"How could the Germans shoot these two young men on such a beautiful day after the war was ended?" asked the Canadian officer who handed them over, perhaps shocked by the consequences of his own unquestioning obedience to orders. "These boys have been deserters," came the response from one of the German officers, "and if they were allowed to go home and have children the minds of the children would be dirty too." It was chilling evidence of how deeply Nazi attitudes still held sway among the defeated forces of Adolf Hitler.

CHAPTER TWENTY-ONE

"FORTUNE IS NOT ALWAYS JOY"

In the Lago di Braies Hotel high in the Italian Alps, Fey von Hassell was having difficulty adjusting to the idea of peace, and liberation had even darkened the shadow hanging over the fate of her children.

She was not the only one in the group who had been forcibly separated from her children. The hand of the SS had reached far and wide in retribution for the attempt on Hitler's life. One of the key members of the plot had been Colonel Caesar von Hofacker, a member of the High Command in Paris, where the conspirators managed to arrest over a thousand SS men before the plot unraveled. He was imprisoned and his three youngest children were taken away by the SS to somewhere in Austria. Ilse-Lotte, their mother, had become one of Fey's closest companions. "It was a tremendous relief," wrote Fey, "to be with someone who could understand the constant torment that such separation caused." Mika von Stauffenberg, Alex's sister-in-law, had also lost her children to the SS, as had Irma, the daughter-in-law of the ill-fated former Mayor of Leipzig, Carl Goerdeler.

All of them besieged Sigismund Payne Best with queries about how they could start searching for their children, but the British intelligence office knew that communications with Germany were so bad that there was little hope of any quick results. "I did what I could to comfort them," he recalled painfully, "but I was feeling so ill myself that I fear on occasion I gave way to impatience." But Fey at least thought he rose to the challenge: he was "very superior" to anyone else she could think of, she later told him.[1]

This was a short breathing space for Fey in which she could slowly adapt to normal life and take her first timid steps towards freedom. Yet it was hard to forget the traumas of the last few months. "Even though I knew it was all over," she confessed, "I somehow found it hard to believe that there would be no more sharp knocks on the door, nor more orders to pack and be ready to leave at once."[2]

God was also much on her mind. A couple of days before the group was finally evacuated from the hotel, she went alone with Alex to the chapel. Like the other Stauffenbergs, he was a Catholic. He sat down and began to play the church's small organ. "Tears rose up in my eyes," Fey wrote. "I felt profoundly touched by the beauty of the sacred music, the silence of the mountains, and the mystical atmosphere of the chapel." They would soon be parting, returning to their separate families, friends and personal relationships. Alex had lost not just his wife, but his brothers. He seemed in many ways so helpless. The thought of leaving him made Fey immensely sad.[3]

Not too long ago she had written a passionate letter to her husband, Detalmo, while she was expecting Roberto:

> You know if I shall die now or after the second baby, I would be immensely sad for leaving you, also because it would be so long before we could meet again. For the rest I would not be sad, for I have had so much happiness in these few years . . . I had a beautiful childhood . . . and I had two years of the most divine and exceptional womanhood. I got to know what real love between a man and a woman means.[4]

But it was hard now to know where her true feelings lay.

VE Day came and went, unremarked and irrelevant, but two days later a convoy of buses arrived to take them away. Fey clambered aboard with her usual traveling companions — Best, the Stauffenbergs and the Schuschniggs — and off they drove on a bumpy four-hour trip down the mountains to Verona and a comfortable room in the Colomba d'Oro Hotel, just off the Piazza Brà and the old Roman arena. As she walked through the lobby, a good-looking Italian in military uniform introduced himself. He was a friend of her sister-in-law Marina, and had seen Fey's name on a list of the freed prisoners. He went out of his way to see she had everything she needed and even sent chocolates and cigarettes to her room. But it felt strange. It was the first time in several months she had had any contact with anyone remotely connected with her life in Italy.

The next morning, they set off in a convoy of jeeps and buses to the Verona airfield, where they boarded three US military planes. It was a clear day, and as they flew over the country Fey enjoyed excellent views. They even passed over Rome and then dipped low over the shell- and bomb-blasted ruins of the great Monte Cassino monastery and battlefield that had claimed so many lives just a year before. Finally, at eleven o'clock in the morning, they landed in Naples.

Here, a shock awaited Fey and the other Germans, who by now had almost forgotten their nationality. They were separated from the rest of the freed prisoners and for a long time no one paid them any notice. They had been used to having Payne Best with them all the time, a friendly and solicitous face, a man who liked Germans and was sympathetic to their individual fates, but as soon as they had arrived he was driven off in a staff car to allied headquarters in nearby Caserta.

Group by national group, the others gradually departed too. In the general confusion, no one bothered to say goodbye. They had been together for so long, and been driven around so much, they all assumed they would see each other again. But the Americans did not seem to know what to do with the Germans, and they hung around for hours. Fey did not even notice when the Hungarians left, even though she had especially enjoyed their company. "We were Germans, people of a defeated nation," she suddenly realized, and their common suffering counted for nothing. In the end, they were bundled across the Bay of Naples to Capri and a small, optimistically named hotel in the village of Anacapri, the Paradiso Eden. The Americans, she learned, wanted to interrogate them. Until then, they could not leave the hotel. Their freedom had seemingly been brief.

However, within a couple of days, the officers in her group were taken away to a military prison in Germany. Among them was Colonel von Bonin, who had saved them from certain death at the hands of the SS by alerting von Vietinghoff to their presence in Villabassa. She was sorry to see him led away under armed guard. But she did not feel the same way about Prince Philipp of Hesse and had no regrets at seeing the back of him. He was a solid Nazi until he was sent to prison, and she could neither forget nor forgive his behavior towards her father.[5]

Once this group had left, the others were told they were free to move around. "Alex and I continued to spend much of our time together," she recorded. "But somehow I sensed that he knew it was over, that I had returned to my adopted country, where all my energies would be devoted to rebuilding my shattered family." Payne Best made a brief reappearance and tried to cheer them all up, urging patience and promising he would do all he could to speed up the reunion with their families. He made a special effort for Fey, whom he could tell was seriously distressed. "She was absolutely distracted about her two little boys," he noted. So at breakfast he introduced her to the US Army major in charge. There was not much the American could do to help, but, remarked Payne Best, "it comforted her to talk about her troubles to someone who appeared to be in authority, and as she was an extremely pretty woman she was given a most sympathetic hearing."[6]

But Fey also took the initiative herself. As soon as she could, she walked to the island's post office and sent a telegram to Detalmo in Rome, giving him her address and asking him to come and take her home. She had no idea if he was still there, or even if he was alive, as they had heard nothing of each other for many months. To her utter joy and amazement, though, the very next day she received a reply saying he was coming to Capri to collect her. That morning, she could hardly contain herself, pacing up and down outside the hotel, anxiously looking for him. Then, suddenly, he was there and they embraced. The words tumbled over themselves as they tried to tell each other what had happened to them over the previous year and a half.

Detalmo was visibly shocked when he heard about the fate of his sons. He had not known they had been taken away so had expected to find them with Fey in the hotel. But he remained calm and tried to reassure her: the Red Cross or the Vatican would surely help find them. Nevertheless, "Though outwardly he seemed convinced about it," she admitted, "I saw in his eyes the same torment that had plagued me for so many months."

That night, after they had moved to a more comfortable hotel, they threw a dinner for Fey's special friends in the group — the Stauffenbergs, the Hofackers and the Hammersteins. Unfortunately, many of them seemed to have little appetite. They were so used to expecting food to run out that they had already eaten at the hotel. However, the evening was a great success. Encouraged by copious amounts of wine, everyone made a speech, including Detalmo, which

Fey thought was one of the best. He concluded by saying that, having met them, he was sorry from the bottom of his heart that he had not been imprisoned alongside them. The force of the comment would only hit home later, when the chasm of experience that now separated husband and wife sometimes became cruelly unbridgeable.

At the end of the dinner, Fey felt a terrible lump arise in her throat. Did she have to leave these people whom she had come to admire so much? Especially Alex. "How could he possibly face the hard life that now confronted him, without wife, family, or home?" she wondered. "The idea was painful for me, but I had to face my own future confidently and renew my life in Italy with Detalmo. I could only hope that Alex understood."[7]

The next morning, Fey and Detalmo left to take the ferry back to the mainland. Alex did not come to say goodbye. But in her hand Fey was clutching a poem, the last of several he wrote for her.

> The moon is shining from a brilliant sky
> Into the pleasure gardens of the South
> And touches my sad heart
> As friends dine, the parting stabs and twists
> Bitterly hidden from the cheerful crowd — the desert
> wind blows strong
>
> Trembling and staggering, two things keep me alive,
> Are my dim light of hope this painful night.
> Thirsty I drink deep
> Your beating heart, deep into my breast
>
> You are mine, I shout it to the winds,
> The sea, as in blue foam, it overwhelms the rocks
> You must hear my call this cruel summer night.
>
> I now dream of a dark time
> When unreal happiness possessed my heart,
> When a nymph, in a Dolomite forest, with magic wand
> Did touch me and give me hope.[8]

As the ferry pulled away from the quayside, she wrote, "I felt my heart breaking into a thousand pieces. My nerves were worn through. For too long I had kept my emotions in check." Now, she finally let go and sobbed uncontrollably. Detalmo could do nothing to comfort her. Behind her lay friendships and love forged so deeply that older relationships paled by comparison. She had learned, as so many had during the hardships of this terrible war, that it was possible to love some people even more deeply than a parent, a husband, a child, a brother or a sister.

To try to help, Detalmo took her for lunch in a small restaurant on the Neapolitan waterfront. Normally, she would have found it charming, but not today. She hated every minute of it. Above all, she loathed the violinist and the way he sang with his "insincere sentimentalism made for tourists, and with false tears in his eyes." The sun was sparkling on the water, the Mediterranean stretched serenely in front of her, and she was finally reunited with her husband. Yet it all felt horribly wrong. "Suffering is not always sadness, Fortune is not always Joy." The words of Goethe, some of Alex's favorite lines, echoed in her mind. Liberation meant she would feel awfully alone for a very long time.[9]

Millions of others across Europe were experiencing similar suffering. Family separation and destruction have always been threads in the cruel tapestry of war, but under the Nazis they were more pronounced than ever before.

In Feldafing, Francesca Wilson was helping pick up the pieces of shattered families and putting them back together. When she succeeded, it felt like a sudden ray of light flashing across a dark landscape of the broken and the lost. She was a firm believer in democracy — not just within the UNRRA organization, where the staff met frequently to discuss issues and hammer out solutions — but with respect to the people they were helping. They should be consulted at every turn, she believed. "Lady Bountiful" attitudes, she wrote with scorn, were long outdated. The cooperation of the refugees themselves should be sought from the start. "Otherwise," she thought, "they will degenerate rapidly into paupers."[10]

One day, a young Polish Jew in the camp named Joseph came to her office and asked for help. His sister and cousin had been living in Budapest, he explained, and he had long thought them dead, but word had reached him that they were alive and living in a camp at an aerodrome near Landsberg, a Bavarian town about fifty miles away. By this time, Francesca had managed to requisition a car from some Germans. "I said I would take him to Landsberg," she wrote. "There was a huge camp there, and I wanted to get a list of its inmates to put up in Feldafing."

They searched the aerodrome for an hour with no luck, then met an American sergeant. "Those two Jewish dames?" he asked. "Why, they left yesterday. They live with peasants in the village. You'd better hunt them up there."

In a stable attached to a farmhouse, Francesca and Joseph found an old couple milking cows. "Is my sister Judith here?" asked Joseph. The old man stopped milking. "Judith, your sister?" he said. "Then"—and he grasped Joseph's hand with spontaneous warmth—"you must be Joseph. She thinks you are dead." Now his wife chimed in: "But only yesterday they left us. They have gone to the dreadful Landsberg barracks because they thought they might get repatriated quicker from there."

The Landsberg barracks consisted of three enormous buildings packed with five thousand people of twenty different nationalities. It was guarded by American sentries, and only a few of the inmates were allowed out at any one time. Francesca could find no trace of the young women on any list, but they went in and searched for them anyway. The task seemed hopeless, "But Joseph was not to be put off," recorded Francesca, "and suddenly we opened a door and there they were, and in a trice brother and sister were in each other's arms."

If Robert Reid had viewed the wanderings of the deportees across Europe in biblical terms, Francesca felt she was experiencing something medieval:

There was something in the scene, which made it belong to the ancient world, or at least to an era before letters, telegrams, trains, all the communications of our modern world existed. And because this ordinary scene—a brother meeting a sister—was so miraculous, making one feel that the lights of the world had gone up again, it seemed to me that it was a measure of the extent to which Europe in our day had gone back into the Dark Ages.

Judith and her cousin, Polly, had been deported from Budapest and spent several months in Dachau. After they were liberated, they lived and worked happily with the two Bavarian peasants on the farm before heading for Landsberg. There was still no sign of repatriations to Hungary starting, so after persuading the two women to return to the farm for the time being, and with a promise that Joseph would join them as soon as he could, Francesca drove them back. "Neither Joseph nor the girls thought it strange that fate had guided them to kindly Germans," she noted. Many Dachau victims, she realized, talked of some German or other who had been good to them. Often, their bitterest feelings were directed against people of their own nationality who had betrayed them. "Of all sins," thought Francesca, "treachery is the hardest to forgive." It was not the first time since landing in Europe that she had come to that conclusion.[11]

The reuniting of Joseph and Judith was a bright interlude in an otherwise dark and difficult May. Good progress was made on many fronts: most of the Western Europeans were rapidly repatriated to Belgium, France or Holland; Francesca's doctor colleague soon had the typhus problem under control, was improving the camp's sanitation and was taking care of the special nutritional needs of the children; and Zina was hard at work with the Russians. But Francesca found much of the work frustrating. The fact of the matter, she quickly realized, was that UNRRA had little independent power. Everything important was still controlled by the military. This was the case everywhere across Europe and had been part of the original arrangement that created the agency in the first place. It was obvious that for the first few months of the peace the army alone would have the means of transport and the equipment to deal with the problems. The humanitarian teams were there to help, not to act as independent units.

At Feldafing, Lieutenant Smith had control of all food and equipment, enjoyed a virtual monopoly on transport, and had at his beck and call a huge staff quite separate from Francesca and her team. In these circumstances she found that some of her training had been little more than pie in the sky. For example, she had been taught how to set up an information bureau. But what, she complained, was the use of that when she had no information to dispense? Every day someone wanted to know how to get a visa for America, Palestine or Australia, or to find their mother, father, sister or brother. She spent hours writing down endless names and details of family members last seen or heard of at Theresienstadt, Auschwitz or some other dreadful place. But as yet, no centralized tracing bureau existed, so the best she could do was circulate her lists among other DP camps in the area.

One of the most heart-rending and unexpected aspects of her work was coming across inmates who did not want to go home. No one had trained her for that. One day she asked a Lithuanian Jew why he did not want to go home. He replied:

I lived in Vilna, and I lived in a little street where we were all Jews together, but they took my brothers and sisters and my parents away, and they were all taken to the gas chambers. I have no relatives left. I don't think I should find any of my friends in that street. I couldn't bear to go back to a place like that with such terrible memories. I want to shake off the dust of Europe and begin a new life somewhere else.[12]

On the last day of May, Francesca sat down at her typewriter and vented her frustrations in her diary. It was a drenching wet day, which added to her profound sense of discouragement. Oddly enough, Lieutenant Smith's dynamism and energy had become part of the problem. He was so organized and determined that there seemed little room for Francesca and the others. That she herself was a strong-willed person made it even worse. "It is difficult to worm one's way in to such a set up, though there are plenty of things to do," she complained. "I have never in my life worked before without having access to one's own stores . . . But there appear to be a whole hierarchy of personnel who control these things and I have no pleasure in going hat in hand to them." She found it especially frustrating that she could not even get a sewing workshop up and running. "It's a queer life," she concluded, "and I have an increasing feeling that Smith does not want us to be there . . ."[13]

There was one hopeful piece of news, though. That day, Captain Paisley drove in from Tutzing with an army friend, another captain, who was in charge of German prisoners of war. So far, the prisoners had been kept behind barbed wire but now, explained the two Americans, many were going to be released so that they could work on the land. The occupying armies were beginning to worry about the food situation in Germany over the coming winter and needed as many hands to put to the harvest as possible. It was a small and hopeful sign of a return to normality.

A few miles away, however, the last act of what had become a terrible normality under the Nazis had just been played out.

Kaufbeuren is a small and picturesque Bavarian city of some forty thousand inhabitants, with a turreted city wall dating back to the twelfth century. One of its best-known historic festivals is the Tanzelfest, a spectacle performed by over fifteen hundred children celebrating a visit to the city by the Emperor Maximilian in 1497. Yet like so many outwardly idyllic places in Hitler's Europe, it concealed a dreadful secret. By some grotesque irony, this also featured children. For its mental institution was one of dozens across Germany where mentally and physically handicapped children, as well as adults, were systematically murdered.

Obsessed with notions of racial purity and physical perfection, the Nazis began killing the handicapped — or "Life Unworthy of Life," as the phrase had it — in the late 1930s. Eventually, the news leaked out and in August 1941 the Catholic Bishop of Münster delivered a blistering sermon denouncing the murders. A public outcry followed, and Hitler stopped the program. But this merely applied to the particular method of killing, which was by gas. The specialists involved simply moved their lethal expertise on to the extermination camps and other centers, such as the Risiera San Sabba in Trieste.

The asylums and hospitals reverted instead to murdering the handicapped through lethal medication and deliberate starvation, and the killing of children went on throughout the war. The director at Kaufbeuren, Dr. Valentin Falthammer, was an especially keen and energetic supporter of the program, and proudly introduced a carefully crafted fat-free diet that guaranteed death to his patients and conveniently economized on pharmaceuticals. The death rate rose so high that the asylum authorities forbade the ringing of church bells at burials, so as not to alert the local population.[14]

Kaufbeuren had a maximum capacity of three thousand people. Its victims, all of them Germans, came from throughout Hitler's Reich. The US Army arrived in the town just six days after Hitler's death and arrested Falthammer, but as there were "Typhus!" warning signs posted, they did not venture inside the facility, and left it strictly alone. Inside, the doctors continued with the euthanasia program, as if VE Day and the German surrender had never happened. On Tuesday 29 May 1945, the head nurse of the children's ward, Sister Worle, approached the bed of a four-year-old boy and killed him by lethal injection. The time of death was recorded as 13:10. The nurse knew what she was doing, as she had already injected more than two hundred children the same way. The boy, whose name was Richard Jenne, had been classified several months before as a "feebleminded idiot," and then deliberately starved to the point of death so as to be ripe for the needle when it came. The cause of death on the certificate was given as typhus. Three weeks after the end of the war waged to destroy Nazism, he was probably the last person to be put to death by the Nazi extermination machine. The hospital lay less than half a mile from the US military government headquarters in the town.

Even more remarkable than the fact that the Nazis went on killing people after the end of the war was that this was not discovered until early July, when American medical personnel finally entered the hospital. "What met their eyes was beyond belief," writes one historian. "Some 1,500 disease-riddled patients confined to the most squalid conditions . . . and a stifling morgue filled with bodies that had not been buried and that could not be disposed of quickly, as the shining new crematorium, finished in November 1944, had been closed down."[15]

"Will anything happen to me?" asked the chief nurse, appearing surprised that anyone could think anything was wrong. By this time, however, the world's press was tired of stories about Nazi atrocities. *The Times*, for example, gave the post-war killings at Kaufbeuren a lurid enough headline — "German Death Camp Found. Murders Still Going On" — but devoted a mere three hundred words to paraphrasing a Reuters report on the story. The mortuary, it noted, contained bodies of men and women who had died between twelve and thirty-six hours beforehand and weighed as little as sixty pounds. Among the children still alive was a ten-year-old boy weighing just twenty-two pounds, with calves only two and a half inches in diameter.[16]

In Germany at the end of the war, there were some twelve million displaced persons to be cared for. Across the rest of Europe, millions more people were malnourished, homeless and searching desperately for lost family members. As Francesca Wilson was learning at Feldafing, and as Fey von Hassell knew from agonizing personal experience, a high proportion of the war's victims were children. Across the continent, feral packs of them scrounged for food, attached themselves to soldiers for handouts, hung around refugee and concentration camps, roamed the countryside and waited to be reunited with their parents. Everywhere, notes one historian, "children who had been hidden for years, sworn to silence and subterfuge, emerged to deal with a strange world. Many who had been sent from occupied countries at a very young age to foster families in the Reich for 'Germanization' would stay hidden until ferreted out, and some would never find out who they really were."[17]

Many of those most directly involved in the euthanasia murders decided to kill themselves rather than face allied justice. At Kaufbeuren, the chief doctor was captured, but his assistant hanged himself the night before the Americans finally entered the asylum. Odilo Globocnik was another case in point. On the last day of May he was captured by British forces in a hut overlooking the Weissensee in Carinthia. Later that same day, he managed to poison himself with a cyanide pill his captors had failed to find.[18] In this, he was following the example of his SS master, Heinrich Himmler.

After he left Doenitz's office at Flensburg, Himmler headed south in the direction of Bavaria. With him were some of his top SS associates, including Dr. Karl Brandt, Hitler's one-time medical adviser, Otto Ohlendorf, head of the Einsatzgruppe killer squads in Russia, and Himmler's own medical adviser, Dr. Karl Gebhardt. In all, the group numbered fifteen. Their false documents identified them as discharged NCOs of the Secret Military Police. Himmler's identity card named him as ex-Sergeant Heinrich Hitzinger of a special armored company attached to the Secret Field Police, demobbed on 3 May 1945.[19]

When they reached the Elbe, they abandoned their cars, paid a ferryman to row them across the river, then carried on by foot. They melded well into the general confusion. Thousands of disarmed German troops were milling around and camping out in the open, so no one took any notice of another group of men in shabby uniforms. And no one seemed to recognize Himmler without his glasses and moustache but sporting his newly acquired eye patch.

Eventually, on Friday 18 May, they reached the small town of Bremervoede, where they lodged for the next four days in a farmhouse. There was a British Army checkpoint on a bridge over the river they needed to cross, and two of the party decided to try to get through. It was a bad place to choose, for the checkpoint was also an intelligence screening point set up by Field Security, which was searching for people named on wanted lists of leading Nazis and war criminals. The group had also made another fatal choice with respect to their fake IDs. The Secret Military Police had come under the control of the Reich Main Security Office Reichssicherheitsdienst, or

RSHA, part of the SS in 1944, and for this reason had been placed on the allied wanted list. Even lowly NCOs fell into the category of those to be immediately arrested when caught.

So when the two men showed their papers, they were taken to a field security post in a nearby flour mill for interrogation by trained intelligence officers. The SS men revealed that others of their group were close by, and allegedly sick. Deliberately lulled into feeling that all was still well, they were sent back to fetch them with an escort and two army trucks. When they returned, they were segregated, separately interrogated, and arrested. That night, they were shipped off to a civil internment camp just south of Lüneberg for further questioning. At this stage, their true identities were still unknown. However, before they left, some of them revealed that three of their number had been left behind in the farmhouse. A search party returned to the site but failed to find them, so Field Security issued a warning to local troops to keep a lookout for them.

One of the three was Himmler. Why he did not board the trucks to cross the river with the others remains a mystery, but perhaps his well-honed security instincts led him to smell a trap. In any case, after lying low for another twenty-four hours, he and his last two escorts set off again on their journey south. By this time, Himmler had changed into civilian clothes and he was wearing a blue raincoat.

It proved to be a short stroll. As they walked down the main street of Bremervoede, a roving army patrol spotted them, picked them up and took them to the mill. When the field security linguist entered the room, he saw the man in the blue raincoat sitting disconsolately on the floor. "He has a bad stomach," declared one of the others. So, in true British Army style, he was brought a cup of tea. That night, the three men slept on the floor of the mill before being trucked to join the others at the civil internment camp.

So far, Himmler had escaped identification, but as he was brought into the internment camp he was recognized by another top Nazi, Karl Kaufmann, the ex-Gauleiter of Hamburg. Himmler now knew the game was up and demanded to see the commandant. When he was ushered into his office, he removed the eye patch, put on his spectacles, and in a quiet voice said simply, "Heinrich Himmler."

Within thirty minutes, a British intelligence staff officer arrived to confirm his identity. Three hours after that, he was bundled into the back of a car and driven the seven miles to Lüneberg and a special house reserved for such top-priority prisoners. He had already been stripped and bodily searched twice. Two small brass cases were found. One contained a glass vial, which was removed; the other was empty. It was suspected that the missing vial might be hidden in his mouth, so it was arranged that an experienced doctor should search him once again when he arrived. In the same building just a few days before another top SS official, Obergruppenführer Hans Prutzmann, head of the Werewolf organization, had committed suicide by swallowing poison hidden in a cigarette lighter.

At 10:45 p.m. on Wednesday 23 May, Himmler was escorted before the army doctor. "I was polite and gentle," recorded the medical officer in his diary, "he was quiet and cooperative." He searched all the bodily orifices and found nothing. Then he casually asked Himmler to open his mouth. Peering in, he immediately spotted "a small blue tit-like object" in the prisoner's cheek. Quickly, he slipped in his finger to sweep it out. But as he did so, Himmler clamped down on the finger, wrenched the doctor's hand away, and swung his head to one side. Then, with a disdainful smile, he crushed the vial between his teeth and took a deep breath. His face immediately contorted, his eyes turned glassy and he crashed to the ground.

Frantic efforts were made to revive him. "We immediately upended the old bastard," recorded the British officer in charge, "and got his mouth into the bowl of water which was there to wash the poison out. There were terrible groans and grunts coming from the swine." The doctor also tried artificial respiration and called urgently for cardiac stimulants. But it was useless. Heinrich Himmler died at 11:14 p.m., just fifteen minutes after crushing the deadly vial.

No one higher up seemed unduly disturbed, and Brigadier Edgar Williams, Montgomery's chief intelligence officer, merely had a drink when he heard the news. This reaction echoed sentiments at the very top. Just three weeks before, when Himmler tried to open negotiations, Churchill had privately declared that they might consider doing that and then "bump him off later"—a view consistent with his firmly held, long-term belief that all the top Nazis should be shot without trial. Himmler had simply saved the British the bother.[20]

The question now was how to get rid of the body. The last thing anyone wanted was for Nazi fanatics to dig it up, for at this stage no one knew if Nazism was truly dead and buried or not. "Put the body under the earth in the morning," ordered Colonel Michael Murphy, chief intelligence officer of the British Second Army. As few people as possible, he instructed, were to know the location.

So, with the body autopsied and extensively photographed, the British commandant and his sergeant wrapped it in a couple of blankets, put two army camouflage nets around it, and trussed up the bundle with telephone wires. Then, "Took the body out in a truck for its last ride," noted the officer laconically in his diary. "Hell of a job to find a lonely spot. Anyhow we did find one and threw the old basket into the hole which we had dug."

That was the end of Heinrich Himmler, tossed casually into an unmarked grave like countless millions of his victims. The building where he killed himself was later converted into an old people's home. Its name was Lebensabend—"Life's Evening."

The world first heard of his death via the BBC on the evening of Thursday 24 May. Appropriately enough, it was the last operational broadcast over the service's high-powered wartime transmitter, MCN ("Mike, Charlie, Nan"), which had been established near Brussels in September 1944 to carry war correspondents' messages to the outside world. Since then, it had transmitted thousands of live reports from British, American, Canadian, Australian, French and Belgian reporters, including the story of the Germans' surrender to Montgomery. "MCN is closing down," announced the renowned BBC reporter Chester Wilmot in its final broadcast the next day. "The war in Europe is finished and its job is done."[21]

But for twenty-three-year-old Leonard Linton, the war was far from finished. Gavin's Eighty-second Airborne Division stayed at Ludwigslust until mid-June, and here the young American continued to help soften the rougher edges of daily relations with the Red Army.

On his second day in the town, he was driving past the palace when he saw a Red Army armored car. Beside it stood a mustached Russian officer, looking lost. Linton drove up and offered him directions in Russian. The officer was surprised and asked him where and how he had learned the language. Linton told him. The Soviet officer recoiled as though he had the plague. "So," he replied aggressively, "they are White Guard traitors."

"They" were Linton's parents. Both were refugees and exiles from the Bolshevik Revolution of 1917. His mother came from Saratov, on the Volga River; his father from near Odessa. They met in Yokohama,

Japan, and Linton was born there on New Year's Day in 1922. Shortly thereafter the family moved to Berlin. His mother was Orthodox Christian, his father Jewish, and after the Nazis came to power they swiftly left for Paris. Five years later, in the late summer of 1938, just before the Munich Crisis, they moved on again. Traveling on "Nansen" passports — documents designed by the Norwegian explorer-turned-humanitarian and Nobel Peace Prize winner Fridtjof Nansen for stateless refugees after the First World War — they sailed on the French liner *Ile de France* from Le Havre, arrived in New York, and settled in Manhattan. There they took the name "Linton." It sounded such an "Anglo" name, plain and simple to just about anyone.

So, if Leonard Linton had a "foreign" language, it was English. In school before 1938 he had learned Oxford English, and he found it tricky to pick up New Yorkese. However, he was quick at languages and was soon at ease. After a spell at New York University, he transferred to Columbia and majored in physics. He was still technically stateless when he was drafted and sent to Camp Wheeler in Macon, Georgia, for basic training. It was only in October 1943, in the US District Court at Macon, that he became a naturalized American citizen. Such was the typically immigrant pedigree of the young and newly minted American now facing off with a Red Army officer in the grounds of Ludwigslust Palace.

Linton was rarely lost for words, but the Red Army officer's hostile response took the breath out of him. So he quickly shifted gear and explained he was in a military government unit. At this, the Soviet officer became a little more civil and explained he had come to fix the demarcation line between the American and Red Army forces. He took a map out of a leather case slung over his shoulder, pulled out a pencil stub from behind his ear, and drew a straight line on the paper. "Let us agree on this demarcation line," he said, "and let each of us step back one kilometre from this line." Linton was shocked. The line ignored basic topographical features such as roads and canals, as well as all administrative boundaries. After a testy discussion, the Soviet officer clambered back into his vehicle, slammed down the cover, and drove off.

It was not a good beginning, and in the end, the issue was settled only after Gavin and his staff invited their opposite numbers over to the palace for talks, champagne and brandy. Then Gavin drove over to the local Soviet command post at Grabow, about five miles away.

"It was an experience," recorded the commander in his diary that day.

> I understand why the Germans did not want to surrender to them. They kicked in store windows, looted, [and] rolled a big keg of wine into the city square, where anybody who came by with a bucket could have a fill. Drunks swarmed about the streets, flagging down vehicles . . . They were very enthusiastic and very rough on the Germans.

He also noted the remarkable quantity of American military equipment the Russians possessed — the results of generous US wartime loans.[22]

Linton had already witnessed the boisterous and alcoholic behavior of Soviet troops himself. The day before, he had almost collided in his jeep with two drunken Russians riding in a newly liberated German military Volkswagen. Going back with them to Grabow, he saw Red Army soldiers and officers staggering in the streets and firing wildly into the air. But not all of them were out of control or inebriated. The next day, when he returned for more discussions about the demarcation line, he saw how everyone smartened up promptly when a neatly uniformed captain wearing green piping in his cap and epaulettes appeared on the scene. This was the NKVD, or secret police, officer. One or more of them were attached to every Red Army unit. "I could see literally how scared the other officers were of the captain," Linton wrote.[23]

With his fluent Russian, Linton found himself dealing as much with the Red Army as with German civilian matters. Mostly it was a case of Soviet soldiers dropping in on social visits. Linton found them intensely curious about life in America. "How do American workers really live?" they would ask. "How much do they earn?" Sometimes they arrived with cameras to take shots of themselves with the Americans to send home. There was always plenty of vodka, bonhomie and smiles. There was also, Linton noted, what Nazi-era German comedians in Berlin had come to call "*der Deutsche Blick*" (the German glance). This was a fearful look over the shoulder for the Gestapo. Whenever the green pips appeared, the ordinary Red soldier simply clammed up.

Linton found it useful himself on occasion to flex muscle. "Linton, there's no juice at divisional headquarters," announced his commanding officer one day after taking an urgent telephone call. "Get it turned on."

He drove to the town's aging power plant and found one or two frowning German technicians poring over a pile of circuit drawings. There had been plenty of stoppages before but they had always been fixed. This one was more serious and tricky, they said. "Who can fix it?" asked Linton.

They shrugged. "Only the chief," came the answer.

The chief lived in Grabow and did not have a pass to cross the demarcation line. Linton sped over to the Soviet command post and asked for the man to be given a permit. He met with a blank refusal. No such passes could be given to civilians, he was told. Permission could come only from higher up.

Frustrated, Linton returned to the power plant and looked again at the circuits. One of those still working, he noticed, fed Grabow. So he ordered it switched off. He waited for a while, then drove back to the Soviet command post, where he found the officer sitting at his desk with a candle burning. Ten minutes later, he got verbal permission to drive the plant chief back to Ludwigslust and the problem was soon solved.

From this early encounter with the Soviets, Linton drew a crucial lesson. "I could not see why anyone had difficulties dealing with the Red Army," he wrote, "unless they failed to propose a worthwhile deal and above all keep the key in their hand; then it [worked]."[24]

But dealing with the Red Army was not all tough bargaining. Occasionally, there were moments of almost surreal exuberance. One day, Linton received yet another urgent phone call. This one told him to get over to the railroad station as soon as possible. A military police patrol had just reported seeing a locomotive under steam and a group of Red Army men terrorizing several German women. Convinced he was about to find a rape and looting session, he slapped on his sidearm and hotfooted it over. But what greeted his eyes was an astonishing and far different scene. In front of a large house with a lawn and big trees stood a steam locomotive bearing a large Russian serial number. The engine was painted a gleaming black and had little red flags on the front. The polished metal of its wheels sparkled brightly in the sunlight. Behind it was a caboose. On the lawn, several Red Army officers were sitting peacefully at a table enjoying food that was being brought to them by women in relays from the house. To one side, Linton could also see a large tub of water where other women were washing Red Army uniforms. It resembled an idyllic scene from a Russian pastoral painting.

Parking his jeep for a quick getaway, Linton warily approached the officers. To his surprise, beaming and laughing, they shook his hand and embraced him. Did they know, he asked politely when the greetings were finally finished, that they were well inside US Army territory? Of course they did, came the laughing reply, but they had just come over to take a look, and found it nice, so they would stay a few days and then go back. Besides, they added, no one would miss them, as they only belonged to a rail transport battalion.

Linton could see no sign of any molestation of the women. On the contrary, he noticed that some of them seemed to be looking at the Russian officers with an appreciative eye. Relaxing, he was invited to share their food. So far, he had spoken in German, but when he accepted the invitation in Russian, pandemonium broke out and they poured him a huge glass of vodka. "Drink to the bottom!" they urged, so he did. What happened after that became hazy. There were more toasts — to Eisenhower, to Zhukov, to Truman, to Stalin — bottles of wine began to appear from the caboose, the women brought out more and more plates of potatoes and sausages, and somehow he forgot to ask when exactly they planned to leave. Afterwards, all he could remember was getting into his jeep, bumping back across the railway tracks, and then waking up many hours later, still fully dressed, with a splitting headache.

Not long after, a rumor began spreading among the higher-ranking German officials he had to deal with that the Eighty-second Airborne was going to leave the area and hand it over to the Red Army. At first he ignored it, but then he was asked the question directly by a police lieutenant with whom he was working closely. Everyone knew that Linton was the main American contact with the Russians on administrative affairs. He had heard nothing of the sort from any of his Red Army contacts, nor had his own brass hats hinted at anything similar, so he replied firmly that there was no substance to the story.

Nevertheless, the rumor continued to grow, fueled not least by the close contacts that Linton himself maintained with his Red Army opposite numbers on many practical issues. One of the most frequent concerned travel permits for German civilians. As conditions normalized, he found himself handing out more and more of these passes. "We heard the most ingenious and unusual reasons," he noted, "for Germans wanting to go somewhere. One day a very pretty girl came with some very sad family story requiring several people to travel and she started crying. I told her nicely to calm down, that we were now giving permits almost automatically; her crying stopped at once and she was all smiles, a great potential actress I thought."[25]

After a few more weeks of increasing normality, Linton was told that the Americans were to be relieved as occupiers by British troops and sent back to their base in France. He and his military government unit stayed on for a couple of days after the main body of Gavin's paratroopers left to hand over control to the British, who annoyingly arrived a couple of days late. Then they lined up in a small convoy, improved by the addition of a looted Mercedes saloon, and headed west. "I left with a heavy heart and concern," he wrote, "how all the people — the good ones, the young girl I had met, and even the bad ones — would fare without our protection and care."

Back at the Eighty-second's European base in France, many of those with sufficient points began to make their way home to the States. Linton wondered when he would be joining them.

CHAPTER TWENTY-TWO

"A GROTESQUE COMEDY"

At 9:30 a.m. on the day that Himmler bit into his suicide pill at Lüneberg, Wednesday 23 May, three gray limousines carrying Wehrmacht license plates left Admiral Doenitz's headquarters at Flensburg and drove to the quayside.[1] Moored alongside was the *Patria*, a luxury German passenger ship of the Hamburg-Amerika Line. On board were the members of a special mission sent by Eisenhower from his headquarters ten days before. With them was a group of Soviet officers. The crew was German.

In the first car rode Doenitz, in the full dress uniform of a grand admiral. Behind followed Admiral von Friedeberg, commander-in-chief of the German Navy, and the third car contained General Jodl, Chief of the Operations Staff of the German High Command. When the convoy reached the quayside, Doenitz's aide-de-camp stepped out smartly and held open the door. Carrying his gold-tipped baton, Doenitz made his way up the gangplank, followed smartly by the others. They were shown into a spacious lounge with a log table covered by a white tablecloth and invited to sit down. Several minutes passed in silence. Then the members of the allied mission entered the room, headed by US Major-General Lowell W. Rooks, followed by his deputy, a British brigadier. The Germans rose to their feet. "Gentlemen," said Rooks, reading from a prepared text, "I am under instructions . . . to tell you that the Supreme Commander, General Eisenhower, has decided, in concert with the Soviet High Command, that today the acting German

Government and the German High Command shall be taken into custody with the several members as prisoners of war. Thereby the acting German Government is dissolved."

Doenitz listened impassively, noted one witness, "turkey-necked and tight-lipped as ever." Jodl's face turned red and he let some papers slip from his hand to the floor. Von Friedeberg looked as though he was on the verge of tears. Rooks asked Doenitz if he had anything to say. "Any word from me," replied the grand admiral curtly, "would be superfluous."

The three Germans, now prisoners, were driven back to their quarters to collect their bags and then taken to the Murwick police building, which was surrounded by a detachment of British troops. Here they were joined by Albert Speer. Hitler's former minister of war production had been arrested at Glucksburg Castle in a simultaneous and carefully planned operation by British forces reinforced by a Belgian field security company who all spoke German. Their swoop was such a surprise to the castle's five dozen inmates that Speer was caught sitting in his bath. "So now the end has come," he remarked. "That's good. It was all only a kind of opera anyway."[2]

Now, seated on a bench with the others, he waited patiently as they were summoned one by one into an adjoining room for a full body search for vials of concealed poison. Afterwards, they were driven in an armed convoy to the nearby airfield for a flight that took them to an allied prison and interrogation center at Bad Mondorf in Luxembourg. The bizarre final chapter of Hitler's Third Reich had at last come to a close.

It was also the end of an awkward interlude for the Western allies. The continued existence of a Nazi enclave within conquered Germany had begun as a curiosity but ended as an embarrassment, reflecting fumbling and uncertainty at the very top of the allied High Command. According to official surrender documents, there was not even supposed to be a German government. Yet, for almost two weeks, allied officers in the area left alone Doenitz and his cabinet. Partly this was to avoid a confrontation with the armed soldiers guarding the Flensburg enclave and any unnecessary deaths. It was also tolerated because Doenitz enjoyed little obvious power or influence outside his tiny domain. This was especially true after British forces seized the radio station from which he was continuing to send broadcasts to the German people.

However, allied leaders were hesitant about dissolving it for other reasons, too. Churchill, at least, thought that Doenitz and his group might prove useful. Millions of German troops were now gathered inside the British zone in and around Schleswig-Holstein, and hundreds of thousands of fully armed German soldiers were still stationed in Denmark and Norway. How were they to be disarmed and managed? More important, how were the German people as a whole to be controlled and directed in the chaos now engulfing Europe? The British Prime Minister talked of "letting things slide" for a while, and of using the Doenitz government, including captured German generals, to help keep order in Germany. "I neither know nor care about Doenitz," he wrote a week after VE Day. "He may be a war criminal . . . the question for me is has he any power to get the Germans to lay down and hand over quickly without any more loss of life? We cannot go running round into every German slum and argue with every German that it is his duty to surrender or we will shoot him. Do you want," he asked the Foreign Office, "to have a handle with which to manipulate the conquered people, or just have to thrust your hands into an agitated ant-heap?"[3]

But any idea of dealing with Hitler's successor was anathema to Eisenhower and was sabotaged by Rooks and the allied mission on board the *Patria* when they decided that the last Nazi Government should be immediately disbanded. It was not just that it was proving useless in carrying out the tasks that Churchill had suggested. It was also that its continued existence was highlighting rifts between Washington and Moscow on how to deal with the Germans. The Americans were still committed to nonfraternization. By contrast, the Soviets were embracing the Germans with comradely abandon, sometimes literally so, and on board the *Patria*, reported Rooks with alarm, a Soviet officer had been drinking and laughing with three German officers in his cabin. Moreover, the press, especially in the United States, was becoming increasingly hostile to the whole Doenitz venture. Even on the news of his succession to Hitler two weeks before the *New York Times* had denounced the grand admiral as "no more trustworthy than Himmler" and the *New York Herald Tribune* was deriding the whole affair as "a grotesque comedy." Even the more staid *Times* in London was by now criticizing any continued dealings with Doenitz.[4]

Worse, the wily Doenitz astutely exploited this. On Sunday 20 May, he had requested a meeting with Rooks and let loose with a diatribe in which he complained bitterly that in the West it was assumed that all Germans were criminals, and that the newspapers were full of reports about concentration camps — stories which, he protested, were "highly exaggerated." By contrast, in their zone, the Russians were being friendly and even offering people cigarettes and sweets. "If you continue to treat the German people as you have done so far," he warned, "they will turn to Russia, and Stalin will undoubtedly seize his chance." Indeed, some pro-Soviet and anti-Western sentiment was already becoming apparent, especially in the German Navy, which had fought mainly against the British and whose officers and men felt that they — unlike the Wehrmacht — had not been defeated in battle. But Doenitz was exaggerating the fact, and using the argument merely as a cynical ploy to gain advantage.

Talk such as this was dangerous. But playing down Nazi atrocities in May 1945 was also foolish, and Doenitz badly overplayed his hand. Remarkably, even unconditional surrender did little to puncture illusions that continued to flourish at Flensburg. Only four days after VE Day, Jodl himself had declared — with no apparent irony — that "the moment will come when we shall play off the Russians against the Anglo-Americans," and a German intelligence briefing that same day announced that "Germany was already again a factor in Europe."[5]

By the time of Doenitz's diatribe towards Rooks, though, an exasperated Eisenhower had already decided to have him and his ministers arrested, and the Soviet High Command agreed. Radio Moscow was also getting restless and broadcasting increasingly fiery denunciations of the Doenitz government. Two days later, Rooks gave the order for Hitler's successor to attend the fateful meeting the next morning on the *Patria*.

One of those who did not make it to the Flensburg airfield was Admiral Hans Georg von Friedeberg, the man who had put his signature to the surrender at Montgomery's headquarters just over two weeks before. While he was collecting his baggage he excused himself to go to the toilet, slammed the door shut, and managed to swallow the cyanide pill he had successfully concealed. His body was laid out on his bunk under a portrait of Doenitz.

But that same day, by way of compensation, allied troops found Alfred Rosenberg. The Nazi racial ideologist, former Minister for the Eastern Territories, and director of the special task force for the methodical plunder of Jewish art, had been hiding in the Flensburg Hospital nursing a sprained ankle suffered during a bout of heavy drinking.

One of the few on the allied side who had reservations about the arrest of Doenitz was Admiral Sir Andrew Cunningham, Britain's First Sea Lord, who was concerned about its possible effect on the thousands of German U-boat crews and naval personnel still at large in Bergen, Norway.

Even as Doenitz was being unceremoniously arrested, a team of allied officers were uncovering the secrets of a practically invulnerable concrete pen that had sheltered his U-boats in the Norwegian port. Some four hundred thousand German troops were still on Norwegian soil, where order depended on continued discipline within the Wehrmacht. At the guardhouse, a young German officer at first refused to open the gate and stared sullenly at the British staff car and its passengers, but eventually he yielded, and they drove down a long drive lined by concrete walls between six and ten feet thick as a protection against shrapnel. In front of them, they saw a vast bunker with an eighteen-foot-thick roof on which workmen had been working just three weeks before. Inside, they discovered seven pens. Some were single, others large enough to take two U-boats moored side by side, and one also served as a dry dock; mobile power lines could carry electric current to the U-boats for welding repairs. The previous October, the Royal Air Force had carried out a devastating attack on Bergen Harbor, but although U-boat operations had been suspended for a while and buildings all around the pens were smashed, the British team could see only a single direct penetration of the bunker itself.

They were impressed. This, they felt, was something for British naval experts to examine. They were also intrigued to learn of the comforts that Doenitz had arranged for his U-boat crews. They had at least fourteen days' leave after each patrol and were taken to hotels in the mountains above Bergen used in peacetime for winter sports. Now, as the British team examined the pens, German Navy personnel watched them, expressionless, as they went about their tasks.[6]

By the end of May, nearly all the top Nazis who had not committed suicide or been killed were behind bars. On allied instructions, Doenitz had been forced to hand over Field Marshal Wilhelm Keitel, Hitler's High Command chief, just a few days before he and his government were arrested. And Rudolf Hess, Hitler's former deputy, had been in British hands since flying to Scotland in a Messerschmitt on a bizarre and deluded one-man peace mission in May 1941.[7] The rest were hunted down, mostly through good intelligence and sharp-eyed allied troops, although it proved a daunting operation given the chaos that was gripping Germany and the dozens of other urgent tasks that faced the occupiers. The Nazis had scattered widely during Hitler's final days in the bunker, mostly to get away from the Russians but also in the hope that they might escape retribution and justice altogether. Extraordinarily, it would be August before the allies could agree on what to do about war crimes and war criminals. But the British and Americans did at least prepare detailed instructions for their troops on how to identify and apprehend those suspected of criminal activities, even though providing last-known addresses proved fairly futile in the circumstances. Those detained were to be sent to internment camps for preliminary interrogation and, if necessary, then for more intensive questioning.[8]

Some were captured almost by chance. Such was the case with Julius Streicher, caught in Bavaria by the Americans on 23 May. After fleeing Nuremberg ahead of Patton's forces, the notorious editor of *Der Stürmer* joined dozens of other Nazis heading in the direction of Berchtesgaden. Then he disappeared. Four weeks later, an officer from the US 101st Airborne Division stopped at a farmhouse hoping to get a drink of fresh milk. A man with a shaggy white beard dressed in a collarless blue striped shirt was sitting by the door next to an easel. "Are you the farmer?" asked the American, speaking his native New Yorker's Yiddish. "No," said the man, "I only live here. I'm an artist." The US officer asked what he thought of the Nazis. The man claimed not to understand such things — he never bothered about politics. "But you look like Julius Streicher!" joked the American, who suddenly saw a resemblance to the Nazi from a photograph on a warrant he had seen. The old man stared at him. "How did you recognize me?" he blurted out, before immediately trying to correct himself. But it was too late. By sheer chance, the infamous Nazi Jew-baiter had been captured by a Jew.

Other Nazis were betrayed by fellow Germans, some of whom were only too keen to ingratiate themselves with their occupiers, others who were fearful of the retribution that would follow if it became clear they had known but not told of their whereabouts, and some because they had at last found the courage to express their true anti-Nazi feelings.

Robert Ley, Hitler's minister of labor infamous for his luxurious lifestyle and gold-tapped bathroom, also fled south to Berchtesgaden, where he hid in a mountain hut south of the town. But after a tip-off by local residents, armed American soldiers broke into it with their automatics at the ready. Inside, they found a man wearing blue pajamas, climbing boots and a Tirolean hat, cowering at the edge of a bed. He adamantly denied he was Ley but was still taken to US Army headquarters in Berchtesgaden for further interrogation. Here, the intelligence officer brought another captured Nazi into the room, an elderly former treasurer of the party. He immediately blurted out, "Well, Dr. Ley, what are you doing here?" and the game was up. It was Ley who had created the "Strength through Joy" movement to organize workers' leisure activities.

Hitler's first foreign minister, Konstantin von Neurath, was captured before VE Day by the French, and on the same day — 6 May — Hans Frank, a middle-class Catholic lawyer from Karlsruhe and one-time governor of occupied Poland known as the "Jew Butcher of Cracow" for presiding over the mass murders there, was identified among a group of two thousand German POWs at Berchtesgaden after he tried to slash his wrists. He then told the Americans that he was "a man of culture" and showed them where he had stashed millions of dollars' worth of stolen art, as well as his thirty-eight-volume diary that detailed the atrocities in Poland. But Auschwitz and Maidanek, he insisted, had been Himmler's work, not his. He had still recorded in his diary, however, that if the Nazis won the war, "as far as I am concerned the Poles and the rest can be turned into mincemeat."[9]

Meanwhile, the Reichskommissar in the Netherlands, Artur Seyss-Inquart, was in British hands. After concluding his negotiations with allied and Dutch officers at the schoolhouse at Achterveld, he was escorted back through German lines and made his way to Schleswig-Holstein to see Doenitz, where, he fondly imagined, he could act as a mediator with the allies. After seeing the grand admiral, he tried to return to Holland by car but got caught up in a huge allied military vehicle traffic jam in Hamburg. When he was stopped by a military policeman and showed his papers, he announced he was on his way to see Montgomery. "You bloody well are," replied the MP. That evening, he found himself under detention in one of Hamburg's hotels.[10]

Late in May, another sensational capture hit the headlines — that of William Joyce, otherwise known as "Lord Haw-Haw," who had spent most of the war broadcasting Nazi propaganda from Berlin. He was a former pro-British Irishman who worked as an informer against Sinn Fein for the notorious "Black and Tans" during the Irish Civil War. But he was also a rabid anti-Semite and avid supporter of Sir Oswald Mosley's British Fascists before departing for Germany in 1939. After a slow start, he emerged as one of the stars of Nazi English-language propaganda broadcasting under his trademark introduction, "Germany Calling! Germany Calling!" It was his high-pitched, nasal drawl that earned him his mocking nickname. He sounded, wrote the American CBS radio correspondent William Shirer, "like a decadent old English blue-blooded aristocrat."

Early in April 1945, Goebbels's Propaganda Ministry ordered that Joyce, along with his wife, Margaret, must at all costs be kept out of allied hands and devised a plan to get them to Sweden. Joyce was given false identity papers naming him as Wilhelm Hansen, a schoolteacher born in Galway, Ireland. On the last day of the month, just hours before Hitler killed himself, a car drove the Joyces from their studio in Hamburg to Flensburg on the first stage of their flight to Stockholm. But in the general chaos the plan broke down and after a few days inside Denmark the couple returned to Flensburg. Then, unable to find a place to live in the crowded city, they moved to a small village nearby and found lodgings with an elderly English widow. There they lived quietly for the next two weeks, undetected.

On Monday 28 May, the couple walked into a neighboring village to buy food. By now, they had fallen to bickering about their predicament and had a quarrel, so Joyce walked home alone through the woods. It was evening, but still light. Suddenly, a couple of British soldiers appeared, driving a truck and looking for firewood for their cooking stove. "There's more wood over there," said Joyce, speaking in French. Then he repeated himself in English. Both soldiers instantly recognized his voice — his broadcasts had never been censored by the British, and had a wide audience. "You wouldn't be William Joyce by any chance, would you?" asked one of them.

At this, Joyce quickly put his left hand in his pocket, reaching for his false identity papers. But the soldiers thought he was reaching for a gun and one of them shot him with his pistol, a German Walther he had confiscated in Hamburg. The bullet went straight through Joyce's buttocks, and he fell to the ground. Asked again who he was, Joyce replied, "Fritz Hansen." Of course, this did not even match the name on his papers, and certainly did not tally with the Wehrmacht pass he was also carrying, in the name of William Joyce. The soldiers dressed his wound as best they could and drove him to the nearest British command post. From there he was driven to Lüneberg Hospital. News had already spread of his capture. As he was taken in on his stretcher, British soldiers shouted out, in cruel mockery of his broadcasts and his accent, "Jairmany Calling! Jairmany Calling!"

There was a double irony in the capture of Joyce, who within months went on trial in London for treason and was hanged. Only by a dubious technicality was he actually British, for he had been born in New York of Irish parents who renounced their British nationality to become Americans. As for the British soldier who shot him, his ID papers revealed him as Lieutenant Geoffrey Perry of the Intelligence Corps. But his birth name was Horst Pinschewer, a German Jew forced to flee Hitler's Reich in 1936. Along with hundreds of other refugee Germans, he joined the Pioneer Corps and changed his name. He was sent to Germany in the war's closing weeks to help with the interrogation of German prisoners, and then hand-picked to start a free German press the minute the war was over. The first edition of the *Hamburger Nachrichtsdienst*, edited by Perry, had appeared the day after VE Day.[11]

So, with Joyce's arrest, one outsider had caught another. And because it was still too sensitive to admit that German nationals had fought in British uniform, Perry's role in the affair was long concealed.

Joyce was only one of many renegade allied nationals who had backed Hitler or Mussolini, a reminder that the appeal of Nazism and Fascism reached far beyond the borders of Germany, Italy and even Europe. Another whose capture that month made headlines was Englishman John Amery. In many ways, his case was even more shocking than that of Joyce, for he was the son of one of Winston Churchill's cabinet ministers.

He was born in 1912, the first son of Leo Amery, a Conservative Member of Parliament who was Secretary of State for the Dominions in the 1920s and as a Churchill loyalist was wartime Secretary of State for India. But the young Amery was trouble from the start. He possessed, as the distinguished writer and journalist Rebecca West once put it, "a character like an automobile that will not hold the road." Twice withdrawn from Harrow School, he lived a life of petty crime, sexual promiscuity and drunkenness in Britain before leaving for

France in the late 1930s. From here, after getting mixed up in far-right anti-Semitic and anti-communist politics in Vichy France, he headed for Berlin.

The arrival in Hitler's capital of the son of a British cabinet minister caused a minor sensation. With the eager support of Foreign Minister Joachim von Ribbentrop, Amery began broadcasting to Britain. The broadcasts, notes Adrian Weale, amounted to little more than "a farrago of ugly, incoherent, anti-semitic drivel." Or, as Rebecca West put it more colorfully, "words flowed from Amery's mouth in the conventional groupings of English culture, but he had no intelligence, only a vacancy round which there rolled a snowball of Fascist chatter."[12] He also helped raise a volunteer force named the "British Legion of St. George" to fight alongside the Wehrmacht against the Red Army and traveled throughout occupied Europe exhorting local collaborators to ever more heroic efforts against the Bolshevik enemy.

He spent the last six months of the war in Italy at Mussolini's invitation, broadcasting on Italian radio, and even met with the dictator just hours before he fled to Lake Como. Mussolini offered to make him a member of the Black Brigades, but Amery declined on the grounds that he did not want to fight against his fellow countrymen. Instead, he said, he would wear a simple Fascist uniform.

Thus clothed, he too left for Como, only to be picked up on the *autostrada* by partisans and returned to Milan. After they broadcast news of his capture, a British officer named Captain Alan Whicker — later to become a distinguished TV journalist — rushed to the city to rescue him from the jail where he was being held. "Thank God you're here," said a relieved and frightened Amery, "I thought they were going to shoot me." A few hours later, though, he effectively put the noose around his own neck when he asked for a typewriter and produced a statement several thousand words long in which he described in detail his wartime activities. He, like Joyce, was put on trial when he got back to Britain, and was hanged. His younger brother, Julian, had served loyally throughout the war as an officer in the Special Operations Executive.[13]

Amery's capture was not the only one in Italy to make headlines. Just a few days later, the American poet Ezra Pound, the most notorious allied pro-Fascist propagandist of all, fell into the hands of US forces in Rapallo.

The fifty-nine-year-old Idaho-born Pound had already made his name as a poet when he settled in Italy in the 1920s. After meeting with Mussolini, however, his political obsessions steadily took over, and in 1941 he began broadcasting against the allies on Radio Rome. Two years later, he was indicted for treason by the US Attorney-General, and American military intelligence in Italy was issued with his FBI photograph and full descriptive details.

Pound's broadcasts were rambling, anti-Semitic tirades denouncing America for waging an "illegal" war, condemning Roosevelt for violating his oath of office, pronouncing that the war was essentially about "gold, usury, and monopoly," and praising both Mussolini and Hitler. After the Italian dictator's overthrow, Pound moved to Rapallo on the Italian Riviera and threw his support behind the Fascist Republic of Salò. Over the next eighteen months, he worked assiduously for Radio Milan as a speech and slogan writer, making occasional fiery broadcasts of his own.

Typical was the one he made in a series aimed at US troops in North Africa and Europe in December 1943. After denouncing the Italians who had turned against Mussolini and urging the execution of Count Ciano, he concluded by stating that "every human being who is not a hopeless idiotic worm should realize that fascism is superior in every way to Russian Jewocracy and that capitalism stinks."[14]

American forces entered Rapallo two days after Mussolini and Clara Petacci were shot. Soon afterwards, communist partisans armed with Tommy guns arrived at Pound's home, handcuffed him and drove him away. After questioning him about bigger Fascist fry they were chasing, they let him go, but then delivered him, at his own request, to the local US military police post. From there, he was driven to the Counter-Intelligence Corps headquarters in nearby Genoa, where he arrived just twenty hours before the German surrender in Italy. Here, he signed several statements about his wartime activities before being transferred to the US Army's detention training center (DTC) close to Pisa on Thursday 24 May. "Hitler was a martyr," he told a reporter who briefly managed to interview him before he was taken away.

The DTC was a dusty, half-mile-square compound surrounded by barbed wire and guard towers. Here were kept the "killers, brawlers, rapists and deserters from line and service outfits, 3,600 of the most hard-headed, recalcitrant soldiery the Army had to offer." Inside its perimeter, detainees not bound for execution or prison were given a last chance to redeem themselves with a year-long program of fourteen-hour-a-day, heavily regimented training. It was, as one biographer of

Pound has put it, "truly the First Circle [of Dante's Hell]." Anyone who tried to escape was shot on sight.

The camp also contained a row of ten wire cages, each measuring six by six and a half feet. These were for the men condemned to death, and stood out in the open with just a tar-paper roof to protect them from the sun and rain. One of them was made ready for Pound. The night before he arrived, it was specially reinforced with galvanized mesh and heavy airstrip steel. This was not so much to prevent Pound from escaping as to thwart any Fascist sympathizers from trying to rescue him. The end of May found Pound sleeping on the cement floor, being fed meager rations once a day, and using a tin can as a toilet. At night, a light was kept shining onto the cage. He was the only civilian in the camp. *The Yank*, the US Army weekly, declared that the DTC was "the toughest training detail in the Army . . . tougher even than frontline combat."[15]

It seems unlikely that Robert Ellis or any other soldier of the US Tenth Mountain Division would have agreed with this assessment given what they had suffered and survived on front-line service in the Apennines. But it was certainly a lot tougher than what they faced now.

At the end of May, allied forces in Italy were still on the alert for a possible new conflict with Tito's Yugoslav Army. On the day that Pound was imprisoned in his wire cage, Ellis and his regiment were moved from their wet and muddy bivouac area on the banks of the Torre River near Udine, close to the disputed Italo-Yugoslav border, to drier land close by, at Tricesimo. The situation was a stand-off, with most of the action taking place behind the scenes in the diplomatic corridors of Washington, London, Belgrade and Moscow. But the American forces still had plenty to do. The mountain troops located all the Osoppo, Garibaldi and Yugoslav troops in their area and mobilized partisans to neutralize a renegade Fascist band still at large which had attacked them. There were minor firefights between the Osoppo (the "green," anti-communist) partisans and Yugoslav forces, and the Yugoslavs and their Garibaldi partisan allies tried hard to draft civilians into their units.

This problem became more serious at the end of May, and instructions were issued that any civilians requiring protection against such efforts were to be placed under armed protection and evacuated out of the region.[16] That serious fighting could still break out was alarmingly brought home to Ellis when regular training was suddenly resumed, and battalions were instructed to find firing ranges and draw down on live ammunition for the carrying out of field exercises.

But in general the situation remained orderly and quiet. Ellis whiled away the time, as most of his companions did, playing softball, reading and enjoying good food. And it had finally stopped raining. So long as he was in Italy and not being shipped out to fight the Japanese, he was content.

In Trieste, Geoffrey Cox likewise remained on the alert. After the Russian-made T34 tanks put on their show of force on the waterfront, all social functions between the New Zealanders and the Yugoslavs were canceled, and allied forces remained on high alert. But both sides seemed keen to avoid any further deterioration in relations. Half the Soviet tanks disappeared almost immediately into the surrounding countryside, and the remainder were never brought into action. Two days later, they too were withdrawn.

In several places, recorded Cox, "harsh words" passed between the Yugoslavs and the New Zealanders, but there was no exchange of fire. The Yugoslavs put up some roadblocks around the city, but when a New Zealand Sherman tank pushed the most troublesome of them aside, nothing happened. Three days later, the Yugoslavs entertained allied officers in Trieste to a banquet in honor of Tito's birthday and fireworks lit up the waterfront. Meanwhile, though, in the city, "political cleansing" remained in full swing.[17]

Across northern Italy, late spring brought peace but no end to the killing. The shooting of Mussolini and his top Fascist associates by partisans was only the most gruesomely visible and dramatic act of retribution and vengeance in what during the lifetime of the Salò Republic had become a virtual civil war. In the gap between the departure of the Germans and the imposition of effective military rule by the allies, a wave of violence and death swept across the region.

Geoffrey Cox and the New Zealanders had bypassed Bologna on their race north, leaving the city to be entered first by Polish troops. Two days later, the head of the Allied Commission for Italy, the future British Prime Minister Harold Macmillan, drove into the city in the back of a jeep wearing his trademark tweed hunting coat and in the company of the American regional commissioner. Climbing into a more appropriate staff car, they then headed for the miraculously undamaged City Hall, where military government officers had already established themselves. Just before fleeing the city, Fascist Black Brigades had shot two well-known political opponents, and the victims were now lying in state in the building, with a tearful crowd filing past the open coffins. "One of the murdered men," scribbled Macmillan in his diary, "was old, white hair, fine well-cut face — obviously a man of character." He could see the bloodstains on the wall where the two men had been shot. It was already covered with photographs of dozens of others, men and women of all ages, who had been slaughtered by the Black Brigades over the previous few months. The Fascist prefect of the city, however, had failed to make his escape in time, and was shot by the partisans next to his last victim. "You could see the brains spattered against the brick," observed Macmillan.[18]

This was graphic evidence of the liquidation of Fascists taking place across northern Italy during the liberation. Bologna was at the center of a particularly murderous region known as the "Red Triangle," a traditionally communist area covering the provinces of Reggio Emilio, Modena, Ferrara and Bologna itself. Throughout this part of the Po Valley there were hundreds of summary executions, as well as thousands of assaults, lynchings, abductions, robberies and beatings. This formidable crime wave was motivated in part by pure revenge, but also by a desire to clear the ground for a wider social and political revolution. Several large landowners were forced to pay large amounts of ransom. Many of the killings and beatings were the products of personal vendettas and the settling of private scores. Some of the violence was organized by local liberation committees, but some was the random and spontaneous "justice of the piazza." In the Po Valley and throughout the region of Emilia-Romagna in particular — the so-called Triangle of Death — the killings went on for the next three years.[19]

But campaigns of retribution and revenge swept through the other big industrial cities of the north as well. The main targets were invariably members of Mussolini's Black Brigades. Here, the end of the war between Germany and the allies was close to irrelevant. Partisans and Black Brigades had been waging open war for months, and liberation merely changed the balance in favor of the former. In Turin, the Black Brigade was named the Ather Capelli. Of its 220 members, 93 were killed by partisans — 55 of these died immediately before the liberation, and 28 in the month that followed. Of its officers, more were killed after the liberation than before. Overall in Piedmont, some two thousand people were estimated to have been killed during the liberation.[20]

Similar killings took place in Milan and Genoa, but often in ways that made it impossible to tally the exact numbers. People just disappeared, and in the mornings their bodies were found heaped in the gutters or dumped at the gates of the local cemetery or in front of the city morgue. Two days after VE Day, the British Ambassador in Rome reported that "about 500" people had been executed in Milan, the majority of them Fascists. In Turin, he claimed, the numbers amounted to "about 1,000." The local British liaison officer with the partisans swore that "no one had been shot who did not deserve it."[21]

The more fortunate among the victims of this wave of retribution ended up in prison. By the middle of May, Milan's San Vittore Prison was packed to overflowing with more than 3,500 political prisoners, many of whom were poking their heads out of the windows and shouting to their families and friends in the street below. The vast Coltano Prison outside Pisa housed over 32,000 men.

But even with so many incarcerated, the killings did not die down gradually. In Milan, after a brief lull, they rose sharply again in the middle of May, and the total of unidentified bodies in the city's morgue since liberation rose to more than four hundred. A sinister feature was that all identification marks had been carefully removed before the victims were shot. "It is therefore difficult to say," reported the British Ambassador, "whether the victims are Fascists executed by partisans, or partisans executed by Fascists, or just victims of personal vendettas." The numbers rose even higher with forty-four killings on Thursday 17 May alone.

Ten days after that, the situation was still chaotic. In some places, special civil assize courts following regular legal procedures were hard at work. In others, semi-legal extraordinary military tribunals were handing out death sentences. Everywhere, partisan liberation committees were issuing orders cutting across those of the allied military government. Finally, on Monday 28 May, a senior US officer called on the chairman of the CLNAI. "This has got to stop," he ordered. From now on, he told the chairman, no order, decree or appointment made by the Italians was to have any force unless it was confirmed by the allies.

But this did not put an end to the killings, and it remained an open question of when — or even whether — public order in Italy would finally be enforced.[22]

Doenitz's Flensburg government was not the only one to be dissolved on Wednesday 23 May. Britain's wartime government had been a coalition of the three major parties — Conservative, Labour and Liberal — and Churchill hoped it would continue in office until after victory over Japan. But the Labour Party rejected the idea, and at noon that day Churchill drove to Buckingham Palace and tendered his resignation to King George VI. A few hours later, though, he returned to the palace and was asked to head a new, purely Conservative administration. Campaigning soon began for a general election.

The day before the Prime Minister's two trips to the palace, the first of Doenitz's surrendered U-boat fleet, U-776, had sailed up the Thames to be moored off Westminster Pier. She was a recently commissioned seven-hundred-tonner, fast and gray, and still carried three anti-aircraft guns abaft her conning tower. The powerful engines carried her swiftly up the river under escort while dense but silent crowds lined the banks and watched. In scenes such as these, observed one spectator, Hitler's navy died.[23]

But was the killing really over? On this same day, Churchill was handed a top-secret report by his personal chief of staff, Sir Hastings Ismay. The Prime Minister was becoming increasingly alarmed about Stalin's plans and the fate of Central European countries now occupied by his troops. The report was an analysis of "Operation Unthinkable," a hypothetical plan for a limited war against the Soviet Union to enforce a "square deal" for Poland. Its firm conclusion was that any such attack would precipitate a general war that was unwinnable, and hence also unthinkable. The only route forward with the Soviets, concluded Churchill, was tough negotiation.

CHAPTER TWENTY-THREE

"AN IRON CURTAIN"

The time of war," muses one historian writing about Europe in the aftermath of the German surrender, "is one of effort, vigil, heroism, suffering. The brief period that follows is the time of determination: whether the struggle will have been just another match between nations . . . or whether it may be seen as the pangs of creation." Did allied victory over Hitler mean the opening up of a new and more peaceful vista? Or did it merely herald the rehearsal for another dismal act in Europe's bloodstained history? The answer, at the end of May 1945, was clear to no one.[1]

Yet Churchill, for one, saw an act unfolding that filled him with gloom and apprehension. Not for nothing did he entitle the final volume of his war memoirs *Triumph and Tragedy*. Even as jubilant city crowds were celebrating VE Day, news reached London that fifteen Polish leaders approved by the West as possible future members of a democratic Polish government had been arrested and taken as prisoners to Moscow. What, feared Churchill, did this portend for democracy elsewhere in Europe?

Five days later, on Saturday 12 May, he penned his thoughts in the lengthy message to Truman that was ostensibly about the events in Trieste but then addressed the future of the whole continent. "I am profoundly concerned about the European situation," he stated flatly, before proceeding to highlight his worry that while allied forces would soon be vastly reduced by withdrawals of American and Canadian forces across the Atlantic, those of Stalin would remain to dominate Europe. Here, he stressed, Soviet power, combined with communist techniques, were already causing deep anxiety.

But what made the future seem even darker, he warned the President — privately deploying a metaphor previously used by Joseph Goebbels which he would make famously public in a speech at Fulton, Missouri, a year later — was that "an iron curtain is drawn down upon their front. We do not know what is going on behind. There seems little doubt that the whole of the regions east of the line Lübeck–Trieste–Corfu will soon be completely in their hands." Even more ominous, he went on, was that the enormous areas of Germany currently occupied by the Americans east of the Elbe would have to be handed over to the Russians because of the wartime agreements that assigned them to the Soviet zone of occupation. This American retreat, he feared, could spark yet another immense flight of refugees westwards. Given Germany's already ruined and prostrate state, this would give the Russians the chance to advance to the North Sea and even the Atlantic.

It was not just events behind the Soviet lines that concerned Churchill. France and Italy, where communist parties had emerged from the war greatly enlarged, were also major causes for worry. Secretly, the day after VE Day, he had told Eisenhower that captured German weapons might yet be needed by the allies in both of these countries.[2] Meanwhile, however, there was a vacuum at the heart of the allies' policy towards the defeated enemy. During the last few months of the war they had drawn up zonal occupation borders, discussed its post-war frontiers, and agreed on basic high-sounding principles such as demilitarization and denazification.

Yet all this meant little until they sat down together as occupying powers and hammered out some agreed practicalities. But here, all was vague. Only a week after VE Day, Churchill told his chiefs of staff that his personal policy towards Germany could be summed up in two words — "disarm" and "dig" — by which he meant that Germany should never again be in a position to start a world war and that its population should be saved from starvation. Unless that were done, he warned, "we might well be faced with Buchenwald conditions on a vast scale, affecting millions instead of thousands, and this would inevitably have repercussions in Great Britain."[3]

But how much longer would American and Canadian troops remain in Europe to balance the millions of Stalin's troops now in Central Europe? How were the allies to manage the German economy, and when would they agree on a joint policy? Germany had always been the economic motor of Europe. If it were to stall, what future could be expected for Europe and its population as a whole? How were people to be housed and fed, and what would happen to the millions of refugees desperate to return home, find work, and rebuild their lives? Was the "iron curtain" destined to become a permanent part of the continent's landscape? If so, what would happen to all those DPs crowded into camps in Germany and Austria who had no desire to return to a life under communist or Soviet rule? And what would become of the millions of ethnic Germans no longer welcome in such places as Poland and Czechoslovakia? Already, events on the ground were providing unsettling answers.

SOE officer Fred Warner's patience with Britain's Red Army allies in Austria was rapidly fraying.

Soviet troops were now in charge of the airfield at Zeltweg. Three days after VE Day, they made it clear that the British group was no longer welcome and forbade it from using its radio transmitting set. They also ordered the Hungarian troops who had been stationed there under the Germans to leave, and suggested they should return home with their families. Provided with an official-looking pass from the senior Soviet officer, the Hungarians moved out in a large convoy of horse-drawn carts piled high with their personal belongings. But it was a cynical trap: the convoy did not get far before it was stopped by a detachment of Russian troops scavenging for food. "They took everything of value the Hungarians had," recorded Warner, "including the horses. I shudder to think what happened to the women." The Hungarians immediately headed back west, towards the protection of British forces.[4]

After being forced to quit the airfield, the SOE group moved south across the Mur River that marked the demarcation line separating Soviet and British troops. Warner was not sorry to leave the airfield and the Russians behind. "By now," he wrote, "most of our illusions regarding them had been destroyed." Nothing that happened over the rest of May would change his mind.

Their new base was Schloss Authal, the residence of Prince von Croy, a Belgian-born naturalized Austrian, and his wife, Countess

Schwarzenberg. Here, Kelly set up his radio set and established contact with SOE headquarters in Siena—the only way they had of receiving instructions in what was proving a fluid and highly combustible transition from war to peace. The castle was packed with refugees and evacuees. Among them were the Count and Countess Andrassy of Hungary and some of their children and grandchildren. The countess was Swedish, and one of her sons-in-law had been stationed as a Hungarian officer at the Zeltweg airfield. One of the children, a small boy, spent much of his time risking life and limb playing with disused weapons he found in the gardens. The Andrassys had fled Hungary to escape the Russians, but the Red Army had now caught up with them anyway. Between them, the Croys and the Andrassys were delighted to welcome Warner and his group, who provided a valuable form of protection.

This proved all too necessary, as the castle was a continuous target for drunken Russian soldiers searching for loot—not surprisingly since its grounds were richly stocked with cattle and poultry. Warner's group therefore mobilized several French prisoners of war to take turns acting as guards day and night. The men had worked on the estate for several months and been well-treated by the Croys, so they willingly obliged.

Although the war in Europe had officially come to an end, it did not feel like that to Warner. Nazi power had evaporated, but fear of the Russians was palpable. "We tried our utmost to keep out all Russian soldiers who continuously strayed across the River Mur," he recorded. "There was a constant coming and going, civilians needing help and advice—among them women who had been raped by the Russians. Others, who feared this might happen, swam across the Mur as the Russians guarded all bridges." The river, in fact, was rapidly turning into a barrier between the allies. On the evening after the SOE group moved to the castle, they were warned that it was dangerous to venture back across in any vehicle flying the British flag as they were liable to be shot at by Soviet troops.[5]

One day, things turned from merely unpleasant to sinister when two grim-looking Soviet commissars turned up on a motorbike and announced they had come to arrest Prince von Croy. The SOE men refused point blank to turn him over. "We stood around in a circle debating furiously," said Warner, "the Prince wearing shorts and an old straw hat and looking anything but princely." Eventually, they persuaded the commissars that they had already arrested the prince themselves. In fact, they had earmarked him as the first potential "*Landeshauptmann*" to govern post-war Styria under the direction of the British.

Another unexpected visit proved more welcome. One evening, two German staff cars pulled up and four German officers clambered out. One of them introduced himself as Captain Niemoller, the nephew of Pastor Martin Niemoller, Fey von Hassell's erstwhile companion during her recent forced odyssey across the Alps. Niemoller had been on the staff of a general who had made his headquarters at the castle and was searching for papers left behind in their hurried evacuation. Hugely relieved to find the British and not the Russians in control, the Germans agreed to stay for dinner. It was, recalled Warner dryly, "a rather international affair with Austrians, Swedes, Hungarians, Germans and British sitting round the Croys' beautiful old dining table. It was laid without a table cloth but with small mats, the British way. Due mostly to the charm of our hostess, this meal was the most pleasant we had experienced since our rather unorthodox arrival on Austrian soil."[6]

At other times, Warner made fruitless visits to the local Red Army headquarters in Zeltweg, trying to put a stop to the continuous raids over the Mur and arranging exchanges of Soviet and British prisoners of war across the demarcation line. By the time he was finished, he had grown used to Russian sentries saluting him wearing half a dozen wristwatches on each arm and with alarm clocks on strings around their necks.

One thing was abundantly clear: the locals had had enough of being occupied. Even those who admitted to having welcomed the Anschluss claimed they had quickly tired of the Nazis. Party bigwigs had moved in, confiscated the best land, and exhorted the locals to emigrate to the east. This had killed off any enthusiasm about the benefits of union with Germany, and strengthened feelings for Austrian independence. As for the Russians, the behavior of the Red Army troops had swiftly extinguished any early enthusiasm for the Soviet Union, even among local communists. For Warner and the British occupiers, however, the honeymoon was still in full swing—if only because they were not Russians.

But the Soviets were still their allies, at least on paper. Shortly after British troops finally arrived on the scene, they agreed to a Soviet request to adjust the demarcation line south of the River Mur, which meant handing over Schloss Authal to the Red Army. Although the agreement forbade any civilians to move, Warner and his friends succeeded in exempting the Andrassys and the Croys from the rule. "We told the Croys," wrote Warner,

> and asked them to warn all the other occupants of the castle. This was done and plans were made for a speedy evacuation. The Andrassys had reached the castle in horse-drawn vehicles, which were now loaded up with theirs and some of the others' property. This was taken to a village south of Judenburg and just outside the area to be taken over by the Russians. We took the Croys a bit further afield to a shooting lodge of theirs in the mountains to the south. They took with them only their most important belongings, but told us to take anything we liked . . . I received a beautiful double-barreled Mauser rifle complete with telescopic sight. Eric [Rhodes], a heavy smoker, got a gold cigarette case and a .22 rifle.[7]

By this time, Warner and the others were acting mostly as interpreters for the Leicestershire Regiment, which was occupying the area. The task meant that they became inextricably mixed up in one of the most notorious operations of the British Army in post-war Austria— the rounding up of Soviet citizens and their forcible return to the Red Army and repatriation to the Soviet Union.

Over the course of the war, several million Soviet citizens fell into German hands. Thanks to Nazi maltreatment, of the six million prisoners of war, only about a million survived. Still alive in May 1945, however, were about two million slave laborers, a million refugees mostly from the Soviet Union's smaller states who had a profound dislike of both Russians and Bolsheviks, plus a million or so men who had actively fought for the Germans against the Red Army. This last group had either been recruited from Russian prisoners of war for service in the Russian Liberation Army of General Andrei Vlassov, who defected to the Germans in 1942, or were deployed in the Wehrmacht proper in the so-called eastern legions, composed of Georgians, Kalmuks, Ukrainians and Cossacks, among others. Having retreated steadily westwards from Russia with the Germans, they spent most of the winter of 1944/5 in northern Italy, but as the allies advanced north, during the spring they retreated over the Alps and into Austria. When the war ended, they surrendered to the British. One British officer recorded:

With their fur Cossack caps, their mournful dundreary whiskers, their knee-high riding boots, and their roughly-made horse-drawn carts bearing their worldly goods and chattels, including wife and family, there could be no mistaking them . . . They were a tableau taken from Russia in 1812. Squadrons of horses galloped hither and thither on the road, impeding our progress as much as the horse-drawn carts. It was useless to give them orders; few spoke German or English and no one who understood seemed inclined to obey.[8]

In Fred Warner's part of Styria, the Cossacks were also running wild. Terrified of falling into Soviet hands, they were also short of food and regularly harassed the local population. Even though they were fine horsemen and loved their animals with a passion, they were now slaughtering them for food. Some of the lucky ones managed to get across the border into Germany. Warner wrote: "I doubt that a worse fate could have befallen them than that which was in store for their colleagues whom we dealt with in Austria."[9]

The Cossacks that he helped round up belonged to the XV Cossack Cavalry Corps, which had been under the command of General Helmuth von Pannwitz, who was now a prisoner of the allies. Most of the corps' officers were also German, and some cooperated with the British in the grim task of rounding up their men and herding them over the zonal border to the Russians. By way of assistance and reward, they were given a special mess of their own next to the officers' mess of the Leicesters, and allocated to small teams of armored cars and trucks led by British officers that scoured the area. Warner reported:

These search parties set off into the mountains and to other places where recce [reconnaissance] parties, Austrian civilians, the police etc. had previously reported the Cossacks . . . These parties were quite successful and rounded up at least 2,000 all ranks who were leaderless and appeared to be pretty fed up, hungry, and dispirited. At the concentration areas the officers were separated from their men. It was quite moving to see the former saying goodbye. The horses and weapons were removed from all ranks, who were allowed to keep all their personal belongings. Some officers, with tears in their eyes, handed over their horses personally to certain Leicester Regiment officers, begging them to take good care of them.

Then the Cossacks were bundled onto British Army trucks and driven under heavy guard to Zeltweg, where they were handed over to the Russians. "From what we heard later," wrote Warner, "the officers were shot immediately on arrival, whilst the approximately 2,000 other ranks were sent to a camp in Russia after being sentenced to 25 years' hard labor."[10]

Warner drew a veil over the details of this handover, but a vivid picture exists of what happened when a group of Cossack officers was turned over at the end of May to the Red Army at nearby Judenburg. Here, the River Mur divides the town. A bridge across the gorge formed the border between the British and Soviet zones. First, the officers were separated from their men, which was done by deceiving them into believing they were being taken to hear personally from Field Marshal Alexander an announcement about their fate. Of course, when they arrived at their destination, they found no field marshal, but a British officer told them abruptly that they were to be handed over to the Russians and that the issue had been decided. They were then interned over night.

The next morning, British Army trucks arrived to transport them across the zonal border, but the Cossacks refused to move and resisted passively by sitting on the ground and linking arms. A platoon of British infantry advanced on them with rifles and bayonets fixed. Still the Cossacks refused to move. Finally, the British soldiers resorted to force and manhandled them onto the trucks. Nicholas Bethell continues the story:

> A river gorge marked the boundary. British armored cars and machine guns lined the approach. One at a time the trucks crossed the bridge over the river to the other side. While the trucks waited for their turn to cross, one Cossack was given permission to use the urinal bucket at the head of the bridge, then suddenly ran forward and jumped over the cliff and fell on the rocks a hundred feet below.

The desperate man was duly recovered, then handed over, mangled and dying, to the Red Army. At least one of the other Cossack officers managed to cut his throat with a razor.

The British could see nothing of what happened when the Cossacks reached the Soviet side, but they could hear well enough. That night and the following day, records Bethell, they heard small-arms fire coming from across the river, to the accompaniment of the finest male voice choir they had ever heard. After each burst of gunfire there would come a large cheer. Clearly, the Cossack officers knew how to die bravely. For several days and nights firing-squads were busy liquidating the Cossack officers in the disused steel mill at Judenburg.[11]

Subsequently, all the remaining Cossacks, along with their wives and children, were also forcibly handed over. Many killed themselves to avoid this fate, while over four thousand fled into the surrounding forests. Here, British patrols combed the mountains for them, sometimes assisted by Soviet Smersh agents. Some thirteen hundred were recaptured, of whom nine hundred were handed over to the Soviets and immediately executed. Altogether in Austria, some fifty thousand Cossacks were handed over. "Of course," wrote Warner, "these men were traitors, but one could not help feeling sorry for them."[12]

Shortly afterwards, the SOE group began to break up. Eric Rhodes joined in the hunt for war criminals, top Nazis and others on the Central Registry of War Criminals and Security Suspects (CROW-CASS) established by Eisenhower's headquarters that spring, and soon he was hot on the trail of Odilo Globocnik. Although the SS officer managed to commit suicide before being captured, two Austrian Gauleiters traveling with him gave themselves up without a fight. One of them had fathered ten children, and his wife had been personally presented by Hitler with a "Mother Cross" made of solid gold. Rhodes duly "liberated" it and gave it to Warner.

By the beginning of June, Warner himself was in Villach, helping with public safety. All the officers involved were British policemen, and none of them, apart from Warner, spoke German. It was his specific task to supervise the translators, all of whom were local Austrian women. It quickly became obvious to him that they were misrepresenting people they disliked and favoring friends to find them enviable jobs with the occupying forces. "We soon came to the conclusion," he wrote, "that these 'ladies' had been chosen . . . because of their looks and not their integrity. The period after the war was rife with corruption. This was the time to settle old scores: we received denunciations and anonymous letters by the dozen."[13]

But being an occupier was not all work. On the first weekend of June, he was invited by a friend to take a trip into the mountains and cross the border into Italy to watch a huge ski race being organized by the US Tenth Mountain Division. With happy memories of his own ski training in Italy, he readily agreed. Driving an open Tatra automobile, he and his friend set off on a glorious journey through the Dolomites to Udine.

One of the ironies of the Tenth Mountain Division's war was that after all the training at Camp Hale, once in Europe they rarely donned skis. Both the terrain — jagged and rocky — and the rainy spring weather put paid to that. The benefits of the grueling mountain training were revealed instead in the unprecedented fitness of the American troops and the intense camaraderie it produced. "A dozen reconnaissance patrols did use skis, but of course no one swooped down slopes," recalled one veteran. "What really counted in combat were the rock-climbing skills."[14]

So the ski meet in the Alps was the first opportunity for the division's top skiers to demonstrate their skills since arriving in Europe. Hundreds of US soldiers were trucked in to watch them and have a good time. Among them was Robert Ellis, who saw the overall contest won by Sergeant Walter Prager, the former ski coach at Dartmouth College, two-time winner of the prestigious Arlberg-Kandahar race held each year in Switzerland, and the 1931 World Champion. Prager was a Swiss instructor who made his name at Davos, and he was one of hundreds of Europeans who had joined the Tenth Mountain. Most were exiles from occupied countries such as Austria and Norway, and had been expert skiers before the war. Their presence in the division, along with their strong anti-Nazi credentials, did much to give it an enviable image in the minds of the public as an elite and fearsome war-fighting unit.[15]

Unfortunately Fred Warner never got to see the race. The night before, he was invited to a big party in Udine where everyone drank "buckets" of champagne. All he remembered later was the presence of a couple of New Zealanders, to whom he talked for a while because two of his sisters were living there. When he awoke next morning on a canvas camp bed, it was to find that he had been stripped of all his valuables and papers, including the watch given to him by SOE before leaving London. Crestfallen and nursing a severe headache, he forgot about the race and returned to Austria.

He now had a new job, at Wolfsberg, vetting police officials, issuing travel permits for civilians, and searching premises for hidden weapons.

On one of these missions he unearthed an old Fiat car in a garage. No one else wanted it because its reverse gear was not working, so he made it his own. Whenever he needed to back up, he simply commandeered a gang of willing local children to push him, and rewarded them with sweets. By mid-summer, he was something of a local celebrity.

The repatriation of the Cossacks was merely a single episode in the gigantic movement of people in Europe in the weeks after VE Day. While forced returns to the Soviet Union inevitably caught the headlines, the vast majority of people going home were only too eager to leave. But this did not necessarily mean that they went full of happiness, as Francesca Wilson was finding out in Bavaria. At the end of May, she was still in the Feldafing camp, doing welfare work with the Jews. "One gets a kind of affection for these people," she wrote in her diary, "but they are many of them poor broken wretches." Three days before, the first group of Czech Jews had left, bound for a reception camp at Pilsen. Nearly all the West Europeans had already left, but this was the first evacuation to the East. She spent hours registering the Czechs individually on carefully printed SHAEF cards that had been produced in the millions. One copy of each card was sent to the destination reception center, while the other was kept in Germany. In addition to basic personal details, the card contained a medical record signed by Francesca's medical colleague.

She liked the job because it helped her get to know the Czechs individually. Yet she also dreaded it. There were too many questions she hated to ask. Are you married? Do you have children? The answer was almost always the same—Auschwitz. She was dealing with people who had lost their wives, their husbands, their children. Even to her, with a lifetime's experience of working with refugees across Europe, it was a sobering experience. "It was this loneliness that made these people seem more unanchored and nakedly exposed than any I have known," she noted. "Even repatriation had no joy."[16]

Sunday 17 June found her sitting in the boathouse in Tutzing, reflecting on events since VE Day. The lake was lapping gently at her feet, the pale gray water occasionally catching a glint of the sun. In the distance, clouds veiled the Alps from her view. It was a peaceful moment after days of turmoil. At the beginning of the month she had started working with the thousands of deportees scattered in towns, villages and farms

433

throughout Upper Bavaria. It was a welcome change. Lieutenant Smith, the commandant at Feldafing, preferred doing things his own way and Francesca eventually felt she was wasting her energies there.

Since then, she had scoured the region trying to bring order out of chaos. More often than not it proved a frustrating task. One of the biggest problems was finding work for the DPs. German soldiers were now being demobilized and the local farmers had more of their own countrymen than they could employ, never mind foreigners. She found plenty of deportees who were skilled engineers and mechanics, but there were hundreds of equally qualified Germans who were queuing up for jobs. And while the military authorities had decreed that displaced persons should have priority over Germans, in practice this was difficult to enforce herself.

On one occasion, Francesca visited a battered aerodrome being reconstructed by the Americans near Munich. "I could employ a hundred DPs," said the US Army captain in charge, "but I can't lodge them. I could send a truck and haul them, if they're not far off. Begin with twenty-five next Monday." Francesca knew of a village only eight miles away with dozens of Russians, mostly engineers and technicians. Finding these few jobs was such a little thing, she mused, but with memories of the mass unemployment of the thirties still fresh in her mind, triumphs such as this felt as precious as gold. But would it happen? The truck was due to turn up at six-thirty the next morning, but she had been frustrated too many times before to raise her hopes too high.[17] The fact was that no one really wanted to make life easy for the DPs and thus encourage them to stay. The Germans feared and disliked them, and increasingly the Americans were wary of dealing with their problems and so devoted their energies to sending them back home, not finding them work. Some of the worst problems involved the Russians, the biggest single group of foreigners at large in Bavaria.

Francesca was still recovering from a fiasco involving some Russians. One morning word suddenly spread that the repatriations, for which everyone had been waiting for weeks, had begun and that four thousand people a day were leaving by train from Munich. But because the city itself held fifty thousand Russians, it was decided that they would leave first, to be followed later by the thousands more scattered throughout Bavaria. But someone, somewhere in the occupation hierarchy, decided to help the Americans in charge of the Starnberg camp, where the Russians had been causing trouble, and it was decided to ship them out straight away. Francesca volunteered to lead the convoy of nineteen trucks into Munich.

The journey itself was a nightmare. No one had bothered to tell the Russians that she was coming, so she found them in one of the barracks squatting around a stove enjoying a meal of stewed rabbit which they insisted on finishing. They were also drinking huge amounts of some ghastly wood alcohol, and when they were finally ready to leave she had to round up some of the more drunken ones from the woods. She also had to persuade them not to leave most of their possessions behind in the hurry to get home, including blankets and overcoats. It was just as well, too, because it started to rain shortly after they left, and the blankets provided at least some cover.

Then came the awful tangle of Munich. The streets were still piled high with rubble on either side and were thronged with thousands of DPs and German civilians, so the going was slow. Francesca was forced to leave the convoy for an hour and a half and go ahead on foot to find out exactly where she was heading. When she got back she was relieved that the Russians had not embarked on some wild round of looting. In the end, she delivered them to their reception point, but news had spread about her convoy, and the US military ordered several hundred Russians to be brought from Feldafing the next morning. However, they had blocked the route ahead of a second convoy out of Starnberg, which had been forced to turn back. By the time it returned, though, the camp had already been transformed into a detention center for Nazi suspects and was surrounded by barbed wire and machine-gun posts. Francesca was tasked with finding alternative housing for the Russians at Feldafing, but Lieutenant Smith insisted that the rooms must be properly disinfected, as there was still typhus in the camp. It was an exhausting and frustrating day.

Francesca felt guilty because if it had not been for her convoy encouraging others to leave, the chaos could have been avoided. On the other hand, she comforted herself, things could have been far worse. After all, none of the nightmares she had conjured up in advance had come true: the Russians had not murdered anyone; and the whirlwind the Germans were reaping as a result of their atrocious treatment of them was still largely confined to stealing.

Anyway, things moved so fast that there was always a new problem to deal with: brooding about old ones did no one any good. One day, she discovered a "whole nest" of DPs at Penzberg, a village about twenty miles away from Tutzing where there was a coal mine. Some were Russian officers who had been forced to work in the mine. Others were Poles, who were held in a separate camp. The problem was that half the Poles were suddenly moved by the Americans, without any warning, to another camp at Oberammagau. Families were arbitrarily separated and trouble broke out. Francesca and a Polish officer, a prisoner in Germany since 1939, drove off to the local US military government headquarters in Murnau to discover what was going on.

A friendly US lieutenant and major were in charge. Francesca liked most of the Americans she met. At their best, she felt, they had something that Europeans lacked. "They are buoyant, their wit is fresh, their speech original and free from clichés," she wrote. "Above all, they are so willing to experiment, to try out your suggestion, not next week but this minute, almost before you have finished making it, that they blow you off your feet."[18]

Now was a case in point. The lieutenant explained that they were trying to clear Penzberg of all DPs. This was because he was trying to get the mine working again, but the Germans had refused to do that until they felt able to leave their homes instead of defending them — and their wives — from "the looting of the free slaves." At least, that was the argument they were using, explained the lieutenant. So he had decided to eliminate their excuse by removing all the foreigners. Where, he asked, could he send the rest of the Poles?

Francesca said she would find out, so she motored with the Polish officer to nearby Oberammagau. It was an exquisite day — Bavaria at its best — with farmers mowing the hay and stacking it in sunny green meadows with the still snow-capped mountains looking down on them. She passed through villages with chalets and brightly painted wooden shutters and balconies bursting with flowers as though there had never been a Hitler, or SS men, or the ruin and human misery that now met her at every turn.

After this, it came as a shock to enter the barracks at Oberammagau. There were no baths, the beds were full of bugs, the plumbing was broken and the roofs leaked. It was a desolate place with not even a flower to be seen. The children were poorly clad and looked sickly. They were living off half a liter of milk a day with no special food. "Very little butter or sugar," Francesca noted down in her diary, "lots of haricot beans. They lack vitamins. Where are the stores we hear of? What about cod liver oil?" Red Cross parcels occasionally got through, but they were hardly enough. She discovered that the camp commandant was a Dutchman, supposedly a former collaborator, and that he was deeply disliked for treating the inmates like prisoners and not allowing them out. So she and the Polish officer immediately drove off and found a far better camp close by with a hospital and school that had room for the Poles. She just hoped the American lieutenant would agree to the move.[19]

More of the unpredictable human debris of war confronted her on the drive back. They stopped to give a lift to an old man with a wrinkled, Mongolian face sitting on a pile of baggage by the roadside. He came from a camp of Kalmucks hidden deep in a nearby valley, so they drove him there and in an instant were surrounded by a crowd of men, women and children all talking at once.

Their history was complicated. Originally a nomadic people from Mongolia, they had settled in southeastern Russia between the Volga and the Don, and were Europe's only Buddhists. They were systematically oppressed by the tsars, but many also fought with the White armies against the Bolsheviks, so Stalin suppressed them even more ruthlessly, destroying their monasteries, killing and harassing their priests, and doing everything in his power to wipe out their religion. Then, in 1944, he exiled all those not fighting in the Red Army to Siberia or to Central Asia. Those in exile as a result of the revolution had previously settled in such countries as France, Bulgaria and Yugoslavia before being forced by the Nazis to work in factories and mines. Others in the group, which numbered some 350, were picked up by the Nazis in Rostov and elsewhere in the Soviet Union. Now, all they wanted to do was stick together and be émigrés — although not, they added hastily, in Germany, where they were treated as a lower order of humanity.

They proudly showed Francesca their little temple decorated with pictures of Buddha and its altar and lamps. She and the Polish officer were the first outsiders ever to show any interest in them. They wondered if they could get permits to travel to Munich to contact the Russian émigré office. She said she would try to help, but knew it was probably hopeless. Maybe those who had worked in France would be able to go back there, but what about the rest? She found it difficult to tear herself away, so desperate were they to have someone listen to them. "Give us horses," they pleaded, "you will see how we can manage them. All beasts — but most of all horses."

"I never saw a more desolate, forgotten group of uprooted people in my life," she wrote in her diary.[20] But there were plenty of others almost equally lost. Soviet citizens were going back, but like the Kalmucks many had no desire to return to Stalin's brutal dictatorship. The policy agreed on by the allies at the Yalta Conference that February was that everyone who was a Soviet citizen in August 1939 had to return, regardless of their wishes. As Fred Warner had seen in Austria, that decision created thousands of victims, and it caused anguish to front-line welfare workers such as Francesca. Repatriation—"going home"—was a heart-warming phrase in anyone's book, as well as in UNRRA pamphlets. But the agency had largely failed to predict that so many of the displaced would not wish to return home. In the end, its greatest task was not repatriation but the care of those who chose *not* to go home. Francesca had been largely unprepared for that. Everything was far more complicated than she had expected.

One day, for example, she found a knot of ten dark-eyed and curly-haired peasants waiting outside her villa. They were Georgians and Armenians from Tiflis who had served in the Wehrmacht—but only, they claimed, because it was either that or death. They had not borne arms, they swore, but had worked for the Todt Organization. Now they wanted to go back to their wives and children but were fearful that they would be shot. Francesca suggested that the Soviet Union needed all the labor it could get for post-war reconstruction so they would probably be fine. And think how awful the alternative would be, she added: statelessness in Germany. "Their large eyes grew sadder and sadder," she noted. "It was harrowing."[21]

She was far from convinced she was giving them good advice. On one occasion she had gone to Dachau to see if she could get certificates proving that the Russians at Feldafing had been sent to the concentration camp for sabotage or some other anti-Nazi misdemeanor, such as trying to escape from a prisoner-of-war camp. This could be a life-or-death issue for them because many Russians had more or less willingly fought in the Wehrmacht and faced death or at least hard labor on their return. Regardless, the Americans seemed eager to send back as many as they could, while the Germans were ecstatic at the prospect of their repatriation, whoever they were. It was not just that they were glad to see the backs of their former slaves: they also needed the space for a new wave of German refugees.

At a meeting with the Mayor of Tutzing he told Francesca that millions of Germans were being expelled by the Czechs from the Sudetenland and would soon be arriving in Germany. Some of them were already on their way with nothing but knapsacks on their backs. Tutzing alone could expect as many as 25,000. Where would they be housed? How would they be fed? Francesca could see that it was an impending nightmare.

The fate of the Sudetens was part of the mass retribution now being visited on some fifteen million ethnic Germans expelled from their former homelands in Eastern and Central Europe. The bulk came from parts of Germany suddenly placed under Polish or Soviet rule, such as East Prussia, Pomerania and Silesia, but about three million hailed from Czechoslovakia. Altogether, it was the largest "ethnic cleansing" in Europe's bloody twentieth-century history.

The Czech government-in-exile worked out its expulsion policy long before liberation, and then won the consent of all the allies for it. Sudeten sympathy and support for Hitler climaxing with the Nazi takeover of the Sudetenland in 1938 had virtually guaranteed that there would be no place for this large and troublesome minority in post-war Czechoslovakia. Although the bulk of ethnic Germans lived in the western border area known as the Sudetenland, significant numbers were in Bohemian cities such as Prague and Brno. Indeed, the University of Prague nurtured claims to be regarded as one of the oldest *German* universities in Europe.

Expulsions began almost as soon as the fighting stopped in May 1945, regardless of age, gender or past political allegiance — a grotesque mirror-image of the racial "cleansing" practiced by the Nazis that indiscriminately included even Germans who had opposed Hitler, such as social democrats and communists. Many Czech Germans saw the writing on the wall and left voluntarily before the end of the fighting, trekking west towards the German frontier in huge horse-drawn convoys. "We read that Hitler was dead," recalled one man. "It was time to leave . . . We left our village at eight in the evening and by four in the morning had reached the western highway. It was crammed, filled, overfilled, with every sort of cart and vehicle that you can imagine."[22]

Embodied in the decision to expel the Germans was the raw reality that many Sudetens played a prominent role in the harsh Nazi rule over the country — such as the notoriously cruel and detested SS General

Karl Hermann Frank from Karslbad, who ran the police and succeeded SS General Reinhard Heydrich as "Protector" of Bohemia and Moravia after the latter's 1942 assassination by Czech agents trained by Britain's SOE. One of the worst Nazi massacres in all of Europe took place at the village of Lidice, not far from Prague, where in direct reprisal for Heydrich's death all the men were shot and the women and children deported to Germany. The village was then razed to the ground and all evidence of its existence eliminated. On 10 June 1945, the Czech President Edward Benes visited the site and made a speech. The blame for Nazi crimes, he thundered, rested with the overwhelming majority of Germans. "Let us not forget," he added, "that the leading instigators, accomplices, and executioners of these crimes were *Bohemian* Germans."[23]

Patton's Third Army occupied much of the western Sudetenland. Here, things remained relatively calm — so much so, indeed, that complaints began to be heard that the Americans were being too friendly with the Germans. But in areas liberated by the Red Army, retribution against ethnic Germans was swift and often violent. In Prague, where the Czech resistance had helped liberate the city, partisans stormed the German-held radio station and began broadcasting calls to "Kill Germans wherever you meet them," making no distinction between soldiers and local German citizens. Throughout most of the city, revolutionary guards rounded up Germans and interned them in prisons, theaters and schools, where they faced starvation, rape and other forms of torture. Thousands of Czech Germans also now found themselves interned in Theresienstadt, the concentration camp used by the SS as a way station to Auschwitz.

A week after VE Day, almost the entire German population of Brno was rounded up and interned. Over the next two weeks, Czech officials went from house to house valuing their contents for confiscation. Then, on the last day of May, the twenty thousand Germans still remaining were force-marched either to holding camps or to the Austrian frontier. Here, though, the guards refused to let them cross. Unable to go back, they sat in a field for days without food or sanitation, and typhus soon broke out.

This was typical of the pogrom mood that swept across Czechoslovakia during the summer of 1945. In one camp for women, armed Czechs and Russians appeared at night, chose their victims by the light of torches, and raped them in public. Czech authorities required all Germans inside or outside the camps to wear white armbands. They could claim only starvation rations, and were forbidden from using local transport.[24]

Back in Bavaria, Francesca Wilson took a trip to see Dachau. She walked through the hospital barracks, still packed with the sick. "God, how lonely the people look," she thought. Some were dying, others were unconscious, and some were recovering. The plan now was to divide the camp in two. One half would consist of the hospital, while the other would become a prison for ten thousand captured SS men. Good retribution, she thought.[25]

At Belsen, in the British zone, conditions were slowly improving and the death rate had declined dramatically: five hundred a day at the camp's liberation, by the middle of May it had fallen to below a hundred. Camp No. 1 — the worst — was being steadily cleared of its inmates, and as each hut fell empty it was burned to the ground. The last four hundred inmates were evacuated on Saturday 19 May, and two days later the last of the huts was ceremonially torched. But twelve thousand sick remained in the hospital, and thousands of others — now classified as displaced persons — were living in Camp No. 2 (for men), and Camp No. 3 (for women).

By June, as the survivors grew fitter, new problems were emerging. Some of the former prisoners, mostly Russians and Poles, started to engage in an orgy of destruction of anything German, and assaults on the German nursing staff were on the rise.[26] The composition of the camp was also beginning to change. Left behind for the most part were Jews, many with no homes to return to and determined to build a new country of their own. For them, in Dachau and other concentration camps as well as Belsen, the liberation had been both the ending of a story and the beginning of a new one.

CHAPTER TWENTY-FOUR

"YOU LOST PEOPLE AS YOU GAINED YOUR FREEDOM"

Through the open window of his hotel bedroom, framed like a picture, Robert Reid could see wooded hills and snow-capped peaks. In the center rose a column of thick black smoke. As night fell, it assumed a reddish tinge as it caught and reflected the flames from a blazing fire beyond his sight. But the BBC man knew what it was. He was in Berchtesgaden, and someone, possibly a homeless deportee, had set fire to one of the buildings surrounding Hitler's Berghof. As soon as *War Report* was shut down after VE Day, he had headed for home, like most other war correspondents. But instead of catching a military transport plane to be ferried sightless across Europe inside a freezing fuselage, he decided to play at being a tourist again, just as he and Vera had traveled in the carefree thirties on their continental tours. It was a nine-hundred-mile journey by jeep to Paris, but he planned to enjoy every minute of it.

Berchtesgaden was the first stop. French troops had reached the town first, but now the place was also swarming with US forces from General Patch's Seventh Army. With a colleague and half a dozen American soldiers, Reid wound his way up the steep and winding bomb-shattered road through fir trees to scramble among the burned-out ruins of Hitler's residence. It had been targeted by RAF Lancaster bombers a couple of weeks before, and the vast drawing room with its great plate-glass window overlooking the Untersberg Mountain (where legend had it that the Emperor Charlemagne lay ready one day to awake and restore the past glories of the German Empire) lay empty and desolate.

Here, unlike Hitler, Reid found nothing to fire his imagination. The scavengers and looters had done their work and there was only a charred and fire-blackened chamber with crumbling plaster and an empty window. As for the great terrace on which Hitler was so often photographed against the dramatic backdrop of the Alps, there remained just a heap of shattered stone, splintered trees, twisted metal, and the smell of a dead body trapped somewhere beneath.

Now, as he watched the smoke rise in the distance, Reid thought of the blaze as more than the result of a carelessly thrown match or deliberate arson. It seemed like the funeral pyre of a nation.

All around the vast complex, other top Nazis had built their homes, and the souvenir hunters and camera-clicking GIs were out in full force. Searchers had found a large part of Hermann Goering's vast collection of stolen art. And everyone seemed to have some small remnant of Hitler's Third Reich to take home, including Reid. In the corner of his room there was a pile of books. He picked up one, a big blue bound volume with the name "Edda" printed on it in gold lettering. Inside were hundreds of photographs of Goering's daughter. He also uncovered half a dozen of Goering's correspondence files, many of them with his scribbled comments and replies. In one, he read letters inviting friends to flee from allied "terror bombing" and stay with him at Karinhall. There were also instructions to the Reichsbank about the sale or purchase of foreign currency, as well as long lists of his art treasures. How these personal belongings of the second most powerful man in Hitler's Reich had got there, Reid could not even guess.[1]

The cameras were flashing in Munich, too, as he went to look at the famous Beer Hall where Hitler had mounted his failed *putsch* in 1923, with people singly or in groups having their pictures taken with a lot of laughter and smiling. Inside, hundreds of people waited silently and stolidly in line to have their jugs, steins and glasses filled with Bavarian beer. It was as though, thought Reid, they were in retreat from the completely topsy-turvy world outside.

Then he drove on through Germany to the Rhine. The roads were bathed in sunshine and heavy with the scent of spring blossom, but the physical wreckage of war was all too visible. Ruined houses, shattered railway stations, blackened factories and roofless churches scarred the landscape. Yet it was the human debris, the nomads of Europe, heading towards home in never-ending streams, that truly caught his attention:

> Russian women in their white kerchiefs, patriarchal, bearded figures in quilted coats, broad-cheeked Mongols with copper skins, swarms of Italian soldiers in full tropical kit, their faces half hidden by their solar topees, German prisoners jumping down from trucks at one end of a village ready to go into captivity, with British and American prisoners of war clambering into trucks at the other end of the village street on the first lap of their journey home.[2]

Finally, he was in Paris again, shining and shimmering in the sunlight, with its crowded boulevards, smartly dressed women, khaki-clad tourists. Here he caught up with friends from the press last seen crouching in some foxhole or other, and yarned and swapped stories well into the night.

It was not his first return to the city after his famous Notre Dame recording: he had taken a forty-eight-hour leave there in February, when the city was liberated but France was still at war. Then he was drawn back to the cathedral out of curiosity, to see if he could find the pillar behind which he had sheltered and gaze at the bullet marks on the stone. Instead, he saw a young woman in her twenties standing mute and silent before the altar of a side chapel where two tall candles burned. Later, he saw her again, rapt and pensive before the figures of Christ and the Wise Men in the tableau of the Nativity. Here, he imagined, was some wife or girlfriend of one of the two million French prisoners of war still in Germany. What thoughts were passing through her mind? The bitter anguish of separation, fear, uncertainty, lost hopes? Such, he mused, were the tragedies of France.[3]

By the end of May, he was in a BBC studio in London being interviewed about his experiences with Patton's men. "I came to love every one of them," he told the listeners, saying he had seen the American troops learning by experience and rapidly adapting to conditions so that by the time they crossed the Rhine "those GIs were some of the toughest, cleverest fighting men . . . anywhere in the world." Another thing that always impressed him about the Americans was their effective mixture of teamwork and individual initiative:

Time and time again, I came across instances of soldiers who had one particular job to do — some specialist job, such as reconnoitring a lane or a river crossing for engineering purposes. Then they'd suddenly come across a strongpoint held by the enemy. Technically it wasn't their job to mop that strongpoint up, but knowing that [it] would have to be mopped up before anything further could be done, they'd sail in and finish the job themselves.

As for Patton, he was probably the "most colorful" soldier Reid had ever met. "I wouldn't like to get in his way," he laughed.

But what had struck him most, he told listeners, was the effect that the uncovering of atrocities had had on the normal GI. He quoted an American lieutenant who had overrun the Ohrdruf camp and told Reid that after seeing it, he would believe anything about the Germans. "The troops who went in there," reported Reid, "were filled with a cold fury at what they saw and from that point onwards they really knew the sort of thing the United Nations [the allies] have been fighting."

As for the problems of post-war Europe, he rated the fate of the displaced persons as close to the top of the list. After that came the reeducation of German children. He told a story to make his point. One day, he was talking to a girl about the same age as his own daughter. He asked her a couple of simple questions. Did she know anything about Britain or the United States? She admitted she knew very little. Who was Hitler? She answered that he was their leader, and the greatest man in the world. Reid then showed her a picture of Himmler. He, too, was the greatest man in the world, she replied. "Where did you learn this?" he asked. At home, from her father, came the reply. "Well," Reid summed it up for the BBC listeners, "there was one warped and twisted young mind ready for the smoothing iron of democracy." Germany was a whole nation of war-mongers. What were the victors going to do, he wondered, about reeducating it and starting all over again from the rock-bottom of decency?[4]

Purifying society of the taint of Nazism was much on the minds of the Dutch, too, as Reg Roy discovered when he returned to Delfzijl after the VE Day celebrations in London.

Liberation in the Netherlands was a passionate but bittersweet affair. The surrender of German forces in Northwest Europe, Denmark and Holland signed at Lüneberg on 4 May came into force the next morning. But when, wondered the nine million desperate and starving Dutch citizens in western Holland, would they finally set eyes on their liberators? The answer was 7 May, the day agreed between General Blaskowitz and General Foulkes for the Canadian forces to enter "Fortress Holland."

However, over the intervening two days, tension steadily mounted. Authority remained in the hands of the Germans, their troops still roamed the streets, a curfew remained in force, and the frustrated Dutch resistance was forbidden to carry arms. "Do I feel free?" asked one Rotterdammer, summing up the national mood. "We still have to be inside, and when we put out the flag we are shot at. The Huns are everywhere."[5] In places, there was isolated shooting and the offices of the Dutch Nazis were looted, but everywhere the SS, unhappy about the surrender, remained a threat.

On the morning of Monday 7 May, as planned, allied soldiers crossed into western Holland and entered Utrecht, the first large city to greet the liberators. In Amsterdam, a huge crowd gathered expectantly on the Dam, the large square in the city center on which stood the huge Royal Palace with its dome and distinctive weather vane in the shape of a ship, the city's symbol, built in the seventeenth century at the glorious height of the Dutch Republic's maritime prosperity. Were they waiting for the Queen, who had already returned to her country, or for the Canadians? No one quite knew. In the meantime, people sang and danced to one of the city's traditional barrel organs.

Suddenly, though, shots rang out from the windows of a building on the corner of the square. People fled in panic, and in a few minutes the square emptied of everyone—except for nineteen dead Dutch civilians and over a hundred wounded compatriots. The shots had come from the windows of the Grote Club, where a group of drunken German naval officers had been drowning their sorrows at the defeat of the Third Reich.

But there was little time for mourning. The next day—VE Day— Canadian troops finally reached the city. The sun was shining brilliantly as the first soldiers entered its outskirts amid a euphoria that astonished the liberators. "The Dutch are a staid race," noted one of them, "but when they broke loose, they simply flung off all restraint." As the first Canadians came into sight, they were mobbed. One transport officer recalled:

As the lorries entered the city, there was a small bridge followed by a sharp turn which necessitated each lorry slowing down to almost a stop. At this point, the people started to climb on the vehicles . . . Some stood, some sat, others just hung on where one would think they couldn't hang on. There were on and in each ten tonner approximately one hundred and twenty-five people . . . even the dispatch riders were forced to put up with three or four people hanging on to their machines.[6]

Such ecstatic scenes were enacted all over western Holland over the next few days. One young woman from The Hague recalled:

I remember standing there, looking down the road. On the third day I saw a tank in the distance, with one soldier's head above it, and the blood drained out of my body, and I thought: Here comes *Liberation*. And as the tank came nearer and nearer, I had no breath left, and the soldier stood up, and he was like a saint. There was a big hush all over the people, and it was suddenly broken by a big scream, as if it was out of the earth. And the people climbed on the tank, and took the soldier out, and they were crying. And we were running with the tanks and the jeeps, all the way into the city.[7]

Yet all was not joy. Among the delirious thousands lining the streets of Amsterdam was a young Jewish woman. Miraculously, she had survived by obtaining false papers, and had lived openly while concealing her true identity. Now, suddenly, she could go out in the streets and use her real name. Recently, she had been living on handouts from the central municipal kitchens — generally just a bowl of watery soup. Her mother had grown so weak on this diet that she could hardly walk. "The Canadians looked so brawny and healthy," she recalled. "One of the first things [they] did was to go to the central kitchens and really spice up the soup we were fed, which was normally made with sugar beets and potato peelings. The next time we got soup, it was fantastic — it had meat and vegetables and rice in it."

But too many mouths were absent for her to experience liberation as an undiluted joy. Most of Amsterdam's Jews, including one of her own brothers, never came back from the camps, and 85 percent of all Dutch Jews perished in the gas chambers. "When you met other Jews," she remembered of the days of liberation, "you didn't dare ask about their families because it was likely they had been killed . . . You lost people as you gained your freedom."[8] The same was true for hundreds

447

of other Dutch families whose sons, brothers, fathers or uncles had been shot by the Germans.

If thousands of Dutch suffered, however, an uncomfortably large minority actively collaborated with the Nazis, and the demand for retribution ran high. If liberation was to lead to democracy, then such elements had to be "cleansed" from the nation. Some 65,000 Dutch collaborators had already fled to Germany.

By the time Reg Roy returned to Delfzijl, the purging of collaborators from all positions of power and authority was well under way. The mass arrests of suspects by Dutch resistance forces started even before allied forces arrived, and between 120,000 and 150,000 men and women were rounded up. In part, this was to protect them from "blitz-justice" or mass lynchings, a reaction so feared by the Dutch government-in-exile that they alerted their secret representatives in the country to deal with it. So did the Roman Catholic Church. In September 1944, when the first allied troops crossed the border from Belgium, it asked priests to open their church buildings as places of refuge for suspected collaborators.

In the event, lynching on a massive scale was largely avoided. Yet in the Groningen area to which Roy returned, feelings ran particularly deep about those who had helped the Nazis. In the town of Winschoten, for example, a crowd dragged the Nazi-appointed Mayor from his office, threw him into the canal, and hurled his portrait of Adolf Hitler and the Dutch Nazi Party (NSB) leader Anton Mussert into the water after him. In the nearby town of Farnum, a mob simply murdered the Mayor, a man also appointed by the Nazis. Lower-level collaborators were humiliated by giving them dirty and menial tasks: Roy saw some of them at work in the Krasnopolsky Hotel when he went on leave to Amsterdam.

Across the Netherlands, special "cleansing committees" were hard at work. Yet only in the weeks after the liberation did the full scale of the problem dawn on the new government, and late in June the Prime Minister began to talk publicly of the "cancerous tumor in our nation." This was when the wave of arrests crested, and suspects were crowded into hundreds of hastily erected internment camps. In the end, some fifty thousand collaborators were given prison sentences, and over a hundred and fifty were condemned to death. Of these, though, only forty were actually executed. Anton Mussert had been found by Canadian soldiers sitting in his office in The Hague. Just a week before, in a defiant mood, he had promised to fight to the death, but in the end he meekly allowed himself to be taken into custody. Exactly a year to the day later, he was executed after a trial for treason.

In and around Groningen, the arrested were held in schools, hotels, cafés, gymnasia and large barns. Some of these improvised camps contained no more than a few dozen internees, while larger ones housed several hundred. These were usually former barracks or compounds used by the Wehrmacht, the Dutch Labour Service or the Todt Organization. In Groningen alone, there were ten large camps, where, at exercise time, gaping spectators came to watch and jeer. There were several camps for women and their children, and the city even established a home especially for the children of NSB members. At the height of the arrest wave, the city had 18,000 internees — 8,500 men, 6,500 women and 3,000 children, a proportion of the population considerably higher than the Dutch national average. Some camps were reasonably comfortable, but overall there was little and bad food, poor hygiene and plenty of dysentery and diarrhea. Conditions were so bad, indeed, that even as the Prime Minister was talking of the "cancerous tumor," newspapers were denouncing them as too harsh.

But after the peak in June, the numbers rapidly declined, and by the end of the summer only twenty out of a hundred such camps were still open in Groningen Province.[9] Nationally, both "restoration" and "renewal" became the order of the day. It was widely accepted that Dutch society had to be reformed, but in an orderly way, and this meant being more strict about who was purged and cooling the radical mood that had developed in the resistance. The first post-war Prime Minister Willem Schermerhorn said he had to find a way "to send it to bed, politically speaking." By the end of the summer of 1945, this had been largely accomplished.[10]

The handling of collaborators was a domestic matter for the Dutch. For the Canadian Army, most of its immediate and urgent tasks involved medical relief, food supply and the repatriation of German prisoners of war. There were also some significant counterintelligence tasks to carry out, as remembered by one of the senior Canadian officers involved:

> In the first three weeks, we managed to get about a hundred thousand German soldiers out of the Netherlands and back into Germany. At each prisoner sorting point, the faces of soldiers were

scanned by a small group of Dutch underground members who could recognise enemy agents, collaborators and others who had served German intelligence. If the German soldier passed through the control point, he was home free and could go on to a demobilisation camp in his own country; if not, he was placed under arrest. Of course, not all those dressed in German uniform were soldiers. Some were Dutchmen trying to escape their own country.

His particular interrogation team could handle dozens of people a day. Yet, even then, he confessed, "it took until September to interrogate all the people arrested in our security area."[11]

But the departure of the Germans was only the beginning of a new story. There were 170,000 Canadian troops in the Netherlands on VE Day. How soon could they be shipped home? The Canadians were competing with hundreds of thousands of Americans also being sent home, and the demand for transatlantic shipping was so great that the queue stretched well into 1946. As they waited, and as the days and weeks stretched into months, impatience grew and morale and discipline began to fray. This problem affected relations with the Dutch. The Canadians arrived as knights, as saints, as liberators, but over the summer of 1945 they turned into occupiers.[12]

The Netherlands at the end of the war was an impoverished country. It had been systematically exploited by the Germans and the Hunger Winter had killed thousands, and left many more at a level of malnutrition from which they found it hard to recover. Railway service was rudimentary, there was no public road transport, and regular employment remained a distant prospect for many. It was hardly surprising that a thriving black market quickly took hold. Two of its main currencies were cigarettes and alcohol. The Canadians were well supplied with both. Troops were under orders not to sell or barter goods with civilians, but this was almost impossible to enforce. It cost a family in Canada a mere three dollars to send a soldier in the Netherlands a thousand cigarettes. On the black market, he could sell them for four hundred dollars or, more likely, barter them for goods and services. Many found it hard to resist the temptation.

Canadian soldiers possessed another highly prized asset. Most Dutch men who had survived the war were badly dressed, undernourished and poor. By contrast, the youthful Canadians possessed muscled good looks, the aura of heroes, an attractive New World courtesy towards women and plenty of food and money. "I don't think we ever met a more willing female population than we did in Holland," said one Canadian soldier of an army that also mixed with the British, the Italians, the French and the Belgians. "They were very warm . . . They seemed so much earthier than most girls we had met previously, and they didn't get uptight about a lot of things." For many in the Netherlands, the summer of 1945 was a wild and crazy time. "Let's face it," remembered one Dutch girl, "after what we had been through the Canadians looked delicious." *Gezelligheid*, a Dutch word implying both coziness and companionability, was extended by whole families to their liberators.

Typical was the experience of one Canadian soldier in Groningen. He and a friend were out one night when they met two girls on the street. They began flirting and one of the girls took them back home to meet her parents, sister and brother. The Canadians quickly nipped back to their camp and returned with chocolate bars, tea, coffee and cigarettes, and they celebrated the liberation late into the night. As the soldiers left, the mother told them they could bring her their laundry. Soon, the daughter of the house was going out on regular dates with one of the Canadians. She spoke no English, and he knew no Dutch, but they managed to communicate with hand signs, smiles and "yes" and "no." It was not long before he asked her to marry him and return with him to Canada. "I nearly fell over and said yes right away," she recalled. "My father liked him, maybe because of the cigarettes." They got the permission of the Mayor and the soldier's commanding officer, each had a health check, and the girl was screened to see that she had not been a collaborator. For the wedding, they rented a café using cigarettes as currency, and hired four horse-drawn carriages for the wedding party. It was one of the first of many "war-bride" marriages in Groningen, and between four and five hundred people crowded into the local church.[13]

Fraternization between soldiers and civilian women in the weeks following liberation was intense, and inhibitions in the traditionally prudish Dutch society fell away. The fighting was over, but a new battlefront now loomed. By the summer of 1945, a medical officer in General Hoffmeister's Fifth Division was confirming a sharp rise in VD rates among the troops. This was despite an efficient campaign to hand out contraceptives and warn the troops about the dangers of unprotected sex. "Perhaps," noted the officer, "it was because the Dutch and

Canadians get along well together." There were no reports of rape in the area.

However, as the summer passed, popular resentment about the behavior of Canadian soldiers and Dutch girls began to rise, and the sight of their women arm in arm with the occupiers started to grate. "Dutch men were beaten militarily in 1940, sexually in 1945," observed one Dutch journalist. Popular songs and doggerel reflected a new mood about the Canadians. "*Meisje let op je zaak*" (Girl, look after yourself) was a typical verse doing the rounds:

> Many who collaborated with the Germans
> Bear the stigma now;
> Girl, you also are a traitor
> Against the honour of the Netherlands!
> People come and go;
> Tommy will do so too
> Don't think that he'll take you with him;
> Girl, have you thought of that?
>
> Then no Dutch boy
> Will even look at you
> Because, so to say,
> You left him out in the cold.
> Be good to our liberators;
> Theirs is a great accomplishment,
> But think, there are limits:
> Girl, look after yourself!

A joke hinting at the number of girls who were "getting into trouble" also began to circulate. "In twenty years, when another world war breaks out, it will not be necessary to send a Canadian expeditionary force to the Netherlands. A few ships loaded with uniforms will be enough."[14]

Other irritations began to arise as well. There were more brawls involving Canadian soldiers, too many cases of looting, too much evidence of Canadians playing the black market, more public drunkenness, too much speeding in army vehicles, too many accidents. By mid-summer, the liberators were beginning to wear out their welcome. That summer *Vrij Nederland*, an important wartime clandestine newspaper that was now legal, published an article on the sexuality of Canadian troops. "We will do anything for the Canadians," it read, "but our girls must stay away from them . . . We will praise God when the Canadians have disappeared to Canada."[15]

Canadian soldiers were beginning to feel the same way. It was time to go.

"At present, other than explore this new town we are in, I am just sitting on my hands, patiently waiting and wondering how soon the word will come for me to pack up and go. Every day is a day nearer, of course, but I hate this sitting around and doing nothing."

It was early July, and Reg Roy was pouring out his frustrations to his parents in a six-page, handwritten letter. The Cape Bretoners had just moved to Bolsward, a small town of seven thousand inhabitants in Friesland. Like many Frisian communities, it owed its existence to shipping, but the steady draining and land reclamation of the Zuider Zee meant it now lay stranded, five miles inland.

Roy was impatient to get home and bored with being an occupier. Even the organized sports, the regular evening dances and the trips to historic sites did little to relieve the monotony of a routine filled with drill, the repairing of vehicles and the much-needed mending of equipment and personal clothing. Once he had even made it to Paris and hit the usual tourist spots, such as the Folies Bergère and Napoleon's tomb. But the visit was all too brief and only made the Netherlands seem more quiet and provincial than ever. True enough, the transfer to Bolsward meant there were some new places to explore, but when all was said and done there was not much to see apart from the magnificent red-brick Town Hall with its elegant Baroque façade. "Tis an old town, and very quiet," he told his parents.

Along with a fellow officer he was billeted in the private home of the local Mennonite minister. His room was nice enough, but the house had no electricity or hot water. The officers' mess, though, was in a comfortable hotel, and at mealtimes he was served by local waiters. Still, time passed slowly, and he wondered a great deal about when he was likely to be shipped out. It did not look good for an early exit to British Columbia, where he was already sending money to his fiancée, Ardith, to buy furniture. There were several problems. One was that his division was second last in line of Canadians to leave for home, and top priority anyway was being given to returning prisoners of war and men who had volunteered for service in the Far East. He definitely was not one of those and could not wait to get out of uniform and back into civilian life. Precisely when you got to go depended, too, on the points system. He was not too badly placed on that front as he had 150 out of a possible score of 250. But here, too, there was a snag. Higher authority had decreed that the regiment should never have fewer than twenty-five officers at any one time. So even if he qualified for fast repatriation on points, if the Highlanders were low on officers, he would have to stay.

Getting home, he confessed to his sister a little later in July, had become "a real hot subject" that was getting more heated by the day. He was sitting in his ascetic little room, bashing away with two fingers on one of the foreign typewriters that the Highlanders had liberated from the Wehrmacht. This one was Italian, he noticed. In the background, Bing Crosby was crooning on the radio. All the division's officers had recently been told that, because of the shipping problem, it would be "about next Easter" before the division returned home. With 26,000 men crossing the Atlantic to Canada every six weeks, Roy could see the problem. So far, out of the 170,000 Canadians in the country on VE Day, only 16,000 had left. "Li'lo Reggie may be out in the cold, cold ground," he typed in the jokey style he liked to adopt with his older sister, "and that may mean I shall not be coming home until next Spring . . . S'help me, if I have to stay over here for any longer, I might as well take out citizenship papers."

There was nothing he could do except silently howl and curse and get on with it. It was all harder to bear because he was anxious to go to college and term began in September. Before then, he would have to get back to Canada, be discharged, move to whichever college would accept him, and—not least—marry Ardith. "It is a poor system," he wrote to his parents, "it makes me mad to think about it even."

In the meantime, he enjoyed the packages his mother continued to send, just as she had during the war, packed with oranges, apples, cookies, tea, shorts and sweatshirts, and dozens of magazines. In return, he promised his father he would be returning with a couple of "Jerry" dress bayonets, a "lovely pair" of binoculars, and a Belgian Browning automatic that he secured with a bottle of Hiram Walker whisky. "I'll be coming home with guns blazing, yunk, yunk," he wrote. " 'Dead Eye' Roy I wuz known as—or was it 'Weakeyes,' haw!" he joked.

He was also proud of some of the photographs snapped in Delfzijl. "They are really good," he promised one and all, "and some are really grim." He was thinking of the picture of his dead Highlander comrades on the battery wall, their bodies neatly wrapped up in cloth ready for burial. Already it seemed like quite a long time ago.[16]

Also in Northwest Europe waiting to move on was British commando Bryan Samain, still based at Eutin in Schleswig-Holstein.

Samain, like Reg Roy, was keen to take back some trophies of war. His chance came one day when a German walked into his office at the Eutin Town Hall. He was wearing a faded Luftwaffe uniform and spoke good English. He had a surprising tale to tell.

The man claimed to be a deserter who was picked up by the SS near Lübeck in 1943. They promised not to turn him in to the Luftwaffe, provided he looked after one of their secret supply stores, which he did for the rest of the war. It was hidden in the countryside near Eutin, concealed in the cellar of an old inn. He offered to take Samain out to see it.

Hopping into his jeep, Samain drove with the man about ten miles out of Eutin along small country roads. Sure enough, in the middle of what appeared to be a deserted hamlet, there were the ruins of an inn. The man led him to a large double trapdoor and down they clambered into a large cellar. It was packed with hundreds of boxes filled with expensive cameras and telescopic lenses. The cameras were all Contax IIIs, each worth a small fortune. In addition, there were dozens of pairs of Zeiss Ikon binoculars as well as crates filled with rolled-up oil paintings and carefully wrapped gold and silver plates.

It had all been scrupulously inventoried. The Luftwaffe man even produced the list carrying an official SS stamp. But what, wondered Samain, was really going on here? Was it truly an SS pile of loot, or was it some elaborate con by the self-proclaimed deserter? Unfortunately, he would never find out, because the whole affair was quickly passed on to more senior officers. But Samain and many of his fellow commandos each returned to Britain with a Contax III camera and a telescopic lens.

During his month as an occupier in Eutin, Samain encountered no serious problems with the local population. Indeed, one of his enduring memories was that from virtually day one of the surrender, German men and women of all ages and conditions were out in the streets clearing up debris, rubble and bomb damage wherever they could. But there was not too much time to observe this. Along with many other British units in Europe, the commandos were now slated for action in the Far East. In early June, he left with a small party of officers and men to drive the unit's trucks and jeeps to Arromanches in Normandy before crossing the Channel back to England. Meanwhile, the rest of 45 Commando sailed to Tilbury out of Hamburg.

Samain was lucky, for throughout the rest of Germany law and order were in short supply. Violence by roaming groups of freed slave laborers troubled the country for months, and remnants of the Werewolves and diehard Nazis continued to cause problems. In remote areas, such as parts of Saxony and the Bavarian Alps, bands of Wehrmacht and SS troops carried out attacks and raids throughout the summer and autumn, until winter forced them out of their hiding-places.

The Werewolves proved less of a headache than allied intelligence had anticipated, but a few groups remained active well after VE Day, especially in Polish-occupied Silesia and the Sudetenland. Some caused trouble in the western zones of Germany, too. The allies had responded to the broadcasts of Radio Werewolf in April by promising that all active Werewolves would be hunted down, captured, judged and, if found · guilty, shot. They kept to that promise, and in the weeks following VE Day scores of Germans were executed for sniping at allied soldiers or for illegally possessing weapons. In Schleswig-Holstein alone, the British executed a dozen Werewolves, with thirty more still awaiting the death penalty at the end of the summer. Over the next few months, allied counterintelligence investigated hundreds of other cases. Denmark proved a surprisingly rich terrain for Nazi resistance groups. Thousands of German refugees fleeing from the Russians sheltered in Jutland while waiting to reenter Germany. In mid-June, evidence emerged that the German Red Cross operating in Denmark was being used as a cover for widespread Nazi activity and for shielding wanted Germans. Both its chief executive and his deputy were arrested. In southwest Germany, a fanatical group of ex-SS men near Stuttgart launched several bombing attacks against "fraternizers" and denazification tribunals before it was rounded up at the end of the following year.[17]

On Thursday 14 June, British intelligence officers captured the last of the big-time Nazis.

Joachim von Ribbentrop was Hitler's foreign minister and a one-time ambassador to Britain. Like many other top Nazis, he had fled north to Flensburg, where he offered his services to Admiral Doenitz. But Hitler's successor chose instead Count Schwerin von Krosigk, a man he thought more likely to prove acceptable to the allies in case of any serious negotiation. Rejected, Ribbentrop made his way to Hamburg. Here, he first sought shelter with a wine merchant he had known in happier days a quarter of a century before when plying the same trade. But he was refused, so he found himself lodgings elsewhere in the city, registering under the name "Herr Reiser." For the next month, he lived the life of a quiet and unobtrusive middle-aged man, taking regular strolls through the streets in an elegant double-breasted suit with a black trilby hat and dark sunglasses.

Meanwhile, British Army Field Security had taken over the city's former Gestapo headquarters, which they found still equipped with telephone-tapping equipment. They were fully briefed on the names of all Nazi intelligence officials in the city — particularly former Abwehr agents — as well as Nazis on the automatic arrest list. Some of these had been officials employed by Goebbels's propaganda machine in the studios of Radio Hamburg, from where William Joyce had frequently broadcast. By now, the British had taken control of the station and were busily denazifying it and getting it running again.

Although Ribbentrop's wine merchant friend had refused him refuge, he kept news of the meeting to himself. But not so the merchant's son, who went to the police to report Ribbentrop's presence in the city. This proved a helpful hint, because for at least the previous two weeks rumors had been rampant that he had already been seized by the Russians.

A three-man field security team led by twenty-nine-year-old Lieutenant J.B. Adam of Paisley, a peacetime schoolteacher, eventually headed to a room on the fifth floor of an apartment block close to the main railway station. They knocked on the door, which was opened by an unkempt young brunette wearing a scanty negligée. Pushing her aside, the soldiers searched the rooms and found a man deeply asleep in bed. Adam shook him by the shoulder for a long time before he woke up. He blinked in the light, gazed incredulously at Adam, then without a word clambered out of bed.

"What is your name?" asked Adam.

"You know very well who I am," answered Ribbentrop, before making a swift bow and adding ironically, "I congratulate you!"

He was carrying a tin of poison which he produced voluntarily before being searched. He was formally identified by both the wine merchant and his own sister, who had been picked up earlier. His son, captured the week before by the Americans in Bavaria, had given no clue as to his father's whereabouts.

"I wanted to stay in Hamburg until British opinion had died down," Ribbentrop told his interrogators. "Then I intended to give myself up and get a fair trial." There was little mistaking the temper of British feeling about him. "This," declared the Glasgow *Evening Citizen*, "is the man who, perhaps more than any other, was responsible for plunging the world into war. He was Hitler's 'evil genius.' Warped with hatred of the British, he poured into his Führer's mind the mistaken judgements which inflamed that megalomaniac and convinced him the world was his for the taking."[18]

The day before Ribbentrop's capture Herman Pister, the commandant of Buchenwald, along with several of his staff officers, had been found in a prisoner-of-war camp near Munich. American intelligence officers had been on his trail since he fled the camp in disguise shortly before US forces liberated the camp.

In Italy, a desperate search of another kind was under way.

After her heart-rending farewell to Alex von Stauffenberg at Capri, Fey von Hassell drove back with Detalmo to Rome.

The capital had slipped as comfortably into the new occupation as it had accommodated itself to its predecessor. Two days after the liberation of the city in June 1944, American officers replaced Germans on the fashionable dinner circuits, and the farewell dinner for Field Marshal Kesselring was quickly followed by the equally hospitable welcome to General Mark Clark. Yet relief that the city had been spared destruction soon gave way to a sobering recognition of the reality that Italy was one of the losers in the war.

VE Day was a somber, downbeat affair. The bars and restaurants were quiet, no more church bells than normal were rung, and while some flags appeared, just a few groups of young Italians paraded in the streets, trying, wrote one observer, "with almost pathetic desperation" to gate-crash the victory party. "But the victory is not theirs," continued Philip Hamburger, an American war correspondent in the city, "and the enthusiasm is hollow." Rome, he wrote, had accepted the news of peace itself "with the helpless and tired shrug of the defeated." For what did peace mean, in practical terms? Little more than a dreary continuation of the misery of fantastic prices, black markets, unemployment, the struggle to regain national pride, and "the even more difficult struggle to get people to think for themselves after two decades of stupefaction."

Personal problems now loomed larger than ever. Hamburger listed some of the typical demands that showered down on him. "How can a young man get to Turin to discover whether his parents survived the German occupation; does the American know someone who will deliver a letter to a lady's husband, a Partisan, in Milan; please, will the United States permit Italians to leave home and settle in the United States." On and on they went.[19]

Fey was soon to find out that she was only one of thousands with such problems that no one seemed able to solve. Her emotions were in turmoil. Everything in Rome was heart-achingly familiar, from the Pirzio-Birlio apartment and Detalmo's family, to the streets and monuments she had loved when her father was German Ambassador there. Yet she now felt dislocated and adrift in a city that had not suffered as so many other places had. "It felt wrong," she remembered. "There was no sign of the horror and destruction that had ravaged the rest of Europe."[20] Detalmo tried hard to distract her, but he had not been party to her misery, and sharing her feelings with him proved impossible.

Above all, though, how could she return to normal peacetime life when her children were still missing? With the war finally over and the Nazis finished, it should have been the best of times, but for Fey it was "the worst time of all."[21]

At least — as far as she knew — her children were still alive, and one day they might all become a family again. Others were not so lucky.

Joseph Goebbels and the Mayor of Leipzig were not the only Nazis to ensure that their children, like themselves, would not survive the collapse of Hitler's Reich. Outside Erfurt, for example, the Americans reported the death of a man, his wife, six children and their nurse. The eldest of the children was aged eight, the youngest just two. "I believe it was their free will to die," said the local doctor, implausibly. Sometimes, children were killed because of Goebbels's dire promises about likely allied behavior towards the Germans, or because the prospect of life in defeat seemed too hard to contemplate. Near Schweinfurt, a young woman who heard that her husband had just been killed at the front poisoned her two small children, then shot herself. Margaret Bourke-White, a photographer for *Life* magazine, was profoundly shocked by the scene. "Making myself photograph these tiny pathetic bodies, victims of forces which should be utterly remote from the life of a child, was one of the most difficult jobs I have ever had," she wrote.[22]

From Rome, Fey and Detalmo tried frantically to trace the boys.[23] They pleaded with officials for permission to travel to Germany and search for them but always met with bureaucratic refusal. Travel was simply too chaotic and they enjoyed no priority. Ironically, despite all her hardships, because she was German and thus an enemy national, she was ineligible for any help from UNRRA — even if they had been able to give it.

Then, by chance, at the end of May, Detalmo met an American officer who was flying to Munich, and he agreed to carry letters to Fey's mother, who was still living in the family home at Ebenhausen. Detalmo's letter was written in English and reflected the exhaustion felt by millions of others when the guns fell silent:

> My thoughts are not too clear. They shift from Christian patience to anarchic rebellion. I am not prepared to accept what has happened to us. If I still feel like fighting and working for a better world, it is only out of loyalty to the sacrifice of those who have shown us the way. Father [i.e. Ulrich von Hassell] has been a great example for us, and we are still under his shadow. It is as if an enduring monument has been raised inside our hearts.

Fey, he added, had shown enormous strength in surviving her ordeal. "I feel like marrying [her] anew," he concluded. "I would marry her ten times if I had ten lives."

In her letter, Fey asked her mother to start looking for the children. But she and Detalmo expected them to be found any day now. Above all, they refused to believe they were dead.

However, still no news came, and soon they resigned themselves to the fact that getting to Germany was impossible. It would be up to Fey's mother to find her grandchildren.

Detalmo was now working as a private secretary to Italy's first postwar prime minister, Ferruccio Parri, one of Italy's leading wartime resistance leaders. When he was not busy with that, he and Fey prepared pamphlets and papers giving details of Corrado and Roberto along with their photographs. They sent them to the Italian, German and International Red Cross, to the American, British and French intelligence services, to Vatican Radio, to all the bishops and archbishops in Germany and Austria. Every leaflet was written in Italian, German, English, French and Russian. But there was no response and Fey increasingly had a sinking feeling. The children were so young, they would now have different names, and perhaps they were lost deep in the Russian zone of Germany or Austria. How could she ever hope to find them in the post-war chaos still engulfing the continent? To distract herself, she began to record everything that had happened to her in the camps.

Meanwhile, her mother had begun to search for the children. Her home in Ebenhausen, like thousands of others at the end of the war, consisted entirely of women. Living with her was her mother — the widow of Admiral von Tirpitz — her unmarried sister, and Fey's sister Almuth. Neither of her sons had returned home. Hans-Dieter had been thrown into prison after the bomb plot before escaping ahead of the Russians to the French zone of occupation. His elder brother, Wolf Ulli, had last been heard of somewhere behind the Russian lines.

For Fey's mother, too, though, it felt like mission impossible. All she knew was that eight months ago, her grandchildren had been taken from their mother at Innsbruck. How on earth was she to carry out a search in a country with no railway services, where the telephone lines were still down, and which was under strict military occupation so you needed a special permit for nearly everything? They were just two small boys, known by false names, among millions of other lost children and orphans in Europe's wasteland. Nazi authority had melted away, and with it the centralized records that might give a clue to their whereabouts. Only the occupiers carried any authority, but they were overwhelmed by the confusion. Besides, they knew nothing about the boys.

Then, early in June, she had a sudden lucky break. While clearing up the debris and searching through buildings, the authorities in Munich found a dark blue abandoned BMW. They were able to identify it as the one confiscated from the von Hassells after the arrest of Fey's father and returned it to the family. Now, at least, Fey's mother had transport of her own. Next, she secured permits for the car, for travel and for petrol. Eventually, her quest led her to the office of Colonel Charles Keegan, the US military governor of Bavaria.

"Charley" Keegan was — in the words of one harsh critic — "a New York Irish politician-turned-soldier with a glad hand and glib gab," and he would later be fired for letting too many ex-Nazis back into office. But Fey's mother found him sympathetic and concerned. He was obviously shocked and disturbed by the chaos and anarchy that greeted him in Germany, and he wanted to help. Solemnly, he wrote out a note asking his subordinates to assist her.

It worked wonders. Armed with the note, she and Almuth carefully planned the route of their search. They relied mostly on rumors and gossip about other missing children in Gestapo hands that were spreading from town to town. They headed first for a children's home in southern Bavaria, but the director there gave them short shrift, saying Fey's children were definitely not among those in her care.

However, after this setback, they received a strong lead directing them to Bad Sachsa. It sounded promising because the Stauffenberg and Goerdeler children had just been located there. The only problem was that it lay just across the border in Czechoslovakia, and it was soon to be taken over from the Americans by the Russians. It took them two hard days' driving to get there. By the time they arrived, it seemed they were too late. Three miles short of the town, they came upon a wooden barrier across the road. A friendly British sergeant on duty first tried to dissuade them from going on because of the Russians. But when Fey's mother insisted, he persuaded her to leave Almuth behind because of what they might do to a young woman. He also told her to leave behind all her papers, money and jewelry, to abandon the car, and complete her journey on foot.

So Fey's mother walked on alone. She was still wearing a black widow's mourning veil in memory of her husband. Eventually, she reached the town, which was almost deserted because most of its German inhabitants had fled. In the Town Hall, she found the Mayor sitting in his office alone and desolate. She explained her mission and he leaped to his feet, took her to his old saloon car, and offered to drive her to the children's home. They could only get there, he explained, when the Russians were changing their guard.

They managed to dodge a Russian patrol and reached a big stone building on a hilltop. Outside, sitting on the porch, they found a woman and a small child playing happily beside her. The woman was the director. She looked at the photographs Fey's mother impatiently pushed in front of her. She was certain that she had never seen them, absolutely certain. "Who's the little one?" asked Fey's mother, pointing to the child. "One of the Goerdeler children," came the reply. It was a dreadful blow.

Fey's mother and sister returned exhausted and dispirited to Ebenhausen. What could they do next? Where were they to look? Germany was simply too big and they had no more leads.

Back in Rome, Fey sweated out June completely in the dark about her mother's efforts. By now, she was desperate to get back to Brazzà. This was not just to escape the capital's stifling summer heat, but to regain some sense of composure. She had always felt safe and happy there. Besides, she could throw herself into getting the estate back in shape and so take her mind off her worries. But here, too, there was a problem: word came through that Brazzà was now occupied by British officers. So she hung on in Rome. Still no word came of the children. As June turned into July, her spirits once again were ebbing away.

CHAPTER TWENTY-FIVE

BERLIN: THE GRAY CITY

For most of May and June, Francesca Wilson remained in the small lakeside town of Tutzing. Almost next door to her lay the villa of Frau Ludendorff, the widow of General Erich Ludendorff, chief of staff to Hindenburg in the First World War and the real power behind the throne during the Kaiser's war. The villa had been requisitioned to house a group of US Army officers, but the Americans allowed the elderly German and her sister to visit during daylight hours, before the start of the night-time curfew.

One evening, Francesca was invited over with other members of the UNRRA team to hear Frau Ludendorff's sister, a well-known pianist, play music by Schumann. It was not a large house, but it was packed with the heavy, solid furnishings of Junker Germany and filled with memorabilia. The general's memoirs lined the bookshelves, and his portraits ringed the walls: Ludendorff as a baby, Ludendorff as a schoolboy, Ludendorff as a soldier. There was even a portrait of Ludendorff looking Napoleonic, wearing a cloak on a battlefield.

After the First World War, he had emerged as a diehard opponent of the new, democratic Weimar Germany, and in 1920 joined hands with Wolfgang Kapp, a fellow right-wing nationalist, to head an attempted coup against the government in Berlin. Three years later, he marched alongside Adolf Hitler during the notorious Munich *putsch*. And he served as a Nazi member of the Reichstag until falling out of favor with the party. On his death in 1937, Hitler gave him a state funeral.

The copies of *Mein Kampf* had already been removed from his library, but as Francesca browsed the shelves, she came across the collected works of Houston Stewart Chamberlain. After settling in Germany, he had joined the Bayreuth circle of nationalist intellectuals influenced by the anti-Semitic ideas of Richard Wagner and married the composer's daughter. His book *The Foundation of the Nineteenth Century* argued that the "white" or "Aryan" race was superior to all others. Hitler praised him as a prophet of the Third Reich.

The widow Ludendorff was a doctor by profession, and famous in the 1920s as a standard-bearer of Hitler's ideas. The author of several books of her own on the fashionable racial theories of the day, she had expounded on the dangers of Catholicism and Judaism, the falseness of Christianity, and the need for a new and "authentic" Teutonic religion. Indeed, Francesca was led to believe, it was because of her influence that her husband threw his weight behind Hitler and his abortive *putsch*. Unlike Hitler, who spent the next six months in prison writing *Mein Kampf*, Ludendorff was acquitted at his ensuing trial.

As she sat and listened to the Schumann, Francesca glanced around the small, oppressive room. Among the select audience of attentive American officers sat Frau Ludendorff herself, dignified and calm, wearing a high-collared dress and looking considerably younger than her age. Probably, thought Francesca, she still believes all that racial theory. But what future, she wondered, could the elderly widow now see for the ideas she had once so earnestly preached, as she sat surrounded by Hitler's "mongrel race" of Americans?[1]

There were other reminders that prewar attitudes had not vanished with Germany's defeat. Soon afterwards, Francesca met a scientist whom she referred to simply as "Dr. X." His small cottage in Bavaria was marked with a huge "off limits" notice. He had worked on the V2 rocket program and was evacuated from Peenemunde when it seemed as though Bavaria might hold out as part of the Alpine Redoubt. She visited him in his modest bed-sitting room that now also served as his laboratory.

Expecting to meet a man of mature years, instead she found a tall, blond young man who spoke with a north German accent. "He looked overgrown and pale," she wrote, "like a plant forced in a cellar, but he was bland and self-possessed." He was also stiff, correct and exceedingly polite. Francesca took an immediate dislike to the detached way he spoke about the Nazi rockets, but she was curious about their range and aim. He admitted that they had not always hit their targets, but, he added, they were far better by the end.

"How are you going to use them now there is peace?" she asked.

"Well," he responded, "there is no reason why there shouldn't be a postal service. It should be possible to shoot letters to New York. They would take about forty minutes."

"But what else?" persisted Francesca.

The scientist said something about Venus and Mars, and his two associates, who were also present, chimed in enthusiastically. After a while, Dr. X interjected that all such speculation was amusing, but not important. "We scientists," he said, "know our limitations now and . . . realize that we are more dangerous than beneficial. Only doctors still retain their nineteenth-century conceit and even imagine that they will produce life some day. Science," he added, "will never create anything uncreated nor can it explain a single mystery. It lives in a quantity world and ignores quality."

No doubt, thought Francesca, this cold man regretted that Hitler's "miracle" weapon had failed to meet its creators' hopes. "When did you know that the war was lost?" she asked abruptly.

"Stalingrad was a landmark," he replied. "But in reality it was lost after Dunkirk with the Battle of Britain." He went on to tell her that the Germans had completely miscalculated the enormous build up of air power in Britain and the United States. As a result, the Third Reich had started to build underground factories far too late. And they relied on supplies such as shell-cases from Upper Silesia. "When that fell to the Russians," he explained, "we were sunk. Nothing to do but wait for the end with hands folded."

Behind him, Francesca noted a small row of stones on a shelf. She told him they reminded her of the collection of pebbles she had as a child. The scientist held a match against a red stone, which ignited, then fell to the floor and burned out harmlessly. It left behind a stifling smell. "It was pleasant to leave to go out into the starlit night," Francesca wrote, "and find the planets still cool and inaccessible, as though there were no Mephistophelian scientists plotting to disturb their inviolability." [2]

There were still plenty of Nazis in Bavaria. Indeed, some of them were already worming their way back into public life. Others had never even left. Under Charles Keegan, denazification and demilitarization were proving something of a mockery.

At the end of May, Keegan appointed Dr. Fritz Schaeffer, a former inmate of Dachau, as Minister-President of Bavaria. But Schaeffer's much-vaunted stay behind Nazi barbed wire had been brief, and his democratic credentials were feeble at best, for he was a veteran of the arch-conservative and ultra-nationalist Bavarian People's Party. No sooner did he take office than he began to appoint unreconstructed nationalists, militarists and even former Nazis to high office. His minister of economics had enriched himself under the Nazis, thanks to his friendship with the local Gauleiter. The head of the Ministry of the Interior had been chief of a pan-German nationalist propaganda front used by the Nazis and the Minister of Education was doing his best to frustrate any fundamental denazification of Bavaria's educational system. Patton was relaxed about all of this, and even went on the offensive against Eisenhower, claiming that denazification was removing too many experienced people from office. The two men were still at odds over the issue as the summer of 1945 came to an end. All too little appeared to have changed in Bavaria.[3]

It wasn't just Nazis in Germany who espoused nationalist or racist ideas and attitudes. Poles, Russians and Slavs in general were still widely despised, even more so now, given the widespread post-war looting and crime wave launched by freed slave workers. And, disturbingly, anti-Semitic views remained entrenched. While some Germans were genuinely horrified by Auschwitz, others continued to regard Jews as a race apart—and definitely unequal. Despite all the revelations about the Nazi death camps, such prejudices could still be found even among the "compassionate" professions, as one Jewish survivor of Auschwitz and Buchenwald learned that summer. After being liberated by the Americans, he found himself living in a camp outside Jena. As a qualified doctor, he was helping fellow survivors recuperate in a hospital staffed by friendly and cooperative German nurses and technicians. One day, he had to take a patient's urine specimen to the lab for analysis. While there, he took off his jacket and rolled up his sleeves, which revealed the Auschwitz number tattooed on his left arm. "What is that?" asked the young female assistant, an attractive girl to whom he had taken a bit of a fancy. He told her. She had heard the American broadcasts about Auschwitz on the radio, but wanted to know if it was true that people had been killed in gas chambers. He confirmed that it was. Her response chilled him to the core: "But those were only Jews, weren't they?"[4]

*

Such attitudes, as well as horrendous wartime experiences, helped explain what Francesca saw happening at the Feldafing camp. More than ever, she was aware that under Lieutenant Smith it was becoming a specifically Jewish camp. She decided that a Jewish woman who could speak Yiddish would carry out the welfare work far better than she herself could.

Zionism was spreading like wildfire through the camp. The majority of the Jews still housed there were Polish. "Palestine was Holy Land" to them, Francesca noted—and it was the only place clamoring for them, too. Convoys of young men left mysteriously in the night, ostensibly bound for Italy, but the word "Palestine" was loudly whispered. Rumors of pogroms in Poland increased the dread of return there and fueled Zionist dreams. The arrival nearby of the Jewish Brigade in late June intensified these feelings among the legions of Jewish DPs scattered throughout Bavaria. The brigade was a five-thousand-strong British Army unit formed of Jewish volunteers who had fought behind the Zionist standard and the star of David.

Throughout Bavaria, similar sentiment was growing rapidly in all the camps. In the eyes of UNRRA, Jews were not considered as a distinct national group, but as Polish, Romanian, or Soviet nationals—and thus they were supposed to return to Poland, Romania or the Soviet Union. But most were unwilling to do so, and with no alternative on offer, feelings of Jewish solidarity deepened and were encouraged by some influential figures. One such was an American military rabbi, Dr. Abraham Klausner, who arrived at Dachau at the end of May and eventually, thanks to UNRRA, set up an office in Munich where he tirelessly pressured the American occupation authorities to recognize the Jews as a distinct group.

With a number of sympathizers such as Lieutenant Smith at Feldafing, it was no surprise that the camp was the scene of a momentous declaration that summer. On Sunday 1 July, forty-three Jewish delegates from across Bavaria met there to formulate a policy for the future. The assembly's final act was to pass a resolution directed at the allied powers who were about to meet at Potsdam, asking that all Jews who wished to emigrate to Palestine should be allowed to do so as the first step towards creating a Jewish state. It was a significant turning point. The story of the liberation from Nazism was ending and a new one was beginning: this was the start of the struggle to create the state of Israel.[5]

*

While Jews in the camps of Europe wrestled with their future, the fate of Trieste was being decided in Italy. Since liberation, life for many Italians under Yugoslav rule in the city had felt more like prison than freedom. By contrast, among many Slovenes both there and in villages throughout Venezia Giulia, enthusiasm for Tito ran high.

So did military tension. The opposing armies remained on the alert while Churchill and Truman demanded that Tito back down and they put heavy diplomatic pressure on Stalin to twist the arm of his ally. It was the first real example of the challenge facing the West as depicted by Churchill in his "iron curtain" telegram to Truman. "This is a small problem," declared the Italian writer Gaetano Salvemini in *The Times*, "but it is a test case of the method by which larger analogous difficulties will be calmed — or envenomed, and World War Three made unavoidable within the next few years."[6]

But Stalin was not yet ready to try the West's resolve by openly defying his allies, and he refused to throw his support behind Tito. This forced the Yugoslav dictator to retreat. Four weeks after VE Day, he finally agreed to withdraw his forces from a large part of the contested province, including the cities of Trieste, Gorizia and Monfalcone.

Within days, the Yugoslavs began to evacuate the territory and abandon the frontier on the Isonzo they had coveted for so long. Geoffrey Cox and the New Zealanders watched as on foot, in motor vehicles and in long horse-drawn convoys thousands of Tito's troops headed sullenly east and south, leaving Trieste behind them. They did not go empty-handed, though. Ignoring the fine print of the agreement, they stripped machinery and accessories from garages, and emptied barracks, hotels and houses of their contents. "The amount of loot," noted one official source, "seemed to be limited only by the paucity of transport."[7] In the areas they quit, the allies moved in quickly to establish military government. "So ended the struggle for Trieste," remarked Cox, still toiling away in the intelligence truck at General Freyberg's headquarters at Miramare Castle.

He was too optimistic. The allies had certainly won the diplomatic war and made the Yugoslav forces withdraw, but a political battle now broke out to rid the city of Tito's influence. During the month that the Yugoslavs occupied Trieste, they purged its administration of unfriendly Italians and placed communists and their sympathizers in dozens of important positions. In the weeks that followed, allied military government struggled hard to counteract their influence. In early

July, two months after VE Day and four weeks after Tito's forces reluctantly straggled out of the city, British intelligence issued a pessimistic report. Throughout the region, it observed, the occupying forces were faced with continuous passive obstruction from local councils of liberation encouraged by hostile propaganda from Belgrade Radio and an unfriendly local press.

In Trieste itself, there were Yugoslav "stay-behind" organizations numbering in total between six and seven thousand people, of whom about half were probably former members of the Yugoslav Army. The *Guardia del Popolo*, or people's militia, was formally dissolved at the end of June amid protests and riots, but it clandestinely retained its identity and its members had caches of arms. Many of them volunteered for the new police force being created by the allies in the hope of penetrating and influencing it.

The scene in Trieste was thus far from simple, and its future certainly was not settled. The past and the present eddied around each other in a witches' brew of ethnic and political antagonism. "Agents-provocateurs, trained propagandists, and toughs are the normal tools of any political party in the Balkans," reported British intelligence. But their activities in Trieste were due to the continuing significance attached to the city by the Yugoslavs and the underground experience they had gained in fighting the Germans. There was also a powerful and legitimate sense of grievance among the Slovenes that was easily exploited by Tito's propagandists. They had been systematically and actively persecuted by the Italians during the twenty years of Mussolini's dictatorship, and the communists had good reason to mistrust a large percentage of the Italian population in the region. After all, as British intelligence recognized, it had "as bad a record of collaboration with both Nazis and Fascists as any area in Italy."[8]

Three days before this report was circulated to allied units in Venezia Giulia, a particularly brutal case of mass murder in an adjacent Italian province showed that settling the score with Fascists remained an issue equally alive in the rest of the country. On the night of Friday 6 July, a group of fifteen masked men approached the prison at Schio, an industrial town in the province of Vicenza. Situated in an otherwise conservative and Catholic area, it had a militant workers' movement and was a hotbed of wartime partisan activity. The men forced the head jailer to hand over the keys, cut the telephone lines and forced the other guards to leave.

Inside were about a hundred prisoners, both men and women, accused of various Fascist misdemeanors. Most were little more than small-time supporters of Mussolini, but at least one was alleged to have sent local anti-Fascists to Mauthausen. As the masked men broke in, chaos broke out. The prisoners refused to organize in groups as ordered and the intruders opened fire. Finally, fifty-four prisoners lay dead, thirteen of them women. The perpetrators were local communist partisans. It was the worst single incident of such violence over the summer of 1945, but it was by no means the last, and killings of Fascists would continue into the following year.

This was yet another reminder that, for Italy, the Second World War was also a civil war scarred deep with fraternal hatred. Yet feelings ran particularly high because of Fascism's intimate links with German Nazism. The massacre at Schio followed closely on the return to the town of a survivor from Mauthausen and the screening of film footage about the liberation of other Nazi camps. Popular outrage, combined with a growing fear that justice might never be done, produced an inflammatory and lynch-mob mood. The post-war Italian government had not yet established control over its people.[9]

The death and violence of war was much on the mind of Robert Ellis. The machine-gun-squad leader in the US Tenth Mountain Division was still stationed near Udine in northeast Italy. His *All Quiet on the Western Front* nightmare of being killed in the last hour of the war had subsided, but left behind were the dreadful scenes of battlefield carnage he had survived. He was a thoughtful and sensitive son who shared many of his deepest feelings frankly with his parents. Many young soldiers writing home kept a relentlessly upbeat tone, so as not to worry their families. Ellis was an exception.

The first day of July was a Sunday. By now, it was getting hot even early in the day, so he sat down and wrote another long letter to his mother and father. He had just turned down the offer of an appointment at West Point Military Academy, having come to despise almost every aspect of army life. "I've seen enough ghastly battles and death to last me a long time," he confessed in an outpouring of feeling. "In a way I'm glad I did see combat for I've got the true picture of what war is like aside from all the hullabaloo and glamour." War for the infantryman was not a pretty sight, he explained. It was no longer a battle of individuals but purely impersonal, machine versus machine. "You never associate the enemy soldier with your hatred," he went on. "You hate the shells screaming overhead, you hate the bullets singing by your ears coming from an unseen force, but you see the enemy only as a distant spot, like a target on the rifle range." War was no longer man against man, spear against spear, but just a "vast holocaust" of destruction through which bewildered soldiers moved like automatons. True, there were moments of heroism, but mostly it was a matter of braving bullets and shells and hoping to emerge alive at the other side. He had probably killed many men, he admitted, but the only one whose face he had seen was the sniper he had shot with his pistol.[10]

With the outbreak of peace, his emotions were riding a roller coaster. The regimental "F" Company reports through June and July spoke blandly of the food being good and the morale high, as though one fed simply off the other. Yet they also recorded events that sent Ellis's spirits plunging. It was hardly reassuring or comforting to attend briefings on "Jap tactics," or to be shown a movie entitled *On the Road to Tokyo*, especially after Tito's backdown removed most of their reason for being in Italy and brought a likely transfer to the Pacific ever closer. Nor did it help to be constantly training for some future ground attack or, for that matter, to be lectured about venereal disease.[11]

There were a few bright spots. Ellis was awarded the Bronze Star, he was playing and winning regular competitive tennis with a partner, and he was finally feeling more comfortable giving orientation lectures to the men. But overall, his mood was edgy. Like dozens of others in the division he wanted out of any future fighting. But all his efforts at shifting into something less dangerous than being an infantryman hauling a machine-gun — such as being assigned to permanent occupation duties, becoming a divisional historian, or joining the military police — came to nothing. Frustrated, he watched as many of his buddies somehow managed the trick while he remained behind.

It hit particularly hard when his best friend in the company, Larry Boyajian, left for military police duty with the Fifth Army in Austria. Ellis had lost a number of good buddies either killed or wounded, and Larry was the only one he could still really talk to. They had survived some amazing experiences together, from the terrifying mortar attack in mid-April and his shooting of the sniper that had won him the Bronze Star to their madcap ride in the German staff car. "He'll never make it to the Pacific now," noted Ellis enviously of his friend.[12]

But what really punched him in the stomach was the letter he received from his girlfriend Pat, who had been the "light of his life" ever since he had left the States. It was the "Dear John" heartbreak letter familiar to thousands of other young men serving overseas. The day after Larry left, Ellis made a laconic entry in his diary: "Pat maintains again she doesn't love me, but hopes to when I return. Beginning to regard the bachelor's life as best. I'm getting used to it."[13]

Getting back into the swing of married and family life was exactly what British ex–war correspondent Robert Reid was happily doing. "Gosh, how good it's going to be watching Dicky riding his bike, and Elizabeth going around like a big girl, and *you* darling," he typed to his wife, Vera, before leaving Austria on his tour home via Berchtesgaden and Paris. It was not just ten-year-old Elizabeth who was growing up fast. Richard, aged eight, had picked up enough of the news to pontificate solemnly on VE Day that only half the war was over and that "we still have to fight the Japs."[14]

In the days following the German surrender, Vera could hardly contain her impatience to have her husband back home. His letter telling her of his plans to return slowly had not yet arrived, so she took matters into her own hands and phoned the Manchester BBC office, asking them to contact London and find out the date of his return. The children's Whitsun holiday was coming up and she certainly did not want to take them to their grandmother's only to find her husband standing at the door when they returned, waiting to get in. But London seemed clueless. "Just come home," she wrote impatiently to Robert a week after VE Day, "it seems to me your job is finished, anyway I should make it so." What clinched it as far as she was concerned was that recently all the news from Patton's Third Army seemed to be coming from Reid's BBC colleague, Frank Gillard, and not from her husband. Her jealous, loyal loathing of Gillard continued. She once even told Robert she would happily strangle the man. It was definitely time for Reid to get home.

By early June, he was. Four years before, he had proudly put on his brand-new uniform with its green and gold shoulder tabs bearing the words "*British War Correspondent*" and the circular green and gold cap badge with the single letter "C" in the center. He also had a blue War Office identity pass containing a slip of paper saying that if he was taken prisoner, he was to be treated like an officer with the rank of captain. Happily, he never had to use it, and now his uniform was already gathering dust. Each morning, instead of clambering into a jeep for a bone-rattling, day-long ride to the battlefront for a story, he was commuting from home near Stockport into Manchester and the BBC regional office to carry out his role as north regional publicity officer. Robert Reid's war was definitely over.

But for American paratrooper Leonard Linton, the most fascinating part of his war was yet to come. Hardly had he arrived back in France than rumors began to fly that the division was destined for Berlin, where its mission was to serve as part of the allied occupation force. For the Eighty-second Airborne, as for every other allied fighting unit in Europe, Hitler's capital had always been the goal. Only a few weeks before, the All-Americans had come close to making a parachute drop into the city before Eisenhower decided otherwise and let the Soviets take the city.

But this did not undo the wartime agreement giving the Western allies post-war control of the three western sectors of the German capital. There had been weeks of high-level negotiation with Stalin about making their arrival in Berlin coincide with their withdrawal from parts of eastern Germany that had been assigned to the Soviets, such as Thuringia and Mecklenburg. Throughout May and June, Churchill urged the Americans not to withdraw their troops from beyond the Elbe before the Potsdam Conference, during which their presence could be used as a bargaining tool with Stalin. But Truman decided otherwise, and late in June the massive shift of forces began, with American forces also leaving those western parts of Czechoslovakia they had entered during the last few days of fighting. There was just one crumb of consolation for Churchill. Soviet forces in the British zone of Austria now also withdrew into their own zone, thus virtually guaranteeing that Austria, at least, would not slip behind the Iron Curtain.

As the Americans left, they took with them hundreds of German scientists, along with their equipment and their families. A few days later, the American chiefs of staff gave their approval to "Operation Overcast," an ambitious program to transfer more than three hundred of Germany and Austria's best scientists to the United States. "Overcast" marked the culmination of efforts that started before D-Day with the drawing up of lists of the main scientific targets in Germany. After entering Germany, a special unit inside SHAEF known as T-Force hunted down targets and removed equipment from such major prizes as the V2 plant at Nordhausen. The allies were astonished to discover how advanced German science and technology was in many different fields. The British chiefs of staff in July 1945 concluded that Germany was "well in advance" of Britain in the fields of high-speed aerodynamics, ballistics and rocketry.[15]

Alarmed by this, the allies' first priority was to determine what had been passed on by the Nazis to the Japanese. Then they bent their efforts to preventing as much as possible from falling into Soviet hands. Finally, they decided to harness as many as possible of the best German scientific brains to their own military and scientific needs. "The more that is learnt of German preparations and progress with new weapons," declared *The Times* at the end of June, "the more apparent is it that the allies ended the war with Germany just in time . . . It is not too much to say that the Germans were in the act of switching from one kind of war to another." It was all the more important, therefore, to recruit Germany's scientists for allied purposes. Wernher von Braun, the youthful genius behind the V2 rocket who gladly turned himself over to the Americans in May 1945, was only one of several dozen German scientists to move almost immediately to America.[16]

As the allies pulled out of eastern Germany, the Soviets withdrew from the western sectors of Berlin. Here, the allies hoped to stage a grand and symbolic entrance into the defeated capital. But Stalin was equally determined to show who was really boss on the ground, and as he controlled access to the city, he found plenty of ways to spoil the show. The result was a delayed and staggered entry.

Linton was one of the first Americans to reach the city, as his unit was designated as an advance guard of the Eighty-second Airborne's occupation force. Luckily, he still had the little Berlin street map picked up in Paris in April, when he thought he would be parachuting into the German capital. His unit set off in convoy along the deserted Hanover-Berlin *autobahn*. They were half expecting to be stopped, but they crossed without trouble through the Soviet checkpoint at the small town of Helmstedt, where rough wooden poles and oil drums marked the makeshift zonal border. At fifteen- or twenty-mile intervals, they passed huge signs in Russian praising Lenin and the Red Army. Linton translated the slogans for the others in his jeep.

At about the same time, eighty press jeeps carrying more than two hundred allied correspondents was also speeding towards the city. This convoy had an unexpected encounter with an advance guard of the Red

Army, which was moving in the opposite direction to replace the Americans withdrawing from Thuringia. The freshly painted and polished allied armored vehicles contrasted sharply with those of the Russians. "The outbound Russians were a rabble," reported one of the Western correspondents.

> Their padded cotton jackets were grease-stained and threadbare, their transport a hodgepodge of antiquated trucks and horse-drawn wagons piled high with looted furniture, and more than half of them traveled on foot. But these were the men who had beaten Hitler's vast armies on the Eastern Front. They looked inured to hardship, and utterly indifferent to the show of mechanized might put on to impress them.

Eventually, Linton's unit reached Potsdam. The great palaces built by Frederick the Great stood empty and wrecked, although their treasures were now being unearthed from salt mines and caves across Germany. But the paratroopers did not stop. Instead, they drove on past burned-out Soviet tanks, deserted and shallow foxholes hastily improvised by the Germans, and increasing piles of rubble. "I could readily visualize the Wehrmacht caught completely off guard by the Red Army," Linton recorded, "after they encircled Berlin."

Finally, they reached the heart of the city itself.[17]

The Americans officially took control of their sector of Berlin on Wednesday 4 July, Independence Day. In a brief ceremony held at the Adolf Hitler Barracks, General Baranov, the local Soviet commander, formally passed responsibility over to General Omar Bradley.

Hours before, an American journalist, James O'Donnell, had flown into the city to establish *Newsweek*'s German bureau in the capital. He was also on an urgent mission to write up the last days of Hitler in the bunker. To get speedily from Tempelhof Airport to the Chancellery, he flagged down a passing jeep, the only moving object he could see in the static urban silence. Its occupants were a couple of Eighty-second Airborne paratroopers, who happily volunteered to show him the Brandenburg Gate — if he could show them where it was. Laboriously, they wound their way through the labyrinths of rubble along the only path cleared for vehicles. They would have gone faster, thought O'Donnell, in a Sherman tank or a bulldozer.[18]

The main body of British troops arrived the next day, marching in under the stony but interested gaze of spectators who lined the route into the city from Spandau. Pride of place was given to men of the Seventh Armored Division, the so-called Desert Rats, men who had started this journey five years before in the North African desert. The ceremony was held in drizzling rain at the foot of the Victory Column, the great statue erected to commemorate Germany's crushing defeat of the French in 1871. The Union Jack was unfurled, and green-uniformed members of the German police force offered a smart salute. The landmark column stood on the great east-west axis running through the Tiergarten that led to the Brandenburg Gate. Beyond, lay Unter den Linden and the Soviet sector. Only a few weeks before, the avenue had served as an emergency landing strip for Nazis as the Red Army tightened its grip around the city. Local British, American, Russian and French commanders watched as the troops marched past, the salute was taken and the national anthem was played.[19]

That same day, electors went to the polls in Britain in the country's first general election since 1935. The British troops in Berlin, as elsewhere across Europe and overseas, were allowed to cast their ballots where they were stationed. Both Conservatives and Labour, the two main parties, felt confident of victory. The day before, Churchill had made a final grand tour of London constituencies and was widely lauded as the man who led his country to victory. But at one meeting, he received a very mixed reception and was booed. It was a straw in the wind.

Leonard Linton's arrival in Berlin was not just a conquest but a home-coming. He got up early the morning after he arrived and headed in his jeep towards the residential district of Schoneberg. The rubble in the streets was piled so high that he had to take endless detours. So many buildings were wrecked or gone altogether that he could not always recognize where he was or the direction in which he was heading, and in the end his little map proved of little use. Instead, he relied on the sun's position to guide him. There was still no petrol supply, water supply was erratic, and many of the city's trams had been turned into barricades. Their derelict hulks still littered the streets and made his progress all the more tortuous. Eventually, though, he found the apart-ment block on Aschaffenburger Strasse where his family had lived before the war. It was here that he had learned the German that he now used every day, and where he had flirted innocently and briefly with the

Hitler Youth. But the building was nothing more than a roofless and hollowed-out shell, with nothing to keep him there but memories.

He had better luck tracing his half-sister, Irene, last seen before the rest of the family fled from the Nazis. William Shirer, the American journalist who was back in the city from where he had reported vividly on the rise of the Nazis, helped Linton track her down to a partially destroyed building. There she was living with Inge Zimmerman, a friend from prewar days, and her family. Two of Inge's brothers had been killed on the Eastern Front, and the third injured. They were all haggard, but insisted they were fine — at least none of them was sick or obviously starving.

Irene had been raped by the Russians when they captured the city. Linton was able to arrange for her to have a prompt medical examination, and to her relief she learned she had not contracted a venereal disease. After a while, he was also able to help her move to the upmarket area of Wannsee. The only thing that jarred was the presence nearby of a Soviet war monument featuring a T34 tank, supposedly the first Red Army tank to enter the city. Linton found it disturbing that its cannon was still facing west.[20]

Irene and her friends were no worse off than most of the Berlin population. Two months after Hitler's suicide, the special correspondent for *The Times* painted a vivid picture of a city still "numbed and prostrate" from the cataclysm that had swept over it. The people who remained were mostly women, children and old men, their energies determinedly focused on getting enough food to eat day by day in order to survive. Compared with the bustling prewar scene, there was barely a flicker of movement along the broad avenues in the center of the city, where people trudged along with bowed heads and burdened backs. On top of the high mounds of rubble from the bombed and shelled buildings, the correspondent reported, great human chains, formed mostly of women, were shifting the debris with buckets that looked ludicrously small for the task. His report was datelined Thursday 5 July, the same day that the news broke of the continued euthanasia killings at the Kaufbeuren Institute in Bavaria.[21]

A young British officer reached Berlin at the same time as Leonard Linton and had an instant and overwhelming reaction to what met his eyes. The city was dominated by a single color. "The ruins were gray, the trees were gray, the houses were gray, even people's faces were gray," wrote Richard Brett-Smith of Hitler's devastated capital. "About all the uprooted dwellings and smashed and acrid rubble hung a thin gray dust which chalked the clothes and faces of those who poked about in them, the prying visitors, the ghouls, and the *Trummerfrauen* or gangs of women sorting bricks." Everywhere, it seemed, despair, apathy and aimlessness seemed to have taken root.[22] Yet the gangs of women sorting bricks were also, paradoxically, a sign of life and renewal. And they were not the only ones hard at work.

One of the minor industries in Berlin was the collecting of cigarette butts. Once these were amalgamated into new cigarettes they acted as valuable currency — perhaps the most important item of barter and exchange that summer. "Enterprising people who had a corner in cigarette paper, or had acquired superfine toilet paper," explained one senior British officer, "employed hundreds of people, children among them, to collect cigarette ends." The collectors were known as *Kippensammler*, and all had their special beats, like prostitutes or beggars. They struck deals with chambermaids, head waiters, and cinema and cabaret managers. Gangs of boys hovered around the entrances to allied messes, troops' clubs and cinemas, ready to pounce when someone stubbed out a cigarette or threw it, still smoking, to the ground. Many waiters collected ends as assiduously as they once had tips. All across the city, small factories sprang up in abandoned or bombed-out buildings, where small armies of men and women sorted the tobacco and rolled and gummed newly formed cigarettes.

The cigarette was small, could be stored in compact containers, was not quickly perishable, and was always in high demand. The most desirable were English and American brands. For the very best, the going rate was between seven and ten marks per cigarette. Discarded cigarette packets were also in high demand. If packed carefully, they could be made to look original and command a higher price.

"It was not long," reported the British officer, "before the Allied soldier realized the vast purchasing and persuasive power he had in his possession of cigarettes." As he was handed out free cigarettes by the army, he could make money out of them, save all his pay, and purchase at knockdown prices a vast array of goods flooding the market, such as fountain pens, jewels, watches, antiques, diamonds and binoculars. "The demand for cigarettes was so great," reported the officer, "that many inveterate smokers rationed themselves, or even gave up smoking, to take advantage of the market."

Another British soldier in Berlin was making so much money that it began to haunt him. "I hid the money in all kinds of places, in my old kit bag, in old socks, in the lining of my tunic," he confessed. "The money began to get on my mind, and I couldn't sleep. I used to go into the latrine and count it. I remember one day counting, to my horror, eight thousand marks. That came to £200, and I had never had more than £5 in my life. I decided that I must get rid of it, and at a faster rate."

Hardly any of the cigarettes were actually smoked by the person who bought them. "They passed from person to person at a profit, or in payment for glass for windows, for wood, food and clothes," noted the British officer. "One packet of cigarettes might change hands a hundred times and, in its travels, bring to a succession of people the things on which their lives or their health depended."[23]

It was no wonder that at least one of the city's nightclubs, the Kabaret Roxy, carried a sign outside its door announcing: "*ALLES FÜR 10 ZIGARETTEN.*" And behind the whole phenomenon there lurked a grim and ironic joke. It had taken Hitler, a non-smoker, to reduce his capital to this.

The allied soldier with an endless supply of cigarettes was a powerful figure. He could also easily buy sex, as the soldier who had begun to lose sleep over his money soon found out. One day, he went to a café where he had been many times before. There, sitting in her usual place, was a German girl of about eighteen. She always sat alone and drank what looked like colored water. This time, the British soldier went over to her and bought her a drink. Until then, he had not taken much notice of any women in Berlin—he had been married only a couple of years. She looked like an English girl of twenty-two or twenty-three, he thought, and was fair with blue eyes, but very pale. She spoke no English, and he spoke no German, but he took her to a dance and paid for her meal. "I felt like a millionaire!" he said. Then he took her home on a tram. After that, they met several more times, going to either the cinema or a dance. All the time, he could see she was hungry.

He began to feel first sorry for her, then responsible for her. "She was nice, so pathetically gay," he explained. She reminded him of a stray dog that would not leave his heels and would starve if he did not take care of her. After a while, they learned how to exchange some words. Once he gave her a bar of chocolate, and she nearly went crazy. At another time, he handed her a piece of soap, which she immediately sold for fifty marks to buy bread on the black market.

One night it was raining. She took him by the arm and led him to the block of flats where she lived. It had been hit by artillery, and the top two floors were burned out. She lived on the third floor and had two rooms and a small kitchen. There was no glass left in the windows, but cloth and boards had been fitted to make the place private. There was a photograph in one room of her mother, who had killed herself when the Russians reached the city. Her father had been killed in the fighting. There was a photograph of him, too.

"I made a sign to ask if there was any food in the house, and she thought I wanted to eat," he said. "She went to a cupboard and I followed her. In the cupboard were a few potatoes, a cupful of flour and some salt. Half a loaf was wrapped in newspaper and she offered me that. I shook my head. It was not easy to make her understand that I did not want to eat anything." Most of the furniture had been taken by the Russians, and there was no coal or wood for heating. The place was cold. In the bedroom, there were no beds, just two settees. She pushed them together. Later, she told him she was going out into the countryside for a couple of days to hunt for potatoes. He could not stand it anymore. Opening his wallet, he handed her four fifty-mark notes. "She did not want them," he said. "She cried."

Sometimes, he felt almost sick about the power he had over her. "She was just like my slave," he said, "she darned my socks and mended things for me." There was no question of marriage, and she knew it. Still, she found him a Leica camera in exchange for cigarettes, and he gave her his money to look after. She told him she knew where she could also find a diamond ring.[24]

This was the Berlin now occupied by the allies. No wonder the city was known as a "sentimental desert." Everywhere, women went about alone. The number of German men in the city had halved since 1939, and there were nearly three women to every man, many of whom were wounded, unemployed or penniless. Marriage bureaus sprang up, but they were of no help to women who could provide no proof that their husbands had been killed in an air raid or at the front. "So, in cellar dives and basements," writes Douglas Botting, "the tribe of Frauleins mingled with the Allied soldiery and plied their trade in half-destroyed rooms among the ruins."[25] This was the city that would soon be hosting Stalin, Truman and Churchill at the "Victory" conference.

CHAPTER TWENTY-SIX

MONDAY, 16 JULY 1945

With his somber "iron curtain" telegram to Truman, Churchill had tried to persuade the President that together they should reach a rapid understanding with Moscow. And for that, he felt strongly, it was vital to have a personal meeting as soon as possible. He hoped that it might be held in London, but if not, then he could envisage some none-too-wrecked city in western Germany.

In the end, however, both men had to yield to Stalin's insistence that it take place in Potsdam, on the outskirts of Hitler's ruined capital, on territory occupied by the Red Army. Deciding on this venue took almost a month—and then, instead of the meeting taking place in June, as Churchill had hoped, it was finally scheduled for the middle of July, more than two months after Germany's surrender. This was because the allied commanders-in-chief did not meet until early June to assume supreme authority in Germany officially, and it took them another month after that to set up the Allied Control Council that was supposed to coordinate policy for the whole of the country.

In the meantime, Churchill's anxiety for Europe's future steadily grew. It was a relief to have Truman support him in his robust stand against Tito's grab for Trieste, but when the Prime Minister met with his chiefs of staff in early June, he was consumed with pessimism. "Winston gave a long and very gloomy review of the situation in Europe," noted Field Marshal Brooke in his diary. "Never in his life had he been more worried about the situation in Europe."

Yet, on the eve of Potsdam, confusion reigned, and a desperate situation was emerging in Germany. A week before the conference opened, General Montgomery sent a warning of the unfolding crisis in the British zone, which included the most heavily industrialized and densely populated regions of the country. He had twenty million Germans to feed, he pointed out, plus uncounted millions of displaced persons and at least two million war veterans. Virtually every major town was a ruin, and country roads were regularly cut off by roadblocks. There was no sign of any serious resistance to the British, but many identity papers were proving false and the occupation was facing serious problems. Not the least of these was the ban on fraternization. This, he thought, should be lifted at once. "We cannot reeducate twenty million people," he insisted, "if we are never to speak to them."

Above all, though, loomed the future of the economy during the next few months, especially the supply of food and fuel. What would happen here depended heavily on how the four allies would manage their four-power control. They had won the war against Hitler, but now they faced another struggle that was almost as tough — the "Battle of Winter." Would they fight this together or divided? Was there to be one Germany or two? "There is in fact," reported Montgomery gloomily, "a complete 'wall' between the Russian zone and the zones of the western allies." A SHAEF intelligence report confirmed this: "We have very little evidence," it stated, "from which to assess Russian policy towards the part of Germany which they occupy."[1]

On Monday 16 July, the American and British Pacific fleets launched their first combined naval action against the Japanese mainland with hundreds of carrier-borne aircraft raiding in and around Tokyo. Meanwhile, three of the biggest US battleships, the *Iowa*, the *Wisconsin* and the *Missouri*, poured hundreds of sixteen-inch shells into the port of Muroran on southern Hokkaido from less than a mile offshore, and fleets of Super-Fortresses struck at numerous other targets. Japan's cities were now ablaze, but Emperor Hirohito still went on the radio to exhort his air force to fight on with all its power to ensure the safety of the throne. There was little sign of peace in the Pacific.

In Britain, however, a peacetime mood was definitely taking hold. For most of the war, city streetlights had remained firmly switched off, but on 15 July, for the first time in six years, London's lights were turned on in a blaze of splendor and thousands of people flooded into the West End and Piccadilly Circus to enjoy the spectacle. That weekend, crowds braved severe thunderstorms and lightning strikes to flock into the capital's mainline train stations, determined to enjoy an escape from the city. Many queued for hours to board packed trains, and seaside resorts became severely overcrowded because dozens of hotels requisitioned for wartime purposes remained closed for business. But those who persisted were rewarded: England's Channel coast was bathed in sunshine and enjoyed temperatures in the mid-eighties. At Hastings, the holiday makers cheered when illuminations along the resort's three-mile-long seafront were switched on at dusk.

Across the Channel, though, much of Europe still felt far from peace. Belgium was embroiled in bitter controversy over the future of King Leopold, who had refused to go into exile during the war and was accused of having been too friendly to the Germans. In Austria, wartime debris and rubbish lay six feet high in the streets and typhus had taken hold. France enjoyed three days of Bastille Day celebrations, the first to be celebrated in freedom since 1939. There was a march down the Champs-Elysées to the Arc de Triomphe headed by General de Lattre de Tassigny, commander of the First French Army, followed by fireworks and street dances into the early hours. But the mood was darkened by growing disquiet over the rough justice still being handed out to collaborators, as well as the execution of "small fry." Meanwhile, Paris itself was preparing for the biggest fish of all—Marshal Pétain. His trial for treason was due to begin the following week.

Francesca Wilson enjoyed Bastille Day. On Saturday 14 July, she was in a small village with a company of French soldiers who had been invited in by the Americans to help with transport. The French were billeted in an old Bavarian inn with a dance hall and Francesca joined in the dancing while the commandant of the troops, a white-haired, elderly man, kissed the girls and "gave jollity and sanction" to the occasion.

Francesca had recently moved from Feldafing to another camp in Bavaria called Föhrenwald, just a few miles away. But in almost every respect it felt like a world away. In 1939, the Nazis had built a model village to house workers in a large munitions plant hidden in the nearby pine woods. It was a classic example of Nazi workers' welfare, with well-designed houses and carefully laid-out streets, and was well equipped with modern kitchens, laundry, baths, a hospital, canteen and theater. By the end of the war, it housed mainly slave laborers. When

Francesca arrived, it was well on its way to becoming one of the largest displaced persons' camps in Germany, with over five thousand inhabitants.

She found it a far happier place than Feldafing, which remained an essentially tragic camp peopled with Holocaust survivors with unsmiling faces and haunted eyes. At Föhrenwald, she responded warmly to Lieutenant Harkness, the camp's quick-witted, energetic and firm young American commandant. He had fought with Patch's Seventh Army in North Africa and Italy and taken part in the conquest of Bavaria. "I told him at once," she wrote, "that we would not interfere with his administration of the camp, and from that moment on, work with him was easy and light-hearted."[2]

The camp's accommodations and the nature of its inhabitants helped as well. Instead of huge impersonal barracks and dormitories, people were living as families in houses, much as they had at home, with each street peopled by a different nationality, so that genuine small neighborhoods developed. There were about a dozen national groups. Strictly speaking, some of them should not have been there because they belonged to "enemy" groups, such as Austrians, Hungarians, and the German-speaking *Volksdeutsch* from Yugoslavia, but the military had put them in the camp to get them out of neighboring villages. They caused little trouble with the other groups, especially when forced to cooperate on solving practical problems, which made Francesca think of the camp as a "little United Nations."

It was not without its problems, however. To keep its high-grade services running, it needed a fairly large staff of German technicians, and for a while this provided cover for SS men on the run along the escapers' highway from Munich to Switzerland. But Germans in the village who were keen to ingratiate themselves with the Americans turned them in, and over thirty were caught.

Francesca witnessed one such catch. A pale young German with unkempt hair was standing in the commandant's office. He was accused of being in the SS. "Take off your shirt," ordered Harkness quietly. The young man did as he was told. "Lift up your arm," commanded the American. When he did so, the small "0" tattooed just above his armpit was revealed. "That's his blood type," explained Harkness. "We've caught thousands that way. Hitler made the job very simple for us." Already, some ten thousand ex-SS men were crowded behind barbed wire at Dachau.

What Francesca really enjoyed at Föhrenwald was working with its eight hundred children. The Americans had not had time to set up any special services for them, so happily left that up to the UNRRA team. Francesca busied herself going about the camp, talking to its occupants about the children's needs, finding teachers, and helping establish schools in six different languages — Polish, Estonian, Lithuanian, Hungarian, Serb and German. The kindergarten and nursery schools proved exceptionally good, and one in particular enchanted Francesca. It was run by a young Estonian woman with a genius for handling small children. Whenever she found that dealing with the occupants' insoluble problems got too much for her, Francesca would escape from her office and watch the woman singing and playing with the children under the pine trees. "She cast a spell over [them]," she wrote. "They sang and they danced, they were bears one minute and birds the next — even babies of two joined in and tried to imitate her gestures."[3]

It was all very innocent and hopeful, a bright spot in an otherwise somber landscape because there were always chilling signs to remind Francesca of how the innocent world of children had been infected by Nazism. One day she went into Munich to search for infant-school textbooks to use in the camp. She found a series that looked promising in beautifully bound covers. But then she opened one and read a math question: "Germany has 100,000 epileptics and 250,000 mental defectives. It costs 2.50 marks a day to keep each of them. How many babies could go to nursery school at a cost of 1 mark daily for the same sum?" In the end, all existing textbooks had to be scrapped and new ones introduced before German schools were allowed to reopen.

Francesca also helped organize entertainment in the camp. The Cossacks had their choir and dancers, the Estonians their folk songs, the Hungarians their waltzes and jazz players, the Austrians good singers. But the star was a Polish violinist named Kasimir Koszelinski, who prewar had played in the highly admired Busch Quartet, then hid a Jew in his Warsaw apartment and played in secret to raise money for the resistance before being caught and sent as a slave laborer to Germany. While he was there, a factory director who had heard him play professionally in Italy before the war gave him a sinecure at the Föhrenwald munitions works. Now, he was playing every Sunday to the camp's freed but still imprisoned inmates.

The Föhrenwald hospital was run by Hungarians, most of whom had fled Budapest in November 1944 when the Fascist leader Ferenc Szálasi took power after Hitler's forces entered the country and Adolf Eichmann arrived to "cleanse" the country of its Jews. They were all specialists, with their own lab technicians and X-ray personnel. In Francesca's words, writing before the establishment of Britain's National Health Service, they transformed the hospital into "the kind of Utopian Health Centre we hope one day to have in England."[4] She made her own contribution to the camp's health by breaking through military red tape and getting milk, vitamins, chocolate and cod-liver oil for the children.

It was all too good to last. One day, an American colonel arrived and ordered the "enemy" DPs to be evacuated because the Austrians, Hungarians and Yugoslav *Volksdeutsch* were a German responsibility and so should be dispersed to German villages. The decree was put into effect almost immediately: the offending groups were driven out of the camp in trucks and dumped into villages all over Upper Bavaria. For days, Francesca was besieged with piteous tales of no beds for the children, no cooking utensils and no work. In the British zone there were plenty of Quaker relief workers ready and willing to look after ex-enemy civilians and ethnic German expellees, but there was no such service in the American zone. For these victims of war, the struggle back to normality was still far from over.

Even worse was the sudden removal of several Lithuanian and Polish families to make way for an unexpected influx of stateless Jews. The Lithuanians, including almost a hundred children and babies, were removed to a dismal barracks with broken windows, beds full of bugs and no drinking water. The Poles had just got their school and kindergarten up and running in Föhrenwald. It made Francesca furious. "I hate the army," she stormed at the red-faced captain in charge of the move. "Why don't you go and fight someone? Why do you meddle with civilians?"

UNRRA's relations with the army had never been clearly defined, but despite Francesca's fury she knew that without the military the situation would have been much worse. Only they, at this stage, had the muscle and the money to organize food supplies. UNRRA's own sources of food were slated for allied countries where starvation was an imminent threat, such as Greece and Yugoslavia, not Germany. And even as she was protesting, her agency's director-general was announcing in Rome that it had been forced to impose severe cutbacks on its imports of supplies into Europe. These included clothing, textiles, fuel, raw materials and essential foodstuffs, such as fats and tinned fish. The problem was no longer one of shipping, as it had been up to now, but hoarding by suppliers anxious about the coming winter.[5]

The happy Föhrenwald camp was a rarity in the usually depressing world of DP camps in the summer of 1945. Millions of inmates were still awaiting repatriation in miserable conditions and food was short. Living amid helpless German civilians, many DPs seized the opportunity to find food, alcohol and women, and sometimes to wreak revenge on their former captors. Cases of murder, rape and looting grew. By July, many DP camps in the British zone were surrounded by barbed wire and sentries, and curfews had been imposed on their inmates.

It even became necessary to rearm the German police. "The Germans," noted one report, "have lost faith in our ability to maintain law and order." There was also violence in the camps between different national groups and among various political groupings. The situation worsened when representatives from the new communist regimes of Eastern Europe, as well as Soviet army officers, urged inmates to return home. Ten days before the Potsdam Conference, there was a fracas in one camp when a Soviet guard shot dead a Russian DP and in turn was lynched by an infuriated mob.[6]

Cape Bretoner Reg Roy was still stranded on the northern shores of the Zuider Zee. But on Friday 13 July, he received a triple boost to his morale. First, a bundle of parcels arrived from his mother packed with tea and magazines. Then, a new officer joined the regiment, raising his hopes that this might allow his early return home. Finally, he got some eagerly awaited leave.

On Monday 16 July, he went off for three days' rest in Amsterdam. It was his first visit to the "Venice of the North," and he was anxious to get there because so many of his buddies had enthused about its pleasures. He trucked it, crossing the twenty-two-mile dead-straight causeway across the mouth of the Zuider Zee and checking into the city's top hotel, the Krasnopolsky, which stood on the Dam, the great square in the center of town. The hotel had been taken over by the Canadian Army for officers on leave. "Boy oh Boy [is] it lovely," gushed Roy. "Hot water and everything." There were dozens of clubs, lots of dances, plenty of cinemas, and he took a boat tour of the city's canals. But the shops were bare and pitiful to see. Still, the people were friendly and he met a very nice "gal"—"and I do mean nice," he emphasized to his parents. "We had a lovely time together. Ah my," he added, remember-ing Ardith, "will I be glad to see my one and only again."

To top it off, when he got back from Amsterdam he learned he was about to be shipped back to Canada almost straight away. "Yep, I am now de-frosted," he typed home ecstatically, "I'll be home in time to taste some of that corn on the cob, to say nothing of Xmas and such."[7]

On the day that Roy arrived in Amsterdam, Robert Ellis sat down in Italy to tell his parents that he, too, was bound for home. But this good news was merely the wrapping round his long-feared nightmare pack-age: official confirmation that the Tenth Mountain Division would soon be bound for the Pacific. The dreaded news had come through just two days before. In addition, he learned that, to fight the Japanese, they would be converted into a regular infantry division.[8]

His regiment was now in Florence, having arrived there late on the night of Saturday 14 July. His mood could not have been more differ-ent from that of Francesca Wilson enjoying the Bastille Day celebrations in Bavaria or of Reg Roy anticipating his leave in Amsterdam. Ironically, his camp was located in a city park right across the street from the GI University that Ellis had once hoped to attend. Now, instead of enjoying its courses, he spent his brief time in the city cleaning his weapons, turning in his equipment, exchanging his heavy woolen uniform for a lighter cotton one, making other preparations for his return to the States, and seeing old friends. He could look for-ward to three weeks' leave when he got there and hoped to see Pat, his erstwhile and possibly future girlfriend, while staying with his parents.

Five days later, he wrote his last letter home from Europe and boarded an ancient Italian train bound for Naples. Although he was packed in a boxcar with two dozen others, and it was boiling hot with the temperature reaching 100 degrees Fahrenheit, and the train took thirty-four hours to travel just 260 miles, and fighting the Japanese was now a confirmed future date, he felt happy. "We were going home," he wrote, "and there was a marvelous feeling of comradeship . . . we laughed and shared memories throughout the trip." As they rattled through Italy, the debris of war was all too visible. The plain below Rome was littered with tanks, shell casings and already-crumbling fox-holes. Towns were battered and the people hungry, poverty-stricken and sometimes living in caves. At night, the men in the boxcar sang spirituals and hymns.

They reached Naples in the moonlight and stayed there for the next ten days, waiting to be shipped out. The city was a ruin and Ellis was repeatedly approached by impoverished swarms of children pimping for their sisters, mothers or aunts. One day, rambling around the city, he stumbled on a huge line of GIs waiting outside a brothel in a dingy alley. As he tried to imagine how anyone could enjoy a woman who had just had sex with dozens of others, he heard someone playing a hauntingly beautiful piano piece by Rachmaninov. The music was coming from a half-ruined building, where a young Italian man was sitting at an undamaged grand piano. For a few minutes Ellis watched and listened, as if in a dream. Then he moved on.

On the last day of July, he boarded the *Marine Fox*, a small troopship, along with the rest of the 85th Regiment, and finally they cast off from Europe. Italy had cost his company and division dear. Only one of its officers who had left the States six months before returned home on the ship. In just over a hundred days of combat, the division lost almost a thousand men killed and over four thousand wounded. But Robert Ellis, just turned twenty-one, survived.

As Ellis was preparing to leave northeast Italy, Fey von Hassell was still trying to return to Brazzà. Rome's summer heat was becoming unbearable and she still had not traced her children.[9] Then, luck intervened. In the middle of July she learned that the head of the British Mediterranean Air Force was visiting Rome. Her father had known him when he was air attaché at the British Embassy before the war, so Detalmo phoned him at his suite in the Grand Hotel and they were invited over for drinks. It was a friendly and convivial evening, and the very next morning the two of them found themselves boarding a military plane bound for Brazzà. A British staff car met them and soon Fey was being driven through the familiar and comforting landscape of Friuli. As they drove up the drive to the gravel courtyard, the domestic staff ran out warmly to greet them.

She was finally home, but the house was still full of British officers, so for the moment she and Detalmo were billeted in a spare bedroom in a nearby house. That evening, they were invited over to the main house for drinks. It felt bizarre to be a guest in her own home, but soon she got used to what became a pleasant evening ritual punctuated with lots of good British humor. The officers enjoyed nicknames like "Pussy" and "Sweetie," and relations grew even friendlier when she was invited to ride with them each morning. The British had captured some horses from a retreating Austrian regiment and stabled them at Brazzà.

Over the next few weeks, she came to love the long morning rides through the park and into the rolling countryside. But her fraternization with the new occupiers of Brazzà did not go unnoticed. In an echo of the reaction inspired by her friendliness with German officers less than a year before, some of her neighbors and friends disapproved. After all, she had lost her father and her children were missing, so to some her behavior seemed frivolous. "But what did they know," she responded with characteristic defiance, "about being cooped up in barracks and cattle cars for months, worrying about one's very survival from one day to the next?"[10]

Soon, she could feel her old energy and vigor returning. Discreetly, though, no one talked about the one item that still dominated her thoughts: the fate of her children. She remained completely in the dark about her mother's efforts to find them because she had heard nothing from Germany since the fighting stopped. Occasionally, great waves of depression about their fate would overwhelm her and she would retreat to her room until they passed. As July ended, she still had no idea where they were.

By this time, British commando Bryan Samain was already back home.[11] After shipping out of Europe in early June, 45 Commando was sent to Petworth House in Sussex, the marshaling area for all commando units, where they spent their time rekitting to make up for the losses of personal equipment suffered since landing in Normandy. In mid-June, he took two weeks' leave and headed straight for London and his pretty WAAF girlfriend. "We were very much in love at the time," he said. He was surprised to find the capital still living in a wartime atmosphere, and at Piccadilly underground station they had to step over beds and sleeping bodies strewn along the platform as though air raids were still a threat.

An added annoyance came on Thursday 5 July, polling day for the general election. This provided the British people with a chance not only to pass judgment on Churchill's leadership in the war but to make their voices heard about the peace ahead. Ironically, the battle-hardened Samain was still only twenty years old and thus ineligible to vote, which was pretty galling. "Too young to vote but not too young to fight," he thought — although he kept his feelings to himself and did not share them with his comrades, nor they with him, for that matter.

After a few blissful days in London, he went to stay with his parents, and when his leave ended he returned to Petworth and a billet with a policeman and his wife in Eastbourne. Here, he and the other commandos did keep-fit exercises and tactical training on the South Downs. Everyone knew that they were bound next for the Far East: probably, rumor had it, for the massive planned invasion of Malaya. Shortly afterwards, he was sent on a jungle training course in the New Forest, which sounded exotic, but turned out to be little more than an elaborate game of hide and seek among the oaks and ferns. It was, he thought, a "complete washout." In mid-July, still in Eastbourne, he was nevertheless preparing himself to fight the Japanese.

In Berlin, Leonard Linton was gradually shifting his attention from occupation duties to finding out more about Red Army troop dispositions in and around the city. He, too, now received the "Dear John" letter so familiar to soldiers serving at the front and far from home. Even before he read the letter, he knew what it was. As he impatiently tore open the envelope, the engagement ring he had given his girlfriend before leaving for Europe fell out onto the floor.[12]

The scenes of utter physical devastation that had greeted him when he arrived in the city told him and the world a story of the irrevocable end of Hitler's Third Reich. This was Germany's "*Stunde Null*" (Zero Hour), the moment when the historical slate was wiped clean and everything started fresh and new again, untainted by the past. At least, that was one version of what happened. Few were more keen to push it than the German communists and their Soviet backers.

Within days of Hitler's suicide, a plane had landed in Berlin carrying the top German communists, who had spent the war in exile in Moscow. Immediately, the Red Army began placing communists and their supporters in influential positions throughout their zone of Germany as well as in every sector of Berlin. From the very beginning, the distribution of food supplies was linked to supervision by "People's Committees," and before Western forces arrived in the city the Soviets authorized the formation of "anti-fascist" political parties and appointed mayors to each of the capital's boroughs.

Two months later, in mid-July, when the Western allies formally took control of their sectors of Berlin, they faced a *fait accompli*. Only the "reddest" of boroughs — such as working-class Wedding — had communist mayors, but that made little difference to the reality on the ground. Wilmersdorf, in the British sector, was a solid middle-class and conservative district and the appointed Mayor was a former member of the old right-wing German People's Party. But his deputy, his chief of police and his education councillor were all communists. On Saturday 14 July, the four main political parties approved by the Soviets agreed to form an "anti-fascist" bloc in the city. Stalin's forces had militarily conquered Hitler's capital and thoroughly ransacked and looted it ever since. Now they were well on the way to completing their victory by taking political control, too. The future of the city, and of the rest of Europe, hung in the balance.[13]

Soviet willingness to deal with the Germans contrasted sharply with the attitude of Western allies. Nonfraternization with the enemy had been a firm SHAEF rule since they had crossed the German frontier some ten months before. But once Germany surrendered, the policy made little sense, and for the next two months SHAEF, in the words of one of the later official histories of the United States Army, "wrestled with itself, trying desperately to enforce [it] and just as desperately, to get rid of it."[14]

Increasingly, the ban was criticized as being both unenforceable and ill-judged, and Montgomery was not the only person becoming exasperated. How else, critics asked, were the allies to rebuild Germany if not by talking, working and socializing with the population? Especially for those Germans who had opposed Hitler and the Nazis and suffered as a consequence, the ban seemed inexplicable. To find themselves treated as outcasts, as something less than human, threatened to remove all incentives to cooperate in building a new, peaceful and democratic Germany. As one British officer reported, a young German typist working for him had pleaded: "Can some British soldier be allowed to talk to me; I cannot bear this silence."[15]

Meanwhile, soldiers continued to be arrested for breaking the ban, and even a handful of US generals were investigated for violating it. Nearly all the offenses involved women. Often, the procedures disintegrated into farce. How, for example, were the authorities to distinguish between a German woman and an allied DP, especially when both spoke German? One bureaucratic wag suggested that allied women should simply be made to wear an armband in their national colors! One American unit tried issuing buttons to the DPs, prompting its newspaper to run the headline: "Button, Button, Who's Got the Button?" Soon, a joke began to do the rounds in Frankfurt, where Eisenhower's heavily guarded headquarters was surrounded by a perimeter of barbed wire. The Americans were a people, said the joke, who built concentration camps and then voluntarily put themselves inside.

Early in June, SHAEF partially accepted defeat and announced that the contraction of venereal disease by troops would not be used, either directly or indirectly, as evidence of fraternization.[16] However, a difficult situation was then made even trickier when US soldiers were granted permission to speak to small children while this remained an offense for British and Canadian soldiers.

But it was the arrival of allied troops in Berlin that finally forced a radical reversal. The Russians had no ban on their troops being friendly to civilians, and the contrast between the two halves of the city became glaringly absurd. "The discovery that there is a nightclub in Berlin where Russians dance with German women," reported The Times in sober criticism, "has given new life to the hard-worked topic of fraternization."[17] Politically, it was now obvious that nonfraternization was hurting the Western allies.

In early July, Montgomery's headquarters produced a highly self-critical report on the situation in the British zone of occupation. So far, it observed, the Germans had learned little from the allies except that they disliked them, and they had been offered virtually nothing in the way of newspapers, political activity or other publications. Willy-nilly, the allies had taken on a good deal of direct rule. So long as they continued to do that, the Germans would be content to sit back, watch and criticize. Overall, the report observed, "the nonfraternization order is becoming a boomerang."[18]

Yet the real pressure to relax the frat ban came from what The Times's correspondent in the German capital referred to coyly as "biological pressure." By this, he meant the impossibility of preventing young, virile, fit and eager allied soldiers from having sex with willing German women. Finally, realism won out: the British cabinet got involved and met to review the ban. While it came to no conclusion itself, it agreed to let the military authorities in Germany make their own decision.[19]

As the Supreme Commander of allied forces, the final decision lay with Eisenhower who had taken a hard line on the ban from the start. How would American wives feel, he fretted constantly, about seeing photographs of relaxed GIs consorting with smiling German women?

Would he be bombarded by a barrage of hostile comment in the press? But finally, on Sunday 15 July, he caved in. From now on, he decreed, conversations between allied forces and adult Germans in streets and public places were permitted. A similar decision was made for allied forces in Austria.

The transformation was immediate. A correspondent for the *New York Times* reported on a scene on the Rhine:

> There was a new watch on the Rhine today — by handholding American GIs and German girls taking advantage of the relaxed restrictions . . . In the hot sunshine of a Sunday afternoon they sat on grassy riverbanks, chugged up and down stream in American boats, and zipped around streets with the zest of a child diving into a box of candy previously accessible only by stealth.

Quibbles remained about details, but to all intents and purposes, the policy was now dead and buried.[20]

Eisenhower made his momentous decision at SHAEF headquarters in Frankfurt. The building it occupied was the perfect symbol of the allies' destruction of Germany's military-industrial war machine. Between 1928 and 1931 I.G. Farben, the giant chemical cartel that provided much of the industrial muscle — and exploited thousands of the slave laborers — for Hitler's Third Reich, had constructed a graceful, ultra-modern glass and concrete headquarters designed by the Bauhaus architect Hans Poelzig in the west end of the city. It escaped allied bombing and stood intact. Rumor had it that this was either because Eisenhower already had his eye on it or because of secret contacts between German and American chemical companies. The more plausible answer, however, was that as an administrative headquarters filled with desks rather than a factory producing chemicals, it was a low-priority bombing target. Whatever the reason, Eisenhower was now occupying the company's former gigantic boardroom. "It should really belong to a sultan or to a movie star," he joked.[21]

But the great SHAEF spectacular was coming to an end. Once the allies had organized the occupation machinery for each of their zones in Germany, Eisenhower's supreme command would be over. Early in June, the Allied Control Council in Berlin assumed full control of Germany. Eisenhower's job was now to shift what had been combined tasks to the separate allied commands.

When that moment came, matters such as fuel, transportation, civil affairs, displaced persons, war criminals, psychological warfare, intelligence, censorship, communications and prisoners of war would be turned over to separate British, French and American commands. The I.G. Farben building would become the headquarters of US forces in Europe, with Eisenhower still as their commanding general. Field Marshal Montgomery would head up the British Army of the Rhine, and General Koening was to be chief of the French occupation forces. Marshal Zhukov assumed a similar role for the Soviets. Throughout July, as thousands of allied troops were redeployed out of Europe, either to the Pacific or home, SHAEF responsibilities and personnel were reassigned to their national commands.

On 13 July, in the officers' club of the great Frankfurt building, Eisenhower addressed his entire staff to thank them for their work. "United in a common cause," read his final order of the day,

> the men and women of Belgium, Czechoslovakia, Denmark, France, Luxembourg, Netherlands and Norway joined with the British Commonwealth of Nations and the United States of America to form a truly Allied team, which in conjunction with the mighty Red Army smashed and obliterated Nazi aggression . . . I pay tribute to every individual who so freely and unselfishly contributed to the limit of his or her ability.[22]

The following morning, at one minute past midnight, SHAEF formally ceased to exist.

Also in mid-July, the *Chicago Daily News* published a startling revelation. For weeks, speculation had been mounting about the exact whereabouts of the top Nazis captured by the British and Americans, and the press had even begun to print stories about their life of "luxury and ease" behind bars. Now, the Chicago newspaper broke the news that they were all being kept at the "Palace" Hotel at Bad Mondorf in Luxembourg, a spa town on the border with France and a mere four miles from the River Mosel and the German frontier. The town was small, easy to guard and possessed ideal accommodation for the prisoners in the six-story Grand (note, not Palace) Hotel, which was reached by a single narrow road. It was temporary home not just to the Nazi grandees, however, but to others who had thrown in their lot with

496

the regime. Among them was Prince Philipp of Hesse, who had accompanied Fey von Hassell on her journey across the Alps.

The hotel did not live up to its name, however. In reality, it provided a shabby and spartan existence for the forty or so Nazis being held there for suspected war crimes. The building had been stripped of its furniture and carpets, was surrounded by two high barbed-wire fences, and the prisoners slept in bunks on straw mattresses. The war was over, and Hitler dead, but the allies remained worried about Nazi Werewolves and possible rescue attempts by SS fanatics. (The dramatic rescue of Mussolini from his mountain prison in 1943 was still fresh in the memory.) So every effort was made to keep the location secret. But once the news was out, Colonel Burton Andrus, the US commander of "Ashcan"—the derogatory code name for the hotel-prison—decided to make the best of it.

On Monday 16 July, he invited members of the world's press to visit Bad Mondorf and see the situation for themselves. "We stand for no mollycoddling here," he told them. "These men are in jail. We have certain rules and these rules are obeyed." The prisoners had a strict regime and diet: breakfast of cereal, soup and coffee was at seven-thirty; lunch was at midday, and provided pea soup, beef hash, and spinach; at the six-thirty supper they were given powdered eggs, potatoes and tea. All, emphasized Andrus, were standard rations for prisoners of war. This, though, did not prevent Radio Moscow from deliberately and shamelessly misrepresenting the facts to suggest that the Western powers were now cuddling up to Hitler's henchmen. The Nazi war leaders, it claimed, were "getting even fatter and more insolent. These notorious war criminals rest in Luxembourg after their sanguinary carnage . . . Nothing but the finest vintage and finest foods will do for them. Servants noiselessly bring delicious wines on silver trays . . . and the latest automobiles are theirs to drive around the grounds."[23]

That same day, President Harry Truman and Prime Minister Winston Churchill were both in Berlin, each having flown in separately the night before for the opening of the Potsdam Conference. Truman had arrived in Antwerp on board the US cruiser *Augusta* to be greeted by Eisenhower and other allied dignitaries before flying from Brussels to the German capital. Churchill had a bumpy flight from Hendaye, a French seaside resort close to the Spanish frontier, where he had spent a few days at a nearby chateau painting and bathing in the Atlantic to recover from the exertions of the recent election campaign. The results were still not known, as the ballots of service personnel overseas were yet to be counted.

Once in Berlin, Churchill was housed in the Villa Urbig, a handsome rose-pink stone house with a lawn sloping down to a lake in the suburb of Babelsberg. Its tree-lined streets and comfortable villas had housed many movie stars and producers working in the nearby UFA studios. But Churchill's house, it was rumored, had once belonged to Hjalmar Schacht, the former Reichsbank president who had joined Fey von Hassell in the last journey of the *Prominente* across the Brenner into Italy.[24]

Churchill woke up to a baking-hot day — "hotter than Hendaye," he grumbled to his wife, Clementine, in a letter — and spent the morning at Truman's residence four hundred yards up the road. The US delegation's house had been the home of a famous German publisher, who had moved in with his family at the start of the battle for Berlin because he thought it would be safer than their previous residence. It was not. His daughters were raped by Red Army soldiers in front of him and his wife, the furniture was smashed, and late in May they were all ordered out at an hour's notice. The Russians then refurbished the house with furniture and carpets taken from elsewhere.

This was the first face-to-face encounter between Churchill and Truman. Already, however, they had taken each other's measure in many transatlantic telegrams that revealed increasing friendliness and respect. The conference was due to start that morning, but Stalin had not yet turned up, and its opening was postponed until the next day.

Mary, Churchill's youngest daughter, was accompanying him. When he emerged from the meeting with Truman, they walked back together to Churchill's residence. The Prime Minister told his daughter that he liked Truman, felt they talked the same language, and was sure he could work with him. "I nearly wept for joy and thankfulness," Mary recorded, "it seemed like divine providence."[25] Truman at first seemed less sure, noting in his diary that night that Churchill "gave me a lot of hooey about how great my country is and how he loved Roosevelt and how he intended to love me." But later he claimed that he liked Churchill from the start.

With time on their hands, the two men separately decided to tour the conquered city. Truman went first, clambering into the back seat of a Chrysler convertible with his chief of staff and secretary of state. As they drove down the *autobahn* into the city, they passed a seemingly endless procession of men, women and children carrying pathetic bundles. Ejected from their homes by the Russians, they reminded Truman of his Confederate grandmother and her family, who had been forced off their Missouri farm by the "Yankees." There were millions like her, he thought, in Europe.

Entering the city, they could smell the stench of corpses. They crossed the battle-torn wasteland of the Tiergarten, which was still strewn with wrecked tanks and other vehicles and completely denuded of its trees. They saw a scarecrow of a woman searching for sticks to make a cooking fire. Along the Sieges Allee (Victory Alley), they spotted a lone garden seat standing miraculously upright. It still bore its sign, "*Nicht für Juden*" (Not for Jews).

Briefly, they stopped to look at the blackened and ruined shell of the Reichstag. "They brought it on themselves," Truman thought, and imagined what Hitler might have done to Washington, DC. Then they drove through the Brandenburg Gate into the Soviet sector, along Unter den Linden, and turned into the Wilhelmstrasse and the wreckage of Hitler's Chancellery. Several accompanying FBI men jumped from the Chrysler's running board as if to escort the President inside the building, but he refused to enter. He did not want to give the impression to the Germans that he was "gloating" over their defeat, he explained. Yet he had little sympathy for the defeated enemy. That night, back in Potsdam, he wrote in his diary that the ruin of Berlin was "Hitler's Folly. He overreached himself by trying to take in too much territory. He had no morals and his people backed him up."[26]

Later, it was Churchill's turn. Wearing a lightweight military uniform, he was accompanied by his daughter, Foreign Secretary Anthony Eden and a small party from the British delegation. Unlike Truman, however, he showed no reluctance to get out and look around. At the Brandenburg Gate, he left the car to take a closer look at the walls of the Reichstag. People stood dumbfounded as if unable to believe their eyes. "It's Churchill — see the cigar," whispered someone, and women held up their children to see him. Grim-faced, and showing no inclination to fraternize, Churchill simply ignored them.

At the Chancellery, he clambered over the debris while Soviet guides showed him around. For security reasons, no notice had been issued about his visit, but there was the usual gaping crowd of onlookers hanging around outside the ruined building. They began to cheer, except for one old man who shook his head disapprovingly. "My hate had died with their surrender," wrote Churchill later, "and I was much moved by their haggard looks and threadbare clothes."

For quite a while, he toured through the empty halls and shattered galleries of the building. "It was frightfully hot milling about in such a crowd," complained one of Churchill's group in his diary, "stumbling over the dusty debris with which all the rooms and passages were littered." Broken glass covered the floors, Iron Crosses lay randomly strewn about, Hitler's desk had been upended, and the map of the world he had hoped to dominate hung in tatters on the wall. "It was a horrible and macabre place," recorded another member of the group, "its evil spirit hanging over the grim city it had destroyed." Olive Christopher, one of Churchill's junior secretaries, noted that both of the great chandeliers in the entrance hall were down. "If one stands very quietly and listens," she wrote, "one can hear the plop, plop of water dripping through. A slight breeze makes a piece of paper flap and a bit of plaster falls off the wall."

Then Churchill was taken to the bunker. Guided by a torch, he carefully descended the flights of steps to the room where Hitler and Eva Braun killed themselves. The air was dank and sour, and already water was beginning to flood some of the lower rooms. In Braun's room there was a vase with a wooden branch still in it — the poignant remains of a spray of spring blossom she must have plucked from the garden just hours before her suicide. "Hitler's room is just a heap of ruins," noted an overawed Olive Christopher, "and this was where the people who planned our destruction lived and worked."

Churchill did not linger long. After a brief glance, he climbed into the welcome fresh air of the garden. The guide pointed to the spot littered with rusty petrol cans where the bodies had been burned and gave the Prime Minister the best first-hand account available of what exactly had happened during those final few moments of Hitler's Reich. Churchill listened intently, cigar in hand. Then he paused for a moment, and without saying a word abruptly turned away with a look of disgust on his face. Spotting a wrecked chair near by, he tested it with his hand and sat down to wait for the others. "Hitler," he mused, "must have come out here to get some air, and heard the guns getting nearer and nearer." When they left the building, he drove straight back to Potsdam. He had had enough of death and destruction.[27]

*

That very day, though, several thousand miles to the west, a terrible new weapon was being born. At 5:30 a.m. — 1:30 p.m. in Berlin — at the Alamogordo test site in the desert of New Mexico, a tremendous pure white flash lit up the sky, followed by a massive shock wave and a mushroom cloud of billowing white smoke surrounded by a spectral glow of blue. The temperature at its center was more than ten thousand times that at the sun's surface. Windows were shattered more than two hundred miles away. The world's first atomic bomb had been successfully tested. The news was waiting for Truman when he got back from his tour of Hitler's ruins.

CHAPTER TWENTY-SEVEN

"OTHER BEASTS IN OTHER LAIRS"

Appropriately code-named "Terminal," the Potsdam Conference was the last of the Big Three's wartime meetings. Yet, although it was held amid the ruins of Hitler's capital, it had little impact on Germany's fate, or indeed that of anywhere else. This was already being decided by events on the ground.

Stalin's will was firmly fixed on stripping the defeated Reich of as much of its wealth as he could. Already, trains and trucks loaded with machinery from Hitler's factories were steaming east to help rebuild the ravaged Soviet economy. In Berlin, special "trophy units" formed by SMERSH were successfully hunting for spoils among the city's museums, galleries and bank vaults. Even as the Potsdam meeting opened, reports from Austria disclosed that, in one Vienna factory, only forty out of five thousand machines were left, and that the city municipality had been stripped of all but twelve of its trucks. Agriculture was being targeted too, with the whole country virtually denuded of its cattle. [1]

The expulsion and killings of the Sudeten Germans of Czechoslovakia also continued apace. Even as the Big Three met, there was an explosion at an ammunition dump near Usti, a Sudeten town known as Aussig, on the River Elbe. Although it was an accident, it was attributed by the local Czech militia to Nazi Werewolves, and a massacre followed: Germans were shot down in the street, women and children were thrown into the river, several hundred people perished, and yet more fled to the West. Some of the bodies were loaded onto trucks and driven to the former Nazi concentration camp at Theresienstadt (Terezin) for cremation.

The Sudeten expulsions were not the only ones. Stalin also sanctioned the mass forced exodus of millions of ethnic Germans from their historic homelands in Silesia and Pomerania, which pushed Poland's border westwards, to the line of the Oder and Neisse rivers, and compensated his communist satellite for his own eager annexation of its eastern territories.

Giving all these mass migrations the polite description of "population transfers," the allies at Potsdam merely asked for them to be "humane and orderly," and requested a moratorium to allow Germany time to absorb the vast influx. The plea was ignored. Over the summer, Berlin's railway stations began to fill up with trainloads of diseased and famine-stricken refugees from Silesia and East Prussia. "They died in hundreds," reported the Australian war correspondent Osmar White,

> lying on platforms awash with filth. I walked through sidings where trucks were piled with corpses, and where women stewed dog meat and turnips in blackened cans beside heaps of human dung. One of them plucked at my jacket sleeve, pointed to her mouth and hissed: *"essen, essen."* I wondered if she, simply because she was German, deserved less pity than the live skeletons down the hill at Buchenwald. I realized then that the war had not ended with the execution and dismemberment of Hitler's Germany. There were other beasts in other lairs.[2]

It wasn't just the railways that delivered their wretched human cargoes. Only ten days after Churchill toured the city, a boat arrived in the West Port of Berlin carrying a cargo of German children aged between two and fourteen. They had been expelled from Pomerania and lay half dead, motionless, stomachs swollen from malnutrition, and eaten up by vermin. That month alone, the figures of such German deportees for successive weeks came to 4,832, 11,343, 14,365 and 14,764. They joined the total of 120,000 others already there when Churchill and Truman arrived in the city.[3]

The capital attracted the expellees like some promised land. "As they trekked daily in their tens of thousands towards this illusory Shangri-la," writes Douglas Botting, "the rumor spread that refugees were met at the station by the Oberburgermeister and taken by bus to their new homes, where they were fed on real coffee and cream cakes."[4]

The reality could hardly have been more different. A British reporter for the *News Chronicle* went to the Stettiner railway station to see things for himself. A train from Danzig loaded with refugees had just arrived after a seven-day journey. One cattle truck had been shunted onto a siding beside Platform 2. The reporter looked inside:

> On one side four forms lay dead under blankets on cane and raffia stretchers. In another corner, four more, all women, were dying. One, in a voice we could hardly hear, was crying for water. Sitting on a stretcher, so weakened by starvation that he could not move his head or mouth, his eyes open in a deranged, uncomprehending stare, was the wasted frame of a man. He was dying too.

On the platform itself, as well as in the booking hall, hundreds of other bundles lay dead, dying and starving.[5]

Just a few miles away from such scenes, the Big Three also agreed on the general principles that should govern their treatment of Germany, such as denazification and demilitarization. Yet there were huge variations in what this meant in practice, and it was by no means clear that the defeat of the Nazis would in itself bring democracy to Germany.

Among ordinary Germans, old attitudes and patterns of behavior died hard. Contrary to the post-war myth, the nation's defeat did not produce some magic "Zero Hour" that swept clean the slate of history to enable a bright new future to emerge instantly. Newsreel pictures and photographs of the acres of bombed-out and deserted buildings fostered a misleading image. For while German cities *were* reconstructed with remarkable determination and speed, and impressively presented a gleamingly modern face to the world, the mindsets of their inhabitants remained largely traditional. Continuity, not change, was the order of the day. A noble minority of Germans faced up to the truth, but the vast majority in 1945 appeared unable or unwilling to accept any causal link between the catastrophe that now overwhelmed them and their all too recent enthusiasm for Hitler and Nazism.

Shortly after VE Day, Count Folke Bernadotte returned to Germany at the invitation of allied headquarters in Frankfurt. Then, he flew in a private plane to Hamburg. As they approached the city, he asked the pilot to circle over the Neuengamme concentration camp, where he had helped its Scandinavian prisoners. Flying low, he looked down to see a large number of people moving about. They were Germans, taken into custody and now having their backgrounds investigated for evidence of Nazism and war crimes. He also asked to be flown over Bismarck's country manor at Friedrichsruh, which the Swedish Red Cross had made its headquarters. He could see that the castle had been almost totally destroyed by allied bombers. The Bismarck family was now living in one of the nearby buildings, used previously as a museum to the founder of modern Germany.

His host in Hamburg was the city's British military commander. That night, he was taken to a theater to attend a performance of *Peer Gynt* presented by the Old Vic Company of London and starred Sybil Thorndike and Laurence Olivier. The orchestra was German. "It was a wonderful performance," recorded Bernadotte, "the first time since the war that I had witnessed collaboration between Englishmen and Germans in a cultural field."

Yet outside lay a much grimmer scene. In late July 1943, Hamburg had been attacked by fleets of British and American bombers. Forty-five thousand people were killed, and half the city's houses totally destroyed. Bernadotte visited the city's largest cemetery, in Ohlsdorf, where the victims lay buried. The mass grave was fashioned in the shape of a giant cross. Across it were laid enormous wooden beams at fixed intervals, listing the different areas of the city where the dead had once lived. At the outer edge of the cemetery lay small private graves which preserved the names of at least a few of the victims. "They tell their own story," recorded Bernadotte. "One man commemorates his wife and his seven children, aged three to fifteen years — his entire family." On another little wooden cross erected in memory of a wife, there was a laconic but eloquent commentary consisting of just one word: "*Warum?*" (Why?).[6]

"Why indeed?" pondered Bernadotte. The question was directed to the whole country. There was no doubting his profound compassion at what lay before his eyes, nor his firm belief that the Germans should be helped, but already he was noticing that many of them were lamenting the "good old days" under Hitler before the war, expressing dislike of the occupiers, and revealing nationalistic feelings. He believed they should face up to the facts:

The German people as a whole never made a serious attempt to cast off the yoke. They never seriously protested against the anti-Semitic policy, against conditions in the occupied countries, or against cruelties in the concentration camps. They have failed. They have allowed themselves to be led by ruthless scoundrels. They must drain the cup of suffering.[7]

He was not the only man of professional compassion who worried that the Germans were in denial. The Reverend David Cairns was a padre with a Scottish division that had fought its way from Normandy to the Baltic. He also witnessed the horrors at Belsen. He believed, as a man of God, that the Germans must be treated fairly, but he was disturbed by what he found. He spent much of the spring and summer of 1945 with the occupation forces in a small village outside Lübeck. When he returned home, he gave a report on his impressions to a meeting of the British Council of Churches.

German civilians, he told it, were obsessed with their own survival and that of their families and friends, and were walking around "as in a dream [where] nothing can move or horrify them any more." But what particularly bothered him was "the lack of understanding for the suffering that Germany has caused other people, and an unawareness of the hatred and contempt that, for example, Holland and Denmark, Poland and Belgium, feel for her." The sense of guilt, he concluded, with masterly understatement, was "rather lacking."[8]

This was an observation shared by numerous others at the time. "I have not found a single German ready to admit his personal guilt in the war," reported the war correspondent Alan Moorehead. "The deeper I go into Germany, the more I am convinced that there is no shred of pity in the hearts of German women for all the misery and suffering their race has brought to the world," wrote another correspondent, Anne Matheson, who was appalled by what she described as the "Who, me?" attitude of Germans when confronted with evidence of Nazi atrocities.[9]

All too soon, evasion of responsibility elided into a sense of victimhood, and Germany's ills were being blamed on the allied occupiers. Voices, some of them distinguished, rose to denounce the allies as little better than those they had defeated. One example was Cardinal Josef Frings, the Catholic Archbishop of Cologne, who declared that the Anglo-American occupation regime was "scarcely different from a totalitarian state." This was an astonishing claim given all that had happened in Germany over the previous twelve years, and a dismaying indicator of how little had been learned from the Hitler years.

Not all Germans agreed with Frings and others like him, though. The *Berliner Tagespiegel* roundly denounced the national mood of denial. In particular, it singled out

the erection of walls to shield oneself against the gruesome crimes against Poles, Jews, and prisoners; the stupidly arrogant ingratitude for the gift of foodstuffs received from America and England; the naïve reproach that others contributed to Hitler's rise by entering into pacts with him; [and] the falsely understood "national solidarity" that will not form an alliance with the truly different Germany.[10]

Yet such self-critical views were an exception. Not for the first — or last — time in history, those who overthrew a dictatorship rapidly fell out of favor with those they liberated. The massive death toll among German civilians caused by allied bombing — some 600,000 — in devastating raids such as those inflicted on Hamburg made denial much easier. After all, it was argued, the Germans were victims too. This attitude was strengthened by the punitive sentences being handed down by allied courts. Early in June, Eisenhower's Paris headquarters announced the execution of two teenagers. Aged sixteen and seventeen, they were Hitler Youth members who had been found guilty of spying on US troops.[11]

Alongside the public screening of newsreels showing other Germans being tied to stakes and shot by firing squads, such punishments began to backfire and turn opinion against the allies. British war correspondent Leonard Mosley toured the Western zones of occupation immediately after the surrender and was dismayed to find how quickly the allies were becoming unpopular — a fact that he blamed on the harshness of nonfraternization. Reporting from the Rhineland a month after VE Day, he told his readers that Nazis who had gone underground were regaining hope and forming blocs again, holding secret meetings and giving instructions.[12]

This was the dilemma for the allies. On the one hand, their occupation had to be firm enough to crush the remnants of Nazism and cement the foundation of victory. On the other, if it was too heavy-handed, they risked fomenting resistance. "All large armies of occupation are disastrous," wrote Francesca Wilson on the strength of her experiences in Bavaria. "They strangle the conquered and demoralise and make helpless the conqueror."[13]

In the summer of 1945, it remained to be seen how, and if, the allies and the conquered alike would resolve the problem. In June, an allied commission was sent to report on how much coal was available to keep Europe fueled over the coming winter. It returned with a gloom-ridden prediction: there would be such a severe famine, it concluded, that it would threaten basic law and order. As far as Germany was concerned, it said that it might be necessary "to preserve order by shooting." Before the year had ended, at least one American intelligence report was noting with alarm a growing reluctance to accept the defeat of Germany as final, and a "bold and unashamed veneration of Hitler and National Socialism."[14]

Alongside the resolute denial of responsibility for the catastrophe, anti-Semitism continued its insidious life. In the initial shock over revelations about the death camps, anti-Jewish feeling became muted. Yet only six months after Hitler's death a survey in the American sector of Germany revealed that, while the majority of those questioned agreed that Hitler's actions against the Jews were in no way justified, fully a fifth believed that "something had to be done to keep them within bounds."

Anti-Semitic views even *rose* in Bavaria. As Francesca Wilson was personally finding out, thousands of Jewish survivors were crowded into dozens of displaced persons camps. Here, just twelve months after Hitler's death, another survey revealed that almost 60 percent of Bavarians exhibited racist, anti-Semitic or "intense anti-Semitic" views. Not surprisingly, Munich, the birthplace of Nazism, demonstrated the highest percentage of anti-Semitism of any city.[15]

But Bavaria was by no means unique. Elsewhere, those who had openly denounced the Jews under Hitler simply donned new clothes and reinvented themselves. One such case was in Eutin, the small and pretty market town in Schleswig-Holstein all too familiar to British commando Bryan Samain. Here, the town's most outspoken prewar opponent of Hitler, a lawyer named Dr. Ernst Evers, was appointed by the British military authorities as a trustee of sequestered Nazi property, as well as a member of the town's first post-war council.

Yet Evers's opposition to the Nazis had sprung from internal rivalries between nationalists on the anti–Weimar Republic right, not from any commitment to liberal democracy. Moreover, as the local chairman of the pre-war German National People's Party (DNVP)—the party supported by Fey's father, Ulrich von Hassell—Evers had signed a stridently anti-Semitic declaration of party policy: "The Jew is a problem the world over . . . Entire nations . . . have so far not been able to defend themselves against this race. Thus the entire world is now looking towards Germany to see what form anti-Semitism will take here." Now, amid the ruins of Hitler's war, Evers also emerged as cofounder of the Eutin branch of the Christian Democratic Party.[16]

In Austria, denial ran as deep, or even deeper. Mostly to kill off any lingering hankerings for the Anschluss, the allies declared the country of Hitler's birth as the "first victim of Nazism." This idea was eagerly embraced by the millions of Austrians who only seven years before had welcomed Hitler's coup with equal enthusiasm.[17] Denying the past also enabled their country to concentrate on securing a future for the new and once-again independent small nation. But on the eve of Potsdam, there was still no fully recognized government in Vienna because Karl Renner's administration had received approval only from the Soviets.

As for Italy, even as Churchill and Truman were touring Berlin, members of the forty-thousand-strong Majella Brigade, the first Italian partisan formation officially to be recognized by the allies—and the only one ever formally entrusted with holding part of the allied line against the Germans—took part in a stand-down ceremony in the town of Brisighella. As eight hundred partisans marched off from their final parade, soldiers of the British Coldstream and Grenadier Guards shouted, "*Viva Italia.*"[18]

Yet what, in reality, was the future for Italy? In the summer of 1945, this was far from clear. The formation in mid-June of a coalition government under one of the main pillars of the wartime resistance, Ferrucci Parri—for whom Fey von Hassell's husband, Detalmo, was now working as a private secretary—extinguished the prospect of a partisan insurrection. Outwardly, life was returning to normal. In Rome, the open-air opera season resumed with the reopening of the ruined Baths of Caracalla for a performance of Verdi's *Aida*. But, as in Germany, it was by no means a certainty that democracy could survive. Disorder and violence still dominated the north of the country. In mid-July, over thirty partisans being held in one of the city's prisons escaped with the help of their guards. And a few days later, a trial of partisans accused of several acts of armed aggression, robbery and murder was disrupted when an angry crowd trying to break into the Palace of Justice in Milan smashed down its glass doors before being repelled.

Italy was politically and geographically fragmented and ravaged physically, financially and economically. It was swamped with illegal arms and half a million refugees, while a million Italians had yet to return home after being deported as slave laborers or kept in prisoner-of-war camps. The country, reported the Rome correspondent of *The Times*, was "at a crisis in her history. Revolted by the results of Fascist rule, the Italian people is clamoring for democracy, with little idea of how to achieve it."[19] Admiral Ellery Stone, the allied high commissioner after Parri's government took office, took an even more gloomy and apocalyptic view. "Italy is at the parting of the ways," he reported. "If present conditions long continue, Communism will triumph — possibly by force."[20] This was alarmist, but it highlighted the uncertain and unstable future now facing Italy.

The Italian popular mood, however, was still one of triumphant anti-Fascism. On Saturday 14 July a huge festival with dancing in the streets of Milan was held in imitation of the Bastille Day events in Paris, while loudspeakers mounted on trucks broadcast the refrain: "Dance, citizens of Milan, it is your day, for Hitler and Mussolini are dead." Shortly before, a band of anti-Fascists had literally danced on the Italian dictator's grave in one of the city's cemeteries. They were accompanied by an accordion and by a woman who stood, legs apart, and urinated contemptuously on the packed earth.

Yet if Mussolini was dead, it quickly became clear that Fascism was not. Less than a year later, over Easter 1946, three neo-Fascists dug up the dictator's grave and concealed his body in a convent. Only when the authorities agreed to give him a Christian burial was his corpse handed back. The leader of the group was a twenty-six-year-old Fascist militant and journalist who was determined to keep Mussolini's memory alive and prove that Fascism had survived.

Later that year, after an amnesty was declared for Fascists, a legal Fascist party, the Movimento Sociale Italiano (MSI), was established with the approval of the Ministry of the Interior and the Vatican. The initials MSI, party militants claimed, also stood for "Mussolini Sempre Immortale" — (Mussolini Ever Immortal).[21]

Mussolini had perished, certainly. But what of Hitler? By now, speculation was rife. Following the identification of his dental remains in early May, Red Army officials in Berlin had firmly stated that Hitler was dead. Yet almost immediately their tune changed. Early in June, Marshal Zhukov backtracked and announced to surprised allied correspondents in the German capital that the dictator's present whereabouts were "unknown." Hitler and Eva Braun could well have flown out of the city at the last moment, he said. His personal view was that Hitler was in Spain.

This abrupt turnaround was entirely due to Stalin. Through a combination of paranoia and political calculation, the Soviet dictator had quickly convinced himself that Hitler was alive and now in hiding. He told this to President Truman's personal adviser Harry Hopkins in Moscow in late May, pointing to reports that German U-boats loaded with Nazi gold and other valuables had headed for Japan. He suggested that Hitler might have been on board one of these. The whole thing, he remarked, was "curious." By this time, a full-scale Soviet disinformation campaign was under way to spread such rumors. Two days after Stalin's remark to Hopkins, *Time* magazine published a deliberately planted story that Hitler had escaped on a trolley that ran on tracks beneath Berlin. Other equally far-fetched tales quickly began to surface. One of the most widely believed was that Hitler had fled from Berlin in a small plane bound for Hamburg that took off from the Tiergarten just minutes before Red Army soldiers arrived.

At Potsdam, the Soviet dictator made it all official. Over lunch on the first day, while Truman sat listening at the table, he told the US Secretary of State James F. Byrnes that Hitler was alive and probably living in Spain or Argentina.[22] The result was that rumors of Hitler's escape were universal over the summer of 1945. Even Count Bernadotte was inclined to believe them, and Eisenhower had doubts about the Nazi dictator's fate. This all played nicely into Stalin's hands. If he could blame his allies for facilitating Hitler's escape, so much the better. It morally compromised the West while diverting attention from his own role as Hitler's partner between 1939 and 1941, which had helped precipitate the war in the first place.

Later in the year, Stalin launched Operation *Mif* (Myth) to propagate the legend even more thoroughly. Directed by his henchman and fellow Georgian Lavrenti Beria, it kept rumors that Hitler was alive and hiding in the West going at full speed for the next decade or so. Germans who had survived the battle for Berlin seemed especially prone to believing them. Easter Sunday 1946 happened to fall on

20 April, Hitler's birthday. A British officer curious about the endurance of the myth informally interviewed twenty educated Berliners on the subject. Only one thought that Hitler was dead. "The other nineteen," reported the officer, "were conscious of the fact that it was their Führer's birthday. They were convinced he was alive, and spoke of him with anything but reproach. I found also that children, who are usually good guides to the beliefs of adults, almost without exception spoke of Onkel Adolf as a living being."[23]

Claiming that London and Washington were secretly sympathetic to Nazism and sheltering or assisting its war criminals became standard Cold War propaganda. Like all such claims, it benefited from a plausible distortion of a modicum of truth, while conveniently omitting how many former Nazis now served the communists. This Moscow line also proved useful to neo-Nazis, who had their own sinister reasons for keeping the myth of Hitler's survival alive and well.

However, the fate of other top Nazis was beyond doubt. Within weeks of Potsdam, the prisoners held at Bad Mondorf were brought to trial in Nuremberg before an allied military tribunal. Absent, apart from Hitler himself, was his secretary Martin Bormann, who had disappeared during the last chaotic hours as Red Army soldiers advanced on the Chancellery. Rumors of his survival were also deliberately kept alive, and only ended when his remains were found many years later under ruins in Berlin. Both Himmler and Goebbels had committed suicide. Goering, though, was brought before the court. During the year-long proceedings at Nuremberg, as befitted the man who had so eagerly strutted before the cameras after his capture, he dominated the proceedings, blustering and playing to the gallery, showing no repentance, proudly proclaiming his Nazi ideals, and often running rings around the prosecutors. "Nobody," wrote one of the British lawyers in his diary, "appears to have been prepared for his immense ability and knowledge and his thorough mastery and understanding of the detail of the captured documents."[24]

He was also too wily and determined to permit the hangman to place a noose around his neck. He asked, as a serving officer in the German armed forces, to be executed by firing squad, but the request was flatly refused—hanging was the deliberately undignified death chosen for Hitler's henchmen. However, throughout his trial, he had managed to keep two poison capsules concealed in his cell. His execution was scheduled for the early hours of 16 October 1946, but just before midnight

Goering swallowed one of the pills and was found dead by a guard just minutes later. In one of several letters found in his cell, he made clear his utter lack of remorse or guilt. "Let me stress once more," it read, "that I feel not the slightest moral or other obligation to submit to a death sentence or execution by my enemies and those of Germany."[25]

Others, though, were hanged that morning, starting at 1:11 a.m. After climbing the thirteen shallow steps to the scaffold, the first to be dispatched by John C. Woods, the American hangman, was Joachim von Ribbentrop, the Foreign Minister found by British troops in a Hamburg boarding house. He was followed in sequence by: Field Marshal Wilhelm Keitel, Hitler's top military adviser; Ernst Kaltenbrunner, Himmler's SS deputy who had fled to the so-called Alpine Redoubt in the futile hope of saving his skin by fomenting a falling-out between the allies; Alfred Rosenberg, Hitler's wartime minister for the occupied Eastern Territories; Hans Frank, governor-general of occupied Poland; Wilhelm Frick, Nazi Minister of the Interior, the fervid promoter of the euthanasia program, and successor to the assassinated Reinhard Heydrich as Protector of Bohemia and Moravia; Julius Streicher, the unrepentant anti-Semite who had escaped from Nuremberg just hours before the arrival of the Americans; General Alfred Jodl, chief of staff and operations of the German High Command; Fritz Sauckel, who had directed the armies of slave labor in the Reich; and finally, Artur Seyss-Inquart, whose last-minute retreat from Hitler's scorched-earth policy failed to redeem his occupation crimes in the Netherlands. His final words before the lever was pulled were: "I believe in Germany."

By 2:45 a.m., it was all over, and by 4 a.m. their bodies, including that of Hermann Goering, were speeding secretly on their way to a crematorium. The allies were terrified of any kind of shrine or place of pilgrimage for unrepentant Nazis, so had agreed that after cremation the ashes would be secretly scattered. Oddly, however, there is no official record of what happened to them. One deeply held belief is that the bodies were driven to Dachau and cremated in the ovens where thousands of the Nazis' victims had been consumed by the flames. This would, indeed, have been an appropriate end. So too, however, would another, claimed by one of the biographers of Goering. After being cremated in Munich, Leonard Mosley writes, the ashes were driven into the countryside, where in pouring rain they were simply tipped into a muddy gutter.[26]

Of the remainder of the top Nazi leaders, Rudolf Hess, one-time close confidant of Hitler and deputy leader of the Nazi Party who had been in prison in Britain for most of the war, was given a life sentence. So were Admiral Erich Raeder, head of Hitler's navy from 1935 to 1943, and Walter Funk, his minister of economics. Albert Speer— Hitler's favorite architect, Minister of Armaments and War Production, and a prominent member of the last Nazi government at Flensburg—was given a twenty-year sentence, as was Baldur von Schirach, former Hitler Youth leader and the Gauleiter of wartime Vienna, who alone of the top Nazis had turned himself in. Early in June, after hearing a report of his death on the BBC and of the arrests of several Hitler Youth leaders, the latter had decided he should take the blame for misleading Germany's youth. Constantin von Neurath, Ribbentrop's predecessor as Foreign Minister and one-time boss to diplomat Ulrich von Hassell, received fifteen years. Ironically, Admiral Karl Doenitz, head of the last Nazi government, received the lightest prison sentence of all—ten years.

Three of the accused were acquitted: Franz von Papen, Hitler's deputy chancellor in 1933–34; Hans Fritzsche, head of Goebbels's radio broadcasting service; and the former Reichsbank president, Hjalmar Schacht, who was furious at having been arrested and charged in the first place. How, he kept asking, could a man imprisoned by the Nazis later be held captive by their enemies? Yet, like too many of his compatriots, he exhibited extraordinary blindness, prejudice and selective amnesia. When someone asked him if he had ever tried to inform himself about the true state of conditions and policies under the Nazis by—for example—listening to the BBC, he dismissed the idea with contempt: "The BBC dealt only in rotten propaganda—Jewish if not in diction in style," he sniffed, "of the kind no decent German would listen to."[27]

After the major trial, several others took place at Nuremberg and elsewhere in Germany, and dozens of lesser disciples of Hitler were either hanged or imprisoned for war crimes, crimes against humanity and other offenses. They included Josef Kramer, the SS commandant at Bergen-Belsen, who was hanged along with eleven others from the camp staff in December 1945. Max Pauly, the commandant at Neuengamme (and previously of Stutthof), the man responsible for sending the several thousand prisoners on the *Cap Arcona* and the other ships to their deaths, went to the gallows in Hamburg along with ten others in October 1946. Between 1945 and 1948, some five hundred defendants appeared before US military courts for war crimes committed at Dachau, Buchenwald, Flossenburg and Mauthausen, and several death sentences and lengthy terms of imprisonment were handed out.

As for Dachau itself, it served as a DP camp for many years after the war, and is now a museum and memorial site. Belsen was also used to house DPs, while Buchenwald had a sinister after-life as a concentration camp for opponents of the communist regime in the Soviet zone of Germany, including social democrats, liberals and Christian dissidents. Several hundred prisoners there were murdered or died of maltreatment and sickness. It, too, is now a memorial site.

The war crimes trials were not perfect: their sentences were sometimes inconsistent, they were tainted by politics and a small number of war criminals escaped, never to be found. A few even notoriously worked for the intelligence services of both sides during the Cold War. Yet, in 1945, these tribunals provided an essential damning verdict against Nazism. With plenty of evidence that underground Nazis were still active, they were deliberately staged to provide a warning to Germans and others tempted to think that Hitler's ideology might still have a future. "We have no choice but to fight fire with fire and blood with blood," pronounced the president of the military court that sentenced the two adolescent boys to death for attacking US troops in the summer of 1945. "You will pay the supreme penalty for your offence, so that Germans will know that we intend to use whatever force is necessary to eradicate completely the blight of German militarism and Nazi ideology from the face of the earth."[28] The avenging sword of justice, rough-edged though it was, did its work.

WHAT HAPPENED TO THEM?

Hunting down Nazis continued to occupy Fred Warner in Austria for several weeks after VE Day, first in Villach, then at Wolfsberg in Styria, where a camp for war criminals was established. Here, he vetted senior police officials, carried out general security tasks, issued passes and permits needed for almost everything by Austrian civilians, and acted as an interpreter. To keep themselves amused during the period of nonfraternization, he and his fellow occupiers organized horse races using animals "liberated" from their owners.

He returned to Britain by ship from Naples just as the Potsdam Conference was getting under way. One day, during a meal in the officers' dining room, he heard the announcement over the radio that Churchill had lost the general election. There was a deathly silence in the room. Then suddenly someone shouted: "They voted against the officer and what did they get? The sergeant-major!"

There was devastating personal news for Warner when he got back to London. Having long feared the worst, it was now confirmed: his parents and younger sister, whom he had last seen in Hamburg before leaving Germany, had been gassed at the Birkenau extermination camp at Auschwitz. On hearing this, he determined not to return to Germany, so it came as an unwelcome surprise to learn that he was being sent to the British Army's War Crimes Group at Bad Oeynhausen. But at least he could help catch some of the criminals responsible for what had happened to his family. "I have often been asked how I felt," he wrote later. "Most certainly not great hilarity, rather sadness and anger over the incredible results which brought about the unspeakable horrors wrought by a small group of evil men. I can honestly say that I was not madly keen to seek revenge."[1]

He worked with this group for three years, during which time he interrogated one of the most notorious SS killers, Otto Ohlendorf, head of one of the *Einsatzgruppen* (special death units) that murdered thousands of Jews in Russia. He also took a witness statement about the Neuengamme concentration camp from one of the few survivors of the *Cap Arcona* disaster, and played a key role in prosecuting Gestapo officials for crimes at the notorious Fuhlstattel Prison in Hamburg. Several of those accused were found guilty and hanged.

After leaving the War Crimes Group in 1948, he took a job with the Intelligence Division of the Control Commission of Germany and spent several years working on the Cold War front line in Lübeck, Hamburg and Berlin. In Lübeck, he met his wife, Annette, and they had a son and a daughter. After retiring in 1984, he returned to live in his home town of Hamburg, from where he continued to correspond with friends from SOE days in Austria, including Walter Freud. He died there in 2005. His wife recalls: "Fred said that although he had no desire ever to become a German again, the fact that Hitler had decided he was not welcome was not a good enough reason to stay away."[2]

Robert Ellis heard the news of the dropping of the atomic bomb on Hiroshima on 6 August over the ship's radio even before he reached New York. But, given the massive casualties the Japanese had already endured without any sign of flinching, neither he nor any of the others in the Tenth Mountain Division believed that this meant a surrender would be coming any time soon. Everyone knew that the invasion of Japan's home islands would almost certainly be a bloodbath on an unprecedented scale, and George C. Marshall had even advised Truman that American casualties might reach a million. Only with the news two days later of the second bomb, dropped on Nagasaki, and of the Russian declaration of war on Japan, did Ellis realize that his war was finally over.

He could hardly wait to embrace the personal freedom that awaited him after his discharge from the United States Army that November. He returned to the University of Chicago, completed an MA in international relations, and later spent twenty-eight years working in the

Research and Analysis Division of the CIA. He married and had two sons. After retiring, he moved to Puget Sound outside Seattle and occupied himself as a wildlife photographer and environmental activist. He published his personal account of the fighting in Italy in 1996, and died in 2002.

In the preface to his memoir, he wrote that while he entered into the military service of his country full of optimism and gullibility, he left it "embittered in many ways and ambivalent about the army and whether the horror we had experienced and the losses undergone — whatever the iniquities of the Hitler and Japanese regimes — were worth the price paid." He did not say or speculate, however, whether the Italians he helped liberate felt the same way.

British commando Bryan Samain's possible fate in fighting the Japanese was also decided by the dropping of the atomic bombs, news of which he heard over the radio in southern England while preparing for action in Southeast Asia. Not much changed immediately, however, and his unit kept up a wearisome round of "training, training."

In the meantime, his personal life took an all-too-familiar wartime twist. The girlfriend he had been dating since Normandy decided it was time to go her own way: she was off to America, she told him. The eighteen months' fighting had also changed him. He had matured fast, but had not been hardened or coarsened by his experiences. On the contrary: "Since I first met you," his girlfriend told him when they split up, "you are much more caring."

Early in 1946, he and his comrades in 45 Commando were shipped out to Hong Kong to help bring law and order to the British colony following the departure of the Japanese. He returned to Britain later that year, was demobilized, spent a brief time in journalism, and then for the next forty years worked in industrial public relations and publicity for such major firms as British Steel, Ford and EMI.

His book, *Commando Men*, first appeared in 1948, dedicated to his good friend Peter Winston and all the other officers and men of the Commando Group who fought and died for an ideal. This was also the year he met his wife, Helen, who had worked as a Wren in the headquarters of Commando Group at Petworth House in Sussex. He now lives with her in Suffolk. They have two sons and several grandchildren.

*

Canadian officer Reg Roy opted not to serve in the Pacific—for Canadians, service overseas was strictly voluntary. On returning to Canada, he left the army, married his fiancée, Ardith, moved to British Columbia, and took a university degree in history. After assisting with research on the Canadian official military histories of the Second World War, he pursued an academic career until retiring as Professor of Military History from the University of Victoria. The author of several regimental and other histories of the Canadian land forces in wartime Europe, he and his wife still live in Victoria, where he continues to write. Although he has toured the D-Day beaches, he has never revisited Delfzijl.

Francesca Wilson stayed at the Föhrenwald camp until she resigned her UNRRA position in September 1945 and went home to England. "Never before in history," she wrote, "[was] there such a meeting place of peoples from all over Europe and from every corner of the globe, as there was in that No Man's land, that Blind Man's Street of defeated Germany."[3] However, she returned to the continent a few months later and spent several weeks working with refugees in Yugoslavia, as well as visiting a number of DP camps near Salzburg in Austria.

She found it a harrowing experience. For most of the inhabitants, the future was no more certain than it had been a year before, and the hopes and excitement of the liberation had long since dissipated. The camp accommodation was frequently makeshift and shabby, and food was poor and scarce. Thousands of Jewish refugees were waiting with increasing impatience to head for Palestine. Some had already returned to the countries from which they had been deported only to find their families dead and their possessions gone.

Meanwhile, three-quarters of a million Poles, Lithuanians, Ukrainians and other national groups from Eastern Europe who refused to return to their homes, which were now under communist rule, also waited aimlessly in the camps. About 400,000 DPs in Austria did not even qualify for UNRRA help because they belonged to ex-enemy nations. They were crowded into towns and villages, where the Austrians frequently proved hostile—even they were in poor straits, existing on just twelve hundred calories a day.

After returning to Britain again, Francesca wrote of her experiences in *Aftermath*, which appeared in 1947, the first insider's account of UNRRA's work in occupied Europe. She settled in London, lectured on refugee matters, occasionally appeared on the BBC's radio talk show *The Brains Trust*, and over the next three decades traveled widely, gave temporary shelter to many young artists, actors and writers from around the world, and wrote four more books, including *They Came as Strangers*, a history of refugees to Britain since the seventeenth century. She died in 1981.

To the end of her long life, she retained her Bohemian panache, her vigorous curiosity about the world, and her ability to entertain visitors with compelling memories of her life. When not in London, she inhabited a small cottage on the coast at Walberswick, Suffolk. One of her relatives visited her there when she was eighty-five. She was sitting in front of a driftwood fire, her feet on the fender, a hot-water bottle at her back, and puffing on a cigarette. Together, they read and discussed Dante's *Inferno*.[4]

By the time of Potsdam, New Zealander Geoffrey Cox was already back in London with his wife and young family — soon to be enlarged by the arrival of twin daughters — and doing what he loved best, working for newspapers. He had left Trieste three weeks after VE Day and on the way home decided to visit Crete, where he and the New Zealanders had first fought the Germans in 1941.[5] They were still there, but now unarmed and awaiting repatriation. Flying into the island's Maleme airfield, where the German paratroopers had landed to seize the island, he went forward to the pilot's cabin and helped guide him in on the route that must, he mused, have looked exactly the same to the enemy just four short years before.

He found post-war London a depressing place where the hopes of a bright and brave new world promised by Labour's election victory were quickly evaporating. "London is full of drabness and frustrations," he scribbled in his notebook in September 1945. "One needs a big heart to keep hope alive amid this tiredness and grime . . . One cannot with any truth speak of a spirit of high endeavour — rather 'tis grim resolution."[6]

Nevertheless, his career prospered. He spent a decade as political editor of the *News Chronicle* before moving into television as news editor of Independent Television News, and in 1967 he founded *News at Ten*, the first half-hour news program on British TV. Knighted for services to television, he later became deputy chairman of Yorkshire TV, chairman of Tyne Tees TV and a director of the *Observer* newspaper.

He also wrote several books on his prewar and wartime experiences, including *The Race for Trieste* (1977), an updated version of his original account published in 1947. He eventually retired to Gloucestershire, where he now lives in a hilltop house with views over the River Severn into Wales.

In January 1946, war correspondent Robert Reid returned to Germany to see for himself what conditions were like. His journey took him to the British zone through Hamburg to Bad Oeynhausen, where Fred Warner was now working with the British Army's War Crimes Group. Nothing Reid witnessed induced any sympathy for the Germans, and he could only contrast their misery with the broken dreams of glory they had happily enjoyed under Hitler. In Hamburg, he watched as a stream of scruffy men and women went in and out of a small shop to barter goods, "the glories and splendor of world domination ending up in the shabby fripperies and hand-to-mouth existence of the exchange mart." The German driver taking him to Bad Oeynhausen had no idea of the route, and even after asking a military policeman he missed the turn until Reid pointed out his mistake. "For six years," he wrote caustically, "his betters had [also] been misreading the signposts." Later, when he was served in a British Army mess by former stewards of the Hamburg-Amerika Line, he mused that "white-coated, sleek, and deferential, that dream of global conquest had for them dissolved into a circular tray, a napkin, and a ready match for an English cigarette."[7]

Soon after this, Reid followed Cox and joined the *News Chronicle*, where he worked as its features editor and befriended the New Zealander. The two men visited Washington, DC, together in 1953, when Cox was on his way to report on the Bermuda summit conference between Churchill and Eisenhower, and Reid was investigating newspaper plants in the United States. Like Cox, too, he later quit the newspaper world for television and returned to the BBC, where he inaugurated the pioneering investigative series *Special Enquiry* with a hard-hitting program about conditions in the Glasgow slums. "The general brief," wrote Reid of the series, "is hard facts and straight talk." It lasted for several years. He kept working as a journalist until he died, aged sixty-nine, in May 1974.

Leonard Linton remained busy with occupation duties in Berlin throughout the Potsdam Conference and beyond. When the rest of the

Eighty-second Airborne Division returned to the United States in late 1945, he transferred to a military intelligence unit, was promoted to sergeant, and stayed on in the city. Based in the middle-class suburb of Zehlendorf, his work increasingly involved monitoring Soviet and communist activities in the city and the Soviet zone of Germany. One early task involved interrogating the thousands of displaced persons in the two UNRRA camps established in west Berlin to house refugees flooding in from the east. Many had no identity papers, some falsely claimed to be from allied countries—hence eligible for support—and others proved to be Soviet agents destined for undercover positions in the West. Refugees also proved to be a gold mine for intelligence about the Red Army. More than a few had once been imprisoned by the NKVD and provided valuable information about its structure and methods.

Early in 1946, he joined a special mission to Romania and Hungary to collect intelligence about developments in what were rapidly turning into Soviet satellites, and shortly afterwards he left the army to join the Counter-Intelligence Corps as a special investigator. One of his many missions was to run an agent inside Walter Ulbricht's SED (communist) Party in eastern Germany.

He left Berlin late in 1946 and returned to civilian life in New York, studied business administration, and founded a multinational chemical fertilizer business. Later, he expanded into the fields of oil and gas exploration. He married, had a son and two daughters, developed a passion for astronomy, and built his own beachfront house on Long Island with an observatory.

When the Cold War ended and Germany was reunited, he went back to Ludwigslust and began collecting information about the victims of the Wobbelin concentration camp he had witnessed in May 1945. In recognition of this work, in 2000 he was unanimously nominated by the city council of Ludwigslust as its first honorary citizen. He died in New York in January 2005.

In August 1945, at her beloved home in Brazzà, Fey von Hassell finally received a letter from her mother in Germany. Impatiently, she tore it open and devoured its contents. She was thrilled because, for the first time, she had proof that her mother was actively searching for the boys. Screaming with joy, she showed it to Detalmo. More somberly, for the first time, too, she learned the full details of her father's trial before the infamous Nazi "People's Court." He was magnificent in standing up to the judge, and just had time to write a moving letter to Fey's mother before being executed. "I pray," she told Fey, "that the sacrifice of his life will show the world that there existed a better Germany, a Germany in despair over the gangsters that oppressed us all." Once again, Fey was moved to tears by the fate of her father. She was also deeply impressed by the strength of character shown by her mother. It gave her renewed courage that she would soon find the children.[8]

Yet the weeks rolled by. Detalmo returned to Rome and no more letters arrived from Germany. Fey felt her anxiety rising again. Perhaps she should simply set off and walk over the mountains into Austria and start looking herself?

Tuesday 11 September marked a full year to the day since she had been arrested. She was outside supervising the gardener in the rose garden close to the chapel. It was late morning. Suddenly, Nonino, the family's coachman, butler and chauffeur, appeared holding a telegram. There was nothing unusual about that since Detalmo was regularly in touch from Rome, so Fey casually tore it open and glanced at the first line. At first she did not take it in. Then she read it again and with a sudden shock the message registered: "Children found they are with your mother," it read. She hardly bothered with the rest before the tears were pouring down her face. Wild with happiness, she shouted out loud to everyone who could hear: "The children! The children! My mother's found them! She's got them!"

That night, the British officers held a dinner for her and raised a toast to the family. At last, after a year of anguish, she knew the boys were safe and her ordeal was over. The news transformed her. "I was full of life and enthusiasm," she wrote. "Whereas I had been shy, I was confident. Whereas I had been silent, I was talkative. The happiness and gratitude that had moved my heart changed me completely."[9]

But how was she to collect her sons? Civilian travel between Italy and Germany was still virtually non-existent. In Rome, Detalmo frantically began pulling strings, but with no effect. A whole agonizing month passed. Then, once again, they had a lucky break. By chance, Detalmo met General Mark Clark at a reception and begged him for help. Twenty-four hours later, travel pass to Germany in hand, Detalmo arrived at Brazzà wearing a US Army uniform and driving a jeep.

At six o'clock the next morning, he and Fey set off, retracing the route over the Brenner Pass into Austria she had taken in the opposite direction six months before. It already seemed far in the distant past. Even the image of Alex von Stauffenberg had begun to fade. So intent were they on getting there safely that they hardly spoke a word: they just stared straight ahead as the miles were eaten up and prayed that no road block would stop their journey. Finally, after ten hours of non-stop driving, they reached Fey's family home at Ebenhausen. As they drove up the dusty drive, she was sick with excitement.

Her mother was standing in the doorway, still wearing her widow's black, and she was far thinner than Fey remembered her. Jumping out of the car, she gave her a hug. "Poor Mutti," she said, and her mother's eyes filled with tears. Her brother Wolf Ulli had turned up, having escaped from the Soviet zone, and he was standing by his mother. Fey embraced him too, and they entered the house.

The children had gone out for a walk with their aunt Almuth, so Fey and Detalmo sat down for tea as though everything were normal and made small talk. But each of them kept staring at the door, wondering how they would react when the boys walked through it. How much would they have changed? What would they say? From time to time, they lapsed into silence, lost in their thoughts.

After a while, they heard footsteps outside and the door flew open. There stood Almuth, with the boys on either side, clinging to her hands. For a few long, agonizing seconds the boys just stood there staring at Fey and Detalmo. "Do you recognize that person?" asked Almuth, pointing at Fey. "Yes, it's Mama," replied Corrado. "And that man there?" she asked. There was a pause, then he shouted excitedly: "Yes, it's Papa! From the photograph!" He broke free, rushed to Detalmo, grabbed hold of his trousers, and stood on his shoes. It was a trick he had always done. Meanwhile, Roberto shyly walked over to Fey, climbed on her lap, and sat there without saying a word. "He seemed the most precious thing in the world," she wrote. "Feeling him next to me, I knew that my nightmare was over."[10]

Later that night, after the children had been put happily to bed, she learned that they had been living at Ebenhausen since July. Only the total lack of communication between Germany and Italy had kept her in agonizing suspense throughout the long, hot summer.

After her earlier frustrating efforts, Fey's mother had decided to search for the boys in Innsbruck, where they had last been seen. At the end of another long journey, she and Almuth drove up to a big stone children's institute deep in a pine forest. Here, she showed photographs of Corrado and Roberto to the governess. After a pause, she said she knew them: they were the "Vorhorf brothers — Conrad and Robert." She led the women up to a bedroom where the two boys were lying in their beds, fast asleep. But when they awoke, only Corrado gave any sign of knowing who the visitors were. Neither boy could understand a word of the Italian being spoken to them, and Roberto looked at the photographs of Brazzà and Fey with no sign of recognition at all. His grandmother even wondered if it was really him. Suddenly, though, he pointed at a small white spot on the photograph and uttered a single word: "Mirko." That was the name of the pony that pulled their little carriage at Brazzà.

As they left the home with the two children in the back of the car, Fey's mother learned that all Nazi children's homes were due to be closed down within the next ten days, and that all unclaimed children were to be handed over for adoption to local peasants. She had arrived just in time.

With the family at last reunited, Fey and Detalmo resumed their normal life. They continued to divide their year between Rome and Brazzà, and in 1948 Fey gave birth to their third child, Vivian.

She also kept in touch with Alex. After his release from Capri, he went to stay with a friend near Lake Constance, and from there he wrote Fey many nostalgic letters about the time they had spent together. In spite of what had happened to him, she wrote, he remained a "true romantic, and I could sense how much he wanted to see me again. On the other hand," she continued, "I have always been a practical and not a sentimental person and had in the meantime become absorbed in life in Italy and bringing up my children." Whatever her feelings once had been, the war was over and now her duty was to Detalmo and the boys. "I don't want to marry him," she declared firmly a year after the liberation, and eventually Alex resumed his teaching post at the University of Munich and remarried. However, "He remained for me a most attractive man," Fey admitted, "so tall, with that head of unruly hair." The last time she saw him was in the early 1960s, when he passed through Rome with a class of students on their way to Sicily, and they dined together in a restaurant. Soon afterwards, he died of cancer, aged fifty-eight.

Fey also kept in touch with Sigismund Payne Best. The British intelligence officer wrote to her within a month of her reunion with her children, and she eagerly responded by bringing him up to date on family matters and passing on news of other members of the *Sippenhafte* group. They had all been saved, she was convinced, by his decisive leadership in the closing stages of their frightening odyssey over the Alps. She also confessed that she badly missed the companionship of the group, and was struggling to cope with the loss of the independence that was forced on her by her ordeal. The war had irrevocably changed not just Germany, but Fey herself. Sometimes, she admitted, she felt very alone.[11]

In due course, her son Corrado became an official with the European Commission, while Roberto practiced as an architect. Detalmo died in 2006 and Fey now spends most of her time at her beloved Brazzà.

NOTES

INTRODUCTION

1 Hitler, quoted in Ian Kershaw, *Hitler*, pages 783–784; Goebbels, quoted in Fey von Hassell, *A Mother's War*, page 193. See also Max Hastings, *Armaggedon*, *passim*, and Michael Burleigh, *The Third Reich*, page 789.

2 John Wheeler-Bennett and Anthony Nicholls, *The Semblance of Peace*; Gregor Dallas, *Poisoned Peace*; Norman Davies, *Europe at War 1939–1945*.

3 Tony Judt, *Postwar*, pages 41, 5.

4 Sebastian Haffner, *Defying Hitler*, page 7.

1 CRUEL SPRING

1 The scene in the bunker during these final days has been described many times. Here, I have drawn on the accounts by Hugh Trevor-Roper, J.P. O'Donnell, Joachim Fest, Antony Beevor and Traudl Junge, whose books are listed in the bibliography. For Eva Braun, see the recent illuminating account by Angela Lambert, *The Lost Life of Eva Braun*, *passim*.

2 Flint Whitlock, *Soldiers on Skis*, quoted in Charles J. Sanders, *The Boys of Winter*, page 135.

3 For the late Robert Ellis's personal story, see his memoir, *See Naples and Die*. John Imbrie, vice-president for Data acquisition and research of the National Association of the Tenth Mountain Division, himself a veteran of the Italian campaign, willingly provided me with extensive material about the division, as well as facilitating my acquisition from the Denver Public Library of copies of the daily morning reports for Company "F" of the 85th Regiment — Ellis's — for the period April–July 1945. He also answered my many questions and suggested further reading. His wife, Barbara, is to be commended for the excellent maps she has produced of the division's campaign in Italy, which I have used extensively. The main additional sources I have used in writing about Ellis and the Tenth Mountain Division are Imbrie's own *Chronology of the 10th Mountain Division in World War Two, 6 January 1945–30 November 1945*, and (with Hugh W. Evans) *Good Times and Bad Times*; John B. Woodruff, *History of the 85th Mountain Infantry Regiment*; Henry J. Hampton, *The Riva Ridge Operation* (US Army, 86th Mountain Infantry HQ, APO 345, 12 June 1945); and the published volumes by Carl V. Cossin, Harris Dusenbery and Wilson Ware, Ernest F. Fisher, McKay

Jenkins, Charles J. Sanders and Peter Shelton, all listed in the Bibliography. On the killing of German prisoners during the battle for Mount Belevedere, see the testimony of Kenyon Cooke in Imbrie and Evans, op. cit., page 60.

4 I am grateful to Bryan Samain for providing me with copies of two private and unpublished histories written for his family and on which I have drawn here: "Family Connection"; and "Going for a Soldier: Notes on Boyhood and an Early Military Life." I have also benefited from many conversations and much correspondence with him.

5 Besides the sources quoted above, the principal source I have used for Samain's experiences is his book, *Commando Men*, first published in 1948 and reprinted many times since. I have used the White Lion edition of 1976.

6 Leonard Mosley, *Report from Germany*, pages 49–50.

7 Longden, *To the Victor the Spoils*, page 280.

8 Barry Turner, *Countdown to Victory*, pages 309–310.

9 Longden, op. cit., pages 282–283.

10 Samain, *Commando Men*, page 150.

11 Samain, "Going for a Soldier," page 60.

12 F. S. V. Donnison, *Civil Affairs and Military Government*, page 217.

13 Ibid., page 218.

14 See Samain, *Commando Men*, pages 170–171. For the scene of the Russian slave laborers in the hospital in Lüneberg, I have drawn on Desmond Flower's *History of the Argyll and Sutherland Highlanders*, and for the history of 45 Commando on David Young's *Four Five*.

15 Malcolm Proudfoot, *European Refugees*, page 144.

16 This and the following quotations and information are taken from Francesca Wilson's "Autobiographical Fragments," in *A Life of Service and Adventure*.

17 J.L. Hammond, "Foreword" to Wilson's *In the Margins of Chaos*.

18 Francesca Wilson's account of her time at Granville is in *Aftermath*, pages 1–29. For further information, I am greatly indebted to her nieces June Horder and Rosalind Priestman. The former generously provided me with fragments of her aunt's diaries and papers in her possession, as well as a copy of *A Life of Service and Adventure*, the family's privately printed memoir and celebration of Francesca's life, which also includes the first part of her autobiography. Rosalind Priestman kindly provided me with a copy of the photograph of Francesca that appears as well as sharing her memories of her aunt. Others who helped include Heather Eggins and Russell Enoch.

For the teething problems of UNRRA, see the official three-volume history by George Woodbridge listed in the Bibliography, as well as Donnison, op. cit., pages 341–358. An excellent recent account of the problems of postwar refugees, especially children, can be found in Lynn Nicholas, *Cruel World*, *passim*.

19 I am deeply grateful to Professor Reginald H. Roy, now of Victoria, British Columbia, Canada, for generously providing me with copies of the many letters he wrote home from the front to various family members in Canada, relevant diary entries, and for responding to my many emailed inquiries following up on this material. The standard history of the Cape Breton Highlanders is to be found in Alex Morrison and Ted Slaney, *The Breed of Manly Men*.

NOTES

20 Earl Ziemke, *The US Army in the Occupation of Germany 1944–1946*, pages 244–245.

21 The scene in Leipzig is described by BBC correspondent Edward Ward and appears in Desmond Hawkins (ed.), *War Report*, pages 304–305. I have supplemented that with the dispatch by Selkirk Panton in the *Daily Express*, 20 April 1945. For accounts of the entry into Nuremberg, I have drawn on the volumes of the official US history of the war by Ziemke, op. cit., page 247, and Charles B. MacDonald, *The Last Offensive*, pages 422–425. For Hitler's response to the suicide of the Leipzig Mayor, see Trevor-Roper, *The Last Days of Hitler*, page 143.

22 For this account of the Nazi Party Rallies, I have drawn mostly on Frederic Spotts, *Hitler and the Power of Aesthetics*, pages 61–70; the quotation is from page 66.

23 Quoted in *Encyclopaedia of the Holocaust* (editor-in-chief Israel Gutman), Vol. 4, page 1415.

24 Many of the buildings were never completed before the outbreak of war in 1939, such as the Congress Hall, whose shell now houses a documentation center. The center's guide, "Fascination and Terror," published by the City of Nuremberg Museum, provides a useful source on the history of the Rally grounds.

25 Peter Heigl, *The US Army in Nuremberg on Hitler's Nazi Party Rally Grounds*, Documentation Centre of the Nazi Party Rally Grounds, 2005; also Ziemke, op. cit., pages 247–248.

2 SORROW AND DARKNESS

1 Michael Burleigh, *The Third Reich*, page 201.

2 Fey von Hassell, *A Mother's War*, page 3. See also n.3, below.

3 Gregor Schollgen, *A Conservative against Hitler*, *passim*; the Thomas Mann quotation appears on page 126.

4 Fey von Hassell has told her story in her book *A Mother's War*, edited by her son-in-law David Forbes Watt, and I am grateful to them both for seeing me in Rome to talk in more detail about her experiences. For a recent broad account of the SS hostages, see Hans-Gunter Richardi, *SS — Geiseln in der Alpenfestung*. For Ulrich von Hassell and the Nazis, see Burleigh, op. cit., pages 693–694 and Ulrich von Hassell, *The Von Hassell Diaries 1938–1944*.

5 Fey von Hassell, op. cit., page 21.

6 Ibid., page 42.

7 Ibid., page 80.

8 Ibid., page 80.

9 Ibid., page 87.

10 Ibid., pages 78–79.

11 Ibid., pages 92–93.

12 Ibid., page 96.

13 Ibid., page 100.

14 For "a big black car," see Lynn Nicholas, *Cruel World*, page 419.

15 Fey von Hassell, op. cit., pages 28–29.

16 Burleigh, op. cit., pages 246, 689.

17 Robert Gellately, *Backing Hitler*, page 248.
18 Burleigh, op. cit., page 783.
19 Fey von Hassell, op. cit., page 133.
20 For the details on Melitta, as well as on the Stauffenberg family, see Peter Hoffman, *Stauffenberg: A Family History*, especially pages 276–278. See also Gerald Posner, *Hitler's Children*, pages 171–172.
21 *Evening Standard*, text of Murrow's report, 16 April 1945.
22 *Ariel*, 12 June 1974.
23 Sian Nicholas, *The Echo of War*, page 216. For Reid's own account, see his *War Correspondent*, pages 56–61.
24 Robert Reid, letter to Vera, 11 February 1945, Reid Papers.
25 Vera, letter to Robert Reid, 20 April 1945, Reid Papers.
26 Elie Wiesel, *Night*, page 134.
27 Ibid., pages 135–136.
28 Christopher Burney, *Dungeon Democracy*, page 83; see also "I was a prisoner in Buchenwald" by Lieutenant Christopher Burney, *Evening Standard*, 18 April 1945.
29 I wish to record my thanks to the late Robert Reid's grandson, my friend and colleague Jeremy Crang of Edinburgh and Dundee, for permitting me to delve through his grandfather's papers, which remain in his family's hands, and for his hospitality while doing so. The quotations are from the typescripts of Reid's dispatches, his typed letters to his wife and her handwritten replies. For SOE and the Newton brothers, see M.R.D. Foot, *SOE in France*, page 213; and for them, Southgate and Burney, see the *Sunday Times*, 1 May 1966. For the story of the Warsaw uprising women, see Reid, WRU C7792, Saturday, 21 April 1945, in Reid Papers.
30 John Oram Thomas, *No Banners*, pages 336–339.

3 AVENGING JUSTICE

1 Fey von Hassell, *A Mother's War*, page 34.
2 For the Pioneer Corps, see Norman Bentwich, *I Understand the Risks*, *passim*; for German and Austrian Jews in the fight against the Nazis, see the article by John P. Fox, "German- and Austrian-Jewish Volunteers in Britain's Armed Forces, 1939–1945," in the *Leo Baeck Institute Year Book 1995*, pages 21–50.
3 Bryan Samain, *Commando Men*, page 118, and his "Going for a Soldier," page 62; for Eric Nathan, as well as other Jewish exiles who fought with allied forces, see Bentwich, op. cit., pages 13–16. Nathan was killed during the battle for Osnabrück. Also, conversation with Bryan Samain, December 2006.
4 Fred Warner, *"Don't You Know There's a War On? A Very Personal Account,"* typescript memoirs in the archives of the Intelligence Corps Museum in Chicksands, Bedfordshire, File No. 2580/A. I am also deeply grateful to the late Fred Warner himself, who kindly invited me to visit him in Hamburg in January 2004 to talk further about his mission, and to his widow, Annette Warner, for generously lending me one of the photographs from his wartime album. For official SOE files on the mission in the National Archives at Kew, see especially HS 7/146, German Directorate History Part 1, Appendix A: "Activities of X Section in Italy," by Captain E.M. Hodgson, MBE, FANY. Also, Appendix E:

NOTES

"Interrogation of Lt. Bryant, Historian Party, 13 May 1945"; and W.J.M. Mackenzie, *The Secret History of SOE 1940–1945*, pages 697–699.

5 Rodney Minott, *The Fortress that Never Was*, pages 17–24.

6 21st Army Group Counter-Intelligence Instruction No. 3 — Operations in Germany, 27 September 1944.

7 Timothy Naftali, "Creating the Myth of the *Alpenfestung*: Allied Intelligence and the Collapse of the Nazi Police-State," page 11. I am grateful to Timothy Naftali for providing me with a copy of this paper. Rodney Minott, op. cit., *passim*.

8 Dulles Radiotelephone Transmission No. 267, 18 January 1945, Document 5–10 in Neal H. Peterson (ed.), *From Hitler's Doorstep*, pages 429–430.

9 For Quinn's report, see the volume in the official history of the US Army in World War Two, European Theatre of Operations, by Charles B. MacDonald, *The Last Offensive*, Chapter 28, "The Myth of the Redoubt," page 407. For the National Redoubt and its impact on allied strategy, there is a considerable literature. The main sources I have used are the following: Earl Ziemke, *The US Army in the Occupation of Germany*, pages 246–256; F.H. Hinsley, *British Intelligence in the Second World War*, Vol. III, Part 2, pages 711–725; Stephen Ambrose, *Eisenhower: Soldier, General of the Army*, pages 392–399; Carlo d'Este, *Eisenhower*, pages 685–698; Omar N. Bradley and Clay Blair, *A General's Life*, pages 416–428; Lionel Frederic Ellis, *Victory of the West*, Appendix X, pages 429–432; Minott, op. cit., *passim*; Peterson, op. cit., *passim*.

10 Hinsley, op. cit., Vol. III, Part 2, page 717.

11 See Nigel Hamilton, *Monty: The Field Marshal*, page 444, and Eisenhower, *Crusade in Europe*, page 397. For a more extended discussion of Eisenhower's strategy and the redoubt, see Stephen Ambrose, *Eisenhower and Berlin*, pages 71–79.

12 Cornelius Ryan, *The Last Battle*, page 214.

13 For Bradley, see Bradley and Blair, op. cit., page 418.

14 Greg Bradshaw, "Nazi Gold: The Merkers Mine Treasure," in *Prologue: Quarterly of the National Archives and Records Administration*, Spring 1999, Vol. 31, No. 1.

15 Quoted in Lynn Nicholas, *The Rape of Europa*, page 312.

16 Margaret Harop to Robert Reid, 13 April 1945, Reid Papers.

17 See Greg Bradshaw, op. cit.; Nicholas, loc. cit.

18 Robert Reid, Dispatches Nos. 140–143, 6–8 April 1945, Reid Papers. See also his *War Correspondent*, pages 79–81.

19 For Patton's dictated memorandum, see Farago, *Patton: Ordeal and Triumph*, pages 809–810; also, Martin Blumenson, *The Patton Papers*, pages 683–684.

20 D'Este, op. cit., page 686; Reid, Dispatch No. 144, 8 April 1945, Reid Papers; Ryan, op. cit., page 329.

21 Hinsley, op. cit., Vol. III, Part 2, page 734.

22 Quoted in J. Bridgman, *The End of the Holocaust*, page 82.

23 Eisenhower, op. cit., pages 408–409.

4 "A CURIOUS PEARLY COLOR"

1 J. Bridgman, *The End of the Holocaust*, page 82.

2 Robert Reid, Dispatch No. 158, 16 April 1945, Reid Papers.

3 Major David Finnie, "The Liberation of Belsen," *The Gunner*, November 2006.

4 Derrick Sington, quoted in Tom Pocock, page 81.

5 Ibid., page 82.

6 Ben Shephard, *After Daybreak*, pages 37–38.

7 Ibid., page 99.

8 Ibid., pages 116–117.

9 Alan Moorehead, *Eclipse*, 222, 224.

10 Shephard, op. cit., page 14.

11 Ibid., page 18.

12 John Gordon, "The Beasts of Europe," *Sunday Express*, 22 April 1945.

13 Shephard, op. cit., page 75.

14 Ronald Monson, "Smug Guards March Out," *Evening Standard*, 20 April 1945.

15 Apart from those already quoted, the principal sources that I have used for this account of Belsen, out of the dozens that exist, are as follows: Paul Kemp, "The British Army and the Liberation of Bergen-Belsen, April 1945," in Joanne Reilly *et al.* (eds.), *Belsen in History and Memory*, pages 133–148, from which the quotations describing medical conditions in the camp are largely taken; "Introduction," in Reilly *et al.* (eds.), op. cit., pages 1–18; Raymond Phillips (ed.), The Belsen Trial, *passim*; "Report on Belsen Camp" by Lt.-Col. R.I.G. Taylor, DSO, MC, in the B.G. Barnet Papers, Liddell Hart Centre of Military Archives, King's College, London, a document which also provides in its Appendix B the terms of the truce negotiated with the German military authorities, as well as a copy of Taylor's handwritten notes on Belsen. The Barnet Papers also include an account of Belsen published as a supplement to the *British Zone Review* of 13 October 1945. Also in the Liddell Hart Archive is an account of the effects of Belsen on his troops by General R.G. Churcher, of the British Eleventh Armored Division. I have also drawn on many contemporary British press clippings about Belsen from a personal collection lent by the late Sydney Hudson, DSO, an officer in the wartime Special Operations Executive. See also, Gena Turgel, *I Light a Candle*, an account by a Belsen victim whose husband, Norman, entered the camp on 15 April 1945 with a field security unit of the British Army, and was responsible for arresting Kramer.

16 Bryan Samain, "Going for a Soldier," page 20.

17 Ibid., page 53.

18 Quoted in Sean Longden, *To the Victor the Spoils*, page 30.

19 Ibid., page 31.

20 Samain, op. cit., pages 64–65.

21 Angela Lambert, *The Lost Life of Eva Braun*, page 420.

22 F. H. Hinsley, *British Intelligence in the Second World War*, Vol. III, Part 2, pages 733–736.

23 Carlo D'Este, *Eisenhower*, page 697; Stephen Ambrose, *Eisenhower and Berlin*, pages 77–78.

24 For the text of Hitler's directive, see Lionel Frederic Ellis, *Victory in the West*, Appendix X, pages 429–432.

5 "TO FALL HEROICALLY"

1 Robin Neillands, *Eighth Army*, pages xxv–xxvi.

2 For Cox's experience, I have drawn on his own account in *The Race for Trieste*,

especially pages 108–117; on his prewar memoir, *Countdown to War;* on a personal discussion with him at his home in Gloucestershire in June 2004; on his original reports for the period held at the Kippenberger Military Archive and Research Library at the Queen Elizabeth II Army Memorial Museum in Waiouru, New Zealand, for which see especially *2NZ Div. Intelligence Summary No. 506, 20 April 1945,* and *Summary No. 507, 21 April 1945* — for providing me with copies of these I am particularly grateful to Dolores Ho; and on his personal papers held in the Alexander Turnbull Library in Wellington, New Zealand. I am grateful to its chief librarian for granting me permission to consult these, and to Peter Cooke for providing me with copies. For general background, see also the relevant volume of the *Official History of New Zealand in the Second World War* by Robert Kay: *From Cassino to Trieste, passim.* The text of Hitler's order of 17 April 1945 can be found on page 491 of that volume. In addition, for Freyberg, see John Tonkin-Colville, "The Salamander's Last Offensive," in *Kia Kaha* (edited by John Crawford), pages 167–172.

3 Typescript note marked "Italy, July 4, 1944," in Cox Papers, Alexander Turnbull Library, 2003–005–05/6; also, Cox, *The Race for Trieste*, page 61.

4 Ibid., pages 65–66.

5 Geoffrey Cox to Peter and Patrick Cox, 27 August 1944, Cox Papers, Alexander Turnbull Library, 2003–005–4/14; also, letter to Peter, 30 March 1945, loc. cit.

6 Cox, *The Race for Trieste*, page 115.

7 For biographies of Mussolini, see those listed in the Bibliography by R.J. Bosworth, Martin Clark, Christopher Hibbert, Denis Mack Smith, Laura Fermi and Sir Ivone Kirkpatrick. See also "Mussolini as War Leader," by Giorgio Rochat, in *Oxford Companion to World War Two*, pages 768–770.

8 For the liberation of Rome, see Raleigh Trevelyan, *Rome '44*, pages 296–326.

9 Cox to Cecily, June 1944, Cox Papers, Alexander Turnbull Library, 2003–005–05/6.

10 Robert Ellis, *See Naples and Die*, page 45.

11 Letter to Margaret, 15 March 1945, quoted in ibid., pages 158–159.

12 Letter to Paul, 15 March 1945, in ibid., page 159.

13 Ibid., pages 111, 144.

6 "ICH WAR IMMER DAGEGEN"

1 Janet Flanner, "Letter from Cologne," in *The New Yorker*, 31 March 1945.

2 For Leonard Linton's Second World War experiences, I am indebted to his unpublished account entitled "Kilroy Was Here," deposited in the archives of the Allied Museum in Berlin. I am similarly grateful to that museum's director, Dr. Helmut Trotnow, for drawing my attention to it. Leonard himself kindly agreed to help me further, but sadly died in New York before we could meet. I am grateful to Sandy Linton, his daughter, for permission to use the photographs I have selected here. For the combat history of the Eighty-second Airborne Division in this period, see Phil Nordyke, *All American All the Way*, pages 736–743.

3 Linton, op. cit., page 48.

4 For the best recent account of what went wrong for Western forces between D-Day and the Battle of the Bulge, see Max Hastings, *Armageddon, passim*; the earlier, classic account of the campaign by the former war correspondent Chester Wilmot, *The Struggle for Europe*, also remains well worth reading.

5 Linton, op. cit., page 56.

6 For Gavin's briefing, see James Gavin, *On to Berlin*, pages 269–270; and Cornelius Ryan, *The Last Battle*, pages 119–123.

7 Linton, op. cit., page 57.

8 Barry Turner, *Countdown to Victory*, page 39.

9 Sean Longden, *To the Victor the Spoils*, page 271.

10 Ibid., page 277.

11 Linton, op. cit., page 83.

12 Ibid., pages 82–83.

13 Longden, op. cit., page 281.

14 Douglas Botting, *In the Ruins of the Reich*, page 189.

15 See, e.g., *Germany 1944: The British Soldier's Pocketbook, passim*. The US Army's order is quoted on page xxiv of the "Introduction" by Edward Hampshire.

16 Botting, op. cit., page 189.

17 Turner, *Countdown to Victory*, page 374.

18 Longden, op. cit., page 95; Botting, op. cit., page 191. For an extended discussion of women in Germany at this time, see Elizabeth Heinemann, *What Difference Does a Husband Make?, passim*.

19 Linton, op. cit., page 87.

20 James Megellas, *All the Way to Berlin*, page 257.

21 Stephen Ambrose, *Eisenhower: Soldier, General of the Army*, page 123; see also Winston Churchill, *Triumph and Tragedy*, pages 515–516, and Martin Gilbert, *Road to Victory*, pages 1302–1303.

22 Omar Bradley, *A Soldier's Story*, pages 433–434.

23 *21 Army Group CI* [Counter-Intelligence] *News Sheet*, No. 20, 25 April 1945, page 4, in WO 106/5924, National Archives, Kew. For the Werewolves in general, I have relied on the recent authoritative study by Perry Biddiscombe, *The Last Nazis*, especially pages 11–60. For the role played by the wolf in the German imagination, as well as that of Hitler personally, see Angela Lambert, *The Lost Life of Eva Braun*, pages 30–31.

24 Linton, op. cit., pages 84–85, 87–91.

25 Nordyke, op. cit., pages 742–743.

7 "A SORT OF ALICE IN WONDERLAND AIR"

1 Francesca Wilson, *Aftermath*, page 19.

2 H. Essame, *Patton*, page 236.

3 Martin Blumenson, *Patton*, page 9; Carlo d'Este, *Patton*, page 400.

4 Robert Reid to his wife, Vera, 17 April 1945, Reid Papers; for the chronology of Patton's advance, see Charles M. Province, *Patton's Third Army, passim*.

5 I.B. Melchior, *Case by Case*, pages 284, 307–308. Melchior was a US counter-intelligence officer in Regensburg.

6 Desmond Hawkins (ed.), *War Report*, page 21.

7 Ibid., pages 24–25.
8 Reid, WRU: C7792, 21 April 1945. For the recording and reporting methods, see Reid's own account in his *War Correspondent*, pages 35–37, and Hawkins, op. cit., pages 24–25.
9 Reid, Dispatch No. 162, 23 April 1945, Reid Papers.
10 J. Coatman to Robert Reid, 10 April 1945, Reid Papers.
11 Vera to Robert Reid, 22 April 1945, Reid Papers.
12 Charles B. MacDonald, *The Last Offensive*, pages 424–425.
13 Reid, letter to Vera, 25 April 1945, and Dispatch No. 163, 23 April 1945, Reid Papers.
14 For the link-up at Torgau, see MacDonald, op. cit., pages 453–456; Antony Beevor, *Berlin*, page 305; Max Hastings, *Armageddon*, pages 503–504; and for Edward Ward, Hawkins, op. cit., pages 330–331.
15 To Robert Reid from Frost BBC, no date, Reid Papers.
16 Vera to Robert Reid, 23 April 1945, Reid Papers.
17 Reid, Dispatches Nos. 170 and 171, 28 and 29 April 1945, Reid Papers.
18 See Martin Blumenson, *The Patton Papers*, pages 693–694.
19 This account of the liberation of Moosburg is taken from John Nichol and Tony Rennell, *The Last Escape*, pages 276–285.
20 Reid, Dispatch No. 174, 30 April 1945 (broadcast 4 May 1945: WRU C11182), Reid Papers.
21 Reid's interview with the Frenchman and the rest of his report on the death march: Reid, Dispatch No. 173, 29 April 1945, Reid Papers.
22 For conditions in Flossenburg see *Headquarters Third United States Army Judge Advocate Section War Crimes Branch*, report to Patton, 21 June 1945, in Avalon Project, Yale Law School, <www.yale.edu/lawweb/avalon/imt/docu-ment/nca_vol 4/2309–ps.htm>.
23 John R. Wilhelm, "The Masters Bury Their Slaves," *Chicago Sun*, 29 April 1945, reproduced in Jack Steinbuck (ed.), *Typewriter Battalion*, page 319; Reid, Dispatch No. 173, 29 April 1945, Reid Papers; for more details of the death march, see the Avalon Project, cited in n. 22, above. For Vera to Robert Reid, see her letter of 22 April 1945, Reid Papers.
24 Reid, Dispatch No. 172, 29 April 1945, Reid Papers.
25 Reid, Dispatch No. 168, 26 April 1945, Reid Papers.
26 See Blumenson, *The Patton Papers*, page 694.

8 "THE MOST DEGENERATE SPECTACLE"

1 *2NZ Div. Intelligence Summary No. 509. Based on information received up to 1800 hours 23 April 45*, in Kippenberger Military Archive and Research Library, Queen Elizabeth II Army Memorial Museum, Waiouru, New Zealand.
2 Monty Soutar, in Ian McGibbon (ed.), *The Oxford Companion to New Zealand Military History*, pages 309–310.
3 Geoffrey Cox, *Race for Trieste*, page 244.
4 Robin Kay, *From Cassino to Trieste*, page 497.
5 Cox, op. cit., page 118.
6 From a battalion diary, quoted in ibid., page 503.

7 *2NZ Div. Intelligence Summary No. 511. Based on Information received up to 1800 hours 25 April 45*, Kippenberger Military Archive, loc. cit.

8 Cox, op. cit., page 123.

9 Geoffrey Cox, *A New Zealand Boyhood, passim.* This brief, fictionalized account of his youth provides a vivid portrait of New Zealand at the time. I am grateful to him for providing me with a copy.

10 Interview with Geoffrey Cox, June 2004.

11 Cox, *Race for Trieste*, page 129.

12 War Diary, G Branch, HQ 2NZ Div. quoted in Kay, op. cit., page 511. See also *2NZ Div. Intelligence Summary No. 512*, Kippenberger Military Archive, loc. cit.

13 Diary Note (typescript), Sunday 29 April 1945, Cox Papers, Alexander Turnbull Library, Wellington, 2003–005–05/6; Cox, *Race for Trieste*, pages 131–135, 141–145; Geoffrey Cox to Cecily Cox, 28 April 1945, Cox Papers, Alexander Turnbull Library, loc. cit., 2003–005–4/14.

14 Kay, op. cit., pages 518–519.

15 Cox, *Race for Trieste*, page 146.

16 Ibid., page 148.

17 *2NZ Div. Intelligence Summary No. 515. Based on information received up to 1800 hours 29 April 45*, Kippenberger Military Archive, loc. cit.

18 James Morris, *Venice*, pages 35, 120, 262.

19 Cox, *Race for Trieste*, page 162.

20 *Daily Telegraph*, 1 May 1945.

21 Ibid., 25 and 27 April 1945.

22 Antony Beevor and Artemis Cooper, *Paris after the Liberation 1944–1949*, pages 166–167.

23 Quoted in Herbert R. Lottman, *The People's Anger*, page 91.

24 Francesca Wilson, *Aftermath*, pages 14–16.

9 DEATH OF A DICTATOR

1 Robert Ellis, *See Naples and Die*, page 200.

2 Ibid., page 18.

3 Frank Harper, *Night Climb*, quoted in ibid., page 30.

4 Ellis, op. cit., pages 32–34.

5 Ibid., page 29.

6 Morning Report, 22 April 1945, Company F, 85th Regiment, Tenth Mountain Division, Denver Public Library, Colorado.

7 John B. Woodruff, *History of the 85th Mountain Infantry Regiment*, page 56.

8 Primo Levi, *If This Is a Man*, pages 22–25, cited in Richard Lamb, *War in Italy*, pages 28–29.

9 On last-minute efforts to surrender by German troops, see Roderick Mackenzie MC, "The End in Italy with the Lowland Gunners: The 178th Medium Regiment RA with the US 10th Mountain Infantry Division 14 April to 2 May 1945." I am indebted to Lt.-Col. Mackenzie for kindly providing me with a copy of this chapter of his memoirs.

10 Ellis, op. cit. ibid., page 194; for excellent maps and diagrams of the campaign, see John Imbrie and Thomas R. Brooks, *10th Mountain Division Campaign in Italy*

NOTES

1945, with battle diagrams by Armand Casini and maps by Barbara Imbrie, *passim*; for von Senger, see McKay Jenkins, *The Last Ridge*, pages 227–228.

11 Ellis's description of this episode is in the "Preamble" to his *See Naples and Die*, pages 5–9; for the quotation from Pyle, see ibid., page 235, and page xiv in the "Introduction" by David Nichols of his edition of Pyle's dispatches — Nichols (ed.), *Ernie's War*.

12 Ibid., pages 32–33.

13 Woodruff, op. cit., page 59.

14 Ernest Fisher, *Cassino to the Alps*, page 504.

15 Jenkins, *The Last Ridge*, page 242; Peter Shelton, *Climb to Conquer*, pages 198–208.

16 Mackenzie, op. cit., page 63.

17 Laura Fermi, *Mussolini*, page 453. There are innumerable accounts of Mussolini's death, often contradictory or inconsistent, and invariably containing a political subtext. For a recent skillful pilot through these treacherous waters, I have been guided by Sergio Luzzatto, *The Body of Il Duce, passim*. I have also consulted the biographies of Mussolini by Robert Bosworth, Denis Mack Smith, Christopher Hibbert and Sir Ivone Kirkpatrick, all listed in the Bibliography.

18 L.K. Truscott, *Command Missions*, page 495.

19 For the conflicting accounts of Mussolini's last few moments, see Luzzatto, op. cit., pages 46–49. As most historical disputes in Italy are, this one is highly politicized.

20 Milton Bracker, "End of the Sawdust Caesar, Milan, April 29 1945"; Steinbuck (ed.), reproduced in *Typewriter Battalion*, pages 315–317; Ernest Ashwick, "Mob Fights to Kick Musso's Body," *Daily Express*, 30 April 1945; Luzzatto, op. cit., pages 61–70.

21 Philip Hamburger, "Letter from Rome, 8 May 1945," in *The New Yorker*, 19 May 1945.

22 Ellis, op. cit., page 207.

23 For the search of Mussolini's villa at Gargagno, see Woodruff, op. cit., pages 60–61, and Jenkins, op. cit., pages 247–249. For this and the larger story of the fate of Mussolini's documents, see Howard McGaw Smyth, *Secrets of the Fascist Era*, pages 168–235.

24 Ellis, op. cit., page 207; for the Tenth Division's casualty rate, see Charles Sanders, *The Boys of Winter*, page 192.

10 HIMMLER'S BID

1 David McCullough, *Truman*, page 377.

2 Count Folke Bernadotte, *The Fall of the Curtain*, pages 20–21.

3 Ibid., page 35.

4 Ibid., pages 56–68; see also Peter Padfield, *Himmler*, page 594.

5 Ibid., page 594.

6 Martin Gilbert, *Road to Victory*, page 1306.

7 Padfield, op. cit., page 596.

8 Gilbert, op. cit., page 1232.

9 Nigel Hamilton, *Monty: The Final Years*, pages 491–495; Clay Blair, *Ridgway's Paratroopers*, pages 488–495.

10 Bryan Samain, *Commando Men*, page 175.

11 Ibid., pages 181–182; David Young, *Four Five*, page 45.

12 Hamilton, op. cit., page 495.

13 Samain, op. cit., pages 182–186.

14 For this and the following, see Leonard Linton, "Kilroy Was Here," his unpublished memoirs, pages 93–139. See also James Gavin, *On to Berlin*, pages 284–290; Phil Nordyke, *All American All the Way*, pages 749–756; and James Megellas, *All the Way to Berlin*, pages 257–269.

11 BOULEVARD OF BROKEN DREAMS

1 David Irving, *Goring*, page 454; Leonard Mosley, *The Reich Marshal*, page 312.

2 James O'Donnell, *The Bunker*, page 131.

3 Mosley, op. cit., page 316; Irving, op. cit., pages 17–18.

4 Angela Lambert, *The Lost Life of Eva Braun*, page 446.

5 For the major sources on Hitler's last days in the bunker, see the references in Chapter 1, n. 1, above. For his remarks to Goebbels, see Kershaw, pages 810–811.

6 Ian Kershaw, *Hitler*, pages 80–82.

7 Lambert, op. cit., page 457.

8 Hugh Trevor-Roper, *The Last Days of Hitler*, pages 140–142.

9 For Albrecht Haushofer's career, as well as the scene that follows, see James Douglas-Hamilton, *The Truth about Rudolf Hess, passim*, but especially pages 218–224.

10 Ibid., pages 221–222.

11 Kershaw, op. cit., pages 817–818.

12 For Bonhoeffer's death, see Eberhard Bethge, *Dietrich Bonhoeffer*, pages 825–831.

13 For Melitta von Stauffenberg's death, see Peter Hoffman, *Stauffenberg*, page 280.

14 For this and other Flossenburg references, see Kurt von Schuschnigg, *Austrian Requiem*, pages 263–271.

15 Fey von Hassell, Diary, 24 March 1937, quoted in idem, *A Mother's War*, page 24.

16 For Niemoller's resistance to Nazism, see his memoirs, *From U-boat to Concentration Camp, passim*; and for his preachings at Dachau, see his *Dachau Sermons*, especially pages 56–57.

17 Quoted by Sigismund Payne Best in *The Venlo Incident*, page 194.

18 Ibid., pages 193–194.

19 M.R.D. Foot, *SOE in France*, page 430. See also Peter Churchill's memoir of his experiences after capture in his book, *The Spirit in the Cage, passim*.

20 Ibid., page 201.

21 Von Hassell, op. cit., page 177. For her later comments on Philipp of Hesse to Payne Best, see her letter to him from Brazzà of 19 April 1946 in the Payne Best Papers, Imperial War Museum, London. For Hesse's wartime art dealings, see Jonathan Petropoulos, *The Faustian Bargain*, pages 106–109, and for an extended analysis of his relations with the Nazis, see idem, *Royals and the Reich, passim*.

22 Schuschnigg, op. cit., page 275.

23 Léon Blum, *L'Oeuvre de Léon Blum*, page 540. Pages 517–544 provide a detailed

account of the journey of the *Prominente* based on his diary. For a life of Blum, see Joel Colton, *Léon Blum*, especially pages 431–444. For the comment by Schuschnigg, see Schuschnigg, op. cit., page 282.

24 Von Hassell, op. cit., page 175; Blum, op. cit., page 538.

25 Churchill, op. cit., page 209.

26 For brief details of the Vermehren affair, see William Shirer, *The Rise and Fall of the Third Reich*, pages 1025–1026; also Hans-Gunter Richardi, *SS — Geiseln in der Alpenfestung*, pages 35–37.

27 Churchill, op. cit., page 210.

28 Red Cushing, *Soldier for Hire*, page 7.

29 Isa Vermehren, *Reise durch den letzten Akt*, pages 202–229 and Cushing, op. cit., pages 261–262. Keeping very much to her own group of fellow prisoners, Fey von Hassell makes no mention in her own account of either Isa Vermehren or Thomas Cushing. For Isa's fiancé, see the letter from Eric Vermehren to Sigismund Payne Best of 10 November 1945, in the Payne Best Papers, Imperial War Museum.

30 Von Hassell, op. cit., page 179, "Italian Refugees," *The Times*, 25 May 1945.

12 ALPINE REFUGE

1 Léon Blum, *L'Oeuvre de Léon Blum*, page 541.

2 Memorandum on his imprisonment written for his SIS superiors immediately after his return to Britain, 22 May 1945, in the Payne Best Papers, Imperial War Museum, London, SPB 1 1/1, page 12. I am grateful to Captain Payne Best's widow for granting me permission to consult her husband's papers.

3 Fey von Hassell, *A Mother's War*, page 182.

4 Francesca Wilson, *A Life of Service and Adventure*, page 20.

5 Francesca Wilson, *Advice to Relief Workers*, page 27.

6 Francesca Wilson, *Aftermath*, pages 13–30.

7 Quoted in Carolyn Burke, *Lee Miller*, page 259.

8 For the liberation of Dachau, see John Bridgman, *The End of the Holocaust*, pages 61–76; also, the chapter by Flint Whitlock, "American Soldiers Recall Their Haunting Experience at Dachau," in Jennifer A. Bussey (ed.), *Events that Changed the World*. This also contains the text of Higgins's report of 1 May 1945 in the *New York Herald Tribune*. For Delestraint, see Blum, op. cit., page 537.

9 Gavriel D. Rosenfeld, *Munich and Memory*, pages 6, 78–79, 349; for "cradle of the Nazi beast," see Rodney Minott, *The Fortress that Never Was*, page 116.

10 Charles B. MacDonald, *The Last Offensive*, pages 435–437.

11 John Toland, *The Last 100 Days*, pages 469–474.

12 MacDonald, op. cit., page 437.

13 Frederic Spotts, *Hitler and the Power of Aesthetics*, page 215.

14 Klaus Mann, quoted in Rosenfeld, op. cit., page 21; for the shelling of SS troops in the city, see MacDonald, op. cit., pages 436–437.

15 Charles Hawley, "The US Soldier Who Liberated Munich Recalls Confronting the Nazi Enemy," *Der Spiegel* Online Special: "The Final Days of World War II," 29 April 2005. (See <http://.spiegel.de/cache/international/>.1518,3554029,00. html>. The American soldier was Wolfgang F. Robinow of the US Forty-second Division.

16 *Daily Telegraph*, 30 April 1945.
17 Sigismund Payne Best, *The Venlo Incident*, page 237. There are some minor inconsistencies of dates in the published accounts of their time at Villabassa by Fey von Hassell, Sigismund Payne Best and Leon Blum. Here, I have relied on the chronology in the synoptic account of their stay in Hans-Gunter Richardi's recent book, *SS — Geiseln in der Alpenfestung*, pages 218–222.

13 "DEATH FLED"

1 Gerald Schwab, *OSS Agents in Hitler's Heartland*, passim.
2 Fred Warner, "Don't You Know There's a War On?," pages 21–30.
3 Ibid., page 54.
4 Ibid., pages 48–55; Major A. W. Freud, "Before the Anti-Climax," unpublished typescript memoir, 1993, Imperial War Museum, London, Papers of Major A. W. Freud, 6, Item 2, pages 46–56. I have checked and complemented these personal accounts with material from the SOE Archives in the National Archives, London, especially HS 7/146, "Activities of X Section in Italy [sic]," Appendix A; "Interrogation of Lt. Bryant, Historian Party, Date 13 May 10.10 Hours," Appendix E of the same document, also in HS 7/146. See also W. J. M. Mackenzie, *The Secret History of SOE 1940–1945*, pages 686–689.
5 For the Bryant group's exploits in the mountains, see HS 7/146, op. cit.
6 Rodney Minott, *The Fortress that Never Was*, page 25.
7 Ibid., pages 25, 38.
8 Peter Black, *Ernst Kaltenbrunner*, page 238.
9 F. H. Hinsley, *British Intelligence in the Second World War*, Vol. III, Part 2, pages 734–736.
10 HW/HW1/3747, National Archives, Kew.
11 The best account in English is by Henri A. van der Zee, *The Hunger Winter*.
12 See *The Times*, 25 November 2003.
13 Van der Zee, op. cit., page 230.
14 Ibid., page 184.
15 Francis De Guingand, *Operation Victory*, page 452.
16 Quoted in David Kaufman and Michiel Horn, *A Liberation Album*, page 105.
17 Van der Zee, op. cit., page 257.
18 F. S. V. Donnison, *Civil Affairs and Military Government*, page 148. See also *The Times*, 28 May 1945.

14 "THE BITTEREST BATTLE"

1 I am grateful to Reg Roy for providing me with the extensive personal details of his service with the Cape Breton Highlanders which appear below. These came largely by way of email contact but also through copies of his diary entries and letters home.
2 Alex Morrison and Ted Slaney, *The Breed of Manly Men*, page 6.
3 Terry Copp, "The Cruellest Month," *Legion Magazine* (Canada), November/December 2003. See also, for the campaign and battle, his *Cinderella Army*.
4 Baudouin Bollaert, "In the Tracks of Simenon to North Cape," *Le Figaro* (Paris) 26 July 2001.

NOTES

5 For information on Delfzijl during the Second World War, I am grateful to local historian Franz Lenselink for very kindly giving me a guided tour of the town in April 2005. I have also relied on his booklet, *Delfzijl 1940–1945: Five Years of War and Occupation in Retrospect*, translated by George van Rossum (Delfzijl 1998) for many of the details here. I am also indebted to Monique Brinks, of the Groningen Archiv, and to Professor Homme Wedman of the University of Groningen, who gave me much-appreciated help relating to the wartime history of the city.

6 M.R.D. Foot, *SOE in the Low Countries*, pages 85, 140.

7 J. Prosser, *Ashes in the Wind*, pages 57–58.

8 For details of the Canadian attack on Delfzijl, see the unpublished thesis by Daniel T. Byers, "Operation 'Canada': The Canadian Attack on Delfzijl, April 23–May 2, 1945," Wilfrid Laurier University, Waterloo, Ontario, April 1991, a copy of which has been kindly supplied to me by Professor Terry Copp, director of the Centre for Military, Strategic, and Disarmament Studies at the university. I have also drawn on Douglas E. Delaney, *The Soldiers' General*, especially pages 343–392, as well as on the history of the British Columbia Dragoons by Reg Roy, *Sinews of Steel*, pages 399–406, and Morrison and Slaney, op. cit., pages 319–329.

9 Byers, op. cit., pages 9–10; Terry Copp, *Cinderella Army*, page 309.

10 Roy, Diary, 21 April 1945; letters to parents, and to Ardith Christie, 7 March 1945.

11 Professor Homme Wedman, letter to author, 8 July 2005.

12 Roy, Diary, 30 April 1945.

13 Roy to author, email, 13 April 2005.

14 Roy to author, emails, 6 April 2005 and 11 December 2006; letter to parents, 9 May 1945.

15 Roy, Diary, 1 May 1945.

15 DEALING WITH NAZIS

1 Chester Wilmot, dispatch of 30 April, quoted in Desmond Hawkins (ed.), *War Report*, pages 322–323.

2 George Blake, *Mountain and Flood*, pages 203–204.

3 Ibid., pages 325–326.

4 "C" [the traditional code name of the head of the SIS — in this case Sir Stewart Menzies] to Prime Minister, 30 April 1945, C9091, in HW1/3793, National Archives, Kew.

5 Hitler order to OKW, 17 April 1945, in HW1/3709, National Archives, Kew.

6 For Churchill's respect for the power of guerrilla warfare and behind-the-lines resistance, see David Stafford, *Churchill and Secret Service*, *passim*.

7 For Kesselring's order of the day, see HW 1/3794; Doenitz message of 1 May 1945, HW1/3752, National Archives, Kew.

8 Gerald Posner, *Hitler's Children*, page 136.

9 Corelli Barnett, *Engage the Enemy More Closely*, pages 852–852; see also F.H. Hinsley, *British Intelligence in World War Two*, Vol. III, Part 2, pages 625–641, and Andrew Williams, *The Battle of the Atlantic*, page 284.

10 Karl Doenitz, *Memoirs*, page 468.

11 Chester Wilmot, *The Struggle for Europe*, pages 689–693; for "rock of resistance," see Williams, op. cit., page 284; Peter Padfield, *Doenitz*, pages 382–403.

12 Doenitz, op. cit., page 445.

13 Bryan Samain, memorandum to author, 27 June 2003. See also his *Commando Men*, pages 186–187.

14 Desmond Flower, *History of the Argyll and Sutherland Highlanders*, page 369.

15 Samain to author, 27 June 2003.

16 Sean Longden, *To the Victor the Spoils*, page 86.

17 Samain to author, 27 June 2003.

18 Samain, *Commando Men*, page 187.

19 For this account of Mills-Roberts's encounter with Milch, I have drawn on his published account in *Clash by Night* as well as on his sworn and unpublished written statement about the incident, dated 8 August 1969, in the Mills-Roberts Papers, Liddell Hart Centre for Military Archives, King's College, London. See also, in the same archival collection, the testimony of his experiences at Neustadt by E.W. Ruston, dated 12 June 1969. Both statements were drawn up during a dispute over the legitimate ownership of Milch's baton, which Mills-Roberts had kept after the war and which Milch's family (unsuccessfully) attempted to recover through court action. The brief account in David Irving's biography of Milch, *Rise and Fall of the Luftwaffe*, pages 295–296, while quoting from Milch's diary, omits any reference to Mills-Roberts. For a pen portrait of the latter, see Bryan Samain, "Derek Mills-Roberts (1909–1980)," in *Personal Encounters*, pages 81–84.

16 THE *CAP ARCONA*

1 *Stern*, 17 March 1983.

2 The story of Michel Hollard, DSO, Croix de Guerre, is told in George Martelli, *Agent Extraordinary*, especially pages 270–276.

3 Ibid., page 273.

4 *Stern*, op. cit.

5 *Titanic* (Germany 1943), directors Herbert Selpin and Werner Klinger, Tobis Productions for UFA films.

6 Martelli, op. cit., page 274.

7 See *No. 83 Group Intelligence Summary No. 138 up to 2359 hours 3rd May* [1945], *Part 1*, page 1. I am grateful to Sebastian Cox, head of the Air Historical Branch, Royal Air Force, Bentley Priory, Stanmore, Middlesex, for providing me with a copy of this report, as well as other material and references relating to the *Cap Arcona* affair. The original report (AIR 25/707) can be found in the National Archives, Kew.

8 Martelli, op. cit., page 276.

9 Hans Arnoldsson, *Natt och dimma*, pages 156–165.

10 *Stern*, 3 March 1983.

11 These quotations are taken from interviews with surviving RAF pilots for a series of articles published in 1983 by *Stern* magazine on the *Cap Arcona* affair. In some important details, however, such as which squadrons were responsible for

attacking which ships, the article is unreliable. See *Stern*, Vols. 10–15, six-part series, "*Cap Arcona*," 3 March–7 April 1983. See also the *Sunday Telegraph*, 13 March 1983. For a more careful, if incomplete, account, see the chapter by Roy Nesbitt in his book, *Failed to Return*, pages 170–178. I have also drawn usefully on the 1992 pamphlet by Wilhelm Lange, "*Cap Arcona*," written for the town of Neustadt and available at the *Cap Arcona* Museum located there.

12 *Stern*, 24 March 1983.

13 Ibid.

14 From the *Cap Arcona* file, Air Historical Branch, Stanmore.

15 For these personal accounts, see ibid.

16 "Report on Investigations," by Major N.O. Till, Investigating Officer, No. 2 War Crimes Investigation Team Headquarters, British Army of the Rhine, WO 309/1592. National Archives, Kew.

17 *Stern*, 30 March 1983.

18 Quoted in Michael Horbach, *Out of the Night*, page 255.

19 Letter by F.G. Parson, former ADC to General Sir Evelyn Barker, Commander of British Army VIII Corps, *Daily Telegraph*, 10 March 1983; and Nesbitt, op. cit., page 178.

20 Samain, letter to author, 27 June 2003. For a pen portrait of de Jonghe, see Ian Dear, *Ten Commando*, pages 182–183.

21 Undated letter from a tank commander (name unknown) in the 23rd Hussars belonging to the British Eleventh Armored Division, in *Cap Arcona* material provided by the Air Historical Branch, Royal Air Force.

22 Gerry Brent, "Brent's Navy," an unpublished manuscript kindly provided by its author, who served with 6 Commando during the Second World War; for "gun flashes," see the unpublished memoir by another 6 Commando soldier, Lance Corporal Cliff Morris, Part 2, page 138, located in the Mills-Roberts Papers, Liddell Hart Centre, King's College, London.

17 "THE DEAD-END OF HITLER'S REICH"

1 For the Canadians at Wismar, see *The 1st Canadian Parachute Battalion in the Low Countries and in Germany: Final Operations. Report No. 17, Historical Section (G.S.) Army Headquarters, Ottawa, 27 October 1947*, Directorate of History and Heritage, Department of National Defence, Ottawa, esp. pages 38–40. Available online at <http://www.forces.gc.ca>. For Wynford Vaughan Thomas's *War Report* dispatch, see Desmond Hawkins (ed.), page 334.

2 Leonard Linton, "Kilroy Was Here," page 109.

3 Ibid., pages 112–113.

4 Ibid., page 112; James Megellas, *All the Way to Berlin*, page 61.

5 Linton, op. cit., page 115.

6 Megellas, op. cit., pages 264–265; Linton, op. cit., page 104.

7 Philip Nordyke, *All American All the Way*, pages 751–752.

8 Quoted in Antony Beevor, *Berlin*, page 28.

9 Ibid., pages 32–33.

10 Ibid., page 67.

11 Linton, op. cit., page 147; Megellas, op. cit., page 267.

12 Elizabeth Heinemann, *What Difference Does a Husband Make?*, page 81; Beevor, op. cit., page 412; Lynn Nicholas, *Cruel World*, page 520.

13 Fey von Hassell, *A Mother's War*, pages 183–184.

14 Sigismund Payne Best to Fey von Hassell, letter of 18 May 1946, Fey von Hassell Collection, Brazzà; with thanks to David Forbes-Watt; see also von Hassell, op. cit., page 285.

15 Léon Blum, *L'Oeuvre de Léon Blum*, page 544; Sigismund Payne Best, *The Venlo Incident*, page 247; von Hassell, op. cit., page 186.

16 Ibid.

17 Douglas Botting, *In the Ruins of the Reich*, pages 115–116.

18 HITLER'S LOOT

1 Ian Kershaw, *Hitler*, pages 834–835. See also Karl Doenitz, *Memoirs*, pages 449–466 and Peter Padfield, *Doenitz*, pages 413–421.

2 Kershaw, op. cit., page 835.

3 Robert Reid, Dispatch No. 175, 1 May 1945, Reid Papers; Charles Province, *Patton's Third Army*, page 275.

4 Letters of Vera to Robert Reid, 29 and 30 April 1945, Reid Papers.

5 Martha Gellhorn, "Das Deutsches Volk," *Collier's*, 26 May 1945.

6 For Hitler, Linz and Bruckner, see Frederic Spotts, *Hitler and the Power of Aesthetics*, pages 62, 87, 187–189, 204, 211–217, 240, 230–233 and 374–378; for "a transcendent aesthetic experience," see ibid., page 4; see also Lynn Nicholas, *The Rape of Europa*, pages 41–49; also, idem, *Cruel World*, page 423, where the date is claimed as 12 April.

7 Reid, telediphone recording, 8 May 1945, WRU 11313, Reid Papers; Reid, report of recording, 8 May 1945, No. 185, loc. cit.; Robert Reid, *War Correspondent*, pages 88–94.

8 Fred Warner, "Don't You Know There's a War On?," pages 55–60.

9 For this and the following, see ibid., as well as Bryant's after-mission debriefing, entitled "Interrogation of Lt. Bryant. Historian Party 13 May 1945," in SOE file HS 7/146, National Archives, Kew, pages 1–29.

10 "Before the Anti-Climax," memoir by A.W. Freud, GB 62/6/2, Imperial War Museum, London, pages 57–61. While a brief report on his mission written immediately afterwards survives, including the text of the radio message he attempted to send from Zeltweg, it differs in several respects from the memoir. Such is the fragility of memory. The novelist Esther Freud, in her novel *The Sea House*, loosely bases the wartime career of her character Lehmann on Walter's experiences with SOE in Austria.

11 Warner, op. cit., page 63; see also Bryant, op. cit. For Globocnik, see Michael Burleigh, *The Third Reich*, page 584; also, Gita Sereny, *The German Trauma*, pages 195, 198.

12 Warner, op. cit., page 66.

13 Catherine Merridale, *Ivan's War*, pages 141, 351.

14 Warner, op. cit., page 67.

15 Quoted in J. Bridgman, *The End of the Holocaust*, page 133.

16 Alison Leslie Gold, *Fiet's Vase*, page 12.

17 For the following, see Nicholas, *The Rape of Europa*, pages 41–49 and 312–317.
18 Spotts, op. cit., pages 215– 218; Nicholas, *Rape*, page 143.
19 Nicholas, ibid., pages 346–350.
20 Thomas C. Howe, *Salt Mines and Castles*, page 143.
21 Nicholas, op. cit., page 348.
22 Ibid., page 360.
23 Ibid., page 282. See also Anne Rothfeld, "Nazi Looted Art," *Prologue* (National Archives, Washington, DC), Fall 2002, Vol. 34, No. 3.

19 "THE DAWN HAS BROKEN THROUGH AT LAST"

1 For this and the following, see Robert Ellis, *See Naples and Die*, pages 210–230; John B. Woodruff, *History of the 85th Mountain Infantry Regiment*, Carl V. Cossin, *I Soldiered with America's Elite*, pages 75–88; and "F" Company morning reports, May–July 1945, Denver Public Library.
2 *The Times*, 26 May 1945.
3 Ellis, op. cit., page 214.
4 Ibid., page 217.
5 Geoffrey Cox, *Race for Trieste*, page 9.
6 Ibid., pages 156–157; Robin Kay, *From Cassino to Trieste*, pages 532–585.
7 Geoffrey Cox, letter to his wife, 6 May 1945, Alexander Turnbull Library, Wellington, New Zealand, 2003–005–4/14.
8 Kay, op. cit., pages 542–543.
9 Cox, op. cit., page 205.
10 "Conference held at main 2NZ Div. at 0830 Hrs, 4th May 1945," in Cox Papers, Kippenberger Military Archive, Waiouru, New Zealand. See also Kay, op. cit., pages 555–556, and Roberto Rabal, "A Hell of a Way to End a War," in John Crawford (ed.), *Kia Kaha*, pages 276–288.
11 *The Times* (London), 15 May 1945.
12 Claudio Magris, *Microcosms*, page 103; and Cox, op. cit., page 158. See also Franklin Lindsay, *Beacons in the Night*, pages 291–312.
13 Michael Burleigh, *Death and Deliverance*, page 237; also, Glenda A. Sluga, "The Risiera di San Sabba: Fascism, Anti-Fascism and Italian Nationalism," *Journal of Italian Studies*, Vol. 1, No. 3, pages 401–412; and *Risiera di San Sabba; Monumento Nazionale*, guide published by the Comune di Trieste.
14 "Quislings in Trieste," *The Times*, 21 May 1945. For "Trojan horse," see Harry Coles and Albert Weinberg, *Civil Affairs*, page 599.
15 Cox, op. cit., pages 18, 150–157, 207.
16 Ibid., page 245; Kay, op. cit., page 558.
17 The account that follows is based on various testimonies to be found in the file FO 371/ 48953, "Venezia Giulia: Yugoslav Atrocities—Investigating Committee Report, 27/9/45, Part 2, Appendix A, 'Foibes,' " National Archives, Kew. At the time of this report, eight whole bodies and a large number of dismembered parts of corpses had been brought to the surface. One body was that of a civilian, the other seven were of German soldiers.
18 John Shillidy to author, 19 January 2005.
19 Cox, op. cit., page 231.

20 David Irving, *Göring*, page 21.

21 Ibid., page 475.

22 See documents 37–39 in *The Papers of Dwight David Eisenhower, Occupation, 1945*, Vol. VI, pages 39–44.

20 VE DAY

1 Juliet Gardiner, *Wartime*, page 573. For VE Day, I have also drawn from the books by Angus Calder, Maureen Waller and Russell Miller listed in the Bibliography. See also Martin Gilbert's comprehensive book, *The Day the War Ended, passim*.

2 Gardiner, op. cit., page 576.

3 Reg Roy, Diary, 2–14 May 1945, and letter to parents, 9 May 1945, Roy Papers.

4 Robert Reid, BBC interview with B. Whitaker, 30 May 1945, WRU C/11616, Reid Papers.

5 *Scotsman*, 8 May 1945.

6 For a brief summary of the work of the Monuments Men, see Anne Rothfeld, "Nazi Looted Art: The Holocaust Records Preservation Project, Part 2," *Prologue*, Fall 2002, Vol. 34, No. 3: Available at <http://www.archives.gov/publications/prologue/2002/summer/nazi-looted-art-2.html>.

7 Walter Hancock, "Experiences of a Monuments Officer in Germany," *College Art Journal*, Vol. V, No. 4, May 1946, page 295.

8 Ibid., page 297. See also Lynn Nicholas, *The Rape of Europa*, pages 338–339.

9 See Anton Joachimsthaler, *The Last Days of Hitler: The Legends, the Evidence, the Truth*, especially pages 231–236. *The Times*, 9 July 1945.

10 Quoted on Benjamin B. Fischer, "The Hitler Archive . . . at Last," *Intelligence and National Security*, Vol. 16, No. 4, Winter 2001, pages 238–247.

11 Hans Frederik Dahl, *Quisling*, pages 354–383.

12 Francesca Wilson, *Aftermath*, pages 29–31.

13 Fey von Hassell, *A Mother's War*, pages 2–3, 33.

14 For the Feldafing SA *Oberschule*, see Lynn Nicholas, *Cruel World*, pages 118–123.

15 Francesca Wilson, Diary, 31 May 1945. I am deeply grateful to Francesca Wilson's niece, June Horder, for providing me with copies of the remnants of her aunt's papers in her possession. Most of the account of her work at Feldafing is based on Wilson, op. cit., pages 31–58. For Salonica, see Mark Mazowar, *Salonica*, pages 392–411.

16 Bryan Samain, note to author, 23 June 2005.

17 Ibid., and David Young, *Four Five*, pages 123–127.

18 Samain, op. cit. For German POWs in Schleswig-Holstein, see *The Times*, 21 May 1945; and for Eutin's political profile, see Lawrence D. Stokes, "Conservative Opposition to Nazism in Eutin, Schleswig-Holstein, 1932–1933," in Francis R. Nicosia and Lawrence Stokes (eds.), *Germans against Nazism*, pages 37–57.

19 Major-General J.B. Churcher, "A Soldier's Story," manuscript in Liddell Hart Centre for Military Archives, King's College, London, pages 74–78.

20 Peter Padfield, *Doenitz*, pages 423–433; Earl M. Ziemke, *The US Army in the Occupation of Germany*, page 262; Joachim Fest, *Speer*, page 277.

21 Ibid., pages 275, 277–278.

22 Padfield, op. cit., pages 423–424.

23 For the following, I have drawn on the article by Chris Madsen, "Victims of Circumstance: The Execution of German Deserters by Surrendered German Troops under Canadian Control in Amsterdam, May 1945," *Canadian Military History*, Vol. 2, No. 1, Spring 1993, pages 93–113. Blaskowitz committed suicide in 1948 before appearing at a Nuremberg war crimes trial.

21 "FORTUNE IS NOT ALWAYS JOY"

1 Fey von Hassell, *A Mother's War*, pages 184–192; S. Payne Best, *The Venlo Incident*, 238; Fey von Hassell, letter to Payne Best, 14 December 1945, Payne Best Papers, Imperial War Museum, London.

2 Von Hassell, op. cit., page 187.

3 Ibid., pages 187–188.

4 Ibid., page 54.

5 Ibid., page 189. See also her letter to Payne Best of 28 July 1946, in Payne Best Papers, loc. cit. For a comprehensive account of Philipp of Hesse's links with the Nazis, see Jonathan Petropoulos, *Royals and the Reich*, *passim*.

6 Payne Best, op. cit., page 252.

7 Von Hassell, op. cit., page 191.

8 Ibid.

9 Ibid., pages 190–192. See also letter to Payne Best, 28 July 1946, Payne Best Papers, loc. cit.

10 Francesca Wilson, *Advice to Relief Workers*, pages 6–7.

11 Francesca Wilson, *Aftermath*, page 54.

12 Quoted by Francesca Wilson in a World Affairs lecture dated 11 January 1950, in her papers.

13 Francesca Wilson, Diary, 31 May 1945, extract in possession of June Horder, to whom many thanks.

14 Michael Burleigh, *Death and Deliverance in Nazi Germany*, especially pages 240–242; Henry Friedlander, *The Origins of Nazi Genocide*, pages 162–163; Lynn Nicholas, *Cruel World*, pages 38–54.

15 Ibid., page 3.

16 Ibid., pages 4–5. See also *The Times*, 5 July 1945.

17 Nicholas, op. cit., page 5.

18 For an account of his suicide, and of the postwar myth that he survived, see Gita Sereny, *The German Trauma*, pages 200–215.

19 The following account is based on material in files of the Intelligence Corps at Chicksands, Bedfordshire, and on the article "Himmler's Suicide," by John Hillyer-Funke and Winston Ramsay in *After the Battle*, No. 14, 1975.

20 Note of 3 May 1945, as quoted in "The Private Thoughts of a Public Man," *New York Times*, 22 January 2006. For Churchill and the summary execution of top Nazis, see Arieh Kochavi, *Prelude to Nuremberg*, page 74.

21 See Desmond Hawkins (ed.), *War Report*, page 38.

22 James Gavin, Diary, 3 May 1945, quoted in Philip Nordyke, *All American All the Way*, page 752.

23 Leonard Linton, "Kilroy Was Here," page 140.
24 Ibid., page 148.
25 Ibid., page 156.

22 "A GROTESQUE COMEDY"

 1 For the story of the arrest of Doenitz, see Major-General J.B. Churcher, "A Soldier's Story," typescript memoir in the Liddell Hart Centre for Military Archives, King's College, London, pages 74–81; also, Earl Ziemke, *The US Army in the Occupation of Germany*, pages 260–263; Peter Padfield, *Doenitz*, pages 424–435; Marlis G. Steinert, *Capitulation*, *passim*.
 2 Joachim Fest, *Speer*, page 280.
 3 Churchill to Foreign Office quoted in Marlis G. Steinert, "The Allied Decision to Arrest the Doenitz Government," *Historical Journal*, Vol. 31, No. 3, September 1988, page 656; Earl Ziemke, *The US Army in the Occupation of Germany*, page 262, n. 23.
 4 Steinert, *Capitulation*, pages 271–275.
 5 Ibid., pages 212–213.
 6 *The War Illustrated*, No. 207, 25 May 1945.
 7 David Stafford (ed.), *Flight From Reality*, *passim*.
 8 Richard Overy, *Interrogations*, page 32; Arieh Kochavi, *Prelude to Nuremberg*, page 74. For the following, see also Joe Heydecker, *The Nuremberg Trials*, pages 1–42.
 9 Anne Tusa and John Tusa, *The Nuremberg Trial*, page 40.
10 Henri van der Zee, *The Hunger Winter*, page 274.
11 For the capture of Joyce, see Adrian Weale, *Renegades*, pages 171–173. On Geoffrey Perry, see Lesley Chamberlain, "Malice through the Looking Glass," *Financial Times Magazine*, 28 February 2004, pages 22–25.
12 Weale, op. cit., page 54; Rebecca West, *The New Meaning of Treason*, page 93.
13 For Amery, see Weale, op. cit., pages 47–62 and West, op. cit., pages 91–108. Also, Adrian Weale, *Patriotic Traitors*, page 225.
14 C. David Heymann, *Ezra Pound*, page 149.
15 Ibid., page 160. For Pound's wartime activities, see also Peter Ackroyd, *Ezra Pound and His World*, pages 85–87; Charles Norman, *Ezra Pound*, pages 386–405; Noel Stock, *The Life of Ezra Pound*, pages 392–415; John Tytell, *Ezra Pound*, pages 268–278.
16 John B. Woodruff, *History of the 85th Mountain Infantry Regiment*, page 70.
17 Geoffrey Cox, *The Race for Trieste*, page 254.
18 Harold Macmillan, *The Blast of War*, page 701; Alfred Connor Bowman, *Zones of Strain*, pages 19–20.
19 C.R.S. Harris, *Allied Military Administration of Italy*, pages 295–316; Luca Alessandrini, "The Option of Violence — Partisan Activity in the Bologna Area 1945–1948," in Jonathan Dunnage (ed.), *After the War*, pages 58–74. For a discussion of the historiography of the period 1943–45, see Richard Bosworth, *The Italian Dictatorship*, pages 180–204.
20 Roy Palmer Domenico, *Italian Fascists on Trial*, page 144; Harris, op. cit., page 305.

NOTES

21 Sir Noel Charles, Rome, to Foreign Office, 11 May 1945, WO 106/3965A/182, National Archives, Kew.

22 Sir Noel Charles, Rome, to Foreign Office, 16 and 25 May 1945, loc. cit.

23 *The War Illustrated*, No. 207, 25 May 1945.

23 "AN IRON CURTAIN"

1 Herbert Feis, *Between War and Peace*, page v.

2 For Churchill's telegram to Truman, see Martin Gilbert, *Winston S. Churchill 1945–1965: "Never Despair,"* pages 6–7; for his concern about France and Germany, see his message to Eisenhower of 9 May, quoted in the *Triumph and Tragedy* volume of war memoirs, page 490.

3 Gilbert, op. cit., page 17.

4 Fred Warner, "Don't You Know There's a War On?," page 66.

5 Ibid., page 69. See also "Interrogation of Lt. Bryant, Historian Party, 13 May 1945," HS7/146, National Archives, Kew, pages 15, 20.

6 Warner, op. cit., page 70.

7 Ibid., page 73.

8 Quoted in Douglas Botting, *In the Ruins of the Reich*, page 124.

9 Warner, op. cit., page 73.

10 Ibid., page 74.

11 Nicholas Bethell, *The Last Secret*, page 166.

12 Botting, op. cit., pages 127–128; Warner, op. cit., page 74. See also Christopher Booker, *A Looking-Glass Tragedy*, passim.

13 Warner, op. cit., page 75.

14 John Imbrie to author, 11 July 2005.

15 McKay Jenkins, *The Last Ridge*, pages 251–252.

16 Francesca Wilson, *Aftermath*, page 55; and Diary, 31 May 1945.

17 Ibid.; on employment, see George Woodbridge, *UNRRA*, Vol. II, page 519.

18 Wilson, op. cit., page 65.

19 For the above, see ibid., pages 71, 80–83; and her Diary for 11 and 17 June 1945.

20 Ibid., 17 June 1945.

21 Mark Wyman, *DPs*, pages 62–63; Wilson, Diary, 31 May 1945. For UNRRA and repatriation, see Woodbridge, op. cit., Vol. II, pages 473–474.

22 Quoted in James Lucas, *Last Days of the Reich*, page 77.

23 Eagle Glassheim, "The Mechanics of Ethnic Cleansing: The Expulsion of Germans from Czechoslovakia 1945–1947," in Philipp Ther and Ana Siljak (eds.), *Redrawing Nations*, page 209. For other accounts, see Alfred de Zayas, *Nemesis at Potsdam*, especially pages 104–120; and Pertti Ahonen, *After the Expulsion*, pages 15–24.

24 Glassheim, op. cit., page 207.

25 Wilson, Diary, 11 June 1945.

26 Paul Kemp, "The British Army and the Liberation of Bergen-Belsen," in Joanne Reilly *et al.* (eds.), *Belsen in History and Memory*, page 144.

24 "YOU LOST PEOPLE AS YOU GAINED YOUR FREEDOM"

1 Robert Reid, "Postscript on Germany," *Yorkshire Post*, 26 June 1945, Reid Papers.

2 Robert Reid, "A Journey by Jeep," *Manchester Guardian*, 19 June 1945, Reid Papers.

3 Robert Reid, "Glimpse of Paris Scene," *Yorkshire Observer*, 5 March 1945.

4 Robert Reid, interview with B. Whittaker, 30 May 1945, WRU C/11616, Reid Papers.

5 Henry van der Zee, *The Hunger Winter*, page 286.

6 David Kaufman and Michiel Horn, *A Liberation Album*, page 112.

7 Ibid., page 117.

8 Ibid., page 120.

9 For collaborators, see Henry L. Mason, *The Purge of the Dutch Quislings*, *passim*; Peter Romijn, " 'Restoration of Confidence': The Purge of Local Government in the Netherlands as a Problem of Postwar Reconstruction," in Istvan Deak *et al.* (eds.), *The Politics of Retribution in Europe*, pages 173–193. For Groningen, see the booklet written to accompany the 2005 exhibition at the University of Groningen Museum, "From Me to May: The First Year after the War in Groningen." I am particularly grateful to the exhibition's curator, Monique Brinks, for providing me with a copy of this, and for talking to me about the exhibition.

10 Peter Romijn, "The Synthesis of the Political Order and the Resistance Movement in the Netherlands in 1945," in Gill Bennett (ed.), *The End of the War in Europe 1945*, pages 139–147.

11 Quoted in Kaufman and Horn, op. cit., page 121.

12 For the following, I have drawn on ibid., especially pages 129–164, and Michiel Horn, "More than Cigarettes, Sex and Chocolate: The Canadian Army in the Netherlands, 1944–1945," *Journal of Canadian Studies*, Vol. 16, Nos. 3 and 4, Fall/Winter 1981, pages 156–173.

13 Kaufman and Horn, op. cit., pages 147–148.

14 Ibid., page 138; and Horn, op. cit., page 167.

15 Ibid., page 168.

16 For the above, see letters from Reg Roy to his parents and his sister of 2, 3, 5, and 7 July 1945, Roy Papers.

17 Perry Biddiscombe, *The Last Nazis*, pages 205, 235.

18 *Evening Citizen*, 15 June 1945. For details of Ribbentrop's capture, see Joe Heydecker, *The Nuremberg Trials*, as well as field security files at the Intelligence Corps Museum, Chicksands, Bedfordshire.

19 Philip Hamburger, "Letter from Rome," 8 May 1945, *The New Yorker*, 19 May 1945.

20 Fey von Hassell, *A Mother's War*, pages 193–194.

21 Fey von Hassell, in discussion with the author, Rome, June 2005.

22 Lynn Nicholas, *Cruel World*, pages 518–519.

23 For the search for the boys, see von Hassell, op. cit., pages 193–204.

25 BERLIN: THE GRAY CITY

1 Francesca Wilson, Diary, undated (July 1945).

2 Francesca Wilson, *Aftermath*, pages 111–115.

3 For Keegan, see Ladislas Farago, *The Last Days of Patton*, pages 73–145; and for

the dispute with Eisenhower, see Stephen Ambrose, *Eisenhower: Soldier, General of the Army*, page 423.

4 Gottfried R. Bloch, *Unfree Associations*, page 236. I am grateful to Frank Bright for bringing this book to my attention.

5 Wilson, op. cit., pages 116–117; see also John Bridgman, "Dachau," idem, in *The End of the Holocaust*, pages 72–73.

6 Quoted in Geoffrey Cox, *The Race for Trieste*, page 260.

7 Robin Kay, *From Cassino to Trieste*, page 565.

8 *13 Corps Periodical Intelligence Summary No. 4*, 9 July 1945, Intelligence Corps Museum, Chicksands, Bedfordshire.

9 Sarah Morgan, "The Schio Killings: A Case Study of Partisan Violence in Post-War Italy," *Modern Italy*, Vol. 5, No. 2, 2000, pages 147–160; also Osvaldo Croci's riposte, "Guilt, Context and the Historian: Debating the Schio Massacre," *Modern Italy*, Vol. 6, No. 2, 2001, pages 223–231. Several of those accused of the massacre fled to Yugoslavia. Seven others were brought to trial before an allied military court and three received death sentences (later commuted).

10 Letter to his parents, 1 July 1945, in Robert Ellis, *See Naples and Die*, pages 224–225. His letters are a valuable corrective to the assertion by Paul Fussell in his book *Wartime* that soldiers' letters home are of little value in providing a realistic view of battle.

11 See "F" Company, 85th Regiment morning reports for May–July 1945, especially those of 8, 15 and 27 June.

12 Letter home, 17 June 1945, in Ellis, op. cit., page 222.

13 Diary entry, 14 June 1945, in ibid., page 221.

14 Robert Reid to Vera, 9 May 1945; Vera to Robert, 14 May 1945, Reid Papers.

15 Quoted in Matthew Utley, "Operation 'Surgeon' and Britain's Post-War Exploitation of Nazi German Aeronautics," *Intelligence and National Security*, Vol. 17, No. 2, Summer 2002, page 1.

16 For the allies and German science, see in general Michel Bar-Zohar, *The Hunt for German Scientists*, and Tom Bower, *The Paperclip Conspiracy*, passim. A recent American account may be found in Wolfgang Samuel, *American Raiders*. For von Braun, see Dennis Piszkiewicz, *Wernher von Braun*, passim.

17 Osmar White, dispatch from Berlin, 3 July 1945, in idem, *Conqueror's Road*, page 119. For fuller details of the US Army's entry into the city, see US Headquarters Berlin District, and HQ First Airborne Army, *History and Report of Operations 8 May–31 December 1945*, Part 2, 27 June 1946, pages 1–13, copy in author's possession. Also, Leonard Linton, "Kilroy Was Here," pages 163–165; and James Megellas, *All the Way to Berlin*, page 272.

18 James P. O'Donnell, *The Bunker*, page 7.

19 "British in Berlin," *The Times*, 4 July 1945; "Union Jack Flies over Berlin," *The Times*, 7 July 1945.

20 Linton, op. cit., pages 166–171.

21 *The Times*, 5 July 1945.

22 Richard Brett-Smith, *Berlin '45*, page 88.

23 W. Byford Jones, *Berlin Twilight*, pages 34–38.

24 Ibid.
25 Douglas Botting, *In the Ruins of the Reich*, page 192.

26 MONDAY, 16 JULY 1945

1 Gregor Dallas, *Poisoned Peace*, page 527.
2 Francesca Wilson, *Aftermath*, page 118.
3 Ibid., page 122.
4 Ibid., page 127.
5 "Big Cuts in UNRRA supplies," *The Times*, 11 July 1945.
6 F.S.V. Donnison, *Civil Affairs*, pages 355–357.
7 Reg Roy to his parents, two letters of 22 July 1945.
8 For this and the following, see Robert Ellis, *See Naples and Die*, pages 227–235.
9 For this and the following, see Fey von Hassell, *A Mother's War*, pages 205–208.
10 Ibid., page 207.
11 For this and the following, see Bryan Samain, letter and enclosure to author, 13 May 2006.
12 Leonard Linton, "Kilroy Was Here," page 191.
13 Philip Windsor, *City on Leave*, pages 32–48; Donnison, op. cit., page 240.
14 Earl Ziemke, *The US Army in the Occupation of Germany*, page 321.
15 Donnison, op. cit., page 238.
16 Ziemke, op. cit., pages 321–324.
17 *The Times*, 9 July 1945.
18 Donnison, op. cit., pages 240–241.
19 *The Times*, loc. cit.; see also Donnison, op. cit., pages 238–239.
20 *New York Times*, 16 July 1945.
21 Stephen Ambrose, *Eisenhower*, page 420.
22 Forrest Pogue, *The Supreme Command*, page 515.
23 Richard Overy, *Interrogations*, pages 60–61; Anne Tusa and John Tusa, *The Nuremberg Trials*, page 44.
24 Charles L. Mee, *Meeting at Potsdam*, page 49.
25 Mary Soames, *Clementine Churchill*, page 384; idem (ed.), *Speaking for Themselves*, page 532.
26 Charles L. Mee, op. cit., page 82; Harry S Truman, *Memoirs*, Vol. I, page 82; David McCullough, *Truman*, pages 413–416.
27 Winston Churchill, *Triumph and Tragedy*, page 539; Douglas Botting, *World War II*, pages 40–41; Joan Bright Astley, *The Inner Circle*, pages 218–219; "Opening of Potsdam Conference," *The Times*, 17 July 1945; Lord Moran, *Churchill*, page 291; for the quotes from Olive Christopher, see Joanna Moody, *From Churchill's War Rooms*, as quoted in *Daily Telegraph*, 19 February 2007, page 19.

27 "OTHER BEASTS IN OTHER LAIRS"

1 *The Times*, 17 July 1945.
2 Osmar White, *Conquerors' Road*, page 136.
3 W. Byford Jones, *Berlin Twilight*, page 56.
4 Douglas Botting, *In the Ruins of the Reich*, page 142.
5 Quoted in ibid., pages 143–144.

NOTES

6 Count Folke Bernadotte, *Instead of Arms*, page 75; see also pages 80–81.

7 Count Folke Bernadotte, *The Fall of the Curtain*, page 82; and idem, *Instead of Arms*, page 63.

8 British Council of Churches, *The German Reaction to Defeat*, copy found with the war diary of the Reverend David Cairns in the National Library of Scotland Documents Collection, Reference No. ACC 5932.

9 Alan Moorehead, "Not One German Has Any Feeling of Guilt," *Daily Express*, 22 April 1945; Anne Matheson, "These Women Have No Pity but for Themselves," *Evening Standard,* 30 April 1945.

10 Quoted in Josef Foschepoth, "German Reaction to Defeat and Occupation," in Robert G. Moeller (ed.), *West Germany under Construction*, page 73.

11 Perry Biddiscombe, *The Last Nazis*, page 235.

12 Leonard Mosley, *Report from Germany*, page 117.

13 Francesca Wilson, *Aftermath*, page 67.

14 Botting, op. cit., page 105; Biddiscombe, op. cit., pages 195, 235–236.

15 See Frank Stern, "The Historic Triangle: Occupiers, Germans and Jews in Postwar Germany," in Moeller, op. cit., page 207; and Constantine Goschler, "The Attitude towards Jews in Bavaria after the Second World War," in ibid., page 232.

16 See Lawrence D. Stokes, "Conservative Opposition to Nazism in Eutin, Schleswig-Holstein, 1932–1933," in Francis R. Nicosia and Lawrence D. Stokes (eds.), *Germans against Nazism*, pages 49–50, 52. At the time of writing, on the sixty-eighth anniversary of Kristallnacht, a survey of opinion in Germany revealed that 18 percent of its citizens believed that the influence of the Jews "is too great." See *The Times*, 10 November 2006.

17 For a recent graphic example of the vigorous after-life of Nazi sentiment and loyalty in Austria, see the extraordinary account by the journalist Martin Pollack of the search for the truth about his father as told in his book, *The Dead Man in the Bunker*.

18 *The Times*, 17 July 1945.

19 Ibid., 14 July 1945.

20 Quoted in David Ellwood, *Italy 1943–1945*, page 198.

21 Sergio Luzzato, *The Body of Il Duce*, pages 99–116.

22 See Benjamin B. Fischer, "The Hitler Archive . . . at Last," *Intelligence and National Security*, Vol. 16, No. 4, Winter 2001, pages 238–247; and Anton Joachimsthaler, *The Last Days of Hitler*, pages 22–28.

23 Byford-Jones, op. cit., page 83.

24 Sir Norman Birkett, quoted in Michael Marrus, *The Nuremberg War Crimes Trial 1945–46*, page 103.

25 David Irving, *Göring*, page 508.

26 Leonard Mosley, *The Reich Marshal*, page 358; for the possible Dachau alternative, see Anne Tusa and John Tusa, *The Nuremberg Trial*, page 486.

27 Ibid., page 42.

28 Biddiscombe, op. cit., page 235.

EPILOGUE: WHAT HAPPENED TO THEM?

1 Fred Warner, "Don't You Know There's a War On?," page 80.

2 Information from ibid., *passim*, from material in the Imperial War Museum,

London, and from an interview with Fred Warner in Hamburg, 2005; also, letter from Annette Warner to the author, 5 January 2007.

3 Francesca Wilson, *Aftermath*, page 147.

4 See Francesca Wilson, *A Life of Service and Adventure*, Part 2, page 13.

5 As told in Geoffrey Cox, *A Tale of Two Battles*.

6 Note of 28 September 1945, Cox Papers.

7 Robert Reid, "Broken Dreams," *Manchester Guardian*, 31 January 1946, Reid Papers.

8 Fey von Hassell, *A Mother's War*, page 208.

9 Ibid., page 210.

10 Ibid., pages 212–213.

11 Ibid., page 225. See also her letter to Sigismund Payne Best in July 1946, Best Papers, Imperial War Museum, London.

BIBLIOGRAPHY

Ackroyd, Peter, *Ezra Pound and His World*, London, Thames and Hudson, 1980.

Ahonen, Pertti, *After the Expulsion: West Germany and Eastern Europe, 1945–1990*, Oxford, Oxford University Press, 2003.

Almond, Gabriel A. (ed.), *The Struggle for Democracy in Germany*, Chapel Hill, University of North Carolina Press, 1949.

Ambrose, Stephen E., *Eisenhower: Soldier, General of the Army, President-Elect 1890–1952*, New York, Simon and Schuster, 1983.

——, *The Victors: Eisenhower and His Boys: The Men of World War II*, New York, Simon and Schuster, 1998.

——, *Eisenhower and Berlin 1945: The Decision to Halt at the Elbe*, New York, W. W. Norton and Company, 2000.

——, *Wild Blue: 741 Squadron — On a Wing and a Prayer over Occupied Europe*, London, Pocket Books, 2002.

Annan, Noel, *Changing Enemies*, London, HarperCollins, 1995.

Anonymous, *A Woman in Berlin*, translated by Philip Boehm, London, Virago, 2005.

Ashman, Charles and Wagman, Robert, *Nazi Hunters*, New York, Pharos Books, 1988.

Astley, Joan Bright, *The Inner Circle*, London, Hutchinson, 1971.

Backer, John H., *Priming the German Economy: American Occupational Policies 1945–48*, Duke University Press, Durham, NC, 1971.

Bainton, Roy, *The Long Patrol*, Edinburgh, Mainstream, 2003.

Balfour, Michael, *Four Power Control in Germany and Austria 1945–6*, Oxford, Oxford University Press, 1956.

Barnett, Corelli, *Engage the Enemy More Closely: The Royal Navy in the Second World War*, London, Penguin, 2000.

Barnouw, Dagmar, *Germany 1945: Views of War and Violence*, Bloomington and Indianapolis, Indiana University Press, 1996.

Bar-Zohar, Michel, *The Hunt for German Scientists*, London, Arthur Barker, 1967.

Beevor, Antony, *Berlin: The Downfall 1945*, London, Viking, 2002.

Beevor, Antony, and Cooper, Artemis, *Paris after the Liberation, 1944–1949*, London, Penguin, 1995.

Bennett, Gill (ed.), *The End of the War in Europe 1945*, London, HMSO, 1996.

Bentwich, Norman De Mattos, *I Understand the Risks: The Story of the Refugees from Nazi Oppression Who Fought in the British Forces in the World War*, London, Victor Gollancz, 1950.

Bernadotte, Count Folke, *The Fall of the Curtain: Last Days of the Third Reich*, London, Cassell and Company, 1945.

——, *Instead of Arms*, London, Hodder and Stoughton, 1949.

Beschloss, Michael, *The Conquerors: Roosevelt, Truman, and the Destruction of Hitler's Germany 1941–1945*, New York, Simon and Schuster, 2002.

Best, Sigismund Payne, *The Venlo Incident*, London, Hutchinson, 1950.

Bethell, Nicholas, *The Last Secret, Forcible Repatriation to Russia 1944–1947*, London, Penguin, 1995.

Bethge, Eberhard, *Dietrich Bonhoeffer*, London, Collins, 1977.

Bezymenski, Lev, *The Death of Adolf Hitler: Unknown Documents from the Soviet Archives*, London, Michael Joseph, 1968.

Biddiscombe, Perry, *The Last Nazis: SS Werewolf Guerrilla Resistance in Europe 1944–1947*, Stroud, Tempus, 2004.

Black, Peter R., *Ernst Kaltenbrunner, Ideological Soldier of the Third Reich*, Princeton, NJ, Princeton University Press, 1984.

Blair, Clay, *Ridgway's Paratroopers: The American Airborne in World War II*, New York, Dial Press/Doubleday, 1985.

——, *Hitler's U-Boat War: The Hunted 1942–1945*, New York, Random House, 1998.

Blake, George, *Mountain and Flood: The History of the 52nd Lowland Division*, Glasgow, Jackson, Son & Co., 1950.

Blaxland, Gregory, *Alexander's Generals: The Italian Campaign 1944–5*, London, William Kimber, 1979.

Bloch, Gottfried R., *Unfree Associations: A Psychoanalyst Recollects the Holocaust*, Los Angeles, CA, Red Hen Press, 1999.

Blum, Léon, *L'Oeuvre de Léon Blum: Mémoires, la prison et le procès, l'échelle humaine, 1940–1945*, Paris, Albin Michel, 1955.

Blumenson, Martin, *Patton: The Man behind the Legend 1885–1945*, New York, William Morrow, 1985.

——, *The Patton Papers 1885–1940*, and *1940–45*, New York, Da Capo Press, 1996 (first published 1972 and 1974).

Booker, Christopher, *A Looking-Glass Tragedy: The Controversy over the Repatriations from Austria in 1945*, London, Duckworth, 1997.

Bosworth, Richard, *The Italian Dictatorship: Problems and Perspectives in the Interpretation of Mussolini and Fascism*, London, Arnold, 1998.

——, *Mussolini*, London, Arnold, 2002.

Botting, Douglas, *World War II: The Aftermath: Europe*, New York, Time-Life Books, 1983.

——, *In the Ruins of the Reich*, London, Allen and Unwin, 1985.

Bower, Tom, *The Pledge Betrayed: America and Britain and the Denazification of Postwar Germany*, Garden City, NY, Doubleday, 1982.

——, *Klaus Barbie*, London, Corgi, 1985.

——, *The Paperclip Conspiracy: The Battle for the Spoils and Secrets of Nazi Germany*, London, Michael Joseph, 1987.

——, *Blind Eye to Murder*, London, Warner Books, 1997.

Bowman, Alfred Connor, *Zones of Strain: A Memoir of the Early Cold War*, Stanford, CA, Hoover Institution Press, 1982.

BIBLIOGRAPHY

Bradley, Omar N., *A Soldier's Story*, New York, Henry Holt and Company, 1951.

Bradley, Omar N., and Blair, Clay, *A General's Life*, New York, Simon and Schuster, 1983.

Breitman, Richard *et al.*, *US Intelligence and the Nazis*, Washington, DC, National Archives Trust Fund Board, 2004.

Brett-Smith, Richard, *Berlin '45: The Grey City*, London, Macmillan, 1966.

Bridge, Ann, *Portrait of My Mother*, London, Chatto and Windus, 1955.

Bridgman, J., *The End of the Holocaust: The Liberation of the Camps*, London, Batsford, 1990.

British Council of Churches, *The German Reaction to Defeat*, London, British Council of Churches, 1945.

Burke, Carolyn, *Lee Miller: A Life*, New York, Alfred A. Knopf, 2005.

Burleigh, Michael, *Death and Deliverance: Euthanasia in Germany 1900–1945*, Cambridge, Cambridge University Press, 1994.

——, *The Third Reich: A New History*, London, Pan Heinemann, 2001.

Burney, Christopher, *The Dungeon Democracy*, London, 1945.

Bussey, Jennifer A. (ed.), *Events that Changed the World: 1940–1960*, Farmington Hills, MI, Greenhaven Press, 2004.

Butler, Ewan and Young, Gordon, *Marshal without Glory: The Life and Death of Hermann Goering*, London, Tandem, 1973.

Calder, Angus, *The People's War: Britain 1939–45*, London, Jonathan Cape, 1969.

Carver, Field Marshal Lord, *War in Italy 1943–1945*, London, Sidgwick and Jackson, 2001.

Cave Brown, Anthony (ed.), *The Secret War Report of the OSS*, New York, Berkley Medallion, 1976.

Chandler, Alfred D., *et al.*, *The Papers of Dwight David Eisenhower*, Baltimore, Johns Hopkins University Press, 1978.

Churchill, Peter, *The Spirit in the Cage*, London, Hodder and Stoughton, 1954.

Churchill, Winston S., *Triumph and Tragedy*, New York, Bantam, 1962.

Clark, Martin, *Mussolini*, Harlow, Pearson, 2005.

Clay, Lucius D., *Decision in Germany*, New York, Doubleday, 1950.

Coles, Harry and Weinberg, Albert K., *Civil Affairs: Soldiers Become Governors*, Washington, DC, Office of the Chief of Military History, Department of the Army, 1964.

Colton, Joel, *Léon Blum: Humanist in Politics*, New York, Alfred A. Knopf, 1966.

Copp, Terry, *Cinderella Army: The Canadians in Northwest Europe 1944–1945*, Toronto, University of Toronto Press, 2006.

Copp, Terry and Vogel, Robert, *Maple Leaf Route: Victory*, Alma, Ontario, Maple Leaf, 1988.

Corbett, Major-General R.J.S, *Berlin and the British Ally, 1945–1990*, Berlin, Zumm Druck and Satz KG, 1991.

Cossin, Carl V., *I Soldiered with America's Elite 10th Mountain Division of W.W. II*, n.p., 1st Books, 2001.

Coutts, Frank, *One Blue Bonnet: A Scottish Soldier Looks Back*, Edinburgh, B&W, 1991.

Cowgill, Anthony, Brimelow, Lord and Booker, Christopher, *The Repatriations from Austria in 1945: The Report of an Enquiry*, London, Sinclair-Stevenson, 1990.

Cox, Geoffrey, *Defence of Madrid*, London, Gollancz, 1937.

——, *The Red Army Moves*, London, Gollancz, 1941.

——, *The Race for Trieste*, London, William Kimber, 1977.

——, *A Tale of Two Battles*, London, William Kimber, 1987.

——, *Countdown to War: A Personal Memoir of Europe 1938–1940*, London, Coronet, 1990.

——, *A New Zealand Boyhood*, Stonehouse, Amadines Press, 2004.

Crawford, John (ed.), *Kia Kaha: New Zealand in the Second World War*, Auckland, Oxford University Press, 2000.

Cushing, Red, *Soldier for Hire*, London, John Calder, 1962.

Dahl, Hans Frederik, *Quisling: A Study in Treachery*, Cambridge, Cambridge University Press, 1999.

Dallas, Gregor, *Poisoned Peace: 1945 — The War that Never Ended*, London, John Murray, 2005.

Dalzel-Job, Patrick, *From Arctic Snow to Dust of Normandy*, Plockton, Nead-an-Eoin, 1992.

Danchev, Alex and Todman, Daniel (eds.), *War Diaries 1939–1945: Field Marshal Lord Alanbrooke*, London, Weidenfeld and Nicolson, 2001.

Davidson, Edward, *Chronology of World War Two*, London, Cassell, 1999.

Davies, Norman, *Europe at War 1939–1945: No Simple Victory*, London, Macmillan 2006.

De Guingaud, Sir Francis, *Operation Victory*, London, Hodder and Stoughton, 1947.

De Lattre de Tassigny, General Jean-Marie, *The History of the First French Army*, London, George Allen and Unwin, 1952.

De Zayas, Alfred, *Nemesis at Potsdam*, London, Routledge and Kegan Paul, 1979.

Deak, Istvan *et al.*, (eds.), *The Politics of Retribution in Europe: World War II and Its Aftermath*, Princeton, NJ, Princeton University Press, 2000.

Deakin, F.W., *The Brutal Friendship: Mussolini, Hitler and the Fall of Italian Fascism*, London, Weidenfeld and Nicolson, 1962.

Dear, Ian, *Ten Commando 1942–1945*, London, Grafton, 1989.

D'Este, Carlo, *Patton: A Genius for War*, New York, Harper Perennial, 1996.

——, *Eisenhower: A Soldier's Life*, New York, Henry Holt, 2002.

Dickens, Arthur Geoffrey, *Lübeck Diary*, London, Victor Gollancz, 1947.

Doenitz, Grand Admiral Karl, *Memoirs: Ten Years and Twenty Days*, Annapolis, MD, Naval Institute Press, 1990.

Domenico, Roy Palmer, *Italian Fascists on Trial: 1943–1948*, Chapel Hill, NC, University of North Carolina Press, 1991.

Donnison, F.S.V., *Civil Affairs and Military Government in North-West Europe 1944–1946*, London, HMSO, 1961.

Douglas-Hamilton, James, *The Truth about Rudolf Hess*, Edinburgh, Mainstream Press, 1993.

Dulles, Allen Welsh, *From Hitler's Doorstep: The Wartime Intelligence Reports of Allen Dulles 1942–1945*, University Park, Pennsylvania State University Press, 1996.

Dunnage, Jonathan (ed.), *After the War: Justice, Continuity and Renewal in Italian Society*, Market Harborough, Troubador, 1999.

BIBLIOGRAPHY

Dusenbery, Harris and Ware, Wilson P., *Ski the High Trail: World War II Ski Troopers in the High Colorado Rockies*, Portland, OR, Binford and Mort Publishing, 1991.

Edwards, Denis, *The Devil's Own Luck: Pegasus Bridge to the Baltic*, London, Leo Cooper, 1999.

Eisenberg, Carolyn Woods, *Drawing the Line: The American Decision to Divide Germany 1944–1949*, New York, Cambridge University Press, 1996.

Eisenhower, David, *Eisenhower at War 1943–1945*, London, Collins, 1986.

Eisenhower, Dwight D., *Crusade in Europe*, New York, Doubleday, 1948.

Ellis, Lionel Frederic, *Victory in the West: The Defeat of Germany (History of the Second World War)*, United Kingdom Military Series, Vol. 2, London, HMSO, 1968.

Ellis, Robert, *See Naples and Die: A Ski Trooper's World War II Memoir*, Jefferson, NC, McFarland and Company, 1996.

Ellwood, David, *Italy 1943–1945*, Leicester, Leicester University Press, 1985.

Enzensberger, Hans Magnus, *Civil War*, London, Granta, 1994.

Essame, H., *Patton: A Study in Command*, New York, Charles Scribner's Sons, 1974.

Farago, Ladislas, *Patton: Ordeal and Triumph*, New York, Ivan Obolensky, 1963.

——, *The Last Days of Patton*, New York, McGraw Hill, 1981.

Feis, Herbert, *Between War and Peace: The Potsdam Conference*, Princeton, NJ, Princeton University Press, 1960.

Fergusson, Niall, *Colossus: The Price of America's Empire*, New York, Penguin Press, 2004.

Fermi, Laura, *Mussolini*, Chicago, University of Chicago Press, 1961.

Fest, Joachim, *Speer: The Final Verdict*, London, Weidenfeld and Nicolson, 2001.

——, *Inside Hitler's Bunker: The Last Days of the Third Reich*, New York, Farrar, Straus and Giroux, 2004.

Fisher, Ernest F., Jr., *Cassino to the Alps, United States Army in World War II: The Mediterranean Theater of Operations*, Washington, DC, Center of Military History, United States Army, 1984.

Flower, Major Desmond, *History of the Argyll and Sutherland Highlanders, 5th Battalion 91st Anti-Tank Regiment*, London, Thomas Nelson, 1950.

Foot, Michael, *The Trial of Mussolini*, London, Left Book Club, 1943.

Foot, M.R.D., *SOE in France*, London, HMSO, 1966.

——, *SOE in the Low Countries*, London, St. Ermin's Press, 2001.

Forfar, John, *From Omaha to the Scheldt: The Story of 47 Royal Marine Commando*, East Linton, Tuckwell Press, 2001.

Freud, Esther, *The Sea House*, London, Penguin, 2004.

Friedlander, Henry, *The Origins of Nazi Genocide: From Euthanasia to the Final Solution*, Chapel Hill, University of North Carolina Press, 1995.

Fussell, Paul, *Wartime: Understanding and Behavior in the Second World War*, New York, Oxford University Press, 1989.

—— (ed.), *The Norton Book of Modern War*, New York, W. W. Norton and Company, 1991.

Gardiner, Juliet, *Wartime: Britain 1939–1945*, London, Headline, 2004.

Gavin, James M., *On to Berlin: Battles of an Airborne Commander 1943–1946*, New York, Viking Press, 1978.

Gellately, Robert, *Backing Hitler: Consent and Coercion in Nazi Germany*, Oxford, Oxford University Press, 2001.

Germany 1944: The British Soldiers' Handbook (foreword by Charles Wheeler), Kew, The National Archives, 2006.

Gilbert, Martin, *Road to Victory: Winston S. Churchill 1941–1945*, London, Minerva, 1989.

——, *Never Despair: Winston S. Churchill 1945–1965*, London, Minerva, 1990.

——, *The Day the War Ended: VE Day in Europe and around the World*, London, HarperCollins, 1995.

——, *Second World War*, London, Phoenix, 1995.

Gimbel, John C., *The American Occupation of Germany: Politics and the Military 1945–1949*, Stanford, CA, Stanford University Press, 1968.

Gold, Alison Leslie, *Fiet's Vase, and Other Stories of Survival*, New York, Penguin, 2003.

Haffner, Sebastian, *Defying Hitler*, London, Phoenix, 2003.

Hamilton, Nigel, *Monty: Master of the Battlefield*, Sevenoaks, Scepter, 1985.

——, *Monty: The Field Marshal 1944–1976*, London, Scepter, 1987.

——, *Monty: The Battles of Field Marshal Bernard Montgomery*, New York, Random House, 1994.

Hammerton, Sir John, *The War Illustrated*, London, The Amalgamated Press Ltd, Vols. 8 and 9.

Harclerode, Peter and Pittaway, Brendan, *The Lost Masters: The Looting of Europe's Treasurehouses*, London, Orion, 2000.

Harris, Charles Reginald Schiller, *Allied Administration of Italy, 1943–1945*, London, HMSO, 1957.

Hastings, Max, *Armageddon: The Battle for Germany 1944–45*, London, Macmillan, 2004.

Hawkins, Desmond (ed.), *War Report: D-Day to V-E Day: Dispatches by the BBC's War Correspondents with the Allied Expeditionary Force 6 June 1944–5 May 1945*, London, Ariel, 1985.

Heinemann, Elizabeth, *What Difference Does a Husband Make?*, Berkeley, University of California Press, 1999.

Hepburn, A.C., *Contested Cities in the Modern West*, London, Palgrave Macmillan, 2004.

Heydecker, Joe, *The Nuremberg Trials*, London, Heinemann, 1962.

Heymann, C. David, *Ezra Pound: The Last Rower*, London, Faber and Faber, 1976.

Hibbert, Christopher, *Benito Mussolini: A Biography*, London, Longmans, 1962.

Hinsley, F.H., *British Intelligence in the Second World War: Its Influence on Strategy and Operations*, Vol. 3, Part 2, London, HMSO, 1988.

Hirshson, Stanley P., *General Patton, a Soldier's Life*, New York, HarperCollins, 2002.

Hoehne, Heinz and Zolling, Hermann, *The General Was a Spy*, New York, Coward, McCann, and Geoghagen, 1972.

Hoffman, Peter, *Stauffenberg: A Family History*, Cambridge, Cambridge University Press, 1995.

Horbach, Michael, *Out of the Night*, London, Vallentine, Mitchell, 1967.

Howe, Thomas Carr Jr., *Salt Mines and Castles: The Discovery and Restitution of Looted European Art*, Indianapolis and New York, Bobbs-Merrill Company, 1946.

Hunt, Irmgard A., *On Hitler's Mountain: Overcoming the Legacy of a Nazi Childhood*, New York, William Morrow, 2005.

BIBLIOGRAPHY

Ikenberry, G. John, *After Victory: Institutions, Strategic Restraint, and the Rebuilding of Order after Major Wars,* Princeton, NJ, Princeton University Press, 2001.

Imbrie, John and Brooks, Thomas R., *10th Mountain Division Campaign in Italy 1945,* Forest Hills, NY, National Association of the 10th Mountain Division, 2002.

Imbrie, John and Evans, Hugh W., *Good Times and Bad Times: A History of C Company of the 85th Mountain Infantry Regiment 10th Mountain Division,* Queechie, Vermont, Vermont Heritage Press, 1995.

Infield, Glenn B., *Skorzeny: Hitler's Commando,* New York, St. Martin's Press, 1981.

Irvine, James, *The Waves Are Free,* Lerwick, Shetland Publishing Company, 1998.

Irving, David, *The Rise and Fall of the Luftwaffe: The Life of Luftwaffe Marshal Erhard Milch,* London, Weidenfeld and Nicolson, 1973.

———, *Göring: A Biography,* London, Macmillan, 1989.

Jenkins, McKay, *The Last Ride: The Epic Story of America's First Mountain Soldiers and the Assault on Hitler's Europe,* New York, Random House, 2003.

Jeschonnek, Friedrich, Riedel, Dieter and Durie, William, *Alliierte in Berlin 1945–1994,* Berlin, Berlin Verlag Arno Spitz GmbH, 2002.

Joachimsthaler, Anton, *The Last Days of Hitler, the Legends, the Evidence, the Truth,* London, Arms and Armour, 1996.

Jones, Wilfred Byford, *Berlin Twilight,* London, Hutchinson, 1949.

Judt, Tony, *Postwar: A History of Europe since 1945,* New York, Penguin Press, 2006.

Junge, Traudl, *Until the Final Hour: Hitler's Last Secretary,* London, Weidenfeld and Nicolson, 2003.

Kaufman, David and Horn, Michiel, *A Liberation Album: Canadians in the Netherlands 1944–45,* Toronto, McGraw-Hill Ryerson, 1980.

Kay, Robin, *From Cassino to Trieste (Official History of New Zealand in the Second World War 1939–45: Italy,* Vol. II), Wellington, Historical Branch, Department of Internal Affairs, 1967.

Kemp, Anthony, *The Secret Hunters,* London, Michael O'Mara, 1986.

Kershaw, Ian, *Hitler 1936–1945: Nemesis,* New York, W. W. Norton and Co., 2000.

Kirby, Norman, *1100 Miles with Monty: Security and Intelligence at TacHQ,* Gloucester, Alan Sutton, 1989.

Kirkpatrick, Sir Ivone, *Mussolini: Study of a Demagogue,* London, Odhams, 1964.

Knightley, Phillip, *The First Casualty: From the Crimea to Vietnam: The War Correspondent as Hero, Propagandist, and Myth Maker,* New York, Harcourt Brace Jovanovich, 1975.

Kochavi, Ariel, *Prelude to Nuremberg: Allied War Crimes Policy and the Question of Punishment,* London, University of North Carolina Press, 1998.

Lamb, Richard, *War in Italy 1943–1945: A Brutal Story,* New York, Da Capo Press, 1996.

———, *Mussolini and the British,* London, John Murray, 1997.

Lambert, Angela, *The Lost Life of Eva Braun,* London, Century, 2006.

Lasby, Clarence, *Project Paperclip: German Scientists and the Cold War,* New York, Atheneum, 1975.

Lehmann, Armin D., with Carroll, Tim, *In Hitler's Bunker,* Edinburgh and London, Mainstream, 2004.

Library of America, *Reporting World War II: Part Two: American Journalism 1944–1946,* New York, Library of America, 1995.

Lindsay, Donald, *Forgotten General: A Life of Andrew Thorne*, Salisbury, Michael Russell, 1987.

Lindsay, Franklin, *Beacons in the Night: With the OSS and Tito's Partisans in Wartime Yugoslavia*, Stanford, CA, Stanford University Press, 1993.

Longden, Sean, *To the Victor the Spoils: D-Day to VE Day: The Reality behind the Heroism*, Moreton-in-Marsh, Arris, 2004.

Lottman, Herbert R., *The People's Anger: Justice and Revenge in Post-Liberation France*, London, Hutchinson, 1986.

Lucas, James, *Last Days of the Reich: The Collapse of Nazi Germany, May 1945*, London, Cassell, 1986.

Luzzatto, Sergio, *The Body of Il Duce: Mussolini's Corpse and the Fortunes of Italy*, New York, Metropolitan Books, Henry Holt and Company, 2005.

Lycett, Andrew, *Ian Fleming*, London, Phoenix, 1995.

MacDonald, Charles B., *The Last Offensive*, Washington DC, 1973.

Mack Smith, Denis, *Mussolini*, London, Weidenfeld and Nicolson, 1981.

Mackenzie, W.J.M., *The Secret History of SOE 1939–1945*, London, St. Ermin's Press, 2000.

Macmillan, Harold, *The Blast of War 1939–45*, London, Macmillan, 1967.

Magris, Claudio, *Microcosms*, London, Harvill, 2000.

Mandle, William D. and Whittier, David H., *Combat Record of the 504th Parachute Infantry Regiment: April 1943–July 1945*, Paris, Draeger Freres, n.d.

Mankowitz, Zeev, *Life between Memory and Hope*, Cambridge, Cambridge University Press, 2002.

Marrus, Michael R. *The Nuremberg War Crimes Trial 1945–46: A Documentary History*, Boston, Bedford Books, 1997.

Marshall, Charles F., *Discovering the Rommel Murder: The Life and Death of the Desert Fox*, Mechanicsburg, PA, Stackpole Books, 1994.

——, *A Ramble through My War: Anzio and Other Joys*, Baton Rouge, Louisiana State University Press, 1998.

Martelli, George, *Agent Extraordinary: The Story of Michel Hollard, DSO, Croix de Guerre*, London, Collins, 1969.

Martin, H.G., *The History of the Fifteenth Scottish Division 1939–1945*, Edinburgh, Blackwell, 1948.

Mason, Henry L., *The Purge of the Dutch Quislings: Emergency Justice in the Netherlands*, The Hague, Martinuus Nijhoff, 1952.

Mazower, Mark, *Dark Continent: Europe's Twentieth Century*, New York, Alfred A. Knopf, 1999.

——, *Salonica, City of Ghosts*, New York, Alfred A. Knopf, 2005.

McBryde, Brenda, *A Nurse's War*, London, Sphere, 1980.

McCullouch, David, *Truman*, New York, Simon and Schuster, 1992.

McGibbon, Ian (ed.), *The Oxford Companion to New Zealand History*, Oxford, Oxford University Press, 2000.

McGovern, James, *Crossbow and Overcast*, New York, William Morrow, 1964.

Mee, Charles L., Jr., *Meeting at Potsdam*, London, André Deutsch, 1975.

Megellas, James, *All the Way to Berlin: A Paratrooper at War in Europe*, New York, Presidio/Ballantine, 2003.

BIBLIOGRAPHY

Meincke, Albert, Jr., *Mountain Troops and Medics: Wartime Stories of a Frontline Surgeon in the US Ski Troops*, Kewadin, MI, Rucksack, 1993.

Melchior, I.B., *Case by Case: A US Army Counter-Intelligence Agent in World War II*, Novato, CA, Presidio Press, 1993.

Merridale, Catherine, *Ivan's War: Life and Death in the Red Army 1939–1945*, New York, Metropolitan, 2006.

Middlebrook, Martin, *The Nuremberg Raid*, London, Cassell, 2000.

Milano, Col. James V. and Brogan, Patrick, *Soldiers, Spies, and the Rat Line: America's Undeclared War against the Soviets*, London, Brassey's, 1995.

Miller, Russell, with Miller, Renate, *Ten Days in May: The People's Story of V-E Day*, London, Michael Joseph, 1995.

Mills-Roberts, Derek, *Clash by Night*, London, William Kimber, 1956.

Minott, Rodney, *The Fortress that Never Was: The Myth of Hitler's Bavarian Stronghold*, New York, Holt, Rinehart and Winston, 1964.

Moeller, Robert G. (ed.), *West Germany under Construction: Politics, Society, and Culture in the Adenauer Era*, Ann Arbor, University of Michigan Press, 1997.

Monahan, Evelyn M. and Neidel-Greenlee, Rosemary, *And If I Perish: Frontline US Army Nurses in World War II*, New York, Alfred A. Knopf, 2003.

Moorehead, Alan, *Eclipse*, London, Hamish Hamilton, 1945.

Moran, Lord, *Churchill: Taken from the Diaries of Lord Moran*, Boston, MA, Houghton Mifflin, 1966.

Morris, James, *Venice*, London, Faber and Faber, 1974.

Morrison, Alex and Slaney, Ted, *The Breed of Manly Men: The History of the Cape Breton Highlanders*, Toronto, Canadian Institute of Strategic Studies, 1994.

Mosley, Leonard, *Report from Germany*, London, Gollancz, 1945.

——, *The Reich Marshal: A Biography of Hermann Goering*, London, Weidenfeld and Nicolson, 1974.

Nansen, Odd, *Day after Day*, London, Putnam, 1949.

Neillands, Robin, *Conquest of the Reich, from D-Day to VE Day: A Soldier's History*, London, Orion, 1996.

——, *Eighth Army: From the Western Desert to the Alps*, Woodstock and New York, Overlook Press, 2004.

Nesbitt, Roy, *Failed to Return: Mysteries of the Air*, London, Patrick Stephens, 1988.

Nichol, John and Rennell, Tony, *The Last Escape: The Untold Story of Allied Prisoners of War in Germany 1944–5*, New York, Viking, 2003.

Nicholas, Lynn H., *The Rape of Europa: The Fate of Europe's Treasures in the Third Reich and the Second World War*, New York, Alfred A. Knopf, 1994.

——, *Cruel World: The Children of Europe in the Nazi Web*, New York, Alfred A. Knopf, 2005.

Nicholas, Sian, *The Echo of War: Home Front Propaganda and the Wartime BBC 1939–1945*, Manchester, Manchester University Press, 1996.

Nichols, David (ed.), *Ernie's War: The Best of Ernie Pyle's World War II Dispatches*, New York, Random House, 1986.

Nicosia, Francis R. and Stokes, Lawrence D. (eds.), *Germans against Nazism: Nonconformity, Opposition and Resistance in the Third Reich*, New York, Berg, 1990.

Niemoller, Martin, *From U-Boat to Concentration Camp*, London, William Hodge, 1939.

———, *Dachau Sermons*, London, Latimer House, 1947.

Noli, Jean, *The Admiral's Wolf Pack*, Garden City, NY, Doubleday and Company, 1974.

Nordyke, Philip, *All American All the Way: The Combat History of the 82nd Airborne Division in World War II*, St. Paul, MI, Zenith Press, 2005.

Norman, Charles, *Ezra Pound*, New York, Macmillan, 1960.

O'Donnell, James P., *The Bunker*, New York, Da Capo Press, 1978.

Orde, Roden, *The Household Cavalry at War: Second Household Cavalry Regiment*, Aldershot, Gale and Polden, 1953.

Ordway, Frederick I., III and Sharpe, Mitchell R., *The Rocket Team*, New York, Thomas Y. Crowell, 1979.

Overy, Richard, *Interrogations: The Nazi Elite in Allied Hands, 1945*, London, Allen Lane/Penguin Press, 2001.

Owen, Ben, *With Popski's Private Army*, London, James, 1993.

Padfield, Peter, *Himmler: ReichsFührer-SS*, New York, Henry Holt and Company, 1990.

———, *Doenitz: The Last Führer*, London, Cassell, 2001.

Parker, Matthew, *Monte Cassino: The Story of the Hardest-Fought Battle of World War Two*, London, Headline, 2003.

Patton, George S., *War as I Knew It*, London, W.H. Allen, 1947.

Peniakoff, Vladimir ("Popski"), *Private Army*, London, Jonathan Cape, 1950.

Persico, Joseph E., *Nuremberg: Infamy on Trial*, New York, Penguin, 1995.

Petersen, Neal H. (ed. with commentary), *From Hitler's Doorstep: The Wartime Intelligence Reports of Allen Dulles, 1942–1945*, University Park, Pennsylvania State University Press, 1996.

Petropoulos, Jonathan, *The Faustian Bargain: The Art World in Nazi Germany*, Oxford, Oxford University Press, 2000.

———, *Royals and the Reich: The Princes von Hessen in Nazi Germany*, New York, Oxford University Press, 2006.

Petrova, Ada and Watson, Peter, *The Death of Hitler: The Full Story with New Evidence from Secret Russian Archives*, New York, W.W. Norton and Company, 1995.

Phibbs, Brendan, *The Other Side of Time: A Combat Surgeon in World War II*, Boston, MA, Little, Brown, 1987.

Phillips, Raymond (ed.), *The Belsen Trial*, London, Hodge, 1947.

Pick, Hella, *Simon Wiesenthal: A Life in Search of Justice*, Boston, MA, Northeastern University Press, 1996.

Piszkiewicz, Dennis, *Wernher von Braun: The Man Who Sold the Moon*, Westport, CT, Praeger, 1998.

Pocock, Tom, *1945: The Dawn Came Up Like Thunder*, London, Collins, 1983.

———, *Alan Moorehead*, London, Pimlico, 1990.

Pogue, Forrest C., *The Supreme Command*, Washington, DC, Department of the Army, Office of the Chief of Military History, 1954.

———, *George C. Marshall: Organizer of Victory*, New York, Viking, 1973.

Pollack, Martin, *The Dead Man in the Bunker*, London, Faber and Faber, 2006.

Posner, Gerald L., *Hitler's Children*, New York, Random House, 1991.

BIBLIOGRAPHY

Prosser, J., *Ashes in the Wind,* London, Souvenir Press, 1965.

Proudfoot, Malcolm Jarvis, *European Refugees 1939–1952* London, Faber and Faber, 1957.

Province, Charles M., *Patton's Third Army: A Chronology of the Third Army Advance, August 1944 to May 1945*, New York, Hippocrene, 1992.

Quartermain, Luisa, *Mussolini's Last Republic: Propaganda and Politics in the Italian Social Republic (R.S.I.) 1943–45*, Exeter, Elm Bank, 2000.

Rabel, Roberto Giorgio, *Between East and West: Trieste, the United States, and the Cold War, 1941–1954*, Durham, NC, Duke University Press, 1988.

Reese, Mary Ellen, *General Reinhard Gehlen: The CIA Connection*, Fairfax, VA, George Mason University Press, 1990.

Reid, Robert, *War Correspondent*, Glasgow, E.J. Arnold and Sons, n.d.

Reilly, Joanne, *Belsen: The Liberation of a Concentration Camp*, London, Routledge, 1998.

Reilly, Joanne, Cesarini, David, Kushner, Tony and Richmond, Colin (eds.), *Belsen in History and Memory*, London, Frank Cass, 1997.

Richardi, Hans-Gunter, *SS — Geiseln in der Alpenfestung*, Bozen, Edition Raetia, 2005.

Richie, Alexandra, *Faust's Metropolis*, London, HarperCollins, 1998.

Rosenfeld, Gavriel David, *Munich and Memory: Architecture, Monuments, and the Legacy of the Third Reich*, Berkeley, University of California Press, 2000.

Roskill, Captain S.W., *The War at Sea*, Vol. III: *The Offensive, Part II: 1st June 1944–14th August 1945*, London, HMSO, 1961.

Roy, Reginald H., *Ready for the Fray (Deas gu cath): The History of the Canadian Scottish Regiment (Princess Mary's) 1920–1955*, Vancouver, The Trustees CSR, 1958.

——, *Sinews of Steel: The History of the British Columbia Dragoons*, Brampton, Charters, 1965.

Ryan, Cornelius, *The Last Battle*, New York, Simon and Schuster, 1966.

Samain, Bryan, *Commando Men: The Story of a Royal Marine Commando in North-West Europe*, London, White Lion, 1976.

——, *Personal Encounters*, Durham, Pentland Press, 2000.

Samuel, Wolfgang, *German Boy*, London, Scepter, 2002.

——, *American Raiders: The Race to Capture the Luftwaffe's Secrets*, Jackson, University of Mississippi Press, 2004.

Sanders, Charles J., *The Boys of Winter: Life and Death in the US: Ski Troops during the Second World War*, Boulder, University Press of Colorado, 2005.

Sayer, Ian and Botting, Douglas, *America's Secret Army: The Untold Story of the Counter-Intelligence Corps*, London, Fontana, 1990.

——, *Nazi Gold: The Story of the World's Greatest Robbery — and Its Aftermath*, Edinburgh, Mainstream, 1998.

Schellenberg, Walter, *The Schellenberg Memoirs: A Record of Nazi Secret Service*, London, André Deutsch, 1956.

Schollgen, Gregor, *A Conservative against Hitler: Ulrich von Hassell*, London Macmillan, 1991.

Schuschnigg, Kurt von, *Austrian Requiem*, New York, G.P. Putnam's Sons, 1946.

Schwab, Gerald, *OSS Agents in Hitler's Heartland: Destination Innsbruck*, Westport, CT, Praeger, 1996.

Senger und Etterlin, General Frido von, *Neither Fear nor Hope*, New York, E.P. Dutton, 1964.

Sereny, Gita, *The German Trauma: Experiences and Reflections 1938–2000*, London, Allen Lane, 2000.

Shelton, Peter, *Climb to Conquer: The Untold Story of World War II's 10th Mountain Division Ski Troops*, New York, Scribner, 2003.

Shephard, Ben, *After Daybreak: The Liberation of Bergen-Belsen 1945*, New York, Schocken, 2005.

Shirer, William L., *The Rise and Fall of the Third Reich: A History of Nazi Germany*, New York, Simon and Schuster, 1960.

Simpson, Elizabeth (ed.), *The Spoils of War: World War II and Its Aftermath*, New York, Harry N. Abram, 1997.

Skinner, Reverend Leslie, *The Man Who Worked on Sundays*, Epsom, Skinner, 1996.

Smith, Bradley F., *The Shadow Warriors: OSS and the Origins of the CIA*, London, André Deutsch, 1983.

Smith, Jean E. (ed.), *The Papers of General Lucius D. Clay: Germany 1945–1949*, Bloomington, Indiana University Press, 1974.

——, *Lucius D. Clay*, New York, Henry Holt, 1990.

Smyth, Howard McGaw, *Secrets of the Fascist Era*, Carbondale and Edwardsville, Southern Illinois University Press, 1975.

Soames, Mary, *Clementine Churchill*, London, Cassell, 1979.

——, (ed.), *Speaking for Themselves*, London, Transworld, 1998.

Speer, Albert, *Inside the Third Reich*, London, Phoenix, 1995.

Spotts, Frederic, *Hitler and the Power of Aesthetics*, Woodstock and New York, Overlook Press, 2003.

Stafford, David, *Britain and European Resistance 1940–1945*, London, Macmillan, 1980.

——, *Churchill and Secret Service*, London, John Murray, 1997.

——, *Ten Days to D-Day*, London, Little, Brown, 2004.

——, (ed.), *Flight from Reality: Rudolf Hess and His Mission to Scotland 1941*, London, Pimlico, 2002.

Steers, Bob, *FSS: Field Security Sections*, Eastlays, Robin Steers, 1996.

Steinbuck, Jack (ed.), *Typewriter Battalion: Dramatic Front-Line Dispatches from World War II*, New York, William Morrow, 1995.

Steinert, Marlis G., *Capitulation 1945, the Story of the Doenitz Regime*, London, Constable, 1969.

Stern, Robert C., *Battle beneath the Waves: The U-Boat War*, London, Arms and Armour, 1999.

Stock, Noel, *The Life of Ezra Pound*, London, Routledge and Kegan Paul, 1970.

Stout, Duncan M., *New Zealand Medical Services in Middle East and Italy*, Wellington, War History Branch, Department of Internal Affairs, 1956.

Stuhlinger, Ernst and Ordway, Frederick I., III, *Wernher von Braun: Crusader for Space*, Malabar, FL, 1994.

Taylor, A.J.P., *How Wars End*, London, Hamish Hamilton, 1985.

Ther, Philipp and Siljak, Ana (eds.), *Redrawing Nations: Ethnic Cleansing in East-Central Europe, 1944–1948*, Oxford, Rowman and Littlefield, 2001.

BIBLIOGRAPHY

Thomas, John Oram, *No Banners: The Story of Alfred and Henry Newton*, London, W.H. Allen, 1955.

Toland, John, *The Last 100 Days*, London, Orion, 1994.

Trevelyan, Raleigh, *Rome '44*, London, Secker and Warburg, 1981.

Trevor-Roper, Hugh, *The Last Days of Hitler*, London, Macmillan, 1956.

Truman, Harry S., *Memoirs*, London, Hodder and Stoughton, 1956.

Truscott, Lt. General L.K., Jr., *Command Missions: A Personal Story*, New York, E.P. Dutton and Company, 1954.

Turgel, Gena, *I Light a Candle*, London, Grafton, 1987.

Turner, Barry, *Countdown to Victory: Soldiers and Civilians Tell the Story of the Final Battles for Europe 1944–45*, London, Hodder, 2004.

Tusa, Anne and Tusa, John, *The Nuremberg Trial*, London, BBC Books, 1995.

Tytell, John, *Ezra Pound: The Solitary Volcano*, New York, Doubleday, 1987.

Van der Zee, Henri A., *The Hunger Winter: Occupied Holland 1944–5*, London, Jill Norman and Hobhouse, 1982.

Vermehren, Isa, *Reise durch den letzten Akt*, Hamburg, Rowohlt Taschenbuch Verlag, 1998.

Vinen, Richard, *A History in Fragments: Europe in the Twentieth Century*, London, Abacus, 2002.

Von Hassell, Fey, *A Mother's War*, London, John Murray, 2003.

Von Hassell, Ulrich, *The Von Hassell Diaries 1938–1944*, London, Hamish Hamilton, 1948.

Waller, Maureen, *London 1945: Life in the Debris of War*, London, John Murray, 2004.

Weale, Adrian, *Patriot Traitors*, London, Viking, 2001.

———, *Renegades: Hitler's Englishmen*, London, Pimlico, 2002.

Webster, David Kenyon, *Parachute Infantry: An American Paratrooper's Memoir of D-Day and the Fall of the Third Reich*, Baton Rouge and London, Louisiana State University Press, 1994.

Weighley, Russell D., *Eisenhower's Lieutenants: The Campaign of France and Germany 1944–5*, Bloomington, Indiana University Press, 1981.

Welch, Samuel Cuthbert Rexford, *The Royal Air Force Medical Services*, London, HMSO, 1954–8.

West, Rebecca, *The New Meaning of Treason*, New York, Viking Press, 1964.

Wheeler-Bennett, Sir John and Nicholls, Anthony, *The Semblance of Peace*, London, Macmillan, 1972.

White, Osmar, *Conquerors' Road: An Eyewitness Report of Germany 1945*, Cambridge, Cambridge University Press, 2003.

White, Peter, *With the Jocks*, Stroud, Sutton, 2001.

Whiting, Charles, *Paths of Death and Glory: The War in Europe, January–May 1945*, Sutton, Severn House, 1997.

Wiesel, Elie, *Night*, New York, Hill and Wang, 2006.

Wilkinson, Peter, *Foreign Fields: The Story of an SOE Operative*, London, I.B. Tauris, 1997.

Williams, Andrew, *The Battle of the Atlantic: Hitler's Gray Wolves of the Sea and the Allies' Desperate Struggle to Defeat Them*, New York, Basic Books, 2003.

Wilmot, Chester, *The Struggle for Europe*, London, Reprint Society, 1954.

Wilson, Francesca, *In the Margins of Chaos*, London, John Murray, 1944.

——, *Advice to Relief Workers*, London, John Murray, 1945.

——, *Aftermath: France, Germany, Austria, Yugoslavia 1945 and 1946*, Harmondsworth, Penguin, 1947.

——, *A Life of Service and Adventure*, privately printed, 1996.

Windsor, Philip, *City on Leave*, London, Chatto and Windus, 1963.

Wolfe, Robert (ed.), *Americans as Proconsuls: United States Military Government in Germany and Japan 1944–1952*, Carbondale, IL, Southern Illinois University Press, 1984.

Woodbridge, George, *UNRRA: The History of the United Nations Relief and Rehabilitation Administration*, 3 vols., New York, Columbia University Press, 1950.

Woodruff, John B., *History of the 85th Mountain Infantry Regiment 4 January 1945– 31 May 1945*, unpublished history, 1945.

Woolf, S.J. (ed.), *The Rebirth of Italy, 1943–50*, London, Longmans, 1972.

Wyman, Mark, *DPs: Europe's Displaced Persons 1945–1951*, Ithaca, NY, Cornell University Press, 1998.

Young, David, *Four Five: The Story of 45 Commando, Royal Marines, 1943–1971*, London, Leo Cooper, 1972.

Ziemke, Earl Frederick, *The US Army in the Occupation of Germany, 1944–1946*, Washington, Center of Military History, United States Army, 1975.

Zweig, Ronald, *The Gold Train*, London, Penguin, 2002.

INDEX

INDEX

Benes, Edward, 440
Berchtesgaden, 67, 442
Bergen, 411
Berger, Gottlob, 216, 257
Beria, Lavrenti, 511
Berlin, 3, 124, 498–9; advance on by Red
   Army, 4, 5, 6, 72, 99, 210, 215, 307;
   allied occupation, 474, 475–81, 492–4;
   cigarette market, 479–80; conditions of
   allied-occupied, 478–81; decision by
   Eisenhower to leave to Russians, 72, 73,
   78, 133; influx of refugees from Silesia
   and Pomerania, 503–4; Soviet sector,
   492; withdrawal of Soviets from western
   half, 475
Bernadotte, Count Folke, 197, 197–200,
   224, 282, 504–5, 505–6, 511
Bernhard, Prince, 260
Bernterode salt mine treasures found in,
   366–9
Best, Captain Sigismund Payne, 223–4,
   231–2, 234, 235–7, 246, 316, 317,
   387–8, 389, 390, 525–6
Black Brigades, 420–1
black market (Netherlands), 450
Blaskowitz, General Johannes, 385, 386
Bletchley Park, 69, 256, 257, 270, 281
Blum, Léon, 224–5, 228, 233, 317
Bologna, 159, 419–20
Bolzano, 341–2
Bonhoeffer, Dietrich, 217, 219–20
Bonhoeffer, Karl, 217
Bonn, 138
Booth-Luce, Clare, 80
Bormann, Martin, 212, 214, 512
Bourke-White, Margaret, 460
Boyajian, Larry, 181, 183, 472
Bradley, General Omar, 71, 73, 78, 134,
   476
Brandt, Dr Karl, 398
Braun, Eva, 3, 5–6, 210–11, 215, 370
Braun, Wernher von, 475
Bregenz, 255
Bremen, 280–1
Brno, 440
Brooke, Field Marshal Sir Alan, 482

Bruck, Dr. Feodor, 370
Brussels, liberation of, 119
Bryant, George, 65, 254, 328, 329–30
Buchenwald camp, 52, 80–2, 445, 515;
   British secret agents at, 55–7, 58–9;
   children at, 54–5; liberation of by
   Americans, 48–50, 58; medical
   experiments carried out at, 45; Polish
   women in, 57–8; prisoners in, 44–5;
   Reid's reports on after liberation of,
   54–6, 57–9, 80–2; run by German
   communists, 48, 56; visited by
   Eisenhower, 79; witnessing of horrors
   after liberation, 80–2
Bulge, Battle of the, 119, 121, 125
Burney, Christopher, 56, 59

Cadorna, General, 188, 194
Canadian Parachute Battalion (1st), 308
Canadians: assault on Delfzijl, 271–5;
   cooperation with German soldiers in
   Netherlands, 384–6; relationship with
   Dutch women, 451–2; see also Cape
   Breton Highlanders
Canaris, Admiral Wilhelm, 219, 229
Cap Arcona, 292–5, 514; attack on and
   sinking of, 299–300, 301–2, 517
Cape Breton Highlanders, 22–3, 264, 265,
   270, 272–5, 453
Celle, 82
Central Registry of War Criminals and
   Security Suspects (CROW CASS), 431
Chamberlain, Houston Stewart, 465
Chartres, 374
Chetniks, 347
Chicago Daily News, 496
children: displaced, 397–8; killed by
   German parents, 459–60; killing of
   handicapped, 396–7
Christian, Gerda, 6
Churcher, Major-General J.B., 381–2
Churchill, Lieutenant-Colonel Jack, 226
Churchill, Mary (daughter of Winston),
   498
Churchill, Captain Peter, 226, 227, 228,
   230, 236

INDEX

INDEX

INDEX

INDEX

INDEX